# World Security

## TRENDS AND CHALLENGES
## AT CENTURY'S END

# World Security

## TRENDS AND CHALLENGES AT CENTURY'S END

*A Project of the Five College Program in Peace and World Security Studies*

**Michael T. Klare**
HAMPSHIRE COLLEGE

**Daniel C. Thomas**
CORNELL UNIVERSITY

ST. MARTIN'S PRESS
NEW YORK

*Senior editor:* Don Reisman
*Managing editor:* Patricia Mansfield
*Project editor:* Elise Bauman
*Production supervisor:* Alan Fischer
*Graphics:* G&H Soho
*Cover design:* Jeheber & Peace, Inc.

For information, write:
St. Martin's Press, Inc.
175 Fifth Avenue
New York, NY 10010

ISBN: 0-312-03747-3

ACKNOWLEDGMENTS

An earlier version of "The Environment and International Security" appeared
in *Foreign Affairs,* Spring 1989, Volume 68, Issue 2. Copyright 1989 by
the Council on Foreign Affairs, Inc.

David Wirth, "Climate Chaos," from *Foreign Policy* 74 (Spring 1989).

*This book is dedicated to the students, faculty, and staff*
*of the Five Colleges of Western Massachusetts*
*and their consortial arm, the Five Colleges, Inc.*

# Preface

*World Security: Trends and Challenges at Century's End* is intended to provide college students and general readers with an introduction to the critical security threats facing the world community in the 1990s. Included in these threats are serious problems that remain from the Cold War era—for example, the continued existence of large nuclear weapons stockpiles with hair-trigger launching systems—as well as environmental and developmental perils whose magnitude has only become apparent in the past few years. In all of these cases, we believe that new and innovative solutions must be sought to overcome the threats involved, and such solutions must address the problems on a *global,* rather than merely national or regional scale.

The original concept for this volume developed out of our work in editing the fifth edition of *Peace and World Order Studies: A Curriculum Guide,* the standard guide for curriculum development in the field of peace studies. In assembling the *Guide,* we inspected literally thousands of syllabi from undergraduate courses in peace studies, international relations, world order studies, and related fields. To our dismay, we discovered that most existing courses on contemporary world security issues lacked sections on such problems as regional conflict, hunger, chronic underdevelopment, and environmental degradation, or lacked up-to-date texts and reading materials on these topics. Because we believe that the study of world security should encompass all significant threats to global peace and well-being, and that students should be made aware of both the nature and the interconnectedness of these threats, we set out to produce a text that would provide faculty and students with a comprehensive and rigorous introduction to the entire span of world security affairs.

In structuring the book, we have attempted to arrange these global perils in some sort of rough chronological order, beginning with those that first arose in the early Cold War era, and then proceeding to others whose urgency has only been recognized in the past few years. Hence, we begin our survey with an assessment of U.S.-Soviet relations, the status of the nuclear arms race, and the prospects for nuclear arms control. Two other manifestations of the Cold War—the arms race in space and the question of European security—are the subject of the following essays. We then examine the dynamics of militarization and violence in the Third World, and consider the relative effectiveness of the United Nations and other international bodies in controlling such violence. Finally, we examine several global problems—hunger, the debt crisis, the violation of human rights, and environmental degradation.

In addressing these threats, we have asked our authors to follow a roughly similar approach: first, to describe the extent and nature of the particular threat as it was manifested in the late 1980s; second, to look at current trends and speculate on the evolution of the threat in the 1990s; and third, to provide a range of possible solutions to the problem—ranging from immediate, concrete steps to long-range and visionary proposals. Our intent, in using this format, is both to indicate the seriousness of the perils involved and to demonstrate that solutions *can* be found if we put our minds to work on the problem.

These problem-oriented essays are set between two other chapters of a more general nature: an introductory essay by Richard Falk of Princeton University on some of the theoretical issues raised by this new constellation of problems, and a concluding essay by Robert Johansen of the University of Notre Dame on policy perspectives for world security. We have included these two chapters because we believe that the discussion of particular security concerns should be viewed in the context of the debate now occurring in the academic and policymaking communities over the basic principles that have heretofore guided U.S. foreign policy. Similarly, we believe that the various proposals advanced by the authors of the other chapters should ultimately be subsumed in a coherent, forward-looking approach to the advancement of world security.

In selecting authors for these essays, we have attempted to choose individuals who are both experts on the particular threats involved and committed to a constructive, problem-solving approach to its amelioration. We do not ask, nor do we expect our readers necessarily to agree with any or all of the particular ideas advanced by these authors. We do believe, however, that these essays can provide a starting point for informed discussion of outstanding world security problems, and of the methods by which they can be brought under effective control. It is not our intention to provide *the* blueprint for world security, but rather to stimulate fresh thinking about these problems. Most of all, we seek to encourage readers to participate fully in the search for new pathways to lasting world peace and security.

Clearly, a project of this scale requires the advice and assistance of a great many people, only some of whom can be adequately thanked here. This list quite properly begins with the authors of the following essays, who devoted considerable time and effort to preparing their manuscripts and to responding to the editors' numerous queries and comments. They are to be lauded for working so hard on their essays solely out of the expectation—

vigorously cultivated by the editors—that this volume will contribute significantly to the discussion of world security issues in the years ahead.

Next, we wish to express our appreciation for the guidance provided by the Faculty Steering Committee of the Five College Program in Peace and World Security Studies (PAWSS), under whose auspices this volume was produced: Jan Dizard, Ronald Tiersky, and William Taubman of Amherst College; Allan Krass, Patricia Romney, and Brian Schultz of Hampshire College; Vincent Ferraro and Anthony Lake of Mount Holyoke College; Thomas Derr, Deborah Lubar, and Thomas Riddell of Smith College; and James Der Derian, Jerome King, and George Levinger of the University of Massachusetts at Amherst. Some of these fine people, it will be noted, did double duty as contributors of essays to the volume.

For offering St. Martin's Press comments about the project in its various stages of development, we would like to thank Carol Edler Baumann, University of Wisconsin–Milwaukee; Mark A. Cichock, The University of Texas at Arlington; June Teufel Dreyer, University of Miami; Robert J. Lieber, Georgetown University; Patrick M. Morgan, Washington State University; Bennett Ramberg, University of California–Los Angeles; J. Philip Rogers, George Washington University; Philip A. Schrodt, The University of Kansas; and Paul Watanabe, University of Massachusetts. We would also like to acknowledge the wonderful cooperation and assistance we have received from the fine people at St. Martin's Press—especially Don Reisman, our editor, and Elise Bauman, the project editor for the book.

Great appreciation is also due to the staff of Five Colleges, Inc., the consortial arm of the five institutions that jointly support the PAWSS program, and to its director, Lorna Peterson. We also wish to acknowledge the tremendous support PAWSS has received through the years from the staff of its host institution, Hampshire College. We particularly wish to thank Adele Simmons and Gregory Prince, the two presidents of Hampshire who have supported our work since PAWSS was established in 1983. Finally, we extend our deepest thanks to the staff of the PAWSS program itself—Adi Bemak and Linda Harris—without whose support and encouragement this project could not have been completed.

Michael T. Klare and Daniel C. Thomas
Amherst, Mass.

# Contents

# World Security

TRENDS AND CHALLENGES
AT CENTURY'S END

# Introduction

Though ten years short of century's end, the onset of the 1990s seemed to herald the beginning of a new era. With the Berlin Wall newly ruptured, strategic nuclear arms control talks making rapid progress, and conflicts in Africa and Central America recently settled, it appeared that the world was entering a new epoch in which peaceful cooperation would triumph over contentious rivalry as the dominant mode of international relations. True, the world community had not succeeded in preventing the Iraqi invasion of Kuwait; nor had the world found common solutions to other outstanding international problems. Still, as we began the countdown to the year 2000, there seemed to be good reasons for optimism regarding the future course of global security. Even the Kuwait crisis provided some grounds for optimism, in that it sparked a near-universal commitment to U.N.-mandated sanctions against the aggressor.

Set against this backdrop of progress, however, were a number of less auspicious trends. These included the continued spread of nuclear and chemical weapons, the further deterioration of economic and environmental conditions in many Third World countries, and the intensification of ethnic and religious warfare on all five continents. Also producing cause for alarm was the emergence of troubling aftereffects of the Cold War: the buildup of toxic wastes from nuclear weapons programs; the outbreak of interethnic violence in Eastern Europe and the USSR; and the diversion of surplus superpower arms to potential belligerents in the Third World. While these various problems did not eliminate all grounds for optimism regarding the future of global security, they did suggest that further progress would require even more effort and ingenuity than had first appeared to be the case. They also served notice that the final years of the twentieth century could entail shocks and crises of types both familiar and unfamiliar.

As we move further into the 1990s, therefore, it appears that the world community has two paramount tasks: first, to continue the progress made over the past few years in resolving international conflicts and in devising means for the collective solution of global problems; and second, to respond effectively to the emerging threats to global security. Clearly, the accomplishment of these tasks will require a renewed commitment to peace and cooperation on the part of all nations, along with the development of new

1

strategies for dealing with global problems of unprecedented scope and severity.

Navigating through these risks and challenges in the 1990s will call for particularly enlightened leadership on the part of the United States. While its international role is likely to be circumscribed by fiscal constraints at home and the emergence of new power centers abroad, the United States remains a major actor in the international community, and a beacon of hope for many in other countries who seek to promote respect for human rights and democratic values. By working with our allies, with former adversaries like China and the Soviet Union, and with international bodies like the United Nations, Washington can play a vital role in devising the new policies and instruments that will be needed to ensure global peace and security in the twenty-first century; if the United States fails to perform this role, the world we inherit in the year 2000 is likely to prove much less serene and healthful.

For the United States to perform the sort of international leadership role that is needed at this time in history, we will have to learn new collaborative skills and unlearn old patterns of dominance. That is, we will have to become more adept at thinking in terms of cooperative solutions, at using persuasion and logic—rather than threats and promises—to gain support for our suggestions, and at acceding to the suggestions and advice of others. As suggested by Secretary of State James Baker during his confirmation hearings in 1989, "U.S. leadership must adjust for a world that has outgrown the postwar era." It must adjust, he noted, to a world with new global challenges "that cannot be managed by one nation alone—no matter how powerful."

Clearly, if the United States is to adjust to this emerging world system, we must all become more knowledgeable about critical global problems and about the various proposals that have been advanced for their amelioration. As we become more familiar with the dynamics of these problems, moreover, we should begin to employ our own inventive skills in the search for more promising solutions. American colleges and universities have an important role to play in this process, by educating students and the community about world security affairs, by conducting research on critical problems, and by devising and testing innovative responses to emerging global hazards.

In this spirit, we have assembled the following collection of essays on world security problems in the 1990s. These essays are intended to provide a "status report" on the current direction and dimensions of the problems, to speculate on future developments in the field, and to consider various strategies for bringing these problems under control. These strategies range from practical steps that can be taken tomorrow to visionary proposals for sweeping international change; all, however, reflect a common desire to harness the creative energies of the world community in the search for constructive solutions to the perils that beset us.

In assembling these essays, we were guided by a number of basic precepts or concerns. These principles were not intended to limit our choice of authors or topics, but rather to lend a sense of purpose and coherence to the enterprise as a whole. Three precepts, in particular, guided our work.

First, the concept of "security" must include protection against all major threats to human survival and well-being, not just military threats. Until now, "security"—usually addressed as "national security"—has meant the maintenance of strong military defenses against enemy invasion and attack. This approach may have served us well in the past, when such attack was seen as the only real threat to national survival; today, however, when airborne poisons released by nuclear and chemical accidents can produce widespread death and sickness (as occurred with the Bhopal and Chernobyl disasters), and when global epidemiological and environmental hazards such as AIDS and the "greenhouse effect" can jeopardize the well-being of the entire planet, this perspective appears increasingly obsolete. As individual economies become ever more enmeshed in the world economy, moreover, every society becomes more vulnerable to a global economic crisis. And, as modern telecommunications brings us all closer together, we are made acutely aware of the pain and suffering of those living under oppression, tyranny, and injustice.

Given the fact that our individual security and well-being will depend to an ever-increasing extent on the world's success in mastering complex political, economic, environmental, and epidemiological problems, we must redefine "security" to embrace all of those efforts taken to enhance the long-term health and welfare of the human family. Defense against military aggression will obviously remain a vital component of security, but it must be joined by defenses against severe environmental degradation, worldwide economic crisis, and massive human suffering. Only by approaching the security dilemma from this multifaceted perspective can we develop the strategies and instruments that will be needed to promote global health and stability.

Second, given the multiplicity of pressing world hazards, the concept of "national security" must be integrated with that of "world security." Until now, most people have tended to rely on the nation-state to provide protection against external threats, and have viewed their own nation's security as being conversely affected by the acquisition of power and wealth by other nations. Thus, in the interests of "national security," nation-states have often engaged in a competitive struggle to enhance their own economic and military strength at the expense of other nations' capabilities. This us-versus-them, zero-sum competition for security is naturally biased toward unilateral solutions to critical problems, frequently entailing military and/or economic coercion. In today's interdependent world, however, the quest for security is rapidly becoming a *positive-sum* process, whereby national well-being is achieved jointly by all countries—or not at all.

The connection between national and international security is perhaps best illustrated by the dilemma of nuclear weapons. Given the unbelievably destructive nature of these weapons, any effort by one nuclear power to enhance its defensive position through the deployment of additional nuclear weapons will inevitably provoke suspicion, fear, and comparable arms acquisitions by its rival(s)—a process that usually leaves the original nation with less rather than more security. Only through *mutual* reductions in nuclear arms—accompanied by joint efforts at confidence building and crisis control—is it possible to promote genuine security in a world of multiple nuclear powers. Similarly, in an integrated world economy, any effort by one country to enhance its economic status through the systematic exploitation of other nations will inevitably produce hostility, indebtedness, and shrinking world markets—a natural recipe for widespread social and economic disorder. Only by promoting economic health and development in the poorer nations can we be assured that there will be a market for the products of the richer, more developed nations. And it is painfully obvious that protection against global environmental and epidemiological hazards can be attained only through joint international effort.

In light of these developments, it is evident that the health and safety of the nation—the traditional goal of national security—cannot be successfully assured in isolation from the quest for world security, broadly defined. This does not mean that the nation-state will lose its responsibility for the pursuit of security—far from it. In the absence of a supreme world government, security affairs will remain a central function of all national governments. But whereas security goals were once pursued through zero-sum, unilateral initiatives, today the attainment of these goals will require multilateral endeavors involving groups or associations of states. Cleaning up the Mediterranean, for instance, will require cooperation among all of the nations bordering on that body of water; protection of the ozone layer will require curbs on certain chemicals by all of the industrial powers; and avoidance of a global economic crisis will require cooperation among both the debtors and creditors in the international system.

Even in the military realm there is a close connection between national and international security. Given the growing worldwide incidence of terrorism, drug trafficking, arms smuggling, and ethnic/religious warfare, it is apparent that increased international collaboration is needed to monitor terrorist and criminal organizations, to prevent the outbreak of regional conflicts, to protect neutral air and sea transportation in the event of war, and to conduct peacekeeping operations once a cease-fire has been arranged. International cooperation on an even larger scale will be needed to prevent the further proliferation of nuclear and chemical weapons, and to control the diffusion of advanced conventional munitions. Clearly, no matter what problem area we examine, the ultimate goals of national security can be successfully attained only through a world security system of some sort.

Finally, in the pursuit of both national and international security objectives, we must never lose sight of basic human values and concerns. Thus, when devising multilateral measures for the solution of a given problem, we must never neglect to weigh the human consequences of any particular action, or agree to a proposal that would place a disproportionate share of the cost or pain of change on any particular community or constituency. Unfortunately, the world has known too many "ideal" solutions that have been imposed through tyrannical rule accompanied by massive human suffering. Hitler's "solution" to Germany's "Jewish problem" and Ceausescu's "solution" to Rumania's "debt problem" are only two of the most recent products of such misguided thinking. Clearly, the avoidance or at least minimalization of human suffering must be the *sine qua non* of all of our efforts on behalf of world security.

It is for this reason that the advancement of fundamental human rights has been included in this volume as a world security concern. Because human rights abuses are both a cause and a consequence of a wide range of global problems, one cannot speak of world security without addressing this issue. In fact, the role of human rights considerations in the policy process is a revealing barometer of progress toward humane governance on a global scale.

Together, these three precepts constitute the conceptual framework for this volume. Not all of the authors we have included would agree with this articulation of the principles involved, and many would probably supply a different set of concerns if they were asked to set the criteria for such a collection. Nevertheless, we are satisfied that the book as a whole does demonstrate the saliency and validity of these three suppositions.

# 1 / Theory, Realism, and World Security

RICHARD A. FALK

Several historical processes climaxed toward the end of the 1980s in ways that bear fundamentally on the outlook for international relations in the years and decades ahead. These developments also raise some serious questions about whether the most influential theory relied upon to interpret international relations is any longer adequate, and if not, what alternatives can be recommended as a basis for understanding, explanation, and prescription. In the United States, the predominant theory of international relations is known as "realism." Although there is a great deal of diversity within the framework of realism, realists generally agree that the state is the prime actor in international political life, that force is widely available and frequently used to adjust relations on the basis of power, and that humanist values offer neither a guide for action nor a basis of appraisal.

Realism has always had its share of critics and detractors, especially among those who believed that war must be overcome and that moral purpose should pertain to every domain of political action, including that of international relations. The argument set forth here, however, is that while such criticism did not amount to very much in the United States during the past fifty years, the new global setting poses a far stronger challenge to realism and increases the need for an alternative framework of interpretation. During the most recent period—a period of extraordinary change—three sets of remarkable developments took place that were not at all foreseeable through the realist lens as recently as the mid–1980s.

First of all, a shift in Soviet leadership produced dramatic changes in Soviet foreign and domestic policy, enabling a reduction of tensions in East-West relations of such magnitude as to support the now widely held view that the Cold War is over, and that, no matter what happens to Gorbachev or to Soviet-American relations, a revival of what we had come to know as the Cold War is highly improbable. As such, the East-West focus that had dominated postwar international relations is now quite marginal to an assessment of the future of world politics. Without the Cold War, and without its attendant arms race and periodic crises arousing fears of nuclear war, the realist focus on the geopolitical and strategic designs of the leading states (and clusters of states) is of far less consequence.

The second, and related, set of developments has involved the rise of a new form of revolutionary mass politics that provided the decisive element in the process of emancipation that occurred in the countries of Eastern Europe in the late 1980s. A somewhat analogous popular movement brought Corazon Aquino to power in the Philippines in 1986, and mounted an historic, if ultimately unsuccessful *democratic* challenge to the Chinese government in early 1989. In all of these cases, a mass mobilization of political opposition occurred without reliance on violent tactics and without any intervention on its behalf by foreign governments. Popular forces, acting creatively, toppled or challenged a series of militarized repressive governments without firing a shot. As the tragedy at Tiananmen Square suggests, not every challenge was successful; and, as Aquino's experience has shown in the Philippines, not every success of "people power" can be translated into a positive political performance—even when control over the state is achieved. What seems evident, however, is the vitality of popular, democratic forces in promoting changes that profoundly alter the character, and even the structure, of international relations. Such an appreciation works against the realist tendency to interpret international relations without giving attention to the social forces within states.

There is another implication of these political surprises of 1989 that has yet been hardly noticed, let alone assessed—namely, the relative inability of the superpowers to control convulsive political change on the level of states and regions within their traditional "spheres of influence." These democratizing movements unfolded in opposition to the political will of the respective dominant superpower, and without any substantial assistance by its adversary. Indeed, these extraordinary changes were brought about largely by movements from below, with help (largely inspirational) coming not from outside the bloc but within—the contagious spread of revolutionary fervor in Eastern Europe during 1989. The hypothesis of bipolarity, relied on to explain the division of Europe and postwar stability, became strangely irrelevant. Also proved ungrounded was the belief that Soviet control over Eastern Europe was rigid and more or less unshakable from within.

Of course, this reaffirmation of populist politics can be carried too far. Intervention from above and from without can frustrate popular forces of change. The United States demonstrated this during the 1980s by its interventions in Grenada, Nicaragua, El Salvador, and Panama. What 1989 does supply, however, is a corrective to a geopolitical view of political development that links stability to governmental control, and change to military intervention and war. The revolutions of 1989 demonstrated that under certain conditions, even in the face of sustained and brutal authoritarian rule, fundamental change can be achieved *nonviolently* from within. Such a demonstration is likely to encourage forces of democratic resistance elsewhere for years to come.

The discrediting and weakening of the Soviet Union is by now widely recognized. President Gorbachev's contribution was to acknowledge these circumstances, and to remove obstacles from the path of the popular movements in Eastern Europe—a contribution that has had a more severe than expected backlash at home, stirring the hot irons of revolutionary nationalist fervor throughout the non-Russian republics of the Soviet Union and even in the Russian heartland itself.

What is less understood is the greatly diminished importance of the United States in Western Europe, given the political dynamics of 1989. During the Cold War years, the United States, as superpower and leader of the Western alliance, exerted a predominant influence on NATO governments, often substantially encroaching on their sovereignty by unilaterally devising doctrines of nuclear war-fighting and targeting. European resentments mounted during the 1980s, leading to discussions about the erosion of the sovereignty of the NATO countries on the most vital decisions affecting war and peace, including the use of nuclear weapons. Now, almost in exaggerated reaction, political discussion on the future of Europe—especially in the Western half—proceeds as if the United States no longer is an important player. It is hard to give a convincing explanation of this new situation. So far it has only rarely been analyzed, and then only to admit that this unanticipated circumstance does indeed exist.

One possible explanation for the abruptness of the shift of view in Europe is an intuitive reading of the 1989 experience. These changes took place in a manner that exceeded the fondest hopes of Western European leaders and peoples: quickly, nonviolently (except in Rumania), and without U.S. intervention. Such an outcome led people to recognize that Europe's destiny is not controlled by the United States, as had previously been assumed. This conclusion is reinforced decisively by the widespread perception that whatever military threat was once posed by the Soviet Union has largely ceased to exist. Europeans are more anxious today about the dangers posed to Europe by a Soviet Union that is quickly becoming weak and unstable at its political center and is increasingly threatened by civil strife as its economy weakens and its regional divisions become more pronounced.

What seems evident from an assessment of these European developments is that the interplay of domestic and international factors is more complicated than is portrayed by realist theory. The domestic political setting—including popular movements and cultural patterns—needs to be included in our conceptualization of international political life. Further, it is now evident that the fit between structural realism and the Cold War depended upon tightly organized and ideologically defined blocs presided over by the two opposed superpowers. Without the special circumstance of these bloc antagonisms, the geopolitical structure may have become far too ambiguous and fluid for the constraints of realist thinking.

The third set of developments that challenge realism involves the spreading realization that environmental decay involves a series of major problems of global scope that cannot be answered by realism's fixation on conflicts between states. Ozone depletion, acid rain, climatic change, ocean pollution, transboundary effects of catastrophic accidents (for example, the Chernobyl nuclear power plant), and toxic waste disposal present challenges to states that can be met over time only through reliance on elaborate arrangements to ensure international cooperation and policy coordination; moreover, unprecedented levels of administrative control would be needed to ensure the implementation of agreed standards of behavior by states, corporations, and individuals. The arrival of the environmental agenda on the global scene was signaled at the start of 1989 when *Time* departed from its practice of naming a "man (or woman) of the year" and named instead "the endangered planet."

Traditional writing on international relations gives no notice whatsoever to environmental concerns. The leading books published up until now by the most respected specialists do not address the environmental dimension of international relations in a systematic fashion. At most, there is an assertion that environmental concerns present a routine series of management problems for states, and not even a problem set demanding any great diversion of public sector resources or imaginative investment. Such a view runs counter to a deepening environmentalist consensus. Whatever else we may feel about reality, we can agree at least that protecting the global environment is necessary for the health and well-being of all peoples, may prove indispensable to the long-term survival of the human species, and presupposes a new system of political relations at the global level.

The realist focus on power dynamics and the interactions of autonomous states does not capture the significance of these three sets of developments. Clearly, a new analytical framework is needed to explain and help us plan for a changing global setting. Accordingly, I will explore in this chapter the theoretical justification for moving from realism to what is called here "world orderism."

Before proceeding, it should be pointed out that "theory" is being used here in a loose way to identify a coherent body of ideas that seeks to explain, predict, and prescribe behavior. Both realism and world orderism can satisfy this loose test of theory, but neither can satisfy more rigorous conceptions that involve testable propositions or a systematic body of tightly interrelated deductive hypotheses. Realism should not be confused with a purchase on *reality*. Every conceptual program or theory claims to be addressing reality more cogently than rival explanations, and realism has no more *inherent* claim to success in this regard than do other theories.

Finally, it bears remembering that widely shared views often turn out to be wrong. (To mention just two familiar instances: most people at one time believed that the sun rotated around a stationary earth and that the earth was flat, not spherical, in its shape.) To retain an outmoded set of ideas after their explanatory power has been eroded is thus common in the history of thought. In this regard, the continuing popularity of realism among political scientists is no exception. But, to rely on realism at this stage for an understanding of international relations is to fall sway to a bad habit, one that is more threatening because it is so widespread.

To challenge the centrality of realism does not imply its total repudiation. States do remain important actors, war does remain profoundly relevant to international relations, and many international settings can be better understood as collisions of interests and antagonistic political forces. But to base our analyses on these observations alone will leave us increasingly ill-prepared to cope with the dramatic changes now occurring on the global horizon.

## THE REALIST CONSENSUS

Understanding the world of sovereign states continues to be the core challenge confronting students of international relations. In recent decades, however, the complexity and fragility of the world have given rise to the search for more durable modes of organizing international life than can be provided by essentially autonomous sovereign states.

The role of theory is crucial, shaping our conceptual categories of what is real and important about political life, but also orienting our political imagination in relation to what it might be reasonable to hope for. Theory, in this regard, always incorporates choices about what is important and what is desirable. These choices can be defended by reference to the past (history), to widely held views about human nature, and to ideas about the place of morality in the behavior of individuals and groups; no theory, however, can convincingly claim to tell the whole truth about international political life. In this regard, all theoretical arguments, no matter how behaviorally grounded or abstractly formulated, should be understood as arguments and appeals that are more or less helpful in grasping reality at a given stage of history.

This interpretation of the contingency of theory is of great importance for evaluating realism in its several dimensions:

1. as a widely shared set of assumptions treated by many political scientists as if it is the only useful and scientific way to conceive of the world;
2. as a methodological pretension that a reliance on analytic devices and an empirical approach to evidence produces a value-free set of scientific conclusions about political behavior; and
3. as a consensus among experts in international relations that seems to be having a detrimental influence on both the struggle for greater decency on a global level and prospects for human survival.

This consensus about theory among international relations professionals is associated with their endorsement of "realism," and draws on a tradition of thought that goes back to Thucydides, and from there forward through Machiavelli and Hobbes, to such contemporary thinkers and political figures as Morgenthau, Kennan, and Kissinger. Realism as a theoretical orientation has the following characteristics:

- an emphasis on the territorial, sovereign state as the dominant political actor in international life;
- a related emphasis on the competitive and conflictual character of the relations among states, with war remaining as an option for the resolution of conflict and with victory in war being treated as the prime criterion of the suitability of policy and leadership;
- a conviction that states are rational actors in pursuit of their own interests; acknowledging that rationality is often distorted by the play of bureaucratic forces within government, without any significant degree of deference to the well-being of other states or of the world system as a whole;[1]
- a strong tendency to neglect the impact of domestic social and political circumstances on the nature of conflict and security in international relations, and to regard objective circumstance of military and economic power as taking precedence over ideology, beliefs, and leadership as the driving forces of international history;
- and, finally, a pessimism about any program of fundamental change with respect to the role of violence in international relations combined with an optimism about the possibility of sustaining global stability even in the face of proliferating nuclear weaponry and the prospect of intensifying conflict between regional powers.

Such a framework of realism, sometimes called classical realism or traditional realism, has been extended by social scientists in at least two directions that are significant within the discipline of international relations. First of all, there is the work of Kenneth Waltz and others that has become known under the rubric of "structural realism." In this refinement of realism, the shaping of international relations is associated with the particular pattern of dominance associated with the role of leading states.[2] Structural realism helpfully moves realism away from an unqualified focus on statism and the formal postulate of the equality of states to the more political circumstance of the inequality of states and the related formation of patterns of hierarchy. This focus on the bloc system administered by the two rival superpowers provided a much more useful framework for interpreting international political life during the Cold War than is provided by the classical realist emphasis on the interaction of sovereign states.

These formulations of structural realism also built upon some of the analytic achievements of systems analysis as applied to international politics. Morton Kaplan had pioneered the study of the geopolitical effects of various systemic arrangements of power (e.g., unipolarity, bipolarity, multi-polarity, unit veto).[3] Unlike structural realism, and its more careful exploration of the analytic conditions of hegemonic stability, the systems approach tended to be ahistorical, and even avoided a direct assessment of the specific character of contemporary developments as they bear on international relations. The Cold War structure was classified as a system based on bipolarity, that is, as dominated by two poles of political power each associated with a superpower. Bipolarity was seen as stable because each side realized that it would suffer grave consequences by provoking war with the other, and alliance structures were tied to ideological affinity as well as to geopolitical calculations.

A closely related application of structural realism, with a more historical twist, was developed out of studies of the international economic order. Students of the Great Depression were agreed that competitive trading blocs following a protectionist logic contributed to the collapse of the world trade system in the 1930s, with adverse consequences for all. Such a condition contrasted with the earlier period of stability provided by British dominance over world monetary and trade policy. In the postwar world, the United States played this hegemonic role in relation to world economic policy up until the early 1970s, providing a reserve currency that was tied to floating exchange rates and presiding over such institutions as the General Agreement on Tariffs and Trade (GATT), the International Monetary Fund (IMF), and the World Bank.[4] The result was the achievement of what is called in the literature "hegemonic stability," which posits as desirable, and perhaps necessary, the predominance of a single state in setting the basic rules of the game for international economic relations. From this perspective of structural realism, there was a concern about the emergence of a multipolar economic order in the late 1970s, and whether it could evolve mechanisms of cooperation that could generate an equivalent stability to that achieved during the immediate postwar period when the United States acted as hegemon.[5]

It is important to contrast the "bipolarity" of geopolitics in the Cold War with the "unipolarity" of geoeconomics during the same span of years. The Soviet Union was never an important player in the policy arenas of the world economy. With the waning of the Cold War and the substantial withdrawal of the Soviet Union as a global actor, the structural circumstance of the 1990s is again one of U.S. predominance in the war/peace setting. At the same time, with security policy of diminished significance in a world of reduced geopolitical tensions, economic relations become more significant, with the superior performances of Japan and West Germany in the recent past creating a more multipolar structure at the core of international relations.

Partly to take account of this international economic order "after hegemony," there emerged a "neorealist" school of thought. These interpreters of the international political scene, although quite diverse on points of emphasis, agreed on several main points:

- Classical realism, at least as modified by the structuralists, was an appropriate focus for the analysis of international security relations.
- International economic policy introduced additional factors, especially a stress on cooperative and managed forms of behavior by states that flow from assumptions about the long-term advantage of participation in frameworks ("regimes") of mutual benefit to regulate critical aspects of international relations.
- The combination of a nuclear stalemate and an increase in the proportion of economic activity that entered world trade led experts in international relations to incorporate these cooperative dimensions into their fundamental conceptualizations of the field.[6]

Neorealism is thus best understood as an expanded realism that is sensitive to the self-interested reciprocities that form a growing dimension of international life.[7] International relations remains state-centric with war as its central preoccupation; rationality of behavior is presupposed; idealistic or altruistic motivations are excluded; and the pursuit of material self-interest is treated as the driving force of human behavior, whether on an individual or a collective basis. The international political–economy side of neorealism has stressed the importance of cooperation, especially given the absence of a hegemon, despite the structure of anarchy that persists in international relations. It also considers "regimes" as significant, involving the array of functional arrangements in various sectors of international life to facilitate routine interaction across state boundaries, to manage complexity, and to foster desired degrees of cooperation. Regimes can be highly institutionalized arrangements such as the IMF or World Bank, or more informal frameworks such as the exchange of ambassadors or rules for maritime safety on the high seas. The underpinnings and policy coherence of regimes can be provided by a hegemonic managing state, or through the more confusing multipolar processes of negotiations and bargaining.

Several conclusions emerge from this analysis. First of all, despite nuclear weaponry and the great increase in the complexity of international life, the war system continues to condition the relations of states in many circumstances. (At the same time, the destructiveness of war—even without nuclear weapons—and the growing difficulty of achieving victory are leading some realist scholars to postulate the obsolescence of war.[8]) Secondly, there is no conviction of the need for or the desirability of overcoming the existing political framework either by strengthening the United Nations or by moving toward drastic forms of disarmament. And thirdly, the basic comprehension of the reality of international relations by neorealists is pre-ecological in character, exhibiting no conceptual or policy adjustment to the challenge of global environmental problems that threaten human health, the viability of the global commons (including the oceans, climate, polar regions, and air quality), and the adequacy of the resource base given the demands of an expanding world population.

## THE RISE OF REALIST THOUGHT

Before venturing to criticize this realist consensus, it would be helpful to understand better why it achieved such prominence in post–World War II theorizing about international relations, particularly here in the United States. It is evident that a basic contention of realism that states rely on war and its threat to shape their relations with one another has a strong grounding in history, and is a position held by other theoretical perspectives. Wars have always occurred fairly frequently, most states' conduct has seemed uninhibited by legal or moral scruples, and states that prevailed in war have exerted greater influences upon international life regardless of whether they had behaved morally or legally.

The United States in the pre-1945 era had not embraced realism to any significant degree. The systematic study of international relations as a distinct field was not very widespread, and much of the writing about international political life was done by those with a law background. It was often prescriptive in tone and content, giving rise to an approach associated with idealism, carrying American claims of "exceptionalism" into foreign policy, claiming the United States to be a country unlike others—namely, a country without geopolitical ambition, but possessed by a missionary zeal for a better world. The modern expression of this idealistic interpretation of international relations centered around the proposals for global reform made by Woodrow Wilson in the context of World War I.

Wilson claimed to favor a new and superior approach to world security resting heavily upon collective procedures administered for the benefit of international society as a whole, and embedded in a global institutional framework. These ideas led to the proposals for the creation of the League of Nations. Wilson advocated a form of collective security that encroached upon the discretionary right of states to wage war and to establish alliance structures that purport to keep the peace through a "balance of power" with a functioning and organized world community that reacts collectively on behalf of victims of aggression. In essence, then, idealism sought to replace "balance of power" thinking as the foundation of international relations with the institutions and rule-based procedures of "collective security."

This early attempt to overcome the power dynamics of the state system failed for several distinct reasons. For one thing, the other major states in the world, mainly the European powers, never believed that it was possible or desirable to abandon balance-of-power approaches to peace and stability, and regarded the American advocacy of collective security arrangements as being disturbingly naive, possibly reflecting U.S. distance from the dangerous rivalries experienced by states in Europe. The failure of the United States to participate in the League, as a result of the failure of the U.S. Senate to approve the Versailles Treaty, undercut decisively whatever moral and political force was embodied in Wilson's attack on balances and alliances. The concept of collective security had until then enjoyed considerable support among the public, as well as U.S. governmental backing, which was significant in light of the decisive role played by U.S. military intervention in shaping the Allied victory in World War I.

Another problem with Wilson's proposals for collective security was their failure to challenge the postulate of sovereignty, thus fashioning institutions that were inherently too feeble to deal credibly with state action that went against the framework of rules and standards embodied in the Covenant of the League of Nations. No centralized peacekeeping capabilities were contemplated for the League, and the League was to operate on the basis of unanimity among all of its members. Besides, neither the League nor its members were obliged to pay the price of protecting victims of aggression. Thus, a weak country confronted by threats could not expect to receive adequate protection by the organized international community, nor were aggressors intimidated by the alleged prospect of a collective international response. The vulnerability of states to aggression became manifest when the League failed in the 1930s to protect Manchuria, Ethiopia, and Czechoslovakia against the unprovoked military onslaughts of the fascist states— Japan, Italy, and Germany—or to react against interventions on behalf of the fascist insurgency in Spain.

Further, the confidence and hopes invested in law and institutions were seen to divert energy away from more constructive and practical approaches to peace and stability. The policies of the democracies associated with the appeasement of Nazi Germany, and culminating in the acceptance in 1939 at Munich of Hitler's aggressive designs against Czechoslovakia, were subsequently repudiated as a failure of pacifism that contributed to the drift toward world war. The lesson of Munich, applied as a central tenet of Western diplomacy in the period of the early Cold War, involved the fundamental idea that an expansionist state can be contained only by the threat of overwhelming and mobilized power in opposition, and the credible willingness to use it at an early stage. The application of such thinking to U.S. foreign policy after 1945 gave emphasis to military preparedness, far-flung security commitments, a low threshold for war and intervention, and close alliance relations with like-minded governments.[9] The Atlantic Community democracies (North America and Western Europe) in the Cold War confronted the Soviet Union with a basic image of political unity backed up by an arsenal of nuclear weapons, and an evident willingness to use such weaponry, if necessary, despite the mutual destructiveness of such a posture.

In this regard, realism was a response by both diplomats and academic specialists to the perceived failures of idealism prior to World War II, as well as to the priority in the nuclear age of preventing the outbreak of major war rather than engaging in war for the sake of victory. Such figures as George Kennan and Dean Acheson emerged as architects of the postwar world. Both of these influential individuals saw law and international institutions as potentially dangerous diversions from the essential need to confront adversaries with the prospect of military defeat and unbearable devastation, especially here in America with its alleged vulnerability to high-minded appeals on the basis of law and morality. To generate popular backing for a peacetime approach to national security that insisted on military preparedness depended upon widespread perceptions of a threatening enemy holding an alien ideology. Mobilizing the American people on behalf of this undertaking helped produce an atmosphere of tension and anxiety that hardened into the Cold War. It is possible, although controversy persists, that if American policymakers were not so anxious about a renewal of isolationism (and an accompanying military demobilization) that some sort of cooperative postwar order might have emerged, averting the Cold War—admittedly at the cost of overlooking the oppressive quality of the Soviet occupation of Eastern Europe and of Soviet domestic politics.

Kennan was particularly concerned to discourage commitments to reformist goals in international relations, such as the promotion of human rights and economic development. Kennan feared a legalistic expansion of commitments based on abstract principles of decency that would distract policymakers from the protection of narrowly conceived U.S. strategic interests and that would impose unsustainable budgetary demands. Kennan's idea was to focus foreign policy and thought about the world narrowly upon the challenge of containing expansionist Soviet power. As it turned out, a far more grandiose and interventionary form of containment than Kennan favored prevailed among U.S. policymakers, as set forth in NSC-68 (National Security Council study number 68, a comprehensive statement of U.S. strategy that called for a major military buildup and an unremitting global struggle against the Soviet Union).

Realist theoreticians believe that realism succeeded in its main objectives during the 1945–90 period, and that this experience, especially when contrasted with the foreign policy failures of the West in the 1918–39 period, constitutes a virtual proof of its validity as a theory of international relations. No general warfare erupted. No nuclear weapons were used.[10] The firmness and durability of the Western alliance helped to expose Soviet weakness, leading eventually to the liberation of the countries in Eastern Europe occupied by the Red Army and climaxing in the late 1980s with the virtual surrender of the Soviet Union as geopolitical challenger.

Surely, comparing this record of realist achievement during the period after World War II with the idealist failures after World War I helps us understand the strength and dogmatism of the realist consensus, and why the study of international relations has gravitated toward realism in the four decades since 1945. Its postulates seem to have been vindicated by practice, while that of idealism, the main contending approach to international relations, has been relegated to ritual roles at the margins of international life. Realism has proved its superiority descriptively (this is the way the world works), and even prescriptively (this is the best way to keep the peace in the nuclear age). Its old theoretical competitor, idealism, seems to have dropped out of political discussion altogether. At the same time, the theoretical terrain of international relations remains slippery and subject to challenge.

## GENUINE AND APPARENT ALTERNATIVES TO REALISM

This chapter admits that theory in international relations is currently dominated by the realist consensus, but it does not accept this situation as necessarily desirable or durable. Rather, the limitations to realist analysis identified earlier suggest the need for consideration of alternative approaches to international relations. In fact, many scholars argue that it is an overstatement to speak of a realist consensus, and argue that "liberalism" and "Marxism" offer fundamentally different ways of viewing the world from that posited by realism.[11]

Liberalism is said to give primacy to the individual rather than to the state, and to regard success in trade as a basis for status in international life alongside the outcome of war.[12] To some extent, this difference in emphasis does call attention to some additional factors of importance in international relations, helping us to grasp the emergence of a concern for the protection of human rights, and to appreciate that the expansion of international trade can under some circumstances bring greater benefit to society than military capabilities, or even victory in war. Yet, in my view, liberalism is better understood as a "liberal tendency" *within* realism, rather than as an alternative to it. To the extent that liberalism is concerned with international relations, it tends to subordinate its distinctive preoccupations with individual well-being to the strategic concerns of the state. Liberals seek to be "practical," and generally accept the need to subordinate their normative goals to perceived "national security" concerns. Beyond this, liberalism has not generated a coherent, full-fledged conception of international relations. At most, as well-argued by Richard Rosecrance, under certain conditions of geopolitical moderation or paralysis—especially recently, as a consequence of the nuclear stalemate—trade expansion offers the best opening for enhancing the position and success of a state.[13] Liberalism thus offers, at most, a subsidiary extension of realism, taking more conceptual account than does mainstream realism of the role of moral purpose (human rights) and commercial advantage (international trade).

Michael Doyle's careful demonstrations that liberally constituted states (that is, market-oriented democracies) do not go to war with one another has exerted considerable influence on international relations theorizing in recent years.[14] It is an important conclusion that cuts against the grain of realist thought to the extent that it stresses domestic political life as a decisive precondition for the quality of international relations. Yet, as seems consistent with our claim that liberalism is subsidiary to realism, realists have called approving attention to Doyle's work so as to reinforce their ideological interest in privileging capitalist-style constitutionalism as the only acceptable and successful form of governance for sovereign states.[15]

Throughout the Cold War years, self-styled liberals as theorists or practitioners of international relations followed the lead of realist policymakers. To be sure, ultra-realists, such as Henry Kissinger and Zbigniew Brzezinski, scorned their liberal counterparts as "soft," by which they meant their greater reluctance to use military power as a foreign policy option or their insertion of moralizing elements in diplomacy. Prototypic liberals, such as Stanley Hoffman among academics and Cyrus Vance among diplomats, shared virtually all of the assumptions about the Cold War and international relations held by the ultra-realists. The differences were generally less matters of substance than of style, although sharp divergences might emerge if policy failure was perceived, as occurred in the later, post–Tet Offensive, stages of the Vietnam War.

The alleged Marxist alternative is identified as different from realism because of its conceptual emphasis on class relations as the basis of political behavior, its ideological commitment to the triumph of socialist revolution, and its consistently anti-imperialist line in foreign policy. As with liberalism in the West, Marxism (taken to include the later Leninist contributions) was also seen by realists as striking a distinctive note, serving as the foundation for foreign policy and international relations on the part of the Soviet bloc countries during the period of the Cold War.

Yet, on closer scrutiny, Marxism provided the rhetoric, but not the policy of the Soviet bloc. Moscow, in particular, relied on the realist consensus to map its actual policy, and did so along pragmatic lines of geopolitical opportunity. Communist jargon about the "correlation of forces" and "objective conditions" is best understood as a variation on the familiar ultra-realist emphasis on the global power equation. The East-West antagonism at the center of the post–World War II experience led to a sharp rivalry between the superpowers, but this rivalry was guided by the dictates of realist statecraft. In this central regard, nuclear weaponry made realists of us all, at least as a basis for action *within* the state system. Nuclear deterrence—the "balance of terror"—provided both Washington and Moscow with guidelines, and created a mutually binding ethos of prudent statecraft. This ethos surfaced at the worst moments of crisis, as during the feverish attempts at communication between the superpowers in 1962, when the Cuban missile crisis seemed to drive the world to the brink of nuclear war.

In fact, Marxism has no theory of international relations of its own, and its concern with the collision of forces leads Marxists to be attentive to a realist calculus of political, military, and economic factors. In operational diplomacy, the Communist governments have turned out to be exceedingly statist in their international relations, even with one another. The bitterness of the Sino-Soviet conflict in the 1970s, as well as the warfare between China and Vietnam, disclosed how little "class solidarity" has meant to the leadership of these countries, and how important have been competing conceptions of state interests. Marxist theory, then, has not developed a distinctive approach to international relations, whereas Marxism in action has been realist in its practice (no matter how many quotations from Lenin are relied upon to justify a given state policy).

The conclusion reached here is that liberalism and Marxism do not provide a genuine alternative to realism, and this is especially true with respect to "security," which is conceptualized in militarist and statist terms by both liberals and Marxists.

## IN SEARCH OF A GENUINE ALTERNATIVE TO REALISM

In one respect, the realist consensus is an inevitable theoretical position in a world of states. So long as warmaking capabilities are retained and used by states, the most prudent approach to stability and security is by way of strategic management (arms control) and balanced military capabilities (deterrence).

There remains ample room for policy disagreements among realists in relation to what the forms and breadth of arms control should be under varying international conditions, what force levels are needed to achieve balance, and what sorts of international situations warrant an interventionary response. For instance, "soft" realists tend to oppose uses of force not directly related to territorial integrity, political independence, or access to vital resources of the state (or its closest allies), whereas ultra-realists take a far more expansive and geopolitical view of "balance" and of "national interest."

One could argue that the realist approach may be far more benign in a phase of international relations not beset by conflict at the core. But the Cold War engendered an expensive and dangerous arms race, interventionary escalation and militarization of Third World conflict, and recurrent crises fraught with geopolitical tension. In the emerging post–Cold War atmosphere, one can expect a moderation of these menacing features of statist rivalry, but tensions may be reinvigorated by the deepening of conflict in certain regional settings. To some extent, bipolarity provided balance and stability in relation to some situations of intense regional antagonism. For example, there has been informed speculation since the muting of the Cold War about the possibility of a new round of warfare between India and Pakistan, conceivably fought this time with nuclear weapons, and real anxiety about escalation in the Middle East with Iraq's chemical weapons pitted against Israel's nuclear weapons.

Even without the Cold War, the world remains dangerous and relations among states problematic. Besides, new types of core conflict could easily reemerge either as a result of regression in the Soviet Union or through a new type of geopolitical antagonism arising from the struggle for shares of the global market, especially in a situation of economic adversity (low growth and high unemployment for major states) on a global scale. Such adversity already exists in many parts of the Third World, but should it spread to the richer countries, the political consequences, although unpredictable, are likely to generate dangerous new antagonisms among leading states, by then possibly arrayed as rival trading blocs.

Beyond these concerns lie the plurality of environmental challenges associated with the ecological agenda. Many of these challenges are of global scope, and cannot be addressed successfully within the structures of statism, or by application of realist logic. The unevenness of states in relation to environmental decay, whether as a result of differing contributions to the harm or differing capacities to pay the costs of such decay, is extremely difficult to adjust in a reliable manner that facilitates sufficient cooperative action.

It is impressive that ninety-three states have agreed as of 1990 to ban all use of CFCs (chlorofluorocarbons, the chemical cause of ozone depletion) by the year 2000, but it remains to be seen whether such promises— although in binding treaty form—will be kept, and if not, what can be done. Environmental arrangements, to date, have been voluntaristic when it comes to implementation, resting essentially on self-enforcement. It will, of course, be encouraging if cooperative action by states succeeds in establishing an effective regime that prevents further ozone depletion, but even such a positive and notable achievement would be misleading. The ozone problem is rare among environmental concerns of a global character—there is substantial agreement as to its severity, cause, and solution, and, what is most important, apparently benign chemical substitutes for CFCs exist at relatively modest cost. In this regard, adjustment costs are not an appreciable burden, and do not require fundamental changes in individuals' life-styles.

But this positive result should not give rise to an optimistic overall assessment. States will not cooperate for the sake of the global interest if major economic and life-style consequences are involved. Worldwatch Institute, a highly respected nongovernmental organization, has produced convincing evidence that implies that only a phaseout of the automobile as a basic mode of transport can prevent global warming from reaching disastrous levels over the next forty years.[16] If adjustments are to be made, it will require a different approach to security than is generated by the postulates of realism. It will require, above all else, substituting an orientation based on the well-being of the whole for the well-being of the part, and a suitable implementing framework of beliefs, procedures, and structures. Credible environmental protection over a period of decades will inevitably require the establishment of some type of limited world government.

Realism rests upon the fragmentation of the world into contending parts, each of which absolutizes its goals without seriously considering the effects on other parts or the whole. Political identity is associated with difference and otherness, and with the fragmentation of the human species into states, nations, races, classes, and genders. Conflict patterns take shape in relation to these categories of fragmentation. A genuine alternative to realism must build upon the possibility of a holistic orientation toward both human identity and the organization of political life and security on the planet. Holistic restructuring, implying structures of authority and political identification (what Robert Jay Lifton has called "species identity") is not inconsistent with the encouragement of cultural diversity.[17] In other words, the unity required for functional purposes is compatible with the flourishing of many varieties of societal organization and with difference affirmed as a basis for fulfillment—provided tolerance and celebration of difference are firmly established.

## TOWARD WORLD SECURITY: REVISIONING THE FUTURE

To achieve world security at this stage of history requires, then, an approach that cannot be undertaken within the frame of realism. It requires a new set of conceptualizations for political life at the global level that is appropriate to the security undertaking for the species as a whole. One attempt to provide such a theoretical foundation has been pursued over the years by the World Order Models Project.[18] As compared to realism, the various strands of WOMP thinking share several common characteristics:

- a strong sense of the unity of human destiny;
- a belief that security encompasses the basic needs of all peoples to have food, shelter, health facilities, education, meaningful work, human rights, and environmental protection;
- a skepticism about the capacity of the war system to provide security, even in the minimal physical sense of protecting territorial states against military attack and other unwanted forms of penetration; and

- a belief that desirable changes in political life throughout history have been largely caused by popular movements and struggles from below, and that democratization and human rights are necessary, but not sufficient, conditions for global reform.

In effect, the continuing WOMP process has attempted to produce a genuine theoretical alternative—here called world orderism—to the realist consensus. This attempt continues to unfold, and has not yet effectively eroded the dominance of realism.[19] In looking toward the future, WOMP has given increasing stress to the role of a transnational social movement built around initiatives taken in specific settings of injustice and peril, altering the political climate within which states act and contributing to the formation of a new reality—a "global civil society." The rise of "green awareness" and global environmentalism is an achievement of this new type of politics.[20] The possibilities for this development depend on deepening and globalizing democracy. In this regard, the grassroots challenge to Soviet state power in Eastern Europe and in the Soviet Union itself are a great source of inspiration, both as evidence of potency and as accomplishing, at least temporarily, a major step in the direction of emancipation from authoritarian rule.

Realism remains the dominant mode of explanation for international relations, and yet any approach to world security that is likely to be beneficial for the peoples of the world will have to proceed on a quite different basis. It will have to take account of two separate conditions that pertain to the political life of the planet: first of all, the nature of problems and policy that exceed the organizational reach of any single state, however strong and rich, and secondly, the relevance for decision and change of domestic social forces that set the climate within which political parties, governments, and corporations act. In effect, the realist paradigm needs to be displaced by what might be called the world order paradigm. A simple table of comparison highlights some of the differences between these two broadly conceived outlooks on the political dimension of international life (see Table 1.1).

The argument offered here is that world orderism is more responsive to the challenges of the 1990s than is realism, although one need not adopt an either/or attitude. Realism helps us grasp continuities with a past in which the predominance of states and hierarchies among them shaped the history of international relations from above, including a central legislative role for wars that helped translate shifts in relative power into new arrangements of benefits and new patterns of influence. In contrast, world orderism provides a framework for nonviolent change and a more cooperative ordering of relations among distinct political communities and civilizations, while facilitating the emergence from below of a value-oriented globalism that combines commitments to human survival with a concern about equity and

Table 1.1 / Realism versus World Orderism

| Parameter | Realism | World Orderism |
|---|---|---|
| Unit of emphasis | state | world/person/group movement |
| Human nature | rational; egocentric | symbolic; culturally shaped |
| Knowledge system | empirical; behavioral | belief, symbol, and value systems; myth and tradition |
| Identity | fragmented | multiple and unified: species mind; life |
| Conflict and peace | balance; deterrence; mobilization for war | disarmament; development; democracy; mobilization from below; mobilization for peace |
| Vision of the future | continuity | transformation or collapse |
| Likely outcome if successful | stability; prosperity of core countries in the north and selected elites in the south | realization of world order values (peace, economic well-being, human rights, environmental balance) for all societies and for the whole of humanity |

participatory forms of governance at all levels of social organization from the family to the world.

## Notes

1. Cf. M. Mastanduno, David A. Lake, and G. John Ikenberry, "Toward a Realist Theory of State Action," *International Studies Quarterly* (1989), pp. 457–474, at 459; see also K. J. Holsti, *The Dividing Discipline: Hegemony and Diversity in International Theory*, Boston, Allen & Unwin, 1985, esp. pp. 1–40; John A. Vasquez, *The Power of Power Politics: A Critique*, New Brunswick, NJ, 1983, esp. pp. 13–37.

2. See Kenneth Waltz, *Theory of International Politics*, Reading, MA, Addison-Wesley, 1979; Robert Gilpin, *War and Change in World Politics*, Cambridge, Eng., Cambridge University Press, 1981.

3. Morton A. Kaplan, *System and Process in International Politics*, New York, John Wiley, 1957.

4. Cf. Robert O. Keohane, *After Hegemony: Cooperation and Discord in the World Political Economy*, Princeton, NJ, Princeton University Press, 1984.

5. Cf. Charles P. Kindleberger, *World in Depression*, Berkeley, University of California Press, 1973; Gilpin, note 2; Keohane, note 4.

6. On various aspects of this theoretical "adjustment" within the "realist" mainstream, Richard Rosecrance, *The Rise of the Trading State*, New York, Basic Books, 1986; Mancur Olson, *The Logic of Collective Action*, Cambridge, MA, Harvard University Press, 1971; Kenneth A. Oye, ed., *Cooperation under Anarchy*, Princeton, NJ, Princeton University Press, 1986.

7. For the range of discussion, see Robert O. Keohane, ed., *Neorealism and Its Critics*, New York, Columbia University Press, 1986.

8. Cf. John Mueller, *Retreat from Doomsday: The Obsolescence of Major War*, New York, Basic Books, 1989; see also qualified endorsement in Carl Kaysen, "Is War Obsolete?" *International Security* 14:42–64 (1990).

9. Such thinking was most appropriately codified in a 1950 document generated by the National Security Council, authored mainly by Paul Nitze, and known as NSC-68. For text, see Thomas H. Etzold and John Lewis Gaddis, eds., *Containment: Documents on American Policy and Strategy, 1945–1950*, New York, Columbia University Press, 1978, pp. 385–442.

10. John Lewis Gaddis, *The Long Peace*, New York, Oxford University Press, 1987; Gaddis, "The Long Peace: Elements of Stability in the Postwar International System," *International Security* 10:99–142 (1986).

11. Cf., e.g., last chapter Robert Gilpin, *U.S. Power and the Multinational Corporation*, New York, Basic Books, 1975.

12. Influentially articulated by Michael Doyle in "Kant, Liberal Legacies, and Foreign Affairs," *Philosophy and Public Affairs* 12:205–235, 12:323–353 (1983).

13. Richard Rosecrance, *The Rise of the Trading State*, New York, Basic Books, 1986.

14. Doyle, note 12.

15. E.g., Francis-Fukuyama, "The End of History?" *National Interest* 16:3–18 (1989).

16. See Lester R. Brown, "The Illusion of Progress," in Brown and Assoc., *State of the World 1990*, New York, Norton, 1990, pp. 3–16; see also pp. 17–38 on global warming.

17. Cf. Robert Jay Lifton, *The Genocidal Mentality*, New York, Basic Books, 1990, pp. 255–279.

18. For a suggestive account of premodern, indigenous sensibilities, see Jamake Highwater, *The Primal Mind: Vision and Reality in Indian America*, New York, Harper and Row, 1981.

19. For representative discussion, see Saul H. Mendlovitz, ed., *On the Creation of a Just World Order*, New York, Free Press, 1975; Rajni Kothari, *Footsteps into the Future*, New York, Free Press, 1974; Richard Falk, *A Study of Future Worlds*, New York, Free Press, 1975.

20. For relatively recent WOMP perspectives, see R.B.J. Walker, *One World, Many Worlds: Struggles for a Just World Peace*, Boulder, Colorado, Lynne Rienner, 1988; Saul H. Mendlovitz and R.B.J. Walker, eds., *Towards a Just World Peace*, London, Butterworths, 1987.

# 2 / Soviet-U.S. Relations: Confrontation, Cooperation, Transformation?

WALTER C. CLEMENS, JR.

A new détente—relaxed tensions—emerged in Soviet-U.S. relations in the late 1980s. But deténte is a fragile flower, easily crushed. There have been many periods of relaxed tensions—in 1955, 1959, 1963, 1967, 1972–75, 1979—none of which lasted more than two or three years.[1] Will the new détente continue in the 1990s, or will it revert to hostile confrontation? Can Soviet-U.S. relations be put on a new basis so that cooperation outweighs conflict?[2] Can these relations be transformed so that—analogous to Canada and the United States—they are rooted in overlapping ties of a complex interdependence? These three alternatives are analyzed in this chapter.

Before looking ahead, we must understand what has happened in the past. What factors propelled the USSR and the United States toward conflict—especially after World War II? What situations pushed them toward détente?

Soviet-U.S. conflict and confrontation derived from many factors. First, Communist ideology challenged the concepts of Western democracy. Second, the Soviet economic system appeared for some decades to be overtaking capitalism. Third, for decades the USSR was ruled by a tyrant—Joseph Stalin—who abused his own people and tried to dominate Russia's neighbors. Even after he died in 1953, his successors, such as Nikita Khrushchev and Leonid Brezhnev, seemed, to the West, unpredictably dangerous, loose cannons on the deck of world politics. Fourth, for decades there was a great geopolitical vacuum between the USSR and the United States. Following World War II, Eastern European countries such as Poland and Hungary became Soviet satellites. Western Europe gradually recovered economically, but—politically divided—was not an independent force. Fifth, the USSR became a military superpower, at least as strong as the United States. All the while, Western responses to these challenges deepened Soviet anxieties, producing a spiral of fear and tension. Despite nuclear terror, each side feared the other might be preparing to attack.

Détente emerged because both sides found confrontation unprofitable and unnecessary. Even Communist Party leader Khrushchev and U.S. President Dwight Eisenhower recognized in the 1950s that nuclear war would be suicidal and that their countries needed arms control and trade more than bitter competition. But the United States and the USSR followed policies that put them back on the upward spiral of tension. Thus, in the mid- and late 1970s the Kremlin dispatched its forces to Angola, Ethiopia, and then Afghanistan. This provoked a massive military buildup in the United States.

By the mid-1980s, both military superpowers had an abundance of nuclear and other weapons, but they showed serious signs of combat fatigue from arms racing and from decades of effort to influence or even dominate other parts of the globe. They had aborted many of their ideals and wasted many of their material and other assets in this competition. An experienced observer compared the superpowers to dinosaurs and wondered whether they could adapt to changing conditions.[3]

The very term "superpower" was thrown into question in the late 1980s by the economic and other troubles confronting the USSR and the United States.[4] Soviet economic growth virtually stopped despite Gorbachev's efforts at *perestroika*—"restructuring" of Soviet economic and social life. Most of Moscow's erstwhile satellites—from Czechoslovakia to Outer Mongolia—kicked off their traces and looked to the West for guidance and support. Next, many constituent republics of the Soviet "Union" groped for liberation from Moscow's domination. In 1990 Lithuania, Estonia, and Latvia demanded independence; even Russia felt itself too encumbered by "Union" and proclaimed its "sovereignty." Gorbachev began to preside over a paper empire existing more in name than reality.[5]

The United States was still a superpower in many dimensions—economic, political, scientific, and cultural as well as military.[6] Its economy was twice the size of Japan's, although smaller than that of Europe as a whole. It still led an alliance system that included most of Europe and Japan. Its scientists dominated Nobel Prize awards and its movies the screens of the world. It matched or surpassed the USSR in strategic nuclear weapons and was unrivaled in force projection, having more than a dozen aircraft carrier battle groups while Moscow had none.

Looked at in objective terms, both the USSR and the United States had no military rivals. No other countries possessed their combined assets: incomparably large and variegated military capabilities; huge territories occupied by large, comparatively well-educated populations; relative self-sufficiency in most resources; large and diversified economies. No other power center could match these assets—not China, not Japan, not Brazil, not the oil-rich Middle East, not even Europe, still far from political union.

Still, the United States as well as the USSR looked to many observers like empires in decline. Both military superpowers faced mounting domestic problems—poor economic growth, declining oil production, floundering educational systems, social alienation, racial strife, crime, drug addiction. By comparison, Japan's sun seemed to be rising, followed by that of Europe.

Both military superpowers seemed to suffer from what the Greeks called *hubris*—excessive pride and confidence. They had erroneously believed that they could have "butter" and "guns" without sacrificing their development in the social, cultural, or scientific spheres. America dissipated many of its strengths in Vietnam; the USSR, in Afghanistan. Both societies suffered from the same faults that Gorbachev in 1986 attributed to many Soviet diplomats: preconceptions, smugness, narrow-mindedness, arrogance.[7]

We cannot answer the major question of this chapter—How will the military superpowers get along with each other?—unless we know how each will get along domestically. Will the USSR disintegrate or recover? Will the United States coast on its laurels, paying others for supplies of oil and narcotics, or will America regain a vitality that once inspired much of humanity?

As in nature, so in superpower relations: everything is interlinked and interdependent. Soviet-U.S. relations depend upon developments within each country; on the world scene generally; and on the texture of their bilateral connections. Each scenario—toward confrontation, cooperation, transformation—hinges on the interaction of these dimensions. More specifically, it depends upon the response of Soviet and U.S. citizens, especially their leaders, to these developments. Had Brezhnev remained in power for another decade, the same problems may have festered without producing any attempt at fresh approaches.

## GORBACHEV'S "NEW THINKING"

Soviet social and economic problems accumulated in what Moscow now calls the "stagnation period" of the 1970s and early 1980s. Mikhail Gorbachev became Communist Party General Secretary in March 1985 and soon called for "new thinking" and bold actions to change Soviet policies at home and abroad.[8] He gradually ousted many old guard Party leaders and brought in like-minded persons such as Foreign Minister Eduard Shevardnadze and policy planner-ideologist Aleksandr Yakovlev. The latter had studied at Columbia University (1958–59), focusing on how Franklin D. Roosevelt had saved the U.S. system by his New Deal reforms; Yakovlev and Gorbachev hoped to rejuvenate the Soviet system by *perestroika*.

Gorbachev became the first Soviet leader to recognize the potential of a world rapidly becoming interdependent. His predecessors had treated "interdependence" as a fig leaf for Western imperialism. Gorbachev made it a positive starting point for Soviet policy. While his predecessors gloated over strategic "parity" with the United States, Gorbachev said that arms could not ensure peace. Rather, he urged radical cuts in armaments, each side cutting forces in which it had superiority. Security, he said, could only be mutual. It could not be based on forces that led others to feel insecure. Gorbachev's predecessors saw the Third World as an arena in which the

USSR could win at the West's expense. Gorbachev instead withdrew Soviet support from most leftist regimes in the Third World and urged them to make peace with their own people and with the West. Gorbachev went far beyond his predecessors in opening the USSR to foreign economic ties. He pushed for joint ventures and wanted to integrate the USSR with the world economy.[9]

Moscow's "new thinkers" portrayed their moves toward arms control and East-West trade as a strategy that would adapt to what Gorbachev often called an "integral but still contradictory world." Their approach found a warm response in the West. Arch anti-Communist Ronald Reagan concluded that the Gorbachev regime was different from its predecessors and that U.S. interests would be well served by improved relations with Moscow.

## ALTERNATIVE FUTURES: MORE CONFRONTATION?

Détente could again collapse. The very word is double-edged, because in French it means "trigger" as well as "relaxation of tensions." In the Middle Ages a *détente* was the bolt that, when released, fired a crossbow, relaxing its pent-up energy. The Russian term *razriadka* also means the discharge of tensions, electric or political. The release achieved by détente or *razriadka* can be short-lived unless steps are taken to make it an ongoing process.

Domestic failures could impel or propel either the USSR or the United States or both toward confrontation. *Perestroika* has generated more chaos than material reward for most Soviet citizens.[10] If this chaos mounts, the USSR may disintegrate still further. Its leaders could accept such changes peacefully, or Russia and whatever republics it still dominates could act like a cornered bear and lash out with brute strength. The Kremlin would then need a foreign bogey to justify its repressive policies and Russia's low living standards. It might want a "victory" in the Third World to show that communism still lives.

A conservative backlash is also possible in the United States. Domestic problems could lead Washington to use Russia and Soviet Communism as scapegoats.[11] Americans may demand that their nominal allies shape up or stand alone against a familiar target: the "evil empire" still dominated by Moscow.

The world system could itself induce Soviet-U.S. confrontation. The Kremlin in 1989–90 acquiesced in the collapse of its Eastern European empire, but a united, potentially aggressive Germany might snap Moscow's tolerance for change. The USSR or its Russian core might feel so isolated, so cut off from the rest of Europe, that it might try to intimidate the West rather than cooperate with it.

If China or Japan became more of a military threat to Russia, and still enjoyed U.S. support, ties between Moscow and Washington would likely suffer. Alternatively, if Beijing again seemed to ally with Moscow, that would sound alarms in Tokyo, Washington, and elsewhere.

If the USSR or residual Russia fails to adapt to the world of commerce and trade, or is spurned by the International Monetary Fund and other such institutions, Moscow may turn inward or try to sabotage the growth of West-West or West-South relations.

Bilateral Soviet-U.S. ties may disappoint both sides and leave a wake of frustration and unpaid debts rather than a growing material base of cooperation. The U.S. Congress may use its power over the purse strings to block long-term credit and East-West trade until the Kremlin has changed its domestic politics and economics entirely in line with American values. Washington may demand not only liberation for Lithuania but for other Soviet republics from the Caucasus to Siberia.

Either military superpower could become disenchanted with arms control accords. These limitations may constrict military potential too much. Alternatively, they may seem meaningless, throttling nuclear weapons but opening the way to intense competition in lasers or other exotic weapons.

In short, there are a thousand and one factors that can disrupt the best efforts of the superpowers to reach an armistice and pursue common interests. Governments are organized to defend sovereignty—not to deplete or share it. Attempts to build a social contract between armed rivals may prove futile.

## BEYOND DÉTENTE: REPLACING CONFLICT WITH COOPERATION

A second alternative future posits that the Soviet-U.S. struggle for power is supplanted by a growing web of shared activities in which both sides find meaning and reward. This growing network gradually diminishes their interests in conflict and heightens their interests in cooperation.

For détente to evolve into wide-scale cooperation, moderate reformers must stay at the helm in both Moscow and Washington. If Gorbachev and his *perestroika* team were replaced by rabid nationalists or dogmatic Communists, all bets would be off. His successors might condemn his "loss" of Eastern Europe and "capitulation" to U.S. imperialism and try to reverse directions.

American attitudes toward the USSR have often vacillated between unrealistic euphoria and bitterness. These moods swings make for an inconstant policy. If America's economic or other problems worsen, U.S. leaders must avoid the temptation to blame these problems on the Soviets, on the Japanese, or on some other foreigners when the root difficulty lies closer to home. Republicans or Democrats might try to divert attention from domestic woes by a foreign confrontation to rally all Americans around the flag.

In short, both Moscow and Washington must manage internal problems skillfully if they are to keep bilateral relations on an upward course. This will be easier to do if Soviet-U.S. trade and arms control bring tangible domestic gains.

The world system, of course, sets the broader stage. The prospect of a uniting Europe offers both opportunity and danger for each superpower. Either could gain increased trade and security; either could also be left out in the cold. How will they cope with residual fears of Germany? Many Western-ers want their NATO alliance to continue as a safeguard against a resurgent Germany as well as Russia. But why keep NATO if the Soviet alliance has collapsed and more than 100 million Eastern Europeans, no longer subject to Moscow, stand between the West and Russia?

Still greater challenges may come from developments in the "South"— proliferation of mass destruction weapons, religious fanaticism, environmen-tal catastrophe, border disputes, rising distinctions between economic "haves" and "have-nots." All these problems could lead Russia and the West toward common positions. But superpower confrontations in the Third World could also undercut the fragile ties of East-West trade and arms control.

Moderation of East-West tensions presupposes resolution of regional conflicts that have pitted Soviet and U.S.-backed forces throughout the Third World. Such confrontations need not all wind down simultaneously, but progress in ending each conflict would make it easier to perpetuate and extend improvement in American-Soviet relations. Superpower stakes are especially high in the Middle East. If a Middle Eastern client of either superpower is endangered, its patron will be pressed to come to the rescue. The most hopeful outcome would be that the superpowers encourage a broad settlement acceptable to the many conflicting parties in the region. Otherwise the United States will feel compelled to stand by Israel, and Moscow will feel reluctant to leave the field.

Given the pressures for the old politics to continue, it is important to strengthen the peacekeeping and peacemaking functions of the United Na-tions. If international organization becomes more effective, leading to "rec-ognized patterns of practice around which expectations converge,"[12] this could reduce the compulsions of the great powers to intervene in local conflicts. There were many positive trends underway in the late 1980s and early 1990s, including changes in Soviet policy and various proposals by Gorbachev for collective security and peacemaking.[13]

Just as important—perhaps more important—would be shared experi-ences in East-West-South cooperation. To make the world system stable and prosperous, the superpowers should seek to supplant zero-sum striving—by themselves and others—with cooperative actions that benefit the First, Sec-ond, and Third Worlds. These actions could be in many spheres—reducing infant mortality through programs to check dehydration; slowing fossil fuel consumption and cultivating alternative energy supplies; establishing seed banks and aquaculture farms.[14] East, West, and South could look for the kinds of three-sided cooperation existing in the 1970s, when Iranian gas was piped to the USSR through lines built with European capital and technology and reimbursed by Soviet gas delivered to Europe. In a constructive spirit, Presidents Bush and Gorbachev agreed in June 1990 that U.S. food would be carried in Soviet planes to starving Ethiopians, and that both Washington and Moscow would promote peace in Ethiopia. Both nations tried also in 1990 to take a common stand against Saddam Hussein, but most forces confronting Iraq were American, with Moscow providing only moral support.

Ultimately the improvement of Soviet-U.S. relations hinges on controlling or diminishing the zero-sum rivalry of high politics and expanding the psychic and material rewards of low politics.[15] Progress in each domain will reinforce and pave the way for greater movement in the other. Thus it is vital to sustain the movement toward arms control. Arms control issues can inflame as well as modulate East-West tensions. Disputes over "who won the most" or compliance could easily interrupt the movement toward arms control.

Many small and large steps are available to continue the momentum toward limiting superpower arsenals. The easiest and most useful are unilateral, beginning with self-restraint. Moscow and Washington can simply avoid behaviors and deployments provocative to the other side. Soviet and U.S. military planners can freeze or reduce spending and production, even without formal agreements.

Another step would be implementing the 1987 INF (intermediate-range nuclear forces) treaty and other accords so as to develop trust and verification experience. The USSR and the United States can also lower the permitted threshold of underground nuclear tests or, more radically, ban all nuclear tests. They can further develop confidence-building measures to develop security against surprise attack. They can make the Nuclear Risk Reduction Centers and other mechanisms for communication and data exchange useful to both sides. They can tighten the nonproliferation treaty with significant rewards and sanctions, and they can reaffirm traditional restraints on ballistic missile defenses.

More difficult but still feasible, Moscow and Washington could avoid weapons modernization mocking the INF treaty. They could shift military deployments, at least in Europe, toward "defensive defense" and away from any kind of offensive planning. They could continue efforts not only to reduce but to eliminate all chemical and biological weapons worldwide. Soviet and U.S. strategic arsenals could be cut by one-half or even three-fourths and a credible "nuclear umbrella" still be retained. Moscow and Washington should engage the other nuclear-weapons states in strategic arms limitations.

As East-West trust increases, worries about loopholes, asymmetries, and breakthroughs may recede. But so long as Moscow and Washington act upon worst-case assumptions about the other side, troublesome questions will obstruct arms control.

Both sides should avoid making arms control more difficult, for example, by proliferating cruise missiles. Valid uses can be conceived for such weapons—especially with conventional warheads—but the long-term problems they portend outweigh their near-term utility. Such deployments also go against the spirit of the INF and other accords of recent years. Given the opportunities of the new détente, the Pentagon and its Soviet counterpart should not conduct business as usual—deploying whatever technology can produce and money procure. Instead they should study how to promote their country's security without adding to the other's insecurity. Self-restraint is needed until mutual restraint becomes negotiable.

The Soviet-U.S. security relationship will probably benefit from positive experiences in less politically sensitive exchanges in commerce, science, and culture. But contacts at any level can lead to misunderstanding or contempt as well as to understanding and affection. In low politics as in high, seeking too much and going too fast could rekindle rather than relax tensions.

## TOWARD "COMPLEX INTERDEPENDENCE"

An optimal response to global problems would be for Moscow and Washington to go beyond moderating their conflicts to building a relationship of "complex interdependence." This would require the emergence of three characteristics:

1. Multiple channels connect Soviet and American societies—interstate, transgovernmental, and transnational; they include not only formal foreign office connections but also informal ties between governmental elites and working relationships between nongovernmental elites in banking, commerce, and science.
2. The agenda of interstate relationships consists of multiple issues not arranged in a clear or consistent hierarchy.
3. Military force and its threat play a declining role in the policies of both countries—at least toward each other.[16]

In contrast to the more familiar world of power politics, the actors linked in complex interdependence do not pursue military security as their dominant goal. Instead, goals vary by issue area. The emergence of transgovernmental politics makes goals difficult to define; transnational actors increasingly pursue their own aims. Actors still bargain and make tradeoffs among issues, but power resources specific to issue areas will be most relevant. International regimes and organizations help to set agendas and induce coalition-formation.[17]

What forces then could transform the Soviet-U.S. relationship from diffidence to complex interdependence?[18]

## Domestic Politics and Economics

"Convergence" of the two countries' economic and political systems is not likely—nor is it necessary or sufficient for them to cooperate in a system of complex interdependence. Convergence is unlikely because of profound differences in the way that each society has been formed and operates. Russian life has been formed by fiat from above; American, by forces rising from below. Even in the late 1980s, *perestroika* and *demokratizatsiia* were initiated and regulated from the Kremlin. While market forces come to play a greater role in Soviet economic life, the CPSU will attempt to maintain state ownership of the means of production; even if the U.S. government does more to promote "industrial competitiveness," most American factories and land will remain privately owned. Each society will adapt and evolve while resisting fundamental or revolutionary change. Parallel evolution of Russia and America is more likely than deep political-economic convergence.[19]

Democracy is probably not a precondition for complex interdependence. Indeed, democracy has its own dangers—illustrated by the frequent competition between America's two major parties to show which is the more patriotic and anticommunist. If a Russian "Patriots' Party" gained power, it might well move to close off the country from Western influences, launch pogroms against Jews and other minorities, and possibly expand abroad to purify others from Western or Asiatic vandalism.

Still, the quality of domestic life certainly has some impact on a country's external behavior. Can a society at war with itself cooperate harmoniously with others? Perhaps a despotism could coexist in a cold peace with another society, but it could not tolerate the varied contacts needed for complex interdependence. Indeed, a model for such relationships was sketched by Immanuel Kant in his essay *On Perpetual Peace*. He argued that national particularism can best be overcome by the growth of representative government, commerce, a common culture, and international law. Where "the consent of the citizenry is required . . . to determine whether there will be war," the citizens will hesitate before entering "so risky a game." A despotic ruler, on the other hand, can "blithely" declare war and leave it to his diplomats to justify the action. The "*spirit of trade*," Kant added, "cannot coexist with war." And while language and religion divide people, gradual progress toward agreement on common principles will be conducive to peace. As community prevails, "a transgression in *one* place in the world is felt *everywhere*. . . ." Since free governments will not tolerate any government over them, they will have to accommodate themsevles to an enlarged body of international law that "will finally include all the people of the earth."[20]

The power of Kant's vision is suggested by the fact that, in the almost 200 years since he wrote, there has been virtually no war between liberal republics.[21] There is little prospect that the USSR will become a liberal republic in this century. The country lurched massively toward self-rule in 1989–90, but strong elements of autocracy remained; the habits of toleration and moderation, essential for self-government, remained alien to most Soviets; and there was little consensus. Instead, Russians tended to divide between nationalist or Communist conservatives and radical liberals, while the USSR as a whole polarized into those favoring a "strong center" and those wishing autonomy for each constituent people. Gorbachev in 1990 had himself elected *president*—not by a popular vote but by the Supreme Soviet, many of whose members had been selected by all-union organizations such as the Communist Party and the Academy of Sciences. Critics suggested that the entire electoral process worked out in 1989 was a sham.[22]

The most positive factor for the long run was that education and *glasnost* were producing a more participant personality in Soviet politics, a person with greater "empathy"—the ability to evaluate distant objects and to incorporate distant values in oneself.[23] These trends reflect and contribute to a more cosmopolitan upbringing; more attention to the media; the growth of "middle-class," urban values; expanded personal freedom; and a greater capacity and desire for self-rule.

As the CPSU monopoly on privileged information and decision making is broken, as views other than the ruling Politburo's come to shape state action, the result should be a less aggressive stance in foreign affairs. As more Soviet budget data are released, popular pressures mount to cut defense spending.

Americans have learned to fear powerful dictators—seeing in each the image of Hitler. If the USSR is not ruled by a dictator, if the ruling Party itself provides a choice for the Soviet people, this would probably reduce American apprehensions. Even if most Soviet factories remain publicly owned, the less anti-capitalist zeal in Russia, the less anti-Communist ardor in America. If the United States moves closer to Kant's ideal republic—consent of all the governed, a spirit of trade, a deeper participation in world culture, more dedication to law—this would also enhance the conditions needed for complex interdependence.

Convergence of values is more likely than convergence of political and economic systems. Even before *glasnost* urbanization and education were tilting the values of Soviet citizens (at least those living in the western and northern regions) toward those of contemporary Westerners. The new openness to outside influences and freedom from internal repression have stimulated the embrace of religion, rock music, political pluralism, avant-garde art, technological fetishism, individualism, and materialism. Even pacifism, ecologism, and national self-determination are asserting themselves openly from Riga to Yerevan. The white three-fourths of the Soviet population must learn to coexist with a rising tide of Muslim and other minority values, just as white Americans have had to adjust to assertions of black, Hispanic, Native American, and now Asian power.

If such trends continue, the two societies may feel that what binds them is more important than what divides them. The experience of sharing and benefiting from interdependence should reduce the nativist tendencies toward xenophobia, black-and-white images of others, and dogmatism. The ultimate attitudinal change conducive to peaceful participation in complex interdependence would be based on a paradigm change like those suggested in Gorbachev's new thinking and in the notion of "value creating" (as opposed to "value claiming," the usual zero-sum approach to power politics).[24] It would place the values of mankind above those of nation, race, class, or creed; assert our collective responsibility to manage the biosphere in ways that enhance—not destroy—life; act on the understanding that the security of each depends on the security of all; and limit military force to last resort self-defense. Mutual aid rather than mutually assured destruction would be the underlying principle.[25]

To reach and maintain complex interdependence, it is essential that each society hold together and function so it contributes to and gains from ties with the other side. If *perestroika* does not halt the USSR's economic decline, nativist fears of foreign influences may revive. Economic collapse could evoke policy extremes such as autarky or aggression. The temptation to lash out at foreign devils may increase.[26] The new rulers may be tempted to play their last trump—military power.

## The World System

Many other great power reconciliations in the past have been spurred by a common enemy. The USSR and America once joined forces against Nazism, but no such threat looms in the foreseeable future. Concern over a rogue Third World government or terrorism does not equate to a shared danger from the Third Reich. But environmental threats are nearly palpable; while they can be pushed off today's agenda, they must surely be faced tomorrow.

Soviet and U.S. cooperation in complex interdependence is possible whether the world system is bipolar, multipolar, supranational, or even "unit-veto" (where many nations exercise a nuclear threat).[27] What is important is that the role of military force recede—at least between the USSR and United States—and that their societies link up through many channels and create values together. It is conceivable that this situation could develop in the context of a bipolar condominium: the superpowers cooperate and use sufficient force to keep others in line. It is less feasible in a situation where one country acquires "unipolar" dominion over all rivals—an unlikely development in any case.

The most feasible scenario for movement toward complex interdependence is that the USSR joins what is now the "Trilateral World" of North America, Europe, and Japan. Nothing in the cards predicts a diminution of European or Japanese material power or, on the other hand, a significant increase in their will for military power. Increasingly the "Trilateral" bloc understands its responsibility for and vulnerability to the Third World. Accordingly, North-South ties deepen. If the USSR over time "joins the North," then East-West tensions should decline while ties of shared experience and value creation mount.

Developments in the Third World and the Pacific Rim are more problematic than in Europe and North America. Will a resurgent China, Japan, India, or Pakistan disrupt the global trend toward cooperation amid diversity? If China retains its nuclear arsenal, will not India or Japan eventually insist on parity? And will not Pakistan or Taiwan some day do the same? So long as Israeli-Arab tensions fester, and Israel maintains some kind of nuclear threat, will not one of its neighbors eventually acquire a "Muslim" bomb? Such prospects *could* stimulate cooperation between Moscow and Washington, but they could also break its back, magnifying Soviet-U.S. tensions just as the Indochina wars added to Chinese-Soviet differences from the 1960s through the 1980s.

Not every local dispute need disrupt Soviet-U.S. cooperation. Even in the 1980s, the Iran-Iraq war raged on, threatening some interests of each superpower but barely casting a shadow over the Gorbachev-Reagan meetings and accords. Ideally the superpowers would combine forces to prevent or quickly settle such disputes, but if that is impossible, they should deal with the disputes in ways that promise no one-sided gain for either Moscow or Washington.

Such problems could be better dealt with by a strengthened United Nations in which all centers of power found representation—from Buenos Aires and Brasilia to New Delhi and Tokyo. The more each country feels a stake in the global system of peaceful settlement and collective security, the less it would be tempted to claim its narrow goals in defiance of the majority.

A network of global economic security would be even more difficult to create, but a sense of movement in that direction would help ameliorate East-West-South tensions. The USSR must, as Gorbachev and his advisers suggest, join the General Agreement on Tariffs and Trade (GATT); make the ruble convertible; and take part in the International Monetary Fund and other institutions of world commerce. The Soviets should join the West in cooperative ventures aimed at creating values for East, West, and South. The most promising vehicles for such cooperation are probably the specialized agencies and regional commissions of the United Nations.

Despite much fanfare about joining in world trade, the USSR will have to overcome many self-imposed as well as external barriers. The country has little capital to invest overseas. Its "multinational" enterprises have been small and basically limited to trading rather than to production. They have operated under the cloud of ideological enmity toward international monopolies. Because the Soviet economy has not been export-driven like the economies of Japan and Korea, there has been little imperative to export manufactured goods in return for raw materials. Communist conservatism and risk-averse Soviet managers will be tempted to stick with familiar ways rather than wager their success in highly competitive world markets.[28] *Prestroika* may break this pattern, for it encourages individual Soviet ministries, firms, and other institutions to deal directly with counterparts abroad.

### Bilateral Issues

Complex interdependence requires extensive Soviet-U.S. interaction in many spheres. Since the early 1970s there has been a broad movement toward the establishment of informal as well as formal ties between Russia and America. Since 1986–87 this movement has increased, promising to create many formal and informal ties between governmental and nongovernmental elites as well as ordinary citizens. Thus, the joint statement issued after the Moscow summit, May 29–June 2, 1988, declared both governments' intention to "intensify" bilateral ties in "transportation science and technology; maritime search and rescue; operational coordination between Soviet and U.S. radionavigation systems in the Northern Pacific and Bering Sea; and mutual fisheries relations." Gorbachev and Reagan welcomed a new accord on civilian nuclear reactor safety under the bilateral agreement on peaceful uses of atomic energy. They instructed their representatives to press ahead to achieve accords on maritime shipping, the Soviet-U.S. maritime boundary, basic scientific research, and emergency pollution clean-up in the Bering and Chukchi seas. They welcomed the start of bilateral discussions on ways to combat narcotic trafficking and consultations on the law of the sea and other areas of mutual interest in the field of law.

A rough content analysis of the long joint statement shows just over four full newspaper columns given to high politics—mostly arms control, with a paragraph on regional issues such as the Horn of Africa and Afghanistan; four columns to cultural and scientific exchanges; one paragraph to human rights and one to trade—the hardest nuts to crack.[29] Thus, high and low politics got roughly equal treatment in the communiqué. Except for INF and Afghanistan, however, high politics in the statement was mostly aspiration; in culture and science, on the other hand, much fruitful progress had already been made and much more was likely. The many projects approved in both domains would produce many contacts for years between officials and other citizens of both countries.

The tendency of low politics to outweigh high security interests was even stronger at the Bush-Gorbachev meeting in May–June 1990. Of twenty-one agreements or joint statements, five dealt with military security: chemical weapons, nuclear testing, European force reductions, nuclear nonproliferation, and strategic arms controls; fourteen dealt with issues of comparatively low political saliency—from grain sales to university student exchanges to a commercial treaty. Two had elements of both high and low security: an accord on the Soviet-U.S. boundary in the northern Pacific and an agreement to supply Ethiopia with food and to work for peace there. On the most delicate issue—strategic offensive arms—the two sides could only issue a joint statement, because serious disagreements still prevented a treaty. But they could "paper over" that impasse with accords to stop drug trafficking, to establish an International Park in the Bering Strait, and to conduct more oceanographic studies.[30]

In a setting of complex interdependence, when the USSR and United States disagree on some issue, bargaining will still take place—but with arms relegated far to the background.[31] Between Ottawa and Washington the threat of coercive power against each other's government is minimal, but the Canadian Navy often uses force against errant U.S. fishermen. As the Canadian-U.S. case also shows, each side will exploit aspects of economic interdependence and transnational actors to gain bargaining leverage.[32]

Trade between Russia and America has always been low relative to each country's GNP and relative to its trade with other countries. Détente and moderation of tensions should lead to an expansion of Soviet-U.S. trade, but it may never reach high levels because the USSR has little to sell to the United States except petroleum. It is not clear that trade would increase a great deal if the Coordinating Committee on Multilateral Export Controls (CoCom) reduced barriers to high-tech exports or if Washington granted Soviet goods most-favored-nation treatment. Even if the Soviet economy modernizes and quality levels increase, the Kremlin may find its natural trading partners elsewhere. The better prospect for material ties is through joint ventures in which Americans and American firms work directly with their Soviet counterparts. The number of Western-Soviet joint ventures shot up dramatically in the late 1980s.[33]

The demands of the scientific-technological revolution summon the complementary strengths of both societies: to preserve and enhance our common habitat and its biosphere; to create cheap, clean, and abundant energy; to feed, house, and care for a much expanded world population living on dwindling space; and to explore the mysteries inside the earth and of outer space together. While the Americans lead in computers and many other essential tools, Soviets bring valuable assets to such work too, such as strength in pure mathematics. Many but not all Americans taking part in East-West studies in recent decades report that they gained as well as contributed.[34] As the USSR liberalizes and becomes more computerized, the quality of Soviet contributions is likely to rise.

The scientific-technological revolution (STR) also provides a vehicle by which the USSR and Eastern Europe can simply join the efforts already uniting North America, Europe, and Japan and—albeit on a lesser scale—

China, India, Israel, and some South American countries. Good science is open and international, thriving on constructive cross-fertilization. Secrets are hard to maintain in this milieu. Military security issues will become less inhibiting if the major countries share a complex interdependence.

Soviet civilian specialists on strategic affairs argue that there is no threat to the USSR from the West; that even a united Germany would not gravitate toward militarism because its prosperity and influence lie in exploiting the STR and international trade; that the nuclear arsenals of France and Britain are maintained more for prestige than because of fear or hostility toward the USSR. Low arms expenditures have benefited Japan and, to a lesser degree, Germany; Soviet analysts want their country to move in similar directions. The Kremlin's achievement of parity with the United States has helped devaluate the utility of nuclear arms, but other countries have gained from this process—not the Soviet Union (or the United States).[35]

Political and economic autonomy for the Baltic states could create a transmission belt linking Russia to what Gorbachev says is its "European home." If Eastern European states and even Russia's border republics become nonaligned, demilitarized, pluralistic market economies, they could ease Russia's struggle to share in the dynamism of the First World.

What about that ultimate guarantee of security and insecurity—deterrence? The place of military force has declined in superpower relations due to risks of escalation and the difficulty of conceiving a winning strategy. Already in 1972 both countries agreed to forswear strategic defenses and live hostage to each other's restraint. But both sides have also recognized that deterrence can fail and so have sought other steps—technical and political—to reduce the danger of deliberate or inadvertent attack.

Despite the cosmopolitanizing and peaceful tendencies posited in the scenario for Soviet-U.S. complex interdependence, it seems unrealistic to advocate absolute nuclear disarmament even for A.D. 2000 or 2020. Neither superpower would be advised to eliminate all nuclear arms. They should reduce but not eliminate their arsenals, keeping them at a sufficiently high level so that cheating—from any quarter—would convey no serious advantage to a potential aggressor. An example of the kind of reductions that might provide deterrence at lower but still stable levels of destructive power might be: for the United States and the USSR, a dyad of one thousand missiles with one warhead; a force one-third to one-half this size for China and for Britain and France (or Europe). The aim of such an arrangement would be to leave all parties better off and no party worse off than it would be absent the pact.

The size and composition of the nuclear umbrella, however, is crucial. Eliminating all stationary land-based missiles would remove a major source of vulnerability and end arguments about needing ABM defenses to shield land-based missiles. But each party must feel that it possesses an invulnerable deterrent capable of dissuading attack from any quarter or quarters. Some Soviet specialists have suggested that the USSR and the United States could get by with a force of two hundred to four hundred invulnerable weapons. (A Soviet general running for the Congress of People's Deputies proposed fifty to seventy!)[36] They downplayed the dangers of cheating so long as the remaining weapons are truly invulnerable; they minimized any problem for the USSR in having to live with a smaller number of weapons than its potential adversaries. Movement to a minimum deterrent, of course, requires some assurance that nuclear weapons are not spreading to additional countries. Soviet specialists are quite aware of the special dangers posed by a Khomeini or Qaddafi armed with some kind of mass destruction terror weapon. This is one reason that they push for treaties to ban chemical and bacteriological weapons with extensive and intensive international verification procedures.

Assuming that East-West-South cooperation becomes strong and stable, some Soviet scholars contemplate transferring the nuclear umbrella from individual nations to the United Nations. This idea probably strikes most Western analysts as impracticable, because it makes excessive demands on international trust. After all, many states (including the USSR and India) have difficulty maintaining "international" peace even within their own borders. Still, that serious scholars consider such scenarios indicates the extent to which they believe military force has lost its meaning in world affairs.

## PROSPECTS FOR TRANSFORMATION

To progress from détente through moderated tensions toward complex interdependence, the United States and the USSR must progress on many fronts, capitalizing on each opportunity that emerges and avoiding the pitfalls and detours that lead back toward cold war and confrontation. They can utilize "graduated reciprocation in tension reduction" (GRIT) and "tit-for-tat" strategies and promote détente and moderate tensions; to move beyond that stage to transform their relationship will take an unprecedented steadiness and scope of vision, one broadly shared within each society and passed on from one generation to another.[37] Cooperation in areas of high and low political saliency will take them toward strategic and functional interdependence.

Is such a transformation possible? An analogous change overtook Europe in less than two generations. The European revolution had to overcome a legacy of hate and bloodshed that is absent in American-Soviet relations. Europe's transformation was aided by a widely shared fear of Soviet Communist dominion and by a need for postwar reconstruction. Even though both pressures have receded, European unification continues. The threat of nuclear or ecological catastrophe facing the United States and the USSR is more pressing (but less apparent) than the problems facing Europe in the late 1940s. Still, today's "world problematique"—from ozone depletion to drought—makes headlines from New Delhi to Cape Town. Chernobyl has made Soviet citizens especially wary of nuclear power; but they are joined by increasing numbers of Ohioans and other Americans worried about nuclear pollution in their own backyards.

Global problems—hunger and many others—bring us back to immediate security issues. The famines threatening Africa and other parts of the world are among the problems too complex to be solved by any one country. More attention to such issues could take the superpowers' attentions away from potential space wars and back to earth, where the challenges of feeding, housing, and educating the globe's billions demand a synthesis of the best insights from Novosibirsk to Palo Alto to Ibadan and Hyderabad, and where none of us stands immune to the quirks of nature which, combined with those of mankind, can suddenly transform abundance to shortfall.

The "value-creating" approach to hard decisions helps bridge the gap between political realism and utopianism.[38] It suggests how narrow self-interest may be enhanced through mutual gain strategies with others. The approach is no panacea and very difficult to apply in practice. But it offers a more useful takeoff point than the zero-sum assumptions of Communist dogmatists and Western "realists" or the "everybody wins" school of optimistic idealists.

## Notes

1. See Richard W. Stevenson, *The Rise and Fall of Détente* (Urbana: University of Illinois Press, 1985); Lincoln P. Bloomfield, Walter C. Clemens, Jr., Franklyn Griffiths, *Khruschev and the Arms Race: Soviet Interests in Arms Control and Disarmament, 1954–1964* (Cambridge, MA.: The M.I.T. Press, 1966).

2. For a systematic effort to learn from the past, see Alexander L. George, Philip J. Farley, Alexander Dallin, eds., *U.S.-Soviet Security Cooperation: Achievements, Failures, Lessons* (New York: Oxford University Press, 1988); also Joseph S. Nye, Jr., "Nuclear Learning and U.S.-Soviet Security Regimes," *International Organization*, XLI, No. 3 (Summer 1987), pp. 371–402.

3. Marshall D. Shulman, "The Superpowers: Dance of the Dinosaurs," *Foreign Affairs*, Vol. 66, No. 3 (1987/88), pp. 494–515.

4. See the recent upsurge of writings on the decline of empires by Mancur Olson and others; for some recent works, see Paul Kennedy, "Can the U.S. Remain Number One?" *New York Review of Books*, XXXVI, No. 4 (March 16, 1989), pp. 36–42; for a critique of "The Persistent Myth of Lost Hegemony," see Susan Strange in *International Organization*, XIL, No. 4 (Autumn 1987), pp. 551–74; also Walter C. Clemens, Jr., "The Superpowers and the Third World: Aborted Ideals and Wasted Assets," in C. W. Kegley and P. J. McGowan, eds., *Sage International Yearbooks in Foreign Policy Studies*, Vol. VII: *Foreign Policy: USA/USSR* (Beverly Hills, CA.: Sage, 1982), pp. 111–35.

5. See Kurt M. Campbell, "Prospects and Consequences of Soviet Decline," in Joseph S. Nye, Jr., Graham T. Allison, Albert Carnesale, eds., *Fateful Visions: Avoiding Nuclear Catastrophe* (Cambridge, MA: Ballinger, 1988), pp. 153–70; Henry S. Rowen and Charles Wolf, Jr., eds., *The Future of the Soviet Empire* (New York: St. Martin's, 1988).

6. Joseph S. Nye, Jr., *Bound to Lead: The Changing Nature of American Power* (New York: Basic Books, 1990).

7. For documentation on statements by Gorbachev and other "new thinkers," see Walter C. Clemens, Jr., *Can Russia Change? The USSR Confronts Global Interdependence* (Boston: Unwin Hyman, 1990), esp. Chap. 7. For an accessible summary, see Mikhail S. Gorbachev, *Perestroika: New Thinking for Our Country and the World* (New York: Harper & Row, 1987). Anthologies of Gorbachev's speeches have been published in New York by Richardson, Steirman & Black and as *Izbrannye rechi i stat'y* in Moscow by Politizdat.

8. For a guide to reading on the USSR today, see Walter C. Clemens, Jr., in *Christianity and Crisis*, 50, 8 (May 28, 1990), pp. 177–78.

9. On Soviet actions to implement the new thinking, see Clemens, *Can Russia Change?*, esp. Chap. 8.

10. See "Gorbachev's Economic Program: Problems Emerge," A Report by the Central Intelligence Agency and the Defense Intelligence Agency to the Subcommittee on National Security Economics, Joint Economic Committee, U.S. Congress, April 13, 1988, Tables 1 and 3. Trade with the developed countries declined in 1985–87 relative to the previous three years. See Table 8. The conclusions of Soviet economist Leonid I. Abalkin were no less dismal than those of the CIA-DIA report. He told the 1988 Party Conference that, despite some positive shifts in the Soviet economy, the first two years of *perestroika* had achieved "no radical breakthrough" and the economy "still remains in a stage of stagnation." National income in the last two years grew at a slower pace than during the stagnation years. Targets for resource savings were not met; indeed, this index performed worse than during the stagnation years. The gap between Soviet science and technology and world levels was continuing to expand, assuming "ominous proportions." Soviet decision makers were continuing to err in favoring quantity over quality, Abalkin charged.

Health Minister Yevgenii I. Chazov outlined the calamitous state of the country's public health record, but noted some improvement in the last two years. For excerpts from these and other statements at the conference, see *New York Times*, July 1, 1988, p. A6.

11. On mood changes in the United States, see Arthur M. Schlesinger, Jr., *The Cycles of American History* (Boston: Houghton Mifflin, 1986). See also J. David Singer and Thomas Cusak, "Periodicity, Inexorability, and Steersmanship in International War," in Richard L. Merritt and Bruce M. Russett, eds., *From National Development to Global Community: Essays in Honor of Karl W. Deutsch* (London: George Allen & Unwin, 1981), pp. 404–22.

12. Oran R. Young, "International Regimes: Problems of Concept Formation," *World Politics*, XXXII, No. 3 (April 1980), pp. 331–56.

13. In 1976–79 the USSR cast two vetoes at the UN Security Council; the U.S., nine. In 1980–85 the USSR, four; the U.S., twenty-five. In 1986–88 the USSR, none; the U.S., thirteen. Tallies from Kevin J. Dunn, "Has Soviet Voting Practice Changed Since Gorbachev?," Boston University term paper, 1988. On Gorbachev's proposals for the United Nations, see Clemens, *Can Russia Change?*, pp. 189–92.

14. The needs and some of the solutions are outlined in the yearly *State of the World* reports by Lester R. Brown et al. of the Worldwatch Institute in Washington, D.C. (1988 and 1989 editions published in New York: W.W. Norton).

15. "Low politics" usually includes issues of trade, environmental protection, and scientific and cultural exchange. "High politics" includes war, peace, and other sensitive issues directly affecting national security. The distinction sometimes blurs in practice, as in "human rights" disputes. For Soviet policies in both domains in the late 1970s and early 1980s, see Clemens, *Can Russia Change?*, Chaps. 4–5.

16. See Robert O. Keohane and Joseph S. Nye, Jr., *Power and Interdependence*, 2d ed. (Glenview, IL and Boston: Scott, Foresman/Little, Brown, 1989), Chap. 2.

17. Ibid., Chaps. 3–7.

18. See also Sean M. Lynn-Jones and Stephen R. Rock, "From Confrontation to Cooperation," in *Fateful Visions*, pp. 111–32 at 126.

19. Zbigniew Brzezinski and Samuel P. Huntington, *Political Power: USA/USSR* (New York: Viking, 1964); for an update, see Zbigniew Brzezinski, *The Grand Failure: The Birth and Death of Communism in the Twentieth Century* (New York: Charles Scribner, 1989).

20. Immanuel Kant, *Perpetual Peace and Other Essays* (Indianapolis: Hackett, 1983), pp. 107–43. Emphasis in the original. Kant praises "republics" but condemns "democracies." He treats all "democracy" as "pure democracy" in which there is no check on the ruler; hence, democracy is another form of despotism.

21. See editors' "Conclusion" in *Fateful Visions*, pp. 215–16.

22. See "An Interview with Andrei Sakharov", *The New York Review of Books*, XXXVI, No. 3 (March 2, 1989), pp. 6, 7.

23. See Daniel Lerner, *The Passing of Traditional Society* (New York: The Free Press, 1958), pp. 47 ff.

24. See David A. Lax and James K. Sebenius, *The Manager as Negotiator: Bargaining for Cooperation and Cooperative Gain* (New York: Free Press, 1986).

25. On mutual aid versus the "survival of the fittest," see Petr Kropotkin, *Mutual Aid* (London, 1902; Boston: Porter Sargent, 1976).

26. The difficulty in countering simplistic chauvinism is illustrated by long-time foreign minister Andrei A. Gromyko's account of how his own "patriotism" began to be formed at birth. See his *Pamiatnoe* (2 vols.; Moscow: Politizdat, 1988), I, 31–35. Anti-Americanism also began early. Gromyko's father used to explain how "America is richer than others . . . because Americans take with their own hands the wealth that belongs to others. Theodore Roosevelt was a crafty president"—to which a neighbor added: "Crafty and intelligent." Ibid., I, 17.

27. See Morton A. Kaplan, *System and Process in International Politics* (New York: John Wiley, 1957), pp. 50–51.

28. Geoffrey Hamilton, "Conclusions," in his edited work, *Red Multinationals or Red Herrings?* (New York: St. Martin's, 1986), pp. 192–93; a more positive appraisal is Carl H. McMillan, *Multinationals from the Second World: Growth of Foreign Investment by Soviet and East European Enterprises* (New York: St. Martin's, 1987).

29. Both governments also pledged support for intensified exchanges in culture and science including "Environmental Protection, Medical Science and Public Health, Artificial Heart Research and Development, Agriculture, and Studies of the World Ocean. . . ." They welcomed the beginning of work on "a conceptual design of an International Thermonuclear Experimental Reactor (ITER)" under IAEA auspices; the imminent institutionalization of the COSPAS/SAR-SAT space-based, life-saving global search and rescue system; and the WHO/UNICEF program to reduce preventable childhood death.

Reagan and Gorbachev endorsed bilateral and multilateral cooperation with respect to environmental protection including conservation of stratospheric ozone and a possible global warming trend. They agreed to expand civil space cooperation by exchanging flight opportunities for scientific instruments and exchanging results of independent national studies of future unmanned solar missions. They welcomed cooperation in the Arctic and Antarctic. They endorsed joint ventures, expanded trade, and expanded relations between Aeroflot and Pan American Airlines. Text of joint statement in Supplement to *Moscow News*, No. 24 (1988), pp. 1–4; also in *Pravda*, June 2, 1988.

30. Releases by Office of the Press Secretary, The White House, late May and early June, 1990. See reportage by Andrew Rosenthal, *New York Times*, June 2 and 4, 1990; Walter S. Mossberg, *Wall Street Journal*, June 8, 1990; and Aleksandr Pulpainskii, *Novoe Vremia*, No. 23 (June 1, 1990), pp. 6–7.

31. For periodic updates on Soviet-U.S. exchanges, see *Surviving Together* (Washington, D.C.: Friends Committee on National Legislation and the Institute for Soviet-American Relations).

32. Keohane and Nye, *Power and Interdependence*, Chap. 7.

33. For a listing of 155 joint Soviet-foreign ventures, see *Interflo*, October 1988 and January 1989; the text of a Council of Ministers Resolution "On Further Developing the Foreign Economic Activity of State, Cooperative, and Other Public Enterprises, Associations, and Organizations" is quoted in the January 1989 *Interflo*, taken from *Ekonomicheskaia gazeta*, No. 52, December 1988 and *Izvestiia*, December 10, 1988.

34. On the views of U.S. participants in the International Institute for Applied Systems Analysis located near Vienna, see letters on file at the American Academy of Arts and Sciences, Cambridge, MA; for analysis of earlier surveys, see Walter C. Clemens, Jr., *The USSR and Global Interdependence: Alternative Futures* (Washington, D.C.: American Enterprise Institute, 1978), pp. 88–99.

35. This complaint is voiced in N. Dolgopolova and A. Kokoshin, "Chemu uchat sud'by velikikh derzhav?" *Kommunist*, No. 17 (November 1988), pp. 115–21 at 120–21. Similar views were expressed by other Soviet scholars interviewed in 1988–89. See Walter C. Clemens, Jr., "Inside Gorbachev's Think Tank," *World Monitor*, II, No. 2 (August 1989), pp. 28–36.

36. Lt. General Dmitrii Volkogonov in *Novoe Vremia*, No. 6 (February 3, 1989), p. 23.

37. On GRIT, see Charles E. Osgood, *An Alternative to War or Surrender* (Urbana, IL: University of Illinois Press, 1962); on tit-for-tat, see Robert Axelrod, *The Evolution of Cooperation* (New York: Basic Books, 1984).

38. See Lax and Sebenius, *Manager as Negotiator;* also, similar ideas expressed by essayists in *Kommunist* in the late 1980s. See, e.g., N. Moiseev, "V. I. Vernadskii i estestvennonauchnaia traditsiia," *Kommunist*, No. 2 (January 1988), pp. 72–81 and the report "Gumanisticheskii vektor nauki," *Kommunist*, No. 14 (September 1987), pp. 74–83.

# 3 / The Future of Nuclear Deterrence

KOSTA TSIPIS

## INTRODUCTION

The concept of deterrence transcends its current usage, which almost always refers to the state of mutual nuclear deterrence between the United States and the Soviet Union. As commonly used today, deterrence refers to the process of convincing a potential enemy, by the threat of nuclear attack, that it is better off not initiating a nuclear attack on you, or your allies.[1] In actuality, deterrence encompasses behavior that is much more common than we usually think. But in all cases, deterrence is based on the principle of self-interest and self-regulation. Examples of deterrence in everyday life that display these traits are legion: I do not drive through a red light, even though I am not prevented physically from doing so, because of the potential harm that such an act may visit upon me, either in the form of physical injury caused by a collision, or of a fine from the lurking police officer. Neither do I buy a bottle of Mouton Rothschild 1968 wine at my vintner's, even though I may have enough money with me, because I consider the cost too high given the level of satisfaction I may anticipate from drinking it and the state of my finances. In all cases, it is my own decision; it is *self-regulation* based on a considered sense of self-interest that, given the cost in each case, deters me from acting in a way that would be highly desirable if the cost were absent.

Mutual deterrence is a mere extension of the principle of self-regulation based on self-interest to a situation involving two parties, each depending on the self-interest of the other to avoid undesirably costly behavior: I drive on the right side of the road and I depend on the driver coming in the opposite direction to do the same in order to avoid a costly collision; the other driver depends on me to do the same for the same reason. Neither of us is physically prevented from driving on the left, but we are both deterred from doing so from self-interest, which determines our behavior—in this case, the way we drive. I also drive on the right in order to place upon the other driver the risk of causing a collision by driving irregularly; my actions place the responsibility of avoiding an accident on the other driver (the situation is, of course, *symmetrical*).

Nuclear deterrence between the United States and Soviet Union is a special case of mutual deterrence. Both countries have made military arrangements so that if one attacks the other, the resulting destruction will be symmetrical in extent and unacceptable in size. These arrangements make such symmetrical destruction almost automatic once one side attacks, in order to enhance their deterring properties. This very *inescapability* of mutual symmetric destruction causes both sides to avoid attacking the other out of self-interest. The savagery of war destruction is avoided by self-regulation, not from direct coercion, which in turn emanates from contemplation of the costs such savagery would impose upon its perpetrator. Thus, the credibility of nuclear deterrence depends on three factors:

1. The effectiveness and invulnerability to preemptive attack of at least a fraction of the nuclear arsenal on each side.
2. The willingness, *as perceived by the other side,* of a nation to use this nuclear arsenal in assured retaliation for an aggressive act— "deterrence is in the eye of the beholder."
3. The *acts* that the threat of retaliation is supposed to deter. Hence, the threat to use our nuclear arsenal in retaliation if the Soviet Union attacks our cities is much more credible than the threat to do so if the Soviets march into the northeastern corner of Turkey.

Given these conceptual underpinnings, both the debate and implementation of nuclear deterrence have revolved around three issues: first, what is an unacceptable cost measured in terms of destroyed socioeconomic capital for either of the two sides; second, how much and what kind of preparation is needed to impose this cost unfailingly; and third, how is the symmetrical character of this cost maintained under all circumstances. The answer to these questions has been expressed in terms of nuclear force structures, and thus the concept of deterrence is analyzed in terms of the number, properties, and command-and-control preparations of nuclear weapons arsenals on each side. For example, the Pentagon has insisted that continuous upgrading of the accuracy of our intercontinental ballistic missiles is essential for the credibility of our deterrent capabilities. Similarly, both the SALT and the START negotiations have sought equivalent limits on the strategic arsenals of both the United States and the Soviet Union, driven by the conviction that numerical asymmetry can erode the deterring capability of arsenals.

But the debate over deterrence is not devoid of parochial factors that have little to do with the deterring credibility of the U.S. or Soviet nuclear arsenals. The structure of the nuclear arsenal of the United States, and in all probability of the Soviet Union as well, has evolved in many instances by the desire of the military services to acquire strategic nuclear weapons for reasons that have little to do with deterrence. For example, the U.S. Navy has acquired consecutive generations of increasingly more accurate submarine-launched ballistic missiles (SLBMs) because it wishes to compete successfully with the Air Force for certain nuclear strategic missions that technology made available first to the Air Force's land-based ballistic missiles. In the Soviet Union, four different missile design bureaus kept cranking out consecutive generations of ever bigger and more accurate land-based ballistic missiles; their competition had hardly anything to do with the credibility of the Soviet nuclear deterrent.

As a consequence, the nuclear arsenals that emerged on both sides often reflect not the logical requirements for a secure deterrent force, but rather the desire of the military on both sides to pursue an escalating arms race and the acquisition of new, increasingly capable weapons systems. Such essentially parochial motives were often couched in arcane syllogisms regarding what constitutes "credible deterrence." For example, to justify the acquisition of increasingly accurate ballistic missiles made available by technological advances, U.S. officials promoted the notion that the only thing that would deter a Soviet surprise attack against the United States would be to threaten their ballistic missiles since, it was claimed, the Soviets valued their ballistic missiles more than their cities and industrial infrastructure. The fact that these missiles would have been used in the feared surprise attack against the United States and therefore could not be attacked did not seem to bother the framers of this theory!

In pursuit of a new generation of intermediate-range ballistic missiles, Western strategic arguments were offered to the effect that the West must possess "escalation dominance" in order to have a credible "extended deterrent"—that is, must possess nuclear systems superior in performance to those of the Soviet Union, from short-range nuclear artillery to intercontinental ballistic missiles throughout the spectrum of ranges. The arguments in favor of consecutive generations of ever more accurate and destructive nuclear weapons revolved around two assertions: first, that "extended deterrence," i.e., the ability of the United States to deter Soviet nuclear (or conventional) attack against our European allies, Japan, or South Korea, required nuclear weapons suitable to attack Soviet military installations, troop concentrations, and transportation and communication centers in the western Soviet Union; and second, that the United States should have retaliatory options other than a spasmodic massive attack against Soviet urban and industrial centers. Neither of these pragmatic requirements, however, necessitate new, more accurate delivery vehicles. "Flexible response," as the requirement for these missions came to be known, could have been fully implemented by a change in the targeting plans and the command and control arrangements of existing nuclear weapons.

The need for such logical acrobatics emerged early in the debate on the type and size of nuclear arsenals because it became tacitly understood that the only practical nuclear doctrine was that of "basic deterrence." With the exception of a few wildly sanguine nuclear theorists,[2] it was generally conceded that nuclear war cannot be won and therefore there is no reason to fight it; instead one must make provisions to avoid it, that is, establish a credible mutual deterrence. Defense—securing one's person and domicile against enemy attack—had to be abandoned as a working concept and replaced by the notion that one is secure only as long as the enemy is deterred from attacking by the prospect of assured retaliation in kind.

This chapter begins by examining the physical factors that make nuclear deterrence possible and affordable while denying the possibility of effective defenses against nuclear attack. Next, it considers what level of retaliation can assuredly be accepted as deterring attack by either side, what combination of nuclear weapons is necessary to ensure such damage, and how the existing nuclear arsenals of the United States and the Soviet Union have been shaped by arguments invoking deterrence. Next, the chapter explores the impact of new weapons technologies on deterrence, as well as the fate of nuclear deterrence in the environment of an abating arms race, vigorous arms control, and increasing disillusionment with confrontational military policies. Finally, the chapter concludes with a heuristic discussion on the future forms that deterrence between the United States and the Soviet Union may assume.

## THE PHYSICAL UNDERPINNINGS OF NUCLEAR DETERRENCE

Military forces that can assuredly deter an opponent from attacking are a relatively new phenomenon that emerged as a result of the development of nuclear weapons. In the pre-nuclear era, it was possible for military planners to conceive of a combination of offensive and defensive forces that could, at once, both limit the damage an opponent could inflict upon one's own socioeconomic infrastructure at home or military forces on the battlefield, and at the same time cause superior damage to the opponent's assets. Thus, it was conceivable that one combatant could, by superior numbers and means, create an asymmetrical final outcome of a war in which one side causes more damage to the other and thus *wins* through victory on the battlefield or by forcing the other side to capitulate in order to avoid further damage at home. In World War II, it was on the battlefield that the Allied forces defeated the Axis forces, by the sheer weight of numbers of soldiers and materiel—on land in Europe, and at sea in the Pacific.

Significantly, even though they possessed overwhelming air superiority, the Allied forces did not manage to cause decisive damage to the industrial and urban infrastructure of Germany and Japan, as postwar analyses of strategic bombing revealed. It is now acknowledged that strategic bombing largely failed to achieve significant damage during World War II. The physical reason for this is that the radius of destruction of a one-ton high-explosive bomb is such that the area it destroys is about a million times smaller than the area of an average urban center. Thus, theoretically a hundred thousand bomber sorties, each carrying ten such bombs, would be needed to destroy such a city completely. It is easy to calculate how the cost and time needed for such a task, especially in the presence of reasonably effective antiaircraft defenses, would be unaffordable. Damage could not be caused under all and any circumstances with certainty. All this changed, of course, with the advent of nuclear explosives. The area of total destruction caused by a single nuclear weapon carried by a single delivery system, be it an aircraft or missile, is comparable to the size of a large city. That simple fact has changed the role of combat and established deterrence as the only practical national defense doctrine.

Combat, and more specifically war, has been a cruel but efficient way to resolve conflict since the dawn of humanity. War is an activity designed to create an asymmetrical final state; a winner and a loser. The former imposes its will on the latter and the conflict is resolved. In this context, a weapon is a tool for winning and resolving conflict, and therefore the more effective the weapons a nation possesses, the higher the probability of winning and resolving the conflict in its favor. Consequently, it has become an axiomatic truth over time that the ability of a nation to impose its political will is somehow proportional to the size and the quality of its arsenal of weapons, and ultimately, to the arsenal's destructive potential.

Nuclear explosives are so quantitatively powerful that they have introduced fundamental *qualitative* changes in the concept of war. Even a small fraction of the nuclear arsenal of the United States or the Soviet Union could wipe out the other. Both the United States and the Soviet Union now possess assuredly invulnerable amounts of nuclear destructive capability larger than each needs to destroy completely the assets of the other. That makes "winning" any form of nuclear combat impossible. At the present time, and into the foreseeable future, neither the United States nor the Soviet Union can reduce the invulnerable portion of each other's deliverable nuclear destructive capability below the level required to annihilate the other's country.

Defenses against nuclear weapons cannot alter this fundamental fact of the nuclear age. Since the defense can only hope to minimize the fraction of offensive nuclear weapons that penetrate it, while the success of a nuclear offense depends on delivering a certain number on enemy territory, the offense can always achieve its catastrophic goal by utilizing such a large number of weapons that the fraction of them that would leak through the defense is equal to the absolute number needed to devastate the opponent's country. Assume, for example, that the Soviet Union can be thoroughly destroyed by four hundred one-megaton nuclear explosives. In the absence of any Soviet defense, the United States could achieve this destruction by launching four hundred such explosives against a number of chosen targets. If the Soviet Union had a defensive system that was ninety percent effective, the United States could still achieve the same catastrophic effect by launching four thousand weapons, ten for each target. On the average, ninety percent would be shot down by the defense, but ten percent, or four hundred, would reach their targets. Anything less than an assuredly *perfect* defense cannot prevent the undesirable effects of nuclear war.

I conclude from all this that nuclear explosives, when used in attacks on cities, are so effective that no defensive system can form the basis of a national policy that could lead to permanent invulnerability to the homicidal properties of nuclear explosives. Therefore, in a nuclear exchange, both countries will be totally destroyed, a symmetrical outcome that precludes the resolution of the conflict by means requiring an asymmetrical winner-loser final state. It would be impossible, in the event of a nuclear exchange, to distinguish a winning side. And even if this somehow could be determined, the "winner" could not impose his political will on the defeated adversary for lack of physical means to do so. At any rate, the devastation would be such as to render the concept of "winning" de facto meaningless. In addition, given the plausibility of recent findings about the long-term meteorological, climatological, environmental, and ecological effects of a large nuclear attack on *either* of the two nations, there is a very good chance that a nuclear attack against one superpower's nuclear arsenal would be literally self-defeating for the attacker *even if the victim did not respond at all.* When it comes to the conflict between the United States and the Soviet Union, nuclear combat cannot yield a winner and therefore cannot resolve their conflicts.

We arrive immediately at two important propositions: first, nuclear explosives are not weapons in the traditional sense since they are not tools that can assist in ensuring victory in combat or yield political gains; and second, accumulating large numbers of them is useless, precisely because they are not weapons. We might as well accumulate gigantic teratomorphic statues in order to scare the opponent into submission.

The pre-nuclear era's axiomatic truth that superior destructive capability leads to victory in combat and therefore can resolve the conflict with an opponent in favor of the militarily superior is no longer true in the nuclear era. The finite size of the earth and its human assets is the inescapable upper limit beyond which further accumulation of destructive capability has no marginal utility in combat: it cannot lead to victory. In the case of conventional weapons—given that their destructive capability is about one million times smaller than nuclear explosives of equal weight, and given that they have only prompt and local effects—there was always something more of the opponent's assets to destroy for every new bomb one accumulated. Such marginal utility quickly disappears with nuclear weapons because the scale in space and time of destruction of nuclear explosives saturates their utility as instruments of policy—including the policy of deterrence—once their number exceeds the number of targets in the opponent nation which, if destroyed, would constitute unacceptable damage for the opponent.

Nor can nuclear explosives be used coercively to achieve "compellance." Coercion (posturing) is an ongoing attempt to resolve an existing conflict by intimidating or coercing an opponent into accepting one's wishes without combat. As such, it imposes specific requirements on the means of posturing: the mechanism of coercion requires the display of *applicable* force (for example, weapons that could effectively and realistically be used in combat) along with a credible threat to use them. The essential condition for successful resolution of conflict by posturing is that the displayed force must be both usable and useful in the context of a potential combat. While the accumulation of large cavalry forces during the nineteenth century could be expected to intimidate a neighboring opponent in proportion to their size, thereby leading to political concessions in favor of the militarily superior power, such forces would be useless as posturing instruments today precisely because they are not applicable in combat between the United States and the Soviet Union. Similarly, since the use of nuclear explosives by one superpower against the other would be suicidal, nuclear explosives are not usable in combat in the practical sense of the word. Therefore, a threat to use them against a nuclear-armed opponent is meaningless and cannot compel a nuclear opponent to abide by our political wishes. Conflict between two nuclear powers cannot be resolved by posturing with nuclear explosives.

"Limited" nuclear war between two nuclear superpowers, like all-out nuclear war and nuclear posturing, also cannot lead to an asymmetrical outcome of winner-loser. The concept of limited nuclear war is predicated on the belief that in a slowly escalating nuclear exchange, one of the two combatants will capitulate in order to avoid further destruction of its homeland, having reached its threshold of acceptable damage. Practically, it is difficult to imagine such a sequence of events. In reality, since neither combatant would know the threshold of unacceptable pain of the other, it is reasonable to assume that they will both attack massively and immediately—rather than in a slow and controlled manner—in the hope of achieving the capitulation of the opponent *first*. Thus, a limited nuclear exchange will be neither limited nor gradual. Instead, it will probably be indistinguishable from a full-blown nuclear exchange and consequently symmetrical in its catastrophic outcome.

It is possible, of course, that nuclear war could be kept limited by the two sides agreeing to stop the escalation before a decisive outcome has been reached. But the risk of failing to control the violence is too great and, at any rate, in such a case the outcome would be inconclusively symmetrical with no resolution of the conflict achieved. Nuclear weapons cannot, therefore, be used to create an asymmetrical final state between two nuclear combatants, and cannot support strategic doctrines for their use that envision asymmetrical final states between combatants. Practically speaking, nuclear weapons can only undergird strategic doctrines for their use that admit symmetrical final states. Of those, only mutual deterrence allows for a nondestructive symmetrical final outcome. Thus deterrence, even though it can be conceived as an analytical strategic doctrine, is in reality *an existential fact*[3] because there is no other choice.

I exclude here the possibility of total nuclear disarmament because it appears politically unattainable and practically unachievable. Even if we allowed for the wildly optimistic chance that all nuclear and near-nuclear nations would agree to a definite date by which they would verifiably destroy all their nuclear weapons, the practical result would be both undesirable and of dubious value. First of all, it is not possible to erase from the collective human intellect the knowledge of how to construct nuclear explosives. The laws of physics are invariant in space and time. Since it is the knowledge of these laws that is necessary (but not quite sufficient) for the creation of nuclear explosives, it is not possible to prevent their reemergence again and again. More importantly, complete nuclear disarmament entails an unavoidable and potentially serious instability. Any nation that, under a prevailing condition of total nuclear disarmament, manages to produce secretly even a small number of deliverable nuclear explosives could achieve decisive political if not military advantage, since a sudden breakout from the prohibition of ownership of nuclear explosives by one nation would not give time to other nations to react effectively. The same instability could be created by a nation revealing the presence of hidden (undestroyed) nuclear weapons retained after the regime of total nuclear disarmament had come into effect.

## WHAT IS NEEDED TO DETER WHAT?

Assured destruction of an opponent country is made possible by two properties of nuclear explosives: they are inexpensive to construct, maintain, and deliver on target; and their area of destruction is comparable to the area of a large city.

In turn, assured destruction makes deterrence both possible and obligatory. The size of the nuclear arsenal that assures immutable deterrence is determined by the saturation effect mentioned earlier: the destructive capacity of a nuclear arsenal saturates when the number of survivable warheads in it exceeds the number of putative enemy targets. Strategic debate, within the Western alliance at least, has revolved over the past forty years over three operational questions:

1. What does the United States want to deter the Soviet Union from doing?
2. How many nuclear weapons are needed in the deterrent nuclear arsenal before the saturation point is reached?
3. What should be the performance characteristics of these weapons?

Logic suggests that nuclear weapons have no appreciable role in deterring conventional wars.[4] The credibility of "extended deterrence" has always been in doubt for the simple reason that a nation that retaliated against its primary opponent with nuclear weapons in response to a conventional attack on one's allies might be attacked with such weapons itself and suffer more than the possible defeat of an ally.[5] We are left then with the only realistic goal of deterrence, i.e., with "basic deterrence" or "minimal deterrence," ensuring that the other side will not attack one's nation with nuclear weapons.

In all probability, what has kept the nuclear powers mutually cautious in their international behavior is not the specific complexion of each other's nuclear arsenals, but the fear of uncontrollable events that can lead to escalation and all-out nuclear war. The question, however, of "how much is enough" to deter has recently taken new urgency as the United States and the Soviet Union struggle to *reduce* their nuclear arsenals. What is the smallest nuclear arsenal that can maintain the symmetry of vulnerability, and thus deter both sides from nuclear adventurism, is a rather timely subject for consideration. In turn, this question can be answered only in the context of what constitutes unacceptable punishment that neither side would be willing to risk, even for the most promising outcome of a nuclear attack on the other.

Over the years the standard of unacceptable damage has varied. In the early 1960s, then Secretary of Defense Robert S. McNamara set the level of destruction that would be unacceptable to the Soviet Union at two-thirds of their industrial capacity and one-third of their population. In his famous article "To Cap the Volcano," McGeorge Bundy considers the destruction of ten cities in a nation as a political disaster of unthinkable magnitude.[6] In a conversation with Western scientists in Moscow in February 1987, Mikhail Gorbachev stated that the destruction of even *one* large Soviet city would be unacceptable to him.[7]

A group of scientists at the Massachusetts Institute of Technology decided in 1983 to examine in some detail the number and performance characteristics of Soviet nuclear weapons that would collapse the U.S. national economy for twenty-five or more years. Since that was a rather conservative criterion of unacceptable damage, it was thought that the arsenal with the potential to achieve such destruction could be safely regarded as deterring.[8] The study was based on a very large computer simulation model of the U.S. economy commissioned by the Federal Emergency Management Agency.[9] It was determined by the M.I.T. scientists that a nuclear attack targeted only on oil refineries, oil import facilities, the strategic oil reserve, and the nodes of the oil, coal-slurry, and gas pipeline systems of the United States would collapse the national economy which, even under the most optimistic assumptions, would not recover twenty-five or more years after the attack. This "counter-energy attack" consists of 85

550-kiloton weapons and 154 200-kiloton weapons, for a total of 239 weapons adding up to 110 equivalent megatons.* The attack would kill immediately only ten percent of the U.S. population and destroy only eight percent of its industry. But it would collapse the transportation system of the United States, and as a result, sixty percent of the remaining U.S. population would die of starvation in the two years following the attack; also, the GNP would dip to twenty-five percent of its pre-attack level by four years after the attack.[10] The M.I.T. study also concluded that the Soviet economy would be even more vulnerable to a U.S. counter-energy attack because of the more fragile economic, social, and industrial conditions in the Soviet Union.[11]

There is analytical evidence then that an arsenal consisting of no more than 250 *invulnerable* nuclear weapons, with a total yield of about 100 megatons, would be an adequate *econolytic* force that could inflict unacceptable damage to an opponent and consequently deter its leaders from mounting a nuclear attack on one's nation. These weapons need not be particularly accurate since their targets would all be "soft" and extended. Beyond this number of nuclear weapons, symmetry of forces becomes irrelevant since symmetry of destruction would have already been obtained. "Making the rubble bounce," in the words of Winston Churchill, does not confer military advantage or political gain.

There has been a school of strategic thinkers who believe that an econolytic arsenal may not deter a determined opponent and may even be unethical since it specifically provides for the mass killing of innocents. This school of thought believes that deterrence can be more assuredly and morally maintained by a *stratolytic* arsenal, one able to attack military installations, facilities, and equipment concentrations. This "countercombat" doctrine[12] requires a larger *number* of nuclear weapons, but not weapons of any specific performance. Several recent studies have estimated that a credible stratolytic arsenal must contain about 1,000 invulnerable nuclear weapons with a total yield of 100 to 200 megatons. Currently, the U.S. strategic arsenal consists of about 10,000 warheads with a total yield of about 4,000 megatons of TNT equivalent, and the Soviet arsenal consists of about 10,000 warheads, totaling more than 7,000 megatons of TNT equivalent.[13] (See Tables 3.1 and 3.2 for tallies of the U.S. and Soviet nuclear arsenals.)

As noted, the key qualification of the weapons either in an econolytic or a stratolytic deterring arsenal is that they must be invulnerable, i.e., that they must be available to counterattack their designated target *after* the arsenal they belong to has suffered a surprise counterforce attack from the other side.

The number of nuclear warheads in an arsenal that would survive a

---

*Equivalent megaton: The amount of energy that would be released by the explosion of a million tons of TNT.

Table 3.1 / United States Current Forces Baseline

| System | Launchers (L) | Warheads (W) |
|---|---|---|
| **ICBMs** | | |
| Minuteman 2 | 450 | 450 |
| Minuteman 3 | 250 | 750 |
| Minuteman 3A | 300 | 900 |
| MX | | |
| Small ICBM | | |
| ICBM Total | 1000 | 2100 |
| Silo total | 1000 | |
| **SLBMs** | | |
| Poseidon C-3 | 288 | 2880 |
| Poseidon/Trident C-4 | 360 | 2880 |
| Trident D-5 | — | — |
| SLBM Total | 648 | 5760 |
| Submarine total | 37 | |
| **Bombers** | | |
| B-52 | 180 | 2160 |
| B-1 | 95 | — |
| Bomber total | 275 | 2160 |
| Force totals | 1923 | 10,020 |

nuclear first strike against them depends on a large number of factors: the basing mode of the warheads, their state of alert, the properties of the attacking weapons, and a myriad of other factors, each adding to the uncertainty of the outcome of the attack. Traditionally, the number of surviving weapons is calculated on the basis of a "worst-case" analysis for the attacked nation; the results are almost always unrealistic, and often driven by some hidden agenda or other. For example, efforts have been made in the past dozen years or so to prove that there existed "a window of vulnerability," a time period during which a Soviet surprise attack would practically disarm the United States. The purpose was to show that the outcome of nuclear war would be "partially asymmetrical," that the Soviet Union could actually "win" by forcing the United States to capitulate. By implication, deterrence was said not to work and therefore we had to resort to the "Star Wars" enterprise to replace it with a perfect defense that would "render nuclear weapons impotent and obsolete."[14] Similar efforts to portray the existence of an asymmetry—usually in favor of the Soviet Union—took the form of various "gaps": the "bomber gap" in the early fifties, the "missile gap" in the early sixties, and so on.

More recently, in an effort to avoid such analytical difficulties and distortions, several groups have used computer simulation studies to estimate by essentially probabilistic calculations the outcomes of nuclear attacks by the

Table 3.2 / Soviet Current Forces Baseline

| System | Launchers (L) | Warheads (W) |
|---|---|---|
| **ICBMs:** | | |
| SS-11 | 448 | 448 |
| SS-13 | 60 | 60 |
| SS-17 | 150 | 600 |
| SS-18 | 308 | 3080 |
| SS-19 | 360 | 2160 |
| SS-25 | 70 | 70 |
| ICBM Total | 1396 | 6418 |
| Silo Total | 1326 | |
| **SLBMs:** | | |
| SS-N-6 | 304 | 304 |
| SS-N-8 | 292 | 292 |
| SS-N-17 | 12 | 12 |
| SS-N-18 | 224 | 1568 |
| SS-N-20 | 80 | 640 |
| SS-N-23 | 32 | 256 |
| SLBM Total | 944 | 3072 |
| Submarine Total | 64 | |
| **Bombers:** | | |
| Bear | 110 | 220 |
| Bear H | 40 | 160 |
| Bison | 30 | 120 |
| Blackjack | 20 | — |
| Bomber Total | 200 | 500 |
| Force Totals | 2540 | 9990 |

United States on the Soviet Union, and vice versa.[15] Ted Corbin and his collaborators used a detailed simulation to determine not only the outcome of counterforce strikes by the Untied States and Soviet Union against each other, but also the degree of uncertainty of these outcomes under a large number of variable assumptions. The study tested the existing arsenals as well as dozens of hypothetical arsenals that could emerge from the START agreement or could be crafted unilaterally by each superpower according to its perceived best interests. The study focused particularly on four attributes of a nuclear arsenal: deterring capability, cost-effectiveness, crisis-stability,* and sensitivity to undetected breakout of the opponent from agreed limits. The results of the study converge on the fact that a well-designed arsenal of three thousand nuclear warheads based on submarines, single-warhead land-based missiles (either mobile or in silos), and nonpenetrating bombers

*A crisis-stable arsenal is one that neither provokes nor threatens a surprise first counterforce strike.

carrying long-range nuclear cruise missiles will always contain a thousand or more surviving re-entry vehicles after a surprise, first-strike attack under all tested circumstances.[16] Therefore these arsenals have assuredly deterring stratolytic capabilities inasmuch as destruction of a thousand militarily significant targets is considered assuredly deterring damage.

The Corbin study also explored the complexion of the smallest, most cost-effective econolytic deterring arsenal. One such arsenal containing 1,000 warheads was studied in detail. It was found that while 1,000 single-warhead land-based mobile missiles offer the most assured second-strike force, this number of single-warhead missiles in silos cannot guarantee 250 survivable second-strike warheads delivered on target. In general, the study showed that "there exist arsenals of this size [1,000 warheads] which display characteristics of absolute crisis stability, assuredly surviving deterrent capability, confident verifiability, and cost-effectiveness favorably comparable to the cost-effectiveness of either the existing or . . . [studied] 3,000 re-entry vehicle arsenals."[17] Given the size of the deployed strategic nuclear arsenals in the United States and Soviet Union (see above), it is clear that nuclear deterrence can be safely maintained in the future by only a fraction of the nuclear weapons the two nations possess today, *if* the technological environment does not change in the future.

## DETERRENCE AND NEW TECHNOLOGIES

The technologies that are currently billed as "new" or "emerging" are based primarily on drastic improvements in the speed and miniaturization of electronic circuits and on newly developed solid-state sensors of electromagnetic radiation.

Almost all weapons systems can be improved in performance, cost, and reliability by incorporating components or devices made possible by new technologies. Delivery systems, munitions, battle management (command, control, communications, and intelligence, referred to as $C^3I$), electronic warfare, and space systems could be decisively changed by the emerging technologies. It remains for the responsible planner, however, to answer two questions:

1. Which of all these new potential capabilities are operationally significant?
2. Which of all the usable options for improvement are desirable, both in the context of costs—money and otherwise—and of the broader implications for stability, deterrence, and the resolution of the East-West conflict?

It is generally accepted that war between the United States and the Soviet Union would lead inevitably to the nuclear devastation of both countries. As outlined earlier in this chapter, the function of war between rational opponents is to resolve the conflict between them with a winner-loser asymmetrical outcome, in which each side hopes to be the winner and thereby enforce its interests. Since mutual devastation is symmetrical and consequently resolves no conflict as it produces no winner, war between two nuclear powers is useless. My position is that the emerging technologies *cannot and do not change this intrinsic stalemate,* no matter what weapons systems they may make possible. Deterrence, the formalized admission that no winning side can emerge from a nuclear war between the United States and the Soviet Union, remains the inescapable steady state in which those two countries find themselves. If deterrence is our only option, are there applications of new technologies that can strengthen it? Alternatively, is it possible to resolve the conflict with the Soviet Union without war, but with the help of these emerging technologies?

A class of analysts believe that new technologies can strengthen "extended deterrence" considerably. According to the theory of U.S.-Soviet competition referred to as "perception theory,"[18] the appearance of superior strength and determination is crucial to deterrence. A subscriber to perception theory would make an entirely different choice of new weapons from another defense planner who is interested only in fielding an efficient, even if unglamorous, system to maximize defense capabilities within given existing constraints. The implications of new weapons systems based on the new technologies are functions of such often unspoken motivations. For example, the development of a new hypersonic bomber or of a "stealthy" bomber—both made possible by the cluster of new technologies—may have crucial implications for a policy of establishing a perceived superiority over the Soviet Union, but no practical significance whatsoever in terms of the ability of the U.S. Air Force to perform deep-interdiction bombing missions against mobile targets in the USSR.

The emerging technologies serve up opportunities for development of new weapons, but which weapon is actually developed is a matter of choice by policymakers. That choice, in turn, is often dictated, or at least supported, by the policymakers' ideological bent and ultimate goal.[19] Thus, in attempting to discover and discuss the implications of new technologies for deterrence, it is prudent to separate the opportunities for weapons innovation that are militarily useful at the operational level from the capabilities, often more theoretical than realistic, that may appear attractive as a means of political posturing for friend and foe alike. In the past, for example, the United States has used its evident technological superiority over the USSR to create a psychological climate, to which both the Allies and the Soviets have been sensitive and responsive, that tends to counter the impression of Soviet superiority in conventional forces. This may be a legitimate use of technology as a bolster to our deterrent, as the 160 tank divisions of the Soviets are to theirs, but it often leads to the development of weapons systems that are militarily and strategically counter-productive to the goal of enhancing the stability and credibility of deterrence.

*Strategic offensive weapons* can profit little from emerging technologies, since their actual performance characteristics—their ability to perform either a counterforce first strike or a retaliatory second strike—are fully established and can be affected only at the margins by applications of new technologies. What new nuclear strategic offensive weapons may be built in the future depends on strategic policy choices and not on technological advances, except in the case of the hypersonic and stealth bombers, which can profit from the development of novel materials. The new technologies cannot and will not affect the offensive stalemate between the Soviet Union and the United States, although the management of offensive strategic weapons may profit from advances in sensors and communications that offer opportunities for practical improvements in their command and control.

One reaches similar conclusions in the case of *strategic area defense* systems (defenses for population and industry), but for exactly the opposite reason. New technologies cannot significantly affect strategic offensive weapons because these are so effective that there is little room for improvement. New technologies cannot significantly affect strategic area defenses intended to protect the population and industry of the United States from nuclear-armed ballistic missiles or aircraft because, as far as can be seen at present, the task is unachievable—nothing can make such defenses efficient enough to be useful.

It is indeed conceivable that new technologies could produce an area defense system that would be more effective than any defensive system that has ever existed; it is also conceivable that such a system could be ten, twenty, or even fifty percent effective against Soviet ICBMs. But even this level of performance is meaningless, on three counts. First, a leakage rate of even one percent would permit an opponent's nuclear ICBMs to destroy the United States. Second, even if an area defense system were one hundred percent effective against one generation of hostile ICBMs, it would soon have to handle the next, improved generation that would certainly be deployed to counter it. And third, no matter what happened to its ICBM attack, the Soviet Union has a multiplicity of other delivery systems such as cruise missiles or depressed-trajectory submarine-launched ballistic missiles that cannot be countered by area defenses. So no matter what technologies emerge in the foreseeable future, area defenses against nuclear ICBMs will remain invariably ineffective. Ultimately, emerging technologies cannot make a meaningful contribution to this class of weapons systems, and consequently the only implication of using these new technologies for defensive systems is that it can generate a novel, endless race between offense and defense in which the offense will always prevail because its mission—destroying cities with nuclear weapons—is operationally simple. Technology will not make the substitution of deterrence with defense in the foreseeable future. Deterrence will remain the only available and viable strategic doctrine.

Where the emergence of new technical capabilities has possible significance is in the field of *point defenses* against nuclear attack. The purpose of defending an important target such as a missile inside a silo, a command post, or other hardened military facility is twofold: first, to increase the uncertainty of the outcome of an attack in the mind of the attacker; and second, to make the destruction of such a point target costly to the attacker, if possible so costly as to make the attack look worthless even if it were to succeed.

The task of point defenses differs in two fundamental ways from the task of area defense. First, the target is a hardened point, protected against the effects of a nuclear blast, so only a small hemisphere around that point, no more than a few thousand feet in radius, needs to be defended. Second, unlike an area defense, a point defense does not need to destroy every nuclear explosive delivered against it, but only enough to make the attack look too costly or too unpredictable to planners on the other side. This reduces the already minute probability of a first strike and thus further strengthens deterrence. It is a significant if costly new option, to be considered along with mobile land-based missiles and drastic reductions of nuclear arsenals through arms control as a means of discouraging a surprise attack against U.S. strategic assets. Of course, the least costly and most sensible way of reducing to virtually nil the probability of a surprise attack against hard targets either in the United States or the Soviet Union would be a carefully crafted mutual reduction of strategic delivery vehicles.[20] But if such arms reduction agreements were not achievable, new technologies do offer the possibility to improve strategic and crisis stability with improved point-defense systems.

Emerging technologies also have potential significance in *antisubmarine warfare* (ASW). The implication of new technological capabilities in the arena of ASW could be disquieting. Detecting, localizing, and killing a submarine is largely a function of signal processing, of being able to resolve the sounds generated by an underwater vehicle that is trying to be as quiet as possible from the ubiquitous ocean noise. The methods the United States has developed to carry out this task require a computational capability previously available only in very bulky (and, as a result, shore-based) computers. But the steady advances in microelectronics have made it possible for individual submarines to possess comparable powers of resolving signal from noise and locating its source, and, as a consequence, attack submarines can become very effective hunter-killers of enemy ballistic-missile submarines (SSBNs). Signal-processing improvements alone cannot accomplish such operational advances, but in combination with quieter and faster ships, more capable torpedoes, and new advanced computers, they could make a significant difference in the ability of U.S. submarines to find and sink Soviet SSBNs.

Implementing such a strategy could have three possible outcomes: over a period of a few days U.S. ASW capabilities could destroy only part of the Soviet missile-submarine fleet; U.S. ASW capabilities could destroy all Soviet missile submarines if the Soviets do not take protective steps; or the United States could assuredly destroy all Soviet missile-carrying submarines no matter what the Soviets do. Since each Soviet ballistic-missile submarine carries over one hundred nuclear warheads capable of reaching U.S. cities, it is questionable whether advances in ASW are worth the cost and effort in the context of the first two results mentioned above. Damage-limitation efforts of this sort have little value in a nuclear exchange involving hundreds, if not thousands, of nuclear explosives. But they would be significant if the arsenals of the superpowers were reduced to one thousand or even three thousand warheads. If the third result were obtained, U.S. ASW capabilities, coupled with a declared doctrine for their early use,[21] would generate a crisis instability that is highly undesirable for the United States: if the Soviet Union were convinced of the vulnerability of their submarines, they would be tempted to use their missiles *before* a war was initiated, during a deepening crisis. Since these missiles do not have the requisite accuracy to attack hardened targets, they would be aimed at soft military targets, and even civilian targets. Thus, improvements of ASW capabilities seem to put in jeopardy U.S. military and industrial centers that otherwise might be spared during a deepening crisis or a U.S.-Soviet war that had not escalated into a full nuclear exchange. Certainly deterrence would be weakened by such developments.

But the more we learn about the oceans and their characteristics, the more it is apparent that in reality, missile-carrying submarines are very difficult to detect and destroy, and therefore they remain, and will remain for the next twenty to thirty years, largely invulnerable.[22] If successful ASW against missile-carrying submarines is neither desirable nor probable, there is serious doubt whether its improvement should be pursued. Unlike antiballistic and antiair defenses, successful strategic ASW mandates *preemptive* use, not against nuclear delivery vehicles that have been launched, but against their launchers. Like the capability to mount a blanketing attack on Soviet missile silos and airfields rather than on missiles or bombers already in flight, the capability to wipe out the opponent's missile-carrying submarine fleet is a counterforce capability that is relevant only as part of an overall *offensive* strategy. Because the relative invulnerability of the submarines makes them the most secure part of the strategic triad, a counterforce threat that makes them even *appear* vulnerable is uniquely destabilizing. Robust deterrence depends centrally, as we have seen, on the invulnerability of a portion of one's arsenal. Up until now, the one unquestionably invulnerable strategic nuclear weapon has been the ballistic-missile submarine. In this case, then, the effects of technological advances are quite marked: the automatic incorporation of improved ASW capability against Soviet ballistic-missile submarines into our naval armamentarium may induce Soviet planners to follow the reasoning of "use them or lose them" early in a conventional clash with the United States. It will introduce an element of crisis instability most undesirable for deterring arsenals.

The most visible contribution to the improvement of air-breathing strategic vehicles is the introduction of "stealth" technology, a combination of passive electronic countermeasures, special shaping of the aerodynamic surfaces of an air vehicle, and the application of suitable surface "paints" that reduce its visibility to selective radar wavelengths. Since radar is the main means for detecting and localizing aircraft in flight, reducing its efficacy automatically shortens the range at which the aircraft can be detected, and therefore increases its theoretical ability to penetrate to its target. But the protection provided by stealth technologies is partial and can be eroded by a sophisticated opponent.

On balance, it can be said that the stealth technology will improve the survivability of penetrating bombers and cruise missiles, but that does not mean that these vehicles will become either undetectable or invulnerable once in the air. The prototype aircraft employing "stealth" technology, the B-2, seems, from the scant unclassified information available, to be encumbered by a number of operational disadvantages—for example, low rate of turn, low speed, limited unfueled endurance. In addition, its exorbitant cost—described as nearly $850 million per copy—and the absence of strategic missions it can perform either uniquely or more cost-effectively than the other strategic delivery systems in the U.S. arsenal,[23] make its production and deployment questionable. Its deployment cannot and will not affect deterrence one way or another.

In conclusion, it is rather easy to imagine how the applicability and utility of deterrence will remain invariant under all technological change that the next two decades may witness. Putative improvements in ASW may impede the trend to smaller arsenals or may win arguments for the U.S. Air Force advocating mobile land-based or new airborne nuclear weapons. But overall we cannot expect that the future of deterrence will be decisively affected by new or future technologies. The real changes will come from the political arena.

## NUCLEAR DETERRENCE AND THE NEW POLITICAL ENVIRONMENT

The recent lessening of tensions between the Western alliance and the Communist world derives fundamentally from the pragmatic recognition that neither combat of any sort nor threats and posturing can ever resolve conflict between the two politico-military conglomerates. Their symmetrical vulnerability to each other's nuclear arsenals derives not from any political decision or ideological precept but from the fundamental physical properties of nuclear explosives.

The immobilizing effects of this symmetrical vulnerability initiated a search for ways other than the zero-sum-game approach to deal with conflict resolution. Three distinct alternatives emerged—the "hardline," the "liberal," and the "pessimistic center" approaches. All three tacitly assume the immutability of nuclear deterrence, while the first two at least anticipate that conflict between the United States and the Soviet Union can be resolved despite it.

The "hardliners" believe that the Soviet Union is bound to lose an all-out political and economic competition with the United States, and that such competition can therefore resolve the conflict between the two nations. Hence, arms control agreements are out, because such agreements would result in reduced arms production, thus benefiting the Soviet Union by letting it off the hook economically. The United States should continue to arms-race the Soviets to the extent possible; put maximum political, diplomatic, and economic pressure on them; deny them technology; oppose them at every opportunity and in every forum; and build nuclear weapons that are always superior to theirs—a situation to which they must respond. Avoid war by all means, but keep maximum pressure on the Soviets, to make sure, at the very least, that a resurgence of Soviet power is prevented, and, at best, to bring about the collapse of the Soviet empire. Sooner or later the Soviet Union will collapse internally: from economic exertion it could not sustain, depletion of its natural resources, disaffection of its citizens and of its allies, and revolution by its various ethnic components. Capitalism will prevail and the Western democracies and the United States will be the winners on the economic and political plane, while nuclear deterrence prevents war from derailing the success of the West.

The "liberal" approach to resolving conflict between the United States and the Soviet Union anticipates an evolutionary solution. This view holds that the internal failures of the centralized communist system will force changes toward a less rigid structure, a more humane polity. With these changes, the goal of converting the world to communism atrophies. The resolution of the U.S.-Soviet conflict can be furthered by helping the Soviet Union to evolve naturally out of its present structure and to integrate itself into the community of nations as a more benign, open, and democratic parliamentary system. This implies that the attitude of the United States, and the West in general, must be one of cooperation rather than of competition. With second-echelon countries—Taiwan, South Korea, Singapore—gaining an economic lead on the Soviets, and the Chinese gradually liberalizing their economy, the Soviet Union must also be anxious to make its economy more efficient and productive. The Gorbachev regime has already started along this path; this explains its desire to attenuate the arms race and establish a stable environment conducive to economic cooperation. The West should grasp this opportunity to resolve the conflict with the Soviet Union by assisting in its movement away from orthodox Marxism.

The "centrists" are distinct from the other two groups. They are pessimistic in believing that the conflict between the United States and the Soviets *cannot* be resolved. It is the traditional conflict between number one and number two in any human assemblage, they say, and therefore irreducible. Hence, attention should focus on how to manage this conflict in order to maintain stability and predictability; how to avoid crises and very large military expenditures that could harm U.S. domestic institutions and standards of living. The United States should strive to minimize the kinds of crises that can lead to war while retaining its present advantages vis-à-vis the Soviet Union. Translated into policy, this means business as usual: military budgets at about current levels; production—after negotiated numerical limits in arms control agreements similar to SALT I and II—of new strategic and conventional weapons systems that ensure stability but create psychological advantages for the United States; and maintenance of a state of managed tension with the Soviet Union. The risk is that the system may run away, deterrence may collapse, and a war may erupt. The centrist position is that it is the best we can do, and perhaps more significantly, it is the only policy with guaranteed political support in the environment created by nuclear deterrence.

The very emergence of these alternatives to military combat is proof that the collapse of the zero-sum-game method of resolving conflict was a fact long before Gorbachev tacitly accepted it as such in instituting the fundamental changes now taking place in the Soviet Union and Eastern Europe. The abandonment of the arms race, which sought to establish partial asymmetry on the perceptual level, was initiated by Gorbachev but would have occurred anyway. Gorbachev decelerated the arms race in the 1980s by being the first to establish policy based on the recognition of the futility of such efforts, and the first to take full advantage of the inescapability, and value, of the symmetrical state of vulnerability we call deterrence.

By actually adopting minimum deterrence as the operative Soviet strategic doctrine, Gorbachev is confident that neither war (whether nuclear or conventional) nor threats of use of nuclear force can successfully promote national interest. The Soviet Union can safely reduce military spending, focus on its economic problems, and allow Eastern Europe to develop independently because there is no external threat to its national security in a relationship with the West dominated by deterrence. Deterrence ultimately immobilizes Western military might even if it were to become asymmetrically more massive than what the Soviet Union could muster at some future time. The current Soviet policy is tangible proof that minimum deterrence actually works as a successful strategic doctrine. The nuclear weapons reductions Soviet officials propose[24] are in line with the size of the minimum arsenals found assuredly deterring by the M.I.T. study described earlier,[25] an indication that the aim of the Gorbachev government may very well be the abandonment of nuclear arms racing and the actual implementation of the doctrine of minimum deterrence.

As a consequence of the Soviet de facto adoption of minimum deterrence, arguments in support of arms-racing doctrines such as "extended deterrence" and "escalation dominance"—which were always considered impractical by the pragmatists—are now obviously flawed even in the eyes of the general public of the West.

What about the future—what could be the role of nuclear deterrence in the years and decades to come? The immutable symmetry of the nuclear powers' vulnerability to each other will, of course, persist. There seem to be neither technological nor political inventions on the horizon that could replace deterrence as the ordering principle among nuclear nations. As a consequence, conflict resolution by combat (the winner-loser, zero-sum-game approach) will remain impractical. This fact has spawned the three alternative approaches mentioned earlier: causing the collapse of the Soviet Union by relentless economic and arms-racing pressure; adopting "win-win" strategies vis-à-vis the Soviet Union in a framework of common security, and resigning to merely managing the conflict into the indefinite future without hope of resolution. Nuclear deterrence has not only made these three approaches necessary, but it is sufficient to maintain them as well.

It is improbable that the United States, while part of the broader Western alliance, will pursue the first alternative. The pessimistic third alternative, popular only a few years ago,[26] seems rather irrelevant as the Cold War abates and the arms race is halting. The most probable future state seems one of rapprochement and cooperation between the nuclear superpowers, of attempts to adopt pragmatic policies that serve common interests,[27] and of the attenuation of geostrategic conflict in the first place. In this more temperate zone, what will be the role of nuclear deterrence?

To begin with, there will certainly be a role for nuclear arsenals, maintaining the symmetrical state of vulnerability that both undergirds, and makes necessary, the new approaches of common security and win-win negotiated resolution of conflict that the nuclear nations—and their allies—are in the process of adopting toward each other. If this trend continues, nuclear deterrence will become decreasingly relevant while a new set of self-interests will impose self-discipline on the political leadership of each nation. The United States and the Soviet Union may forego war in the future, not just because nuclear deterrence will prevent them, but probably because economic or common geopolitical interests will make war irrelevant. Hence, the United States and England refrain from making war on each other, not because they both possess nuclear arsenals, but because they have established institutional and procedural frameworks within which they can negotiate their differences; they are deterred from war with each other not because of the fear of annihilation resident in their nuclear arsenals, but because of other motivations beyond mere survival. Nuclear deterrence between the United States and the Soviet Union may evolve in a similar manner into simple mutual deterrence not unlike the one we are practicing when we do not drive on the wrong side of the road. Motives such as a desire for international stability, economic gain, common defense against common threats, and the numerous other expressions of national self-interest that bind sovereign states into "international regimes" may replace the motivating core of nuclear deterrence, i.e., the avoidance of assured destruction.

Nuclear deterrence will always remain an existential state of being for the nuclear powers, a fact of their national lives; but it will cease being the link between their foreign and military policies, or the determinant factor that "sizes" their arsenals. But while nuclear deterrence can continue to exclude combat as the arbiter of international conflict, it is powerless in the face of internecine strife. The turbulence or even anarchy that could ensue from the collapse of *perestroika* into ethnic violence in the Soviet Union cannot be deterred by Moscow's, or any other nation's, nuclear arsenal. In the end, nuclear deterrence may become irrelevant—at the international level, because it may be supplanted by a calculus of self-interest based on economic considerations, and in the domestic arena, because ethnic strife cannot be arrested with nuclear weapons.

## Notes

1. For a broader definition of deterrence, see A. Carnesale et al., *Living with Nuclear Weapons*, (Cambridge: Harvard University Press, 1983), p. 32.

2. See, for example, Robert Scheer, *With Enough Shovels* (New York: Random House, 1982).

3. McGeorge Bundy, "Existential deterrence and its consequences," in D. Maclean, ed., *The Security Gamble* (Totowa, N.Y.: Rowman and Allanheld, 1984).

4. See Joseph S. Nye, *Nuclear Ethics* (New York: Free Press, 1986), p. 103.

5. Carnesale, *Nuclear Weapons*, p. 34.

6. McGeorge Bundy, "To Cap a Volcano," *Foreign Affairs*, 48 (October 1969).

7. Mikhail Gorbachev, interview by J. Wiesner, 1987.

8. M. Anjeli Sastry et al., "Nuclear Crash," *Program in Science and Technology for International Security*, Rprt. 17, June 1987.

9. Economic model commissioned by Federal Emergency Management Agency as described in "Development of a dynamic model to evaluate economic recovery following a nuclear attack," final Rprt., Vol. I, *Description and Simulations*, (Cambridge, MA: Pugh-Roberts Associates, Inc., Nov. 1980).

10. Sastry, "Nuclear Crash," p. 90ff.

11. Ibid., p. 107.

12. Carnesale, *Nuclear Weapons*, p. 114.

13. May, et al, "Strategic arsenals after START", *International Security*, Summer 88.

14. Ronald Reagan, televised address to the nation, 23 March, 1983.

15. Ted Corbin et al., "Nuclear Arsenals for the 21st Century," P. S. T. I. S. report #22, Cambridge, MA, September 1989. See also May, "Strategic Arsenals."

16. Corbin, "Nuclear Arsenals," p. 50 ff.

17. Ibid, p. 83.

18. Steven Kull, "Nuclear Nonsense," *Foreign Policy* 58 (Spring 1985).

19. Kosta Tsipis, *New Technologies: Defense Policy and Arms Control* (New York: Harper & Row, 1989).

20. Corbin, "Nuclear Arsenals," p. 82 f.f.

21. Admiral James D. Watkins, "The Maritime Strategy," (U.S. Naval Institute, January 1986).

22. Tom Stephanic, *Strategic ASW and Naval Strategy* (Lexington, MA: Lexington Books, 1987).

23. Mark Anderson, "The B-2 Bomber: A Comparative Assessment," *Program in Science and Technology for International Security*, Rprt. 21, July 1989.

24. Andrei Kokoshin, "A soviet view on radical weapons cuts," *Bulletin of the Atomic Scientists* (March 1988) p. 14 ff.

25. Corbin, "Nuclear Arsenals."

26. Carnesale, *Nuclear Weapons.*

27. Consider, for example, the U.S. and French government statements in effect approving of Soviet intervention in Rumania, *New York Times*, 25 Dec. 1989.

# 4 / Death and Transfiguration: Nuclear Arms Control in the 1980s and 1990s

ALLAN S. KRASS

## INTRODUCTION

Arms control suffered its deepest crisis in the 1980s but reemerged at the end of the decade with renewed vitality across the entire spectrum of weapons. There are as many explanations for this rejuvenation as there are political axes to grind. To the Reagan administration, it was an unwavering commitment to a policy of "peace through strength" that brought the Soviets back to the bargaining table. To others, it was the advent of Mikhail Gorbachev and his "new thinking" that transformed Soviet foreign policy and pulled the rug out from under Reagan's military buildup. Still others credit the Western European antinuclear movement and the U.S. nuclear weapons "freeze" campaign for moving public and Congressional opinion away from confrontation and toward negotiation. Finally it can be argued that Gorbachev and Reagan were simply yielding to the inescapable reality that the arms race is no longer affordable for either side. While the United States and the Soviet Union squandered their human and financial resources on increasingly expensive and useless weapons, other countries like Japan and West Germany were laughing all the way to the bank.

This chapter does not presume to reach a definitive judgment on which of the above explanations is correct. Arms control is a complex, political, and often logically contradictory enterprise. Although it is usually discussed in technical terms by technical people, no one has yet offered a coherent set of principles for it that can be applied in all situations. And even if such principles did exist, international, domestic, Congressional, and bureaucratic pressures would never allow them fully to determine negotiating positions. Still, the 1980s demonstrated convincingly that arms control, for all its incoherence and frustrations, is here to stay. It is important, therefore, that we survey the events of the 1980s in order to see what they might tell us about how arms control will evolve in the 1990s.

# THE THEORY AND PRACTICE OF ARMS CONTROL

What we today call arms control has a long but half-hearted history, going back at least to the early nineteenth century, when the United States and Great Britain agreed to restrictions on the sizes and numbers of guns on ships on the Great Lakes.[1] But it was not until the advent of nuclear weapons that arms control took on the urgency and persistence that it has today. Grotesque and horrifying images of the destruction of Hiroshima and Nagasaki, the threat of accidental war resulting from a mistaken radar image or unauthorized attack, and the prospect of an endless arms race at ever escalating cost have all combined to make nuclear arms control a compelling goal.

The first impulse of many after World War II was to call for the total elimination of nuclear weapons. But after fifteen years of largely empty rhetoric and sterile negotiations, nuclear disarmament seemed to many an impossible objective—and to others an undesirable one. To the latter group, nuclear weapons were an essential deterrent to war, so the proper goal was not to get rid of them but to stabilize and make as efficient as possible their deterrent function. This could be done both unilaterally and in collaboration with potential adversaries, who would presumably share the desire to avoid accidental wars and unnecessary arms competition.

The modern definition of arms control was formulated in 1961 by Thomas Schelling and Morton Halperin. It entails, in their words, "all the forms of military cooperation between potential enemies in the interest of reducing the likelihood of war, its scope and violence if it occurs, and the political and economic costs of being prepared for it."[2] These forms of cooperation can range all the way from formal treaties requiring elaborate verification procedures to informal or tacit agreements intended to increase mutual confidence. To reduce the likelihood of war, in particular accidental or unwanted war, nuclear postures must be "stable," that is, there must be no incentive to strike first in a crisis. To reduce the scope and violence of war, weapons and strategies must be designed to avoid unnecessary damage, and there must be reliable command and control of nuclear forces on both sides and good communication between the adversaries even after a war starts. To control the costs of preparations for war, the adversaries should be able to agree that some number of weapons is "enough" to provide mutual deterrence and that it is futile to endlessly expand their nuclear arsenals.

These goals are to some degree reflected in the agreements that have been reached in the twenty-nine years since Schelling and Halperin wrote. After the nerve-wracking Cuban missile crisis of 1962, the United States and the Soviet Union agreed to create a "hot line," a teletype connection between the Kremlin and the White House intended to prevent future crises from escalating because of misunderstandings or false warnings. This connection has been upgraded several times since and is considered one of the important and durable achievements of arms control. The desire to limit expenditures on weapons is reflected in the SALT I and II treaties,[3] which put numerical limits on certain classes of weapons the two sides could deploy. It is harder to find examples of agreements that would limit the scope and violence of nuclear war. Nuclear weapons are so numerous and powerful, and the uncertainties of controlling them in an actual war so enormous, that there can be no confidence that once a nuclear war began it could be kept from wreaking widespread devastation. Indeed, some argue that it is wrong even to attempt to limit the devastation of nuclear war, since this could make nuclear war appear a more "thinkable" option.

Schelling and Halperin's definition of arms control is as clear and precise as one can find, but as the preceding paragraph makes clear it has some logical inconsistencies. It also misses another essential aspect of arms control, at least as it is practiced in the United States. Almost from the beginning, arms control negotiations have served to legitimize U.S. nuclear programs and to protect them from public criticism and Congressional budget-cutting. We can see the roots of this function of arms control as far back as 1950, in a report to President Truman's National Security Council. The report, usually called NSC-68, called for a massive U.S. military buildup to counter the Soviet threat, but it recognized that such a buildup would be expensive and politically controversial. So it advocated the use of disarmament proposals as a "tactic." In the words of NSC-68, "A sound negotiating position is therefore an essential element in the [U.S.-Soviet] ideological conflict. [I]t may be desirable to pursue this tactic both to gain public support for the [military] program and to minimize the immediate risks of war."[4]

The insight that an attractive negotiating position, however insincerely held, could gain public support for military programs has remained one of the most durable and resilient features of arms control. In the opinion of the late I.F. Stone, a persistent critic of U.S. military policy, SALT spelled "fraud" because its only purpose in his view was to protect Richard Nixon's antiballistic missile (ABM) system from Congressional attack.[5] While this may overstate the case, it does contain a strong element of truth.

The interaction between negotiations and weapons can be made to work in two directions, giving the president more freedom to maneuver. The weapons serve as "bargaining chips" to put pressure on the Soviets at the negotiating table, while the promise of imminent progress in the negotiations serves to inhibit Congressional interference with the weapons. The development of arms control in the 1980s can be understood only if this "double-track" aspect is added to the others listed by Schelling and Halperin.

# DEATH: 1980–84

The 1970s had seen a U.S.-Soviet détente and the signing of two major nuclear arms control agreements, SALT I in 1972 and SALT II in 1979. SALT I placed interim limits on ballistic missiles and strong permanent limits on antiballistic missile defenses. SALT II extended the limits on ballistic missiles and added strategic bombers to the list of restricted weapons. The treaties symbolized a hopeful trend in superpower relations that encouraged the United Nations to look forward to the 1980s as the "Second Disarmament Decade." But the first four years of the decade turned out to be anything but hopeful as the delicate structure of nuclear stability began to crumble under resurgent U.S.-Soviet hostility and suspicion.

## The Last Days of Jimmy Carter

The new decade opened on a most inauspicious note when on January 3, 1980, President Jimmy Carter withdrew the SALT II treaty from consideration for ratification by the Senate. The treaty had been signed by Carter and Soviet President Brezhnev in June 1979 after seven years of tough negotiations by three U.S. administrations. But from the moment Carter delivered it to the Senate for advice and consent, it was clear that the required two-thirds vote for ratification would be difficult to achieve. Domestic politics had undergone a rightward shift in the late 1970s, and the Carter administration's foreign policy was under pressure from people who believed that the Soviet Union had taken advantage of past arms control agreements to gain a military edge on the United States.

Along with growing public and Congressional suspicion of Soviet motives, Carter found himself being held responsible for the long captivity of the Americans held hostage in the U.S. embassy in Tehran, and for managing the response to the Soviet invasion of Afghanistan. The invasion, which took place in December 1979, was the last straw for Carter, who confessed that the Soviet action had "made a more dramatic change in my own opinion of what the Soviets' ultimate goals are than anything they've done in the previous time I've been in office."[6] In his memoirs Carter lamented that "the worst disappointment to me personally was the immediate and automatic loss of any chance for early ratification of the SALT II treaty."[7]

But even if the invasion had never occurred, ratification of SALT II would have been a long shot. Opposition to the treaty, and the U.S.-Soviet "détente" it represented, had been growing since the mid-1970s, led by conservative groups such as the Committee on the Present Danger (CPD).[8] A remarkable number of members of this group, including Paul Nitze, Eugene Rostow, Richard Pipes, and Ronald Reagan himself, were to become key arms control policymakers in the Reagan administration. In 1980 they were still on the outside but had found sympathetic ears in the media and in

Congress. In the opinion of the CPD, SALT had paved the way for a massive Soviet nuclear buildup that had neutralized if not surpassed U.S. strategic nuclear power.[9]

Carter had entered office in 1977 with a promise to cut the military budget by $15 billion and to promote arms control. He left it asking for substantial increases in the Pentagon's budget—increases that were retained and then raised again by the incoming Reagan administration.[10] In his final year in office, Carter also announced the hitherto secret development of the so-called "stealth" or B-2 bomber and signed Presidential Directive 59 (PD-59), a modified nuclear war-fighting plan that called for selective strikes on Soviet government and military installations as part of a controlled, protracted use of nuclear force.[11] This feverish, last-ditch attempt by Carter to appease the right has led historian Raymond Garthoff to conclude that "the main turning point [in U.S.-Soviet relations] in many respects, and especially in the Soviet view, was not January 1981 so much as January 1980."[12]

## The Ascendancy of Ronald Reagan

Reagan's campaign promises were the exact opposite of Carter's. U.S. military strength was to be built up and Soviet power challenged wherever in the world it appeared. Arms control as it had been practiced by his predecessors was "fatally flawed," and further negotiations with the Soviet Union would have to await the rebuilding of U.S. power. That rebuilding would involve a 600-ship navy, modernization of all three legs of the strategic triad (bombers, submarine-launched ballistic missiles, and intercontinental ballistic missiles), and massive investments in command, control, and communications for sustained nuclear war fighting. Two years later would come the commitment to the Strategic Defense Initiative, to which we will return shortly. All of this was accompanied in the first three years of Reagan's presidency by a strident and confrontational anti-Soviet rhetoric. In his first presidential press conference Reagan characterized the Soviet leaders as men who reserve "the right to commit any crime, to lie, to cheat,"[13] and by March 1983 he was calling them "the focus of evil in the modern world."[14]

Reagan's rhetoric and policies were initially popular with the American people. According to Daniel Yankelovich and John Doble, "The public mood was characterized by injured national pride, unqualified support for increasing the defense budget, and a general desire to see American power become more assertive."[15] One group of public opinion polls, taken between November 1978 and February 1981, showed that an average of 44.7 percent of Americans believed that too little was being spent on the military, while only one-third as many (15.3 percent) thought too much was being spent. The rest thought it was about right or had no opinion.[16]

But it is remarkable how quickly Reagan's confrontational style lost its appeal. By the time he had been in office only one year, public attitudes on military spending had practically reversed. A poll taken in March 1982 showed 36 percent believing that military spending was too high and only 19 percent, barely half as many, believing that it was too low.[17] Thus, in only a year in office Reagan had turned a 3-1 approval for his rapid escalation of military spending into a 2-1 disapproval. By 1984, surveys indicated that while Americans were still somewhat concerned about "losing the arms race," they were "convinced that it is time for negotiations, not confrontations, with the Soviets"; that the U.S. attitude toward the Soviet Union should be "live and let live"; that "a national reconsideration of the strategic role for nuclear weapons is badly needed"; and that "certain risks for peace" were warranted.[18]

Precursors of this rapid shift in public opinion can be seen even before Reagan took office. The nuclear freeze movement, a demand for mutual cessation of production, testing, and deployment of nuclear weapons, began in the late 1970s among a small coterie of peace activists, but it was already big enough in 1980 to put freeze referenda on the election ballots of sixty-two New England towns. The freeze won in fifty-nine of them, polling the same margin of victory as Reagan did over Carter.[19] So, even as the Reagan program appeared to be endorsed by his substantial election victory, signs of ambivalence in the voting public toward his promised military buildup were already evident.

The freeze movement was to grow dramatically over the next two years, culminating in an antinuclear demonstration in New York City on June 12, 1982, that drew nearly a million people, and in the passage of supportive resolutions in both houses of Congress.[20] But it was not only the American people who were alarmed by Reagan administration rhetoric. Since the 1979 NATO decision to deploy intermediate-range nuclear forces (INF) in Europe, Western Europeans had become increasingly apprehensive about U.S. nuclear strategy, and the Reagan administration's bellicose posture exacerbated these concerns. As 1981 unfolded, Reagan authorized production of the neutron bomb in August and in October admitted to a group of newspaper editors that he could see how a nuclear war could be limited to European territory. Three weeks later his Secretary of State, Alexander Haig, revealed in Senate testimony that NATO war plans included the firing of "demonstration" nuclear shots to deter Soviet aggression in Europe. The insensitivity of these statements to European concerns was stunning, and as if in direct response, between 250,000 and 300,000 protesters took to the streets in Bonn on October 10, followed by 400,000 in Amsterdam on November 21.[21]

The growing public unrest forced Reagan to return to the bargaining table well before he had intended to, if indeed he had intended to at all. On November 30, 1981, in response to pressure from allied governments, who themselves were under enormous pressure from their own people, the United States resumed INF negotiations with the Soviet Union in Geneva.

Negotiations on strategic weapons, rechristened the Strategic Arms Reduction Talks (START) to distinguish them from Strategic Arms Limitation Talks (SALT), resumed in June 1982. However, bureaucratic and ideological divisions within the Reagan administration prevented any realistic, or even coherent, negotiating positions from being developed.[22] Nevertheless, just the resumption of negotiations went a long way toward neutralizing both the Western European and American protest movements, both of which began to deflate in 1983.

Meanwhile, Soviet policy had stagnated because of a chronic leadership crisis. Leonid Brezhnev, already weakened by poor health for several years, died in November 1982 and was replaced by Yuri Andropov, who in turn found himself terminally ill only a few months later. Andropov's death in February 1984 led to the ascension of an old Brezhnev crony, Konstantin Chernenko—another tired, sick, and weak leader who lived only until March 1985.[23] Thus, even if the Reagan administration had been able to define a coherent arms control policy, productive negotiations with this succession of sick and dying Soviet leaders would have been difficult.

However bad the arms control situation had become by the spring of 1983, it was made far worse by President Reagan's startling announcement of his Strategic Defense Initiative (SDI) in a televised speech on March 23. The bedrock of the SALT process had been the ABM treaty, and SDI posed a direct threat to that treaty. In agreeing not to deploy nationwide ABM defenses, the superpowers had acknowledged the inescapable reality of their mutual vulnerability and had agreed that if offensive forces were to be frozen and ultimately reduced, an essential prerequisite would be to prevent the deployment of strategic defenses.[24] By resurrecting the prospect of nationwide defenses against ballistic missiles, SDI threatened to regenerate an open-ended offense-defense competition that would exploit U.S. technological superiority. The Soviet leadership reacted with anger to its announcement, denouncing SDI as part of a U.S. effort to sabotage the agreements of the 1970s and to acquire a nuclear first-strike capability.[25]

Prospects for arms control continued to deteriorate as 1983 unfolded. On July 20, the Reagan administration announced that it would not resume the negotiations on a comprehensive nuclear test ban that had been left in a relatively advanced state by the Carter administration. According to the new administration, a vigorous underground testing program would be required as long as the United States depended on nuclear weapons for its security. By implication this meant that an end to testing could be achieved only in connection with total nuclear disarmament, a position vigorously disputed by many nuclear scientists and strategists.

Arms control reached its nadir at the end of the year, when on November 23, the Soviets walked out of the INF negotiations in protest over the U.S. deployments of Pershing-II and ground-launched cruise missiles in Western

Europe. Two weeks later, they extended their boycott to the START negotiations. Yet the public pressures for superpower accommodation remained strong, now finding increased expression in Congressional opposition to a number of Reagan military programs, including antisatellite weapons, chemical weapons, the MX missile, and even SDI. And while the peak of the anti-INF protests had passed in Europe, the controversy had left behind deep political divisions in a number of countries and a need for the United States to refurbish its image with its allies by demonstrating a willingness to negotiate with the Soviets.

With the beginning of election year 1984, Reagan showed his awareness of these pressures. In January he made a conciliatory speech opening the Stockholm Conference on Confidence- and Security-Building Measures and Disarmament in Europe.[26] Following this speech the tone, if not the substance, of Reagan's rhetoric became more positive. The Soviet walkout had been a serious tactical error, and Reagan was able to capitalize on it by emphasizing his willingness to negotiate and by repeatedly calling on the Soviets to come back to Geneva. By mid-1984 the Reagan administration had rediscovered what all previous administrations since Kennedy had already learned, that arms control negotiations are an essential component of U.S. national security policy. In order to gain approval for the INF deployments, the United States had to pursue a "double-track" policy, the other track being negotiations. And now, in order to protect his strategic modernization program from Congressional budget cuts, Reagan would have to find some way to negotiate strategic arms limitations with the Soviets. The dilemma was summed up neatly by presidential adviser Kenneth Duberstein when, referring to Congressional arms control advocates like House Armed Services Committee Chairman Les Aspin and Senator Albert Gore, he advised the president, "we've got to give those guys something, or we'll lose the MX."[27]

## TRANSFIGURATION: 1985–89

Ronald Reagan was returned to office by an overwhelming vote in the 1984 elections, but this time it was clear that it was his apparent openness to negotiation that got him votes rather than the militant rhetoric of 1980. However, his second administration retained many committed opponents of arms control in high-level positions, and Reagan's own commitment to SDI and a full-scale modernization of U.S. strategic nuclear forces remained as strong as ever. This meant that unless substantial changes took place in Soviet attitudes and actions, little real progress would be possible. As President Reagan took his second oath of office in January 1985, no one could imagine how dramatic and revolutionary those Soviet changes would be.

## Enter Mikhail Gorbachev

Konstantin Chernenko died on March 10, 1985, and the following day Mikhail Gorbachev became the new General Secretary of the Soviet Communist Party, ending over five years of paralysis in the Soviet leadership. Coincidentally, U.S.-Soviet arms control negotiations resumed the very next day in Geneva. Gorbachev wasted no time in seizing the initiative. In April, he announced a unilateral suspension of deployments of SS-20 intermediate-range missiles in Europe, and in July he announced a five-month unilateral moratorium on Soviet nuclear weapon tests. The moratorium was to be extended twice, and ended up lasting over eighteen months, until February 1987.

The Reagan administration refused to reciprocate either gesture and continued to pursue a confused and ambivalent arms control agenda. Hardliners at the Pentagon and other agencies were able to prevent any constructive changes in U.S. positions. For example, even as Reagan was agreeing to meet Gorbachev at the summit, his National Security Adviser was announcing a new interpretation of the ABM treaty that would allegedly permit the United States to test and develop space-based components for ballistic missile defense.[28] The treaty explicitly forbids such tests, but some pro-SDI officials claimed to have found a loophole that would exempt so-called exotic technologies, like lasers and particle-beam weapons, from the restrictions. To the vast majority of arms control experts, including all but one of the Americans who had negotiated the ABM treaty, this new interpretation was patently fraudulent. And to Senators Sam Nunn and Carl Levin it represented an unconstitutional attempt by the executive to override the role of the Senate in treaty making. All of this opposition forced the administration to state that while it reserved the right to implement the new interpretation, it would continue for the time being to abide by the traditional interpretation. But by the end of the decade, the reinterpretation dispute had not been resolved, and the threat of U.S. violations of the ABM treaty as new SDI components were readied for testing remained a key issue between President Bush and the Congress, not to mention the Soviet Union.[29]

Political indecision and bureaucratic infighting characterized the Reagan approach to arms control for the remainder of his tenure, while Gorbachev's policies became increasingly bold, imaginative, and challenging. He made it clear almost from the beginning that he was interested in "new thinking" about arms control and military strategy, and he connected the necessity for this new thinking to the desperate needs of the Soviet Union for social and economic *perestroika*, or restructuring.[30] Gorbachev's energy, intelligence, and mastery of the media won over Western Europeans and Americans alike, and his relentless propaganda pressure, marked by frequent unilateral initiatives, both symbolic and substantive, made it increasingly difficult for the hardliners in the Reagan administration to block new superpower agreements.

Reagan and Gorbachev met in Geneva in November 1985 and agreed that "a nuclear war cannot be won and must never be fought," an almost direct repudiation of the rhetoric of the first Reagan administration. This summit was followed by three more: in Reykjavík, Iceland, in October 1986, where the two leaders came to the brink of agreeing to eliminate all nuclear-armed ballistic missiles (or by some accounts all nuclear weapons) by the end of the century; in Washington in December 1987, where they signed the INF treaty and committed their countries to deep cuts in strategic offensive weapons; and in Moscow in June 1988, where they formally put the INF treaty into force. These meetings resulted in the creation of a comprehensive framework for negotiations, a framework that will guide the progress of arms control throughout the 1990s.

## The Lessons of the 1980s

What have we learned from the experience of the 1980s in arms control? First, we have learned that a good political relationship is far more likely to result in arms control agreements than arms control agreements are to improve a bad relationship. Secondly, we have learned that public opinion—first in Western Europe, then in the United States, and now, at long last, in the Soviet Union and Eastern Europe—will not tolerate sustained deviations from the general trend toward relaxation of East-West tensions. Reagan's first-term attempt to revive the Cold War hostility and intense nuclear competition of the 1950s turned out to be a short-lived aberration, much more related to the frustrations of U.S. domestic politics and Third World foreign policy than to any irreconcilable U.S.-Soviet conflicts. Thirdly, we have learned how heavily the Western desire for nuclear armaments depended on the secrecy, dogmatism, and ruthlessness of previous Soviet regimes and how different the arms race can look in the context of a crumbling Warsaw Pact and a Soviet leadership genuinely committed to *glasnost, perestroika,* and *demokratizatsiia.* Finally, it has become increasingly obvious to everyone how economically and socially debilitating the arms race has been for the societies involved. The "zero-sum" nature of the domestic versus military spending game emerged with unprecedented clarity in the late 1980s, and neither the United States nor the Soviet Union is likely for the foreseeable future to have the resources to make a bid for military dominance over the other without risking major damage to its economy and social cohesion.[31]

## The New Framework

The Reagan-Gorbachev summit meetings resulted in a restructuring of nuclear arms control in the form of the Nuclear and Space Talks (NST) in

Geneva. The NST framework encompassed three separate but related areas: intermediate-range forces, strategic offensive forces, and strategic defense and space weapons. Separate from these, but also resumed in 1985 as a result of the public relations success of Gorbachev's moratorium, were discussions on nuclear testing limitations.

**Intermediate Nuclear Forces**  By far the most successful of the four efforts has been the INF negotiations, which culminated in the signing of the INF treaty in December 1987 and its entry into force in June 1988. It was the first arms control treaty ratified by the U.S. Senate in seventeen years, and there is little doubt that its endorsement by a conservative Republican president substantially improved its chances for ratification. The ABM treaty had benefited similarly from Richard Nixon's reputation as a tough anticommunist. There is not enough of a historical record to permit broad generalizations, but the record so far is consistent with the hypothesis that while Democratic presidents may be more interested in reaching arms control agreements, Republican presidents have a better chance of getting them ratified.

The problem with Republican presidents is in getting them interested in the first place. With Nixon, it was the pressure of the Vietnam War and the accompanying rise in antimilitary sentiment it engendered among the American people. With Reagan, as we have seen, public pressure was also a factor. But until the end of 1986, the changes in U.S. policy were more rhetorical than substantive. It was then that the Iran-Contra scandal broke, providing the Reagan administration with a powerful incentive to achieve a foreign policy victory. And Gorbachev was willing to help. He astounded most Western observers by accepting the so-called zero option, a proposal that would force him to get rid of almost three times as many intermediate-range missiles as the United States and to give them up in Asia as well as in Europe. This highly asymmetrical proposal had originally been put forward by hardliners in the Pentagon precisely because they believed it would be unacceptable to the Soviets.[32] Gorbachev's willingness to make this unprecedented concession, in combination with Reagan's need to distract attention from Iran-Contra, produced an irresistible momentum toward agreement.

The INF treaty broke significant new ground in arms reductions and especially in verification (see below). It established the precedent of asymmetrical cuts and entirely eliminated several classes of missiles. All U.S. and Soviet land-based ballistic and cruise missiles with ranges between 500 and 5,500 kilometers were to be eliminated. Also to be destroyed, dismantled, and shut down were the launch vehicles, support structures, test and training facilities, and production lines for these systems. By June 1, 1991, all of these weapons should be gone, resulting in the removal of over two thousand nuclear warheads from Europe and Asia. Progress toward this goal has been steady and nearly trouble-free. As of September 20, 1990, all of the older Soviet missiles, and 561 of their 654 modern SS-20s had already been destroyed. The United States had destroyed 256 of its 443 ground-launched cruise missiles and 150 of its 234 Pershing-II ballistic missiles.[33] And all of this had taken place under an on-site inspection regime whose intrusiveness and comprehensiveness would have been unimaginable for most of the history of international relations.

**Strategic Arms Reductions**    With a full year remaining in his administration at the signing of the INF treaty, Reagan appeared to many to have a golden opportunity to move on to a START treaty. But for several reasons this was not to be. One is the great complexity of the treaty itself. The weapons covered comprise a wide range of types, including fixed and mobile land-based missiles, submarine-launched ballistic and cruise missiles, and long-range bombers carrying a variety of payloads. Since none of these is to be completely eliminated, verification of the precise numbers allotted to each side will be more difficult than for INF.[34] And the weapons themselves are seen by both sides as more vital to their deterrent or war-fighting postures than the shorter-range and less numerous weapons deployed in Europe.

While these problems are real ones, they are not the most important reasons for the failure to achieve a START agreement during the Reagan administration. More fundamental were the inability of the president, the Congress, and the Pentagon to reach a consensus on the modernization of U.S. land-based missile forces; the Soviet insistence on limits on sea-launched cruise missiles (SLCMs); and, to be discussed shortly, Reagan's unyielding commitment to SDI. In the end, despite what appeared to be a genuine desire on the part of both leaders to reach an agreement, these issues stymied the START negotiations during Reagan's last year in office.

The land-based missile problem goes back to the early 1970s, when the accuracy of Soviet ICBMs, especially their ten-warhead SS-18, improved to the point where they could theoretically wipe out most of the U.S. ICBM force in a surprise or preemptive strike. This hypothetical threat, usually called the window of vulnerability, has made elimination of the SS-18 the highest priority of U.S. arms control policy for many years. Unfortunately, the U.S. position is not as straightforward as it sounds because of the often contradictory views on nuclear strategy and stability held by U.S. analysts, policymakers, and members of Congress.[35]

The basic concept of crisis stability requires that the two sides' nuclear deterrent forces be invulnerable to preemptive strikes by the other side. On this basis the United States has every right to be concerned by the SS-18, whose accurate warheads threaten U.S. land-based missiles and whose basing in fixed silos invites a U.S. preemptive strike in a crisis. But even as they condemn the destabilizing threat of accurate Soviet ICBMs, U.S. military planners have tried to retain the capability to attack Soviet ICBMs by deploying the new and more accurate MX ICBM and Trident D-5 SLBM. The

Soviet response to these systems has been to make their new generation of ICBMs, the SS-24 and SS-25, mobile. The ten-warhead SS-24s are being deployed on railroad cars and the single-warhead SS-25s on trucks. Theoretically such deployments reduce the possibility of a preemptive attack and are therefore desirable. But because they interfere with U.S. targeting plans, and because they make the verification of deployments more complicated, the Reagan administration held to a formal demand that all mobile ICBMs be banned, even as it struggled to gain Congressional approval of funding for a railroad-basing plan for the MX and a new single-warhead truck-mounted ICBM called Midgetman.

**Space Weapons**  The ABM treaty formally established the intimate connection between strategic offenses and strategic defenses, and despite years of effort by the Reagan administration to disestablish it, the connection remains firm in the minds of a majority of U.S. analysts and members of Congress, as well as of Soviet leaders. The preservation, and if possible the strengthening, of the ABM treaty was a primary goal of Soviet arms control policy throughout the 1980s, and a commitment by the United States to adhere to the traditional interpretation of the treaty for at least ten years was a constant prerequisite for Soviet agreement to START. But to Ronald Reagan, SDI was the best way out of what he saw as the immoral policy of "mutual assured destruction," in which the two sides kept the "peace" by threatening each other's society with total annihilation. Reagan maintained to the end of his administration that SDI was purely defensive and non-threatening and never seemed fully to grasp the ABM treaty's basic premise that offensive reductions could be achieved only after a defensive race was renounced by both sides. His last words on the subject to Mikhail Gorbachev during the Moscow summit were, "But it would not kill or hurt anyone." Gorbachev, having by that time given up trying to change Reagan's mind on SDI, replied, "Let's talk about something else."[36]

Throughout the remainder of the Reagan administration, the U.S. negotiating team was not even allowed to discuss possible compromises on SDI despite the potential impact on the ABM treaty of technological advances in sensors and directed energy weapons. Reagan also refused negotiations on antisatellite (ASAT) weapons, despite the arguments of many weapons analysts that because of its greater reliance on sophisticated satellites, the United States had more to lose from an ASAT arms race than the Soviets. In 1983 then General Secretary Andropov declared a unilateral moratorium on tests of a primitive and unreliable Soviet ASAT system, and his successors have held to it. The Reagan administration fought against growing pressure for the United States to respond in kind, but the Congress took matters into its own hands and for three consecutive years refused funding for tests of the U.S. ASAT. The program was finally canceled by the Air Force in 1987, and no tests of an antisatellite weapon were conducted for the rest of the decade.[37]

Unfortunately, this does not mean that the threat of an ASAT arms race has passed. The Defense Intelligence Agency continues to accuse the Soviet Union of developing ground-based lasers with the capability to damage low-orbit satellites, and the Pentagon has created its own shopping list of new ASAT technologies for which it wants substantial research and development funding. As the decade ended, the two sides had still not discussed in any serious way the possibility of a treaty limiting the development, testing, and deployment of ASAT weapons.

**Nuclear Weapon Tests** As already noted, the Reagan administration had little interest in nuclear testing limitations but found itself compelled by public and Congressional pressure to respond in some way to Gorbachev's extended moratorium and repeated calls for negotiations on further testing limits. The response was to resurrect an old treaty that had been signed in 1974 by the Nixon administration, but never ratified by the Senate. The Threshold Test Ban Treaty (TTBT) limited both sides to underground tests of less than 150 kilotons explosive yield and incorporated the most advanced verification provisions of its time.[38] Most important was the Soviet agreement to provide the United States with detailed geological data on its underground test sites and actual yields of some nuclear explosions. This information would have allowed seismologists to calibrate the network of seismic stations in countries bordering the Soviet Union and to obtain more accurate and precise yield measurements of Soviet tests. But the treaty was never ratified, so the information has not been supplied, and American seismologists have had to develop improved methods for analyzing seismic records without access to Soviet geological and yield data. These methods now enable the United States to monitor Soviet underground tests with high confidence, and in particular they show that the Soviets have almost certainly complied with the TTBT, despite persistent charges by the Reagan administration that there have been "likely" violations.[39]

The Soviets have consistently argued that there is no reason to doubt the adequacy of the monitoring measures already incorporated in the 1974 treaty. However, Gorbachev agreed at the December 1987 summit to a joint verification experiment in which each side would use both seismic and on-site methods to measure the yields of explosions at both the U.S. and Soviet test sites. These experiments were carried out in August and September 1988, and while the Reagan administration refused to release the results, they were leaked to the press almost immediately. They showed no significant difference in accuracy between the seismic methods proposed by the Soviets and the on-site CORRTEX method favored by the United States.[40] Still, the experiments apparently satisfied both sides and presidents Bush and Gorbachev signed the verification protocols on June 1, 1990.

**Compliance**   Two important questions underlie the possibility of progress in all of the above areas. First, have the Soviets complied with the agreements they have signed, and second, how well does the United States know whether they have or not? Both of these questions figured prominently in the arms control debates of the 1980s, when the conservative argument against SALT relied heavily on accusations of Soviet cheating and the alleged weaknesses of U.S. monitoring systems and compliance policies.[41] The questions have been particularly relevant to the problem of gaining ratification of treaties in the Senate, and while the INF treaty was ratified by a comfortable majority, a number of senators have made it clear that they would hold START to a much higher standard of verifiability than INF.

Allegations of Soviet cheating on arms control agreements began almost before the ink was dry on the 1972 SALT I agreements, and as U.S. politics swung further to the right in the late 1970s, they gained increasing currency and credibility. By 1980, the Republican Party platform would "deplore the attempts of the Carter administration to cover up Soviet noncompliance with arms control agreements."[42] Carter had issued a generally favorable report on Soviet compliance with SALT I as part of his effort to gain ratification of SALT II.[43] It listed a number of compliance issues that had arisen during the 1970s, but concluded that all had been satisfactorily resolved through discussions by U.S. and Soviet experts in the Standing Consultative Commission (SCC), a body created by the SALT I agreements for just this purpose. To SALT opponents, however, the Carter report was a whitewash and the SCC "an Orwellian memory hole into which our concerns have been dumped like yesterday's trash."[44]

Despite the conviction of several of his administration's most influential members that Soviet violations were a serious problem, Reagan's compliance policy was ambivalent. His first noncompliance report was not sent to the Congress until January 1984, and it was precipitated by Congressional anger over the Soviet downing in September 1983 of an off-course Korean airliner with 269 people on board, including U.S. Representative Larry McDonald. The noncompliance report charged that the Soviet Union "is violating," "has almost certainly violated," "is probably violating," or "is likely to have violated" various provisions of SALT II, the ABM treaty, and the TTBT, among others.[45] The Soviets wasted no time in responding in kind, issuing one week later an *aide-mémoire* accusing the United States of numerous violations of both the letter and spirit of the same list of agreements.[46]

Reagan's 1984 report was followed by four others at roughly one-year intervals, and in each one the number of alleged Soviet violations increased. However, even as this "pattern" of Soviet deception and bad faith was growing, so was the interest of the Reagan administration in negotiating new agreements. The illogic of this policy did not escape conservative opponents of arms control,[47] but it did not appear to slow down Reagan's pursuit of the INF treaty. In the late 1980s a number of independent analyses of the cheating allegations demonstrated that the evidence for many of them was weak or nonexistent. For example, the alleged "yellow rain" chemical warfare attacks in Cambodia turned out to be clouds of bee excrement dropped in hive-cleaning flights, and the few Soviet underground nuclear tests categorized as "likely violations" of the TTBT by the Reagan administration have been shown by careful geological and statistical analysis to be almost certainly within the 150-kiloton limit.[48]

Even allegations for which a strong case existed, such as the Krasnoyarsk radar, posed no significant threat to U.S. security. First photographed by U.S. satellites in 1983, the partially completed radar was one of a type singled out for special restrictions in the ABM treaty. Such radars, when intended for purposes of early warning of ballistic-missile attack, are supposed to be located on the periphery of the national territory facing outward. This helps to distinguish them from ABM battle-management radars, which are more usefully deployed inland, closer to the targets they are defending. The Krasnoyarsk radar was more than two thousand miles from the nearest coastline and relatively close to several ICBM bases, suggesting a battle-management role. But its lack of hardening or defenses against nuclear attack and its relatively low operating frequency suggested an early-warning mission. Either way it was a violation of the ABM treaty, and most independent U.S. analysts agreed with this conclusion.

But few agreed with the Reagan administration's more alarming conclusion that the Krasnoyarsk radar, when taken together with several other ambiguous ABM-related activities, constituted evidence that "the Soviet Union may be preparing an ABM defense of its national territory." So serious was the radar violation in Reagan's view that until it had been fully dismantled it would be "impossible to conclude future arms control agreements in the START or Defense and Space areas."[49] The Bush administration wasted no time in reaffirming this position.

The Soviet Union took a number of steps to address American concerns about the radar. Gorbachev ordered construction suspended in 1987 and then invited a delegation of three U.S. Representatives, accompanied by scientific experts and journalists, to inspect the installation.[50] Finally, in September 1989 the Soviets agreed to dismantle the radar unilaterally without preconditions, and a month later Soviet Foreign Minister Eduard Shevardnadze admitted that the radar was "to put it bluntly, a violation of the ABM treaty."[51] By May 1990, U.S. intelligence was reported to have photographic evidence that dismantling work had begun on the radar.[52]

The Krasnoyarsk radar episode leaves much to be regretted on both sides. The Soviets allowed short-sighted economic and engineering considerations to override their treaty commitments, while high-ranking Reagan administration officials blatantly exaggerated the significance of the violation to further their own assault on the ABM treaty. At the same time, it is important to recognize that neither the violation nor the response were strong enough to destroy the treaty, which survived intact into the 1990s. The question of its continued survival, one of the major ongoing issues in arms control, will be considered in the next section.

**Verification**  The United States monitors Soviet arms control compliance with the most comprehensive, sophisticated, intrusive, and expensive military intelligence effort ever undertaken. The overall intelligence budget is classified, but $20 billion per year would not be an extreme estimate of its cost. The territory of the Soviet Union, its troop deployments in Eastern Europe, and its naval maneuvers at sea are watched from space by optical, infrared, and radar imagers. Soviet communications are tapped into by antennas based on land and sea, and in air and space. Soviet nuclear tests are monitored by sensitive seismic detectors deployed throughout the world, and Soviet submarines and ships are tracked by sonar networks deployed under the oceans at strategic locations. Armies of U.S. analysts monitor Soviet economic and social data; read Soviet newspapers and military, professional, and scientific journals; listen to Soviet radio broadcasts; watch Soviet television; and debrief tourists and business and professional visitors. U.S. intelligence agencies exchange information with their counterparts in allied countries and recruit informers, defectors, and spies within the Soviet Union itself.[53]

Until the INF treaty went into force in June 1988, these so-called national technical means were all the United States had to monitor agreements, although earlier agreements had incorporated an increasing number of "cooperative measures." The most important of them was the Standing Consultative Commission already mentioned. Others involved exchanges of data bases, counting rules for missile warheads, agreements on observable characteristics of certain weapons, and commitments not to interfere with the other side's national technical means or to engage in deliberate concealment measures on treaty-related activities. But with the signing of the INF treaty, the two sides achieved the ultimate cooperative measure: on-site inspections. The intrusiveness of these inspections would have been unthinkable in the pre-Gorbachev era.

A memorandum of understanding accompanying the INF treaty provides detailed data on the numbers, characteristics, and locations of treaty-limited items on both sides, and other annexes provide specific procedures for eliminating these systems and conducting on-site inspections. There are actually five kinds of on-site inspections in the treaty: baseline inspections to verify the exchanged data; observation of the elimination of all items; close-out inspections to confirm the shutting down of facilities or bases; short-notice reinspections to verify that no prohibited activities have been resumed at inactive locations; and continuous portal monitoring at one production facility in each country. Until 2001, a team of thirty American inspectors will be continuously stationed about six hundred miles east of Moscow at the Votkinsk Machine Building Plant, where SS-20 missiles were once manufactured (and SS-25 missiles still are). A similar Soviet team will monitor the Hercules plant at Magna, Utah, where Pershing-II missiles were made, using a variety of instruments to inspect train and truck traffic into and out of the plant for the presence of prohibited items.[54]

In their first two years of operation, the inspections worked well, experiencing only minor difficulties.[55] Surveys show that the American people are aware of the breakthrough in on-site inspection and that it has helped reassure them that arms reductions can be undertaken with minimal risk.[56] But there are many things the United States wants to know about Soviet military activities that on-site inspections cannot reveal. So national technical means are still the heart of the verification effort, and considerable resources are being devoted to modernizing and expanding them.[57]

## THE BUSH ADMINISTRATION AND THE 1990s

The arms control situation facing the incoming Bush administration could hardly have been more different from the one encountered by Ronald Reagan. When Reagan took office in 1981, arms control was a shambles, and many in the new administration, if not the president himself, saw as their objective the delivery of the *coup de grâce* that would put it out of its misery. In contrast, George Bush found arms control flourishing—indeed, threatening to spiral out of control under the constant prodding of a dynamic, imaginative, and persistent Soviet leader, a Western European public hungry for an end to the forty-five-year-old military stalemate, and a U.S. Congress searching relentlessly for ways to reduce the legacy of massive budget deficits left by the tax cuts and military spending of the 1980s.

There is one important similarity between the Reagan and Bush administrations: both inherited an across-the-board modernization program for U.S. strategic weapons. Reagan did add some new items to the Carter military program, such as restoring the B-1 bomber, introducing the Small ICBM (SICBM or Midgetman) and, most importantly, launching SDI. But many of the strategic programs that are now the subject of intense debate in Congress—the Trident D-5 SLBM, the B-2 ("stealth") bomber, the MX missile, and the sea-launched cruise missile—were originally Carter programs that were continued by Reagan. These programs involve large amounts of money, thousands of jobs in the districts of influential members of Congress, and political commitments to key military and industrial constituencies. They also embody a strategic concept, the "triad," that has been at the heart of U.S. nuclear weapons policy for more than thirty years and has acquired the status of unassailable dogma.

The problem for George Bush is that while the basic rationale for that dogma—the Soviet threat to initiate nuclear conflict—is evaporating, the weapons commitments made in its name will be difficult to break. This defines the basic dilemma for Bush's arms control policies in the 1990s: how can he preserve as much as possible of the U.S. strategic modernization plan in the face of decreasing perceptions of Soviet threat and declining military budgets? To resolve this dilemma, Bush will have to negotiate simultaneously with the Soviet Union, the NATO allies, the U.S. Congress, and the Joint Chiefs of Staff—four powerful actors whose interests will not often coincide. Added to this formidable array of interests is public opinion, which, while often passive and manipulatable, can, as Ronald Reagan learned in his first administration, be unpredictable and volatile. In such a fluid and contradictory situation it would be foolish to predict rapid progress toward coherently defined goals. It would be equally foolish, however, to predict continued stagnation and stalemate. As the saying goes, "something's got to give," and this reality is bound to make U.S. arms control policy a fascinating spectator sport for the entire decade. The following sections focus on the components of the arms control framework introduced above and attempt to identify the key issues likely to determine progress (or the lack of it) in each one.

## European-based Nuclear Forces

The INF treaty removed over two thousand nuclear weapons from Europe, but many thousands remain deployed on aircraft, short-range ballistic missiles, artillery shells, submarines, and surface ships. The indiscriminately destructive nature of nuclear weapons has always made their use in the "defense" of Europe, whether Eastern or Western, a bizarre concept. Yet the deep political division of Europe and the memories of surprise attacks and total war in the twentieth century have made nuclear deterrence appear essential to many to prevent a third European war. Today the primary argument for retaining nuclear weapons in Europe, articulated most often by Britain and the United States, is that they have prevented war for more than forty years and should continue to do so for the foreseeable future.

It is certainly true that the presence of nuclear weapons in Europe has been associated with the absence of war between the two alliances. But association is not causality, and some have always questioned whether it was necessary to base nuclear weapons on European soil to prevent war.[58] Critics have also pointed to a strong *political* interest on the part of the United States in maintaining a nuclear presence in Europe. Except for the relatively small independent forces of France and Great Britain, all nuclear weapons in Europe have remained under U.S. control and provided a unique kind of political leverage for the United States in European affairs.[59] It is not surprising, therefore, that it is the United States and Great Britain, the two powers whose influence on the continent has traditionally been strongest in times of conflict and weakest in times of peace, who are most reluctant to acknowledge that the political changes sweeping Europe may call into question the future need for nuclear weapons there.

The INF treaty was a *fait accompli* when George Bush took office in January 1989, and there were strong political pressures coming from Europe to eliminate even more nuclear weapons. The only remaining U.S. ground-based missile was the short-range (under three hundred miles) Lance, and the only targets it could shoot at were in Eastern Europe, especially East Germany. West Germans had always seen the nuclear targeting of East Germany as at best a necessary evil, but with the declining Soviet threat and the emergence of more democratic politics in East Germany, the "evil" began to appear far more prominent than the "necessity." A popular slogan of the antinuclear forces in West Germany became "the shorter the range, the deader the Germans." But the Bush administration held fast to its plans to modernize U.S. short-range nuclear forces (SNF) by deploying a follow-on to the Lance. Development funds for the Lance follow-on were dramatically increased in the fiscal year 1991 U.S. military budget, and Bush, supported strongly by British Prime Minister Margaret Thatcher, insisted that there could be no further reductions in European nuclear deployments until substantial reductions in conventional forces had been achieved. His first major initiative in arms control involved a unilateral reduction of 30,000 in U.S. troops in Europe and a concession to Soviet demands to include combat aircraft in conventional force reductions. These concessions were made to appease West German demands for progress in European arms reductions and helped temporarily to take the heat off SNF and avoid an embarrassing intra-alliance conflict at the June 1989 NATO summit.[60]

But the collapse of the Berlin Wall in November 1989 and the breathtaking movement toward German reunification that followed it swept away this fragile compromise. Suddenly the notion of aiming short-range nuclear weapons from West to East Germany looked analogous to aiming them from Missouri to Illinois. Nor did Czechoslovakia, Poland, and Hungary, with their budding democracies and free-market economies, look like promising targets for NATO nuclear weapons. In fact, these countries were already negotiating with the Soviet Union for the removal of all Soviet troops from their territory.

German reunification, the coming Western European economic integration, the emergence of political democracy and economic reform in Eastern Europe, and the growing preoccupation of Soviet leaders with internal economic and political problems have worked together to undermine the rationale for U.S. nuclear weapons in Europe. By May 1990, President Bush had to acknowledge that there would be no follow-on to Lance, and that plans to modernize U.S. nuclear artillery were to be scrapped as well. The next, and possibly last, line of defense for a U.S. nuclear presence in Europe is the so-called tactical air-to-surface missile (TASM) to be based on U.S. aircraft.

But it will be several years before the critical deployment decisions have to be made on this weapon, and in the meantime it is likely that every traditional rationale for nuclear deterrence in Europe will have been overtaken by events. It is hard to envision any Western European country accepting new deployments of U.S. nuclear weapons in 1995, when the TASMs are supposed to be ready. It is also difficult to imagine the U.S. Congress continuing to spend hundreds of millions of dollars a year developing a weapon that it will become increasingly evident is not wanted by the people it is designed to defend.

The 1990s is likely to see the issue of U.S. and Soviet nuclear weapons in Europe become increasingly irrelevant. An interesting result of this will likely be more attention paid to British and French nuclear weapons, especially if U.S.-Soviet reductions in strategic weapons continue beyond the initial cuts mandated by START (see below). Proposals for unilateral nuclear disarmament have been politically unpopular in Britain and literally unthinkable in France. The legitimacy of these forces has always been buttressed by the possession of far greater arsenals by the superpowers, and membership in the "nuclear club" has been an important contributor to French and British national self-esteem. However, if political relaxation and economic integration continue to evolve along current lines in Europe, it is possible that meaningful challenges to British and French nuclear forces could emerge.

## START

The Reagan administration left a nearly complete START agreement for the Bush administration. Already agreed-to were major cuts in the number of strategic warheads deployed by the two sides, including a fifty percent cut in the heavy, accurate ten-warhead SS-18, the Soviet weapon most feared by U.S. military planners. However, negotiators on both sides had been careful to protect all of the weapons in their strategic modernization programs, so the Soviets would be free to deploy more mobile ICBMs while the United States could go ahead with the Trident SLBM, the Midgetman ICBM, the "stealth" bomber, and both air-launched and sea-launched cruise missiles. Taking into account various "discounts" and "counting rules," the actual cuts in deployed warheads on both sides would be closer to twenty-five percent than the fifty percent often used to characterize the agreement.[61] Nevertheless, even twenty-five percent reductions would result in the destruction of thousands of nuclear weapons and, through the precedents it set in implementation and verification, help to pave the way for deeper cuts.

Despite the advanced state of negotiations, Bush relegated START to a relatively low priority during his first year in office. Public fear of nuclear war had declined sharply in light of Soviet reforms and Eastern European political changes, and consequently public interest and pressure for nuclear arms control had also decreased. On the other hand, the success of the INF treaty had alarmed many conservatives who insisted that further nuclear reductions should be held up until agreements on conventional force reductions in Europe were achieved.

The Bush administration's initial proposals at the Vienna Conventional Forces in Europe (CFE) and Geneva START negotiations were consistent with these relative priorities. The Vienna proposals were bold, substantive, and apparently intended to move the negotiations forward, while his opening proposals in Geneva were weak and superficial. They completely sidestepped the substantive obstacles to a START agreement—namely the future of SDI and controls on sea-launched cruise missiles—and dealt instead with relatively minor verification issues on mobile ICBMs and warhead counting.[62]

But by the time Bush and Gorbachev met in Washington at the end of May 1990, events had forced a reassessment of Bush's agenda. The CFE talks had stalled because of Soviet uncertainties about a variety of problems ranging from worries about the resurgent power of a united Germany to how its crippled economy could absorb the hundreds of thousands of soldiers to be demobilized under CFE. Meanwhile, Gorbachev had made more concessions in START, yielding to U.S. proposals on sea-launched cruise missiles and accepting U.S.-proposed counting rules for air-launched cruise missiles. The Bush administration, facing the embarassing possibility of a summit meeting with nothing of importance to achieve, also made some concessions when Secretary of State James Baker visited Moscow in mid-May. The United States accepted the Soviet limit on the range of cruise missiles covered by the agreement and dropped its demand for no further flight testing of the SS-18, incurring the wrath of some right-wing commentators who accused Secretary Baker of caving in to Soviet trickery.[63]

The summit itself was disappointing from the point of view of strategic arms control. The leaders were able to issue a joint statement agreeing on most of the important START issues, but they had still not settled the question of SS-18 flight tests, the status of the Soviet "backfire" bomber—a plane the United States has insisted be counted a strategic weapon but which the Soviets call an intermediate-range weapon—and the issue of U.S. transfers of strategic weapons to its allies. These and a myriad of minor details on definition, implementation, and verification had still not been resolved by the end of the summit. Hope was expressed by both sides that the agreement would be ready for signing by the end of the year, but any number of things could occur in the interval to further delay a treaty that had already been under negotiation for more than eight years.[64]

The prospect of a START agreement raises the question of next steps, and a remarkable consensus among former U.S. Pentagon officials appeared to be emerging in favor of even deeper cuts in a future agreement. Former Secretaries of Defense Robert McNamara, Harold Brown, and James Schlesinger, as well as former Assistant Secretary of Defense Richard Perle, one of the prime "hawks" of the Reagan administration, were all urging further cuts amounting to another fifty percent or even more.[65] Adding to the pressure were Congressional Democrats who saw big-ticket strategic weapons programs as prime candidates for major budget cuts to reduce the deficit.

On the other side were Secretary of Defense Richard Cheney, the Joint Chiefs of Staff, and a number of Congressional Republicans who threatened to delay or oppose ratification of a START treaty and to fight against further cuts. The Pentagon was trying to draw the line on further cuts in order to preserve what they could of their most prestigious and expensive strategic weapon programs. The B-2 bomber, the MX missile, and sea-launched cruise missiles were promised to the Joint Chiefs of Staff in return for their support of START, so when the B-2 was threatened by budget cuts in 1989, the Air Force Chief of Staff hurried to Capitol Hill to warn the Congress, "I find it largely inconceivable that we could continue with current negotiating positions without the B-2."[66] By the time of the summit the Air Force had already agreed to a cut in B-2 procurements from 132 to 75, but it was not at all clear that Congress would be satisfied even with this number. The final FY 1991 budget was hard on the B-2, authorizing no new planes and including only enough money to pay the cost overruns on already-ordered aircraft.

The future of strategic arms control is uncertain for a number of other reasons. Agreements are becoming increasingly complex and difficult to negotiate because of the variety of weapons covered and the constant pressure of technological innovation. The relatively simple INF treaty required almost three hundred pages of text, and the current draft of the START treaty is reported to require more than a thousand pages. Verification provisions are becoming more comprehensive, intrusive, and expensive, and in 1990 some commentators began to notice that the costs of monitoring future agreements could escalate dramatically in future years. And public interest in the arcane and frustrating process of arms control is noticeably decreasing relative to more immediate political and social issues like drugs, the economy, and the environment. It now seems clear that it was the fear of nuclear war that generated the powerful antinuclear movements of the early 1980s, and that as that fear waned in the late 1980s, public pressure for new arms control agreements also waned.[67] As the new decade began, it seemed likely that the most important negotiations on arms control in the 1990s would be driven by economic concerns and involve the president and the Congress rather than the traditional U.S.-Soviet negotiations driven by political activists and world public opinion. Clearly, the U.S. and Soviet governments could help each other deal with their domestic problems by agreeing to further cuts, but the history of arms control suggests that the process may be too slow and cumbersome and too subject to political distractions and game playing to achieve the rapid reductions in military spending dictated by political relaxation and required by the two economies. The 1990s may see a kind of "mutual unilateralism" replacing the traditional bilateral arms control negotiations of the 1970s and 1980s.

## Strategic Defense and Space

In the seven years between President Reagan's 1983 "Star Wars" speech and the 1990 Bush-Gorbachev summit, the Strategic Defense Initiative had fallen on increasingly hard times. What began as a "peace shield" destined to render nuclear weapons "impotent and obsolete" had become an object of deep skepticism, frequent ridicule, and increasingly deep budget cuts. In an effort to sustain public and Congressional support, the program had pinned its hopes on a series of technologies, each of which lasted no more than a year before it was replaced by an even more fanciful one. The technology of 1990 was "brilliant pebbles," a word play on a previous incarnation called "smart rocks." The difference was that while smart rocks would be launched on missiles from space-based platforms and guided with help from radars, brilliant pebbles would be permanently deployed by the thousands in space, totally enveloping the earth at an altitude of about 250 miles. Each interceptor would be about one meter long, carry the computing power of a Cray supercomputer, and cost only about a million dollars, yet be capable on its own of detecting, tracking, and attacking an enemy ballistic missile from space. To George Bush brilliant pebbles was "one of the most promising concepts" in the history of SDI, but to two Pentagon scientific advisory panels it posed several "critical" unresolved technological problems. Nor were the optimistic cost estimates of the SDI organization taken seriously by independent analysts.[68]

Not only had SDI lost credibility among U.S. policymakers, it had also lost its power to frighten the Soviet leadership. When Gorbachev came to power in 1985, it would have been unthinkable for the Soviet Union to have agreed to sizable cuts in its offensive nuclear forces while allowing the United States to develop a defense against those forces. But by the spring of 1990, Gorbachev had stopped insisting that no START agreement could be concluded without a U.S. commitment to adhere to the ABM treaty for an extended period. However, the Soviets reserved the right to reassess their adherence to START if the U.S. SDI program ever reached a point that threatened the credibility of their nuclear deterrent. In other words, the Soviets had not abandoned the basic premise of the ABM treaty that offensive forces could be reduced only if limits were placed on defenses.

Meanwhile, the Bush administration maintained the public position that "in the 1990s, strategic defense makes sense more than ever before,"[69] and continued to support the discredited "broad" interpretation of the ABM treaty contrived by the Reagan administration (see above). The 1991 budget request for SDI was over $4.5 billion and included funding for a number of tests that would bring into question U.S. compliance with the ABM treaty. These include, among many others, tests of the Airborne Optical Adjunct, an infrared sensor mounted on an aircraft that could possibly substitute for ABM radars, and the Zenith Star space-based laser that could attack booster rockets or satellites. Just how many of these tests would be carried out would be determined by a complex mix of technical, political, and economic factors that is difficult to evaluate from the vantage point of 1990. However, it seems highly probable that Congress will continue to make sizable cuts in the SDI budget requests and will continue to hold the administration to the traditional interpretation of the ABM treaty.[70] The actual appropriation for SDI in the FY 1991 budget was only $2.9 billion, representing a real reduction from FY 1990 levels, the first such reduction in the program's history.

At the same time, it would be foolish to predict the imminent demise of the SDI program. It has become a conservative political touchstone, and many in Congress who oppose deployment of an ABM system still support an active research program to prevent technological surprise and to stimulate innovation in other areas, both military and civilian. Nor will the Bush administration willingly enter negotiations with the Soviet Union on clarifying the terms of the ABM treaty and limiting research and development of new ABM technologies. The Soviets have repeatedly offered such negotiations, and many U.S. analysts have warned of the political consequences of unrestrained development of SDI, but after two years in office, President Bush has shown no more interest in such talks than his predecessor.

Even lower on the priority list of the Bush administration is a treaty banning or limiting antisatellite weapons, even though there is much in the way of desirability, negotiability, and verifiability to recommend one. The Soviet moratorium on ASAT tests was still in force in mid-1990, and no U.S. programs were anywhere near deployment, although the Pentagon was asking for a major increase in funding for a new ASAT to be tested by 1992 and deployed in 1994. Several programs funded under SDI also threatened to spin off into ASAT weapons, since the technical demands of shooting at satellites are similar in kind but often simpler in execution than shooting at ballistic missiles or warheads.[71]

ASAT arms control did not have the same ideological content as SDI, so the Bush administration appeared more ambivalent about it. One influential administration official, National Security Adviser Brent Scowcroft, had favored some kinds of ASAT arms control before joining the administration and had expressed some skepticism about the value of some kinds of ASAT weapons.[72] However, others in the administration strongly supported a U.S. ASAT capability and were likely to see even a limited ASAT agreement as a "slippery slope" to be avoided if possible. The Congress can—and probably will—cut or restrict funding for ASAT development, but it remains an open question whether Congressional and/or public pressure can force the administration to negotiate in good faith toward a ban on ASAT weapons if it does not want to.

All of this suggests that space arms control negotiations face a dim future in the 1990s. Negotiations to update the ABM treaty appear unlikely, and it appears far more likely that unilateral decisions dictated by domestic politics and economic constraints will govern the development of space weapons. This is not necessarily a bad thing; politics and economics could place even more stringent limits on such weapons than negotiated agreements. But the absence of clear, legally binding, and verifiable agreements on strategic defenses and ASATs does make the future less predictable and keeps alive the threat of technological breakthroughs that could upset the equilibrium achieved by offensive arms limitations.

**Nuclear Testing** A comprehensive nuclear test ban is supported by a wide range of American arms control groups, and is even more strongly advocated by other countries—especially those that have renounced their own nuclear option by signing the nonproliferation treaty.[73] Yet the Bush administration has stayed with the Reagan policy of insisting on intrusive new verification procedures for the obsolete Threshold Test Ban Treaty before it will even discuss progress toward a comprehensive ban or a reduction in the threshold.

A major event of the 1990s will be the 25-year review conference for the nonproliferation treaty in 1995. The treaty is scheduled to expire if the signatory nations do not take positive action to renew it, and continued nuclear testing by the United States and Soviet Union is likely to be a major issue raised by non-nuclear states at the conference (see Chapter 7). The nuclear weapon states are committed under the nonproliferation treaty to "good faith" efforts to end the nuclear arms race, and a comprehensive test ban is seen by most of the world as the most significant step the superpowers could take to fulfill that obligation. It is also the most readily and accurately verifiable of any of the agreements now under consideration.

However, from the administration's point of view, a comprehensive test ban is undesirable because it would cut off research and development on new technologies—an area in which the U.S. has traditionally held a substantial advantage over the Soviet Union.[74] In addition, bureaucratic interests in the nuclear weapons industry have traditionally opposed limits on nuclear testing with great effect. These interests dug in their heels in April 1990 when Secretary of Energy James Watkins informed the Senate Armed Services Committee that it would take at least ten more years for the United States to determine whether any further limits on nuclear testing would serve U.S. interests.[75] A further impediment to a test ban arose in the spring of 1990 when safety problems were revealed in a number of U.S. nuclear weapons.[76] This is certain to buttress the arguments of test ban opponents that further testing is essential to improve the safety of U.S. nuclear weapons.

As long as these controversies persist, and as long as public and Congressional concern remain relatively quiescent, bans on nuclear testing and development of new weapon types will be difficult to achieve. However, if the administration continues to resist a comprehensive test ban, its commitment to the nonproliferation treaty will certainly be called into question at the 1995 conference, threatening the survival of a treaty that the United States has always seen to be in its national interest. The key question for the 1990s, therefore, is whether pressure from world opinion and an increased threat of unconstrained nuclear proliferation can bring about a change in Washington's attitude toward a nuclear test ban.

**Verification, Compliance, and Confidence Building**   Verification will be one of the key issues of the 1990s. The verification provisions of the INF treaty and the bureaucracy created to implement them were the most elaborate of their kind in history, but they pale beside the effort and expense that will be required to apply similar or higher standards to START and a wide range of other treaties on conventional, chemical, and space weapons. It seems likely, therefore, that in the 1990s the question of diminishing returns on investments in verification will arise. The new generation of photo-reconnaissance and radar satellites cost at least one billion dollars each, and the number of high-priced technicians and analysts required to operate these systems and to process the staggering amounts of information they generate will be substantial. A rapidly expanding on-site inspection bureaucracy will become increasingly expensive and raise questions of industrial espionage and financial burden-sharing between industry and government. As the 1990s began, some experts on verification were already urging "a rigorous net assessment of the benefits and costs of . . . verification regimes; more specifically, the question of who benefits from the increased use of [on-site inspection] should be raised and answered."[77] There is at present no rational basis for such a net assessment, and at the start of the decade most policymakers and senators appeared to believe that more verification is better, and still more is better still. Clearly this attitude will have to change, but when and how and by what logic cannot be predicted.

Meanwhile, the Soviet Union will almost certainly be on its best compliance behavior during the 1990s. It is extremely unlikely that they would engage in the sort of ambiguous and irritating activities at the margins of treaty limits that marked Soviet behavior in the late 1970s and early 1980s. On the contrary, Gorbachev has gone to extraordinary lengths to reassure Americans of Moscow's good intentions. The Congressional inspection of the Krasnoyarsk radar was only one of a series of such invitations by Gorbachev to American groups. The National Resources Defense Council (NRDC) and the Soviet Academy of Sciences collaborated on a seismic monitoring project near the two countries' nuclear test sites, and another NRDC-led group traveled to the Soviet Union in July 1989 to conduct a simulated on-board inspection of a Soviet ship to see if nuclear weapons could be detected. On the same trip, the group of three members of Congress, two physicists, and several journalists visited the Soviet nuclear materials production complex at Kyshtym and a laser space-tracking facility at Sary Shagan.[78] When the Reagan administration charged in 1987 that two old Soviet radars that had been moved to an electronics plant at Gomel were in violation of the ABM treaty, Gorbachev invited official American inspectors to come and verify that they were inoperative. The administration accepted the invitation but did not reveal what it learned and did not change its position that the radars constituted a violation.[79] Nevertheless, the on-site inspection reassured most American observers that Gorbachev had nothing to be embarrassed about and the United States nothing to fear.

All of these efforts by Gorbachev have had a significant impact on Western public opinion, but they do not appear to have diminished in any important way the demands by the Senate for airtight, precise, and intrusive verification of future arms control treaties. What has given the senators pause has been the prospect of providing Soviet inspectors with all of the rights in the United States that U.S. inspectors get in the Soviet Union. American aerospace firms do not want Soviet inspectors learning industrial secrets; American military leaders do not want Soviet personnel prowling around their sensitive installations; and American politicians do not want to force these things on recalcitrant constituents. It is more likely to be rising costs and American secrecy restrictions, rather than Soviet foot dragging, that will limit the extent of on-site inspections in future treaties.

One area in which more rapid progress might be expected is in the management of crises and the prevention of accidental war. An impressive series of so-called confidence- and security-building measures was negotiated during the 1980s. One group, dealing with the problem of surprise attack in Europe, was implemented in connection with the 1986 Stockholm agreements and involves prenotifications of major military activities and on-site observations of military maneuvers.[80] In the nuclear area, new crisis management efforts included the upgrading of the 1963 "hotline" to full-fledged Nuclear Risk Reduction Centers in the State Department and Kremlin. Continuously staffed by military and diplomatic personnel, the two centers exchange information on upcoming missile tests, provide data relevant to implementation of the INF treaty, and send emergency messages to avert misunderstandings and overreactions in periods of tension.

Confidence building was extended even further in June 1989 when Admiral William Crowe, Chairman of the Joint Chiefs of Staff, joined his Soviet counterpart, General Mikhail Moiseyev, in signing an agreement to prevent accidental military encounters from escalating into war. Both military establishments appear to appreciate the value of such contacts and agreements, which, according to one high-ranking U.S. officer, represented "a new level of trust" between the militaries of the two states.[81] One arms control analyst has argued that confidence-building measures are more workable and productive than complex and difficult to verify agreements like START.[82] There is considerable validity in this argument, and arms control in the 1990s could come to rest more on progressive mutual confidence building than on elaborate arms reduction agreements.

## CONCLUSION

Georgi Arbatov, a prominent Soviet strategic analyst, captured the essence of George Bush's dilemma in his often-quoted warning to Americans: "We will do a terrible thing to you. We will deprive you of an enemy." By the summer of 1990, there seemed to be little doubt that the Soviet Union would carry out this threat, forcing Americans to face a brand new world, a world for which nothing has prepared them. And among the first questions that will emerge in this new world are: What are nuclear weapons for? If nuclear weapons are for "deterrence," then what is it that needs to be deterred? If nuclear weapons are for war fighting, than with whom shall we prepare to fight? How many and what kinds of nuclear weapons do we need in a world in which no military threats exist to our national survival? Traditionally, arms control has served both to manage and to legitimate the superpower military competition. What happens when one side refuses to compete? Can arms control, which *presumes* a military competition, contribute to the elimination of its own foundation? Or is it time again to talk of disarmament, as people did when nuclear weapons first exploded on the scene?

The arms race is best understood as a rising spiral of action and reaction: political tensions lead to increases in armaments, which increase suspicions and fears, leading to further increases in armaments. But the process could just as well go the other way. Political relaxation can lead to cooperative decreases in armaments, which can further reduce suspicion and fear, leading to further destruction of armaments. But for the spiral to go very far in this direction, the legitimacy and perceived utility of nuclear weapons as rational implements of national power and security must be challenged. Such a challenge appears to be an integral part of Gorbachev's new thinking, but it has created deep anxiety in significant segments of the American political spectrum and possibly among Soviet conservatives and military leaders as well. For these people, nuclear weapons have been the bedrock of superpower strategy, a vital symbol of national power, and the primary guarantor of peace for over forty years. It is hardly surprising that people who believe this find it difficult to conceive of a stable world without nuclear weapons.

The great contribution of the 1980s has been to resurrect the debate over whether the world can ever again be free of nuclear weapons. Deep philosophical divisions separate those who believe it can from those who believe it cannot. The most exciting prospect of the 1990s is the playing out of this debate in a context of growing social, economic, and political intercourse between the traditionally hostile NATO and Warsaw Treaty blocs. While the beginning of the decade saw an emerging consensus that far fewer nuclear weapons would be needed to keep the peace, it was still clearly unrealistic to imagine, as Gorbachev and Reagan did at Reykjavík, a world free of nuclear weapons at the turn of the century. But it is not at all unrealistic to imagine that when we reach that symbolic moment, if the number of nuclear weapons in the world has in fact been substantially reduced, a nuclear-free world could appear far more realistic than it did in 1990. Residents of small, remote towns often remark that "this may not be the end of the world, but you can see it from here." A paraphrase that suggests itself for nuclear arms control in the 1990s is that while the year 2000 may not mark the end of the nuclear confrontation, we might just be able to see it from there.

## Notes

1. James Eayrs, "Arms Control on the Great Lakes," *Disarmament and Arms Control,* Vol. 2, No. 4, Autumn 1964, pp. 373–404.
2. Thomas C. Schelling and Morton H. Halperin, *Strategy and Arms Control* (Washington, Pergamon-Brassey's, 1985), p. 2.
3. SALT stands for Strategic Arms Limitation Talks, and the weapons it covers are the so-called "strategic" weapons. These include intercontinental ballistic missiles (ICBMs), submarine-launched ballistic missiles (SLBMs), and long-range bombers like the US B-1 or the Soviet Blackjack.
4. United States Objectives and Programs for National Security, NSC-68, April 14, Thomas H. Etzold and John Lewis Gaddis, eds., 1950, reprinted in *Containment: Documents on American Policy and Strategy, 1945–1950* (New York, Columbia University Press, 1978), pp. 423–24.
5. I.F. Stone, "Why SALT Spells Fraud," in *Polemics and Prophecies: 1967–1970* (NY, Vintage, 1972), pp. 241–48.
6. Quoted in Raymond Garthoff, *Détente and Confrontation: American-Soviet Relations from Nixon to Reagan* (Washington, Brookings Institution, 1985), p. 950.
7. Ibid., p. 946.
8. Jerry Sanders, *Peddlers of Crisis: The Committee on the Present Danger and the Politics of Containment* (Boston, South End Press, 1983).
9. The position of the CPD was most clearly stated by its Chairman, Eugene V. Rostow, in "The Case Against SALT II," *Commentary,* Feb. 1979, pp. 23–32. See also "Ten Questions about SALT II," *Commentary,* Aug. 1979, pp. 21–32.
10. "Ronald Reagan's military budget dreams," *Bulletin of the Atomic Scientists,* Dec. 1988, p. 52.
11. PD-59 is described and analyzed in Louis René Beres, "Tilting Toward Thanatos: America's 'Countervailing Nuclear Strategy'," *World Politics,* Oct. 1981, pp. 25–46, and in Thomas Powers, "Choosing a Strategy for World War III," *The Atlantic Monthly,* Nov. 1982, pp. 82–110.
12. Garthoff, p. 1009.
13. Strobe Talbott, *Deadly Gambits* (New York, Knopf, 1984), p. 8.
14. Garthoff, p. 1010.
15. Daniel Yankelovich and John Doble, "The Public Mood: Nuclear Weapons and the U.S.S.R.," *Foreign Affairs,* Fall 1984, p. 35.
16. Data from Sean M. Lynn-Jones, "Lulling and Stimulating Effects of Arms Control," in Albert Carnesale and Richard M. Haass, eds., *Superpower Arms Control: Setting the Record Straight* (Cambridge MA, Ballinger, 1987), p. 237.

17. Ibid.

18. Yankelovich and Doble, pp. 43–46.

19. Pam Solo, *From Protest To Policy: Beyond the Freeze to Common Security* (Cambridge MA, Ballinger, 1988), pp. 49–50.

20. Douglas C. Waller, *Congress and the Nuclear Freeze*, (Amherst, MA, University of Massachusetts Press, 1987).

21. Information in this paragraph is taken from the "Chronology of Major Events Related to Arms Control Issues," *World Armaments and Disarmament: SIPRI Yearbook 1982* (London, Taylor & Francis, 1982), pp. 499–504.

22. Talbott, *Deadly Gambits*, pp. 300–52.

23. For a useful history of this period of uncertainty and drift in Soviet policy, see Dusko Doder, *Shadows and Whispers: Power Politics Inside the Kremlin from Brezhnev to Gorbachev* (New York, Random House, 1986).

24. For the argument that SDI and arms control are mutually contradictory objectives, see McGeorge Bundy, George F. Kennan, Robert S. McNamara, and Gerard Smith, "The President's Choice: Star Wars or Arms Control," *Foreign Affairs*, Winter 1984/85, pp. 264–78. See also Peter A. Clausen, "Transition Improbable: Arms Control and SDI," in Union of Concerned Scientists, *Empty Promise: The Growing Case Against Star Wars* (Boston, Beacon Press, 1986), pp. 181–202.

25. Garthoff, pp. 1026–28.

26. Public Papers of the Presidents of the United States, Ronald Reagan, 1984 (Washington, U.S. Government Printing Office, 1986) Book I, pp. 40–44.

27. Quoted in Talbott, *Deadly Gambits*, p. 337.

28. Strobe Talbott, *The Master of the Game, Paul Nitze and the Nuclear Peace* (New York, Knopf, 1988) pp. 239–48.

29. Matthew Bunn, "Star Wars Testing and the ABM Treaty," *Arms Control Today*, April 1988, pp. 11–19.

30. For an excellent analysis of the domestic roots of Gorbachev's arms control and military policies, see Alan B. Sherr, *The Other Side of Arms Control: Soviet Objectives in the Gorbachev Era* (Boston, Unwin Hyman, 1988).

31. A zero-sum game is one in which all winnings by one side represent losses by the other.

32. Talbott, *Deadly Gambits*, pp. 56–70.

33. Fact Sheet, U.S. On-Site Inspection Agency, Office of Public Affairs, September 20, 1990.

34. For a detailed analysis of the verification issues in START and other negotiations, see Allan Krass, *The Verification Revolution* (Cambridge MA, Union of Concerned Scientists, July 1989).

35. For a revealing study of the deep confusion and ambivalence of U.S. and Soviet nuclear strategists, see Steven Kull, *Minds At War: Nuclear Reality and the Inner Conflicts of Defense Policymakers* (New York, Basic Books, 1988).

36. Talbott, *The Master of the Game*, p. 390.

37. For an introduction to the foundations of U.S. and Soviet ASAT policy, see Paul B. Stares, *Space and National Security* (Washington, Brookings Institution, 1987).

38. A companion to the TTBT is the Peaceful Nuclear Explosions Treaty (PNET) signed by President Ford in 1976. Even though the United States abandoned PNEs years ago, the Soviet Union continued until recently to use them for natural gas exploration and possibly other purposes as well. The PNET has not been as controversial as the TTBT, so it will not be discussed further here.

39. For the most comprehensive analysis of seismic yield measurements and Soviet testing behavior, see U.S. Congress, Office of Technology Assessment, *Seismic Verification of Nuclear Testing Treaties*, OTA-ISC-361 (Washington, U.S. Government Printing Office, May 1988).

40. CORRTEX stands for Continuous Reflectometry for Radius versus Time Measurements. For a description of the CORRTEX method, see the OTA report, pp. 129–39. For press reports on the joint verification experiment results, see Michael R. Gordon, "Atomic Test Data Weaken U.S. View," *New York Times*, Sept. 11, 1988, p. 11; "Soviet Test Data Rekindle Dispute," *New York Times*, Oct. 30, 1988, p. 15; "U.S. Opposes Release of Soviet Nuclear Test Data," *New York Times*, March 23, 1989, p. A7.

41. See, for example, Walter Slocombe, "A SALT Debate: Hard But Fair Bargaining" and David S. Sullivan, "A SALT Debate: Continued Soviet Deception," *Strategic Review*, Fall 1979, pp. 22–38; David S. Sullivan, "The Legacy of SALT I: Soviet Deception and U.S. Retreat," *Strategic Review*, Winter 1979, pp. 26–41; Malcolm Wallop, "Soviet Violations of Arms Control Agreements: So What?" *Strategic Review*, Summer 1983, pp. 11–20.

42. Donald Bruce Johnson, *National Party Platforms of 1980* (Urbana, IL, University of Illinois Press, 1982), p. 211.

43. "SALT ONE: Compliance," Selected Documents No. 7, U.S. Department of State, Bureau of Public Affairs, Washington, Feb. 21, 1978, pp. 3–10.

44. Caspar Weinberger, *Responding to Soviet Violations Policy* (RSVP) Study, Memorandum for the President, Nov. 13, 1985, p. 9.

45. Public Papers of the Presidents of the United States, Ronald Reagan, 1984 (Washington, U.S. Government Printing Office, 1986) Book I, pp. 72–76.

46. "The United States Violates Its International Commitments," *News and Views from the USSR*, Soviet Embassy Information Department, Washington, Jan. 30, 1984.

47. See, for example, "Soviet Treaty Violations and U.S. Compliance Policy," American Heritage Society National Security Record, Washington, December 1983, p. 2.

48. Two independent analyses of Soviet compliance behavior and U.S. compliance policy are Allan Krass and Catherine Girrier, *Disproportionate Response: American Policy and Alleged Soviet Treaty Violations* (Cambridge MA, Union of Concerned Scientists, 1987) and Gloria Duffy et al., *Compliance and the Future of Arms Control*, Report of a project sponsored by the Center for International Security and Arms Control, Stanford University, and Global Outlook (Cambridge MA, Ballinger, 1988).

49. Quotes from "The President's unclassified report on Soviet noncompliance with arms control agreements," White House Office of Public Information, Dec. 2, 1988.

50. William J. Broad, "Soviet Radar on Display," *New York Times*, Sept. 9, 1987, p. 1.

51. Matthew Bunn, "Soviets Admit ABM Violation," *Arms Control Today*, Nov. 1989, p. 27.

52. Don Oberdorfer and Ann Devroy, "Soviets Dismantle Disputed Radar," *Washington Post*, May 29, pp. 1,11.

53. For a thorough survey of U.S. intelligence efforts directed against the Soviet Union, see Jeffrey Richelson, *American Espionage and the Soviet Target* (New York, William Morrow, 1987). For descriptions of many of the technologies employed and their interaction with the politics of verification, see Allan Krass, *Verification: How Much Is Enough?* (Lexington MA, Lexington Books, 1985). A good history and excellent descriptions of U.S. space surveillance can be found in William E. Burrows, *Deep Black: Space Espionage and National Security* (New York, Random House, 1986). The best descriptions of U.S. communications intelligence are in James Bamford, *The Puzzle Palace: A Report on NSA, America's Most Secret Agency* (Boston, Houghton Mifflin, 1982) and Seymour Hersh, *The Target Is Destroyed: What Really Happened To Flight 007 and What America Knew About It* (New York, Random House, 1986).

54. "Insights of an On-Site Inspector," Interview with Brigadier General Roland Lajoie, head of the U.S. On-Site Inspection Agency, *Arms Control Today*, November 1988, pp. 3–10.

55. "Soviet Noncompliance with Arms Control Agreements," Unclassified version of Annual Report of the President to Congress, White House Office of the Press Secretary, Feb. 23, 1990, pp. 9–12.

56. Yankelovich and Smoke, "America's New Thinking," pp. 15–16.

57. Matthew Bunn, "Spy Satellite Controversy Resolved," *Arms Control Today*, May 1989, p. 23.

58. See, for example, *Defence Without the Bomb*, Report of the Alternative Defence Commission (London, Taylor & Francis, 1983).

59. Mary Kaldor, "The Role of Nuclear Weapons in Western Relations," in *Disarming Europe*, Mary Kaldor and Dan Smith, eds., (London, Merlin Press, 1982) pp. 105–25.

60. Bernard Weinraub, "Arms Plan: How Frustrated Bush Took Page from Gorbachev's Play Book," *New York Times*, May 30, 1989, p. A12.

61. According to the U.S. Strategic Air Command, the U.S. could cut its deployments by as little as 10 percent and still comply with the treaty. Matthew Bunn, "SAC Force Proposal: 11,700 Warheads Under START?" *Arms Control Today*, February 1990, p. 31.

62. R. Jeffrey Smith, "U.S. to Propose Monitoring Arms Plants Prior to Treaty," *Washington Post*, June 20, 1989, p. A1; "U.S. Makes Six Proposals on Monitoring Strategic Pact," *Washington Post*, June 22, 1989, p. A30.

63. William Safire, "Taking Baker to the Cleaners," *New York Times*, May 21, 1990, p. A21.

64. Dunbar Lockwood, "START Talks Stalled, 1990 Finish in Jeopardy," *Arms Control Today*, September 1990, pp. 17, 21.

65. Michael R. Gordon, "Stocking the Atomic Arsenal: How Much Deterrence to Buy?" *New York Times*, May 23, 1990, pp. A1, 26.

66. Richard Halloran, "Stealth Bomber is Key to Arms Talks, Administration Warns," *New York Times*, July 22, 1989, p. 6.

67. Michael Oreskes, "American Fear of Soviets Declines, Survey Finds," *New York Times*, May 30, 1990, p. A12.

68. James R. Asker, "SDIO Believes Brilliant Pebbles Could Cut Cost of Missile Defense by $14 billion," *Aviation Week & Space Technology*, Feb. 26, 1990, pp. 62–63; Colin Norman, "SDI Heads for Fiscal Crash," *Science*, March 16, 1990, pp. 1283–85.

69. Quoted in James R. Asker, p. 62.

70. For a comprehensive review of the ABM treaty and its prospects for the 1990s, see Matthew Bunn, *Foundation for the Future: The ABM Treaty and National Security*, (Washington, Arms Control Association, 1990).

71. For a good review of ASAT technology and arms control issues, see Paul B. Stares, *Space and National Security*.

72. William J. Perry, Brent Scowcroft, Joseph S. Nye, Jr., and James A. Schear, "Anti-Satellite Weapons and U.S. Military Space Policy: An Introduction," in *Seeking Stability in Space: Anti-Satellite Weapons and the Evolving Space Regime*, Joseph S. Nye, Jr., and James A. Schear, eds. (Lanham, MD, Aspen Institute for Humanistic Studies, 1987), pp. 1–28.

73. For a clear statement of the pro-CTB position, see "Phasing Out Nuclear Weapons Tests: A Report to the President and Congress from the Belmont Conference on Nuclear Test Ban Policy" (Washington, Natural Resources Defense Council, 1989). For an excellent technical introduction to the problems of a CTB, see Steve Fetter, *Toward a Comprehensive Test Ban* (Cambridge, MA, Ballinger, 1988).

74. *Discriminate Deterrence*, Report of The Commission on Integrated Long-Term Strategy, Fred C. Iklé, and Albert Wohlstetter (co-chairs) (Washington, U.S. Government Printing Office, Superintendent of Documents, January 1988), p. 42.

75. R. Jeffrey Smith, "DOE Says Decade Is Needed to Weigh More A-Test Curbs," *Washington Post*, April 9, 1990, p. A10.

76. Keith Schneider, "Flawed Nuclear Arms Repaired Secretly," *New York Times*, May 24, 1990, p. A18.

77. Patricia Bliss McFate and Sidney N. Graybeal, "The Revolution in Verification," in *New Technologies for Security & Arms Control: Threats and Promise* (Washington, American Association for the Advancement of Science, 1989), pp. 139–45.

78. Bill Keller, "Rare Test by U.S. Scientists of Soviet Missile at Sea," *New York Times*, July 6, 1989, p. A1; "American Team Gets Close Look at Soviet Secret," *New York Times*, July 9, 1989, p. 1.

79. Matthew Bunn, "New Administration Report Charges Soviet ABM Violation," *Arms Control Today*, Dec. 1987, p. 25.

80. For the text of the Stockholm document and an interview with the Chief of the U.S. delegation, see *Arms Control Today*, Nov. 1986, pp. 13–24. For an update of U.S. participation in the Stockholm process, see "Military Confidence- and Security-Building Measures in Europe: Strengthening Stability Through Openness," U.S. State Department, Bureau of Public Affairs, Washington, April 1989.

81. Francis X. Clines, "U.S.-Soviet Accord Cuts Risk of War," *New York Times*, June 12, 1989, p. A12.

82. Bruce D. Berkowitz, *Calculated Risks: A Century of Arms Control, Why It Has Failed, and How It Can Be Made to Work* (New York, Simon & Schuster, 1987).

# 5 / The High Frontier of Outer Space in the 1990s: Star Wars or Spaceship Earth?

DANIEL DEUDNEY

## INTRODUCTION: COSMIC VISIONS AND EARTHLY REALITIES

The cosmos beyond the earth's atmosphere transcends the grasp of the human mind. Yet the regions of space around the earth have increasingly become the scene of human activity during the thirty-five years since humans first sent objects into orbit. Beginning a hundred miles or so above the earth's surface, where the atmosphere trails into a near vacuum, outer space is perhaps the most inherently global of the extraterritorial regions that technology has made accessible to humans. As such it is an arena where the ambitions of state security apparatuses clash most sharply with the imperatives of global interdependence.

The main possibilities for space travel and exploitation were first envisioned by science fiction writers and other futurists in the late nineteenth and early twentieth centuries.[1] The first halting steps of humans beyond the earth, what the great Russian space visionary Konstantin Tsiolkovsky called "humanity's cradle," have been accompanied by tremendous excitement and an intoxicating sense of unlimited possibilities. Like pioneers at previous frontiers, today's "high frontier" visionaries hold bold hopes that accelerated space technological development, like manna from heaven, can deliver humans from their terrestrial predicaments of nuclear vulnerability, resource shortages, overpopulation, and political oppression.[2]

Unfortunately the reality of space development has been far more sordid and mundane, more a mirror of terrestrial human maladies than an escape from them or a solution to them. By far the most significant exploitation of space technologies has been by the militaries of the nuclear superpowers, who have exploited rocket and satellite technologies into their globe-spanning capacities to obliterate industrial civilization. In any cosmic ledger book, this role of space technology in darkening the prospects for human survival outweighs all others thus far.

The most visible space activities, the manned space programs of the United States and the Soviet Union, are mainly circus and symbol, consuming tens of billions of dollars of public funds, while generating negligible scientific and economic benefits. Like the giant monuments and spectacular ceremonies of earlier ages, the manned space programs are gambits in the symbolic gamesmanship of national rivalries.

Apart from the perils of space war and the pageantry of manned space exploration, a myriad of space endeavors—the robotic exploration of other celestial bodies, communication satellites, and remote sensing of the earth's environment—have had far-reaching effects upon the human situation. More beneficial and less expensive than military and manned space activities, these endeavors have considerable untapped potential to make positive contributions to global well-being. Ensuring that space technologies and activities with positive contributions to make to global security and welfare become more the norm than the exception requires a shifting of priorities.

Although the militarist, nationalist, and escapist visions of the space age continue to shape world space priorities, an alternative "whole earth" or "greenpeace" vision of space implies a different lesson and agenda. For many environmentalists and globalists, the "whole earth" photograph—the first picture of humanity's home in the cosmos—has come to symbolize the lesson of limits and the need for cooperation and stewardship.[3] In the vast sterility of the cosmos revealed by modern science, the earth and its life are extraordinarily rare, precious, and precarious. In this "whole earth" perspective, the borders between human communities on earth must be rearranged to promote the sustainable stewardship of the life-support system on "spaceship earth." Human survival depends upon how rapidly a global mentality can spread and how soundly institutions of global governance can be erected.

The question of whether space technology will be employed to continue and accelerate the global security predicament or directed toward more positive purposes remains to be decided. Technology creates opportunities and constraints, not inevitabilities. The "Star Wars" effort of the Reagan administration to intensify space weapons development, still a cherished goal of the right wing of the Republican party, is on a collision course with the existing arms control regime. On the other hand, the waning of the Cold War and the new foreign policy approach of the Gorbachev administration open new possibilities for shoring up the space arms control regime and for increasing international cooperation in civilian space activities that can make a vital contribution to a sustainable "spaceship earth."

# SPACE AND MILITARY SECURITY:
# A BRIEF HISTORY

Since the beginning of the space age thirty years ago, the progress of space technology and the military rivalry between the United States and the Soviet Union have been inextricably linked. Military organizations built the first rockets capable of lofting objects beyond the earth's atmosphere and into orbit around the earth. The superpower militaries have been the foremost exploiters of space technology, and space technology remains of central importance to the nuclear delivery and information systems of the superpowers.[4]

The military exploitation of space has passed through three phases, the first marked by ballistic missiles, the second by reconnaissance and surveillance satellites, and the third by space-based "force multiplier" satellites that enhance weapons capability. The emergence of these uses has had a far-reaching impact upon the course of the arms race and superpower relations.

The first and still most important military space technology is the rocket or ballistic missile. Employing the empty regions beyond the earth's atmosphere for frictionless—and thus high-speed—movement, ballistic missiles make possible intercontinental bombardment. During the 1920s, enthusiastic civilian advocates of rocket development approached the major governments for support, but only the German army, seeking to evade the Versailles treaty limits on artillery, backed the conversion of vision into hardware.[5] During World War II these efforts bore fruit in the V-2, which was used in the psychologically terrifying, but strategically ineffective bombardment of Britain. Building on Nazi technology, Soviet and American engineers pushed ahead during the 1950s to develop more powerful and better guided rockets.

The real beginning of the space age was October 1957, when the Soviet Union electrified the world by using a large rocket to launch into orbit around the earth an artificial satellite, or "sputnik," demonstrating that Soviet communism had emerged as a contender for world technological leadership. Although the satellite was itself of little military value, the rocket that launched it into orbit had profound military significance, since it was powerful enough to carry a nuclear weapon from deep within the Eurasian interior to any point in North America in half an hour, thus making the United States vulnerable to devastating, unstoppable, and sudden attack. Caught unprepared for the tremendous psychological impact of the Soviet feat, the public and Congress became caught up in a crisis mentality, and the Eisenhower administration responded with a far-reaching reconstruction of the relationship between the government and science and technology, including the establishment of NASA, a vast increase in federal funding for science education, and the establishment of a White House apparatus for independent scientific advice.[6]

The ballistic missile has had several ramifications for the global security situation. Although the United States fielded a reliable nuclear rocket force before the Soviet Union, the long-range missile was initially of much greater strategic value to the Soviets, for it permitted them to offset American advantages in long-range air power and overseas bases. The ballistic missile profoundly altered the global security situation by narrowing the time frame for nuclear decision making while greatly increasing the geographic scope of the nuclear deployments. Whether based on submarines, in ground silos, or in railcars, the ballistic missile/nuclear warhead combination remains at the center of the superpower strategic equation.

As with nuclear technology, there has been a steady diffusion of rocket capability to other countries. Despite the occasional use of rockets to launch a civilian satellite, the main purpose of many of the world's "space programs" is military. The close connection between nuclear weaponry and space launch capability, begun by the United States and the USSR, is reflected in the fact that the members of the nuclear and space "clubs" closely overlap. Of space-faring states, only Japan has forgone nuclear development. The last three countries to enter the nuclear club—China, India, and Israel—have all developed rockets powerful enough to place satellites into orbit.

And as with nuclear technology, the spread of rocket launch capability has been marked by a schizophrenic attempt on the part of the superpowers to share civilian uses of the technology to advance peaceful relations, while keeping the technology from falling into the "wrong hands." During the 1960s and 1970s the United States gave or sold rocket and satellite technology to many other countries, some of whom have subsequently built extensive space launch programs. In the late 1980s, in order to stop the spread of missile technology to smaller states, particularly Islamic countries in the Middle East and South Asia, the major industrialized nations negotiated a nuclear missile control regime. However, the prospects for these limits are dim for several reasons: several states with missile technology to sell are not part of the regime; several states party to the agreement are circumventing it; and considerable technology was transferred before the agreement.[7]

Information-producing satellites are the second most important type of military space vehicle. Like a hill overlooking a battlefield, orbital space is a "high ground" ideal for observation and communication. Since the early 1960s the superpowers have deployed a wide array of increasingly complex, capable, and expensive satellites for surveillance, navigation, communication, damage assessment, and early warning.[8] The current American surveillance satellite, the KH (Keyhole) satellite is the size of a railroad boxcar, costs an estimated $1.5 billion, and is reportedly capable of collecting images of objects inches in size and sending them back to earth nearly instantly. The ballistic missile left both superpowers naked to attack; the surveillance satellite has left them naked to inspection.

The emergence of orbital surveillance capability benefited the United States more than the Soviet Union, for Soviet society was much more closed and secretive than the American. Satellites permitted the United States to maintain "open skies" over the Soviet Union after the Soviets developed rockets capable of shooting down high-flying U-2 aerial reconnaissance aircraft. In the early days of the Kennedy administration, early satellite photographs of Soviet missile facilities disproved the "missile gap" and helped limit a crash U.S. missile deployment program.

During the 1960s and early 1970s satellite reconnaissance and surveillance generally helped stabilize the superpower military competition, encouraging both unilateral restraint and bilateral treaties. By providing both sides with a high degree of confidence that they knew the numbers and locations of the other side's missile and bomber forces, these observation satellites also played a key role in the emergence of the first halting steps during the late 1960s to control the nuclear arms race. Satellites, known as "national technical means of verification," are the main tools for verifying the SALT agreements. With the acceptance of extensive on-site inspection in the INF treaty of 1986 and the START negotiations, satellites still provide wide-area surveillance necessary to detect locations for on-site inspections.[9]

Because satellite reconnaissance and surveillance have played such an important role in arms control between the United States and the Soviet Union, many have urged the creation of an international organization equipped with satellites.[10] Such an organization could monitor compliance with the various multilateral treaties that currently lack such capacities, provide the Secretary General of the United Nations with up-to-date information for peacekeeping missions, and provide the world community with a source of satellite information not dependent upon the United States and the Soviet Union. In 1978, a UN study committee—opposed by both the United States and the Soviet Union—concluded that an International Satellite Monitoring Agency (ISMA) was both feasible and useful. It would cost an estimated $1 billion, a sum roughly equaling the entire UN budget but less than a third of one percent of annual U.S. military expenditure.[11] To make such a "peace-satellite" organization feasible, difficult decisions about access to information would have to be resolved.

During the 1970s and 1980s satellite information systems of the superpowers began to help make possible the deployment of nuclear forces intended for a flexible range of war-fighting options. Satellites used for tasks such as military communication, collection of geodetic data, and target location are "force multipliers." Like sights on a gun, these systems are not themselves weapons, but make weapons more capable. For example, anomalies in the earth's gravitational field cause ballistic missiles traveling over intercontinental distances to deviate from expected trajectories by several miles. Using exacting measurements made from geodetic satellites, missile flight paths have been adjusted for these factors, thus enabling intercontinental accuracies of hundreds of feet, close enough for missiles to destroy hardened missile silos and command centers. And navigational satellites have helped improve the accuracy of sea-based ballistic missiles to the point where they rival land-based missiles in accuracy. As the volume and quality of information available from satellites has increased, it has become increasingly possible to integrate them directly into military operations.[12] As with ballistic missiles, numerous other states are beginning to deploy observation satellites for military purposes.[13]

Unfortunately for arms control purposes, such "force-multiplier" satellites are often difficult to distinguish from important civilian applications. For example, navigational satellites have many civilian applications. And some types of information—such as accurate mapping of the earth's gravitational anomalies—are impossible to eliminate once acquired. The cumulative effect of these diverse systems is difficult to measure, but the capabilities they have provided have seriously undercut the security gains from the arms control process by making the remaining weapons much more militarily capable. The difficulty in regulating such space-based information technologies reinforces the need to control nuclear weapons and their delivery vehicles.

# THE "STAR WARS" VISION AND GLOBAL SECURITY

In the last decade there has been renewed American and Soviet activity to develop and deploy weapons capable of destroying satellites and ballistic missiles in space. Orbital space is already extensively *militarized;* if these new antisatellite weapons (ASATs) and antiballistic missile systems (ABMs) are deployed, space will be *weaponized.* The debate over these emerging capabilities has been acrimonious. Its outcome in the years ahead will have far-reaching consequences for superpower military relations and world security.

Before weighing the case for and against space weapons, it is necessary to review the historical and technical background to this impending space arms race, first of ASATs, then of ABMs.

### Antisatellite Weapons

Because satellites travel in predictable orbits at extremely high speeds and are fragile, they can be destroyed in several ways: either by other "killer" satellites that maneuver into proximity for attack (or mutual self-destruction), or by missiles launched from the earth to intercept them.

During the early years of the space era, the superpowers largely eschewed ASATs. Through a process of informal or implicit bargaining, an

ASAT race was avoided, despite Khrushchev's threat to treat satellites as intruders of Soviet territory.[14] While space remained relatively free of weapons, various marginal ASAT capabilities were developed, generating considerable suspicions on both sides.[15] As observation and communication satellites have become more capable and integrated into military operations during the 1970s and 1980s, military planners have had increasing interest in developing the ability to attack and destroy them.

During the 1960s, the United States tested and deployed an ASAT employing nuclear explosives that was intended to neutralize a Soviet orbital nuclear delivery system. But the nuclear ASAT proved indiscriminately destructive and could no longer be tested after the Nuclear Test Ban Treaty of 1963 outlawed nuclear explosions in space, so the system was dismantled with little fanfare in 1976.

Apparently fearing the military capability of the U.S. space shuttle and the first Chinese reconnaissance satellites, the Soviet Union tested about two dozen times a rather slow and cumbersome co-orbital ASAT capable of attacking satellites in low-earth orbit. In attacking targets, the Soviet ASAT goes into orbit near its target and then explodes, showering its target with debris. Western fears that the Soviet Union had developed a ground-based laser capable of attacking satellites were put to rest by a *glasnost* tour of the Soviet site by independent American scientists.

As a response to the Soviet ASAT, and as a means to destroy Soviet ocean reconnaissance satellites designed to target American naval vessels, the United States began development in the late 1970s of a more versatile direct-ascent ASAT that destroys its target through the collision of a small homing vehicle launched from a high-flying fighter aircraft. After several tests, this system was canceled due to strong Congressional opposition and rising costs. In its place, the United States is developing at White Sands, New Mexico, a powerful ground-based laser which will be used to disable satellites.[16]

Opponents of ASATs argue that the existence of weapons designed to attack vital early warning and reconnaissance satellites increases the danger that a crisis situation will spiral into war and makes escalation more likely. By blinding and deafening one's adversaries during a crisis, ASATs reduce the prospects for effective control of nuclear forces and negotiated cease-fires. ASAT critics argue that a ban on ASATs would be easier to verify if agreed to before extensive testing and deployment take place.[17]

Since the early years of the Reagan administration, the antisatellite weapons question has been increasingly overshadowed by, and entangled with, the renewed debate over antiballistic missile systems. Even a limited ABM capability would have substantial ASAT potential. An extensive ASAT system would have limited ABM potential, thus eroding confidence in the ABM treaty regime. On the other hand, a ban on ASAT testing would effectively eliminate all ABM research beyond the laboratory.[18]

## Intercepting Ballistic Missiles

Due to the central role of the ballistic missile in the superpower military equation, the question of antiballistic missile technology has been among the most complex and politically charged of the Cold War era. Before considering the case for and against extensive deployment of space-based weapons, it is useful to review the basic facts of ICBM interception and the history of efforts to develop and constrain such technology.

Between launch and arrival at a target, a ballistic missile passes through three distinct phases, each of which imposes constraints and opportunities for interception. These phases—the boost, midcourse, and terminal—correspond roughly to the parts of the flight that are in the atmosphere over the launch site, in the free-fall trajectory through space, and in the atmospheric reentry over the target. A technology effective in one phase of a missile's trajectory will seldom work in another, thus requiring a full-scale defensive system composed of three interrelated but quite distinct "layers," each with different strengths and weaknesses.[19]

A rocket in the boost phase of its flight is easy to detect and target because of its bright burning engines, its slow speed, and its large size. A missile in boost phase is also an inviting target because it will typically contain many independently targeted warheads. However, boost phase lasts only about two minutes and takes place in the atmosphere, where energy beams are obstructed and scattered by air molecules, making them much less effective than in the void of space.

The second phase of an ICBM's flight—midcourse—poses a different, but no less challenging task for an interception scheme. For missiles traveling between the interiors of Eurasia and North America, the midcourse free-fall through space takes nearly half an hour. This affords a more leisured response time, but by midcourse the attacking missiles have released a vast flock of independently targeted warheads and decoys that are small, rapidly moving, and hard to distinguish against the background of space. The final—terminal—phase of flight is shorter even than the boost phase and occurs over the target, thus placing constraints on the violence of the means of interception.

During the 1960s, both the Soviet Union and the United States extensively researched and began deployment of ground-based interceptors equipped with nuclear warheads that were intended to intercept ballistic missile warheads very late in the midcourse and in the terminal phase of flight. However, an attacker could overwhelm a terminal or point defense system by proliferating the number of attacking warheads. And the radars necessary for target acquisition, kill confirmation, and interceptor vectoring would not survive in an environment of nuclear explosions. Since the interception "kill-mechanism" was a nuclear warhead, the system tended to be self-defeating, as well as untestable. At most it appeared such systems would add only briefly to the life of hardened military targets. Doubts about technical feasibility and public safety, combined with fears of a costly antimissile race, led the superpowers to agree to a complex and stringent set of constraints in the ABM treaty of 1972.[20] Perhaps the most militarily significant U.S.-Soviet arms agreement, the ABM treaty specifies a complex set of prohibitions designed to prevent the deployment and testing of capabilities to intercept ballistic missiles.

### President Reagan's "Star Wars" Vision

The ABM issue again burst into the center of public debate on March 23, 1983, when President Reagan, surprising both the Pentagon and his national security advisers, proclaimed the beginning of a major research effort to "render nuclear weapons impotent and obsolete" by developing and deploying space-based antiballistic missile systems.[21] Thus was launched the Strategic Defense Initiative (SDI), which cost about $25 billion in the first five years of its existence and was projected by the Reagan administration to consume $125 billion by 1992.[22]

The debate over ABM deployment and treaty restraints in the late 1960s and early 1970s concerned ground-based interceptors designed to intercept an attacking force in the final seconds of flight. Today's debate is about a multitiered or layered system, including new versions of terminal defense employing nonnuclear, rapidly accelerating interceptors based on the ground. The renewed interest in ABM systems stems from the perceived opportunities for boost-phase and midcourse interception by weapons based in space. The focus of interest has thus shifted from the last-ditch defense of a target with interceptors based nearby, to the forward defense of space-based interceptors designed to strike into the upper atmosphere and dominate vast regions of near-earth orbital space.

Several political and technical developments helped produce this visionary venture. The right wing of the Republican party had long opposed arms agreements with the Soviets and the ABM treaty in particular. They argued that anticipated restraints on offensive missiles intended to complement the ABM treaty had not materialized, and that it was therefore immoral and illogical for the superpowers to constrain defensive systems rather than offensive ones. Far-right activists such as Senator Malcom Wallop of Wyoming and Lyndon LaRouche, conspiratorial far-right presidential candidate, claimed the increasing power of lasers and other exotic beam weapons had made the complex task of missile interception technically possible for the first time.[23]

The "Star Wars" initiative was also in part a response to the political problems of the Reagan administration's nuclear arms buildup. From the left and center, the arms buildup was being undercut by the Catholic bishops' pastoral letter on nuclear deterrence and by the nuclear freeze movement. By proposing an arms development program to counter nuclear weapons, Reagan was holding out the prospect that the solution to the nuclear peril lay in the next phase of arms development rather than in an end to the arms race.

Defenders of President Reagan's space-weapons vision make arguments on strategy and doctrine, morality, technology, and politics. In the realm of strategy, advocates of the SDI program insist that the mutual hostage relationship between the superpowers can be transformed into one dominated by defense rather than offense. The direction of these proposed "defensive transitions" vary greatly. Some argue that the insular protection that the United States enjoyed before the advent of nuclear explosives and ballistic missiles can be recovered through technological advance pursued unilaterally, making both arms control and political accommodation with the Soviet Union or other states unnecessary.[24] Others envision a buildup of defensive weapons coupled with a negotiated builddown of offensive nuclear weapons.[25] In this view, space weapons are coupled with and help reinforce arms control by ensuring that small, postdisarmament arsenals can be protected from surprise attack. Others argue that mastery of space will enable the United States to protect itself and its allies, and to have decisive military advantage over potential adversaries, making possible an American global military imperium frustrated for so long by the vulnerability of the United States to nuclear attack.[26] And finally, advocates claim that even a thin system incapable of protecting against a full-scale attack could usefully intercept an accidental missile launch or an attack by a Third World country such as Libya.

Advocates also insist that advances in several important fields of technology—computers, sensors, and lasers in particular—give new hope that large-scale interceptions could be accomplished. As the power of small computers has expanded exponentially over the last decade, the enormously complex task of sensing missiles, aiming interceptors, assessing damage, and coordinating defenders in extremely short periods of time has become more plausible. Advances in information and thus accuracy have in turn stimulated interest in nonnuclear means of disabling oncoming missiles and warheads. In one scenario—favored by the Bush administration and dubbed "brilliant pebbles" by its proponents—compact computers would be exploited as the basis for large numbers of small and cheap interceptors that would operate on their own against targets, thus eliminating the need for complex and vulnerable centralized coordination.

Advances in laser-directed energy technology have also been great. The idea of using intense beams of energy in war has long been a staple of military science fiction, but over the last two decades the power of laboratory lasers has steadily risen. Advocates hope that progress will continue, and that lasers soon will be powerful enough for the task of missile interception. As more discriminating technologies of destruction emerge, the tendency for systems to blind themselves has become less of a barrier.

Third, SDI proponents insist that the Soviet Union, which has traditionally invested much more in strategic defensive systems, is violating key provisions of the ABM treaty and enjoys a major head start toward nationwide deployment of a system.[27] Because the Soviets are seen as ahead in development and deployment, but weak on the technological bases for sustained and rapid advance, the classic American approach of a technological "end-run" again seems attractive.

On the issue of economics, some proponents claim that an extensive ballistic missile intercept capability can be purchased for as little as several tens of billions of dollars. Some proponents of SDI also argue that development and deployment of space weapons will stimulate a broad technical revolution, with broadly stimulative economic effects. In this view, space weaponization is the cutting edge of a "high frontier" strategy of extensive industrialization and colonization of space. More modestly, others hope that the resources spent on advanced research will help stimulate the lagging international competitiveness of the United States.[28]

## The Case against "Star Wars"

The arguments against "Star Wars" are also diverse and can be conveniently grouped under seven headings.

First, and most decisively, critics point out that even if the most extravagant claims of proponents are true, the superpowers will still be in a nuclear mutual hostage relationship due to the vast number and tremendous destructiveness of nuclear explosives. No complex system ever works perfectly. Even a strategic antiballistic missile system that was 99 percent effective against the approximately 10,000 existing Soviet nuclear warheads would still permit enough warheads to reach their targets to obliterate the United States. Even an impossible-to-achieve 100 percent effectiveness against ballistic missiles would still leave each side vulnerable to air delivery by cruise missiles and bombers. In short, space weapons can never render "nuclear weapons impotent and obsolete." At best they restrain only one mode of delivery.

Nor are all space weapons nonnuclear. The SDI initiative was inspired in part by the proposals of Edward Teller (the reputed father of the H-bomb) for the development of so-called third-generation nuclear weapons, such as the X-ray laser, that channel the energies of a nuclear explosion into intense radiation beams designed to destroy objects nearly instantaneously at great distances. Instead of ending the nuclear arms race, President Reagan's space weapons initiative has spurred the development of such exotic new types of nuclear weapons.[29]

Second, critics point out that space weapons are intrinsically offensive in character. Based closer to Soviet territory, and with more rapid striking power than any other weapon, space weapons could form the cutting edge of a first strike by quickly destroying Soviet early warning systems. Indeed, even referring to space weapons as ballistic missile defense (BMD), as is often done, confuses function with intent. Even if space weapons capable of intercepting ballistic missiles are themselves judged defensive, such weapons used in coordination with existing weapons such as SLBMs and ICBMs could help make a nuclear force structure much more offensively capable: accurate ballistic missiles could destroy much of the Soviet missile force, and then space weapons could destroy the remaining Soviet missiles as they are launched. Critics point out that even a modest ABM capability could serve to augment an offensive first strike since Soviet retaliation is likely to be relatively uncoordinated.

Third, critics point out that there are a wide variety of potentially effective, but relatively inexpensive, ways to reconfigure ballistic missiles so as to make them more difficult to intercept. The boost phase can be shortened; clouds of metal foil balloons shaped like warheads can be dispersed in midcourse. And missiles and warheads can be hardened against the effects of beam weapons.[30] The same advances in computing and sensing technologies exploited by the "brilliant pebbles" interceptors could also be exploited to make "brilliant reentry vehicles," which would be able to maneuver to avoid interception.

Fourth, the various components of a space-based ABM system are themselves vulnerable to attack. Orbital battle stations equipped with beam weapons will be expensive, large, and difficult to secure against ASATs, other orbiting weapons, or "space mines."[31] The weapons based in orbit will have to communicate with each other and command authorities on the ground and will depend upon elaborate sensors and computers. These complex nerves, eyes, and brains of space weapons will be tempting targets to attack and difficult to protect.[32] The deployment of space weapons is likely to trigger a measure-countermeasure race rather than an end to the arms race.

Fifth, critics point out that the testing and deployment of space weapons will destroy the existing arms control order in space. Testing third-generation nuclear weapons such as the X-ray laser in space is outlawed under the Limited Test Ban Treaty of 1963. Since testing and deployment of a space-based ABM system is proscribed by the ABM treaty of 1972, it seems to some arms control advocates that SDI is a more effective weapon against existing arms control treaties than against Soviet missiles.[33]

Sixth, the deployment of space weapons will impose health and environmental risks upon all the inhabitants of the earth. Powering space weapons will require numerous nuclear reactors in orbit, and some of these reactors will surely reenter the atmosphere, spreading radioactive debris over large areas. To combat this danger to public health, a group of Soviet and U.S. scientists have proposed a treaty banning reactors from near-earth orbit.[34]

Space weapons development also promises to add to the "space junk" problem, and thus to make civilian and manned space activity more hazardous.[35]

Seventh, critics argue that space weapons deployment and the ensuing space arms race will have severe economic effects. Solid estimates of space weapons deployment vary greatly, depending upon the type of system envisioned, and the extent of Soviet countermeasures. But it seems likely that deployment of an extensive ensemble of space weapons will cost into the hundreds of billions of dollars. Furthermore, critics argue that space weaponization will divert the critically short supply of scientists and engineers from other pressing social needs. Because of secrecy, any "spin-off" technologies are unlikely to help U.S. high-technology industries against fast-moving industrial competitors in East Asia and Europe.[36]

The Bush administration, while not as enthusiastic about SDI as the Reagan administration, continues to support space weapons development and maintains a general verbal commitment to deployment. The right wing of the Republican party remains deeply committed to space weapons.

Thus far the SDI program has been concerned mainly with research and development, with visions of the future, not options for the present. The first tests of hardware against objects in space, however, will begin in the 1990s. Once these tests have been performed, it will be much more difficult to construct an arms control regime in which test constraints play an important role.

## COMPETITION AND COOPERATION IN CIVILIAN SPACE DEVELOPMENT

Although the military exploitation of space technology has been the most significant for superpower relations and world order, a wide range of civilian space activities, most importantly manned space exploration, scientific exploration with robots, communication satellites, and remote earth sensing satellites has occurred. The different areas of civilian space development have followed divergent, even clashing, directions. Civil space development has been marked by a complex mixture of international competition and cooperation. The early monopoly of space activity by the United States and the Soviet Union has been broken by the emergence of strong civilian space programs in Europe and Japan, opening both new competitive pressures and new cooperative possibilities.

### Humans in Space

Sending humans beyond the earth's atmosphere into orbit and to the moon has been by far the most expensive, publicly visible, and politically important civilian space activity. So far, only the Soviet Union and the United States have developed the ability to send humans into space, although both countries have carried foreign nationals into orbit in recent years. Although military organizations have contributed to these ventures, and in the Soviet Union operated the manned space programs until recently, humans in space have yet to demonstrate significant military value beyond servicing and retrieving satellites.

Opinion about the value of sending humans into space is sharply divided. For many space enthusiasts, the expansion of the human habitat beyond the earth is an overriding goal valuable as an end in itself. Others argue that sending humans into space is a waste of resources because almost all of the actual benefits of space technology can be realized much more simply and cheaply by unmanned vehicles. In both the United States and the Soviet Union, the scientific community has vocally opposed the focus of national space efforts on human space flight.

Thus far the manned space efforts have been motivated mainly by a Cold War rivalry for prestige between the United States and the Soviet Union. During the 1960s and early 1970s the Soviet Union and the United States vied with each other for spectacular space "firsts," such as the first man in orbit (Soviet) and the first lunar landing (U.S.). Project Apollo, the U.S. effort to place astronauts on the moon, was begun by President Kennedy as a way of competing peacefully with the Soviet Union.[37]

After the moon race, the sense of both urgency and competition diminished considerably. The Soviet Union has concentrated its energies on a steady program of space station development, extending from the *Soyuz* stations that were little more than space capsules to the current *Salyut* stations capable of supporting several cosmonauts for missions lasting several months.[38] In the post-Apollo era, NASA has concentrated its energies on the creation of a fleet of reusable manned space shuttles, to ferry materials to and from orbital space, an effort which has absorbed over $30 billion. The objective of the shuttle program was to make access to near-earth orbit more flexible and routine, and less expensive for both civilian and military users.[39] The U.S. shuttle program, and with it the entire U.S. space program, was dealt a crippling blow in January 1986 when a launch of the space shuttle *Challenger* catastrophically failed, killing seven astronauts and destroying the billion-dollar vehicle.[40] Subsequent investigation of the disaster by a presidential commission and others revealed that public and political expectations for routine launches were so great that important safety procedures had been compromised.[41] The *Challenger* disaster demonstrates that human access to near-earth orbit is still in a risky pioneering phase and is not yet routine or inexpensive. Risk assessments project that there is a 50 percent chance of another catastrophic accident over the next decade.[42]

Despite these problems, the Reagan and Bush administrations have endorsed an ambitious set of national space goals, including the construction of an earth-orbiting space station several times larger than Soviet *Salyut* stations (estimated in 1990 to cost $40 billion to build, and another $80 billion to operate), a manned lunar base (at a cost of $100 billion or more), and a manned landing on Mars by the year 2019 (perhaps costing as much as $500 billion).

Due to the vast cost and limited tangible benefits of this manned space exploration agenda, and the waning of the political tensions of the Cold War, large-scale international space cooperation has gained increasing plausibility and support. Leading space figures such as Roald Sagdeyev, former head of the Soviet Space Sciences Institute, and Carl Sagan, Cornell University astronomer and president of the largest citizen space lobby, the 100,000-member Planetary Society, have endorsed major joint ventures.[43] Like President Reagan's "Star Wars" proposal, large-scale cooperation in space is a vision, with several distinct justifications, alternative implementation scenarios, and problems.[44]

The first argument for space cooperation is economic. By proceeding cooperatively to reach the major next steps in manned human space exploration, duplication can be avoided, and the immense costs can be spread among more countries, making possible missions that would otherwise be unaffordable.

Advocates of cooperation also argue that joint space activities are a natural complement to arms control agreements. The aerospace industries in both the United States and the Soviet Union are heavily dependent upon military orders to sustain them, which generates political resistance to arms control and disarmament. Cooperative space activities can help solve this problem by channeling the aerospace resources into peaceful activities. Furthermore, an effective program of large-scale space cooperation can help create constituencies for the continuation of good relations between the superpowers. In contrast, effective arms control or disarmament does not directly employ people and industries in activities that depend upon a continuation of good relations. But once extensive projects have begun, a powerful "space peace industrial complex" will have been created.

Although expensive and less productive of tangible benefits than other areas of potential cooperation, space cooperation may have an effect upon the superpower relationship that is disproportionate to the resources expended, since both the United States and the Soviet Union attach great symbolic significance to space activities. Space explorers in both countries are hailed as heroes, and the leaders of both countries routinely refer to space as the frontier of the future. Closely interconnected activities in space will link this powerful political symbolism to international reconciliation. By colonizing the space frontier for cooperative goals, a major step toward colonizing the future for peace could be taken.

Large-scale space cooperation may also help close off further avenues for military competition. The emergence of a demilitarized Antarctica is an example of the impact of pioneering scientific cooperation upon regime formation in remote areas. After Antarctica was extensively explored during the International Geophysical Year of 1957, the great powers negotiated the Antarctica Treaty in 1959, deferring national territorial claims and keeping the continent completely free of weapons.[45] The treaty permits short-notice visits under the guise of "scientific exchange," providing an effective means of on-site inspection during the height of the Cold War. Applying the same logic, the moon will be easier to keep demilitarized if the first lunar base is an international science research facility rather than a base for the supply of orbital battle stations.

The cooperative exploration of deep space could begin with a coordination of existing unmanned missions and lead up to joint manned missions for exploring and the establishment of small bases for scientific research. Cosmonaut-astronaut exchanges and joint operations between the U.S. space shuttle and the Soviet space station could begin almost immediately, and build toward the creation of an in-orbit infrastructure for supporting larger long-duration missions into deep space.[46]

How such missions are organized will have great bearing on their political impacts. A Mars mission, for example, could be composed of separate space vehicles contributed by various countries, in which case the coordination problems would be minimal and the ability for one country to continue alone would be great. Such an approach could easily become more competitive than cooperative. Alternatively, if different countries contributed components on one vehicle or class of vehicles, then continued cooperation would be necessary for a mission actually to occur.

## Science in Space

The gathering of scientific knowledge by unmanned space probes in the last thirty years has greatly expanded human knowledge of the cosmos and the earth's place in it. Probes have been sent to the moon, Venus, and Mars. The soft-landing of the *Viking* probes on Mars in 1976 gave strong indication that life does not exist on Mars, the one planet besides the earth where life as we know it might survive or once have existed. The highly successful *Pioneer* and *Voyager* spacecraft also have made a preliminary reconnaissance of the four gas giants of the outer solar system. And a series of astronomical observatories, placed in earth-orbit to escape the distorting and filtering effects of the atmosphere, are enabling scientists to peer vastly farther and more clearly into the cosmos.

Although the most scientifically productive of space activities, planetary and astronomical space exploration has received far less funding than manned activities. Since the 1970s, however, European and then Japanese space probes have been launched, making possible extensive multilateral space science coordination and cooperation.[47] In 1982, for example, spacecraft from three countries coordinated their flights to the comet Halley. Dozens of other missions, to survey the planets and asteroids more closely, to return samples for study, to perform resource surveys, and to locate preferred manned landing sites, are in preparation or seeking funding.[48]

Although deep-space science is often far removed from practical terrestrial needs, the deep-space robotic reconnaissance of asteroidal bodies could help preserve the habitability of the earth. Scientists have located thousands of asteroidal bodies large enough to cause as much damage as a major nuclear war should they collide with the earth, and many more are suspected to be flying undetected through the solar system. Over the last several billion years, the earth has been repeatedly struck by such objects, and there is strong scientific evidence that such an event wiped out the dinosaurs some 65 million years ago. A "space watch" systematic survey of the solar system in order to map such objects would be relatively inexpensive to perform and could provide the warning time needed to take corrective action.[49]

## Comsats and the Global Village

So far the only space activity that has paid its own way and produced substantial profit has been the use of satellites as relay stations for long-distance communications. Such satellites typically are placed in an orbit 22,500 miles above the equator. These geosynchronous satellites orbit the earth in exactly the same amount of time it takes the earth to turn on its axis, thus remaining stationary relative to the earth's surface. More than two dozen civil communications satellites are in use, and worldwide this industry is a multibillion dollar enterprise.[50] Communication satellites have helped create a "global village" in which large quantities of information—telephone calls, business and scientific data, and television news—are routinely transmitted nearly instantly, knitting human activities together on a global scale. A variety of additional satellite communications services—notably direct broadcast of satellite television signals and networks of satellites providing mobile telephone services everywhere—are technically feasible, but face economic and regulatory hurdles.

International cooperation is an important feature of the satellite communications business. The single largest communications operation is INTELSAT, an international consortium owned in part by more than sixty countries, but largely controlled by the Western industrial countries. The general trend, however, is away from centralized management, and numerous private companies and individual countries have deployed their own communication satellites.[51]

Potential resource scarcities regarding space communications exist because satellites in geosynchronous orbit must be spaced apart in order to avoid signal interference with each other, thus limiting the number of satellites orbiting there. Because it oversees the allocation of radio frequencies, the International Telecommunications Union (ITU), a specialized UN organization, has been in effect regulating the global satellite industry.[52] Third World countries have objected to the "first come, first served" pattern of ITU allocations, arguing that developing countries just beginning intensive communication uses are being cheated out of their fair share of the valuable and limited geosynchronous orbit resource. Such resource conflicts pitting developed and developing countries have loomed on the horizon for over a decade, but have thus far been resolved readily. This emerging resource conflict may be mitigated further by the growing use of fiber optics cables, which are reducing the demand for communication satellites.

## Missions to Planet Earth

The fourth main area of civil space activity, observation of the earth from satellites, is of increasing importance to scientists studying the earth and its environment. Because they provide synoptic data of vast areas, satellites are indispensable tools for studying such diverse phenomena as continental drift, ocean weather and current patterns, atmospheric processes and pollution, and patterns of deforestation. In addition to expanding scientific knowledge of the earth, remote sensing satellites are being routinely employed for resource management. The world's weather services make heavy use of satellites and routinely pool satellite data to achieve global coverage. On a more ad hoc basis, satellite imagery has been employed for monitoring illegal burning of the Amazon rain forests, exploring for oil, and keeping tabs on major food crops.

Despite the proven technology and the growing need for better information about earth resources, efforts to establish a routinely operating remote sensing system have been plagued by administrative and financial difficulties. The U.S. Landsat satellites pioneered many remote sensing technologies, but nearly a decade of effort to transfer this technology to the private sector has failed to bear fruit. With strong government financial backing, the French SPOT remote sensing satellite has begun to produce images with ten-meter resolution (i.e., the smallest object visible is ten meters). And the Soviet Union has begun marketing images with five-meter resolution. Whether any one of these systems can operate on an economically sustainable basis remains to be seen.

Although monitoring the earth from space has yielded vital scientific and practical benefits, such monitoring is far from realizing its potential. Recent concern over such global environmental problems as the destruction of the stratospheric ozone layer and the greenhouse effect has spurred a major global effort to employ space technology for earth habitability monitoring on a larger scale and more regular basis.[53] Known variously as Global Change, Global Habitability, or Mission to Planet Earth, these global research programs have been conceived and coordinated by a group of distinguished scientists from many countries under the auspices of the

International Congress of Scientific Unions. To contribute to this effort, NASA plans to spend around $30 billion in the 1990s for a network of satellites, known as the Earth Observation System, or Eos, the Greek goddess of the wind and stars. Vast amounts of data about the earth will be produced, and special centers for data storage and study will be created for international scientific study. However, scientists complain that NASA's approach of using the space shuttle to launch a few large satellites with many sensor platforms is much more expensive, less scientifically productive, and less reliable than orbiting a large number of satellites with cheap, expendable rockets. It is hoped that the information gained from these global satellite studies will bring about improved understanding of the complex whole earth systems, thus laying the basis for major corrective actions.

## CONCLUSIONS: OUTER SPACE AND WORLD ORDER

Today the superpowers face a stark and simple choice in space: will they give new life to the arms race and Cold War by embarking upon the development and deployment of space weapons? Or will they redeploy and redirect their activities in space toward the creation of a more robust global security system, the expansion of human knowledge, and the preservation of the earth's habitability? Behind these two competing visions of space lie fundamentally opposed views of the nature of national security at century's end.

For the advocates of extensive space weaponization, the nuclear era and its unpleasant security vulnerability is temporary, soon to be eliminated by the advance of technology. They hope to recover security again through unilateral strength and national assertiveness. With security recovered through space control, the "American Century" envisioned by Henry Luce will finally be realized.

Alternatively, the superpowers could signal their acceptance of the realities of security interdependence on "spaceship earth" by joining together to lead international cooperative space missions. By linking the most technologically advanced and symbolically significant sectors of their societies together in cooperative space missions, the superpowers could lay the foundations for a more enduring peace and take important steps toward maintaining the habitability of "spaceship earth."

A decisive point of decision is fast-approaching. Are the superpowers really ready to turn the recent progress toward ending the Cold War into actual agreements that halt and reverse the arms race? Because they are so potentially volatile technologically, and collide so directly with the existing arms control regime, space weapons programs could perpetuate the Cold

War and undermine the recent improvement in superpower relations. As long as the world stands perched precariously on the verge of a new arms race in space, the Cold War—or worse—will be ready to break out again.


## Notes

1. For an overview of the complex relationship between science fiction and the development of space technology and programs, see Eugene Emme, ed., *Science Fiction and Space Futures: Past and Present* (San Diego: American Astronautical Society, 1982).

2. The most influential escapist and utopian space vision has been developed by Gerard O'Neill and his followers. See *The High Frontier* (Garden City, NY: Anchor/Doubleday, 1982) and *2081: A Hopeful View of the Human Future* (New York: Simon and Schuster, 1981). For a critique, see Daniel Deudney, "Space: A Mirage of Abundance," *The Futurist,* Fall 1982.

3. For this interpretation, see Daniel Deudney, "Space: The High Frontier in Perspective," *Worldwatch Paper 50,* August 1982, and Eugene Hargrove, *Beyond Spaceship Earth: Environmental Ethics and the Solar System* (San Francisco, CA: Sierra Club Books, 1986).

4. For illustrated overviews of the history of military activity in space, see Curtis Peebles, *Battle for Space* (New York: Beaufort Books, 1983) and David Baker, *The Shape of Wars to Come* (Cambridge, MA: Patrick Stephens, 1981).

5. William Bainbridge, *The Spaceflight Revolution* (New York: John Wiley & Sons, 1976).

6. For a vivid political history of the early military space race and its Cold War setting, see Walter A. McDougall, *The Heavens and the Earth: A Political History of the Space Age* (New York: Basic Books, 1985).

7. For an overview of ballistic missile proliferation, see Aaron Karp, "The Frantic Third World Quest for Ballistic Missiles," *Bulletin of the Atomic Scientists,* June 1988.

8. The most up-to-date and judicious work on satellite observation is William Burrows, *Deep Black* (New York: Murrow, 1986).

9. Allan Krass, *Verification: How Much Is Enough?* (Lexington, MA: Lexington Books, 1985).

10. Walter Dorn, "Peace-Keeping Satellites," *Peace Research Reviews,* Vol. 10, No. 5 and 6, 1987.

11. *Study on the Implications of Establishing an International Satellite Monitoring Agency,* Report of the Secretary General, Preparatory Committee for the Second Special Session of the UN General Assembly Devoted to Disarmament, August 1981.

12. For an overview of force multipliers, see Thomas Karas, *The New High Ground: Strategies and Weapons of Space-Age War* (New York: Simon and Schuster, 1983).

13. Michael Krepon, Peter Zimmerman, Leonard Spector, and Mary Unberger, eds., *Commercial Observation Satellites and International Security* (New York: St. Martin's Press, 1990).

14. Gerald Steinberg, *Satellite Reconnaissance: The Role of Informal Bargaining* (New York: Praeger, 1983).

15. An in-depth history of early U.S. policy on the ASAT question is found in Paul Stares, *The Militarization of Space, U.S. Policy, 1945–1984* (Ithaca, NY: Cornell University Press, 1985), particularly Chapters 6 and 7.

16. The capabilities of different ASAT systems and their implications for the survival of military satellites is examined at length in Paul Stares, *Space and National Security* (Washington, DC: The Brookings Institution, 1987) and Office of Technology Assessment, *Anti-Satellite Weapons, Countermeasures and Arms Control* (Washington, DC: GPO, 1985).

17. The case for an ASAT treaty is made in Union of Concerned Scientists, *The Fallacy of Star Wars* (New York: Vintage, 1984), particularly Part III.

18. The ASAT-ABM interaction is described in Aston Carter, "The Relationship of ASAT and BMD Systems," in Franklin Long, ed., *Weapons in Space* (New York: Norton, 1986).

19. For a detailed analysis of the technical and strategic issues involved in extensive space weapons deployment, see Office of Technology Assessment, *Ballistic Missile Defense Technologies* (Washington DC: GPO, 1985).

20. The technologies of the 1960s ABM are described in Richard Garwin and Hans Bethe, "Anti-Ballistic Missile Systems," *Scientific American*, March 1968. The role of citizen action in hindering ABM deployment in the United States during the 1960s is described in Joel Primack and Frank von Hippel, "Invoking the Experts: The Antiballistic Missile Debate," in *Advice and Dissent* (New York: Basic Books, 1974).

21. These unusual origins are described in Greg Herken, "The Earthly Origins of Star Wars," *Bulletin of the Atomic Scientists*, October 1987, pp. 20–28.

22. President Reagan's "Star Wars" speech and related SDI documents are reprinted in Steven Miller and Stephen Van Evera, eds., *The Star Wars Controversy* (Princeton: Princeton University Press, 1986).

23. For LaRouche's claims, see Fusion Energy Foundation, *Beam Defense: An Alternative to Nuclear Destruction* (Fallbrook, CA: Aero Publishers, 1983).

24. General Daniel Graham, *The Non-Nuclear Defense of Cities* (Cambridge MA: Abt Books, 1983).

25. Colin S. Gray, "The Transition from Offense to Defense," *Washington Quarterly*, Summer 1983, pp. 59–72.

26. G. Harry Stine, *Confrontation for Space* (Englewood Cliffs, NJ: Prentice Hall, 1981).

27. The question of whether the Soviet Union is violating the ABM treaty is debated in Colin Gray, "Moscow Is Cheating," and Michael Krepon, "Both Sides Are Hedging," *Foreign Policy*, No. 56, Fall 1984.

28. Daniel Graham, *The High Frontier: A New National Strategy* (Washington, DC: High Frontier, Inc., 1982).

29. For an overview of the X-ray laser and other beam weapons, see Jeff Hecht, *Beam Weapons: The Next Arms Race* (New York: Plenum, 1984).

30. These strategies are discussed at length in OTA, *Ballistic Missile Defense Technologies*.

31. For an extensive discussion of countermeasures, see ibid.

32. A detailed discussion of the C-cubed dimensions of space weapons is provided by Office of Technology Assessment, *SDI: Technology, Survivability, and Software* (Washington DC: GPO, 1988).

33. Arms control aspects of space weapons are discussed in Stares, op. cit., and in all the OTA studies mentioned. See also United Nations Institute for Disarmament Research, *Disarmament: Problems Related to Outer Space* (New York: United Nations, 1987).

34. Steve Aftergood, "Nuclear Space Mishaps and Star Wars," *Bulletin of the Atomic Scientists*, October 1986.

35. Bhupendra Jasani and Martin Rees, "The Junkyard in Orbit," *Bulletin of the Atomic Scientists*, October 1989.

36. The potentially negative impacts of space weaponization on the U.S. economy are described in William Hartung et al., *The Strategic Defense Initiative: Costs, Contractors and Consequences* (New York: Council on Economic Priorities, 1985).

37. For an analysis of the political origins of the Apollo Project, see John Logsdon, *The Decision to Go to the Moon* (Chicago: University of Chicago Press, 1970).

38. For an overview of the Soviet space program, see James Oberg, *Red Star in Orbit* (New York: Random House, 1981).

39. For an overview of the hopes for the shuttle, see Jerry Grey, *Enterprise* (New York: Morrow, 1979).

40. Richard Lewis, *Challenger: The Final Voyage* (New York: Columbia University Press, 1988).

41. *Report of the Presidential Commission on the Space Shuttle Challenger Accident* (Washington, DC: GPO, June 1986).

42. Office of Technology Assessment, *Round Trip to Orbit, Human Spaceflight Alternatives* (Washington DC: GPO, 1989).

43. Roald Sagdeyev, "To Mars Together—A Soviet Proposal," *Washington Post*, December 13, 1987, and Carl Sagan, "A Proposal for a Joint U.S./Soviet Expedition," *Parade Magazine*, February 2, 1986.

44. For an overview of the case for large-scale space cooperation, see Daniel Deudney, "Forging Missiles into Spaceships," *World Policy Journal*, Spring 1985. A vivid and detailed account of one cooperative Mars mission is described in Brian O'Leary, *Mars 1999* (Harrisburg, PA: Stockpole Books, 1987).

45. Harold Bullis, "The Political Legacy of the International Geophysical Year," in U.S. Congress, *Science, Technology, and American Diplomacy* (Washington, DC: GPO, 1977).

46. James Oberg, "A Shuttle-Salyut Joint Mission," in Oberg, ed., *The New Race for Space* (Harrisburg, PA: Stockpole Books, 1984).

47. For an overview of space programs emerging outside the United States and the Soviet Union, see Office of Technology Assessment, *International Cooperation and Competition in Civilian Space Activities* (Washington DC: GPO, 1985).

48. For detailed discussion of the many facets of Mars exploration, see Christopher McKay, ed., *The Case for Mars II* (San Diego: American Astronautical Society, 1985).

49. Clark Chapman and David Morrison, *Cosmic Catastrophes* (New York: Plenum, 1989).

50. The development of satellite communications is described in Delbert Smith, *Communication via Satellite: A Vision in Retrospect* (Boston, MA: A.W. Sijtoff, 1976). Prospects and impacts are described in Joseph Pelton, *Global Talk* (Rockville, MS: Sijthoff & Noordhoff, 1981).

51. Policy issues concerning satellite communications are described in Donna Demac, ed., *Tracing New Orbits, Cooperation and Competition in Global Satellite Development* (New York: Columbia University Press, 1986).

52. An overview of the ITU and its workings is provided in Office of Technology Assessment, *Radiofrequency Use and Management* (Washington, DC: GPO, 1981).

53. T.F. Malone and J.G. Roederer, eds., *Global Change* (Cambridge: Cambridge University Press, 1985).

# 6 / From Mutual Containment to Common Security: Europe during and after the Cold War

THOMAS RISSE-KAPPEN

## INTRODUCTION[1]

The Cold War finally ended on November 9, 1989. When the Berlin Wall came tumbling down, even the most skeptical observers had to admit that the post–World War II structure in Europe was changing. The bipolar order, which allegedly preserved the peace in Europe for more than forty years by dividing the continent and freezing the social and political structures, collapsed within a couple of months. When the world entered the 1990s, the Eastern and Central European members of what used to be the Warsaw Treaty Organization (WTO) were released from the Soviet-imposed regimes and in transition to liberal democracies. The Soviet Union was negotiating the withdrawal of its troops from Eastern Europe, not only with NATO, but, more important, with its own former allies.

An important debate is now under way in politics as well as in academia as to who won the Cold War. Among the self-proclaimed victors is the West, particularly the United States, whose strategy of containment supposedly worked. Others praise the new Soviet leadership under President Mikhail Gorbachev for having accepted an alternative approach to security and redefined Soviet interests in Europe, thus setting the stage for a strategic withdrawal from Eastern Europe. Or are the ultimate victors democracy and people's power, as the citizens of Poland, Hungary, East Germany, Czechoslovakia, Bulgaria, and Rumania staged democratic revolutions in their countries?

Efforts at interpreting the events of the late 1980s are closely linked to the evaluation of the European future. Those who believed in the stability of the Cold War order offer the gloomiest outlook and predict that a powerful united Germany together with nationalist movements in Eastern Europe will create a multipolar environment filled with all sorts of unstable and war-prone situations. Others believe in the inherent peacefulness of liberal democracies and, therefore, predict a stable, democratic, and prosperous Europe. In between are those who believe that the transition to a European peace order can be managed by building upon existing institutions, such as the European Community (EC), the North Atlantic Treaty Organization (NATO), and the Conference on Security and Cooperation in Europe (CSCE), commonly referred to as the "Helsinki process."

This chapter attempts to shed some light on these questions. However, one has first to explain the past in order to understand the present and to make predictions about the future. Moreover, analytical tools are needed to guide the interpretation of events and to prevent ad hoc explanations. Such tools are provided by various theories of international politics.[2]

# THREE APPROACHES
# TO INTERNATIONAL RELATIONS

## Realism

Realism is still by far the most prominent approach to the study of international relations, at least in the United States. The approach is based on the following assumptions:[3]

- States are the key actors in international relations. They behave rationally by calculating ends and means in order to maximize expected utility.
- States try to maintain and/or to expand their relative power position in the international system.
- The international system is anarchical, since there is no central authority creating order.

Kenneth Waltz's *Theory of International Politics* (1979) describes international relations as a self-help system in which states struggle to survive by balancing the power of the other actors. The structure of the international system is explicable in terms of the distribution of power—economic and military—among the various actors. According to Waltz, bipolar orders tend to be more stable than multipolar systems in which the actors more frequently shift alliances and are more independent from each other.

Robert Gilpin's *War and Change in World Politics* (1981) adds to this analysis the explanation of change in the international system as a result of shifts in the distribution of power between the states. Power capabilities grow at an uneven rate due to differences in economies and technology. As a result, imbalances occur in the system and it becomes harder for the hegemonial powers to maintain the status quo. Gilpin predicts that wars are likely in the transition period from a system in disequilibrium to a new international balance of power.

In sum, the relative distribution of power among states is the central variable of the realist paradigm to explain outcomes in international relations. Ideologies, belief systems, and domestic politics count only insofar as they make states more or less efficient in their struggle for power.

## Liberalism

The liberal theory of foreign policy disagrees with the core assumptions of realism. It posits a causal relationship between the internal political and/or economic organization of states and their external behavior. Adam Smith and David Ricardo, for example, argued that capitalism and free trade are the best guarantees for international peace. Joseph Schumpeter—in contrast to Marxist thinking—added that the welfare orientation of modern industrial societies reduces the strive for expansionism and for aggressive behavior in the world.[4]

Another version of the liberal approach links the foreign policy of democracies to their political structures.[5] Liberal democracies are thought to pursue a more peaceful foreign policy than authoritarian regimes because the norm of peaceful conflict resolution that governs democracies internally also guides their external behavior. In addition, it is argued that the costs of aggressive behavior run counter to the welfare orientations of citizens, who are therefore less willing to support such policies except in cases in which their immediate survival is at stake.

In sum, the more democractic a state's domestic structure, the less inclined it will be to use or threaten to use force in international politics. International conflicts result largely from clashes between competing ideologies and from disputes between antagonistic economic and political systems.

## The "Security Dilemma" and Neoliberal Institutionalism

An intermediate position between realism and liberalism is taken by approaches that challenge the rationality assumption of both realists and liberals by pointing to the effects of domestic politics, misperceptions, and cognitive biases on the part of the decision-makers involved.[6] Tensions arise, more often than not, as a result of domestic politics and/or perceived threats in the international environment. Defensive motivations on both sides can lead to international crises and wars because of the nature of the "security dilemma": State A is uncertain about State B's defensiveness and decides to play it safe and accumulate power to defend against B. This behavior is perceived as threatening by B, which reacts by also building up its defenses. A vicious cycle is thus set in motion because of a lack of certainty about either side's peaceful intentions.

However, the "security dilemma" can be overcome. States can reduce the uncertainty through cooperation. Neoliberal institutionalists try to explain why and under what conditions such cooperation occurs despite hegemonic rivalries and/or antagonistic political and economic systems. They argue that international agreements and institutions—"regimes"—create international norms that transform the foreign policy goals of states in favor of cooperation. As a result, the international environment becomes more predictable and uncertainty is reduced.[7]

# ORIGINS OF THE COLD WAR: THREAT PERCEPTIONS AND COMPETING INTERESTS

"In these circumstances it is clear that the main element of any United States policy toward the Soviet Union must be that of a long-term, patient but firm and vigilant containment of Russian expansive tendencies." ("X" [George F. Kennan], "The Sources of Soviet Conduct," July 1947)[8]

"The more the war recedes into the past, the more distinct become two major trends in post-war international policy, corresponding to the division of the political forces operating on the international arena into two major camps: the imperialist and anti-democratic camp, on the one hand, and the anti-imperialist and democratic camp, on the other." (Andrei Zhdanov, "Report on the International Situation to the Cominform," September 22, 1947)[9]

From a realist perspective, the East-West conflict was another great power rivalry, a conflict about spheres of influence that quickly reached a global scale. Once the German attempt to establish world hegemony had been defeated in World War II, the U.S.-Soviet confrontation was almost inevitable, since they were the only two remaining great powers. The U.S. economic position was virtually undisputed; as a result, the postwar international economic order was largely built according to a U.S. design. Militarily, the U.S. nuclear monopoly—and later overwhelming superiority— could be matched only by the Soviet Union's conventional superiority in Europe.[10]

Soviet behavior in Eastern Europe was equally explicable.[11] First, having been invaded twice in the twentieth century, any Russian government would have been concerned about secure frontiers. The absorption of the Baltic republics and of territory in East Poland, the annexation of Carpathian Ruthenia, Bessarabia, and Northern Bukovina nearly restored Russia's frontiers to their 1914 position. Second, Stalin's policy of securing a sphere of influence and "friendly neighbors" in Eastern Europe can also be explained as a result of the Soviet Union's geostrategic position as a land power.

There are problems with this explanation, though. A policy of securing spheres of influence does not necessarily imply that the domestic political and socioeconomic orders of the neighboring countries have to conform to the hegemon's model. In other words, how is the *Sovietization* of Eastern Europe to be explained? Why was it that only Finland was allowed to choose its domestic order, while accepting a security alliance with the USSR? For all the other European states bordering the Soviet Union, Stalin's policy meant not only that their foreign policies were dictated by Moscow, but also that communist systems were imposed on them. Between 1946 and 1948, Bulgaria, Rumania, Hungary, Poland, and Czechoslovakia were all Sovietized by more or less forceful means. Moreover, when the occupation regime of the four allies over Germany had broken down as a result of the emerging Cold War, the country was divided. The USSR imposed a communist system on its occupation zone in East Germany, leading to the creation of the German Democratic Republic in October 1949.

The Western response to Soviet policies after World War II cannot be fully explained, either, if one emphasizes nothing but relative power capabilities. Why would the Western Europeans join the United States in an anti-Soviet alliance when the United States had nuclear superiority and the world's strongest economy? Stephen Walt suggests modifying the realist "balance of power" concept by "balance of threats." He argues that geographic proximity and offensive military power are among the major factors constituting threats to other states, which helps explain why the Western Europeans balanced against the Soviet Union.[12]

The liberal theory of foreign policy also has a straightforward interpretation of both Soviet behavior in Eastern Europe and the Western reaction to it. From this point of view, the East-West conflict was not so much about hegemonic rivalries, but resulted from the basic antagonism between liberal democracies and market capitalism on the one hand, and authoritarian regimes and centrally planned economies on the other. At the roots was a basic disagreement about individual human rights.

Liberal theorists explain the Sovietization of Eastern Europe as resulting from Marxist-Leninist ideology and/or from the fact that authoritarian regimes feel threatened by liberal democracies surrounding them. They also argue that the "Soviet threat" to Western Europe was not so much the USSR's military power or geographic proximity, but, above all, the brutality with which the Sovietization of Eastern Europe was carried out.[13] Had the Soviet Union just "Finlandized" Eastern Europe, rather than "Sovietizing" it, i.e., had it allowed the Eastern Europeans to choose their own domestic system, a "Cold War consensus" on the containment of Soviet expansionism would probably not have emerged in the West.

How did this consensus evolve? From the mid-1940s on, a growing group of government officials and other members of the political and business elites in Washington, London, and Paris (later joined by Chancellor Adenauer in West Germany) became convinced that containment of Soviet power should be the new grand strategy for the West.[14] In the United States, a coalition emerged between the foreign policy elite arguing that centrally planned economies and authoritarian regimes lead to instability and war, and prominent sectors in the business community who favored free trade to further their economic interests. However, there was only reluctant domestic support for their viewpoint in the beginning. Even in 1947–48 the U.S. public continued to adhere to isolationist attitudes. It was Soviet political and military actions in Eastern Europe that led to increased threat perceptions in Western Europe and the United States, thereby creating a "window of opportunity" for those elite groups who were long convinced of the necessity to contain Soviet power. For example, the Soviet blockade of Berlin in June 1948 tipped the balance in favor of those in Washington who advocated a positive response to European demands that the United States join a transatlantic alliance. As a result, the North Atlantic Treaty was signed in April 1949.

At the time, however, NATO was a political alliance without a military organization. While military planners and senior government officials on both sides of the Atlantic were convinced that NATO needed a military organization, they lacked the domestic support for a costly defense buildup. The militarization of the Western alliance occurred only after the Korean War and Stalin's backing for Kim Il Sung's invasion of South Korea. These events triggered the Cold War defense buildup of the United States, the transformation of NATO into a military organization, and the rearmament of West Germany.[15]

However, by emphasizing that the West mainly reacted to a perceived Soviet threat, the liberal explanation fails to take into account that the United States and the Western Europeans shared responsibility for the increased level of tensions, too. This explanation by and large takes the Western *perception* of the reality for the reality itself.

The strategy of containment—meant to be defensive—could well be perceived as offensive by the Soviet Union. Here, the "security dilemma" comes into play.[16] After all, it was the United States that enjoyed undisputed nuclear superiority and economic hegemony on the world markets, while the Soviet Union lay decimated by the war. The Marshal Plan, which was meant to foster European economic cooperation and rebuild its devastated economies, was perceived by the Soviet leadership as an American attempt to "make the world safe for capitalism."[17] In a similar way, the Berlin blockade can be seen as a Soviet (over-)reaction to the currency reform in the Western occupation zones of Germany, which was interpreted by Stalin as creating a *fait accompli*.

To conclude, a modified version of the liberal theory, taking into account perceptions, misperceptions, and competing interests, seems to be best suited to explain the origins of the Cold War. Western threat perceptions, which legitimized the strategy of containment as well as the defense

Table 6.1 / U.S. Military Spending, 1930–90 (in billions of 1990 dollars)

| YEAR | OUTLAYS | YEAR | OUTLAYS | YEAR | OUTLAYS |
|------|---------|------|---------|------|---------|
| 1930 | 11.4 | 1952 | 299.6 | 1975 | 209.9 |
| 1940 | 22.2 | 1953 | 330.8 | 1980 | 221.0 |
| 1941 | 73.4 | 1955 | 268.7 | 1982 | 250.7 |
| 1943 | 594.7 | 1960 | 248.0 | 1984 | 284.9 |
| 1945 | 803.9 | 1965 | 236.7 | 1986 | 308.6 |
| 1947 | 113.6 | 1967 | 296.5 | 1988 | 314.4 |
| 1950 | 105.9 | 1969 | 314.5 | 1990 | 300.0 |
| 1951 | 166.7 | 1970 | 289.8 | | |

Source: William Kaufmann, "A Plan to Cut Military Spending in Half," *Bulletin of the Atomic Scientists*, Vol. 46, No. 2, March 1990, pp. 35–39.

buildup, largely reacted to the Stalinist ideology and to Soviet behavior in Eastern Europe as well as in Korea. On the other hand, the Western "Cold War consensus" contributed to a climate of mutual hostility that endured throughout the 1950s and prevented a relaxation of tensions prior to the Cuban missile crisis of 1962. Defense expenditures in both the United States and Western Europe skyrocketed in the early 1950s and institutionalized the military, economic, and bureaucratic apparatus, which President Eisenhower later called the "military-industrial complex" (see Table 6.1).

# CONTAINMENT AND DÉTENTE: EUROPEAN SECURITY FROM 1955 TO 1985

"The Atlantic Alliance has two main functions. Its first function is to maintain adequate military strength and political solidarity to deter aggression and other forms of pressure and to defend the territory of member countries if aggression should occur. . . . In this climate the Alliance can carry out its second function, to pursue the search for progress towards a more stable relationship in which the underlying political issues can be solved. Military security and a policy of détente are not contradictory but complementary." ("The Future Tasks of the Atlantic Alliance," Harmel Report, December 14, 1967)[18]

By 1955, the bipolar order in Europe was firmly established, with the Federal Republic of Germany entering NATO and the German Democratic Republic becoming a member of the newly founded WTO. The two Germanies became the area with the largest concentration of troops in the world (see Figure 6.1). In addition, thousands of nuclear weapons with ranges from fifteen to several thousand miles were deployed in or targeted against Central Europe.[19]

Given the militarization of the East-West conflict in Europe, it is remark-

Figure 6.1. / Combat-Ready NATO and Warsaw Pact Ground Force Divisions on the Central Front, 1986.

Source: Jonathan Dean, *Watershed in Europe* (Lexington, MA: Lexington Books, 1987), p. 43.

able that from the early 1960s on (i.e., after the Berlin crises of the late 1950s, the building of the Berlin Wall in August 1961, and the Cuban missile crisis in October 1962), there was no serious crisis or confrontation between the two alliances in Central Europe. While the U.S.-Soviet confrontation continued in the Third World and led to numerous proxy wars, Europe seemed to remain an island of stability during much of the Cold War. In fact, NATO and the WTO embarked upon a process of political and military détente. In 1967, NATO formally adopted the above-quoted Harmel Report, which based its policies on both deterrence and détente. In 1975, thirty-three European nations plus the United States and Canada met in Helsinki to sign the Final Act of the Conference on Security and Cooperation in Europe, including the recognition of the territorial and political status quo in Europe, an affirmation of human rights for each European citizen, and a framework for economic and humanitarian cooperation between the blocs.[20]

The détente process also affected bilateral relations between individual Western European countries and the East. In 1969, for example, West German Chancellor Willy Brandt began his *Ostpolitik,* the improvement of relations with the Soviet Union, the GDR, and the other nations of Eastern Europe.[21] He concluded treaties with the East that recognized the status quo in Europe, including the division of Germany. Throughout the 1970s, a firm domestic consensus emerged in favor of these policies. Cooperation with the East became an accepted goal of West German foreign policy. *Ostpolitik* even survived the deterioration of the superpower relationship after the 1979 Soviet intervention in Afghanistan.

How are the political stability in Europe and the emergence of détente and arms control to be explained? One interpretation holds that political stability in Europe was the result of the two sides confronting each other armed to the teeth. The integration of nuclear and conventional weapons in the force postures of both sides introduced the risk that any confrontation would lead to nuclear escalation. By the same token, when the United States and the Soviet Union achieved nuclear parity and secure nuclear second-strike capabilities in the 1960s, they recognized their common interest in avoiding (nuclear) war and increasing crisis stability. The turn toward arms control and détente resulted from this reevaluation of the national interest, say the realists.[22]

However, the détente process in Europe, while improving the political relationship, only marginally affected the military confrontation. European arms control did not produce tangible results prior to 1985 (i.e., before the leadership change in the Soviet Union). The conventional troop reduction talks in Vienna, which started in 1973, were stalemated for fifteen years.[23] Negotiations on nuclear weapons in Europe did not begin until 1981, and were equally stalemated until Mikhail Gorbachev entered the scene.

Moreover, arms control did not have much impact on the defense policies of both alliances. The logic of arms control and détente assumed that nuclear weapons are too dangerous to be treated as "normal" military weapons and that they are essentially nonusable as means of warfighting. In 1967, however, when NATO adopted arms control as the second pillar of its security policy, it also accepted a military strategy known as flexible response, which was based on the assumption that tactical nuclear weapons could be used to limit damage in an ongoing conflict and that the control of nuclear escalation would be possible.[24]

There are two explanations for the ambiguities in the approaches of both sides to arms control and détente. First, the "security dilemma," which provides incentives for opponents to cooperate in order to reduce uncertainties about each other's intentions, also limits the scope of cooperation, in particular when it comes to national security.[25] Accordingly, while East and West were prepared to cooperate politically and to embark upon arms control negotiations, they did not trust each other enough to allow the process to dominate their defense policies. In other words, the détente process of the 1970s failed to establish "common security" as the principle governing the East-West relationship. "Common security" means that, in the nuclear age, neither side can feel secure if one side feels threatened. As a result, the system of deterrence, which is based on mutual distrust, has to be gradually replaced by a system of mutual reassurance about each other's defensive motives.[26]

A second explanation adds domestic politics in East and West to the "security dilemma" interpretation. To begin with, the stagnation of Soviet policy in the late Brezhnev era has to be taken into account.[27] Brezhnev's power in the Politburo was apparently based on a coalition with the military and those in charge of heavy industry; both groups resisted arms cuts. While the Soviet Union used the détente process to gain Western acceptance of strategic parity and the status quo in Europe, it was not prepared to address the military confrontation. Moreover, the USSR continued to modernize its already superior conventional forces, thereby raising suspicions in the West. Moreover, in 1976, the Soviet Union began to deploy the SS-20, a new medium-range missile that added considerably to its nuclear capabilities against Western Europe. Moscow was told by almost every European government that the West would react if the Soviets continued this buildup. Finally, in December 1979, NATO adopted the "dual-track decision" calling for the modernization of its intermediate-range nuclear forces (INF), but also for negotiations with the USSR aiming at the elimination of all land-based INF. It was not until 1986—after four years of deadlocked negotiations—that the USSR reacted favorably to this proposal. In December 1987, the INF treaty signed by the USSR and the United States implemented the "zero option."[28]

Moreover, domestic politics in the West has to be taken into account, too. In the United States, the domestic support for détente began to erode from the mid-1970s on.[29] The repression of human rights in the Soviet Union and Moscow's actions in the Third World created a "window of opportunity" for those groups in Washington who had never believed in détente and arms control. The Committee on the Present Danger, for example, was able to form a powerful coalition that severely reduced the domestic support basis for President Carter's arms control policy. When the USSR invaded Afghanistan in December 1979, this spelled the end of détente for the U.S. public, at least for the time being. The superpower relationship quickly deteriorated, and President Reagan was elected on a firm anti–arms control platform. Thus, U.S.-Soviet relations from the mid-1970s on did not create a favorable environment for European arms control.

However, the Western Europeans did not give up the concept of détente in reaction to the Soviet arms buildup and the change in U.S. policies. As argued above, détente, which was strongly supported by public opinion, had become an accepted norm for the conduct of East-West relations in Western

Europe, particularly in West Germany. In the mid-1970s, parts of the political elites in Western Europe, above all the Social Democrats, advocated increased arms control efforts in Europe. They also introduced the concept of "common security" into the East-West debate. Ten years later, the idea had become conventional wisdom in many Western European countries.[30]

As a result of these domestic processes, the Europeans—East and West—tried to preserve détente even after the superpower relationship deteriorated. The CSCE survived the difficult 1980–83 Madrid review conference largely through European efforts. Moreover, new peace movements emerged in Europe in the early 1980s protesting the East-West arms race,[31] and the level of public attention to security issues rose considerably. When Mikhail Gorbachev reoriented Soviet foreign policy toward Western Europe and embraced the Social Democratic concept of "common security," he became the hero of many Europeans, particularly the West Germans. The ten years from 1975 to 1985 had essentially been wasted in terms of putting the East-West relationship in Europe on a more stable footing, first because of the late Brezhnev's stubbornness, later because of Reagan's (over-)reaction to it.

In sum, realist theory can explain why the overarching interests of both sides to survive eventually led to a considerable relaxation of tensions after the Cuban missile crisis. However, it can account neither for the ambiguities of the first détente period nor for the different approaches by the Europeans as compared to the superpowers. Neoliberal institutionalism, which starts from the "security dilemma" but takes domestic politics seriously, seems to be better suited to explain the ups and downs of the East-West relationship during the 1970s and early 1980s.

## WHEN THE WALL CAME TUMBLING DOWN: THE END OF THE COLD WAR

"*Wahnsinn!*"
("Just crazy!" Exclamation of Germans when the Berlin Wall was opened on November 9, 1989)

"We are the people!"
(Slogan of demonstrators all over Eastern Europe in the fall of 1989)

When the 1990s began, the bipolar order, which had dominated the strategic environment in Europe for forty years, was gone. One by one, communist regimes in Poland, Hungary, East Germany, Czechoslovakia, Bulgaria, and even Rumania were overthrown by democratic revolutions. Eastern Europe was in transition to democracy and market economy, while the Soviet Union continued to struggle with the most profound transformation of its political, economic, and social system since the October Revolution of 1917.

How did the Cold War, or "long peace,"[32] end within a three-month period? There are two versions of a realist explanation for the transformation of the European order. First, conventional wisdom held by many policymakers and scholars alike suggests that the Western strategy of containment had worked. The end of the Cold War, it is claimed, is the result of Western "peace through strength."[33] There are indeed indications that the new Soviet leadership took Western firmness into account during its reevaluation of Moscow's foreign policy in 1985–86. However, the "peace through strength" theme fails to explain why the change began only after Mikhail Gorbachev assumed the Soviet leadership and not, say, during the 1970s or even earlier. Why, for example, was Khrushchev not able to convince his Politburo thirty years ago—in the aftermath of Western firmness during the Berlin crises—that Soviet expansionism would lead nowhere?

A more sophisticated version of the realist argument claims the end of the Soviet bloc as the result of "imperial overstretch."[34] If states overextend themselves, the costs of maintaining their empire will eventually outweigh the gains extracted from it. The decline of the British empire is a frequently cited example of this phenomenon. The Soviet Union had simply overextended itself after World War II. The burden of maintaining an empire that was not integrated into the world economy, of supporting authoritarian regimes that lacked support from their populations, and of pursuing a costly arms race with the West finally overwhelmed the already inefficient Soviet economy. Minor adjustments would not help anymore; a profound turnaround of Moscow's domestic and foreign policies was needed.

The "imperial overstretch" argument has a powerful point to make with respect to the underlying causes of the politics of *perestroika,* since it relates the origins of the Gorbachev revolution to the crisis of the Soviet system. Thus, unlike the "peace through strength" viewpoint, it explains why it took the Soviet Union so long to realize the failure of its system. The Soviet decisions to withdraw from Afghanistan and to renounce the "Brezhnev doctrine," which had reserved the right for WTO troops to intervene in Eastern Europe whenever a communist regime was in trouble, are also in line with this argument. However, to rely exclusively on "imperial overextension" in the Soviet case masks in fact a domestic structure approach. The USSR's failure to maintain its hegemony had less to do with an "objective" lack of resources than with the inefficiency of a centrally planned economy perpetuated for ideological reasons despite its irrational consequences. The same is true for the need to support regimes in Eastern Europe that lacked domestic legitimacy, by the presence of Soviet troops. This strain on badly needed resources would have been avoided had the Eastern Europeans enjoyed basic human rights.

Furthermore, the realist approach does not explain why the Soviet leadership under Gorbachev did not just embark on a program of technocratic reforms without touching the authoritarian political structure—as the Chinese did under Deng Xiaoping. The politics of *perestroika* included *glasnost,* or "openness," i.e., the democratization of the Soviet political structure. Social and political forces were unleashed that Gorbachev was increasingly unable to control.

Finally, the rapidity with which the authoritarian regimes in Eastern Europe collapsed when Soviet tanks ceased to back them anymore is equally beyond the explanatory power of realism. Just as the Sovietization of Eastern Europe in the late 1940s is explicable only if the assumptions of liberal theory are taken into account, so is the return of these countries to democracy. It ultimately proved that the Giereks, Kádárs, Honeckers, Husáks, and Zhivkovs were kept in power only by Soviet tanks.

The events of 1989 as well as the differences between the countries become understandable if one looks back to the evolution of Eastern European societies since at least the 1970s. As mentioned before, the Helsinki accords of 1975 established human rights as an international norm in Europe. Dissident groups emerged in various Eastern European countries, including the Soviet Union, and explicitly used the CSCE to legitimize their demands. They were supported in this effort by the West, which constantly reminded the Soviet bloc of its obligations under these accords.

As a consequence, civil societies developed in Eastern Europe underneath the frozen structures of the Cold War that only needed an outside catalyst to transform the political regimes. Democratic cultures were already in place, before the political structures changed.[35] In Poland, *Solidarnosc* emerged in 1980 as the first independent trade union in Eastern Europe. While the movement was forced into illegality after General Jaruzelski's military coup, it nevertheless survived and largely maintained its structure with the support of the powerful Polish Catholic church. At about the same time and influenced by the West German peace movements, small independent peace groups emerged in East Germany, equally protected by the Protestant churches. Similar developments occurred in Hungary and Czechoslovakia—in the latter case the memories of the "Prague Spring" of 1968 were still alive. These developments, which were facilitated by the détente period of the 1970s,[36] explain the extraordinary peacefulness of the transformation processes once Gorbachev had repudiated the Brezhnev doctrine and had made it clear that the USSR would not use force to defend its communist allies in Eastern Europe. The exception of Rumania, in which a particularly brutal neo-Stalinist regime was overthrown only by violence, confirms the rule.

To conclude, the sudden end of the Cold War does not represent the victory of the Western containment strategy or of the United States in the hegemonic rivalry with the Soviet Union. If anything, it is the triumph of liberal democracy and human rights. This is what the Cold War ultimately was about. The USSR has lost the competition about the more attractive political system. This conclusion should not obscure, however, the losses incurred by the West. First, conducting the Cold War cost both sides trillions of dollars urgently needed to fulfill societal needs. Second, more often than not, Western policies overreacted to perceived threats instead of adopting the right mix of containment and the offer to ease the tensions. The militarization of the East-West conflict in Europe resulted as much from NATO's policies as from the USSR's.

## ANARCHY OR PERPETUAL PEACE? EUROPEAN SECURITY AFTER THE COLD WAR

"A liberated Eastern Europe will not necessarily be a peaceful place. Irredentist grievances, ethnic rivalries and religious antagonisms abound. Once these begin to manifest themselves, the Helsinki process, if that is the only structure we have in place to deal with them, is apt to have all the authority of a voluntarily enforced 55 mile-per-hour speed limit on America's interstate highways." (John Lewis Gaddis, "One Germany—in Both Alliances," *New York Times*, March 21, 1990)

"It is our goal to create a European peace order on the basis of a security partnership of the existing military alliances which ultimately overcomes these blocs." (*For a New Strategy of the Alliance*, Party Platform of the West German Social Democratic Party, as resolved on the Party Congress, Essen, May 17–21, 1984)

Europe is in a transition phase. While the bipolar order of the Cold War no more exists, a new security environment is not yet in place. The remnants of the past forty years, the two alliances and much of their military equipment, for example, are still around. Bits and pieces of a new order are emerging, however. The two Germanies are united since the East Germans overwhelmingly voted for a rapid merger with the Federal Republic of Germany in their first free elections on March 18, 1990. The European Community is moving toward increased economic and political integration. The thirty-four nations involved in the CSCE have agreed to move on to strengthen existing all-European institutions.

What will a new European security environment look like? Will it grant its members not only external stability, but also human rights and economic prosperity? Or will the European order quickly disintegrate and give way to new conflicts and new grievances? The three approaches to international relations discussed above not only offer different interpretations of the past, but also suggest diverging outlooks into the future.

Realists offer the most pessimistic scenario. According to them, the bipolar order in Europe and the imposition of Soviet and American spheres of influence after World War II have kept the peace in the Northern Hemisphere so far. "A global ideological and military rivalry had the effect, for the four and one-half decades that followed 1945, of suppressing the regional rivalries that had propelled Europe into two world wars in the three decades that preceded 1945," says the historian John Lewis Gaddis.[37] Since a multipolar world does not create the predictability of behavior that guarantees stability in an anarchical international system, Europe is likely to return to the rivalries of the late nineteenth century.[38]

In order to prove the argument, one could point to the reemerging ethnic and nationalist rivalries, in particular in the Balkan states and the Soviet Union itself. Rumanians have been at the verge of a civil war with the Hungarian minority ever since dictator Ceausescu's ouster. Yugoslavia's unity is threatened by intense rivalries between the Serbs and the Croats. The Soviet Union is faced with civil war in several of its southern republics; the Baltic states are struggling for their independence from Moscow.

Finally, the consequences of a united Germany have to be considered. After all, one major purpose of the two alliances has always been to solve the "German question" once and for all, which had resulted in two World Wars and the Holocaust against the Jews. Even before unification, West Germany had already emerged as the predominant economic power in the European Community. The *Bundeswehr* has been one of the strongest, best-equipped, and best-trained conventional armies in Central Europe. Thus, many people fear that German unity could reestablish the country's hegemony in Europe. It might even lead to a resurgence of German militarism, which in the past had caused so much bloodshed on the continent. Finally, what will prevent a united Germany from acquiring nuclear weapons, the ultimate symbol of national sovereignty in the modern age?

Liberal theorists profoundly disagree with this analysis. First, supporters of the bipolar "long peace" are reminded that peoples on both sides of what used to be the Iron Curtain had to pay a high price for the alleged stability of the Cold War order. Half the Europeans were deprived from basic human rights and democratic freedoms; Europe was militarized. While war was prevented in the Northern Hemisphere, the superpower rivalry in the Third World led to or prolonged numerous military conflicts in the southern part of the globe. In sum, the notion of "long peace" describes only part of the reality of the Cold War.

Second, there is some reason for an optimistic outlook toward the European future. Since 1815, democracies have not gone to war against each other.[39] After 1945, the world of the Western industrialized democracies has been by far the most peaceful region on the globe. Century-old enmities such as the hostility between the French and the Germans have been turned into lasting friendships and alliances, once both countries had become democracies. To view a post–Cold War Europe in light of the nineteenth century would, therefore, miss the point. There would be no comparison between the great power rivalry of mostly authoritarian states and a democratic

Europe entering the twenty-first century "whole and free," as President Bush says.

While realists point to Rumania, Yugoslavia, and the USSR's southern republics to underline their arguments, liberals point out that the transition in Eastern Europe to democracy and independence from Moscow has thus far proceeded rather peacefully. The new government in Prague has been able to temper the tensions between Czechs and Slovaks by integrating both groups into the new democracy under the charismatic leadership of President Vaclav Havel. The moderateness and the orderliness with which drastic domestic changes in Eastern Europe have been carried out are all the more significant in light of the numerous economic incentives for social turmoil. Poland, for example, has been remarkably stable despite rising unemployment and growing social insecurity due to the rapid introduction of a market economy.

Finally, many people argue that the united Germany of the twenty-first century will look entirely different than the German Reich of the late nineteenth century. Unification has not meant that a new domestic structure is in the making, but that the democratic political, economic, and social institutions of the Federal Republic of Germany have been extended into what was once East Germany. For example, the West German "basic law," drafted in 1949, contains stronger guarantees of human rights than other Western constitutions. Moreover, forty years of democracy in West Germany have firmly embedded liberal values among the population, while nationalist feelings are far less common than in other Western countries.[40] As far as foreign policy is concerned, the West Germans have learned to pursue their goals via policy coordination in the European Community and in NATO. Cooperation with the Western and Eastern neighbors is among the highest priorities of the German policymakers, and enjoys overwhelming domestic support. There is no sign that a united Germany would change the way the Federal Republic conducts its foreign policy, providing its neighbors with ample opportunities to influence the country's actions.

However, there are problems with the argument. Its prediction of "perpetual peace" among liberal democracies and market economies is less relevant for the transition period, in which elements of the old realm and the new order still coexist within as well as between the countries. This is precisely the situation Europe is facing in the 1990s. As a result, peace in Europe will not automatically break out, simply because Eastern Europe and the Soviet Union are in transition to liberal democracies. Efforts have to be made to prevent instabilities, institutions have to be created or expanded that temper possible tensions between the countries and facilitate the kind of domestic and international changes that guarantee further peace. In sum, the transition period toward a greater Europe "whole and free," from Vladivostok to San Francisco, has to be managed. This is where neoliberal institutionalism enters the scene. It argues that international institutions and regimes, by creating norms of cooperation, predictability of behavior, and stability of expectations, change the foreign policy behavior of states, away from unilateralism.

Luckily enough, such institutions do not have to be created from scratch in post–Cold War Europe; they already exist. But they have to be adapted to new roles. First, as far as economic policies are concerned, there is the European Community (EC). In 1992, the Single Market will integrate the economies of the twelve member states, leading to even closer political coordination among the Western Europeans. The EC will be the main instrument to contain the economic power of the united Germany, forcing it to continue to adjust to the demands of its partners.[41] The EC will also be the main instrument to help rebuild the economies of the new Eastern Europe. The necessary funds will be provided partly through individual contributions by Western countries, and partly through the new European Bank for Reconstruction and Development specifically designed for these purposes.[42] In addition, individual Eastern European states may negotiate associate membership status with the EC, which would provide them with the benefits of the Single Market without exposing them prematurely to the pressures of free trade.

In the security area, the détente era of the 1970s created a partial security regime for Europe by changing the decision rules of the main actors in favor of international cooperation and arms control. Until now, however, the Helsinki process has had very weak enforcement mechanisms. The only binding CSCE agreements thus far concern confidence- and security-building measures such as the mutual announcement of military exercises and the exchange of observers.[43] But there is no reason why an expansion and further institutionalization of the CSCE should not be feasible. The Helsinki process is an all-European structure comprising not only the members of NATO and the WTO but also the neutral and nonaligned European states and the two superpowers. A strengthened CSCE with binding agreements among the members could serve as the starting point for a future European peace order to be based on collective security arrangements guaranteed by the two superpowers. For example, the CSCE could work out guarantees for the existing borders in Europe so as to reassure in particular the Eastern European countries against possible aspirations of their neighbors. The CSCE already served to codify the international arrangements worked out between the Germanies and the allied powers regarding German unity. Thus, the Helsinki process could be a forum for the European states to discuss possible grievances regarding the German issue. Finally, as the United States suggested, the CSCE's provisions concerning human rights issues could be reorganized to assist the process of democratization in Eastern Europe.[44]

While the CSCE can provide the "superstructure" of a future European peace order, NATO will continue to have a role to play in the new Europe, at least throughout the 1990s. However, its function will drastically change from a predominantly military into a political organization. Throughout the

Cold War, NATO's main purpose was to contain the Soviet Union. The new priority will be to reassure Moscow of the West's peaceful intentions.[45]

First, NATO and—as long as it continues to exist—the Warsaw Pact will assume a major role in the demilitarization of Europe. European arms control will codify the changed security environment, and restructure existing military forces toward "nonoffensive" postures.[46] The two alliances will also provide the means for the implementation of arms control accords and for the necessary on-site inspections.

Second, the Western alliance will continue to play a major role in containing a united Germany, which will remain in NATO until the dissolution of the two alliances is agreed upon by their members. This might even become NATO's most important political task in the future. Reassurances have been worked out regarding the demilitarization of the former East Germany, and the united Germany's troop strength is far below the level of former West Germany's army. U.S. troops will continue to stay in the Western part of the country, although at fairly reduced force levels, to provide security guarantees for Germany's European neighbors. As long as Germany participates in implementing these arrangements, there is no reason to assume that it would not accept them. After all, the two former German states had been used to much stronger restrictions on their national sovereignty. These restrictions ceased to exist when the rights of the four allied powers expired with German unification.

In conclusion, each of the three approaches to international relations offers a different outlook on the future of the new Europe. It is impossible to predict which viewpoint will carry the day; political scientists should be particularly careful, since nobody foresaw that the Soviet Union would stage a strategic withdrawal from Eastern Europe in 1989 or that the Cold War order would be undone so rapidly by people's power. However, this chapter has argued that liberal theory modified by institutionalist explanations offers a more plausible account for the history and the end of the Cold War than insights based solely on realist assumptions. If this evaluation makes sense, there is reason to hope that a Hobbesian Europe in which everybody fights against everybody else can be prevented and a peace order guaranteeing human rights and stability can be established.

### Notes

1. For very helpful comments to the draft of this paper, I thank Matthew Evangelista, Peter Katzenstein, and Daniel Thomas.
2. This approach was inspired by Jack Snyder, "Averting Anarchy in the New Europe," *International Security*, Vol. 14, No. 4, Spring 1990, pp. 5–41.
3. See Robert O. Keohane, "Theory of World Politics," in Keohane, ed., *Neorealism and Its Critics* (New York: Columbia University Press, 1986), pp. 158–203. Standard realist works are Hans Morgenthau, *Politics Among Nations* (New York: Knopf, 1948); Kenneth Waltz, *Theory of International Politics* (Reading, MA: Addison-Wesley, 1979); Robert Gilpin, *War and Change in World Politics* (New York: Cambridge University Press, 1981).

4. See Joseph Schumpeter, *Imperialism and Social Classes* (New York: Augustus M. Kelley, 1951). First published in 1919. For an overview, see Jack S. Levy, "The Causes of War: A Review of Theories and Evidence," in Philip E. Tetlock et al., eds., *Behavior, Society, and Nuclear War*, Vol. 1 (New York: Oxford University Press, 1989), pp. 209–333, pp. 260–262; also Michael Doyle, "Liberalism and World Politics," *American Political Science Review*, Vol. 80, No. 4, December 1986, pp. 1151–1169. The liberal theory of international politics comes to the opposite conclusions as the Marxist theory of imperialism, which asserts that international conflicts are caused by the internal dynamics of capitalist economies. See, for example, Rudolf Hilferding, *Finance Capital* [1910] (London: Routledge, 1981).

5. This approach goes back to the German philosopher Immanuel Kant. See his *Eternal Peace*, first published in 1795. For reviews, see Doyle, "Liberalism," note 4; same author, "Kant, Liberal Legacies and Foreign Affairs," *Philosophy and Public Affairs*, Vol. 12, No. 4, 1983, pp. 323–353; Bruce Russett, *Controlling the Sword: The Democratic Governance of Nuclear Weapons* (Cambridge, MA: Harvard University Press, 1990), Chapter 5.

6. On the effects of perceptions and cognitive biases, see Robert Jervis, *Perception and Misperception in International Politics* (Princeton, NJ: Princeton University Press, 1976); Jervis, "Cooperation under the Security Dilemma," *World Politics*, Vol. 30, No. 2, January 1978, pp. 167–214; Richard N. Lebow, *Between Peace and War: The Nature of International Crisis* (Baltimore, MD: Johns Hopkins University Press, 1981). For an approach that explains foreign policy by the domestic structure of states, see Peter Katzenstein, ed., *Between Power and Plenty* (Madison, WI: University of Wisconsin Press, 1978).

7. See, for example, Stephen Krasner, ed., *International Regimes* (Ithaca, NY: Cornell University Press, 1983); Robert O. Keohane, *International Institutions and State Power* (Boulder, CO: Westview, 1989); Ken Oye, ed., *Cooperation Under Anarchy, World Politics*, Special Issue, October 1985; Oran Young, *International Cooperation* (Ithaca, NY: Cornell University Press, 1989).

8. Kennan's famous article originally appeared in *Foreign Affairs*, July 1947, here quoted from Jeffrey Porro et al., eds., *The Nuclear Age Reader* (New York: Knopf, 1989), p. 46.

9. Quoted from ibid., p. 47.

10. For this interpretation, see Paul Kennedy, *The Rise and Fall of the Great Powers* (New York: Random House, 1987), pp. 357–372.

11. See for the following A.W. DePorte, *Europe Between the Superpowers*, 2nd ed. (New Haven: Yale University Press, 1986), pp. 62–74.

12. See Stephen Walt, *The Origins of Alliances* (Ithaca, NY: Cornell University Press, 1987).

13. While most of the historical studies on the origins of the Western alliance are implicitly based on liberal assumptions about what constituted the "Soviet threat," they are rarely explicit regarding their theoretical approaches. See, for example, Don Cook, *Forging the Alliance: NATO, 1945–1950* (New York: Arbor House/William Morrow, 1989); Lawrence S. Kaplan, *NATO and the United States* (Boston: Twague, 1988).

14. For evidence, see Richard Best, *Cooperation with Like-minded People: British Influence on American Security Policy 1945–1949* (New York: Greenwood, 1986); Fred Block, *The Origins of International Economic Disorder: A Study of United States International Monetary Policy from World War II to the Present* (Berkeley, CA: University of California Press, 1977); Cook, *Forging the Alliance*, note 13. For analyses of the Cold War in general and the emergence of the NATO alliance, see John Lewis Gaddis, *Russia, the Soviet Union, and the United States* (New York: John Wiley & Sons, 1978); Gaddis, *The Long Peace: Inquiries into the History of the Cold War* (New York: Oxford University Press, 1987); Alfred Grosser, *The Western Alliance* (New York: Continuum, 1980); Walter LaFeber, *America, Russia, and the Cold War*, 5th ed., (New York: Knopf, 1985).

15. On the Korean War, see Rosemary Foot, *The Wrong War: American Policy and the Dimensions of the Korean Conflict, 1950–1953* (Ithaca, NY: Cornell University Press, 1985). On German rearmament, see Robert McGeehan, *The German Rearmament Question* (Urbana: University of Illinois Press, 1971); Olav Riste, ed., *Western Security: The Formative Years: European and Atlantic Defense, 1947–1953* (New York: Columbia University Press, 1985).

16. On Soviet postwar foreign policy in general, see Vojtech Mastny, *Russia's Road to the Cold War* (New York: Columbia University Press, 1979); William Taubman, *Stalin's America Policy: From Détente to Entente to Cold War* (New York: Norton, 1982); Thomas W. Wolfe,

*Soviet Power and Europe: 1945–1970* (Baltimore, MD: Johns Hopkins University Press, 1970). For the following see also Daniel Yergin, *Shattered Peace: The Origins of the Cold War and the National Security State* (Boston: Houghton Mifflin, 1977).

17. On the origins of the Marshall Plan, see Charles L. Mee, Jr., *The Marshall Plan: The Launching of the Pax Americana* (New York: Simon and Schuster, 1984); Emmanuel Wexler, *The Marshall Plan Revisited* (Westport, CT: Greenwood, 1983).

18. Quoted from NATO Information Service, *NATO: Facts and Figures* (Brussels: 1978).

19. For data, see the respective editions of IISS, *The Military Balance* (London: 1972ff). See also Jonathan Dean, *Watershed in Europe* (Lexington, MA: Lexington Books, 1987), pp. 29–59.

20. There is no comprehensive account of the European détente process. See, however, Jonathan Dean, *Watershed in Europe*, note 19; Raymond Garthoff, *Détente and Confrontation: American-Soviet Relations from Nixon to Reagan* (Washington DC: Brookings, 1985), pp. 473–501; John J. Maresca, *To Helsinki: The Conference on Security and Cooperation in Europe, 1973–1975* (Durham, NC: Duke University Press, 1985).

21. For a general discussion of West German *Ostpolitik*, see Helga Haftendorn, *Security and Détente: The Foreign Policy of the Federal Republic of Germany, 1955–1982* (New York: Praeger, 1984).

22. This argument is the realist foundation of the arms control school. See, for example, Hedley Bull, *The Control of the Arms Race* (New York: Praeger, 1961); Morton Halperin/ Thomas Schelling, *Strategy and Arms Control* (New York: Pergamon, 1961).

23. See John G. Keliher, *The Negotiations on Mutual and Balanced Force Reductions* (New York: Pergamon, 1980); Dean, *Watershed in Europe*, note 19, pp. 153–184.

24. On "flexible response," see Jane E. Stromseth, *The Origins of Flexible Response: NATO's Debate over Strategy in the 1960s* (New York: St. Martin's Press, 1988). For a discussion of NATO's nuclear problems, see David N. Schwartz, *NATO's Nuclear Dilemmas* (Washington DC: Brookings, 1983).

25. See Jervis, "Cooperation," note 6. See also George W. Downs et al., "Arms Races and Cooperation," *World Politics*, Vol. 38, October 1985, pp. 118–146.

26. For the concept of "common security," see the "Palme Report" of 1982: Independent Commission on Disarmament and Security Issues ("Palme Commission"), *Common Security* (London: Pan Books, 1982).

27. For details, see Garthoff, *Détente*, note 20; Harry Gelman, *The Brezhnev Politburo and the Decline of Détente* (Ithaca, NY: Cornell University Press, 1984); Stephen Larrabee, "Gorbachev and the Soviet Military," *Foreign Affairs*, Vol. 66, No. 5, Summer 1988, pp. 1002–1026.

28. For details, see Jonathan Haslam, *The Soviet Union and the Politics of Nuclear Weapons in Europe, 1969–1987* (London: Macmillan, 1989); Thomas Risse-Kappen, *The Zero Option: INF, West Germany, and Arms Control* (Boulder, CO: Westview, 1988).

29. For the following see Garthoff, *Détente*, note 20; Jerry W. Sanders, *Peddlers of Crisis: The Committee on the Present Danger* (Boston: South End Press, 1983).

30. For West Germany, see Barry Blechman et al., *The Silent Partner: West Germany and Arms Control* (Cambridge, MA: Ballinger, 1988); Thomas Risse-Kappen, "Anti-Nuclear and Pro-Détente? The Evolution of the West German Security Debate," in Don Munton/Hans Rattinger, eds., *Debating National Security* (New York: Lang Publisher, 1990).

31. On the emergence and the effects of the peace movements, see Thomas Rochon, *The Politics of the Peace Movements in Western Europe* (Princeton, NJ: Princeton University Press, 1988). On European public opinion and security policy in general, see Richard Eichenberg, *Public Opinion and National Security in Western Europe* (Ithaca, NY: Cornell University Press, 1989).

32. See Gaddis, *Long Peace*, note 14, especially pp. 215–245. For a detailed account of the events in East Germany see Elizabeth Pond, "A Wall Destroyed: The Dynamics of German Unification in the GDR," *International Security*, Vol. 15, No. 2, Fall 1990, pp. 35–66.

33. "What made the start of [arms] reductions possible was the willingness of the democracies to maintain an adequate deterrence posture. What will sustain the process of reductions is the willingness to ensure that at every level of reductions, deterrence is maintained and preferably strengthened." Valéry Giscard d'Estaing/Yasuhiro Nakasone/Henry A. Kissinger, "East-West Relations," *Foreign Affairs*, Vol. 68, No. 3, Summer 1989, pp. 1–21, 8/9.

34. For the following see Kennedy, *Rise and Fall*, note 10. For a slightly different argument that focuses on the costs of hegemony, see Gilpin, *War and Change*, note 3.

35. For an overview, see Vladimir Tismaneanu, "Eastern Europe: The Story the Media Missed," *Bulletin of the Atomic Scientists*, Vol. 46, No. 2, March 1990, pp. 17–21; Tismaneanu, ed., *In Search of Civil Society: Independent Peace Movements in the Soviet Bloc* (forthcoming).

36. It should be remembered that these effects were indeed intended by Western politicians. West German Social Democrats, for example, adopted the concept of "change through rapprochement," which was meant to induce political changes in Eastern Europe through a process of East-West détente, as early as 1963.

37. Gaddis, "One Germany—in Both Alliances," *New York Times*, March 21, 1990. See also his *Long Peace*, note 14.

38. For this argument, see John J. Mearsheimer, "Back to the Future: Instability in Europe After the Cold War," *International Security*, Vol. 15, No. 1, Summer 1990, pp. 5–56.

39. For details, see the sources quoted in note 5.

40. For evidence, see Kendall Baker et al., *Germany Transformed: Political Culture and the New Politics* (Cambridge, MA: Harvard University Press, 1981); David P. Conradt, *The German Polity* (New York: Longman, 1982); Gebhardt Schweigler, *National Consciousness in Divided Germany* (Beverly Hills-London: Sage, 1975).

41. The economic strength of a united Germany should not be overestimated. The Gross National Product of the two Germanies in 1989 roughly equaled that of France plus the Benelux states. It was still only half of the Japanese GNP. Data according to Meinhard Miegel, "Kein kolossaler Wirtschaftsgigant," *Frankfurter Allgemeine Zeitung*, February 15, 1990 (translated in *The German Tribune*, March 4, 1990, p. 5).

42. See "New Bank to Help East Bloc Revive its Economy," *New York Times*, January 14, 1990.

43. See John Borawski, *From the Atlantic to the Urals: Negotiating Arms Control at the Stockholm Conference* (Washington DC: Pergamon-Brassey's, 1988).

44. See Secretary of State James Baker's speech in Berlin, December 12, 1989, quoted from *New York Times*, December 13, 1989.

45. For an outline of the future role of NATO, see J. Baker's speech in Berlin, note 44.

46. An overview on the different concepts of "nonoffensive defense" is provided by "New European Defense," *Bulletin of the Atomic Scientists*, Vol. 44, September 1988. On conventional arms control in general, see Jonathan Dean, *Meeting Gorbachev's Challenge. How to Build Down the NATO-Warsaw Pact Confrontation* (New York: St. Martin's Press, 1989).

# 7 / Nuclear Proliferation in the 1980s and 1990s

PETER A. CLAUSEN

## INTRODUCTION

In the final decade of the century, nuclear weapons continue to pose the greatest immediate danger to world security. But the nuclear threat is in flux, and the next few years may be decisive for efforts to bring it under control. Historically, these efforts have spanned two broad dimensions: controlling the U.S.-Soviet arms race, and preventing the spread or "proliferation" of nuclear weapons to additional countries. While progress in superpower relations holds out hope for a winding down of their nuclear confrontation, prospects for halting proliferation are less reassuring.

The dangers of proliferation are clear. As nuclear weapons are obtained by more nations, the likelihood of their use will almost surely increase. Attacks with these weapons would be the first since 1945; they would not only inflict massive death and destruction in their own right but could trigger wider conflicts involving the superpowers. Proliferation also multiplies the chances that atomic bombs will be fired accidentally or without authorization (especially in light of the domestic instability of many of the would-be nuclear powers), or will fall into the hands of terrorists.

For these reasons, there has long been a strong international consensus against the spread of nuclear weapons.[1] Moreover, efforts to avert proliferation have had considerable success. Early in the nuclear age, predictions that the bomb would rapidly spread to twenty or more nations were common. Yet there are still only five acknowledged nuclear powers (Great Britain, France, and China in addition to the two superpowers), and no country has openly joined the nuclear club since China's entry in 1964.

But this record of success is in some ways misleading, and does not justify complacency about the future. Proliferation has less been stopped than driven underground. Over the last two decades four countries—Israel, India, Pakistan, and South Africa—have acquired de facto if unavowed nuclear weapons capabilities. Several others, including both parties and nonparties to the 1970 Nonproliferation Treaty (NPT) harbor clear nuclear ambitions, or have in the recent past (see Figure 7.1). Meanwhile, the steady diffusion of nuclear capability is now paired with a burgeoning spread of

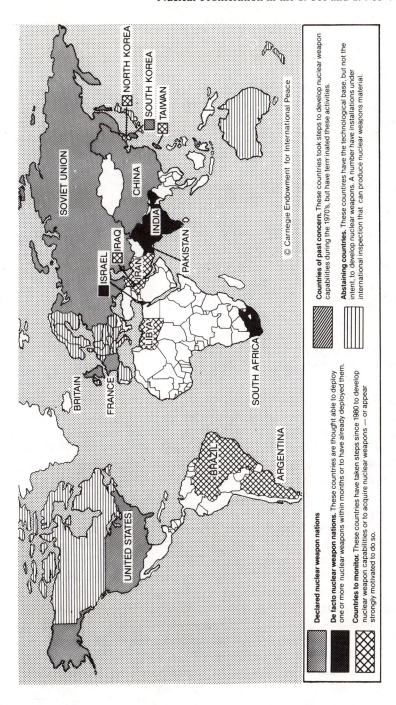

Figure 7.1 / The Spread of Nuclear Weapons, 1989–90

© Carnegie Endowment for International Peace

**Declared nuclear weapon nations**

**De facto nuclear weapon nations.** These countries are thought able to deploy one or more nuclear weapons within months or to have already deployed them.

**Countries to monitor.** These countries have taken steps since 1980 to develop nuclear weapon capabilities or to acquire nuclear weapons — or appear strongly motivated to do so.

**Countries of past concern.** These countries took steps to develop nuclear weapon capabilities during the 1970's, but have terminated these activities.

**Abstaining countries.** These countries have the technological base, but not the intent, to develop nuclear weapons. A number have installations under international inspection that can produce nuclear weapons material.

missile technology that compounds the dangers of each. Against this background, the NPT is due for renewal in 1995, when its twenty-five year term ends. The approach of this deadline may intensify strains in the global nonproliferation "regime" of which the NPT is the centerpiece.

These trends, together with the ending of the Cold War, are likely to move the proliferation issue toward the forefront of international politics in the 1990s. Indeed, if East-West tensions continue to recede, proliferation can be expected to emerge as a primary threat to world order. At the same time, the changed international landscape may create new opportunities to forestall the spread of nuclear weapons through closer superpower cooperation and the settlement of regional conflicts. U.S.-Soviet arms cuts and a waning of Cold War rivalry in the Third World could help ease the cross-pressures and double standards that have often undercut nonproliferation policies in the past. This outcome is by no means assured, however; it is also possible that superpower détente and retrenchment will unleash new centrifugal forces in world politics, including further proliferation. Here, the 1990 takeover of Kuwait by Iraq—an aspiring nuclear power—could be a portent of the future.

## BACKGROUND: PROLIFERATION AND RESPONSE

The spread of nuclear weapons was probably inevitable from the time the United States developed and used the first atomic bombs in World War II. Then, as now, proliferation was a matter of capabilities and incentives. The ability to make the bomb could not be monopolized by the United States, given the natural diffusion of scientific and technological knowledge; and the rapid emergence of postwar tensions and conflicts assured that other nations, especially the Soviet Union, would be determined to deny the United States a nuclear monopoly.

In this setting, the first U.S. effort to forestall proliferation—the 1946 Baruch Plan—was doomed to failure.[2] The plan called for establishing international control of atomic energy, but on U.S. terms. It would have allowed the United States to retain the bomb until the end of the process, while the Soviets were required to abandon their own nuclear program and submit to inspections at the outset. Predictably, the plan was rejected by Moscow, becoming an early victim of the Cold War. The United States then adopted a nonproliferation policy based on strict nuclear secrecy and denial. This policy applied to civil as well as military applications of nuclear energy, and to allies and adversaries alike. But within a few years the Soviets had tested a bomb—well ahead of U.S. expectations—and several other countries had embarked on nuclear programs.

## Atoms for Peace and War

In the 1950s the United States revised its nuclear policy, laying the foundations of the current nonproliferation regime. The new policy was heralded by President Eisenhower's Atoms for Peace initiative. Its core idea was that the promotion of nuclear energy for peaceful purposes could be used to elicit nonproliferation commitments from recipient nations. In what became known as the nuclear bargain, nuclear reactors and fuel were widely disseminated subject to assurances that they would not be diverted to military uses. These assurances were to be verified by "safeguards"—inspections and other accounting procedures—applied by the International Atomic Energy Agency (IAEA), established in 1957.

Atoms for Peace was a mix of self-interest (the lure of a global nuclear market), idealism (faith in nuclear power as a key to economic modernization), and fatalism (the belief that the only alternative was an uncontrolled spread of national nuclear programs). In retrospect, the policy oversold the benefits of atomic energy while accelerating the diffusion of knowledge and technology relevant to nuclear weapons. In addition, the early safeguards system contained loopholes and ambiguities that made it a shaky bulwark against proliferation. Nonetheless, Atoms for Peace established the basic framework of international nuclear cooperation on which later efforts to strengthen the regime were built.

Meanwhile, both superpowers faced pressures for proliferation from within their own alliances. Great Britain, which had participated in the U.S. bomb program until cut off by the 1946 Atomic Energy Act, proceeded independently and tested a weapon in 1953. France decided to acquire nuclear weapons in the wake of the 1956 Suez crisis and tested its first bomb in 1960. In both countries, nuclear programs were motivated by a combination of doubts about U.S. reliability and a desire for increased influence with Washington.[3] The U.S. response to these developments was ambivalent. Though he opposed the spread of independent nuclear forces within NATO, Eisenhower sympathized with the allies' desire for greater access to nuclear weapons and sought a loosening of restrictions on allied nuclear collaboration. In 1958, the United States restored full cooperation with Britain in weapons development, but rejected French President de Gaulle's bid for equal treatment.[4]

The Soviet Union also flirted with "selective proliferation" during this time. It offered extensive nuclear assistance to China, but then had second thoughts as tensions between the two communist nations increased. In the late 1950s, Moscow ended all nuclear cooperation with China, and the latter, like France, adopted an independent nuclear policy marked by harsh criticism of the superpowers' attempts at nuclear "hegemony." China became the fifth nuclear-weapon state with an underground test in 1964.[5]

## The NPT

By the early 1960s, the two superpowers were beginning to acknowledge a shared interest in nonproliferation.[6] Both saw that the spread of nuclear weapons could reduce their influence and freedom of action, increase the likelihood of nuclear war, and undercut efforts to stabilize the nuclear balance through arms control and crisis management. They especially feared that the actions of a nuclear-armed ally or client state might trigger a U.S.-Soviet nuclear confrontation. These convergent interests led the superpowers to cooperate—in the face of considerable resistance from their allies—in negotiating the NPT.[7]

The treaty was completed in 1968 and took effect two years later with a term of twenty-five years. Its central provisions (Articles I and II) are pledges by the nuclear powers (defined as states having exploded a nuclear device prior to 1967) not to transfer explosive devices to other states, and by the nonnuclear states not to acquire such devices. Nonnuclear parties must accept IAEA safeguards on all their nuclear facilities (so-called fullscope safeguards), rather than just on imported materials as under Atoms for Peace. Two other key provisions, both subjects of perennial controversy, are Article IV, pledging unfettered international cooperation in peaceful nuclear energy, and Article VI, promising good faith efforts toward arms control and disarmament by the existing nuclear powers.

The NPT helped create an international norm of nonproliferation, in effect delegitimizing the acquisition of nuclear arms by new countries. But despite broad acceptance (it now has some 140 parties), the NPT was rejected by the main candidates for proliferation. An outspoken critic was India (newly threatened by the Chinese bomb), which protested the NPT's discriminatory nature and its failure to provide security guarantees to nonnuclear states. Joining India in rejecting the treaty were Pakistan, Israel, South Africa, Brazil, Argentina, and nuclear powers France and China.[8]

## Upgrading the Regime

Within a few years of the NPT's entry into force, weaknesses in the regime became evident. A series of developments in the mid-1970s indicated that the danger of proliferation was increasing. First, India tested a nuclear device (calling it a "peaceful" explosive rather than a weapon), using plutonium from a reactor supplied by Canada under an early Atoms for Peace project. Second, West Germany and France, emerging as challengers to the former U.S. near-monopoly on nuclear exports, agreed to supply the most sensitive nuclear technologies—those required to produce weapons-grade plutonium and uranium—to customers in the Third World.[9] Germany offered reprocessing and enrichment technology (used, respectively, to extract plutonium from used reactor fuel and to raise the proportion of the fissile isotope U-235 in uranium) to Brazil as part of a multi-reactor sale; France agreed to supply reprocessing plants to Pakistan and South Korea. Third, the oil crisis of the mid-1970s stimulated new interest in nuclear power, including the development of so-called fast-breeder reactors. The latter, fueled by recycled plutonium, held a strong attraction for many industrial countries as a route to greater energy self-sufficiency. But unlike conventional nuclear reactors, breeders would involve the direct handling of weapons-grade material in large quantities.

These trends signaled a blurring of the line between peaceful and military uses of nuclear energy. With access to sensitive technologies and weapons-grade materials, countries could obtain a virtual nuclear weapons capability under the guise of a civil program. Moreover, they might be able to assemble nuclear bombs so quickly that safeguards inspections would be devalued as a deterrent to proliferation and a source of warning to the international community.[10]

Another development at this time cast further doubt on the adequacy of the NPT's conceptual approach—Israel's apparent acquisition of a covert nuclear weapons capability. In 1974, the CIA concluded that Israel, having pursued a highly secret program throughout the 1960s, had produced atomic weapons but was unlikely to test openly or otherwise confirm its nuclear status. Together with India's "peaceful" explosion and the spread of sensitive technologies, the Israeli case showed that the NPT's sharp distinction between nuclear and nonnuclear powers failed to capture the increasingly complex reality of proliferation.

These events prompted a concerted effort, led by the United States, to strengthen nonproliferation policies. (However, Washington carefully avoided criticism of Israel, which became a tacit exception to U.S. policy.) In spirit, the reforms were a partial reversion to the denial strategy—an attempt to reinforce the eroding separation between peaceful and weapons activities by curtailing nuclear trade and development.[11] The leading exporters formed a Nuclear Suppliers Group and adopted stricter guidelines for nuclear sales and safeguards, including restraint in future sales of enrichment and reprocessing technology. Although the German-Brazilian contract went forward despite U.S. protests, pressure and persuasion from the United States won cancellation of the Korean and Pakistani reprocessing deals.

The United States also adopted new legislative restrictions. The Glenn and Symington amendments to the Foreign Assistance Act called for a cutoff of American aid to countries that acquired reprocessing or enrichment plants without accepting NPT-type fullscope safeguards.[12] The 1978 Nuclear Nonproliferation Act imposed tighter conditions on U.S. nuclear trade, including a demand that all recipients of U.S. reactors and fuel submit to fullscope safeguards; this requirement eventually led to the termination of U.S. nuclear cooperation with India, South Africa, and Brazil. (Not all suppliers followed the U.S. lead on safeguards, however, so non-NPT states continued to obtain foreign assistance to their civil nuclear programs.) Finally, the Carter administration urged a deferral of plans for commercial reprocessing and use of plutonium fuels, but faced strong resistance from Western Europe and Japan, where such plans were central to future energy strategy.

As the 1970s ended, the nonproliferation regime was beset with multiple strains. The industrial countries were at odds over domestic nuclear development and export policy. Third World nations were resentful of attempts to curb their access to nuclear technology. And evidence of proliferation continued to accumulate. In 1977, the superpowers detected apparent preparations for an underground nuclear test by South Africa. Pretoria agreed to dismantle the site, but continued to pursue a nuclear weapons option. Two years later, the United States discovered that Pakistan was building a secret enrichment plant at Kahuta, based on plans stolen in Europe and an elaborate network of clandestine technology purchases. The discovery led to cutoff of U.S. aid under the Symington amendment.

## RECENT TRENDS

On the surface, the 1980s were a period of comparative calm for the nonproliferation regime after the turbulence of the previous decade. No new countries openly obtained nuclear weapons, and disputes over plutonium and export policies abated in the wake of policy changes (in particular, the Reagan administration's friendlier approach to European and Japanese plutonium use) and the declining fortunes of nuclear energy. The visibility and priority of proliferation issues declined as the drama of superpower relations—a revival of East-West tensions followed by the virtual ending of the Cold War—dominated security policies.

This eclipse of the proliferation issue was deceptive, however. While world attention was directed elsewhere, South Africa and Pakistan joined Israel and India as de facto nuclear powers, and these four countries accrued growing stocks of uncontrolled weapons material. This development drew only a half-hearted and ineffective international response. The 1980s also revealed serious defects in export controls, and saw an overall erosion in the power of supplier countries to curb proliferation. As the 1990s began, the ominous implications of these trends were dramatized by rising nuclear tensions in the Middle East and South Asia, the two most volatile flashpoints for proliferation (see Figure 7.2).

### The Emerging Nuclear Powers

**South Asia**  India and Pakistan stand at the brink of an open nuclear arms race. Though neither country is known to have yet assembled nuclear

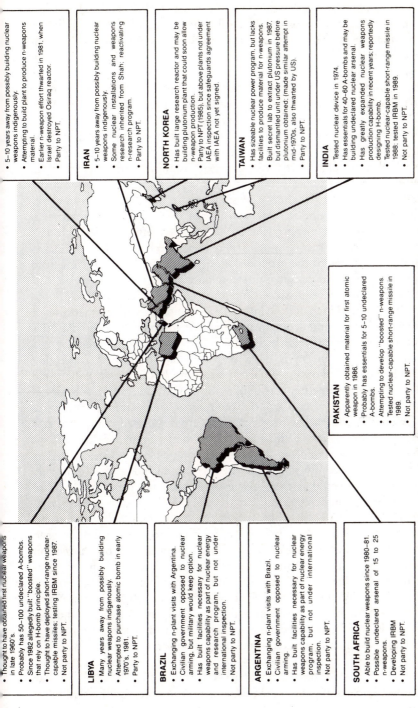

- 5-10 years away from possibly building nuclear weapons indigenously.
- Attempting to build plant to produce n-weapons material.
- Earlier n-weapon effort thwarted in 1981, when Israel destroyed Osiraq reactor.
- Party to NPT.

**IRAN**
- 5-10 years away from possibly building nuclear weapons indigenously.
- Some nuclear installations and weapons research inherited from Shah: reactivating n-research program.
- Party to NPT.

**NORTH KOREA**
- Has built large research reactor and may be building plutonium plant that could soon allow n-weapon production.
- Party to NPT (1985), but above plants not under IAEA inspection since safeguards agreement with IAEA not yet signed.

**TAIWAN**
- Has sizeable nuclear power program, but lacks facilities to produce material for n-weapons.
- Built secret lab to extract plutonium in 1987, but dismantled unit under US pressure before plutonium obtained. (made similar attempt in mid-1970s, also thwarted by US).
- Party to NPT.

**INDIA**
- Tested nuclear device in 1974.
- Has essentials for 40–60 A-bombs and may be building undeclared nuclear arsenal.
- Has greatly expanded nuclear weapons production capability in recent years; reportedly designing H-bomb.
- Tested nuclear-capable short-range missile in 1988; tested IRBM in 1989.
- Not party to NPT.

- Thought to have obtained first nuclear weapons in late 1960's.
- Probably has 50–100 undeclared A-bombs.
- Since 1982 allegedly built "boosted" weapons that rely on H-bomb principle.
- Thought to have deployed short-range nuclear-capable missiles: testing IRBM since 1987.
- Not party to NPT.

**LIBYA**
- Many years away from possibly building nuclear weapons indigenously.
- Attempted to purchase atomic bomb in early 1970's, 1981.
- Party to NPT.

**BRAZIL**
- Exchanging n-plant visits with Argentina.
- Civilian government opposed to nuclear arming, but military would keep option.
- Has built facilities necessary for nuclear weapons capability as part of nuclear energy and research program, but not under international inspection.
- Not party to NPT.

**ARGENTINA**
- Exchanging n-plant visits with Brazil.
- Civilian government opposed to nuclear arming.
- Has built facilities necessary for nuclear weapons capability as part of nuclear energy program, but not under international inspection.
- Not party to NPT.

**SOUTH AFRICA**
- Able to build nuclear weapons since 1980–81.
- Possible undeclared arsenal of 15 to 25 n-weapons.
- Developing IRBM
- Not party to NPT.

**PAKISTAN**
- Apparently obtained material for first atomic weapon in 1986.
- Probably has essentials for 5–10 undeclared A-bombs.
- Attempting to develop "boosted" n-weapons.
- Tested nuclear-capable short-range missile in 1989.
- Not party to NPT.

**NPT—The Nuclear Non-Proliferation Treaty.** Requires all nuclear installations in a signatory country to be placed under International Atomic Energy Agency inspection.

Carnegie Endowment for International Peace

**Figure 7.2 / Emerging Nuclear Weapon Nations, 1989–90**

151

weapons or deployed them with its military forces, there is little doubt that both could take these steps quickly following a decision to do so.[13] In a serious crisis or conflict between these two adversaries, as a result, the prospect of nuclear threats or attacks would have to be taken seriously by both sides. Though a kind of implicit nuclear deterrence has begun to emerge in South Asia, it is a fragile balance that could easily fail under stress. This danger was apparent to all sides when the chronic Indo-Pakistani dispute over the territory of Kashmir flared up again in 1990.[14]

The immediate threat in South Asia is Pakistan's determined drive to acquire a nuclear capability. This effort reached a key milestone in the late 1980s when Pakistan achieved weapons-grade uranium enrichment levels at its Kahuta plant. The plant is thought capable of producing material for up to a few bombs a year, creating a possible arsenal of eight to sixteen weapons through 1990. Although Pakistan claims that its nuclear program is devoted only to peaceful purposes, its leaders have affirmed the country's ability to produce nuclear weapons. There have also been persistent reports of Chinese assistance to the program, in areas ranging from enrichment to the sharing of warhead design and testing data.

Pakistan's progress has caused India to reconsider its own nuclear options. New Delhi did not follow up its 1974 explosion with further tests or weapons production and deployment, though it continued to reject the NPT and refuse fullscope safeguards. But this policy of restraint is increasingly strained and would probably collapse in the face of firm evidence that Pakistan had deployed or tested nuclear weapons. In that event, India could dwarf Pakistan's production capabilities and quickly assemble a substantial nuclear arsenal. With several reactors and reprocessing plants operating free of IAEA controls, India has been amassing unsafeguarded plutonium at a rate sufficient for as many as fifteen to thirty bombs annually. New Delhi is also believed to be exploring advanced thermonuclear warheads. It has tested short- and medium-range ballistic missiles, including the 1,500-mile range Agni, which could carry a nuclear warhead as far as Beijing.[15]

The growing South Asian nuclear threat reflects not only the bitter rivalry between the two sides, but also the failure of external pressures for nonproliferation. The latter, in turn, owes much to the tension between nonproliferation and other superpower interests in the region—a tension that became acute for the United States during the Soviet war in Afghanistan. Pakistan's value as a U.S. strategic partner rose sharply as it became the main conduit for Western aid to the anti-Soviet Afghan rebels, leading Washington to abandon nonproliferation sanctions. Early in the Reagan administration, the United States waived the Symington amendment to permit a new multibillion dollar aid package—including F-16 attack aircraft with the potential to deliver nuclear weapons—for Islamabad. Halfhearted attempts by the administration and Congress to link this aid to Pakistani nuclear restraint were defied with impunity, dealing a serious blow to the credibility of U.S. nonproliferation policy.[16] Nor has the Soviet Union pressured India on the nuclear issue, despite the potential leverge afforded by the military, economic, and civil nuclear ties between the two countries.

There is some hope for a deescalation of the nuclear rivalry in South Asia. Prior to the 1990 Kashmir crisis, there were signs of a thaw in relations between the two countries, including an agreement barring attack on each other's nuclear facilities. But the undeclared nuclear standoff between India and Pakistan remains precarious. Both countries entered the 1990s with unsettled domestic politics, and accountability and control over nuclear weapons programs are uncertain. While neither side's interest lies in provoking an open arms race, their latent bomb capabilities and the short lead times for deploying operational weapons would severely test mutual restraint in a crisis.

In addition, there are daunting obstacles to a true nuclear settlement in South Asia, rooted in basic conflicts betweeen the two sides' nuclear perspectives and objectives. Pakistan has linked its policy directly to that of India, offering to join in any arrangement—including the NPT or a bilateral nonnuclear pledge backed by inspections—accepted by New Delhi. India, however, is determined to be recognized as a great power and the region's paramount state, and rejects formulas that imply equality with Pakistan. And while the threat from Pakistan dominates India's immediate nuclear calculations, China remains a key point of reference for its overall approach to nonproliferation. Thus New Delhi insists on Beijing's participation in any regional solution and, more broadly, continues to demand a softening of the discrimination between nuclear and nonnuclear states that marks the global regime.

**The Middle East**   The nuclear threat in the Middle East is different but no less volatile than in South Asia. Israel is the region's only de facto nuclear power, with no near challenger among its Arab adversaries. But Israel's capability continues to fuel the Arab nuclear ambitions and poses a threat of nuclear escalation in a future Middle East war. The dangers have increased with the rapid spread of ballistic missiles and chemical weapons in the region and the sharp rise in tensions following the Iraqi invasion of Kuwait in 1990.

Israel has long maintained a deliberate ambiguity about its nuclear status. While claiming it would not be the first country to "introduce" nuclear weapons into the Middle East, it has not discouraged the widespread assumption that these weapons would be readily at hand should Israeli security require them. This approach has the advantage of providing implicit nuclear deterrence against all-out Arab aggression (and also, perhaps, against Soviet intervention in support of the Arabs), while avoiding the harsh regional and international reactions that might be provoked by an open demonstration of nuclear capability.[17]

Since the 1986 revelations of Mordechai Vanunu, a former technician at Israel's Dimona nuclear reactor, this strategy of nuclear ambiguity has been stretched thin. According to Vanunu, Israel possesses a large arsenal of sophisticated nuclear warheads and delivery systems. Experts now estimate that Israel has from fifty to sixty to over one hundred weapons, some incorporating the principle of nuclear fusion employed in the H-bomb (and thus many times more powerful than fission bombs), and that they have been integrated into the nation's military forces and strategy.[18]

No other country in the Middle East could gain nuclear weapons in the immediate future (barring theft or black-market purchase of warheads), but several aspire to this goal despite nominal adherence to the NPT. Iraq's program was set back by the 1981 Israeli bombing of the Osiraq reactor (which, though under IAEA safeguards, was suspected by Israel and others of having a military purpose), but was energetically revived several years later. Following Pakistan's example, Iran has acquired components for a centrifuge enrichment facility, although it is thought by most experts to be several years away from a weapons capability. The Kuwait crisis focused belated international attention on Baghdad's nuclear ambitions, which were cited by the Bush administration as a leading rationale for military action against Iraq. Other Middle East nations with nuclear ambitions—but no near-term prospects for obtaining weapons—are Iran and Libya.

Adding to the Middle East nuclear threat is the growing regional prominence of ballistic missiles. While these missiles have been present in the area for some time, the last few years have seen a dramatic increase in their numbers, sophistication, and range.[20] The 900-mile range of Israel's latest Jericho missile, assumed to be designed for nuclear delivery, puts not only the Arab world but the southern Soviet Union within reach. An even longer-range delivery capability—extending as far as Moscow—was signaled by Israel's use of a modified Jericho to launch satellites into orbit in 1988 and 1990. The second launch came in the wake of a threat by Iraq's President Saddam Hussein to destroy "half of Israel" with chemical weapons should Tel Aviv attack his country.[21] Iraq and a number of other Arab countries also possess improving ballistic missile capabilities. These are based mainly on rockets acquired from the Soviet Union and China (which sold the 1,600-mile-range nuclear-capable East Wind missile to Saudi Arabia) and, increasingly, on indigenous development programs.

Ballistic missile proliferation could profoundly alter the dynamics of future Middle East crises or conflicts. The short flight times of these weapons, and the lack of effective defenses against them, will increase fears of surprise attack and pressures for preemption during tense periods. Should war break out, missile attacks, potentially delivering chemical as well as conventional warheads, would quickly raise the level of violence and destruction.[22] In these circumstances, the danger of escalation to the nuclear level would be heightened. Indeed, Israel may increasingly regard its nuclear forces as a necessary counter to a growing Arab missile and chemical threat. Conversely, the Arab states have justified their interest in chemical weapons as a response to Israel's nuclear capability, arguing that a ban on chemical proliferation should be linked to Israeli nuclear controls.[23] Another escalation danger is posed by the longer-range missiles appearing in the region, especially those capable of reaching European and Soviet territory. They inherently raise the potential scope and stakes of a future Middle East conflict and increase the risks of superpower involvement.

Despite these dangers, the superpowers have failed to respond forcefully to the Middle East proliferation threat. As in South Asia, their influence is limited by the intractable nature of local conflicts and security dilemmas. Equally important, the superpowers' response to the threat has been inhibited by their own rivalry in the region, which has encouraged solicitude toward their respective allies and clients.[24] After early attempts to turn off Israel's nuclear-weapons program were rebuffed, the United States virtually dropped the issue from its bilateral agenda with Tel Aviv. This policy remained unshaken even in the wake of the Vanunu revelations; subsequent reports of nuclear cooperation between Israel and South Africa elicited U.S. protests but apparently no warning that Israel's nuclear activities might endanger its relations with the United States.[25] The Soviet Union, though unwilling to aid the Arab states in matching Israel's nuclear capability, has failed to exert strong pressure to discourage their own efforts and only recently has acknowledged the threat of missile proliferation in the region.

**South Africa**    South Africa mastered the production of weapons-grade uranium—produced in a pilot-scale, unsafeguarded enrichment plant—in the early 1980s. With an assumed production rate of a few bombs worth of fissile material per year, this facility would have given South Africa a potential nuclear arsenal of several tens of weapons by 1990. Early in that year, however, Pretoria announced the closing of the plant and indicated that it was considering signing the NPT. South African adherence to the treaty would bring the nation's new commercial-scale enrichment plant (potentially a much larger source of weapons material) under IAEA safeguards and would be a major political boost for the nonproliferation regime.

The turnaround in South African nuclear policy is clearly related to dramatic political changes that may signal the demise of the country's long-entrenched apartheid system of racial segregation and white domination. Until recently, the beleaguered and internationally isolated Pretoria regime had found it advantageous to maintain an ambiguous nuclear posture similar to that of Israel. The nuclear option was seen as a last-resort deterrent against an invasion from neighboring states aimed at overturning the white regime, and as a possible diplomatic bargaining card in negotiations over South Africa's future.[26]

The trend toward reform in South Africa has brightened the prospects for nonproliferation there in two ways, by reducing the country's motives for nuclear weapons and by making it easier for the outside world to reward Pretoria for submitting to nuclear controls. For example, the United States and European states may agree to lift their ban on nuclear energy cooperation with Pretoria—a step that would have been politically unthinkable at the height of apartheid. Nevertheless, the nuclear threat in South Africa could reemerge if white resistance to racial reform should plunge the country into domestic instability and violence. Another problem that will arise if South Africa does accede to the NPT is to account reliably for the weapons material that Pretoria may already have produced and assure that it can be adequately safeguarded.

**South America** Proliferation threats have also diminished in Brazil and Argentina. Although these countries lack the strong security incentives for nuclear weapons that mark South Asia and the Middle East, national rivalry and prestige motives have long fed military interest in the nuclear option. During the 1980s, both countries revealed that they had mastered sophisticated enrichment technologies, giving them the potential to produce weapons-grade uranium.[27]

Under civilian leadership, however, Brazil and Argentina have recently moderated their nuclear rivalry. Officials of the two countries have exchanged visits to nuclear facilities and have begun to shift their relationship from competition to cooperation. In Brazil, the government announced in 1990 that it would close down a secret military program to build nuclear weapons. Subsequently, both Brazil and Argentina formally renounced the pursuit of nuclear weapons and declared their willingness to negotiate full-scope safeguard agreements with the IAEA.

**East Asia** East Asia, a major focus of nonproliferation efforts in the mid-1970s, has resurfaced as a region of concern. In the earlier period, the United States used its strong political and military leverage to squelch apparent nuclear weapons programs in South Korea and Taiwan. In the late 1980s, however, Washington learned of renewed Taiwanese activities suggesting clandestine plans to extract plutonium produced in a large research reactor supplied by Canada. Again under U.S. pressure, Taiwan agreed to dismantle the reactor and to halt construction of the plutonium facility.[28]

North Korea's nuclear policy has also come under suspicion. Though it joined the NPT in 1985, North Korea has stalled on concluding the required fullscope safeguards agreement with the IAEA. The country operates a large research reactor of a type well suited for producing weapons-grade pluto-nium and has reportedly constructed a reprocessing plant as well. The United States has protested the situation and urged the Soviet Union to pressure North Korea to meet its NPT obligations. An obvious danger is that North Korean activities could revive South Korea's interest in nuclear weapons. A nuclearized Korean peninsula, in turn, would risk opening a serious debate on the nuclear option in Japan.

## Nuclear Markets and Supply Policies

If dealing with the "problem countries" is the overriding task of nonprolif-eration policies in the 1990s, changes in the political-economic setting of world nuclear relations also pose serious challenges to the regime. These changes have reshaped the proliferation problem, with implications for the relevance and effectiveness of earlier strategies from Atoms for Peace to the reforms of the 1970s.

**Shrinking Nuclear Markets**   The prospects for nuclear power declined sharply during the last decade. Ambitious plans for reactor construction were scaled back in both industrial and developing countries amid growing economic, political, and safety concerns. This trend, already well under way at the time of the 1986 Chernobyl nuclear accident in the Soviet Union, accelerated in the wake of the accident. New reactor orders dwindled, and many previous orders were canceled. While the IAEA projected in the mid-1970s that several thousand reactors would be operating worldwide by the turn of the century, the forecast has now shrunk to a few hundred. Reactor exports have also virtually dried up, failing to compensate industrial suppli-ers for the shrinkage of their domestic markets. Plans for rapid nuclear growth in Brazil, Mexico, and China raised supplier hopes for lucrative new markets only to collapse in the face of economic realities.

These developments have mixed meanings for the proliferation threat, making it more manageable in some respects and less so in others. On the positive side, the market downturn has slowed the global diffusion of nu-clear energy technology and undercut the rationale for a transition to pluto-nium fuels. Uranium, once expected to become scarce and expensive, is abundant and cheap. (The price of uranium hexafluoride, from which reac-tor fuel is fabricated, dropped from around fifty dollars a pound in the late 1970s to ten dollars a pound a decade later.) As a result, the separation of plutonium from spent reactor fuel for use as a fuel in its own right has become clearly cost-ineffective. Breeder-reactor programs in Europe have slipped or been abandoned, and reprocessing plans in West Germany have been canceled. While such programs are still proceeding in Japan, they face an inauspicious economic future. Thus, the harsh realities of the market have largely brought about the deferral of commercial plutonium use that the Carter administration vainly sought in the diplomatic arena.

The shrinking export market has also eased some earlier strains in the nonproliferation regime. Reduced demand has helped mute Third World complaints about abridged access to nuclear technology. On the supply side, while keener competition for exports might have produced a relaxation of nonproliferation standards, for the most part this has not occurred. Fears that suppliers would vie for reactor orders by offering enrichment or reprocessing technology as a "sweetener" have not materialized. Such pressures could still reappear, but at present the scarcity of nuclear customers seems to limit the scope for a breakdown of supplier restraint. Unfortunately, it may also prevent a significant upgrading of export conditions.

**Declining Supplier Leverage** Accompanying the nuclear market downturn in the 1980s has been a general decline in the role of nuclear trade and supply policy, historically central to the regime, in the dynamics of weapons proliferation. The result is an erosion of nonproliferation strategies relying on supply power—whether in the positive sense (nuclear cooperation as an inducement to nonproliferation, as in Atoms for Peace) or the negative one (supplier restraint as a preventive to proliferation, as in the Nuclear Suppliers Group).

On the one hand, the nuclear recession has reduced the vitality of the traditional "nuclear bargain," whose nonproliferation logic assumed an expanding market in which nuclear power was highly valued and the web of nuclear interdependence created strong incentives for compliance. At the same time, the efficacy of supplier restraint and denial has declined with the loosening of the link between civil nuclear and weapons programs. The proliferation scenarios that inspired the supplier reforms of the 1970s— diversion from civil nuclear programs, transfers of sensitive nuclear facilities, and the rush to use plutonium fuel—have become increasingly marginal to the threat posed by the undeclared nuclear powers and their would-be emulators.

Two other trends aggravate the decline of supplier leverage. First, the indigenous technical capabilities of the undeclared nuclear powers and other developing countries have steadily improved, reducing their dependence on outside sources. The mastery by Argentina and Brazil of enrichment technology, long assumed to be within reach of only the most advanced industrial countries, epitomizes this trend. Second, the export market has become more diversified. A number of countries outside the Nuclear Suppliers Group are now able to offer nuclear equipment and technology abroad. Argentina and China are becoming important suppliers, and could be joined in the future by Brazil, India, Pakistan and others. So far, the new suppliers have indicated that they will require IAEA safeguards on their exports. But in many cases their commitment to the nonproliferation regime is weak at best, and their growing activity threatens to make the international export control system more porous.[29]

**Supplier Responses**　The tasks of supplier cooperation have evolved in response to this changed setting. The main goal of export control has shifted from regulating overt nuclear commerce and government-sponsored cooperation to uncovering and preventing clandestine acquisitions of technology. As direct access to sensitive technologies has been closed off, aspiring nuclear powers have increasingly exploited gaps and loopholes in export control systems to obtain components for weapons programs. An array of clandestine and deceptive tactics—including falsified licensing documents and the use of front companies to acquire dual-use technologies (those with legitimate civilian applications as well as relevance to weapons programs)—have posed a severe challenge to supplier controls. The problem is magnified by national differences in export control laws and by the willingness of some firms and brokers in supplier countries to abet illegal nuclear trade.[30]

Missile proliferation has become another area of supplier action. Concern about this problem reflects the accelerating spread of missile technology to the developing world, and the rising importance of delivery systems in regional nuclear scenarios. In the past, the production of fissile material (plutonium or enriched uranium) has been considered the key technical hurdle facing a would-be nuclear power. But as a growing number of countries surmount this barrier, nonproliferation policy increasingly must focus on preventing the development of operational, deliverable weapons. Missiles are especially threatening, as noted earlier, because their speed, range, and ability to penetrate defenses give them a highly destabilizing potential.

Supplier efforts to come to grips with this threat have been belated and limited in scope. In 1987, seven Western supplier countries established a Missile Technology Control Regime (MTCR), setting guidelines for restricting exports in this area. The regime applies to missiles able to carry a 500-kilogram (1,100-pound) payload over a range of 300 kilometers (186 miles)—criteria chosen to cover nuclear-capable missiles that would have military significance in a region like the Middle East. Controlled items are divided into two categories—a more sensitive one (including complete rockets and large components such as rocket stages, engines, and guidance systems), where there is a presumption that exports will be denied; and a less sensitive one (including fuels and various ancillary equipment and materials), where export is at the discretion of the supplier.

Though a constructive beginning, the MTCR is a weak reed for stemming missile exports. As a voluntary, nonbinding arrangement, it carries no enforcement procedures or sanctions against violators. Numerous disputes have arisen—for example, over French exports to Brazil and Iraq—on the coverage and implementation of the regime's guidelines. As with nuclear export control, dual-use technologies pose a difficult problem, especially because of the similarities between booster rockets used in civilian space programs (which the MTCR attempts not to impede) and military ballistic missiles. Finally, some missile-exporting countries have not participated in the regime. The Soviet Union, the main supplier of missiles to the Arab world, remained aloof until 1990, when it began to adopt a more cooperative policy. But China has so far refused to curb missile exports, despite U.S. protests, and has become a leading supplier to the Middle East. Nor have emerging and potential missile exporters such as Israel, South Africa, Brazil, Argentina, and Israel joined in the regime.

## CHALLENGES AND POLICIES FOR THE 1990s

The requirements of nonproliferation policy in the decade ahead can be broadly defined in terms of three challenges. First, the problem of the de facto nuclear states will have to be addressed more directly. If these countries cannot be induced to curtail their weapons programs, there is a strong chance that the 1990s will see deployments of new national nuclear forces—and a heightened threat of regional nuclear wars. Second, the institutions of the nonproliferation regime will face a dual task—more effective supplier cooperation and renewal of the Nonproliferation Treaty in 1995. Third, the transformation of U.S.-Soviet relations will have major implications for nonproliferation efforts, creating both new opportunities and new hazards. To meet these challenges, the United States and other governments will have to move nonproliferation policy beyond its typically narrow confines, raising the priority of the issue and treating it as an integral part of foreign and national security policy.

### Dealing with Undeclared Proliferation

The de facto nuclear powers defy the formal categories of the NPT regime, demonstrating that "going nuclear" is not a simple yes-or-no proposition. Proliferation is better seen as a ladder with several rungs—including the production of fissile materials, the making of actual nuclear devices or components that could be quickly assembled into bombs, the deployment of operational weapons, and the development of advanced warheads and delivery systems. Explosive testing—once the hallmark of entry into the nuclear club—is not essential, at least for the construction of basic fission weapons. Even for more advanced warheads (such as fusion weapons), access to another nation's design and test data or to sophisticated computer capabilities may reduce the need for testing.

This lack of a clear boundary between nuclear and nonnuclear status is partly responsible for the international community's inability to respond coherently or effectively to the undeclared nuclear powers. Indeed, it raises basic questions about the goals and criteria for success of nonproliferation policy. When the prevention of new nuclear capabilities has failed, should energies be directed at reversing the process, holding the line against further moves up the proliferation ladder, or smoothing the entry of de facto weapon states into the nuclear club?

The last approach, often called "proliferation management," is advocated by some. They argue that nuclear status of the undeclared powers should be accepted and formalized, and that the goal of policy should be to assimilate new members of the club in a stable fashion.[31] Assistance might even be offered to help make nascent nuclear arsenals safer and more secure through improvements in command and control arrangements, basing, and other aspects of managing nuclear weapons.

But while this strategy may become prudent as a last resort in some cases, it is unwise as a general approach to the undeclared nuclear powers. First, it is premature: the emergence of these states as full-fledged nuclear powers is not inevitable and should not be treated as such. This is all the more true in view of the trend toward reductions and deemphasis of nuclear weapons by the existing weapon states. And the examples of South Africa, Argentina, and Brazil suggests that even the most entrenched nuclear programs may be brought under control as political conditions change. Second, legitimizing the de facto nuclear states would severely undercut the nonproliferation regime—on the eve of the NPT renewal date—by rewarding countries for pursuing a nuclear option.

Third, and most important, the "management" strategy is too sanguine about the chances for stable nuclear deterrence among new Third World nuclear powers. For a number of reasons, it is very doubtful that a nuclearized Middle East or South Asia would match the stability of the superpower nuclear balance. Unlike the United States and the Soviet Union, antagonists in these regions have a history of recurrent armed conflict over deeply rooted religious and territorial disputes. Far from mellowing, these disputes could erupt into open warfare at almost any time. The threat is compounded by the high incidence of terrorist activity—especially in the Middle East—and by the domestic instability and strong military influence characteristic of many Third World regimes. In short, the danger that nuclear weapons once deployed would actually be used, or would invite preemptive attacks by threatened target states, is all too plausible in these regions.

These considerations argue strongly against a policy of fatalistic acceptance of proliferation. At the same time, realism demands a modest, incremental strategy for bringing undeclared nuclear powers under control. While keeping the ultimate goal of reversing these nuclear weapons programs, initial efforts should focus on freezing them in place and then gradually subjecting them to increasingly rigorous controls. This approach calls for a mix of policies ranging from export controls to wider diplomatic and security initiatives to alleviate the long-standing regional conflicts that feed nuclear ambitions. A basic requirement is that the superpowers take non-proliferation seriously. In the hard cases, the United States and the Soviet Union have typically been unwilling to pay the costs of a vigorous assault on proliferation; as a result, would-be nuclear powers have rarely incurred high costs for their actions.

Highest priority should go to stopping further advances towards nuclear weapons in South Asia and the Middle East. India and Pakistan must be dissuaded from taking actions, such as nuclear testing or deployment, that would unleash an open-ended nuclear arms race between them. Beyond this, the two countries should be pressed to adopt a step-by-step program of controls and confidence-building measures to reduce their mutual nuclear suspicions and fears. These could include exchanges of visits to nuclear installations, inspections (either reciprocal or by an outside party) of sensitive facilities, a freeze on producing fissile material for a specified time, and—eventually—formal nonproliferation pledges.[32]

This strategy would need active support from the superpowers, using a careful balance of carrots and sticks to help ease underlying security fears in the region while making clear that weapons activities cannot be pursued cost-free. Any future U.S. aid to Pakistan should be clearly tied to specified nonproliferation conditions. The Soviets, for their part, should use their influence with India to strengthen that country's nonproliferation commitments. They should cease offering nuclear cooperation (such as the lease of nuclear submarines and sale of reactors) without demanding nonproliferation concessions in return. Both superpowers should insist on verifiable assurances that advanced aircraft transferred to the region will not be used as nuclear delivery vehicles. China also has a key role to play in defusing South Asian nuclear tensions, by giving assurances of nonaggression to India and halting further nuclear assistance to Pakistan.

In the Middle East, Israel's monopoly on nuclear capability (and the tacit acceptance of it by the United States) has until recently created the impression that the proliferation threat is not urgent. But changing circumstances—greater public knowledge of the Israeli weapons program, rising concern about missiles and chemical weapons in the region, and the Persian Gulf crisis—have altered this perception. A serious attack on the problem will require the United States to press for Israeli nuclear restraint more convincingly than in the past. While Washington cannot credibly threaten to cut all ties to Israel (a threat that would only backfire by increasing the latter's nuclear incentives), it can and should make clear that Israel's present nuclear course will increasingly corrode bilateral relations between the two countries. To be effective, pressure on Israel must be accompanied by parallel moves, with strong Soviet involvement, to restrain Arab nuclear, missile, and chemical programs. In the long term, lasting nonproliferation arrangements in the region depend upon, and should be made a part of, broader initiatives for a Middle East peace settlement.

Elsewhere, strong efforts should be applied to institutionalizing nuclear restraint in Latin America and to avoiding an unraveling of the situation in East Asia. In the former region, Brazil and Argentina should be pressed to move beyond informal nuclear détente to official nonproliferation commitments backed by inspections of their unsafeguarded nuclear plants. In East Asia, an immediate priority is to obtain IAEA safeguards on North Korea's program and prevent a revival of nuclear ambitions in South Korea. In addition, Taiwan's nuclear aspirations, which could grow amid China's turn toward internal repression and increased tensions with the West, could again become a serious concern in the 1990s.

## Extending the Nonproliferation Regime

**Supplier Controls**   Curbs on the spread of nuclear technology remain essential despite their declining potency in stopping proliferation. Even if they ultimately fail to prevent countries from obtaining a nuclear capability, experience has shown that these curbs can significantly slow the progress and raise the costs of weapons. As such they send a useful signal to other would-be proliferators (and may strengthen bomb opponents in these countries), while buying time for domestic and regional developments that may dampen the drive for nuclear weapons in the target nations themselves. Thus, technology controls are not a substitute for policies aimed at the political and strategic roots of proliferation, but can be a valuable complement to them.

The agenda for strengthening supply policies includes several priority items. First, emerging non-Western suppliers need to be enlisted in efforts to restrict technology exports, although their formal adherence to the Nuclear Suppliers Group is unlikely in most cases. In spite of their hostility to aspects of the nonproliferation regime, countries like India and Argentina may become persuaded (as were the original nuclear powers) that the uncontrolled spread of nuclear technology is contrary to their own security interests. Second, closer oversight and cooperation in controlling dual-use technology transfers should be established. Currently these items too easily slip through export-control nets.[33] Suppliers should create a list of critical dual-use items relevant to the nuclear programs of problem countries; exports of these items should be tied to the recipient's acceptance of nonproliferation obligations and to credible assurances that the end-use of the items in question is nonnuclear. Third, the missile control regime badly needs to be reinforced. Members of the MTCR should clarify ambiguities and fill gaps in the regime's coverage, and nonmembers like China should be pressured to join.

Civilian nuclear cooperation and commerce, despite their diminished role in weapons proliferation, also need continuing attention. (A major revival of nuclear power in response to the global warming threat—which dictates alternatives to fossil-fueled energy—could restore this issue to its former prominence; but such a revival is unlikely, at least within the next decade.) Although few reactor export deals are on the horizon, it is important to maintain rigorous standards when export opportunities do appear. Recent offers of reactor sales to India (by the Soviet Union) and Pakistan (by France) without a requirement for NPT-type fullscope safeguards fall short of these standards. Such deals devalue NPT membership and forfeit opportunities to apply nonproliferation leverage on the recipient countries.

Another area of concern is commerce in plutonium fuel. Though the economic basis for commercializing breeder reactors has collapsed, Japan and several European countries continue to reprocess their spent reactor fuel, in part to defer the politically explosive issue of nuclear waste disposal. The result is a growing "overhang" of separated plutonium in amounts far exceeding the needs of nuclear energy programs. This development will place severe strains on the capacity of IAEA safeguards and domestic security forces to guard against diversions, thefts, or accidents involving weapons-grade material.[34]

**Maintaining the NPT**   In 1995, the Nonproliferation Treaty will reach the end of its twenty-five-year term. At that time, a conference must be convened to approve the treaty's renewal (by a majority vote of the parties) either for a specified period or indefinitely. In theory, the NPT could terminate if no proposal for renewal is able to command majority support; but this outcome—which would be tantamount to a collapse of the nonproliferation regime—is unlikely.

Though the nonnuclear parties remain discontented with aspects of the treaty and the performance of the nuclear-weapon states under it, most believe that on balance the NPT serves their national interests by helping contain a spread of nuclear weapons that would lessen their security. The outlook is thus more favorable than it was several years ago, when the nonproliferation regime and the IAEA were threatened by the debilitating North-South politicization that has plagued some other international agencies.[35] Since then, assessments of the regime have become somewhat more pragmatic and less ideological. However, unexpected shocks—such as an outbreak of overt proliferation or a breakdown of East-West détente—could change this outlook and threaten the chances for renewing the treaty.

In the absence of such dramatic shocks, trouble could still come from two directions. First, the Israeli nuclear program (and South Africa's, should Pretoria backslide from its recent policy change) could become a flashpoint for nonnuclear state protests, especially among the Arab and African states. Second, there may be attempts to hold the NPT hostage to other objectives, particularly superpower disarmament. This might be done by linking renewal to explicit arms-control benchmarks—for example, a comprehensive nuclear test ban or specific nuclear force reduction targets—to be met by the superpowers. This possibility was underscored when the 1990 NPT review conference failed to reach a consensus because of disagreements over the test ban issue.[36] Another approach, advocated by India at the 1988 UN Special Session on Disarmament, would replace the NPT with a new, nondiscriminatory regime requiring the elimination of existing nuclear arsenals by an agreed date in tandem with nonproliferation commitments by the nonnuclear and undeclared nuclear powers. (Although non-NPT states like India and Argentina will not be directly involved in the renewal conference, they still may exert considerable influence among Third World NPT parties.)

Such strategies are unlikely to succeed, given the certain opposition of the nuclear-weapon states, and if pursued energetically they could endanger NPT renewal. A more prudent strategy would be to extend the NPT as is, while continuing to pursue nuclear-power arms control as a parallel—but not explicitly linked—process. Not only is this strategy more realistic than the linkage approach, but it is justified on its merits since the NPT offers its members real security benefits in its own right and the superpowers are at last discussing serious arms reductions.

## Nonproliferation after the Cold War

The decline of the Cold War dramatically alters the global setting of the nonproliferation regime, with consequences that cannot be foreseen with certainty but are likely to be far-reaching. Superpower rivalry, after all, has been a powerful force in shaping nonproliferation policies throughout the postwar period.

Significantly, this rivalry has had two contrary impacts. On the one hand, it has provided a basic motive for curbing access to the nuclear club (and, since the 1960s, in cooperating to that end) to reduce the risks of the superpowers' global competition. On the other hand, it has impeded nonproliferation initiatives that would threaten the superpowers' nuclear prerogatives or endanger ties with allies and client states. From the Baruch Plan to U.S. waivers of the Symington amendment on behalf of Pakistan four decades later, nonproliferation policies have often fallen victim to Cold War priorities.

It is likely, then, that the ending of the Cold War will also have mixed implications for nonproliferation. In several respects it could create new opportunities to strengthen the regime. For example, it could ease superpower cross-pressures in dealing with regional allies seeking to acquire nuclear weapons. Thus, the Soviet withdrawal from Afghanistan reduces Pakistan's leverage over Washington and could make the latter more willing to attach meaningful nonproliferation strings to its military and economic aid. The Soviets, in turn, might deal more firmly with suspect nuclear activities by Arab states or North Korea if Middle East and Asian conflicts are no longer seen as tests of superpower rivalry and influence. By the same token, better U.S.-Soviet relations may improve the prospects for resolving the regional conflicts that drive proliferation. As their own regional conflicts of interest recede, the scope for superpower cooperation in support of peace initiatives in areas threatened by proliferation may increase.

Finally, superpower arms reductions could strengthen the nonproliferation regime by softening the double standard that has always hurt the regime's legitimacy. The Strategic Arms Reduction Treaty (START) and subsequent arms control agreements will for the first time demonstrate more than token compliance with the superpowers' commitments under NPT, Article VI, improving the chances for a successful renewal of the treaty in 1995. And, while U.S.-Soviet reductions will not directly assuage the motives of the undeclared nuclear powers, over time they may alter perceptions of the utility, relevance, and prestige value of nuclear weapons. This perceptual change could weigh heavily, and constructively, in the calculations of states considering a nuclear option.

But the Cold War's end may also have a negative side for nonproliferation policies. The bipolar Cold War world, for all its risks and inequalities, did provide a degree of hierarchy, structure, and predictability that on balance dampened pressures for proliferation. The emergence of a more fluid, fragmented, and multipolar system could, in contrast, unleash new forces for proliferation. Traditional alliance ties and commitments may be weakened, creating new insecurities and uncertainties among states formerly enjoying the patronage of the Cold War antagonists. This trend could be aggravated by two other developments—retrenchment for economic reasons from the overextended security roles the superpowers have taken on during the Cole War, and the possibility of growing instability in the USSR and a disintegrating Soviet bloc.

These shifts could produce new incentives for nuclear weapons in East and South Asia and the Middle East, while simultaneously reducing U.S. and Soviet influence over potential proliferators. A related danger is that, as the superpowers disengage from Third World conflicts, their sense of urgency about the proliferation threat may diminish. In that case, the superpower response to proliferation in the Middle East or South Asia could be a "decoupling" from these regions, rather than more active involvement aimed at nuclear restraint.

These scenarios underscore the proliferation risks of a disorderly collapse of the postwar world order, and the importance of managing the transition to a new order with these risks firmly in mind. The superpowers must recognize that in an age of economic interdependence and long-range missiles, they cannot insulate themselves from the dangers of regional proliferation. As their conflict abates and their dominance of world politics declines, they must not abdicate responsibility for containing nuclear proliferation.

At the same time, the task of maintaining a strong nonproliferation regime will have to be spread more widely. The regime's traditional guarantors—the superpowers and the industrial supplier nations—will increasingly have to enlist the cooperation of other actors. In this more decentralized regime, the major developing countries will have a larger role to play, as will international organizations. A strengthening of the IAEA and its safeguards system is crucial, but other institutions can make an even more important, if indirect, contribution. In the security field, an enhanced UN role in conflict-resolution and peacekeeping, joined by new regional peace initiatives, can help reduce proliferation incentives. And in the field of economics and technology, development programs can reduce the symbolic appeal of nuclear weapons, reinforcing the message—already evident in the industrial world—that in the emerging world order the bomb is an obsolescent source of status and influence.

## Notes

1. Early works on the subject include Leonard Beaton and John Maddox, *The Spread of Nuclear Weapons* (London: Chatto and Windus, 1962); Richard Rosecrance, ed., *The Dispersion of Nuclear Weapons* (NY: Columbia University Press, 1964); and Alastair Buchan, ed., *A World of Nuclear Powers?* (Englewood Cliffs, NJ: Prentice-Hall, 1966). A minority opinion holds that proliferation might actually promote peace. The clearest statement of this argument, which essentially analogizes from the U.S.-Soviet nuclear standoff, is Kenneth Waltz, "The Spread of Nuclear Weapons: More May be Better," *Adelphi Papers*, no. 171 (London: International Institute for Strategic Studies, 1981).

2. On the early years of atomic energy diplomacy, see Gregg Herken, *The Winning Weapon* (New York: Vintage Books, 1982).

3. In other respects, the two cases were quite different. See Andrew Pierre, *Nuclear Politics: The British Experience with an Independent Strategic Force* (London: Oxford University Press, 1972); and Wilfred Kohl, *French Nuclear Diplomacy* (Princeton: Princeton University Press, 1971).

4. See William Bader, *The United States and the Spread of Nuclear Weapons* (New York: Pegasus Books, 1968); and John Steinbruner, *The Cybernetic Theory of Decision* (Princeton: Princeton University Press, 1974).

5. See John Wilson Lewis and Xue Litai, *China Builds the Bomb* (Stanford, CA: Stanford University Press, 1988).

6. See Joseph S. Nye, Jr., "The Superpowers and the Non-Proliferation Treaty," in Albert Carnesale and Richard N. Haass, eds., *Superpower Arms Control: Setting the Record Straight* (Cambridge, MA: Ballinger, 1987).

7. The NPT negotiations imposed severe strains on U.S. relations with Europe, and especially West Germany, in part because the treaty foreclosed the option for a NATO Multilateral Force (MLF) in which the allies could share control over alliance nuclear forces. On this controversy and other aspects of the negotiations, see Glenn Seaborg and Benjamin Loeb, *Stemming the Tide: Arms Control in the Johnson Years* (Lexington, MA: Lexington Books, 1987).

8. On national policies toward the NPT, see George Quester, *The Politics of Nuclear Proliferation* (Baltimore: Johns Hopkins University Press, 1973).

9. Atomic bombs can be made from two fissile materials, plutonium and uranium-235. Plutonium does not exist in nature, but is created as a byproduct of a nuclear reactor fueled with uranium. It can be chemically separated from the other waste products of the reactor by dissolving the irradiated or "spent" reactor fuel and feeding it through a "reprocessing" plant. Uranium-235 is present as a very small fraction (0.7%) of naturally occurring uranium, which is predominantly composed of the nonfissile isotope uranium-238. The proportion of uranium-235 can be increased (normally to 90% or more for nuclear weapons) through a process of "enrichment," which uses sophisticated technology to separate isotopes on the basis of their

minute difference in mass. In addition to their role in weapons development, reprocessing and enrichment both may play a role in civilian nuclear energy programs—the former to produce plutonium-based reactor fuels and the latter to produce the low-enriched uranium (about 3% uranium-235) with which most current power reactors are fueled.

10. On these dangers, see Albert Wohlstetter, "Spreading the Bomb Without Quite Breaking the Rules," *Foreign Policy*, Winter 1976–7; and Joseph Nye, "Non-Proliferation: A Long-Term Strategy," *Foreign Affairs*, April 1978.

11. For a thorough account of U.S. reforms, emphasizing bureaucratic politics, see Michael J. Brenner, *Nuclear Power and Non-Proliferation: The Remaking of U.S. Policy* (New York: Cambridge University Press, 1981).

12. These amendments were invoked against Pakistan's nuclear activities in the late 1970s but, as discussed below, were later waived to allow a resumption of U.S. aid. See Leonard S. Spector, *The Undeclared Bomb* (Cambridge, MA: Ballinger, 1988), pp. 474–76.

13. See Spector, *The Undeclared Bomb*, note 12, Chapter III; and David Albright and Tom Zamora, "India, Pakistan's Nuclear Weapons: All the Pieces in Place," *Bulletin of the Atomic Scientists*, June 1989, p. 20.

14. See Leonard S. Spector, "India-Pakistan War: It Could Be Nuclear," *New York Times*, June 7, 1990, p. 23; Michael Gordon, "War over Kashmir is Feared by U.S.," *New York Times*, June 17, 1990, p. 15.

15. See Gary Milhollin, "India's Missiles—With A Little Help From Our Friends," *Bulletin of the Atomic Scientists*, Nov. 1989, p. 31.

16. Nevertheless, the fear of losing U.S. aid may have helped deter Islamabad from open nuclear testing. Since 1985, U.S. aid has been subject to an annual presidential certification that Pakistan does not possess nuclear weapons. In 1990, the Bush administration was unable to make this certification, leading to at least a temporary suspension of aid. See Michael Gordon, "Nuclear Issue Slows US Aid to Pakistan," *New York Times*, Oct. 1, 1990, p. 3. For background, see Charles Van Doren, "Pakistan, Congress, and the Nonproliferation Challenge," *Arms Control Today*, November 1987, p. 6.

17. On Israeli nuclear motives and strategies, see Shai Feldman, *Israeli Nuclear Deterrence: A Strategy for the 1980s* (New York: Columbia University Press, 1982); and Louis Rene Beres, ed., *Security or Armageddon: Israel's Nuclear Strategy* (Lexington, MA: Lexington Books, 1986).

18. For details and historical background, see Spector, *The Undeclared Bomb*, note 12, pp. 164–95. The Dimona reactor, acquired in a secret deal with France in the 1950s, produces plutonium for Israeli weapons. There is also strong evidence that Israel surreptitiously obtained enriched uranium for bombs from an American company in the 1960s. It may also have received enriched uranium from South Africa in return for missile technology, according to 1989 press reports. Israel is not known to have tested a nuclear device, although there is speculation that a still-unexplained "flash" in 1979 over the South Atlantic (picked up by a U.S. nuclear-detection satellite) was an Israeli-South African test of a tactical nuclear warhead. Israel is also assumed by many analysts to have received data from the first French nuclear tests.

19. See Malcolm Browne, "Unless Stopped, Iraq Could Have A-Arms in Ten Years, Experts Say," *New York Times*, Nov. 11, 1990, p. 1. U.S. concern about a more immediate threat centers on 13 kg. of highly enriched uranium fuel—intended for the destroyed Osirak reactor—in Baghdad's possession but subject to IAEA inspection. See Michael Gordon, " U.S. Aides Press Iraqi Nuclear Threat," *New York Times*, Nov. 26, 1990.

20. See Martin S. Navias, "Ballistic Proliferation in the Middle East," *Survival*, May–June 1989.

21. Joel Brinkley, "Israel Puts a Satellite in Orbit a Day After Threat by Iraqis," *New York Times*, April 4, 1990, p. 6.

22. Chemical weapons are believed to be held by Iraq, Israel, Egypt, Libya, Syria, and Iran. They were used by Iraq in its war against Iran, which also saw extensive missile attacks against each side's cities. See Elisa D. Harris, "Chemical Weapons Proliferation," in Aspen Strategy Group, *New Threats: Responding to the Proliferation of Nuclear, Chemical, and Delivery Capabilities in the Third World* (Lanham, MD: University Press of America, 1990).

23. Edward Cody, "Talks Show Growing Arab Consensus That Chemical Arms Balance Nuclear," *Washington Post*, January 13, 1989, p. A24.

24. See Shai Feldman, "Superpower Nonproliferation Policies: The Case of the Middle

East," in Steven L. Spiegel, et al., *Soviet-American Competition in the Middle East* (Lexington, MA: Lexington Books, 1988), and Helena Cobban, "Israel's Nuclear Game: The U.S. Stake," *World Policy Journal*, Summer 1988.

25. See David B. Ottaway and R. Jeffrey Smith, "U.S. Knew of 2 Nations' Missile Work," *Washington Post*, October 27, 1989, p. 1.

26. See Richard Betts, "A Diplomatic Bomb for South Africa?" *International Security*, Fall 1979; and Michele A. Flournoy and Kurt M. Campbell, "South Africa's Bomb: A Military Option?" *Orbis*, Summer 1988.

27. See Shirley Christian, "Argentina and Brazil Renounce Atomic Weapons," *New York Times*, Nov. 11, 1990, p. 1, For background, see David Albright, "Bomb Potential for South America," *Bulletin of the Atomic Scientists*, May 1989, p. 16. Brazil's secret weapons effort was separate from the safeguarded nuclear program—now virtually moribund due to technical and economic setbacks—pursuant to the 1975 German-Brazilian deal.

28. Stephen Engelberg and Michael Gordon, "Taipei Halts Work on Secret Plant to Make Nuclear Bomb Material," *New York Times*, March 23, 1988, p. 1; Spector, *The Undeclared Bomb*, note 12, pp. 75–79.

29. William C. Potter, ed., *International Nuclear Trade and Nonproliferation: The Challenge of the Emerging Suppliers* (Lexington, MA: Lexington Books, 1990).

30. The complicity of German companies in numerous secret nuclear transactions involving Pakistan, India, and other problem countries was revealed in 1988–89. See Dan Charles, "Exporting Trouble—West Germany's Freewheeling Nuclear Business," *Bulletin of the Atomic Scientists*, April 1989, p. 21. For a detailed assessment of clandestine nuclear trade and its contribution to proliferation, see Leonard S. Spector, *Nuclear Exports: The Problem of Control* (Washington, DC: Carnegie Endowment for International Peace, April 1990).

31. See, for example, Kenneth Waltz, "The Spread of Nuclear Weapons," note 1; and Shai Feldman, "Managing Nuclear Proliferation," in Jed Snyder and Samuel Wells, Jr., eds., *Limiting Nuclear Proliferation* (Cambridge, MA: Ballinger, 1985).

32. For elaboration of these ideas, see the report of the Carnegie Task Force on Non-Proliferation and South Asian Security, *Nuclear Weapons and South Asian Security* (Washington, DC: Carnegie Endowment for International Peace, 1988); and *Nuclear Proliferation in South Asia: Containing the Threat*, Staff Report to the Senate Foreign Relations Committee (Washington, DC: GPO, 1988).

33. For example, see Jeffrey Smith and Benjamin Weizer, "Commerce Dept. Urged Sale to Iraq," *Washington Post*, Sept. 13, 1990 p. 1.

34. See Frans Berkhout et al., "The Approaching Plutonium Surplus: A Japanese-European Predicament," *International Affairs* 66, 3 (1990). The Reagan administration, softening its predecessor's opposition to plutonium, adopted a policy of blanket approval for Japan and Western Europe to reprocess reactor fuel supplied by the United States and to use the resulting plutonium in civilian power and research programs.

35. This trend, which paralleled the growing presence and influence of the "Group of 77" developing countries in international organizations, led to a curtailment of South African participation, and reached its peak after the Israeli bombing of Iraq's nuclear reactor in 1981. A year later, the IAEA General Conference rejected Israel's credentials, prompting a temporary U.S. walk-out from the agency. See Lawrence Scheinman, *The IAEA and World Nuclear Order* (Washington, DC: Resources for the Future, 1987), pp. 209–25.

36. See Leonard Spector and Jacqueline Smith, "Treaty Review: Deadlock Damages Nonproliferation," *Bulletin of the Atomic Scientists*, Dec. 1990.

# 8 / Deadly Convergence: The Arms Trade, Nuclear/Chemical/Missile Proliferation, and Regional Conflict in the 1990s

MICHAEL T. KLARE

As the 1980s drew to a close, there were many signs that the world was headed in the direction of greater peace and stability. In the space of just a few years, the United States and the Soviet Union concluded several new arms control agreements, the two halves of Europe began to dismantle the military systems that had divided them for forty years, and the United Nations helped to negotiate peaceful solutions to a number of regional disputes. But while these and other such developments produced a significant reduction in international tensions, the world also experienced a number of less promising developments. These included the further proliferation of nuclear and chemical weapons, the intensification of ethnic/religious conflict in Africa and Asia, and, only six months into the new decade, the Iraqi invasion of Kuwait. Thus, as we proceed further into the 1990s, it appears that the decline in East-West hostilities is being counterbalanced by an increase in regional Third World conflicts, and that wars of this type will be fought at ever-increasing levels of violence and destructiveness.

The risk of escalating violence is further underlined by data on conventional arms transfers to the Third World, and on the acquisition by emerging powers such as India, Iraq, and Israel of advanced arms-making technologies. According to the Congressional Research Service (CRS) of the Library of Congress, the developing nations spent an estimated $341 billion (in constant 1988 dollars) on imported arms and military systems between 1981 and 1988. Included in this largesse were 11,341 tanks and self-propelled cannon; 20,355 artillery pieces; 3,731 combat aircraft; 513 warships; and 37,180 surface-to-air missiles.[1] To augment these imported systems, many Third World countries stepped up the production of arms and military equipment in their own industrial facilities. According to the Stockholm International Peace Research Institute (SIPRI), twelve Third World countries now produce combat aircraft, eleven produce armored vehicles, twelve produce major fighting ships, and about forty produce small arms and ammunition.[2] Together, these imported and domestically produced arms have endowed many Third World nations with a formidable war-making capability.

Most of the weapons acquired by Third World countries in the 1980s have, of course, been used to replace outmoded equipment presently in their military stockpiles, and to otherwise enhance their ability to deter or resist external attack. However, a significant proportion of these arms were employed in actual shooting wars, inasmuch as the Third World was wracked by a wave of local, regional, and internal conflicts. Thus, to sustain their bloody eight-year war in the Persian Gulf, Iran and Iraq together spent an estimated $60 billion on imported arms.[3] Vast quantities of arms were also consumed in the Afghanistan war, the Falklands conflict, the Angolan civil war, and other regional conflicts of the 1980s.

As significant as the quantity of arms expended in battle is the nature of these weapons, and the manner in which they were employed. Thus, in looking at the Iran-Iraq war, one is struck not only by the vast carnage wreaked on each side but also by the deliberate use of terror weapons—principally ballistic missiles and chemical munitions—to sap the morale of the noncombatant population. Both sides also used modern guided missiles to strike at neutral ships and oil facilities in the Persian Gulf region, including vessels belonging to or under the protection of the United States. Indeed, what is most striking about the conduct of the two belligerents in the eight-year Gulf war was the progressive erosion of constraints on the use of ever more destructive and destabilizing weapons.[4]

In anticipation of future conflicts of this magnitude, the large and medium powers of the Third World are stockpiling large quantities of modern arms and enhancing their capacity for the domestic production of modern weapons. Many of them, moreover, are acquiring the capability to produce weapons of mass destruction—that is, nuclear or chemical weapons—along with the capability to deliver such munitions over considerable distances. As a result, many developing nations have been caught up in regional arms races that exhibit the same dynamics long evident in the military competition between the United States and the Soviet Union. And while the U.S.-Soviet competition now appears to be winding down, there is no evidence that these parallel arms races in the Third World are experiencing a similar relaxation.

Indeed, the most likely prospect for the 1990s is a continued buildup of military capabilities in areas of tension, accompanied by the periodic outbreak of local, regional, and internal conflict. Many of these wars will be of limited scale, and of purely local significance; some, however, are likely to equal or exceed the destructive intensity of the Iran-Iraq conflict. This is disturbing enough; what makes this prospect especially worrisome, however, is the fact that more and more Third World countries are likely to acquire weapons of mass destruction in the years ahead, along with ballastic missiles of intercontinental or continental range. What this means, in effect, is that future regional conflicts in the Third World will increasingly pose a threat of uncontrolled escalation, bringing the world closer to the brink of nuclear war.

To appreciate the potency of this threat, it is necessary to identify a number of converging military trends. These trends first became apparent in the late 1980s, and are likely to become significantly more pronounced in the later 1990s.[5]

The first trend entails the steady accumulation of large stockpiles of sophisticated conventional arms by highly militarized states in areas of potential conflict. Thus, of the $341 billion worth of arms sold to developing countries between 1981 and 1988, some $235 billion worth, or 69 percent, were purchased by countries in the Middle East and South Asia.[6] Among the biggest spenders in this group were India, Iran, Iraq, Israel, Libya, Pakistan, and Syria—countries that went to war in this period and/or participated in regional arms races with contentious neighbors. Large military purchases were also made by other parties to regional disputes, including China and Taiwan, Algeria and Morocco, and the two Koreas. In all of these cases, moreover, the countries involved sought access to the most modern and capable weapons available—among them, F-15 and F-16 aircraft from the United States, MiG-27 and -29 aircraft from the Soviet Union, and Mirage-2000 aircraft from France.[7]

The second trend is the continuing proliferation of nuclear and chemical weapons technology to emerging Third World powers. Although the rate of nuclear proliferation has not been as great as some analysts had feared, the 1980s witnessed some very significant breaches in the international regime established in the 1960s and 1970s to prevent the diffusion of nuclear weapons capabilities. Most ominous in this regard was the apparent success of India, Israel, Pakistan, and South Africa in obtaining materials and technology for the manufacture of nuclear munitions. It is also thought that several other countries, including Argentina, Brazil, Iraq, North Korea, South Korea, and Taiwan, conducted secret nuclear projects with a possible military application.[8] The 1980s also witnessed a significant diffusion of chemical weapons technology to the developing countries, with some thirteen nations—China, Egypt, Ethiopia, Iran, Iraq, Israel, Libya, Syria, Taiwan, Thailand, Vietnam, and the two Koreas—obtaining chemical munitions or the wherewithal to manufacture them.[9] (See Table 8.1.)

The third trend is the acquisition by nations with nuclear and/or chemical weapons of sophisticated aircraft and missiles capable of delivering such munitions over considerable distances. Most notable in this category are long-range strike aircraft with the capacity to deliver bombs and rockets deep into a neighbor's territory. Such aircraft include the American F-15 and F-16, the Soviet MiG-21 and MiG-23, the British Jaguar, and various models of the French Mirage—examples of which can be found in the inventories of most of the countries listed above with a nuclear or chemical arsenal.[10] Furthermore, many of these nations also acquired ballistic missiles with the ability to deliver nuclear and chemical warheads over ranges of several hundred or even thousands of miles. These missiles include the Soviet Scud-B, SS-12, and SS-21 (now in the arsenals of Afghanistan, Egypt, Iran, Iraq, Libya, North Korea, South Yemen, and Syria), the Chinese CSS-2 (sold to Saudi Arabia), and several weapons of indigenous design (the Indian Agni, the Iraqi al-Husayn, the Israeli Jericho-I and -II.[11]

Clearly, the convergence of these three trends is producing a military environment of great risk and instability. It is not hard to imagine, for instance, how this convergence could transform a small local conflict into a

Table 8.1 / Emerging Third World Superpowers

| Country | Arms Imports 1982–86 (in $U.S. millions)[a] | Domestic Arms Production[a] | Nuclear Devices/ Unregulated Reactors[b] | Chemical weapons[c] | Ballistic missiles[c] |
|---|---|---|---|---|---|
| Argentina | 1,960 | IW,AR,AV,JF,ML | no/yes | NR | yes |
| Brazil | 330 | IW,AR,AV,JF,ML | no/yes | NR | yes |
| Egypt | 7,640 | IW,AR,AV,ML | no/no | yes | yes |
| India | 9,275 | IW,AR,AV,JF,ML | yes/yes | NR | yes |
| Iran | 8,405 | IW,AR | no/no | yes | yes |
| Iraq | 31,740 | IW,AR | no/no | yes | yes |
| Israel | 3,700 | IW,AR,AV,JF,ML | yes/yes | yes | yes |
| Libya | 10,160 | IW | no/no | yes | yes |
| North Korea | 1,410 | IW,AR,AV | no/yes | yes | yes |
| Pakistan | 2,225 | IW | yes/yes | NR | UD |
| Saudi Arabia | 16,715 | IW | no/no | NR | yes |
| South Africa | 20 | IW,AR,AV,ML | yes/yes | yes | UD |
| South Korea | 2,160 | IW,AR,AV,JF | no/no | yes | UD |
| Syria | 10,830 | | no/no | yes | yes |
| Taiwan | 2,500 | IW,AR,AV,JF,ML | no/no | yes | UD |

Key: AR = Artillery, AV = Armored vehicles, IW = Infantry weapons (small arms, mortars, antitank guns), JF = Jet fighters, ML = Tactical missiles, NR = None reported, and UD = Under development.

Sources:

[a] U.S. Arms Control and Disarmament Agency, *World Military Expenditures and Arms Transfers 1987* (Washington, 1988), augmented by other sources.

[b] Leonard Spector, *The Undeclared Bomb* (Cambridge, MA, 1988). Unregulated reactor refers to research reactor, enrichment plant, or reprocessing plant not under IAEA safeguards.

[c] Robert Shuey, et al., *Missile Proliferation*, Congressional Research Service, October 3, 1988.

major regional conflagration. Conflicts of this intensity could pose a threat of catastrophic defeat to one side or the other, thus prompting the loser to employ chemical or even nuclear weapons to avert disaster. And, once any one side in a conflict used weapons of mass destruction in combat, we can assume that the other nations involved would feel free to retaliate in kind—thus igniting a regional nuclear war that could easily spread to other countries and possibly draw in the superpowers.

Despite this terrifying prospect, the major military suppliers made virtually no progress in curbing the conventional arms trade or in further restricting the proliferation of nuclear and chemical weapons in the 1980s. The only significant negotiations on arms transfer restraint, the Conventional Arms Transfer Talks (CATT) of 1977–78, were suspended by President Carter in 1979 and have not been revived since.[12] Some efforts were made to tighten the restrictions embodied in the Nuclear Nonproliferation Treaty (NPT) and other nuclear nonproliferation instruments, but these initiatives clearly failed to prevent the acquisition of critical nuclear technology and materials by India, Israel, Pakistan, and South Africa (see Chapter 7). Nor do we see much evidence of effective international action in halting the spread of chemical weapons. In one area only—the control of ballistic missile exports—was a new agreement signed in the 1980s, and even this agreement, the Missile Technology Control Regime (MTCR) of 1987, does not include China or the Soviet Union, and entails no mandatory enforcement procedures.[13]

Given this convergence of worrisome trends and the lack of effective international control, it appears that we face a very perilous security situation that can only grow more hazardous in the years ahead. While it is possible that the United States and the Soviet Union will make further progress in the area of strategic nuclear arms control (see Chapter 4), there are no multilateral talks currently under way aimed at controlling arms transfers to the Third World. Unless the world community responds to the three trends described above in a vigorous and cooperative manner, there will be little real improvement in the world security environment. We must, therefore, pay close attention to the international arms trade and begin to develop effective international controls on the worldwide diffusion of sophisticated conventional weapons.

## THE STATE OF THE TRADE

To begin this process, let us review the behavior of the arms traffic in the 1980s and consider its likely evolution in the 1990s. Four basic parameters delineate the basic contours of the weapons trade: the *volume* of transfers (usually measured in dollars); the various *commodities* supplied through these channels; the major *suppliers* of these commodities; and the *recipients* of arms.[14]

## Volume

When measured in dollars, the annual volume of arms purchases by Third World nations exhibited a steady increase from the early 1970s to the mid-1980s. From an average of $4 billion to $5 billion per year in the 1960s and early 1970s, military sales to Third World countries rose to $20 billion per year in the 1973–79 period and $40 billion annually in 1980–84.[15] After reaching peak levels in the early 1980s, arms sales dropped to an annual level of approximately $36 billion in 1985–89 (in current dollars). This still represents a very significant increase over the $20 billion level of the late 1970s, but it does suggest that there was some retrenchment in Third World arms spending. Still to be determined is whether this retrenchment is merely temporary—the result of secular economic and technical factors—or whether it will persist in the 1990s.

Arguing in favor of a temporary decline in Third World arms purchases is the fact that many of these countries accumulated a huge debt burden in the early 1980s, thus inhibiting their capacity to acquire imported arms later in the decade. As suggested by Stephanie Neuman of Columbia University, "The growing indebtedness of these states, combined with high interest rates and the reluctance of lending institutions to extend more credit to them, sharply curtailed their buying power."[16] The sharp drop in oil prices, meanwhile, diminished the national income of the oil-producing states, and thus forced a cutback in their defense expenditures. As we entered the 1990s, however, the debt crisis was beginning to subside and there was evidence of a long-term trend toward higher oil prices; if these trends persist, the purchasing power of many Third World countries will grow, and thus we are likely to see an increase in their arms buying.

In addition to these economic factors, there are other considerations that point to a temporary rather than permanent decline in Third World arms spending. Foremost among these is the "crisis of absorption" brought about by the acquisition of large numbers of sophisticated arms in the early 1980s. While possessed of great ambition, many Third World countries found that they lacked the technical military capacity to operate, repair, and maintain so many new weapons at once. As suggested by former State Department arms analyst Morton S. Miller, "Many of the weapons systems purchased [in the early 1980s] were far too ambitious for the acquiring countries' weak infrastructures of operational and maintenance facilities and far too small pools of trained manpower."[17] These absorption problems occupied many Third World countries in the late 1980s, thus diminishing their appetite for additional weapons; as this crisis abates in the 1990s, however, we can expect a revived demand for sophisticated and costly arms.

The overseas demand for sophisticated weapons also received a substantial boost from the 1990 Iraqi invasion of Kuwait, which sent a shockwave of anxiety across the Middle East. In response to the invasion, Saudi Arabia placed an emergency $25 billion order for American arms—the largest such purchase ever recorded. Included in the Saudi order (which was divided up into several separate packages by U.S. officials in order to allay Congressional concerns about such a massive transfer of weaponry) were F-15 aircraft, M-1A2 tanks, M-2 Bradley fighting vehicles, AH-64 Apache helicopter gunships, and Patriot air-defense missiles. The Saudi purchase was succeeded, in the days that followed, by substantial arms orders from Egypt, Israel, and the United Arab Emirates. Most of these orders were received by the United States, but France and Great Britain also received substantial orders from traditional clients in the region. And while Moscow was not an immediate beneficiary of this spending spree, it is likely that increased arms purchases by the conservative Arab governments will eventually lead to comparable orders for Soviet arms from such states as Algeria, Libya, Syria, and Yemen—thus pushing up total Middle Eastern arms imports to record highs.

If this analysis proves correct, we are likely to see a significant increase in the volume of Third World arms purchases. However, while the annual sales statistics compiled by the CRS and other U.S. agencies are likely to exhibit steady growth, it is unclear that these tallies will accurately reflect the full extent of Third World military purchases. Such doubts arise because of the growing complexity of the arms traffic, entailing increased sales of products and services that are not easily captured by the standard statistical sources. Thus, as indicated earlier, many Third World countries are now producing weapons in their own factories rather than relying entirely on imported supplies; to sustain these production ventures, these countries regularly import materials, machine tools, technical services, and other specialized products from the established suppliers—products that contribute directly to the military potential of these nations, but are rarely counted in the statistics on arms transfers.

These figures also tend to underestimate exports of ammunition and spare parts for previously supplied weapons. Such items are obviously harder to keep track of than sales of finished military systems, and thus are not always fully counted in the annual tallies of arms transfers. Similarly, the standard figures tend to leave out or underestimate sales of "upgrade kits" for the enhancement of older-model weapons. Such kits—usually consisting of upgraded guns, engines, and electronics—have become an increasingly important factor in the arms traffic as Third World nations seek to extend the usable lifetime of arms presently in their inventories.

At this point, it is impossible to calculate just how much is being left out of the standard figures on international arms trafficking, but it is likely that the discrepancy is substantial. "Since there probably are now fewer major weapons and more services and small items in the worldwide arms sales mix," Miller noted in 1988, "it is likely that current arms sales to Third World countries are more understated."[18] And because sales of technology, services, ammunition, spare parts, and upgrade kits are likely to continue their growth well into the 1990s, this discrepancy could grow wider in the years ahead.

## Commodities

The international arms trade encompasses a broad range of weapons and military systems, ranging from small arms and ammunition at one end of the spectrum to tanks, aircraft, and warships at the other. Also included in this spectrum are combat-support systems (communications devices, radar systems, transport vehicles, and so on), uniforms and other quartermaster supplies, military technical services, and technology for the manufacture of arms. All of these commodities are likely to be included in the international arms flow in any given year, but the proportional *mix* between these various categories is constantly shifting in response to changing military and economic conditions.

In the 1970s and early 1980s, Third World buyers exhibited a strong desire for major front-line combat systems—notably heavy tanks, modern jet fighters, and missile-armed warships—as they sought to modernize all branches of their military establishment in a short space of time. During this period, it was not uncommon for Third World leaders to place multiple orders for costly front-line systems, thus pushing military trade levels to record heights. Between 1980 and 1983 alone, the developing nations acquired 7,889 tanks and self-propelled guns (SPGs); 2,258 supersonic combat aircraft; 83 major surface warships; and 1,300 helicopters.[19] In the mid-1980s, however, the demand for major combat systems of this sort dropped off significantly. Thus, in 1984–87, deliveries of supersonic combat aircraft fell by 47 percent from the 1980–83 figure, while deliveries of tanks and SPGs fell by 49 percent,[20] And, because "big-ticket" items of this sort account for such a large share of the dollar value of arms transfers, the slackened demand for front-line systems produced a corresponding decline in annual trade figures.

Several factors account for the decline in orders for major front-line systems in the mid-1980s. Some of these, of course, were economic in nature: as the global debt crisis intensified and the income of oil-producing countries diminished, many Third World countries curtailed their purchases of big-ticket items and spent what remained of their military funds on upgrade kits, spare parts, and ammunition for previously acquired systems. The aforementioned "crisis of absorption" also inhibited the demand for sophisticated front-line systems. But economic and structural factors were not the only causes of the reduced demand for front-line systems. Indeed, the debt crisis and the absorption crisis occurred at the same time that many Third World military officials were reassessing their requirements for different types of military equipment, placing less emphasis on high-performance front-line systems and more emphasis on ordinary guns and cannon, ammunition stockpiles, communications and logistical gear, and other basic combat-support equipment.

To a great extent, this reassessment was the product of "lessons learned" from the Iran-Iraq war and other armed conflicts of the 1980s. Prior to the onset of the Iran-Iraq conflict, most military analysts assumed that future engagements of this sort would be decided quickly—as was the October War of 1973—in a series of intense air, land, and sea engagements involving high-technology weapons of the type then being sold on the world market. Instead, the Persian Gulf war evolved into a prolonged war of attrition in which the *quantity* of arms on each side, rather than their quality, often proved decisive. "The Gulf war quickly stalemated into an infantryman's and an artilleryman's war, reminiscent of World War I," Miller wrote. This outcome, he noted, "created a market for huge quantities of low-technology arms and combat-consumables."[21] Iran and Iraq each spent many billions of dollars on such hardware during their eight-year war with one another, and other countries, fearful of being caught in a similar situation, made comparable purchases of their own.

The conflicts of the 1980s also demonstrated the extreme sensitivity of high-performance weapons to the harsh climatic and operational conditions found in many developing areas. The most dramatic example of this, perhaps, was the failure of the 1980 U.S. rescue mission at "Desert One" in the Iranian interior—a failure caused largely by helicopter malfunctions brought about by a blinding sandstorm. The Iranians, for their part, experienced great difficulty in maintaining their U.S.-supplied high-tech weapons once the United States cut off deliveries of spare parts and technical assistance. As a result of these and other such experiences, many Third World military officers have become somewhat skeptical about the proclaimed advantages of high-tech systems, and have tended to look more favorably at less sophisticated (and less costly) variants.[22]

In counterpoise to this general trend, one category of modern weapons—guided missiles—did acquire increased popularity as a result of recent conflicts. Thus the Falklands conflict, and later the Iran-Iraq war, convincingly demonstrated the lethal effectiveness of precision-guided antiship missiles like the French Exocet—used by Argentina to sink the British destroyer HMS *Sheffield* and later by Iraq to cripple the USS *Stark*. In Afghanistan, the military fortunes of the anti-Soviet *mujahedeen* were reversed almost overnight by the introduction of shoulder-fired Stinger antiaircraft missiles. Much larger (if somewhat less accurate) surface-to-surface missiles were used by both Iran and Iraq during the so-called "war of the cities" to attack each other's civilian populations. These, and other such experiences, have led many Third World countries to place great emphasis on the acquisition of modern missiles, even while cutting back on purchases of other combat systems.

The Iran-Iraq experience has also led many Third World countries to place greater emphasis on the acquisition of arms-making technologies, as distinct from the purchase of finished military systems. Because Iran was the subject of a global arms embargo—Operation Staunch—organized by the United States and thus was compelled to make do with whatever bits and pieces of equipment it could obtain on the black market, Iranian leaders launched a crash program to establish domestic facilities for the production of a wide variety of basic combat systems. This, in turn, has inspired many other Third World nations to build up their own arms-production capabilities, lest they, too, be caught in such a dilemma.

The Third World's drive for increased self-sufficiency in military production is, of course, being fueled by a number of motives in addition to the fear of an embargo. Principal among these are a desire to diminish outlays on imported weapons, and to stimulate the development of a high-tech industrial sector. In line with these goals, the emerging Third World producers have usually cut back on purchases of finished weapons in order to conserve funds for the import of machine tools, specialized components, and other systems needed for domestic arms-production ventures. And while many analysts have questioned whether such efforts—dependent as they are on imported technology—will actually result in lasting military and economic benefit, a growing roster of Third World nations are proceeding with elaborate plans for the expansion of their military-industrial infrastructure.[23]

The character of the arms flow in the 1980s was also influenced by the growing incidence of insurgency, ethnic conflict, and other forms of "low-intensity conflict" in the Third World. These wars rarely produce major battles of the sort witnessed in the Persian Gulf, but have nevertheless produced significant loss of life in such areas as Central America, sub-Saharan Africa, Southwest Asia, and the Middle East. To contain these conflicts, Third World governments ordered vast quantities of small arms, infantry weapons, off-road vehicles, and other types of counterinsurgency equipment.

As a result of all these developments, the arms flow of the early 1990s will look considerably different from that of the 1970s and early 1980s. While many developing countries will continue to rely on the traditional suppliers for deliveries of major military systems, such acquisitions will increasingly be accompanied by transfers of materials and technology for the production of arms. Thus Turkey, which plans to spend at least $10 billion on military modernization in the early 1990s, will devote most of these funds to the acquisition of technology for the manufacture of modern aircraft, rockets, and armored vehicles.[24] Similarly, both South Korea and Taiwan plan to manufacture modern jet aircraft using parts and technology supplied by the United States, while India plans to produce MIG-27 fighters and T-72 tanks with Soviet technical assistance.

The 1990s are also likely to witness a further proliferation of nuclear weapons, chemical munitions, and long-range ballistic missiles. As emerging

Third World powers strive to achieve local dominance and/or to counter the military gains of their rivals, they are increasingly seeking "strategic" weapons that can be used in attacks on the urban centers of their adversaries, or to deter such attacks against their own cities.[25] Thus, as the 1990s commenced, several Third World countries were engaged in nuclear research programs that have suspected weapons applications, while a somewhat larger group of nations is believed to be working on the development of chemical weapons. Most of these nations, moreover, were reportedly engaged in efforts to develop or improve ballistic missiles capable of carrying nuclear and/or chemical warheads over substantial distances.[26]

Finally, at the other end of the technology scale, the 1990s are likely to witness increased procurement of small arms and counterinsurgency gear in response to the growing incidence of low-intensity conflict. "It is possible that the decade of the 1990s will be the decade of civil wars," Abdel Monem Said Aly of Egypt told the Pugwash Conference on Science and World Affairs in 1989. With the growing economic hardship being experienced by many developing nations, he noted, there is a "rise of social and political tensions"—and thus a corresponding increase in the demand for internal security hardware.[27]

## Suppliers

Until very recently, the sale of arms to the developing countries was a highly concentrated enterprise, with the two superpowers and a handful of other industrial powers accounting for a very large percentage of the total world traffic. Thus in 1975–82, six nations—the United States, the Soviet Union, Great Britain, France, West Germany, and Italy—together supplied 84 percent (in dollar terms) of all munitions sold to Third World nations. Within this exclusive group, moreover, the two superpowers enjoyed an especially privileged position, accounting together for approximately two-thirds of all military sales to the Third World.[28]

As the decade progressed, however, the market share enjoyed by the "Big Six" began to shrink as other producers, eager to profit from the booming arms business, offered comparable systems of their own at competitive rates. As a result, the share of Third World orders claimed by the Big Six declined somewhat in the mid-1980s, to approximately 75 percent of the total.[29] Dividing up the remaining one-fourth of the market were a number of "second-tier" suppliers in Europe (notably Belgium, Czechoslovakia, the Netherlands, Poland, Spain, Sweden, and Switzerland), along with several emerging producers in the Third World (particularly China, Brazil, Israel, and the two Koreas). These smaller suppliers cannot always compete with the Big Six in all categories of high-tech weaponry, but they have succeeded in selling less-sophisticated versions that are well suited to Third World needs and budgets.

Probably the most dramatic development of the past decade was the emergence of Brazil and China as world-class military suppliers. While both had engaged in some arms trafficking in previous years, it was only in the 1980s that they showed up as significant factors in the international arms traffic. Thus, according to the U.S. Arms Control and Disarmament Agency (ACDA), military sales by Brazil grew from $670 million in 1976–81 to $2.6 billion in 1982–87 (an increase of 288 percent), while sales by China soared from $1.25 billion to $7.8 billion (an increase of 524 percent).[30] Both of these countries now manufacture a wide range of basic combat gear (armored vehicles, rockets and missiles, artillery pieces, and light combat aircraft), and both have pursued a common strategy of offering reliable, no-nonsense weapons at prices considerably lower than those charged by the traditional suppliers for comparable systems.[31]

While not quite in the same league as Brazil and China, several other Third World producers posted significant export gains in the 1980s. Notable examples include North Korea and Israel (each with 1982–87 sales of $2.4 billion), South Korea (with sales of $2.1 billion), and Egypt (with sales of $770 million).[32] These countries, along with Brazil and China, found an especially lucrative market for their products in the Persian Gulf area, where both Iran and Iraq spent billions of dollars on imported munitions during their eight-year conflict. According to the ACDA, approximately half of all the arms acquired by Iran between 1980 and 1987 were supplied by other Third World countries.[33]

By the beginning of the 1990s, it had become apparent that the supply side of the munitions traffic was much more crowded and complex than it had been in previous decades. What we are seeing, in effect, is the emergence of a multitiered supply system, with both old and new producers striving to expand their existing share of the market.

At the apex of this system—occupying the first tier—are the two superpowers and the major industrial powers of Europe. Because these countries continue to lead the rest of the world in the development of high-technology weapons, they will continue to find customers for their products among those Third World nations that seek (and can afford to pay for) the most advanced systems available. For the superpowers, this will mean the continuing exploitation of domestic research and development (R&D) capabilities in order to develop new weapons systems at the cutting edge of technology. For the Europeans, this will probably entail increased collaboration across national boundaries as individual companies pool their R&D capabilities with those of others in order to better compete with the two superpowers.[34]

Next in line are the second-tier suppliers, consisting of the smaller European nations that have succeeded in finding a distinctive market "niche" for a particular type of product (as Sweden has done with antiaircraft guns, and the Netherlands with naval systems), along with the emerging producers in the Third World that have found a receptive market for low- and medium-technology products. Many of these suppliers recorded significant sales gains in the 1980s, but most are likely to face increased competition from aggressive newcomers in the 1990s.

Finally, there is a third tier, consisting of private dealers and brokers—some operating on the fringes of the law—that sell secondhand and surplus equipment, spare parts, and, in some cases, stolen guns and ammunition. These suppliers played a relatively minor role in the international arms traffic prior to 1980, but received a significant boost from the Iran-Iraq war, which generated an enormous demand for black-market arms. Sales have been somewhat sluggish for this group since the end of the Iran-Iraq war, but could rise again in the years ahead due to increased demand from insurgent groups in Africa, Asia, and Latin America.[35]

This picture is likely to become even more complex in the 1990s, as still other Third World nations seek to carve out a niche in the weapons market and as other producers combine forces to compete better in a crowded field. Thus, among the countries that have pursued plans to enter the military export trade in the current decade are India, Indonesia, Pakistan, Taiwan, and Turkey.[36] At the same time, many of the smaller and medium-sized producers in Europe are joining forces with larger firms to establish multinational pan-European companies with a capacity to compete with the superpowers in the development of costly high-performance systems.

The emergence of so many new military suppliers, along with the emergence of multinational arms companies, is dramatically altering the dynamics of international arms trafficking. Previously, in the 1960s and 1970s, the major suppliers enjoyed a seller's market in which they could determine the quality, numbers, and prices of the items put on sale; today, the arms trade confronts a buyer's market, with the terms of trade determined accordingly. In practice, this has meant a substantial erosion in the various restraints—whether political or technological—that had previously constrained the export of arms.

Politically, the erosion of arms export restraint is seen in the abrogation of restrictions on sales to areas of conflict, or to governments charged with human rights violations. Hence, many of the Western European suppliers that previously banned the sale of weapons to areas of conflict have gradually relaxed such constraints, or chosen to overlook them.[37] This pattern was especially noticeable during the Iran-Iraq conflict, when many of America's closest allies in Europe—including France, West Germany, and Italy—chose to ignore Operation Staunch in order to sell arms to the two belligerents.[38] Similarly, many suppliers have elected to ignore embargoes on military sales to South Africa, Libya, and other international "pariahs."[39]

In the technological sphere, diminished international restraint is reflected in the export of increasingly sophisticated arms, and in expanded sales of technology for the production of arms. The trend toward sophistication is especially evident in the case of the two superpowers, which in years past had been reluctant to sell their most advanced weapons to clients in the Third World. For the United States, the most notable example of such relaxation is the sale of F-15 fighters and AWACS radar patrol planes to Saudi Arabia; for the Soviet Union, the most notable examples are the sale of MiG-29 aircraft and SS-21 surface-to-surface missiles to Syria, and the leasing of nuclear-powered submarines to India.

The two superpowers have also provided significant arms-making technologies to favored clients—the United States to Egypt, Israel, South Korea, and Turkey; the Soviets to India. The European suppliers have been even more permissive in the sale of military technology to the developing nations. Thus West Germany is helping Brazil, India, and South Korea to build a fleet of submarines, while France is helping Egypt to establish a modern aircraft and helicopter industry.[40] As a result of all this, the emerging military producers of the Third World will be even better poised to compete with the traditional suppliers in the decades ahead.

## Recipients

Although more and more Third World countries are now producing at least some weapons in domestic factories, most of the developing countries continue to rely on the international market for a significant share of their arms requirements. According to the ACDA, a total of 107 Third World countries purchased at least $1 million worth of imported arms each between 1983 and 1987; of these 107 countries, 43 were located in Africa, 24 in Latin America, 16 in the Middle East, 15 in East Asia and the Pacific, and 6 in South Asia.[41]

Despite the relative abundance of recipients, however, the statistics on arms transfers indicate that a relatively small number of countries are responsible for a very large proportion of the total value of all arms transfers to the Third World. Thus, again using ACDA data, we find that only fifteen nations—Afghanistan, Algeria, Angola, Cuba, Egypt, Ethiopia, India, Iran, Iraq, Israel, Libya, Saudi Arabia, Syria, Turkey, and Vietnam—accounted for 72.9 percent of all arms transfers to the Third World between 1983 and 1987.[42] (See Table 8.2.)

An assessment of the major arms-importing countries reveals a number of common features: these countries have either engaged in armed combat within the past decade (Afghanistan, Angola, Cuba, Ethiopia, Iran, Iraq, Israel, Libya, Syria, Vietnam) or participated in a regional arms race with a neighboring rival (India vs. China; India vs. Pakistan; Israel vs. Egypt; Egypt vs. Syria; Syria vs. Iraq; Iraq vs. Iran; Iran vs. Saudi Arabia), or both. In addition, most of these countries possess large supplies of petroleum or, as in the case of Afghanistan, Angola, Ethiopia, Cuba, Egypt, Israel, and Vietnam, are closely linked to one of the superpowers and thus receive substantial military subsidies from them. It is, in fact, this combination of means

Table 8.2 / Major Third World Recipients of Imported Arms, 1983–87, in Rank Order

| Country | Arms imports 1983–87 (in $U.S. millions) | Percentage of all Third World imports |
|---|---|---|
| Iraq | 29,895 | 15.9 |
| Saudi Arabia | 18,320 | 9.7 |
| India | 10,990 | 5.8 |
| Syria | 10,450 | 5.6 |
| Iran | 8,865 | 4.7 |
| Vietnam | 8,650 | 4.6 |
| Cuba | 8,380 | 4.5 |
| Egypt | 7,820 | 4.2 |
| Libya | 7,730 | 4.1 |
| Angola | 6,350 | 3.4 |
| Ethiopia | 4,830 | 2.6 |
| Israel | 4,300 | 2.3 |
| Afghanistan | 4,070 | 2.2 |
| Algeria | 3,230 | 1.7 |
| Turkey | 2,935 | 1.6 |
| Total | 136,815 | 72.9 |

Source: U.S. Arms Control and Disarmament Agency, *World Military Expenditures and Arms Transfers 1988* (Washington, D.C., 1989), pp. 111–14.

and motive that carried these nations to the top of the list of Third World arms importers in the 1980s.[43]

As we move into the 1990s, it is likely that the list of major Third World arms recipients will continue to show a high degree of concentration, although the composition of the list may change periodically as wars are started or settled, and as economic conditions change. Thus it is likely that major recipients of Soviet aid—including Angola, Cuba, Ethiopia, and Vietnam—will move down the list as Moscow cuts back on its military assistance programs (largely to conserve funds for economic revitalization in the USSR itself). At the same time, major fluctuations in the price of oil could affect the relative standing on the chart of such countries as Iran, Iraq, Libya, and Saudi Arabia.

However, while it is entirely possible that some of the top military spenders of the 1980s will be compelled to reduce their spending in the 1990s, it is also likely that we will see an increase in military spending by a number of other Third World nations. Of particular significance is the surge in military spending by the emerging economic powers of the Pacific Rim—notably South Korea, Taiwan, Thailand, Malaysia, Indonesia, and Singapore. As the trade revenues and national incomes of these nations have risen, they have devoted more and more money to the modernization of their military forces.[44] South Korea, for instance, increased its military spending from $2.9 billion in 1980 to $5.6 billion in 1987, while Taiwan's defense expenditures jumped from $2.8 billion to $4.7 billion. Military spending in Singapore and Malaysia has been rising at an equally brisk pace, pushing defense expenditures in these countries to well over $1 billion per year.[45]

Also fueling the arms trade in the 1990s will be the efforts of a number of Third World countries to improve their overall military capabilities and thereby to enhance their status as major regional powers. Especially prominent in this category are Egypt, India, Iraq, and Turkey—all of which have embarked on ambitious efforts to modernize the combat capabilities of their sizable military forces. India, which seeks to play a major military role in South Asia and the Indian Ocean area, became the world's number one arms importer in the late 1980s, and is likely to remain high on the list of major recipients throughout the 1990s. Iraq and Egypt have both engaged in major efforts to enhance their domestic arms-production capabilities, and in some cases have cooperated in the development of new weapons. And Turkey, which has long been eclipsed by the other powers in NATO, has ordered 120 F-16 fighters from the United States and plans to spend some $10 billion on imported arms and military technology over the next few years.

Also to be found on the list of major recipients in the 1990s will be those Third World countries that are facing major insurgent or ethnic conflicts. Among those likely to be included in this group are such countries as Afghanistan, Angola, El Salvador, Mozambique, Peru, the Philippines, and Sudan, which face continuing internal wars left over from the 1980s, as well as other nations that are just beginning to experience widespread insurgent and ethnic unrest. And while the purchasing power of these countries is likely to be constrained by domestic economic conditions and the diminished military aid programs of the superpowers, they are likely to seek large supplies of infantry arms, helicopters, and other counterinsurgency weapons in the years ahead.

## IMPLICATIONS FOR ARMS CONTROL AND INTERNATIONAL SECURITY

As we have seen, the 1980s witnessed a steady erosion in international control over the conventional arms trade. Emblematic of this trend was Ronald Reagan's decision, soon after taking office as president in 1981, to rescind Jimmy Carter's arms transfer restraint policy—a policy which, while limited in scope, was seen by Reagan as an unacceptable obstacle to U.S. efforts to bolster the military strength of friendly Third World countries.[46] With the emergence of a buyers' market, moreover, most of the other major military suppliers have abandoned or diluted their restrictions on arms exports to areas of tension. And while many world leaders have spoken out against the dangers embodied in an uncontrolled arms traffic, no government has yet taken the initiative in convening negotiations aimed at curbing the arms flow.

The consequences of this laissez-faire approach to the international arms traffic have been grave. Even though economic hardships have cut into sales of some high-tech munitions, the 1980s nonetheless witnessed a steady increase in the variety and sophistication of weapons available to Third World buyers. As a consequence, nations that were once equipped solely with the obsolete hand-me-downs of the major powers are now able to conduct wars of great intensity, duration, and reach. Such conflicts can erupt with little or no warning—witness the rapid Iraqi takeover of Kuwait in August 1990—and, once initiated, can escalate rapidly into major regional conflagrations. As the Iran-Iraq conflict demonstrated, moreover, nations at war can now turn to an expanding network of military suppliers to sustain and even to escalate their military operations.

No one, of course, can state categorically that the growing availability of conventional arms is leading to an increase in the frequency of armed conflicts. Recent experience suggests, however, that the growing accumulation of advanced weaponry in Third World arsenals has encouraged potential belligerents to seek a military rather than political solution to outstanding disputes. Hence, in all three of the major wars of the 1980s—the Iran-Iraq war, the 1982 Falklands conflict, and the 1982 Israeli-Syrian encounter in Lebanon—the initial protagonists (Iraq, Argentina, and Israel, respectively) had previously built up large stockpiles of military supplies and apparently acted on the assumption that such provisioning would ensure their success in battle. Similarly, the growing abundance of black-market arms has made it easier for ethnic and religious minorities to launch armed struggles against the regime in power.

Once armed combat has erupted, moreover, the widespread availability of arms has made it easier for belligerents to conduct wars of great magnitude and duration. The Iran-Iraq war lasted eight years, consumed $60 billion worth of imported arms and ammunition, and resulted in the death or injury of an estimated 1,250,000 people.[47] To satisfy the belligerents' mammoth need for weaponry, moreover, a total of forty-one countries sold arms or ammunition to at least one side between 1980 and 1987, while twenty-eight of them supplied such hardware to both.[48] These deliveries included not only the many tons of bombs and shells used in the drawn-out battles for key towns and positions, but also the mines used to sink neutral vessels and the missiles used to strike at population centers.

Other recent conflicts, while not quite as devastating as the Iran-Iraq war, are also notable for the high levels of death and destruction engendered by imported weapons. The fighting in Afghanistan, for instance, produced an estimated 500,000 deaths over a ten-year period, and resulted in the virtual annihilation (through bombing and rocket attacks) of many provincial towns and villages. In Lebanon, heavily armed militias and sectarian armies have produced thousands of casualties each year in a seemingly unquenchable fratricidal conflict. And in El Salvador, where both sides have periodically been resupplied with fresh weapons, the death toll had reached 60,000 by 1990.[49] These and other recent conflicts suggest that even the so-called low-intensity conflicts of the 1990s are likely to entail high levels of violence and bloodshed.

Arms transfers have also contributed to the escalatory potential of regional wars, as graphically demonstrated by the eight-year history of the Iran-Iraq war. After countless battles failed to produce a decisive victory for either side, both Iran and Iraq escalated their military efforts in a number of ways. Hence, in an effort to curb the oil exports of their adversary (exports that produced the income needed to buy military supplies), both sides struck at ships and oil facilities located far from the front lines of battle. Both sides, moreover, used ballistic missiles to pummel each other's urban centers, and both used chemical weapons in attacks on enemy civilians and military personnel.

Fortunately, neither Iran nor Iraq took the fateful step of using their ballistic missiles to deliver chemical warheads on enemy cities—a step that undoubtedly would have produced many thousands of civilian fatalities. It is important to note, however, that the technology to employ missiles for this purpose is in the hands of potential Middle Eastern belligerents. Syria, for instance, has reportedly developed chemical warheads for its Soviet-supplied Scud-Bs and SS-21s, and several other countries are believed to possess a similar capability.[50] Such weapons, if used in battle, would almost certainly provoke retaliation with weapons of equal—if not greater—destructive power. Indeed, if the target of such attacks proves to be one of the Third World's nascent nuclear powers, we could conceivably witness the first use of nuclear weapons since 1945.

At present, the most likely locale for such a catastrophe is the Middle East, where nuclear-armed Israel is ringed by Arab states equipped with both chemical weapons and ballistic missiles. Even in the absence of active hostilities, the proliferation of such capabilities could provide the sparks for a regional conflagration by inviting preemptive attacks on missiles sites and chemical weapons factories by fearful adversaries. Indeed, Israeli officials have already threatened to launch a preemptive attack on Syria or Iraq if they have any reason to believe that either country was readying chemical-armed missiles for attacks on Israel.[51] Even more frightening to contemplate is Israel's likely reaction in the event that Syria or Iraq actually struck Israeli cities with chemical weapons. "If, heaven forbid, they dare to employ these means," Israeli Defense Minister Yitzhak Rabin declared in 1988, "the response [by Israel] will be one hundred times stronger"[52]—an obvious allusion to nuclear retaliation.

Nor is an Israeli-Syrian or Israeli-Iraqi clash the only encounters that could spur nuclear escalation in the decades ahead. The growing proliferation of nuclear weapons, chemical munitions, ballistic missiles, and high-technology conventional arms is fueling regional arms races in several Third World areas where mutually hostile powers face each other across disputed boundaries and/or unstable territories. Coupled adversaries of this sort include India and Pakistan, China and Taiwan, North and South Korea, and Argentina and Brazil—all being nations that presently possess nuclear weapons or are believed to harbor the technical capacity and infrastructure to produce such munitions if a decision were made to do so. These pairings may of course change in the years ahead, and other emerging powers may forge new adversarial relationships, but the risk of nuclear escalation can only grow more potent as the number of such rivalries increases.

If this analysis is correct, then it should be obvious to all that the "deadly convergence" of arms transfers, nuclear and chemical proliferation, and missile exports represents a very significant threat to international peace and security—in fact, this may prove to be the *greatest* threat to world stability in the years ahead. It is essential, therefore, that existing restraints on nuclear and chemical proliferation be tightened, and that new negotiations—involving both suppliers and recipients—be undertaken to establish multilateral constraints on the transfer of sophisticated weapons, ballistic missiles, and conventional arms-making technologies.

Before such efforts can proceed, however, government officials of both North and South will have to approach the arms trade from a new perspective—seeing it as part of a generalized threat to world security rather than as a bilateral transaction between buyer and seller. Until now, arms transfers have been viewed in Washington and in other national capitals as a tool of convenience—as a foreign policy "instrument" that can be freely wielded to enhance the seller's political influence and the recipient's military power. Experience suggests, however, that the leverage gained by the seller through arms transfers is relatively short-lived, and that any military advantage gained by the recipient from such transactions is eventually negated by similar acquisitions on the part of its neighbors and rivals. Hence, all of the arms supplied by the United States to Israel and by the Soviet Union to Syria have not provided either superpower with lasting control over the political and military actions of their clients; nor, moreover, have these supplies provided either Israel or Syria with any sense of lasting security.[53]

What is needed, in place of this outmoded view of arms exports as a tool of power and influence, is a perception among policymakers that *every* transfer of military equipment—whatever its original motive—adds to the global deluge of war-making paraphernalia that is inundating volatile Third World areas. While no single transfer may tip the balance toward war, the accumulation of such transfers, year after year, is producing an increasingly dangerous and unstable situation. As suggested by Senator William Proxmire in 1979, the delivery of any particular weapon to potential Third World belligerents may not be the same as "throwing a lighted match into a gasoline tank," but it is "like adding more gasoline to a tank that has exploded in flaming destruction over and over in the past few years."[54]

Fortunately, there is some evidence that the major powers are beginning to think in these terms. President Bush has spoken on several occasions of the need to constrain the flow of sophisticated weapons, and as part of the "new thinking" advocated by President Gorbachev, Soviet leaders have indicated a willingness to discuss mutual curbs on conventional arms exports. "A growing number of nations are acquiring advanced and highly destructive capabilities," Bush warned in a 1989 speech, and thus "we must work to curb the proliferation of advanced weaponry."[55] Similarly, in a 1988 speech before the UN General Assembly, Soviet delegate V. F. Petrovsky declared that efforts should be made for "preventing the proliferation of the most destructive types [of conventional arms]." By taking such action, he noted, "the international community would thereby contribute to stopping bloodshed and destruction in the hotbeds of conflict."[56]

It is also significant that more and more Third World leaders are expressing such views. Thus, Indonesian delegate Nana S. Sutresna told the United Nations in 1988 that "the astronomical costs [of modern arms] . . . and the potential for conflicts waged with conventional weapons escalating into nuclear confrontation have rightly convinced many states of the need to control and curb the development, production, and transfer of conventional weapons." Similarly, the representative of Nigeria, I. O. S. Nwachukwu, expressed the hope that the world community would adopt "an unambiguous statement to the effect that an essential element of the disarmament process is an undertaking by the major exporters of conventional arms to progressively reduce arms exports to the Third World."[57] Such statements are all the more significant because Third World leaders have generally opposed such restraints in the past, viewing them as an effort by the former imperial powers to perpetuate the inferior military status of the developing nations.

Finally, it is worth noting that the enormous cost of high-tech conventional weapons is creating an atmosphere that could prove conducive to the negotiation of arms transfer restraints. Because the costs of sophisticated arms have risen so high in recent years, nations ranging from China and Israel to South Africa and Peru have had to abandon or cut back on major military projects. Costly military ventures have also diverted funds from other budget priorities, thus slowing the pace of economic development in many Third World countries. "It is clear," the Colombian government noted in 1989, "that the conventional arms race absorbs many of the resources, both national and international, which would otherwise be directed towards social welfare and economic development."[58] Given this perception, it appears to be an auspicious moment for the initiation of talks on restraining the arms trade.

# A PROGRAM FOR ACTION

Now that many world leaders are beginning to approach the problem of conventional arms transfers with a heightened appreciation of their destructive potential and economic costs, it is time to develop constructive proposals for controlling the arms flow. Finding the right approach to this task will not be easy, given the complexity of the trade and the large numbers of actors involved. Rather than attempting to devise one overarching global system for the control of arms transfers (as in the case of the NPT), it might be more efficacious to consider a number of individual measures that address particular aspects or dimensions of the trade—aspects that could prove amenable to remedial action—and from these particular measures to fashion a comprehensive approach to arms transfer restraint.

Before considering such proposals, however, it is necessary to recognize that any successful effort to curb the arms trade will ultimately require the cooperation of Third World nations, whether in their guise as recipients or as suppliers of arms. It is essential, therefore, that we take into account Third World concerns regarding the dynamics of arms control.[59] Hence, it is unrealistic to expect Third World nations to scale back their military forces unless the developed nations also agree to make significant reductions of their own; likewise, it is unreasonable to ask Third World countries to dilute their defense capabilities unless existing mechanisms for international mediation and peacekeeping are significantly strengthened. Any proposals for restricting the arms trade must, therefore, be considered within the context of a comprehensive approach to world security—one that entails substantial reductions in superpower arsenals, the dissolution of the Cold War military blocs, and the strengthening of international institutions for mediation and peacekeeping. (For discussion of such a framework, see Chapter 18.)

In this spirit, we can proceed to a discussion of possible arms export control measures. Four specific proposals are offered here as possible models for cooperative international action in this regard.[60]

1. *Resume and expand the CATT negotiations.* As the only U.S.-Soviet negotiations ever undertaken in this field, the Conventional Arms Transfer Talks (CATT) of 1977–78 provided a useful forum that should now be revived. While no formal treaty documents were produced by the talks, the CATT negotiators reportedly reached agreement on many of the terms and conditions to be incorporated into such an agreement—the restoration of which could save many months of future meetings and consultations.[61] The resumption of the CATT talks would also send a powerful signal to the world that the two superpowers—and the two leading suppliers of arms— had reached agreement on the need for new constraints.

Obviously, an agreement involving the two superpowers alone will not solve the arms trade problem so long as other major suppliers—especially France, Britain, West Germany, and China—continue to export arms without restraint. Hence, to succeed in controlling the weapons traffic, it will ultimately be necessary to integrate these other suppliers into an expanded CATT process. It is unlikely, however, that these countries will fully engage in such a process until the two superpowers have reached agreement on the need to restrain their own exports. The best way to proceed, therefore, would be for the United States and the Soviet Union to reconvene the CATT talks, to clarify and reaffirm the progress made in 1977–78, and then to adopt a number of bilateral measures that could serve as a framework for expanded multilateral cooperation in this area.

Assuming that the CATT talks are resumed, what should U.S. and Soviet negotiators seek to accomplish in the first stage of a bilateral control system? It is probably too much to expect a massive cut in superpower sales, but it might be possible to set an annual ceiling on arms transfers—say, $8 billion to $10 billion per nation—and then to negotiate lower levels in subsequent talks, when experience has been gained in verification, and when the CATT regime has been expanded to include other suppliers.

How would such agreements be monitored and verified? This is an important question that will require extensive discussion by specialists from the major powers. However, while the problems involved may appear daunting, the fact is that much thought has already been given to the resolution of these questions.[62] Thus, considerable experience has been gained over the years by SIPRI and by other international bodies in monitoring the flow of major military systems—experience that could be tapped in developing mechanisms for verification. Following this lead, the United Nations has discussed plans for the establishment of an international register of arms transfers, and a number of countries, including the Soviet Union, have expressed interest in such an initiative.[63]

2. *Expand and enhance the MTCR.* The Missile Technology Control Regime, established in 1987 to restrict exports of ballistic missile technology, represents an important precedent for multilateral action in this area. Seven nations—Britain, Canada, France, Italy, Japan, West Germany, and the United States—signed the agreement, which essentially bans the transfer of missiles that could carry a nuclear warhead (i.e., a payload of 500 kilograms or more) and calls for strict oversight of exports of parts and technology that could be used in the manufacture of such missiles. Enforcement of the MTCR is left up to the signatories of the agreement.[64]

While the MTCR represents an important step forward, it has many critical defects. It does not, for instance, include several nations—including Brazil, China, and the Soviet Union—that have played a conspicuous role in supplying missiles to Third World belligerents. Furthermore, it generally exempts technologies that are used in producing missiles for space exploration—missiles that can be converted to military use. Finally, it fails to establish any verification and enforcement machinery such as that provided by the International Atomic Energy Agency (IAEA) for implementation of the NPT.[65]

To be truly effective, therefore, the MTCR needs to be substantially strengthened. Inclusion of the Soviet Union among the signatory nations should be the most immediate priority, particularly as Soviet officials have already met with their U.S. counterparts to discuss possible cooperation in this area.[66] Once the Soviet Union has come on board, it will be easier to approach some of the other holdouts and persuade them to join. Since all of these countries seek U.S. aid and technology, further delivery of such assistance should be made contingent on participation in the MTCR. Efforts should also be made to tighten the constraints on transfers of space-related technology, and to ban any such exports to nations that fail to ratify and observe the NPT.[67]

3. *Establish quadrilateral negotiations involving pairs of rivals and their respective superpower suppliers.* Assuming that the United States and the Soviet Union have resumed the CATT process and are willing to cooperate in reducing regional tensions, it might be possible for Washington and Moscow to convene four-way arms control talks with pairs of mutually antagonistic Third World nations that rely heavily on superpower military assistance. Such a formula could, for instance, be tried with North and South Korea, both of which depend on one of the superpowers for their military supplies. In such a setting, it might be possible to adopt mutual restraints on arms imports into the Korean Peninsula, backed up by a joint superpower pledge of cooperation in verifying such an agreement.

The same formula could be tried with India and Pakistan, and with Israel and Syria. In each of these cases, the two countries involved face their greatest security threat from the other member of the pair, and each is highly dependent on one of the two superpowers for military assistance. While these countries have resisted such negotiations before, they might find such agreements more attractive if they involved an equitable and mutual reduction of transfers on both sides and if the superpowers agreed to cooperate in preventing aggressive action by their respective clients. Subsequently, if these pairs of adversaries can be persuaded to adopt such agreements, it might be possible to establish more comprehensive agreements covering several nations in a region, and thence to bring in the other major military suppliers.

4. *Tie development aid and technology transfers to arms-import restraint.* Ultimately, any progress in curbing arms transfers will require cooperation on the part of the recipient countries. So long as these nations continue to seek large quantities of modern arms, they will find some suppliers willing to risk international censure by providing such products. It is essential, therefore, that some means be found to enlist Third World countries in an international arms transfer control regime.

Clearly, any effort to include Third World nations in such a regime will have to make allowance for the legitimate security needs of these nations. It is too much to expect them to forgo arms imports on their own when potential rivals are not so restrained. The first step, therefore, is to initiate quadrilateral and regional negotiations of the sort described above aimed at adopting mutual import restrictions, backed up by a pledge of superpower cooperation and by other international guarantees. Once these countries conclude that they can restrain their arms imports without incurring a reduction in security, it will be possible to institute other measures intended to promote and reward self-restraint in this area.

One such approach that could be adopted on either a unilateral or multilateral basis would be to tie development assistance and multilateral bank loans to progress on arms-import restraint. Economic and technical assistance could be increased to those countries that agree to curb their imports of arms (in the context of a regional agreement of some sort), and decreased to those countries that eschew such agreements. To encourage cooperation by Third World arms suppliers, moreover, future North-to-South transfers of nonmilitary technology should be made contingent on recipient restraint in the export of arms to other Third World countries.

Would these various measures succeed in substantially reducing the international trade in conventional armaments? Could they make the world a safer place? Certainly in the absence of such measures the arms trade will continue to develop in the manner described above and the world will assuredly become a more dangerous place. On the other hand, these four proposals, if fully implemented, would contribute to a significant contraction of the international arms flow. It is important to recognize, however, that each proposal is intended to address a particular aspect of the arms trade problem; if adopted individually, each could probably secure improvement in some areas but leave the other aspects of the problem unaffected. Given the complex nature of this issue, a *comprehensive* approach—involving all of these measures—is most likely to yield the maximum results.

In addition, it is essential that the arms trade problem be addressed in concert with the other perils described above, so as to initiate an integrated strategy for global stability. Unless these problems are dealt with in unison, we face the imminent convergence of several hazardous trends that jointly threaten to sabotage international security in the 1990s and beyond. Without substantial progress in the field of arms transfers control, nuclear nonproliferation, and chemical weapons disarmament, the world will remain poised for tragic and needless catastrophe.

## Notes

1. Richard F. Grimmett, *Trends in Conventional Arms Transfers to the Third World by Major Supplier, 1981–1988* (Washington, DC: Congressional Research Service, 1988), pp. 34, 57. (Hereinafter cited as CRS, *Trends 1981–88*.)

2. Stockholm International Peace Research Institute, *SIPRI Yearbook 1985: World Armaments and Disarmament* (London and Philadelphia, 1985), pp. 331–33. (Hereinafter cited as *SIPRI Yearbook 1985*.)

3. CRS, *Trends 1981–88*, pp. 50–51.

4. For discussion, see Philip A.G. Sabin and Efraim Karsh, "Escalation and the Iran-Iraq War," *Survival*, May–June 1989, pp. 241–54.

5. These trends were first discussed in Michael Klare, "Deadly Convergence: The Perils of the Arms Trade," *World Policy Journal*, Vol. VI, No. 1 (Winter 1988–89), pp. 141–68.

6. CRS, *Trends 1981–88*, p. 36.

7. See the register of arms transfers in *SIPRI Yearbook 1989*, pp. 244–68, and in earlier editions.

8. See Leonard S. Spector, *The Undeclared Bomb: The Spread of Nuclear Weapons 1987–88* (Cambridge, MA: Ballinger, 1987). See also the other studies published by Spector on nuclear proliferation, including *Going Nuclear* (1987) and *The New Nuclear Nations* (1986).

9. Robert D. Shuey, et al., *Missile Proliferation: Survey of Emerging Missile Forces*, CRS Report for Congress, Congressional Research Service, Washington, DC, October 3, 1988, p. 35. See also *SIPRI Yearbook 1987*, pp. 110–13.

10. See Leonard S. Spector, "Foreign-Supplied Combat Aircraft: Will They Drop the Third World Bomb?" *Journal of International Affairs* (Summer 1986), pp. 142–58. The military holdings of all Third World countries are itemized in International Institute for Strategic Studies, *The Military Balance 1989–90* (London, 1989).

11. Shuey, et al., *Missile Proliferation*, pp. 38–42. See also *SIPRI Yearbook 1989*, pp. 287–318; and Spector, *The Undeclared Bomb*, pp. 60–66.

12. For an account of the CATT talks and an analysis of their failure, see Jo L. Husbands and Anne Hessing Cahn, "The Conventional Arms Transfer Talks: An Experiment in Mutual Arms Trade Restraint," in Thomas Ohlson, ed., *Arms Transfer Limitations and Third World Security* (Oxford and New York: Oxford University Press, 1988), pp. 110–25.

13. See Aaron Karp, "The Frantic Third World Quest for Ballistic Missiles," *Bulletin of the Atomic Scientists*, June 1987, pp. 17–18.

14. Such an analysis was first attempted in Michael Klare, *American Arms Supermarket* (Austin: University of Texas Press, 1984), pp. 1–25. Revised assessments were subsequently supplied in "The State of the Trade," *Journal of International Affairs*, Vol. 40, No. 1 (Summer 1986), pp. 1–21; "The Arms Trade: Changing Patterns in the 1980s," *Third World Quarterly*, Vol. 9, No. 4 (October 1987), pp. 1257–81, and "Who's Arming Who? The Arms Trade in the 1990s," *Technology Review*, May–June 1990, pp. 43–50.

15. CRS, *Trends 1981–88*, p. 33. (All figures in current dollars.)

16. Stephanie Neuman, "The Arms Market: Who's on Top?" *Orbis*, Fall 1989, p. 516.

17. Morton S. Miller, "Conventional Arms Trade in the Developing World, 1976–86: Reflections on a Decade," in U.S. Arms Control and Disarmament Agency, *World Military Expenditures and Arms Transfers 1987* (Washington, DC, 1988), p. 19. (Hereinafter cited as ACDA, *WME&AT 1987*.)

18. Ibid. For further discussion of this point, see William Hartung, "Nations Vie for Arms Markets," *Bulletin of the Atomic Scientists* (December 1987), pp. 27–35; and Klare, "The State of the Trade," pp. 10–12.

19. CRS, *Trends 1980–87*, p. 65.

20. Ibid.

21. Miller, "Conventional Arms Trade," p. 21.

22. For discussion, see Neuman, "The Arms Market," pp. 518–19.

23. For background on and discussion of these endeavors, see Michael Brzoska and Thomas Ohlson, *Arms Production in the Third World* (London and Philadelphia: Taylor and Francis, 1986). See also Klare, *American Arms Supermarket*, pp. 163–82.

24. See "Turkey's 10-Year Shopping List," *Armed Forces Journal*, June 1989, pp. 56–58.

25. For discussion of this trend, see Rodney W. Jones and Steven A. Hildreth, *Modern Weapons and Third World Powers* (Boulder, CO: Westview Press, 1984).

26. See Shuey, et al., *Missile Proliferation*; and *SIPRI Yearbook 1989*, pp. 104–112, 287–318.

27. Abdel Monem Said Aly, "The Arms Trade and Regional Conflict," paper prepared for the 39th Pugwash Conference on Science and World Affairs, Cambridge, MA, July 23–28, 1989.

28. CRS, *Trends 1975–82*, p. 10.

29. CRS, *Trends 1981–88*, p. 34.

30. ACDA, *WME&AT 1988*, pp. 77, 80. (All figures in current dollars.)

31. See Miller, "Conventional Arms Trade," pp. 20–22. On the Brazilian arms industry, see Brzoska and Ohlson, *Arms Production in the Third World*, pp. 79–104; Clovis Brigagao, "The Brazilian Arms Industry," *Journal of International Affairs*, Vol. 40, No. 1 (Summer 1986), pp. 101–14.

32. ACDA, *WME&AT 1988*, pp. 83, 89, 91. See also Brzoska and Ohlson, *Arms Production in the Third World*, pp. 105–24, 163–92, 215–32, and 260–64.

33. ACDA, *WME&AT 1988*, p. 22.

34. For discussion of this technological competition, see Neuman, "The Arms Market," pp. 518–29. On European joint ventures, see Carole A. Shifrin, "Lower East-West Tensions May Boost Joint European Defense Projects," *Aviation Week and Space Technology*, March 19, 1990, pp. 86–88.

35. For discussion of this phenomenon, see "Violence: A Buyer's Market," *Jane's Defence Weekly*, May 12, 1990, pp. 909–11; and Michael Klare, "The Thriving Black Market for Weapons," *Bulletin of the Atomic Scientists*, April 1988, pp. 16–24.

36. See *New York Times*, February 5, 1989 (on India) and February 6, 1989 (on Pakistan). See also Alex Gliksman, "Arms Production in the Pacific," *National Defense*, December 1989, pp. 41–43; and Alex Gliksman and Jack Nunn, "Military Aerospace in the Pacific Rim," *National Defense*, April 1990, pp. 49–53.

37. For discussion, see Jean Klein, "Arms Sales, Development, Disarmament," *Bulletin of Peace Proposals*, Vol. 14, No. 2 (1983), pp. 160–61; and *SIPRI Yearbook 1984*, pp. 188–90.

38. For discussion, see "How the World Keeps the Iran-Iraq War Going," *Business Week*, December 29, 1986, pp. 46–48; Michael Brzoska, "Profiteering on the Iran-Iraq War," *Bulletin of the Atomic Scientists*, June 1987, pp. 42–45; Pranay Gupte, "Rhetoric and Reality in the Iranian Arms Trade," *Forbes*, October 19, 1987, pp. 32–35; and Kenneth R. Timmerman, "Europe's Arms Pipeline to Iran," *The Nation*, July 18–25, 1987, pp. 47–52.

39. On clandestine arms sales to South Africa, see Thomas Conrad, "South Africa Circumvents Embargo," *Bulletin of the Atomic Scientists*, March 1986, pp. 8–13; *New York Times*, October 27, 1989; and *Washington Post*, March 28, 1987.

40. See *SIPRI Yearbook 1989*, pp. 204–207. For a complete list of arms produced in the Third World under license from the major suppliers, see ibid., pp. 274–77.

41. ACDA, *WME&AT 1988*, pp. 111–14.

42. Ibid.

43. For discussion, see Rodney W. Jones and Steven A. Hildreth, eds., *Emerging Powers: Defense and Security in the Third World* (New York: Praeger, 1986); and Frederic S. Pearson, "The Correlates of Arms Importation," *Bulletin of Peace Proposals*, Vol. 26, No. 2 (1989), pp. 153–63.

44. For discussion, see "Proposed Superpower Arms Cut in Asia Could Spark Rise in Regional Spending," *Aviation Week and Space Technology*, February 12, 1990, pp. 83–90; and P. Lewis Young, "Strong Southeast Asian Budgets Attracting Widespread Industry Interest," *Armed Forces Journal*, March 1990, p. 38.

45. ACDA, *WME&AT 1988*, pp. 38, 49, 52, 60. (All figures in current dollars.)

46. For discussion of the Carter policy, its implementation, and Reagan's objections to it, see Klare, *American Arms Supermarket*, pp. 43–53.

47. See: "High Costs of the Persian Gulf War," in ACDA, *WME&AT 1988*, pp. 21–23.

48. Ibid., p. 22.

49. For data on casualties in recent wars, see *SIPRI Yearbook 1989*, pp. 339–55.

50. Shuey, et al., *Missile Proliferation*, pp. 3, 54, 68.

51. Ibid., p. 69.

52. Cited in ibid.

53. For discussion, see Klare, *American Arms Supermarket*, pp. 127–62.

54. From a statement reproduced in the *Congressional Record*, May 14, 1979, p. S5726.

55. Address by President George Bush at the U.S. Coast Guard Academy, New London, CT, May 24, 1989 (White House Press Office transcript).

56. Statement by V.P. Petrovsky at the U.N. General Assembly, October 18, 1988 (transcript provided by USSR Mission to the UN).

57. From collection of statements on arms transfers at the 43rd General Assembly and at the Third Special Session on Disarmament; compiled by the Quaker Office at the United Nations (xerox).

58. United Nations General Assembly, *Complete and General Disarmament: International Arms Transfers,* Information Received from Governments, Report No. A/44/444, August 14, 1989, p. 5.

59. For further discussion of these concerns, see Michael T. Klare, "An Arms Control Agenda for the Third World," *Arms Control Today,* April 1990, pp. 8–12.

60. These proposals were first advanced in Klare, "Deadly Convergence," pp. 160–65.

61. For an assessment of progress made by the CATT negotiators, see Husbands and Cahn, "The Conventional Arms Transfer Talks," pp. 117–19.

62. See Michael Brzoska, "Third World Arms Control: Problems of Verification," *Bulletin of the Atomic Scientists,* Vol. 14, No. 2 (1983), pp. 165–73.

63. For discussion of the UN register idea, see *The International Trade in Arms: Problems and Prospects,* a Conference Report by Keith Krause, Canadian Institute for International Peace and Security, Ottawa, 1987. For the Soviet view, see October 18, 1988, remarks by Petrovsky, cited above.

64. See: Karp, "The Frantic Third World Quest," pp. 15–16.

65. Ibid., pp. 17–18. See also Janne E. Nolan, "Ballistic Missiles in the Third World—The Limits of Nonproliferation," *Arms Control Today,* November 1989, pp. 12–13.

66. See *New York Times,* September 27, 1988.

67. For elaboration of these proposals, see Karp, "The Frantic Third World Quest," pp. 19–20.

# 9 / Militarized States in the Third World

NICOLE BALL

## INTRODUCTION[1]

In his address to the joint World Bank-International Monetary Fund annual meeting in Washington, D.C., at the end of September 1989, Bank President Barber Conable argued, "It is important to place military spending decisions on the same footing as other fiscal decisions . . . and to explore ways to bring military spending into better balance with development priorities."[2] This marked the first time that a World Bank president had commented publicly on the resources allocated by Third World governments to their security forces since Robert McNamara had made a similar statement in 1973. In the 1970s, McNamara's comments appeared to raise no echo, either within the Bank or within other development financing organizations. In 1990, there are signs that the Bretton Woods organizations are preparing to face this once-taboo subject head on. A willingness on the part of major funders and governments to address an issue as closely associated with the basic sovereign rights of governments as military expenditure is overdue given the large proportion of their budgets that many Third World governments allocate to their security forces.

Although many Third World governments have allocated a significant portion of their budgets to the security sector for the last twenty or thirty years or more, until relatively recently only a small number of individuals have been concerned about the political and developmental implications of these budgetary decisions. Governments and multilateral organizations have, for the most part, been silent on this issue. This is, at least in part, because the East-West conflict has tended to override and, in the minds of some, justify the situation in the Third World. High military budgets and politically active armed forces were seen as necessary evils in the fight against communism (or capitalism, depending on the side of the Iron Curtain). Now, all of that is changing, largely because one individual set in motion a much-needed tide of domestic and international reform.

It was clear almost from the beginning of his tenure that Mikhail Gorbachev would be a very different leader from his predecessors. Few, however, could have foreseen the seriousness and resolve with which the

Soviet government under his guidance would pursue domestic reforms, arms control, and the resolution of conflicts outside Soviet borders. And no one could have anticipated the degree of freedom of choice that Gorbachev was willing to permit the Soviet Union's Eastern European allies in determining their own political future. The 1980s, which had begun with the Soviet invasion and occupation of Afghanistan, ended with the inauguration of a democratically elected noncommunist government in Poland, the opening of the Berlin Wall, and the popular revolt against the Stalinist regime in Rumania. The beginning of the 1990s has witnessed the apparent abandonment by the Soviet Union of a major ally in the Persian Gulf, Iraq, and unprecedented cooperation among the major powers and many other governments in the United Nations in the search for a peaceful solution to the crisis engendered by Iraq's annexation of Kuwait.

The reforms occurring in the Soviet Union and Eastern Europe will, as the Gulf crisis illustrates, have an effect far beyond the borders of these countries, and the 1990s have the potential for ushering in a period of significant political change at all levels and in all regions of the world. Where Soviet-bloc governments have offered the chance for participation in the political process, ordinary citizens have been more than eager to grasp the opportunity. In countries such as China and Rumania where communist governments did not offer the chance, citizens showed themselves willing to confront the state security forces in an attempt to seize the right to self-determination.

While the fragility and lack of legitimacy of the Eastern European communist governments should have come as no surprise, the decision by the Soviet government not only to cease supporting them any longer but in fact to hasten their dissolution was unexpected. Yet it is clear that for the Soviet Union and Eastern European countries to overcome the severe economic problems confronting them, a movement toward more open, participatory political systems was necessary.

For Third World countries, there are opportunities and lessons in the events of the late 1980s in Eastern Europe and the Soviet Union. Opportunities arise out of the reduction in tensions between East and West and the encouragement of the peaceful resolution of conflicts, which should have a direct impact on local and regional security. Lessons are to be learned from the link between domestic political reforms and successful economic development.

Just as the existence of communist governments in Eastern Europe depended on the security apparatus, particularly the Soviet security apparatus, the governments in many Third World countries rely heavily on military forces to remain in power. Indeed, in many cases, the security forces are the dominant political force in society. In the past, militarized states have posed a serious obstacle to political development in the Third World, preserving as they have elite-dominated political systems. They have also on many occasions complicated the resolution of domestic and international conflicts by seeking military solutions to problems that are inherently political and economic in nature, even *creating* conflict by their refusal to countenance economic and political pluralism.

There are several criteria by which a militarized state can be defined: the security forces play an active political role; a large share of government resources is devoted to the security sector; the government seeks military, rather than political, solutions to domestic and inter-state disputes.

On the first criterion alone, most countries in the Third World could have been characterized as militarized in the last forty years since security forces have ruled—directly or indirectly—approximately three quarters of the countries in Africa, Asia, South and Central America, and the Middle East since 1945. With respect to the second, we find that the proportion of global security expenditure accounted for by Third World governments has grown substantially over the last four decades. The Third World accounted for approximately 6 percent of world military expenditure as measured by the Stockholm International Peace Research Institute (SIPRI) in 1955, and for about 17 percent as measured by the U.S. Arms Control and Disarmament Agency (ACDA) in 1987.[3] Finally, although precise figures are hard to come by, there have been some 250 wars and conflicts in the Third World since the end of World War II. A portion of these have been exacerbated, if not actually caused, by the involvement of the great powers, particularly the United States and the Soviet Union, as well as of other developing countries, but one can nevertheless demonstrate that pressures indigenous to the Third World underlie many of these conflicts.

The trend toward decreased superpower support for and intervention in Third World conflicts, which began in the late 1980s, is an important first step in reducing the incidence of armed conflict in this part of the world, but it is by no means an indication that disputes will be resolved peacefully since many Third World governments may well continue to seek to dominate domestic and regional opponents militarily. Indeed, it is possible that an increased preoccupation on the part of the Soviet government with domestic issues and on the part of Western governments with developments within the Warsaw Pact countries will make it easier for Third World governments to pursue local and regional conflicts unimpeded by external constraints. Even if these conflicts were not to run quite the same danger of igniting an East-West war, the effects at the local and regional levels in terms of retarding both political and economic development will be substantial and undesirable.[4]

Throughout the post–World War II period, relatively little emphasis has been given to political development by Third World governments or by Western governments and development experts. The experience of countries such as South Korea and Taiwan during most of the postwar period encouraged the belief that substantial economic development could occur without the need to expand the political base of Third World governments and that Third World populations would be politically quiescent if the output of a growing economy were reasonably equitably distributed. The fallacy of this notion will only become more evident as domestic reforms within the Eastern bloc gain momentum. The record of Third World governments controlled or dominated by security forces in promoting popular participation in the decision-making process is poor. The continued existence of militarized states can only make the transition to participatory government more costly and painful. Yet this transition must occur if the challenges of the 1990s are to be met.

## THE EXPANSION OF THIRD WORLD SECURITY SECTORS

While the share and volume of Third World security expenditure have increased substantially over the last forty-five years and these outlays have absorbed a significant proportion of the resources of certain states, it is important to understand why Third World security sectors have expanded.

There are several reasons for assuming that *some* natural growth should have taken place since the 1950s. First, the number of independent countries has increased threefold since 1950. Second, many Third World countries, particularly those that did not have to fight to gain their freedom, had virtually no indigenous armed forces at independence. For these two reasons alone, even if each newly independent country spent only a minimal amount on its security forces, Third World security sectors would have expanded. Contributing to the rise in the Third World's share of security expenditure (although not necessarily to the growth of global outlays for security purposes or the size of forces) are both the decline in security assistance provided by established powers and the shift from grant aid to loans that began in the late 1960s. Both of these phenomena have required many Third World governments to devote a larger proportion of their own resources to the security sector.

Theoretically, the level and composition of security expenditure should be determined by an assessment both of the likely security threats confronting a country and the most effective means of meeting these threats and of the resources available to the government. In reality, other factors unrelated to the security environment affect the allocation of resources to the security sector. These include domestic bureaucratic and budgetary factors, the influence of the security forces themselves, and the role of the major powers. To clarify the context within which security expenditure occurs and security forces are maintained, the major determinants of security expenditure will be reviewed before examining the economic and political roles of the armed forces and evaluating the domestic and international implications of these roles.

### External Conflicts

Protection against external aggression provides the *raison d'être* for all armed forces, and external security considerations are most often used to justify increases in security expenditure. A number of Third World countries are involved in unresolved conflicts with neighboring states which, with greater or lesser frequency, flare into active combat. With one or two exceptions, all interstate wars since the end of World War II have taken place in the Third World, although there have been industrialized participants in some of these conflicts. The governments of countries engaged in external conflicts tend to have the largest security sectors in the Third World, with security outlays regularly absorbing 20 percent or more of state expenditure. In the 1980s, these included Syria, Saudi Arabia, Israel, Egypt, North Korea, Pakistan, Iran, and Iraq, among others.[5]

Despite all this, the vast majority of Third World countries face few, if any, serious threats from abroad. The noncommunist countries of Southeast Asia are typical of many developing countries in this respect. Despite fears of Vietnamese aggression following Vietnam's reunification in 1975, political and military elites in Thailand, the Philippines, Malaysia, Indonesia, and Singapore have not considered their countries to be in any danger of direct external aggression since the late 1970s. Instead, concern tends to be directed toward what is described as "aggression" from abroad in the cultural and economic spheres, but even here the level of concern has not been very high. Interviews with Asian elites most commonly elicit the response that "external threats are nonexistent or limited, but that 'the real threats are internal—and more economic than military.' "[6] A successful resolution of the Kampuchea conflict would presumably reduce threat perceptions in the region even further.[7]

At the same time, it must be recognized that accommodation between the two superpowers and a reduction in military support for regional allies might not suffice to put an end to regional conflicts or local conflicts that spill over into the region. Indeed, reduced interest on the part of the superpowers in a region, for example South Asia, might provide the signal for the regional powers to vie for local domination. A country such as India, which has always had hegemonic aspirations, is likely to view the end of the Cold War as an opportunity to continue its efforts to dominate the smaller countries on the subcontinent, including Pakistan, and may become even more unwilling than in the past to seek political solutions to conflicts such as those over Jammu and Kashmir. Thus, external conflicts, particularly those among the larger powers within a region, could increase during the 1990s. One question that must be answered, however, before it is possible to make a serious evaluation of the likelihood of increased regional conflicts is the effect that the withdrawal or significant reduction in military assistance will have on the pursuit of conflict by Third World governments. If the Indian government can no longer barter raw materials and domestic manufactures for Soviet arms and weapons-production technology and must instead purchase these with hard currency, its ability to wage war may be impaired. India is, of course, not unique in this respect. Other parties to long-standing regional conflicts may discover during the 1990s that the support offered by their major power patrons is severely diminished and their ability to wage war significantly reduced.

## Internal Security

Lowered perceptions of external threats do not automatically lead to smaller security forces or budgets. Some Third World countries that have not engaged in conflict for many years and are under no obvious external threat still allocate considerable portions of state and national resources to the security sector. In addition, countries for which external threats have diminished substantially have continued to allocate substantial sums to the security forces. These seemingly contradictory conditions reflect the need to preserve internal security and the fact that the foremost task of many armed forces in the Third World is to protect governments and elite groups from the mass of the population.[8]

In many parts of the world, political systems are dominated by a relatively small number of elite groups (distinguished by characteristics such as class, race, ethnicity, religion, and occupation). These groups seek to dominate the economy and restrict access to power in both the economic and political spheres. The general public has little or no opportunity to participate in the policy-making process or in the formal economic system. Under these conditions, conflicts among the different elites as they vie for power and between the ruling elite and groups suffering discrimination or repression are inevitable.

When governments decline to seek political solutions to such conflicts, they require the assistance of the armed forces, the police, and/or paramilitary groups to maintain some semblance of order and to remain in power. For over thirty years, military-dominated governments in Burma have been fighting non-Burmese ethnic groups—Shan, Karen, and Kachin—who oppose absorption into a political unit dominated by ethnic Burmese. The overwhelming disregard on the part of the Israeli government for the economic and political rights of Israeli citizens of Palestinian background has most recently given rise to the *intifada*—a popular revolt employing minimal force that has been answered by significant Israeli violations of human rights, including several hundred deaths, in its first three years. By seeking military solutions to political disputes such as these, governments both ensure that a substantial proportion of their budgets is allocated to the security sector and make it more likely that the armed forces will play a central role in the process of government itself.

The predominantly internal role of the armed forces is especially evident in South America, where interstate conflict has occurred infrequently over the last century but military establishments continue to flourish. Throughout this region, armed forces have promoted the doctrine of national security, which assigns a central role to the security forces not only in guaranteeing external security but also in defining and protecting internal security and in promoting economic development. According to this doctrine, national security depends on a strong economy and a unified society. These in turn require strong government and an efficient planning apparatus. Social control and the need to respect hierarchical authority are necessary attributes of this system. Pluralism is seen as a divisive factor. This system is designed to protect the political and economic prerogatives of Latin American elites against attack from other societal groups, whether these be defined by level of income, religious or ethnic affiliation, or some other characteristic.

Similar doctrines have been developed in Asia and in Africa. In view of the ethnic conflicts that have divided Burma since the end of World War II, it should come as no surprise that the Burmese armed forces developed the "National Ideology of the Defense Services" at about the same time as the doctrine of national security was enunciated in Latin America. Like the doctrine of national security, it equates national security both with defense against external enemies and maintenance of the integrity of the country and with the implementation of successful development programs. The Indonesian armed forces developed the *dwi fungsi* (dual function) doctrine, which gave the army the permanent right to intervene in the "ideological, political, social, economic, cultural, and religious" aspects of Indonesian life.[9]

It is not clear that conditions giving rise to internal security problems have worsened in recent years. There are some who look at the situation in places such as Israel, Kashmir, and Sri Lanka and argue that ethnic and religious disputes are intensifying and will be a major determinant of the level of military expenditure in the 1990s. There can be no doubt that some internal conflicts have become more severe in recent years, and it is likely that others will intensify over the next decade. Most of these conflicts, however, have been with us for twenty, thirty, or forty years, flaring up from time to time but never dying out because their root causes have never been addressed. It is probable that the reduction in "background noise" from the East-West conflict has brought local conflicts and the domestic role of the armed forces into sharper relief. Nonetheless, internal political considerations have been extremely important throughout the postwar period in determining the allocation of resources to Third World security sectors.

## Domestic Bureaucratic and Budgetary Factors

The outer limits of all public expenditure are ultimately determined by the availability of resources, and security expenditure is no exception. It is not only the existence of a series of unresolved regional and domestic conflicts that has caused countries in the Middle East and Northern Africa to lead the annual list of major Third World arms importers. The rise in the price of oil and other petroleum products that occurred in the 1970s was also a key factor in enabling governments in these regions to equip their forces with sizable amounts of sophisticated military equipment and to continue to seek military solutions to conflicts.

Similarly, a lack of resources has not infrequently forced governments to reduce the size of their security forces or to reduce outlays on the security sector. Resources can become constrained for a variety of reasons. For Third World countries during the 1980s, two of the more important constraints were a decline in the value (both relative and absolute) of their major exports, leading to a reduction in export earnings, and ever-increasing debt burdens, brought on in part by indiscriminate lending during the 1970s. For example, the popularity of the Nigerian armed forces at the end of the civil war and the vastly increased state revenues generated by income from oil enabled Nigerian governments to avoid demobilizing large portions of the armed forces and to reverse a decline in the share of state budgets allocated to the security sector in the mid-1970s. However, a glut in the international oil market and the effects of overambitious and ill-conceived development plans contributed to a decline in the security budget and the size of the Nigerian armed forces in the late 1970s and early 1980s.

Once the broad parameters of resource availability are set, there is a tendency for inertia to set in. Macroeconomic surveys have found that two-thirds or more of the variance in security expenditure for any given year can be explained by the level of security expenditure in the previous year. This appears to be particularly true for operating (day-to-day) expenditure.[10] Intuitively, a close relationship between prior and current expenditure levels makes sense because large portions of Third World security budgets are composed of operating costs. These can be expected to increase incrementally through pay or pension increases or normal price increases for items such as fuel, food, electricity, education, and office supplies. Barring rapid changes in the size of the security establishment, a large portion of a government's security budget will be predetermined as troops are paid, fed, clothed, and housed and as the basic requirements of the command and administrative apparatus are met.

Despite this, the growth of security expenditure does not always occur in an orderly fashion. It has been suggested that a substantial proportion of the year-to-year variations in security-related outlays is determined by bureaucratic expenditure requirements: inflation, salary and pension rises, equipment replacement, and so on. In Liberia in the early 1980s, following the overthrow of the Tolbert government and the imposition of military rule, the Liberian armed forces awarded themselves substantial increases in pay. Since over half the Liberian security budget was allocated to salaries and wages, the (on average) doubling of military salaries that occurred in 1980 had the effect of doubling the share of security spending in both state and national resources between 1980 and 1981.[11]

## Role of the Military Establishment

The security forces are frequently seen as the single most important actor in determining security expenditure. In organizational terms, the security forces are concerned with maintaining their share of government allocations, ensuring that their members (at least the officer corps) are compensated as well as other comparable societal groups, and creating as well equipped a force as possible. The regular armed forces seek to avoid being at a disadvantage to paramilitary forces in terms of pay and equipment, and the different services within the regular forces may compete with each other for allocations. This can drive up total security outlays and the amount of weaponry purchased by a government.

As individuals, military officers seek to enhance their own status and wealth. This can be done by ensuring that budgeted salaries are high and that health and education benefits are provided not only to military officers but also to their families. The personal status and wealth of military officers can also be enhanced by accepting rake-offs from arms import contracts or funneling other kinds of military procurement and construction contracts to firms with which the officer in question or a member of his family has close ties. There are few countries in the Third World where military corruption is not a problem, but it has reached major proportions in countries such as Indonesia and Thailand. Corruption is frequently the glue that holds military-dominated governments in Third World countries together or helps prevent challenges to the prevailing order by keeping officers busy lining their own pockets rather than seeking to overthrow their superiors.[12]

The security forces have a greater chance of influencing the budgetary process when they control the government. There is not, however, a straightforward correlation between military coups d'état and military governments on the one hand, and higher levels of military spending on the other. Nor, as discussed above, are governments controlled by the military exempt from reductions in the security budget during times of economic crisis. The military government's proposed economic policies and the relative strength of the country's economy are important factors in determining whether a coup will result in an immediate rise in security outlays and whether such a rise can be sustained for more than a year or two.[13]

## The Role of External Powers

Third World countries engaged in external disputes tend to have the largest security sectors. External powers frequently play an important role in the creation and exacerbation of conflict in the Third World: as colonial powers, as interventionary forces, as promoters of coups d'état, as providers of military assistance, and as arms sellers. Most frequently, it has been the two superpowers and their allies that have played this role, but governments of Third World countries have become increasingly active over the last decade. The post-1973 oil price rises were important in enabling countries such as Libya, Saudi Arabia, Kuwait, Algeria, Iran, Iraq, and the United Arab Emirates to send expeditionary forces to Third World countries or to help friendly governments purchase weapons and hire technicians and other specialists to operate and maintain these weapons. Cuba, Israel, Pakistan, South Africa, North Korea, and India have also intervened in the affairs of other Third World countries.[14]

Indochina provides a tragic example of how a region can be transformed by external intervention and how historic animosities can be given a new and deadly lease on life as a result. Colonized by the French in the latter half of the nineteenth century, Indochina was occupied by the Japanese in 1941. During World War II, a communist-dominated united front organization, the League for the Independence of Vietnam (known as the Viet Minh), was created. At the end of the war in August 1945, when the Japanese forces were in retreat, this group created the Democratic Republic of Vietnam (DRV) under the leadership of Ho Chi Minh. French troops, rearmed by the British and assisted in the initial stages by British-Indian and Japanese troops, sought to reconquer the former colony. By 1954, the French forces were defeated.

Under strong pressure from its Soviet and Chinese allies and the promise of national elections, the Democratic Republic of Vietnam agreed at the 1954 Geneva Convention to allow the country to be partitioned at the seventeenth parallel (although the DRV actually controlled territory south of the seventeenth parallel). The DRV was in control in the north, and a French-backed government controlled the south. Supported by the United States, Prime Minister Ngo Dinh Diem gained control of the government in the south (initially led by the French puppet, Bao Dai) and proclaimed the establishment of the Republic of Vietnam in October 1955.

Despite repeated attempts by the Ho government, Diem never agreed to hold the election promised by the Geneva Accords. Rather, he sought to consolidate his control of the south by increasingly repressive means. Supporters of the Viet Minh in the south, members of the National Liberation Front, began an insurgency against the Diem government in 1961. This conflict ultimately grew to involve the United States, the Democratic Republic of Vietnam, the People's Republic of China, and the Soviet Union, as well the contesting parties within the south. Before it ended in 1975, it had spilled over into Cambodia and had affected neighboring Thailand, where the United States had important air bases.

Enormous amounts of every imaginable kind of military and economic assistance were provided to the combatants by their major power patrons. The government in the south was essentially a creation of the United States. U.S. economic and military assistance enabled Ngo Dinh Diem to consolidate and maintain his position; later, U.S. troops fought the war for the Diem government. Millions of Vietnamese, from north and south, were killed, wounded, or missing in action. It has been estimated that 90 percent or more of the deaths in Indochina during this period were civilian deaths. In Cambodia, whose neutrality the United States had violated in 1969 by bombing enemy sanctuaries and whose government was overthrown—possibly with U.S. assistance—in March 1970, nearly three-quarters of a million civilians were killed or wounded by March 1975.

But peace did not return to Indochina in April 1975 when North Vietnamese troops entered Saigon (now Ho Chi Minh City) and the communist Khmer Rouge forces of Pol Pot drove the Lon Nol government from Phnom Penh. New fighting broke out almost immediately as the new governments in Cambodia and Vietnam contested border areas and offshore islands in early May 1975. By December 1977, this conflict had become a serious border dispute between the two countries. In December 1978, the Vietnamese government announced the creation of a new organization to liberate Cambodia and launched a full-scale invasion of the country. In February 1979, China, expressing its historical concern for Vietnamese attempts to gain hegemony over Indochina and its opposition to the treatment of Vietnam's ethnic Chinese citizens, launched a limited but intensive attack on Vietnam. By the end of that year, an uneasy truce was reached.

Also by the end of that year, a pro-Vietnamese government had been installed in Phnom Penh. Some 200,000 Vietnamese troops occupied Cambodia for a decade. (There were also some 30,000 Vietnamese troops stationed in Laos at the end of the 1970s.) The withdrawal of Vietnamese troops has not brought peace to Cambodia however, as various domestic factions continue to vie for power. Attempts, led by the French government, to mediate this conflict had not produced a solution by mid-1990, at least in part because the Chinese government has not been willing to abandon the Khmer Rouge.[15]

Unresolved external conflicts, which frequently imply the intervention of external powers, have been a major factor in the increase in Third World security expenditure since the early 1950s. For most countries in the Third World, however, the importance of external conflicts has been relatively minor. Instead, the imperatives of internal or regime security, bureaucratic factors such as budgetary inertia, and the political role of the armed forces have contributed substantially to the growth in resources allocated to the security sector by Third World governments.

# THE MILITARY IN POLITICS

The security forces have played an important role in the political systems of a large number of countries in Asia, Africa, the Middle East, and Latin America during the post–World War II period. It is not, however, only since 1945 that the armed forces in these regions have participated in politics. Military governments and rule by caudillos (military leaders who set themselves up as dictators) have been a central aspect of Latin American politics since the first Latin American countries attained independence in the early nineteenth century. The first military coup in Thailand, which established a pattern of government that endures to this day, occurred in 1932.

Despite this history of military involvement in politics in the Third World, the degree to which Third World security forces have assumed a political role in the postwar period may seem surprising, given the stress that has been placed by the United Nations and Western governments on decolonization and democratization. In reality, the governments of the former colonial powers were more interested in the rhetoric of democracy and independence than in ensuring that countries became fully independent and that functioning democracies were established. Decolonization was promoted at least in part by the government of the United States, for example, to enable U.S. political and economic influence to spread to areas that were once the more or less exclusive preserve of European colonial powers.

Democratization was frequently viewed as a means of preventing the spread of communism to newly independent areas. Western governments, especially the U.S. government, preferred to support what could be defined as "strong," anticommunist governments in the Third World, which were often led by the armed forces.

In the late 1950s and during the 1960s, American social scientists emphasized the need to prevent the spread of communism and argued that strong leadership, good organization, and moral authority were the keystone of both successful government and successful modernization programs in the Third World—attributes they believed could be found in the leadership of the security forces. Nationalist (often left-wing) politicians who had inherited power from the departing colonial states were viewed by these analysts as "too weak" to withstand pressure from communist groups, which were characterized as well organized and highly purposeful. The former required time to learn to "manage" the democratic process—that is, to control dissent and limit participation. In the interim, strong governments had to be created that would be capable of preventing communist groups from stepping into the power vacuum created by ineffective nationalist governments.[16] The outcome was a proposed course of action that, in order to "save" democracy, would effectively destroy it by supporting military governments. On the economic front, it was assumed that military-led governments would provide the direction necessary to implement development programs and guarantee the efficient functioning of the economy.

Interestingly, the Soviet Union has also found ideological justifications for supporting military governments in the Third World. Prior to the mid-1960s, the official Soviet view had been that the armed forces in Third World countries were subordinate to and always reflected the political orientation of the ruling group, irrespective of whether that group was "bourgeois" or "socialist." However, following the 1966 ouster of the "socialist" Ghanaian leader Nkrumah by "reactionary" military officers, the Soviet line underwent a radical change. Third World armed forces began to be described as "the best-organized force in public life." Once military officers with a more progressive orientation began to take power in the Third World in the late 1960s and early 1970s, writers expressing the official Soviet line ceased to speak of creating (civilian) vanguard parties and started to discuss the benefits of military rule more openly. One Soviet writer went so far as to call the army the "vanguard of the nation," with not only "military, political and administrative-police functions, but also important national-economic, ideological and educational functions."[17]

This assessment of the security forces as a central actor in the domestic unity, political and economic development, and external security of Third World countries strengthened the arguments of policymakers who sought to channel more funds to Third World armed forces. It could be argued that such aid was beneficial economically, strategically, and politically for the recipient. However, these predictions have, for the most part, not been borne out by reality.

Even relatively early on, in the mid-1960s, there were analysts who questioned whether the security forces were really models of efficiency, leadership, and moral authority.[18] That the answers to these questions appear to have been ignored by most U.S. administrations in the postwar period makes them no less pertinent. Indeed, in view of the number of Third World countries that have been ruled by the armed forces during the last four decades, it is important to understand the strengths and weaknesses of military officers as formulators and implementers of policy. Discipline and organizational capacity should never be confused with the ability to direct the development process. Although military officers may be able to run their own affairs efficiently—or so it is usually assumed—there is no guarantee that they can formulate and coordinate broader government policies as successfully.

One important shortcoming of military officers is that they frequently lack the bargaining skills necessary to reach the political compromises essential to governing pluralistic societies. When South Korean officers were surveyed in the early 1980s, for example, they scored well in terms of honor, justice, responsibility, and anticommunism. They scored less well on management capability, flexibility, and adaptability.[19] Military officers in charge of governments frequently attempt to avoid compromise and expect that once they have decided on a policy, it will be implemented without further discussion. No military can govern entirely on its own—if for no other reason than that it lacks sufficient manpower to staff all bureaucratic posts—and an alliance between military officers, bureaucrats, and technical advisers is of necessity created when the military rules. Some military governments, such as the Velasco government in Peru (1968–75), fail to follow the recommendations of their own advisers, at least in part because military officers are not accustomed to functioning in an environment where policies are subject to critical appraisal by subordinates. Others, such as the Park Chung Hee government in South Korea (1961–79), recognize their limitations and rely heavily on civilian advisers, particularly in the economic sphere.

It is important to view politics in the Third World as the interaction of elite groups and examine the political role of the security forces within this context. It has been suggested that Third World armed forces act as the defender of middle-class interests (and, by definition, capitalism). Attempts have been made to link such behavior to the class background of military officers. Such attempts have not been very successful, partly because class background is but one factor influencing the behavior of members of the armed forces. In some cases, class interest provides a good explanation of civil-military relations, but in others, it does not. Third World armed forces do frequently support civilians in their attempts to exclude the mass of the population from the political and economic decision-making process. One reason for this exclusion is that civilian and military elites fear that increased participation by the poor would lead to alterations in existing political and economic structures that would be inimical to their own interests.

This can be true even for military governments that ostensibly promote greater participation, such as the Velasco government, which came to power in Peru in 1968. The Velasco government's public pronouncements, particularly in its early years, strongly favored the economically disadvantaged groups: peasants, urban workers, shop employees, and other low-paid individuals. In reality, however, the government strongly opposed the creation of grassroots organizations by these groups, fearing that such organizations could be used by communist activists to further their own ends. The Velasco government therefore created a government agency to direct and control "social mobilization." As a result, despite the rhetoric, the main beneficiaries of Peruvian military rule in the 1970s, even before it became more conservative under Morales Bermudez, were local industrialists and bankers, the public sector, and foreign firms.[20]

It is important to understand, however, that Third World elites seek not only to guard against the dissolution of a political and economic system that has enabled them to amass considerable personal wealth and power, but also to maintain their preeminent position within that system. The "middle class" is by no means a homogeneous entity whose members all share precisely the same beliefs and all benefit to exactly the same extent from the operation of the capitalist system. Furthermore, there are socialist elites, feudalist elites, and semi-feudalist elites. Each of these classes of elites can be divided according to occupational differences, ethnic divisions, generational gaps, regional divisions, racial differences, and hierarchical disputes. Each of these subgroups can, in turn, pursue policies that are disadvantageous to members of the same class. There are many instances of civilians seeking military support in order to exclude other political and economic elites from positions of power even when the groups involved all share similar class backgrounds and operate within essentially the same economic framework.

In a country such as Thailand, where cliques are the basic building blocks of all political activity, different military groups ally with different civilian groups, and each major coalition attempts to gain as much power and wealth as possible for itself; but this all occurs within the same economic system. Since 1932, Thailand has experienced at least six successful coups d'états, many unsuccessful ones, and several elections of varying degrees of fairness. Yet none of this has produced any serious alteration in the Thai elite.[21]

Civil-military relations are profoundly affected by these various divisions. Like any large grouping of people, the security forces reflect the divisions within society as a whole. When civilians seek the cooperation of the military, they most often do not seek the cooperation of all elements of the security forces. They deal almost exclusively with the officer corps, generally at the highest level. Then they build alliances with individual services, with factions within the security forces as a whole, or within the services. Civil-military relations often involve interactions between several civilian groups and several military groups. Coalition formation is of the greatest importance.

When the Brazilian armed forces overthrew President João Goulart in early April 1964, they had the support of three governors—Carlos Lacerda of Guanabara, Adhemar de Barros of São Paulo, and Magalhães Pinto of Minas Gerais—several leading daily papers, and a network of government opponents called IPES. IPES was particularly interesting because it was composed of businessmen, lawyers, technocrats, and military officers. Its members had created a shadow government, studied a broad range of social and economic issues, and even published their own economic statistics because they felt those produced by the government were unreliable.

Goulart was a left-of-center politician who had been removed as Labor Minister by President Getúlio Vargas in February 1954 in an attempt to restore the confidence of the public and, most important, the armed forces in his government, which faced severe economic problems and was perceived as "pro-communist." Goulart was not removed from the political scene, however, because in 1960 he was elected vice president at the same time Jânio Quadros became president. When Quadros ran into serious political difficulties (having moved sharply and suddenly to the left) in 1961, he resigned. Under the constitution, the vice president, in this case Goulart, was to be named president. Three military ministers in the Quadros government attempted, however, to block Goulart's accession. They failed when a "legality" campaign, supported by centrists as well as those on the left, succeeded in arguing that the legal mechanisms of the constitution should be upheld. (It should be noted that many military officers held the same position, even though they were not favorably disposed to Goulart.)

Faced with an economy in serious trouble, Goulart implemented an economic stabilization program that included reducing public-sector employment, freezing wages, and devaluing Brazil's currency (thereby effectively raising prices for imported goods such as wheat and oil). After six months, the costs of this program were deemed to be too costly to Goulart and to the left, and Goulart adopted a radical nationalist economic program. On the domestic front, this program called for reforms in the area of land ownership, taxation, education, and housing. Goulart's opponents, members of the conservative União Democrático Nacional and some military officers, sought the president's impeachment, on the grounds that he had violated the 1964 constitution.

Although this strategy failed because the necessary majority in the Chamber of Deputies could not be gained, Goulart did not have sufficient support in the Chamber to win passage for his reforms. As the end of his five-year term rapidly approached, Goulart accepted the advice of his radical nationalist advisers to take his program "to the people," which would, it was hoped, generate substantial popular support for the program and force the legislators to approve it. Encouraged by the popular support he encountered in his travels around Brazil, Goulart began issuing presidential decrees implementing his reform program. By March 1964, as the number of decrees mounted and Goulart appeared to be moving farther left, his military-civilian opponents were also very active, and military commanders who had previously been wary of joining a coup against the government reversed their decision. Goulart was overthrown shortly thereafter. The military conspirators then made a coup within a coup. They declared an end to direct presidential elections for the time being and changed the constitution so that military officers became eligible to hold elective office. This series of events paved the way for General Castelo Branco, leader of the conspiracy against Goulart, to be elected president by the Congress on April 11, 1964, inaugurating a period of military rule that lasted until 1985.[22]

Any assessment of what civilians expect to gain by the involvement of the security forces in politics must specify which civilian group(s) ally with which group(s) within the security forces and just what each group expects to obtain from the collaboration. And as the Brazilian example shows, it cannot be forgotten that the security forces are increasingly an independent player in elite politics, as well as in the economic sphere.

In assessing the political role played by security forces, it is useful to ask whom the security forces are protecting and from whom these individuals and groups are being protected. When security forces claim for themselves a role in guaranteeing internal security for a society, they are not, in most cases, seeking to make all citizens equally secure. Indeed, their actions often create greater instability. All too often, the security forces are not even protecting a majority of the population from a minority bent on pursuing its own political and economic objectives without reference to the needs of the majority. Rather, they seek to enable the ruling elite to remain in power and to sustain a socioeconomic system under which a relatively small elite (of which the military is frequently a part) enriches itself at the expense of a majority of the population. Instead of "internal security," the security forces seek to guarantee "regime security" (which often means "military regime security").[23]

Because rulers can represent the class and group interests of a very small segment of the population of a country, regimes may not be very stable, leading to a situation in which governments replace each other with great regularity. An extreme example, Bolivia has had nearly two hundred governments since it became independent in 1825. Even with a lower rate of government turnover, it is difficult to formulate and implement policies that will promote economic and political development. The losers in such situations have invariably been the poor and powerless.

## THE ECONOMIC IMPACT OF SECURITY FORCES

The development of political systems responsive to the needs of pluralistic societies has been a low priority for all governments, industrialized and developing, East as well as West. Rather, as we saw in the previous section, elite groups have vied with each other for control over governments, and support from the security apparatus—or portions of it—has often been instrumental in winning and maintaining power in the Third World. Not only has this process stunted the development of democratic institutions, but it has also helped to prevent the development of economic systems capable of a rational and equitable allocation of resources in many parts of the Third World. Control over government implies control over state resources in countries where the public sector plays a central role in the economy, as it has in so much of the Third World. Even in the era of privatization, the proportion of national resources controlled by Third World governments can be substantial. By being in a position to determine or strongly influence the allocation of state resources, security forces can influence the way in which the economy as a whole develops.

The most direct route by which the security forces can influence economic development is through the security budget itself. In common with other forms of public expenditure, outlays in the security sector can both promote and hinder economic growth. They will tend to encourage economic growth, for example, if resources that were previously idle are employed or if the balance between resources consumed and resources invested is altered in favor of investment. To the extent that expenditure in the security sector contributes to inflation, reduces the rate of saving, causes the misallocation of resources, or increases a country's debt, it will hinder economic growth.

It is difficult to generalize about the relative weight that should be accorded these effects because the situation varies both among countries and within individual countries over time. For example, while security expenditure might increase aggregate demand, the benefits are most likely to be felt where excess capacity exists. Increased demand from the security sector may not, however, enable that excess capacity to be employed, since output may be restricted by factors unrelated to the level of demand, such as a lack of foreign exchange to purchase production inputs from abroad. Alternatively, increased demand may stimulate production in one sector but be rendered ineffective by bottlenecks in other sectors. Similarly, the size of a country's security budget and the level of its military-related imports are not a sufficient guide in and of themselves to the magnitude of its military-related debt. Some countries, such as Saudi Arabia, spend a considerable share of their national budget in the security sector and import a large quantity of weapons and related equipment but have adequate supplies of foreign exchange to finance these purchases without recourse to borrowing. Others, such as India, have bartered weapons for goods produced domestically, substantially reducing their outlays of foreign exchange. Still others, such as Israel and Cuba, have received large parts of their military-related purchases free of charge from their major power patrons, the United States and the Soviet Union.

To understand the effects of security expenditure on the economies of Third World countries thus requires considerable knowledge of each country's economy and the composition of its security expenditure.[24] It is not sufficient, for example, to argue that by increasing the amount of investment in the economy through expenditure on military industries, security budgets promote economic growth. Merely investing in the military industrial sector does not guarantee that a viable arms industry will be created. Countries without a strong, integrated industrial base already in existence will not succeed in creating a viable arms industry of any size.[25] In order to reap the benefits of investment in the military industrial sector, an economy must be able to produce certain kinds of goods or, at a minimum, rapidly acquire that capability. This requires the mastery of many, often complex, technologies so that they can be reproduced domestically. A country cannot import "turn-key" plants and expect that by merely operating these plants the technology they embody will automatically be mastered. Conscious efforts must be made to learn how and why plant and machinery function as they do. This involves creating a well-trained body of scientific and technical manpower capable of maintaining, altering, and reproducing the imported technology.

Many governments, for example, that of the Shah of Iran during the 1970s, have misunderstood or ignored this necessary progression. They have believed that importing arms-production technology provides a short-cut to modernizing their economies. In Iran, for example, the military-industrial sector was poorly integrated into the economy. Almost all inputs for the defense industries had to be imported. Not only did this reduce backward linkages to the civilian economy, but it increased the foreign exchange costs of domestic production substantially.[26] The true beneficiaries of Iran's military industrialization program were foreign corporations.

Another avenue by which security forces affect Third World economies is by influencing the allocation of resources outside the security sector. In Chile, for example, following the coup that toppled the constitutionally elected Allende government in 1973, public investment was cut back sharply as responsibility for investment was shifted to the private sector. Outlays in the public housing and health sectors fell dramatically during the mid- to late 1970s, while expenditure in the security sector rose substantially.[27]

While Third World armed forces have the most direct influence over allocations outside the security sector when they control the government, their influence can extend beyond the security sector even when the government is nominally under civilian control. Promotion of military industries, for example, not only increases the likelihood that the industrial sector will receive substantial outlays from the government or that economic policies favorable to the industrial sector will be implemented (often at the expense of the agricultural sector), but also increases the likelihood that capital- rather than labor-intensive industrial techniques will be chosen, which has serious implications for countries with high levels of unemployment and underemployment. Furthermore, those industrial sectors that are crucial for defense production are not always those sectors that should be strengthened and expanded if the basic needs of Third World populations are to be met.

Finally, Third World security forces have increasingly participated directly in the economy by engaging in economic activities, often owning and running businesses. In many cases they have assumed this economic role in order to find nongovernmental sources of revenue for the security budget. But the patronage that such a system enables a government to dispense to members of the armed forces has clear political advantages as well. The Indonesian armed forces used their martial law powers to place Dutch enterprises under military control in late 1957, after nationalist demonstrators responded to an adverse vote in the United Nations on the West Irian issue by taking over some of these concerns. When these firms were subsequently nationalized, the armed forces continued to be involved in their management. In 1965, British enterprises were placed under military supervision. In addition, the armed forces began to establish their own companies, often as joint ventures with Chinese businessmen. Perhaps the best known of these was the oil corporation Pertamina, but by the late 1970s, the Indonesian armed forces were at the center of an extensive network of firms engaged in activities as diverse as shipping, forestry, fishing, tourism, banking, and air transport.[28] The income generated by these military-run enterprises has enabled the Suharto government to keep budgetary outlays for the armed forces at perhaps 50 percent of actual expenditure. Bringing the income of these companies into the public coffers, putting all security spending on-budget, and using the remainder of the income in the civil sector, while economically advantageous, would certainly prove to be politically counter-productive for the Suharto regime and, for that reason, is not likely to occur.

There are many reasons why a large proportion of Third World economies function poorly. The allocation of resources to the security sector and the misuse of resources by the security forces are often two of these reasons, but they are by no means the only or even always the most important ones. Based on the history of the last forty years, however, it is fair to state that the countries that allocate a large share of their national resources to the security sector and that allow the security forces to become actively involved in the economy are less likely to have economies that provide the entire population with the basic requirements of food, shelter, clothing, and social services.

It can be extremely difficult to determine when a government is spending "too much" in the security sector, since this involves a somewhat subjective evaluation of a country's security requirements. Most governments and international organizations that provide development assistance or loans to the Third World have in the past avoided making this evaluation, preferring not to leave themselves open to charges of interference in the internal affairs of Third World countries. As discussed at the beginning of this chapter, there are signs that this attitude may be undergoing a change, at least within the World Bank and the IMF and at least for countries that have been consistently spending a sizable portion of their resources in the security sector. Increasing the willingness of aid donors and major lenders to raise concerns about high levels of military expenditure in the Third World will be one of the challenges of the 1990s.

## Into the 1990s

There can be no doubt that the end of the 1980s constituted a turning point in history. The potential for restructuring political relations within and among countries is now greater than at any time since the end of World War II. The question before us is whether we can, individually and collectively, grasp the opportunity before us. For the Third World, a number of the trends that appeared to be emerging at the end of the 1980s could, if continued, contribute to a slowdown of militarization. The share of the Third World in global security expenditure, which had exceeded 20 percent in the late 1970s and early 1980s, had dropped to 17 percent in 1987. In certain regions, notably South America, the number of governments directly controlled by the military declined significantly during the 1980s. A process of conflict resolution supported by the major powers was inaugurated in the late 1980s, designed to resolve specific conflicts such as those in Afghanistan, Angola/Namibia, and Cambodia.

Clearly, fewer regional conflicts, fewer military governments, and lower security budgets would mean fewer heavily militarized states. The chances that conflicts would be resolved peacefully by political means would be increased. The likelihood that the external powers would be drawn into regional conflicts would decline, thereby promoting not only local and regional stability but also a reduction of tensions at the international level. The opportunities for economic and political development would also increase. But what can be expected to occur? Will these trends be sustained into the 1990s?

It is, unfortunately, extremely difficult to foresee with any accuracy the direction governments will take in these areas. The number of military governments in the Third World has waxed and waned throughout the postwar period. In Latin America, only four countries (Guyana, Mexico, Costa Rica, and Belize) have not been ruled directly by the armed forces at some point since 1945. In 1954, twelve of the twenty countries in the region were under direct military rule. By mid-1961, only one country had a military government. Seven coups occurred between 1962 and 1964. By 1975, the military ruled directly in twelve countries. Ten years later, that number had fallen to three. The historical evidence, therefore, does not provide much hope that political disengagement by Third World militaries will endure.

The decline in the Third World's share of global military expenditure reflects the difficult economic conditions that have faced Third World governments during the mid- to late 1980s. Were economic conditions to improve in the 1990s, it seems likely that some Third World governments would choose to spend a larger share of their resources in the security sector. What is more, all Third World regions did not experience a decline in military spending during the 1980s. In South Asia, for example, military expenditure grew by nearly 7 percent (according to ACDA figures) between 1982 and 1987, and East Asian military spending grew by nearly 2 percent.[29] The rise in oil prices following Iraq's invasion of Kuwait in August 1990 means that some countries will enjoy greater income, as long as these prices remain high, but many oil-importing Third World countries will not.

Efforts to settle regional conflicts have also not proceeded smoothly. In the summer of 1989, the settlement of the Angolan conflict appeared to have broken down and have placed the resolution of the Namibian conflict in jeopardy. By the end of 1990, the United States and the Soviet Union had renewed their efforts to find a negotiated solution to the conflict in Angola. The Cambodian peace conference held in Paris in August 1989 ended in a stalemate, with all sides fearing the outbreak of renewed violence. Apart from these specific regional conflicts, the likelihood exists that, as the United States and the Soviet Union increasingly learn to resolve their conflicts peacefully and do not feel the need to confront each other through Third World intermediaries, the larger powers in the Third World will increasingly seek to play a dominant role in their regions. This could give rise to increased interstate conflict. The apparent preoccupation of both the United States and the Soviet Union with domestic and bilateral issues may have been one element in Saddam Hussein's decision to invade and annex Kuwait.

Countries engaged in ongoing external conflicts tend to rank highest in terms of resources devoted to the security sector. At the same time, however, governments in countries that are not facing significant external threats can spend a considerable amount on the security forces in order to guarantee internal or regime security. A countertrend to the decline in security expenditure noted in a portion of the Third World in the 1980s was the increase in arms transfers that occurred at the end of the 1980s. A decrease in external conflicts should reduce the requirement for weapons, but again it is a question of degree. Even in the absence of specific threats, some governments purchase weapons to bolster their claims to regional-power status. The Shah of Iran, for example, envisaged his country becoming "the guardian of the Gulf" and purchased arms accordingly during the 1970s. During the same period, Nigerian governments argued that their country had a "claim to regional dominance" and should be viewed "as an arbiter in the region."[30] Just as in the industrialized countries, Third World militaries experience interservice rivalries that may lead to the acquisition of more weapons than are required to meet internal and external security needs.

The fragility of Third World political systems and the concentration of political and economic power in the hands of relatively few individuals have frequently created situations in which governments have had to rely on the armed forces to remain in power. One means of gaining or rewarding this support has been by purchasing weapons and keeping the troops, particularly the officer corps, well paid. The imposition of nonrepresentative forms of government often requires the use of force, although the kinds of weapons most useful for repression tend to be of the small, less expensive variety. Thus, the resolution of external conflicts will almost certainly not, in and of itself, lead to lower expenditure in the security sector. Both external and internal conflicts must be resolved if lasting cuts in security expenditure are to occur.

The resolution of domestic conflicts is, however, an extremely sensitive issue. No government welcomes what it would define as interference in its internal affairs or challenges to its sovereignty. Nonetheless, internal conflicts must be resolved peacefully if the basis is to be laid for significant political and economic development. In the past, ethnic, religious, and racial differences have defined "in" and "out" groups in Third World societies.

Although it is difficult to determine whether conflicts based on cultural difference are increasing in the 1990s, there is no evidence that they are abating.

As long as domestic conflicts remain unresolved, the security forces will continue to be able to justify their involvement in the political life of Third World countries. What is more, these conflicts and the continual intervention of the security forces in politics undermine the stability and legitimacy of governments and make political development that much more difficult to achieve.

In elite-dominated political systems, the general public tends to have little or no opportunity to influence the policy-making process or participate in the economic system. These domestic inequalities, along with an international economic system not designed to operate in the interests of Third World countries, are at the root of underdevelopment.

It was argued at the end of the 1970s that "there is now agreement across a wide political spectrum that the central development problems for most LDCs (less developed countries) are internal . . . that the real solution of the development problem lies in the capacity of each of the developing countries to mobilize its resources and energies."[31] A decade later, the central role of domestic priorities and capabilities is perhaps clearer than ever, but the experience of most Third World countries over the last thirty years strongly suggests that the domination of the economic and political systems by a small proportion of the population is not the best way to mobilize "resources and energies" for development. Rather, it has proved to be an open invitation for the few—distinguished by characteristics such as class, ethnicity, religion, and occupation—to exploit the many. In Latin America, this process has been in evidence for over 160 years.

The inability or unwillingness of many governments to deal with the primary causes of underdevelopment has led them to arm themselves against their own people, as well as against potential external enemies. By relying on the armed forces to remain in power or by producing political and economic conditions that provide the military with the justification for intervention, many governments have facilitated the entry of the armed forces into the political arena.

If political development that meets the needs of all social groups is to take place, there must be, among other things, a relatively equitable distribution of resources and a political system that both allows all groups to articulate their demands and is capable of producing workable compromises between competing interests. The greater the political power of the armed forces, the less likely it is that these requirements will be met. Most Third World security forces have not supported the growth of participatory forms of government or the implementation of development strategies designed to promote the well-being of the poorer segments of the population. Rather, they have become important both as mediators between different elite groups and as guarantors of elite-dominated political and economic systems. By helping to maintain a system in which the state is seen as a source of wealth to be tapped by a privileged minority of the population, the security forces seriously complicate the task of implementing structural changes necessary for the attainment of self-sustaining growth and the improvement of the lives of the poorest groups in society.

This is not, however, the only way in which politically active military institutions can hinder development and create instability. Although military governments frequently raise security expenditure on taking power, they are often unable to sustain these higher levels for more than a year or two. For the Third World as a whole, there is no clearly identifiable tendency on the part of military governments to spend more in the security sector than civilian governments. What may occur, however, and certainly has occurred in individual cases, is that a politically active military may drive up the level of security expenditure in civilian regimes as the civilians attempt to guarantee the loyalty of the security forces, or portions of it, by increasing security-related outlays. Similarly, the greater the political strength of the armed forces, the more likely the government would be to act on military requests for the establishment or expansion of a domestic arms-production capability and for the procurement of military equipment from abroad. It may also be that governments dominated by the armed forces will engage in conflict against external or domestic opponents more readily than those dominated by civilians. All this means that the negative effects of security expenditure would be felt.

It is incumbent on governments and intergovernmental organizations to take a hard look at their priorities and devise policies that will promote reduced tensions and increased development at all levels. This will require compromises to be struck, both domestically and among states. Industrialized-country governments must begin to reassess their security needs and the kinds of weapons and defense systems needed to meet these needs. As long as these governments continue to define their defense requirements as they have in the past, it will be difficult if not actually impossible to obtain a reevaluation on the part of Third World governments and the reversal of local arms races. Many Third World governments feel strongly that it is impossible to apply one set of politico-military doctrines to the Third World and another to the industrialized world. They argue that if industrialized countries require certain categories of weapons (for example, ballistic missiles) to ensure their defense, the same weapons should be at the disposal of Third World governments.[32]

More use must be made of international and regional organizations, such as the United Nations, the Organization of American States, Association of South East Asian Nations, and the Organization of African Unity, in examining areas of conflict and finding solutions that protect the vital interests of concerned parties and at the same time promote stability and development. The unprecedentedly strong and unified response on the part of the United Nations in defense of Kuwaiti sovereignty in the autumn of 1990 clearly moderated the response of the U.S. government to the Iraqi invasion and may provide a model for collective international action in the future. If it ultimately proves necessary to use force to resolve the Gulf crisis, it is infinitely preferable for it to be employed in the name of and under the direction of the United Nations than under a single country or even a group of countries led by the most powerful among them. The choices that governments will have to make are difficult ones, but if they are not made, the outlook for many people in the Third World—indeed, throughout the world—in the 1990s and beyond is dim.

The 1990s bring many opportunities. The size of the military forces of NATO countries and members of the Warsaw Pact are almost certainly going to decline during the decade, perhaps substantially. The interventionary capacity of these forces will decrease accordingly, and the political desire to intervene on the part of the major powers, the U.S. intervention in Panama in December 1989 and the situation in the Gulf notwithstanding, is also declining. To the extent possible, it is incumbent upon the governments of the major industrialized powers, particularly the United States and the Soviet Union, to encourage the peaceful resolution of conflicts and to encourage the implementation of economic and political reforms that will give all segments of society in the Third World the opportunity to have an input into the decision-making process and benefit from economic development. But it is ultimately the people and the governments of Third World countries that must seize the opportunities presented by the changes occurring in East-West relations and create a more equitable future for themselves.

## Notes

1. This chapter draws extensively on Nicole Ball, *Security and Economy in the Third World* (Princeton, NJ: Princeton University Press, 1988), and, to a lesser extent, on Nicole Ball, "The Military in Politics: Who Benefits and How," *World Development* 9:6 (1981): 569–582. The views expressed in this chapter are those of the author and should not be interpreted as an expression of opinion on the part of The National Security Archive.

2. Hobart Rowen, "Conable Warns Poor Nations on Arms," *Washington Post*, September 27, 1989. See also "World Bank Lending Study," *New York Times*, November 8, 1989, which reported a speech by Conable to a meeting of the International Planned Parenthood Federation in Ottawa in which the Bank's president indicated that the World Bank would examine its lending policies to countries such as Ethiopia, Somalia, and the Sudan, which devote upwards of 50 percent of the national budgets to the security sector.

3. The ACDA figures by and large omit expenditure on police and paramilitary forces, while SIPRI makes an effort to include them. In the early and mid-1980s, the Third World accounted for 20 percent or more of global military outlays. Although it is not advisable to mix sources since definitions of military expenditure vary, as the issue of expenditure on police and paramilitary forces indicates, there are no ACDA figures available for the 1950s and SIPRI data for the late 1980s are incomplete. For ACDA data, see the *World Military Expenditure and Arms Transfer (WMEAT)* series. For SIPRI data, see the *World Armaments and Disarmament*

yearbook series. For the definitions of military expenditure employed by the International Monetary Fund, ACDA, and SIPRI, see Ball, *Security and Economy,* Appendix 2, pp. 403–404.

A relatively few countries have accounted for a large share of Third World military expenditure. Until quite recently, China was consistently responsible for between one-quarter and one-half of all Third World military expenditure. After 1975 or so, the Middle East contributed another one-third, while East Asian countries have been responsible for another 10 to 15 percent during the 1980s. Within these regions, a number of countries can be singled out as major spenders, for example, North and South Korea in East Asia.

4. If, however, there were substantial reductions in arms transfers and military assistance to Third World governments from the major suppliers, it would become more difficult for Third World governments to pursue these conflicts.

5. ACDA, *World Military Expenditures and Arms Transfers,* 1988, Publication 131 (Washington, DC: U.S. Government Printing Office, June 1989), Table 1.

6. Franklin B. Weinstein, "The Meaning of National Security in Southeast Asia", *The Bulletin of the Atomic Scientists* (November 1978): 23. See also Harold W. Maynard, "Views of the Indonesian and Philippine Military Elites," pp. 148–150, in *The Military and Security in the Third World: Domestic and International Impacts,* ed. Sheldon W. Simon, (Boulder, CO: Westview Press, 1978). The internal and external components of security threats faced by fourteen major Third World countries are discussed in Edward A. Kolodziej and Robert E. Harkavy, eds., *Security Policies of Developing Countries* (Lexington, MA: Lexington Books, 1982).

7. See the interview with Malaysian Prime Minister Mahathir on Southeast Asian security issues in Keith B. Richburg, "Malaysian Premier Backs U.S. Bases in Philippines," *Washington Post,* August 13, 1989, p. A24.

8. "Internal security" is something of a misnomer since the objective is rarely to make all citizens equally secure. Rather, the point is frequently to enable the ruling elite—whether civilian, military or, most likely, some combination—to remain in power and to sustain a socioeconomic system under which the elite enriches itself at the expense of the vast majority of the population. In these cases it is more accurate to speak of "regime security" or "elite security." See the discussion in the section entitled, "The Military in Politics," pp. 208–213.

9. For further reading on the doctrine of national security in its various forms, see Alfred Stepan, *The Military in Politics: Changing Patterns in Brazil* (Princeton, NJ: Princeton University Press, 1971), pp. 172–183; Alfred Stepan, "The New Professionalism of Internal Warfare and Military Role Expansion," pp. 47–53 in *Authoritarian Brazil,* ed. Alfred Stepan, (New Haven: Yale University Press, 1973); Moshe Lissak, "Military Roles in Modernization: Thailand and Burma," pp. 455–462, in *The Political Influence of the Military: A Comparative Reader,* eds. Amos Perlmutter and Valerie Plave Bennett, (New Haven and London: Yale University Press, 1980); and Harold Crouch, "Generals and Business in Indonesia," *Pacific Affairs* 48 (Winter 1975–1976):519–520.

10. See Barry Ames and Ed Goff, "Education and Defense Expenditures in Latin America: 1948–1958," pp. 181–184, in *Comparative Public Policy: Issues, Theories and Methods,* eds. Craig Liske, William Loehr, and John McCamant, (New York: Halstead Press/John Wiley, 1975); and Philippe C. Schmitter, "Foreign Military Assistance, National Military Spending and Military Rule in Latin America," pp. 159–163, in *Military Rule in Latin America: Function, Consequences and Perspectives,* ed. Philippe C. Schmitter, Vol. III, Sage Research Progress Series on War, Revolution and Peacekeeping (Beverly Hills, CA: Sage, 1983).

11. Mark Webster, "Liberia Pays the Price for Change," *Financial Times,* May 30, 1980; "Les nouveaux dirigeants n'ont pas réussi a emporter l'adhésion de la population" *Le Monde,* September 4, 1980; and U.S. Arms Control and Disarmament Agency, *World Military Expenditures and Arms Transfers, 1985,* Publication 123, (Washington, DC: U.S. Government Printing Office, August 1985), p. 71.

12. See, for example, Ansil Ramsay, "Thailand 1978: Kriangsak—The Thai Who Binds," *Asian Survey* 19 (February 1979): 105–106; Henry Bienen and David Morell, "Transition from Military Rule: Thailand's Experience," in *Political-Military Systems: Comparative Perspectives,* ed. Catherine M. Kelleher, (Beverly Hills, CA: Sage, 1978); J. Stephen Hoadley, "Thailand: Kings, Coups and Cliques," pp. 9–24, in *The Military in the Politics of Southeast Asia: A Comparative Perspective,* ed. J. Stephen Hoadley, (Cambridge, MA: Schenkman, 1985); Crouch, "Generals and Business"; and David Jenkins, "The Military in Business," *Far Eastern Economic Review* 99 (January 13, 1978):24.

13. A survey of seventeen coups d'états in fifteen Latin American countries between 1950 and 1980 by this author suggested that security spending is more likely to increase than to decrease immediately following a coup, but the initial rise will not necessarily be translated into a permanent increase or upward trend. See the data provided in Nicole Ball, *Third-World Security Expenditure: A Statistical Compendium*, C-10250-M5, (Stockholm: National Defence Research Institute, 1984), pp. 181–248.

14. The Indian government for many years had supplied Tamil rebels with weapons to use in their fight against the Sri Lankan government. In July 1987, Rajiv Gandhi's government sent some 45,000 troops to Sri Lanka to attempt to disarm the Tamil separatists after having forced the government in Colombo to sign an agreement "requesting" this intervention. Cuba's extra-territorial involvements are, of necessity, financed by the Soviet Union, but Cuban officials insist that they in no way contradict Cuban foreign policy goals. The Pakistanis are primarily interested in earning foreign exchange and Pakistani forces have been involved in the Middle East and Libya.

For a survey of postwar intervention, see Milton Leitenberg, "The Impact of the World-wide Confrontation of the Great Powers: Aspects of Military Intervention and the Projection of Military Power," in *Armaments-Development-Human Rights-Disarmament*, ed. G. Fischer, (Brussels: Etablissement Bruylant, 1985).

15. There are numerous accounts of the conflicts in Indochina. A useful source is Richard Dean Burns and Milton Leitenberg, *The Wars in Vietnam, Cambodia and Laos, 1945–1982: A Bibliographic Guide*, War/Peace Bibliography Series #18 (Santa Barbara, CA: ABC-Clio, 1984), which lists over 6,000 works. This brief rendition has drawn upon George McTurnan Kahin and John W. Lewis, *The United States in Vietnam: An Analysis in Depth of the History of America's Involvement in Vietnam*, revised edition (New York: Dell, 1969); The Committee of Concerned Asian Scholars, *The Indochina Story* (New York: Pantheon, 1970); and William Shawcross, *Sideshow: Kissinger, Nixon and the Destruction of Cambodia* (New York: Pocket Books, 1979).

16. See, for example, Guy Pauker, "Southeast Asia as a Problem Area in the Next Decade," *World Politics* 11 (April 1959): 325–345.

17. By the late 1970s, the Soviet government began once again to stress the need to establish vanguard parties. Charles C. Petersen, *Third World Military Elites in Soviet Perspective*, Professional Paper 262 (Alexandria, VA: Center for Naval Analyses, November 1979). See especially pp. 10, 20, 33. See also Francis Fukuyama, "Gorbachev and the Third World," *Foreign Affairs* 64 (Spring 1986):715–731.

18. See, for example, Ann Ruth Willner, "The Underdeveloped Study of Political Development," *World Politics* 16 (April 1964), and Morris Janowitz, *The Military in the Political Development of New Nations* (Chicago and London: Phoenix Books, 1964). Another useful article is Ann Ruth Willner, "Perspectives on Military Elites as Rulers and Wielders of Power," *Journal of Comparative Administration* 2 (November 1970):261–276.

19. See Jong-chun Baek, "The Role of the Republic of Korea Armed Forces in National Development: Past and Future," *The Journal of East Asian Affairs* 3:2 (Fall/Winter 1983), and Do Young Chang, "The Republic of Korea Army and Its Role in National Development" (Paper prepared for the Biennial International Conference of the Inter-University Seminar on Armed Forces and Society, Chicago, October 18–20, 1985, mimeograph), p. 9.

20. See Cynthia McClintock, "Velasco, Officers, and Citizens: The Politics of Stealth," pp. 275–208, and Luis Pasara, "When the Military Dreams," pp. 309–343, in *The Peruvian Experiment Reconsidered*, ed. Cynthia McClintock and Abraham F. Lowenthal (Princeton, NJ: Princeton University Press, 1983).

21. David A. Wilson, "The Military in Thai Politics," pp. 253–254 in *The Role of the Military in Underdeveloped Countries*, ed. John J. Johnson (Princeton, NJ: Princeton University Press, 1962); David Elliott, *Thailand: Origins of Military Rule* (London: Zed Press, 1978); and Hoadley, "Thailand: Kings, Coups and Cliques." An interesting exposition of this point as it relates to Ghana is found in Eboe Hutchful, "A Tale of Two Regimes: Imperialism, the Military and Class in Ghana," *Review of African Political Economy*, no. 14 (January–April 1979):36–55.

22. Thomas E. Skidmore, *The Politics of Military Rule in Brazil, 1964–85* (New York and Oxford: Oxford University Press, 1988). Thailand offers another excellent example of the importance of coalition (clique) building. See Hoadley, "Thailand: Kings, Coups and Cliques."

23. For a recent article on the situation in El Salvador as it pertains to this issue, see Joel Millman, "El Salvador's Army: A Force Unto Itself," *New York Times Magazine*, December 10, 1989, pp. 46–47, 95, 97.

24. Disaggregated security expenditure is difficult to come by. Most sources that regularly report Third World security expenditure provide only one aggregated figure. Some data are available in Ball, *Security and Economy*, Appendix 2, pp. 396–402, and in Ball, *Third-World Security Expenditure*. For information not included in either of these publications, researchers are advised to consult national budget documents available at the Joint World Bank-International Monetary Fund Library in Washington, DC, and produce their own breakdown of expenditure.

25. See Michael Brzoska and Thomas Ohlson, eds., *Arms Production in the Third World* (London and Philadelphia: Taylor & Francis, for SIPRI, 1986), esp. pp. 281–282; and Ball, *Security and Economy*, pp. 335–385.

26. See Ann Tibbitts Schulz, *Buying Security, Iran Under the Monarchy* (Boulder, CO: Westview Press, 1989), pp. 101–115. The Military Industries Organization was the largest single purchaser of machine tools in Iran; three-quarters of the metallurgical and metal-working machinery sold in Iran during the 1970s was imported. Military demand for plastics had to be met by imports as well because the domestic plastic industry manufactured primarily consumer goods.

27. Carlos Portales and Augusto Varas, "The Role of Military Expenditure in the Development Process. Chile 1952–1983 and 1983–1980: Two Contrasting Cases," *Ibero Americana* 12:1–2 (1983): pp. 48–49.

28. See, for example, David Jenkins, "The Military's Secret Cache," *Far Eastern Economic Review* 107 (February 8, 1980): 70–72; Jenkins, "The Military in Business"; Crouch, "Generals and Business"; and Alexis Rieffel and Aninda S. Wirjasuputra, "Military Enterprises," *Bulletin of Indonesian Economic Studies* (July 1972): 106.

29. Arms transfers, which had declined or stagnated in most regions of the Third World (with the exception of South Asia) since the mid-1980s, increased in 1987 in Third World regions, particularly the Middle East and Latin America. See U.S. Arms Control and Disarmament Agency, *WMEAT, 1988*.

30. See J.M. Ostheimer and G.J. Buckley, "Nigeria," p. 290, and Ann T. Schultz, "Iran," p. 253, both in Kolodziej and Harkavy, eds., *Security Policies of Developing Countries*.

31. Geoffrey Barraclough, "The Struggle for the Third World," *New York Review of Books*, November 9, 1979, p. 53.

32. See, for example, "Report on Working Group 5: The Arms Trade and Regional Conflict," *Pugwash Newsletter* 27:2 (October 1989):89–90.

# 10 / Ethnic and Nationalist Conflicts

DONALD L. HOROWITZ

From Montreal to Mombasa, from the Karen areas of Burma to the Basque country of Spain, a new wave of ethnic sentiment seems to have been sweeping across the continents in the last twenty-five years. Very few countries in the world are inhabited by a single ethnic group. Many are severely divided among groups that differ from each other in language, religion, color or appearance, regional affiliation, or some other attribute of origin. Such groups have been advancing political claims that have brought them into conflict with neighboring ethnic groups.

These conflicts are frequently accompanied by human rights abuses, often of a particularly brutal sort. They also have the potential for escalating into warfare that can produce famine and other forms of suffering, as well as major negative effects on development (destroyed infrastructure, diversion of governmental resources, and the like). If warfare does break out, that is typically because one or both sides of the conflict have attracted international support, but the international consequences do not necessarily end there. What begins as an internal conflict can become a very dangerous international one.

## ETHNICITY: UBIQUITOUS, OFTEN DANGEROUS

The most severe manifestation of ethnic conflict has, of course, been violence: from riots to terrorism to wars of secession to international warfare. There are, however, many other examples of the pervasive force of ethnicity in daily political life in all regions of the world.

To gauge the formidable ability of ethnic affiliations to permeate public life, consider a few illustrations, drawing from many countries and many spheres of social and political activity.

The census, thought in stable, more or less homogeneous countries to be a dreary demographic exercise, is a bone of contention in many others. In Iraq, Nigeria, Lebanon, Kenya, and Pakistan, among others, the census has long been a delicate political issue, because the apportionment of legislative seats, revenue, and other public goods among various ethnic groups depends on what the census results show. Sometimes no census at all can be conducted for this reason. Lebanon has had no census since 1932. Sometimes the wording of the census questions is disputed. Very often the results are contested, especially if they show, as they did in Kenya in 1981, that the population of one ethnic group has increased dramatically, to the apparent disadvantage of others.

Occasionally, the census triggers warfare. In Assam, a state in northeast India, census results showing small changes in the proportion of Bengalis to Assamese in the 1970s paved the way for a violent reaction to an increase in Bengali names on electoral rolls later in the decade. Thousands died as a result. The census can become a life-or-death matter in an ethnically divided society.

The question of indigenousness is often a delicate one as well, and immigrant status can continue for generations. In France and Britain, North Africans and Asians, respectively, are referred to as "immigrants," even if they and their parents were born in the country. In Sri Lanka, Sinhalese are inclined to think that they are entitled to priority in the country, over Sri Lankan Tamils. Malays are called *Bumiputera,* a term meaning "sons of the soil."

Policy follows such conceptions. Indonesia and Kenya have adopted plans to promote indigenous ownership of businesses controlled by immigrant groups. Britain has tightened its immigration laws, Switzerland has held a referendum on foreign workers, and Uganda has expelled nearly all of its Asian population. Like a number of other countries, Malaysia has adopted far-reaching programs to redress economic imbalances between ethnic groups, defined in terms of indigenous Malays and immigrant Chinese and Indians. Targets for share ownership, employment, and education have been set up and enforced.[1]

In many countries, an array of organizations having no formal connection to ethnicity are in fact monoethnic. This applies to clubs, sports teams, cooperative societies, chambers of commerce, trade unions, political parties, and even revolutionary insurgencies. In Northern Ireland, people speak, only half in jest, of Catholic beers and Protestant beers, which are drunk in Catholic pubs and Protestant pubs. In Fiji, there are two teachers' unions, one Fijian and one Indian. In Angola, the government has been dominated by one ethnic group; the guerrillas fighting it, by another. This is the common pattern in such warfare all over Asia and Africa.

Political parties based essentially on ethnic groups may seem strange phenomena to those accustomed to the broadly aggregative parties of Great Britain and the United States. Nevertheless, this is a very common propensity in divided societies, because the parties, reflecting what are seen to be incompatible group claims, can bridge the gap created by those claims. Ethnically based parties are, however, very dangerous to political stability, because they open the possibility that a party representing only one group can gain power and exclude from power or influence any group that supports a different party. Where this happens, it tends to pave the way for violence. Some military coups have reflected the grievances of those ethnic groups that are better represented in the army than in the civilian government. Where groups are territorially separate, exclusion from power may stimulate the growth of secessionist movements. In country after country, wherever one group gains control of the apparatus of the state, the legitimacy of government is contested.

In divided societies around the world, regional and ethnic disparities in wealth and in the distribution of government resources have become major political issues. But ethnic conflict does not merely involve disputes over material goods. Disputes over seemingly symbolic issues, such as recognition of one or another language as the official language or one design or another in a national flag, are, if anything, more severe.

There is, in ethnic conflict, an irreducible element of intergroup competition for an official declaration of relative group worth, and there is also an inescapable dimension of intergroup antipathy. Rationalist and materialist explanations for ethnic conflict have had great difficulty coming to grips with the struggle of ethnic groups for symbols that acknowledge group prestige and group legitimacy.

The element of antipathy is well illustrated by ethnic riots, in which members of one group set out to kill members of another. There have been hundreds of such riots in the last decade alone, ranging from the Azeri killings of Armenians in the Soviet Union in 1989 to the Sinhalese killings of Tamils in Sri Lanka in 1983 to the Krahn killings of Mano and Gio in Liberia in 1990. In such riots, hundreds, sometimes thousands, of victims die. The manner in which they are killed typically involves burning, hacking, or spearing, rather than shooting. Atrocities and mutilations are common. But such an episode does not involve random violence. Rather, victims are carefully chosen by ethnic affiliation, and the victimized group is generally one against which there is considerable animosity.

Given the widespread character of ethnic conflict, efforts to reduce it are common. (However, since many governments are dominated by some groups, at the expense of others, the policies of a good many governments exacerbate rather than mitigate ethnic tensions.) Belgium and Spain have adopted regional autonomy plans to counter conflict and secessionist sentiment. In Canada, there has been a proposal for the Canadian constitution to recognize Quebec as "a distinct society," with certain special powers lodged in the provincial governments. Czechoslovakia has long been a binational state, joining Czechs and Slovaks, but that has not prevented a recent upsurge of Slovak separatism. A regional autonomy plan in the Sudan was essentially repealed in 1983. This repeal resulted in a new and deadly round of armed insurrection—the latest of several, beginning in 1955. Burma, a mostly heterogeneous state that could certainly benefit from regional autonomy, has had no such program. Instead, the central government has been at war with ethnic groups, such as the Karen, steadily since independence in 1948.

Although different political systems handle ethnic problems differently—or not all—the existence of the problems is not confined to any region or any system, democratic or undemocratic.[2] Western Europe and North America, sometimes thought to have "outgrown" ethnic differences, are, like Asian and African states, experiencing a revival of ethnic consciousness. Latin America, with more muted ethnic problems, nevertheless has produced a number of militant Indian movements and experienced some racial tensions in countries, such as Brazil, that formerly had economies based on slavery. Eastern Europe has long been an area of ethnic tension and continues to be today. The movement toward democracy has created numerous opportunities for the expression of ethnic aspirations and antipathies. In Rumania, there has been violence in the Transylvanian region, inhabited by many Hungarians. Bulgaria has expelled thousands of Turks. The Soviet Union has had to contend with separatist movements, not only in the Baltic states, but also in Georgia, the Ukraine, and potentially in the Central Asian republics.[3] Yugoslavia has experienced serious conflict between Serbs and Albanians in Kosovo, and more prosperous Yugoslav republics, such as Slovenia and Croatia, have strong separatist tendencies. The next decades will see continued ethnic strife.

## THE ROOTS OF ETHNIC CONFLICT

To say that ethnic conflict is ubiquitous is not to explain its sources. What are the roots of ethnic conflict? And why does it seem to ebb and flow?

In accounting for the origins of ethnic sentiment, it is important to recognize its dual character. Ethnicity has meant conflict and violence, but it has also meant kinship and community. Without ethnic nationalism, after all, most of the modern states of Western Europe would not have come into being. The depth of ethnic loyalties suggests that they respond to some rather basic needs. In times of rapid change, ethnic ties can provide a basis for interpersonal trust and affection when people move from the families that customarily meet these needs. When political systems seem new, alien, or remote, ethnic affinities between leaders and those led can provide assurance that the interests of group members are being protected, attaching people to political institutions that would otherwise have dubious legitimacy.

No doubt, in a great many countries, these functions have been not only performed but overperformed. Some groups have been given so much security as to make others restless. Ethnic allocations that convince one group of a regime's benign intentions have served to persuade others of its unfairness. Nevertheless, it is necessary to bear in mind the functions ethnic ties serve, as well as the dangers they pose. Keeping ethnicity within manageable bounds may be a desirable goal; suppressing ethnic ties altogether may not.

In seeking the explanation for a phenomenon as intense and widespread as ethnic conflict is in the world today, it is natural to suppose that many forces, at many different levels, have contributed to its growth. This, indeed, turns out to be true.

At the broadest level, international currents provide an environment that is or is not favorable to the advancement of ethnic claims. Ethnic tensions tend to be submerged in times of world war, only to reemerge afterward. When states are at war, domestic differences tend to be suppressed for the sake of the greater effort. There are exceptions, of course. Ethnic tensions grew in Yugoslavia and in Burma during World War II, as armed groups fought each other. But, by and large, the periods after the First and Second World Wars were times for the revival of ethnic sentiment. The policy of President Woodrow Wilson, after World War I, favoring the "self-determination of nations," added to the postwar ethnic upsurge, and not just in Europe. Among others, the Kurdish movement in Iraq can be traced to this period. Following World War II, the Cold War impeded for a time the emergence of ethnic tensions in Eastern and Western Europe. But as the sense of immediate external danger abated, ethnic demands were increasingly heard.

Something comparable occurred in the new states of Asia and Africa. The nationalist movements that sought independence from the colonial powers from the 1940s onward were not always wholly representative of all the ethnic groups in their territories. Some groups that were not so well represented attempted to slow down the pace of the march toward independence. But, overall, until the anticolonial movements attained independence, ethnic differences tended to be muted.

Following independence, however, the context and the issues changed. No longer was the struggle against external powers paramount; no longer was colonial domination the issue. With independence secured, the question was who within the new state would control it.

As this issue began to emerge, the independence of Asia and Africa was being felt in Europe and America. The grant of independence to the former Belgian territories in Africa (Zaire, Rwanda, and Burundi) helped stimulate the ethnic movement among Flemings in Belgium itself. If, they said, tiny Burundi can have an autonomous political life, why should we be deprived of the same privilege? The emancipation of Africa, of course, had an impact on Afro-Americans, and it probably made the system of racial segregation seem anomalous to many other Americans. In Canada, some French-speaking Quebeckers also cited African independence as a precedent for their own.

International conditions and foreign examples create a setting that makes ethnic demands seem timely and realistic, but such influences cannot create a conflict where one does not exist. The existence of ethnic conflict depends instead on a tangled skein of objective and subjective conditions—the relative position of groups and how they feel about that position.

Broadly speaking, two types of ethnic relationship can be distinguished. In the first, there is fairly complete subordination of one group by another. In the second, there may be inequalities of wealth, status, and prestige, but not complete subordination.

On a global scale, ethnic subordination is clearly in decline. The spread of egalitarian values has helped undermine caste untouchability in India and apartheid in South Africa, just as it undermined racial segregation in the United States South.[4] The two movements that qualify as genuine revolutions in postcolonial Africa—in Rwanda and Zanzibar—were both violent reactions to ethnic subordination. Where subordination continues, there are further struggles ahead. But there is a widely shared feeling that subordination based on ethnic criteria is illegitimate. This illegitimacy accounts for the strength of the movements against subordination.

Ethnic conflict does not, however, always derive from clear-cut superior-subordinate relations. On a world scale, conflicts between ethnic groups, neither of which has been subordinated, are far more common and likely to prove enduring than those that derive from a desire to escape the stigma and deprivation of inferior status. Here nationalist aspirations and uncertainty about relative group position, where two or more groups are located in a single state, spur antagonism. In such conflicts, it is often difficult to tell who has the advantage. Is it the educated Ibo or the more populous Hausa? The politically influential Malays or the economically well-off Chinese? The Basques who are powerful in commerce or the Castilians who control the state bureaucracy?

Not only is it difficult in such cases to make judgments about the justice of group claims, but it is also sometimes difficult to sort out the exact claims being made. Still, there are some patterns.

Consider, for example, the role of immigration. As indicated earlier, in many countries, groups that claim to be indigenous have asserted their entitlement to priority over immigrants. (Never mind that most such "indigenous" groups were preceded by others, now usually identified as "aboriginal.") What is sometimes not immediately clear is that the "immigrants" may have come many centuries ago. The Turks have been on Cyprus since about 1571, but the Greeks have been there longer. The Scots and English who migrated to Northern Ireland and now form the nucleus of the Protestant population there arrived in the seventeenth century. The Ceylon Tamils came to Sri Lanka from India on the average perhaps a thousand years ago. In each case, there are lingering notions of priority based on earlier occupation.

Geography, as well as history, figures in ethnic psychology. Groups that have a strong position in domestic politics sometimes act the part of the weak and oppressed, often because they are looking beyond their borders to the ethnic balance of power in their region. Southern Sudanese do not wish to be merged into the Arab world. Some Quebecois fear being swamped in an Anglophone North America, just as Ulster Protestants entertain comparable fears about the Catholics in the Irish Republic. The Sinhalese of Sri Lanka look apprehensively at the large Tamil population in South India, and the Maronites of Lebanon are uneasy about the large Muslim majorities in neighboring countries. The potential intrusion of international forces complicates domestic ethnic politics.[5]

Some ethnic conflicts are contemporary manifestations of ancient problems that were never resolved. Others stem from entirely new contacts between groups that had no prior experience with each other. This is particularly true in the new states, where independence has often brought peoples into competitive contact. It is also true in Northern Europe, where Turks, Italians, and Yugoslavs have come to work in recent decades. Still other conflicts result, paradoxically, from the reaction of ethnic groups to their previously successful assimilation in the majority culture. A number of powerful separatist movements—those of the Basques and the Kurds, for example—were begun by professionals or intellectuals who had either lost the use of their mother tongue or become deeply concerned about the group's general loss of cultural distinctiveness.[6]

A common source of conflict is the competition of educated elites for secure, rewarding jobs in the state bureaucracy. Many disputes over language policy are related to this competition. If one language is given official status, then bureaucrats will have to be proficient in it. This puts speakers of the nonofficial language at a disadvantage.

Yet disputes over official languages and religions also involve people with no conceivable interest in civil service jobs. They seem to be emotionally committed, because the status of a language denotes the status of the group that speaks it. One of the objects of ethnic conflict seems to be official confirmation of group status. In the modern world, where nearly everything is politicized, the state's stamp of approval has both monetary and psychological value.

## THE INTERNATIONAL SECURITY IMPLICATIONS OF ETHNIC CONFLICT

The present resurgence of ethnicity has not yet run its course. The claims of some groups continue to provide an example for others. A Canadian commission appointed in the 1960s to study bilingualism and biculturalism (French and English) ended by endorsing bilingualism and *multiculturalism*. It was not possible to recognize only two cultures. In Spain, other groups have followed the lead of the Basques and Catalans in demanding autonomy. Spanish-speaking Americans, American Indians, and a variety of Americans of Central European origin have emulated Afro-Americans in organizing to improve their lot. The same has been true virtually everywhere. Ethiopia, which for years contended only with a secessionist movement in Eritrea—indeed, a movement supported by only one part of the Eritrean population—ended up fighting several ethnic civil wars simultaneously.

Whether the worldwide upsurge in ethnic conflict will produce a healthy period of modest self-assertion and adjustment of group interests or dangerous instability and upheaval depends on both international and domestic forces. Their interplay is a complex matter.

The most common threats to state borders are secessionist movements and irredentist movements (to annex territory populated by ethnic kin). Although irredentism has been a recurrent fear of those concerned with international stability, the fear is misplaced. Irredentism has not been a serious threat in most areas so far and probably will not become one, because most states that are potential annexationists are themselves multi-ethnic. Embarking upon such international adventures jeopardizes ethnic balances at home.[7] There are prominent exceptions—such as Somalia, which has a longstanding claim on parts of Ethiopia inhabited by Somalis—but the exceptions are few. Moreover, given a choice between annexing one's region to an adjoining state or seceding to create an independent state out of such a region, most politicians would prefer to control an independent state.[8]

Secession is therefore a wholly different matter. There are dozens of secessionist movements around the world, and there will surely be more. Secessionist movements arise because of domestic grievances, but they cannot succeed without international help. So far, with the exception of Bangladesh, sufficient help has not been forthcoming. But, in some regions, restraints on international involvement in ethnic disputes may be declining. If states feel freer than they have felt to support the claims of ethnic groups across borders, the present period of extraordinary boundary stability may be coming to an end.

The motives that induce foreign states to provide aid to secessionists are various. They begin with the global interests of major powers. The United States and the Soviet Union were on the side of the central government in the war of the attempted Biafran secession, but France supported the Ibo secessionists. The United States and China were allied with Pakistan at the time of the Bangladesh secession, but the USSR was aligned with India, which supported the Bengali secessionists.

If global power balances can play a role, it stands to reason that regional and local balances can play an even bigger role. This is assuredly the case, as the support of Ethiopia and the Sudan for secessionists in each other's territory attests. Beyond this, a desire for a specific quid pro quo motivates many assisting states. Iran supported a Kurdish separatist insurgency in Iraq in order to secure Iraqi concessions about a disputed waterway. Malaysia was hospitable to Moro secessionists in the Philippines in order to induce the Philippine government to abandon its territorial claim on the Malaysian state of Sabah. Support for armed separatists seems an inexpensive way to pursue the interests of a state.

To such national interests must be added the powerful force of ethnic affinity. Arab states have supported kindred Muslim separatists in Eritrea. The Ugandan regime of Idi Amin aided southern Sudanese in the early 1970s; the southerners were related to a number of ethnic groups in the north of Uganda. Where transborder ethnic affinities exist, there is considerable potential for separatism to flourish. Even if the neighboring state is wary of supplying the insurgents, it may find itself embarrassed in domestic politics if it attempts to deny them sanctuary.

Nevertheless, there are some important limits to the external assistance most secessionists can expect to receive. The international interests of neighboring states, even those that foment or assist the secession, can prove to be surprisingly ephemeral. If the central government of the threatened state is prepared to offer a quid pro quo to the state assisting the separatists, the assistance may end precipitously. This is what the Kurds in Iraq discovered when Iraq offered to settle its waterway dispute with Iran in 1975. The Kurdish insurgency simply collapsed.

Moreover, the central government of a state threatened with separatist warfare has other weapons. If the state assisting the secessionists has other enemies, they may come to the aid of the threatened state. If the state assisting the secessionists has potential separatists of its own, the threatened state may assist them in turn, until some modus vivendi is worked out. Separatist warfare typically takes a long time to achieve results. During that time, there are many ways in which assisting states can be induced to forbear giving further assistance. Many states will meddle for a while in a secessionist insurgency. Few will stay with assistance to a successful conclusion. That is an important reason why most separatists fail to achieve independence.

In fact, many states can be deterred from assisting separatists in neighboring countries in the first place. With its large, discontented Kurdish minority, Turkey has refrained from aiding Kurdish separatism even in states with which it did not have particularly good relations. Changing patterns of alliance and interest, the consummation of an agreement on an unrelated matter, and the fear of either retaliation or demonstration effects at home are all forces that point to restraint.

On the other hand, the conjunction of ethnic affinity and strong regional rivalry can produce a dangerous propensity to intervention. It is notable that the one successful case of secession in the postwar world is Bangladesh.[9] Seceding from Pakistan, Bangladesh obtained its independence through the intervention of the Indian army. That intervention had triple roots. First of all, for India, it accomplished cleanly and quickly what two previous wars with Pakistan had not accomplished: a change in the balance of power between regional rivals. Second, it responded to the aspirations of the well-situated Bengalis in India to aid their cousins across the border. Third, by quickly establishing an independent Bangladesh, the intervention thwarted any possible attempt to create instead a Bengali irredenta that might join Bangladesh to India, thereby upsetting ethnic and religious balances within India—or, worse, any attempt to create a movement for an independent pan-Bengali state that would detach Bengali areas from both India and Pakistan.

There are equivalent possibilities now in Pakistan. The Pakistanis have encouraged Sikh separatism in India. Like the Sikhs, most Pakistanis speak Punjabi, and so they can claim—and perhaps feel—an affinity across the border.[10] Perhaps more dangerous are Pakistani efforts directed at the pre-dominantly Muslim state of Kashmir. Detaching Kashmir from India might also affect the Indo-Pakistani balance of power, and it would satisfy Muslim sensibilities in Pakistan as well. Cases like Kashmir may be few, but they are very dangerous. Since Kashmir borders, not merely Pakistan and India, but Pakistan's ally, China, there is a serious chance of escalation into international warfare.

To be sure, changing international conditions may facilitate efforts like those of the Pakistanis in Kashmir in many parts of the world. With the decline of the Cold War, the global rivalry of the major powers does not extend everywhere. For secession, this cuts both ways. Every secessionist movement does not present opportunities for gains by the Soviet Union or the United States. To that extent, external support will probably decline. On the other hand, neighboring states, unrestrained by the major powers, may become freer, for their own various motives, to assist secessionists. If that is so, there will be more opportunities for low-level warfare in support of separatist objectives.

This does not mean, however, that there will necessarily be more successful irredentas or secessions. The restraints on irredentas remain intact, and the forces that render the assistance of neighboring states liable to be terminated at any moment are also unaffected by these considerations. If anything is clear about separatism, it is that a secessionist movement cannot attain independence without a generous measure of sustained external support. That is a lesson that the Lithuanians learned rather quickly in 1989–90. Yet separatist sentiment, with its roots in all of the factors considered earlier, is unaffected by this iron law of success and failure. Consequently, there are likely to be many low-level secessionist insurgencies, some of which, like those in Burma and the Sudan, may endure for decades. They and the military campaigns mounted against them can take an enormous toll in destroying lives and the productive capacity of whole countries, as the Sudanese and Ethiopian cases, among many others, illustrate. Yet few are likely to succeed through warfare.

What is still not known, however, is how many can succeed through consent. Until now, the modern territorial state, extremely jealous of its sovereignty, has rarely been willing to permit secessionists to withdraw peacefully. One reason has been that such states almost never have just one potential secessionist movement within their borders. As a result, if they permit one region to secede, they fear the demonstration effect on other separatists, and they suspect there will be no stopping, short of disintegration of the state. In some multinational states like the Soviet Union, however, it now seems at least possible that separatist regions may be permitted to withdraw in an orderly fashion, by mutual consent. If that should happen in the USSR, the implications for the proliferation of new states around the world would be enormous. And if it should happen, then, ironically enough, ethnic separatists would have achieved by consent what few if any of them could ever have achieved by warfare.

The Soviet case underscores the direct relationship between the domestic and international sources of conflict and accommodation. Accommodation can take many forms; it certainly does not imply a willingness to permit secession. But it has taken many countries a long time to recognize the need to come to grips with ethnic demands. Suppression and artificially generated "consensus" have been—and still are—more common. Nonetheless, some countries are putting their experience to work in constructive ways. For some states, one promising course is for groups to move somewhat apart without severing ties altogether. Regional autonomy schemes may make this possible. Another serious problem is the existence of political parties organized along ethnic lines, as they are in the most deeply divided societies. As indicated earlier, ethnically based parties are usually impediments to compromise. It is possible to foster the growth of multiethnic parties in democratic ways. Usually this involves skillful constitutional engineering, with special attention to the electoral system and the apportionment of territory, particularly in federal systems.

Ethnicity, of course, poses great challenges to political creativity. The political leaders who are required to put in place the institutions of accommodation are, more often than not, subject to conflict-intensifying demands from within the groups they represent. If, despite these demands, conflict management capabilities increase within states, there will be fewer dangers of international involvement in ethnic conflict.

## Notes

1. For a recent comparative critique of such programs, see Thomas Sowell, *Preferential Policies: An International Perspective* (New York: Morrow, 1990). For the origins and effects of the Malaysian programs, see Donald L. Horowitz, "Cause and Consequence in Public Policy Theory: Ethnic Policy and System Transformation in Malaysia," *Policy Sciences,* Vol. 22, nos. 3–4 (November 1989), pp. 249–87. For some similar measures, based on indigenousness, see Myron Weiner, *Sons of the Soil: Migration and Ethnic Conflict in India* (Princeton: Princeton University Press, 1978).

2. For a sense of worldwide commonalities and variations, see Crawford Young, *The Politics of Cultural Pluralism* (Madison: University of Wisconsin Press, 1976).

3. On ethnicity in the Soviet Union, see Alexander J. Motyl, ed., *Building Bridges: Soviet Nationalities in Comparative Perspective* (New York: Columbia University Press, 1991); Alexander J. Motyl, *Will the Non-Russians Rebel?* (Ithaca: Cornell University Press, 1987); Rasma Karklins, *Ethnic Relations in the USSR* (Boston: Allen & Unwin, 1986); Geoffrey Wheeler, *Racial Problems in Soviet Muslim Asia* (London: Oxford University Press, 1962).

4. For a study of South Africa in comparative perspective, see Donald L. Horowitz, *A Democratic South Africa? Constitutional Engineering in a Divided Society* (Berkeley and Los Angeles: University of California Press, 1991).

5. See Astri Suhrke and Lela Garner Noble, eds., *Ethnic Conflict in International Relations* (New York: Praeger, 1977).

6. For the origins of separatist movements, see Donald L. Horowitz, *Ethnic Groups in Conflict* (Berkeley and Los Angeles: University of California Press, 1985), pp. 229–81.

7. For a more careful explanation of why irredentism is not a serious world problem, see ibid., pp. 281–88.

8. The logic of this calculation is more complex than I have depicted it here. I have expounded it in more detail in an essay entitled "Irredentas and Secessions: Adjacent Phenomena, Neglected Connections," in Naomi Chazan, editor, *Irredentism and International Politics* (Boulder, CO: Lynne Rienner, 1990).

9. Singapore, often cited as a case of secession, was in fact expelled from Malaysia in 1965.

10. This is an extremely ironic turn of events. In 1947, when India and Pakistan were partitioned, there were horrendous reciprocal massacres of Sikhs and Muslims. See, e.g., Penderel Moon, *Divide and Quit* (Berkeley and Los Angeles: University of California Press, 1962).

# 11 / The Terrorist Discourse: Signs, States, and Systems of Global Political Violence

JAMES DER DERIAN

From the 1978 news photograph of the kidnapped Italian Prime Minister Aldo Moro sitting under the banner of the *Brigate Rosse,* to the 1989 videomurder of Lieutenant Colonel William Higgins by the Organization of the Oppressed on Earth in Lebanon, terrorism has attracted much public attention, a great deal of media commentary, and very little critical theory. After a decade marked by a rising number of incidents, the proliferation of terrorist studies, and the escalation of rhetoric by U.S. presidents, terrorism remains as resistant to comprehension as it is to remediation.[1]

This is not for the lack of intellectual effort. To explain the terrorist predicament, a welter of articles, academic books, professional reports, and special news programs have been produced. The predominant focus of the expert field has been on the psychological and organizational side of terrorism—its often fanatical motivations, unpredictable nature, and twisted techniques—resulting in models that range from complex and insightful to the crude and IdentiKit.[2] Another group, popular in both journalistic and literary circles, has sought out—presumably for the purpose of retaliation and extirpation—the invisible hand that supplies and controls terrorism. Especially vocal are the counterterrorist conspirators, who see behind every Carlos, Agca, Abu Nidal (or the latest terrorist exemplar) the Soviet Union, Libya, Iran (or some other pariah state), acting as the central command of international terrorism.[3] Found somewhere between these camps are the liberal commentators, who study the particular features of democracies— an aversion to the use of naked force, an unrestrained media, hand-tying checks and balances—that make them appealing and vulnerable targets for terrorism. Generally more astute about the various religious, social, and economic causes of terrorism, the liberal theorists vacillate between remedies like better law enforcement and selective use of antiterrorist forces.[4]

# THE MATTER OF METHOD

For all the academic, professional, and journalistic efforts of the last ten years, we seem far from a general theory of terrorism and farther yet from any credible or generally acceptable plan for eradicating terrorism in the decade ahead. To be sure, the "terrorist specialists" are not the only nor the most culpable party. Our ability to think and make judgments about terrorism has suffered from a corrosive mix of official opportunism, media hype, and public hysteria. The essential link between detached analysis and policy-making has become as attenuated as a fuse wire, ready to blow at the mere threat of a terrorist attack.

It is fairly easy—that is, politically expedient— to single out particular individuals as responsible for this state of affairs. Current candidates would include the political leader preoccupied with the "wimp factor," the media magnate with an eye on profit margins, or the think-tank courtier eagerly working the space between. But such an assessment of blame is to mimic the very cardboard construction of terrorist identities that presently preempts any serious attempt to comprehend terrorism.

It is more difficult—and certainly less popular—to assess the intellectual and structural obstacles blocking an inquiry into terrorism. The first obstacle is *epistemological:* even the most conscientious and independent student of terrorism faces a narrowly bounded discipline of thought. Over the last ten years, terrorist studies has become a fortress-haven at the edge of the social sciences, a positivist's armory of definitions, typologies, and databases to be wielded as much against the methodological critic as the actual terrorist who might call into question the sovereign reason and borders of the nation-state. The second obstacle is *ideological:* to gain official entry into the terrorist debate, one must check critical weapons at the door and join in the chorus of condemnation—or risk suspicion of having sympathy for the terrorist devil. What this means is that following a rash of terrorist incidents—at the moments of highest tension, when sober thinking is most needed—responses other than instant excoriation and threats of retaliation are seen as "soft," or worse, collaborationist. As others have noted, this is very reminiscent of the regimentation of critical thinking by threat-mongering that marked Cold War I in the 1940s and 1950s and the most morbid moments of Cold War II in the early 1980s. "It is very important," Oliver North recently (and repeatedly) reminded us, "for the American people to understand that this a dangerous world, that we live at risk and this nation is at risk in a dangerous world."[5] However, as Gorbachev works hard to improve relations with the United States, and as the Soviet bloc begins to disintegrate, it is proving increasingly difficult to find, let alone maintain the credibility of, an alien, uniform foe. In the decade ahead there will indeed be external dangers, but it is our national identity, not our nation, that is truly at risk. Here lies the third, *ontological,* reason for the intractability of terrorism: it has been subsumed by the traditional gambit of defining and unifying our own indentity through the alien-ation and actions of others. Despite the odds that we are more likely to die from a lightning strike, an automobile accident, or even a bee sting, many have come to accept the terrorist threat as ubiquitous and constant, and have come to take on the identity of its victims.

Yet, even in polls taken immediately after a terrorist strike, the majority of Americans are reluctant to endorse military retaliation.[6] Common sense probably plays a conservative role: if polled, most Americans would proba-bly not (for similar reasons) endorse surgical air strikes on automobile plants or bee colonies to lessen the chances of an unlikely death. But I suspect something beyond common sense is at work. Reflecting the diverse and highly individualistic forces behind terrorism, we are not—nor can we be—of one mind, of one identity, or of one course of action when it comes time to think and act collectively against the terrorist threat. What the polls probably reflect is that after Vietnam (and before another Lebanon debacle), many prefer the *non*identity of a silent but safe majority when it comes to taking on an enemy that is fearsome but faceless, anywhere and nowhere.

This is not to claim that one must sympathize with terrorism in order to understand it, although this chapter does attempt a better understanding of the terrorist *in situ*. Nor is it to pretend that a total comprehension of terrorism is possible, remedial, or even preferable, although this chapter does try to reconstruct our knowledge and critique current practices of terrorism and antiterrorism. Rather, it is to argue at the outset that any productive reading of terrorism requires a difficult, even contorted feat, of stepping outside the one-dimensional identities that terrorism and the na-tional security culture have implanted in both sides of the conflict.[7]

For some, this kind of intellectual activity might be considered subver-sive. Indeed, former Secretary of State George Shultz in a major policy address on terrorism stated that the United States cannot effectively respond to terrorism unless Americans are of one mind on the subject: "Our nation cannot summon the will to act without firm public understanding and sup-port." Without such a consensus, we risk becoming, in Schultz's words, "the Hamlet of nations, worrying endlessly over whether and how to respond."[8] I believe, however, that it is time to take up a position of detachment toward terrorism that international relations theorist Hedley Bull approvingly re-ferred to as "political nihilism."[9] After all, "when times are out of joint," as they were for Hamlet and as they appear to be for us as this decade takes a radical turn, we might find in Hamlet—who through his passionate yet intellectual introspection discovered just how rotten the declining state could be—a better guide than, say, Henry V—who, "because he did not know how to govern his own kingdom, determined to make war upon his neighbors."[10] We might also discover that there are more things in heaven and earth than are dreamt of in the official view of terrorism, perhaps even the uncomfortable truth that there is some of the terrorist in us, and some of us in the terrorist. My response, then, to Shultz is more diplomatic than politic: the estrangement of international relations *requires* that we endlessly mediate the terrorist act and the response to it with a deeper and broader knowledge of *all* practices of global political violence. Otherwise, the will to act becomes inseparable from the will to know, and terrorism becomes indistinguishable from counterterrorism.

Moreover, an alternative approach is needed because the problem of terrorism is implicated by a profound predicament that now confronts advanced societies. Call it late capitalism, postmodernism, postwarring, or, as I shall later, neomedievalism, it is a disturbing, anxiety-inducing condition in which traditional modes of knowledge and formations of identity no longer seem up to the task of representing, let alone managing, international relations. Nation-states never enjoyed a true monopoly on the use of force, but now more than in any other post-Westphalian time*—and certainly at an accelerated pace—the legitimacy of that monopoly has come under serious challenges from social, economic, technical, and military changes. Interdependent economies, global ecological concerns, penetration by surveillance and media technologies, the three-dimensionality and nuclearization of warfare—they have all been recognized as growing forces undermining the sovereign privileges and obligations of the territorial state.[11]

Less noticed and understood is the emergence of a *terrorist discourse*, by which I refer to a global semiotic activity where violent powers and insurgent meanings clash.[12] With a nuclear stalemate curtailing super-power based on military might, and a global information economy boosting sign-power based on cultural hegemony, it is increasingly in the discursive realm of terrorism that the "crises" of political legitimacy, national identity, and practical knowledge are being played out. Simultaneously brutalizing, repugnant, and fascinating, the terrorist repertoire—kidnapping, hijackings, and assassination—cannot alone account for its rise to the singular status of international crisis. In terrorist discourse a less visible battle is being fought—most desperately between the vanguards of aspiring great powers and the rear-guards of others—to reinscribe the boundaries of legitimacy in international relations.

In short, four important yet neglected theoretical points are being made here. In the study of terrorism, method matters: but very little critical consciousness of just how much it matters has been demonstrated in the field. Second, method *is* matter: given the symbolic practices of terrorism, the limitations of physical antiterrorism, and the simulacrum projection of terrorism by the media, the representations of terrorism have taken on a powerful materiality. Third, because of changing configurations of power that rival traditional claims of international legitimacy, new critical methods are

---

*Time since the end of the Thirty Years' War in 1648.

called for. Fourth, method alone cannot substitute for an ontological step that anyone seriously seeking truths about terrorism must take: questioning how our own identity is implicated and constituted by the terrorist discourse must precede any study of terrorism.

These critical considerations inform the analysis of modern forms of terrorism that follows. Taking into account the sheer volume of the terrorist archive, I can make no claims for comprehensiveness. My strategy is deconstructive *and* reconstructive: to provide a method that might displace, critique, and historicize received accounts of terrorism and, simultaneously, to present an alternative primer for reading terrorism in its multiple, deterritorialized forms.[13] What I wish to avoid is the subtextual ploy found in much of the terrorism literature where the theoretical organization of an inchoate body of thought pretends to reconcile the differences and contradictions of terrorism, thus "taming" rather than interpreting a heavily conflicted field.[14] At best, I hope to leave the reader with a critical method and minimal amount of historical knowledge necessary to distinguish the politically dispossessed from the violently possessed, and to imagine possible forms of coexistence with the former, while galvanizing collective action against the latter.

## RITES OF PASSAGE

First, a necessary diversion. Entry onto the grounds of the terrorist discourse requires an initiating ritual of purification—otherwise known as definition. It is a difficult ritual, given that much of the semantic confusion as well as the urge for terminological purity is enmeshed in the discursive operations of terrorism and antiterrorism. How are we to distinguish the terrorist from the bandit, criminal, or freedom fighter? What sets terrorism off from other forms of violent conflict? Why is one state's violence considered terrorist, while another's is antiterrorist?

On the violence spectrum, terrorism is clearly somewhere between a rumble and a war. Or is it? In 1985 Secretary of Defense Caspar Weinberger called the TWA hijacking and hostage taking "a war and it is the beginning of war."[15] What appears to be a logical trap—if terrorism is war, why isn't war terrorism?—or at the very least a chronological distortion—does terrorism precede its beginnings?—could also be interpreted as a calculated definitional maneuver to invoke the strategies of war for a phenomenon that by definition resists such strategies. By first making terrorism identical with war, Weinberger attaches justification for a military response, and then seeks to add credibility by declaring "it is the beginning of war." If the taking of the hostages becomes identical to war, then it also is the "beginning of war," because the United States can and will use military force in retaliation for a form of conflict that, in fact, defies "traditional" beginnings, in the sense of hostilities with an extended duration or an official declaration between belligerents. Faced by the spasmodic immediacy of terrorism, Weinberger—who much preferred the *threat* of retaliation to the real thing—equates terrorism with war in the desire to install a compensatory, *deterrent* strategy.[16]

Other sources of confusion intrude. War clearly has its terrorist element: Dresden, Hiroshima, My Lai, Afghanistan all testify to the ability of states in an age of total war to sanction the killing and maiming of large numbers of civilians. Conversely, many terrorist groups employ the nomenclature of war (the Red *Army* Faction, the *Armed Forces* of National Liberation, the Red *Brigades*, the Provisional Irish Republican *Army*, the Holy *War*), communiqués full of military jargon, and many of the tactics of war, like tactical surprise, diversionary attacks, and psychological operations.

But ultimately, I believe, the definitional distinction between war and terrorism holds. War is a form of organized violence conducted by states, with commonly accepted (if not always observed) rules against bombing, assassination, armed assaults, kidnapping, hostage taking, and hijacking of civilians—the type of actions that make up 95 percent of what is most often described as terrorism.[17] Terrorism, moreover, relies on unpredictable, random violence to achieve its various objectives.[18] However, the nature or type of violence utilized by terrorists does not provide sufficient criteria to define terrorism. Outgunned, outmanned, and outlawed by states, terrorists rely more on the intangible power of menacing symbols than on techniques of physical violence to achieve their goals. So, typologies and definitions of terrorism perform much like the airport security systems that seek to prevent terrorism: finely calibrated, they alert the reader to dangers that can prove to be so much loose change; crudely set, they might miss entirely the nonferrous, free-floating *immaterial* threats that make up much of the terrorist arsenal; but regardless of the setting, they are supposed to work as much through deterrence as through detection.

This chapter eschews the intellectual equivalent of an antiterrorist security system. It does not seek to define or detect, to stereotype or deter the terrorist. It takes an alternative route of plotting the many philosophical, historical, and cultural differences that have made the multiple forms of terrorism so difficult to understand and so resistant to remedy. To this end, I have interpreted terrorism as a strategy of intimidation and violence that can be delimited into eight formations: mytho-terrorism, anarcho-terrorism, socio-terrorism, ethno-terrorism, narco-terrorism, state terrorism, antiterrorism, and pure terrorism. These formations should be read as an *array:* like soldiers on parade, this intellectual marshalling does not pretend to reproduce or capture the horror, uncertainty, and savagery of terrorism—it just temporarily represents and gives some order to it for the purpose of a critical review.

# MYTHO-TERRORISM

The first (if not primal) form is *mytho-terrorism*. At the root of much terrorism lies fear, desire, and violence—all the makings of myth. There is the reciprocal fear that comes from a relationship in which the less powerful simultaneously need and feel alienated from the more powerful. There is the desire for national, class, or simply *more* power to make a different world from the one inherited. And there is the violence that erupts when the desires of the alienated confront each other in mimesis and can no longer be negotiated, displaced, or ritualized away.[19]

Mythology and terrorism fuse when imagined solutions to intractable problems are pursued through new or unconventional rituals of violence. Mytho-terrorism has similar characteristics to other forms of ritual violence, like wars or general strikes, that bind together the deprived, the weak, the resentful, the repressed, or just the temporarily disadvantaged in a violent encounter with more powerful others.[20] The difference, however—and this is the difference that both gives mytho-terrorism its power and anticipates its failure—is that its targets are identified by others as innocent victims, not guilty surrogates. What is tactically effective against the more powerful is strategically disastrous because terrorism's mythical justifications are sufficient to arouse the fears and antiterrorism of the authorities, but not to assure the support of the mythical "people" in whose name the terrorist strikes. Executed in the name of an imagined group-identity, looking backward to a prior golden age, or anticipating a future utopia, mytho-terrorism can undermine an order through violence but is unable on its own to generate the necessary ritual substitutes for violence (in contrast, for instance, to the Eucharist, or the rules and customs of diplomacy or jurisprudence).

The most potent forces behind mytho-terrorism are usually eschatological and millenarianistic: that is, they join redemption, social change, and cathartic violence in the pursuit of a new era. The eschatological millenarianism of the Crusades, the *jihad*, the Anabaptist insurrections of the sixteenth century, and indeed, the more radical forms of Catholic liberation theology and Islamic fundamentalism of today have inspired or sanctioned mytho-terrorism. The attempt to construct the kingdom of heaven on earth has been marked by assassinations, violent uprisings, and all kinds of martyrdom. Understandably, many historians have turned once again to the Middle East to study possible transhistorical links between myth and terrorism.[21]

Even a superficial scan clearly shows that no one nationalist religion or religious nationalism has had a monopoly on mytho-terrorism. From the random killings of the messianic Zealots in their first-century struggle against the Romans, to the Assassin *fidayeen* seeking to purify Islam in the twelfth and thirteenth centuries; from the terrorist attacks of the twentieth century, of the Jewish Irgun blowing up British occupiers, to Christian

Phalangists massacring Palestinians, to the Islamic Hizballah car-bombing American and French soldiers; all have appealed to myth and resorted to violence to attain their other worldly aims. Indeed, in our own backyard, such groups as the Order, the Covenant, and the Sword and the Arms of the Lord (CSA) have targeted American judges and FBI agents for assassination in their apocalyptic pursuit of a second Christian millennium.

In mytho-terrorism as well as the other types of terrorism that follow, there is no clear-cut boundary of motivation or targets. Obviously, social, ethnic, ideological, and other factors weigh heavily on any consideration of why people turn to terrorism. A short history of the Provisional Irish Republican Army would be a case in point. But it is important to recognize the power of the mythological element that binds and motivates a variety of terrorist groups with multiple grievances—and how this might handicap a purely reasonable inquiry or reaction. In the modern states system, the pale of power is marked by mytho-terrorism, the boundary where legitimate, rational use of violence to attain goals comes up against the illegitimate, irrational use of violence. On this borderline, the intelligibility of terrorism is more likely to be discerned by a mythical reading than a rational analysis.

## ANARCHO-TERRORISM

A statement reprinted in the *New York Times* underscores the spreading threat posed by yet another form of terrorism: "It was soon recognized at the Rome conference that very little could be done in the matter by diplomatic means. I, therefore, took the earliest opportunity in the course of the conference of proposing that the sixteen chief officers of police of different nations who were present or their representatives should be formed into a special committee secretly to consider with closed doors and without minutes or written reports what steps could most advantageously be taken."[22] These uncomfortably familiar remarks were made by Sir Vincent Howard, Great Britain's representative at the Rome Anti-Anarchist Conference, convened in 1906. The assassination of Czar Alexander II by the *Narodnaya Volia* (the People's Will) in 1881, the Haymarket Square killings in 1886, an assassination attempt on Henry Clay Frick of Carnegie Steel by a Russian anarchist in 1892, the murder of the president of France by an Italian anarchist in 1894, the assassination of the king of Italy in 1900, the shooting of President McKinley by a follower of Emma Goldman in 1901, the assassination of the Empress Elizabeth of Austria: this is just a sampling of the rise of a new kind of international political violence, the amalgamation of anarchism and terrorism, or *anarcho-terrorism*.

Captured by the rapidly growing mass dailies, the anarchist archetype of the nineteenth-century terrorist—eyes borderline mad, revolver in one hand, bomb in the other—lingers long after its ideological origins have been forgotten, its technology antiquated. Certainly any elision of anarchism and terrorism risks simplifying the subject of a major political debate among some very heavy thinkers of nineteenth-century radicalism—including Proudhon, Bakunin, Marx, and Kropotkin—and furthering the modern slide into the false equation that anarchism=communism=terrorism. But at least a cursory knowledge of the original forces behind antistate political violence is needed if we are to understand much of the history of Euro-terrorism, for the anarchist message was to resonate in the discourse of, among others, the German Red Army Faction, the Italian Red Brigades, and the French Direct Action. Moreover, the antianarchist reaction at the turn of the century has certainly found its echo in the antiterrorism summit conferences of the 1980s.

The common element of anarchism is violence against the state. The politics of reform is not an option, for its instruments of debate and persuasion are too weak when confronted by the cloaked violence of the state. Words are corruptible and ambiguous: violent deeds are pure and to the point. While vengeance, hate, and despair might secretly reside in the anarchist's heart and motivate his or her actions, there is an open and often overlooked archive of the destructionist intent of anarchism.[23] Most notorious is Sergey Nechaev's 1869 *Catechism of the Revolutionist*. In twenty-one points he constructs the identity of the anarcho-revolutionary: "a doomed man . . . an implacable enemy of this world . . . he knows only one science, the science of destruction."[24] Anarchist manifestos proliferated in this period, but in the series of increasingly vehement debates between Nechaev and Bakunin against Marx and Engels we can locate the heroic, individualist terrorist ethic that was rejected by socialists yet persists in the anarchoterrorism of modern Euro-terrorist groups like the small but deadly French Direct Action and Belgian Communist Combatant Cells.[25]

## SOCIO-TERRORISM

Terrorism acquired its modern meaning in the French Revolution, when Robespierre, Saint-Just, and other Jacobins advocated the use of systematic social violence "to make right and reason respected"—and to get rid of some factional enemies in the process.[26] Originally a word with some positive social connotations, the heavy use of the guillotine and the internationalization of the French Revolution radically transformed the term. By 1795 *terrorist* had entered the lexicon as a clearly pejorative term when Edmund Burke referred to the "thousands of those hellhounds called terrorists."[27] Ever since, the word has been part of a socio-political game—a kind of "pin-the-term-on-the-class"—to condemn some forms of social violence and legitimize others.

The debate over who were the "real" socio-terrorists, those who endorse and conduct class warfare, erupted again in France in 1871. It is an important debate because it had a profound influence on future socialist and Marxist-Leninist positions on terrorism. After workers of the Paris Commune were charged by the British press with terrorist "incendiarism," Marx countered with cases of when the "British troops wantonly set fire to the Capitol at Washington and to the summer palace of the Chinese emperor," and "the vandalism of Haussmann, razing historic Paris to make place for the Paris of the sightseer."[28] But Marx's major concern was not explicating the class character of pyromania or urban planning. He was attempting to rebut the accusation that a revolutionary party in power was inherently terrorist, as was suggested by the Communards' execution of sixty-four hostages, including clergy and the Archbishop of Paris. Marx's reply bears quotation, not only because it is a seminal statement for future socialist positions on terrorism, but also because it makes short shrift of the bowdlerized *Reader's Digest*-ation of Marx that has gone on for the last ten years to prove that communism equals terrorism.

Marx first historically establishes that revolutionary socialists and colonial subjects have never been protected by the rules of war: "The bourgeoisie and its army, in June 1848, re-established a custom which had long disappeared from the practice of war—the shooting of their defenceless prisoners. This brutal custom has since been more or less strictly adhered to by the suppressors of all popular commotions in Europe and India; thus proving that it constitutes a real 'progress of civilization'!"

In the disputed case of the Communards, Marx claims they were responding in kind to others, like the Prussians and the French statesman Thiers, who initiated the taking of hostages. Moreover, the Communard's efforts to negotiate a hostage-exchange were rebuffed, which Marx believed to have exposed "the unscrupulous ferocity of bourgeois governments": "The real murderer of Archbishop Darboy is Thiers. The Commune again and again had offered to exchange the archbishop, and ever so many priests in the bargain, against the single Blanqui, then in the hands of Thiers. Thiers obstinately refused. He knew that with Blanqui he would give to the Commune a head while the archbishop would serve his purpose best in the shape of a corpse."[29]

Future theorists of socialism would draw on Marx's analysis both to condemn terrorism and to justify the extreme occasions when the use of terror against terror is necessary. At the height of the Russian civil war, Leon Trotsky, as head of the Red Army wrote: "The revolution 'logically' does not demand terrorism, just as 'logically' it does not demand an armed insurrection. What a profound commonplace! But the revolution does require of the revolutionary class that it should attain its end by all methods at its disposal—if necessary, by an armed rising; if required, by terrorism."[30] Trotsky's defense of terrorism comes across as a mix of the class analysis of Marx, the strategic theory of Clausewitz, and the *Realpolitik* of Bismarck.

Terrorism in itself is "helpless" as a political instrument unless adopted as a temporary measure against a reactionary class. "Intimidation," says Trotsky, "is a powerful weapon of policy, both internationally and internally,"; and "war, like revolution, is founded upon intimidation."[31] The niceties of morality do not obtain in such extreme moments; or as he coldly puts it, "we were never concerned with the Kantian-priestly and vegetarian-Quaker prattle about the 'sacredness of human life.' " However, Trotsky is not one to make a virtue out of a necessity. The expedient use of terrorism must not obscure the higher aims of Marxism: "To make the individual sacred we must destroy the social order which crucifies him . . . and this problem can be solved only by blood and iron."[32]

Lenin was just as straightforward in his attitude toward terrorism. Early in the fight against czarism, Lenin sought to distance the social democratic movement from the *Narodnaya Volia* as well as other populists and anarchists who were advocating or practicing terrorism and assassination against czarist officials (often successfully, with the 1881 assassination of Czar Alexander II the most notable). Writing for party paper *Iskra* in 1901, Lenin criticized the growing wave of terrorism: "In principle we have never rejected, and cannot reject, terror. Terror is one of the forms of military action that may be perfectly suitable and even essential at a definite juncture in the battle, given a definite state of the troops and the existence of definite conditions. But the important point is that terror, at the present time, is by no means suggested as an operation for the army in the field, an operation closely connected with and integrated into the entire system of struggle, but as an independent form of occasional attack unrelated to any army. . . . Far be it from us to deny the significance of heroic individual blows, but it is our duty to sound a vigorous warning against becoming infatuated with terror, against taking it to be the chief and basic means of struggle, as so many people strongly incline to do at the present."[33]

But once in power and besieged by war and famine, Lenin found terrorism defensible. In August 1918 he wrote a "Letter to American Workers" for *Pravda;* "How humane and righteous the bourgeoisie are! Their servants accuse us of resorting to terror. . . . The British bourgeoisie have forgotten their 1649, the French bourgeoisie their 1793. Terror was just and legitimate when the bourgeoisie resorted to it for their own benefit against feudalism. Terror became monstrous and criminal when the workers and poor peasants dare to use it against the bourgeoisie!"[34] A few years later, Lenin was attacking the actions of the Social Revolutionary Party as anarchist and terrorist.[35] And Trotsky, exiled by a man who would make wide and brutal use of both internal and international terrorism, soon found himself in the position of defending his earlier use of terrorism against Stalin's.[36]

What does this prove? Only a minimal amount of the writings and history of socialism is required to dismiss the accusation that Marxism is identical to terrorism. A slightly more sophisticated charge is that Marxism promotes the kind of relativism that condones terrorism. A more accurate, and I beleive realistic, assessment would be that Marx, Lenin, and Trotsky endorsed a historicist perspective to make difficult and complex judgments on the effectiveness and justifiability of terrorism. It is another question, begged by Stalin's unchecked use of terrorism, whether they got it right. But this analysis of terrorism on a historical and social level can, I believe, contribute a better understanding of the motivations and actions of modern counterparts like the Farabundo Martí National Liberation Front (FMLN) in El Salvador, the New People's Army (NPA) in the Philippines, and the *Sendero Luminoso* in Peru, who exploit (and are exploited by) the ambiguous boundary between social revolutionary and terrorist politics.

## ETHNO-TERRORISM

The pursuit of honor and justice, wealth and territory have been recurrent and seemingly eternal causes of violence in the history of the states-system. But from the dynastic rights of the "prince" to the popular rights of the nation there has been an evolution in the legitimacy of violence. The multiple, sometimes conflicting, even extraterrestrial loyalties of medieval feudatories, and the "jealousies" and often capricious alliances of the royal houses made for unpredictable, unaccountable, or what today we would call "irrational" political violence. It might be historically dubious—as well as morally specious—to consider it a sign of progress that when push comes to legal shove in the contemporary international system, a peoples' war is more likely now to determine the outcome than, say, individual trial by combat. But the tandem rise of the principles of national self-determination and nonintervention with the rights of war has brought a degree of *formally* democratic benefits to the international order.

Ironically, they have also abetted the rise of *ethno-terrorism:* the violent efforts of a national, communal, or ethnic group to acquire the status of a state. There are many nations or groups acting in the name of a nation, still pursuing the legitimacy and protection of statehood, like the Kurds or the Palestinians. There are nation-states that have lost—or have failed to acquire fully—the rights of self-determination because of enduring conditions of suzerainty that the great powers have installed at one time or another, as has been the case at different times in Central America and Eastern Europe. And the history (and still unfinished process) of decolonization in which social and ethnic forms of terrorism merge into a violent prelude for state formation has been well documented.[37] Indeed, some radical analysts, like Franz Fanon writing of the Northern African case in *The Wretched of the Earth,* consider terrorism to be an essential element of decolonization, both to liberate the physical territory and to free the colonized subject from years of psychic repression.[38]

The next explosion of ethno-terrorism, however, is more likely to be on the peripheries of the Soviet Union than in the Western or developing regions of the world. Lost in the antiterrorist din of the last decade is the fact that it has been over five years since a major terrorist group has emerged in North America or Europe (the Communist Combatant Cells, or the CCC, in Belgium). In the meantime, the potential for ethno-terrorism in the disintegrating Soviet bloc has been willfully neglected by those on the right who persistently viewed the Soviet Union as an unchanging totalitarian monolith, as well as by those on the left who considered the United States to be the only imperial power of significance in the postwar system. The ingredients for a violent combustion are plentiful: 104 discrete nationalities in 15 republics, 20 autonomous republics, and 18 national districts; a radical reconfiguration of power at the center of the Soviet Union; and at the fringes of power, mass movements in Latvia, Lithuania, Estonia, Moldavia, Georgia, Armenia, Azerbaijan, the Ukraine, and other regions where expectations for autonomy and democracy have been rising. The prospect for outbreaks of ethno-terrorism in this area—whether by impatient minority groups (like the Baltic or Caucasian peoples in the Soviet Union) or newly subordinated majorities (like Russians in Estonia and Moldavia)—has yet to be seriously studied.

It must be acknowledged that these positive developments—the breaking up of a monolithic Marxist-Leninist system (which had created conditions of totalitarian terrorism), the repudiation of the Brezhnev Doctrine (which had provided *ex post facto* justification for Soviet intervention in Czechoslovakia), the open rejection of the secret protocols of the 1939 Nazi-Soviet pact (which had led to the annexation of the Baltic Republics)—have a darker side. Alongside—and sometimes within—the display of progressive nationalism in the Baltic, Georgian, Azerbaijani, and Armenian Republics there lies an atavistic chauvinism. For instance, at the same time that Estonians declared their virtual sovereignty, they disenfranchised a sizable portion of their Russian population, prompting widespread strikes and increased tensions. Christian Armenians and Muslim Azerbaijanis killed each other over their claims to the autonomous region of Nagorno-Karabakh, resulting in martial law. And in the Republic of Georgia, Soviet troops used shovels and toxic gas against nationalist protestors who were taking seriously Gorbachev's slogans of *perestroika* and *glasnost*. Elsewhere, in Rumania, Yugoslavia, Bulgaria, Uzbekistan, and the Ukraine, the volatile ingredients for ethno-terrorism—territorial disputes (between Rumania and Hungary), economic disparities (in Yugoslavia between ethnic groups), cultural differences (between Slav and Turk in Bulgaria)—have also begun to surface after many years of repression.

Full of historical disparities, the experiences of the Jews, Basques, Irish, Sikhs, and others who waged long campaigns of ethno-terrorism against hegemonic powers nonetheless offer some insights for what might lie ahead for the Soviet Union and its neighbors. Why some terrorist groups succeeded in their bids for statehood while others failed seems linked to their ability to mobilize and subsume social cross-sections of native populations against occupying or dominant powers that have lost the will and/or the way to rule. The mytho-terrorism of the Jewish Irgun, the anarcho-terrorism of the Serbian Black Hand, or the socio-terrorism of the Irish Republican Army alone were not sufficient to achieve their respective goals. It is ethno-terrorism, once legitimized as a stage in the transformation of nations into states, that has the best historical record among terrorist movements in achieving its goals.

However, this very ability to mount and sustain a long-term campaign of political violence makes ethno-terrorism a favored target of external manipulation, as well as a potential trigger for systemic, inter-state violence. Throughout history, ethno-terrorist groups have acted—sometimes as the vanguard, at other times as proxies—for transnational rivalries that have ended in global conflicts, such as the friction generated by pan-Slavic and pan-Germanic terrorism in the Balkans before the first world war, and the racial supremacist violence that fueled Italian, Japanese, and German fascism before the second world war. Parallels could be drawn with the hydra offshoots of pan-Shiism like the Revolutionary Justice Organization, Organization of the Oppressed on Earth, and other groups under the umbrella of Hizballah that have proven their ability to light fuses that stretch far beyond the Middle East.

## NARCO-TERRORISM

It is difficult to pin a date on the origins of *narco-terrorism,* the violent blending of illicit drug trade and political intimidation. In the early 1980s, Peruvian officials began to popularize the term by linking the *Sendero Luminoso* (Shining Path) insurgency to the narcotics trade; soon after, the military arm of the Medellin drug cartel was similarly labeled. The war *against* narco-terrorism is better marked, with Nancy and Ronald Reagan sitting on a sofa in the White House a few years back, giving the American public the first high-level televised debriefing of the "war on drugs." At a time when Gorbachev seemed intent on unilaterally calling off the Cold War, and Qaddafi preferred to sulk in his tent rather than execute his threat to bring terrorism home to the United States, narco-terrorism moved up the ranks to become our most immediate and dire foreign threat. The charges flew: Colombian cartels were using drug profits to suborn left-wing guerrillas, the Syrians were growing opiates in the Bekaa Valley to fund Palestinian militias, the Nicaraguan Sandinistas were providing transshipment for cocaine and using the money to back El Salvadoran rebels. Our popular culture was selling a similar narrative, although the good guys and bad buys were often reversed: t.v. drama *Miami Vice,* and movies *Lethal Weapon* and

*Above the Law* took the first step in this reversal by dredging up the drug-running forays of the CIA-proprietary *Air America* in Southeast Asia, and reinstating their clandestine operations to Latin America.[39]

The discursive tactic of "just say no" quickly proved inadequate in the war against the new public enemy number one. A volatile combination emerged: internal terrorism in U.S. cities, led by Jamaican, Colombian, and the expansionist gangs of Los Angeles, the Crips and the Bloods; international terrorism, by the Mexican *narcos* who killed DEA agents and the Medellin "Extraditables" who assassinated Colombian judges and other officials; and media overrepresentation, topped by the video *verité/simulé* of *Cops* and *America's Most Wanted*. Our national security and the American way of life now being at risk, narco-terrorism took on the qualities of a synergistic threat. In response, then-Mayor Koch of New York advocated an air attack on Medellin, and Daryl Gates—the chief of the Los Angeles Police who had become infamous for his anti-drug sweeps of the city with helicopters and armored vehicles—outdid Koch by calling for an outright invasion of Colombia. Military AWACs began to patrol the Caribbean; the State Department was supplied with over 150 fixed-wing aircraft and Huey helicopters for use in Colombia, Bolivia, and Peru; the Customs Service and Coast Guard set up a Command, Control, Communications and Intelligence Center ($C^3I$) in Miami and lined the Mexican border with radar-equipped blimps; and the Green Berets set off to train paramilitary forces in Latin America for the war against narco-terrorism. It was only a matter of time before stealth technology was introduced, as a front page article from the *Arizona Republic* reported that "National Guardsmen in Texas could be fighting the war on drugs dressed as cactuses, sneaking up on smugglers under the cover of night and prickly needles, according to a proposal submitted to the Defense Department."[40]

How did narco-terrorism come to claim precedence over all other forms of terrorism? One history, the official history, is made up of what President Reagan once referred to as "stupid facts," by which he meant the stubborn facts that U.S. users spend between $100 and $150 billion a year on narcotics, creating a demand that—according to the State Department's 1989 International Narcotics Strategic Control Strategy Report—over fifty-six countries are ready to service in the capacity of growers, manufacturers, traffickers, or money launderers.[41] Again, we should not allow the data to obscure the most important fact, that illegal drugs ruin and kill people. But we have heard all this so often that they have become not stupid but stupefying facts: they incur an inertia of helplessness, a mass mood that accepts the official view that only the experts, the police, the forces of law and order can handle the drug problem. But the problem clearly exceeds the capabilities of the best-trained TNT (Tactical Narcotics Team) units, which sweep a neighborhood clean of dealers one week only to lose it the next, or the Drug Enforcement Agency, which was recently forced out of Medellin, Colombia.

The problem is that we have so demonized the drug problem that we have lost sight of its all too human face.

To compensate, some alternative facts and histories are needed. Tobacco, an addictive drug, kills over 300,000 people a year, alcohol kills 100,000 (including those killed by drunk drivers), while the use of all illegal drugs combined—cocaine, heroin, marijuana, angel dust, LSD, etc.—accounted for fewer than 4,000 deaths in 1987.[42] From the latest figures (1989), the use of illegal drugs in the United States is declining. Yet the war on drugs continues to escalate. This can be explained, I believe, only in the larger context of past examples of when U.S. strategic interests intersected with the interests of the drug trade. Some would claim that the United States became entangled in the drug web; others that we helped spin it.[43] The web-spinning theorists claim that we not only inherited the Vietnam war from the French, but also the opium trade that the French intelligence service, SDECE, had used to finance and win the support of Hmong tribesmen from the Vietnamese highlands in the struggle against the Viet Minh guerrillas. Even earlier, from 1948 on, the CIA had supposedly used drug-smuggling routes and trade in the Golden Triangle to disguise intelligence and paramilitary operations against the Chinese communists. It is also claimed that some of the players who later showed up in the Iran-Contra affair first perfected the guns-drugs-secret warfare matrix in Laos in the 1960s, when Theodore Shackley was station chief of the CIA in Vientiane, General John Singlaub was chief of the Studies and Operations Group (SOG), which carried out secret raids into Laos, and Thomas Clines, also of the CIA, worked with Lieutenant Colonel Secord to run covert air-supply missions. The Iran-Contra hearings also revealed other drug connections, with the DEA involved in the hostage ransom attempt in Lebanon, and the CIA use of the Santa Elena airstrip in Costa Rica for the transshipment of illegal drugs and weapons.[44] There is a substantial body of evidence that agencies of the U.S. government have at various times colluded with narcotics trafficking. At the very least, over the last thirty years, narco-terrorism has been mainly perceived as a minor strategic threat and as a sometime ally in the battle against (what was seen then as) the much larger danger of communism.[45]

My own suspicion is that narco-terrorism is being taken seriously—if not hysterically—because it has now taken on characteristics of a major transnational conglomerate rather than primitive capitalism, with a commensurate increase in political power.[46] In Colombia, the source of 80 percent of the cocaine that reaches the United States, right-wing paramilitary squads, Marxist guerilla groups, and two major drug cartels have used drug profits to build up power bases that seriously challenge the sovereignty of the Colombian government. We have heard much of how the *narcotraficantes* have killed over two hundred judges and court employees since 1981, and most recently, assassinated several candidates for president. Less often reported is the number of jobs, homes, health services, soccer fields, earthquake relief, and schools supplied by the *narcos*—amenities that the state cannot provide.[47] For many peasants they provide a cash crop, and more importantly, a transportation system that can get "produce" to its far-flung markets. The *narcos* do not—could not—rule by terror alone. As war is for most states, terrorism is for the *narcos* the *ultima ratio* of their burgeoning agri-business empire. Providing a relatively lucrative living for everyone from the subsistence farmer to the ghetto dealer—along with bribes for the underpaid police or military officer—is as important a source of power as the threat or use of terrorism.

Hence, the much ballyhooed solution of beating narco-terrorism by antiterrorism is certain to fail, as are schemes to make interdiction and eradication the top priority.[48] The same plan was used with marijuana, which simply resulted in an increase in domestic production as well as in the potency of the marijuana supply. There are already signs that the Colombian drug cartels, feeling the heat, are moving operations into the Brazilian jungles. And even if we could someday develop the equivalent of a Narcotics Defense Initiative to shield the United States from foreign-produced narcotics, designer and synthetic drugs could quickly fill the void.[49] Narco-terrorism will not be stopped until the supply *and* demand of illegal narcotics are stopped, which means that the United States must provide treatment and education, substitute businesses and jobs in the American cities, and crop alternatives to coca as well as an infrastructure of credit and roads in the Latin American countries. For political and economic reasons, that is unlikely to happen in the near future. The worst-case scenario, then, would be for incarceration, the preferred drug treatment program in the United States, to be exported as foreign policy. The legal principle of *posse comitatus* against the military making arrests as well as taking on policing duties will be further eroded as actions are taken, through sanctions, surveillance, and even perhaps blockades, to imprison "criminal" nation-states.

## STATE TERRORISM

If one were to parachute back into the early 1980s, attend a White House briefing, sit through a State Department news conference, or read the *New York Times,* one could walk away with the impression that terrorism was solely a violent activity orchestrated, supplied, and executed by a semipermanent coterie of pariah states, among them Libya, North Korea, Iran, Syria, and the Soviet Union. In this period, "terrorism," overused and lacking rhetorical sufficiency, had begun to show all the signs of semantic bleaching. Conservative spokespersons like Jeane Kirkpatrick, mainstream wordsmiths like Claire Sterling, and White House spin-masters reissued and circulated a new term: *state terrorism,* by which they meant—among many other things—"premeditated, politically motivated violence perpetrated against noncombatant targets by clandestine state agents."[50]

What got lost in this ideological/semantical shuffle was a long history of state rule by terror: in modern times, Hitlerite Germany, Stalinist Russia, Suharto's Indonesia, Argentina's "Dirty War," Idi Amin's Uganda, Pol Pot's Khmer Rouge . . . the list goes on. And today, South Korea, South Africa, and the People's Republic of China stand out as examples of how states—communist or capitalist in their economy but politically dictatorial—regularly resort to violent intimidation and political murder to maintain and further their power. Enhanced by a security, police, or military apparatus, internal state violence—or what we might generally call *endo-terrorism*—has achieved a much higher body count than any other form of terrorism. But Kirkpatrick and "Antiterrorism, Inc.," have a different form of terrorism in mind: state *exo-terrorism*. Defined as state-supported kidnapping, hostage-taking, or murder by proxy terrorists, state exo-terrorism is for the most part seen as a Middle Eastern continuation of war by condemnatory means: the motivations and actions of the terrorist groups that bombed the Labelle discotheque in Berlin, seized the *Achille Lauro* and killed Leon Klinghoffer, hijacked TWA Flight 847 and killed Navy diver Robert Stethem, and kidnapped and killed Marine Lieutenant Colonel Higgins are defined and countered through their links to Libya's Qaddafi, Syrian intelligence, Iranian fundamentalist leaders, or with Moscow in the background. Secretary of State Shultz put it bluntly in a policy address: "States that support and sponsor terrorist actions have managed in recent years to co-opt and manipulate the terrorist phenomenon in pursuit of their own strategic goals."[51]

But if we stick to the strict definition of state exo-terrorism, would we not also need to include U.S. sponsorship of the contras, the delivery of missiles to the *mujahedeen,* the 1985 mid-air "hijacking" by F-14's of the Egyptian airliner carrying the *Achille Lauro* terrorists, the 1986 "assassination" attempt on Qaddafi by U.S. F-111's, the 1987 "kidnapping" of suspected terrorist Fawaz Younis in international waters off Cyprus?[52] Is it only a matter of scale that separates legitimate state violence from illegitimate state terrorism? The official position is that U.S. violence is defensive, retaliatory, and—hopefully—deterring. But can a mere prefix—the *anti* before "our" terrorism—support the distinction?

## ANTI-TERRORISM

The construction and maintenance of an unambiguous boundary between terrorism and antiterrorism has become a preeminent function of the modern state. In the 1985 policy address, an indefinite "we" are told by Secretary of State Shultz that the distinction is self-evident, once "we" settle on "our" definition of terrorism: "We cannot afford to let an Orwellian corruption of language obscure our understanding of terrorism. We know the difference between terrorists and freedom fighters, and as we look around the world, we have no trouble telling one from the other."[53] If the definition of terrorism is the primary semantic battlefield in the struggle for international legitimacy, the delimitation of terrorism from antiterrorism has become its bloodiest strategic site.[54] The official side of this struggle is embodied in the proliferation of antiterrorist forces. Just about all of the major as well as many of the smaller powers have developed such elite antiterrorist units: the Israeli *Sayaret Matkal,* the German *Grenzschutzgruppe 9* (Border Protection Group 9) or GSG9, and the British Special Air Service or SAS are among the more successful ones—if we are to judge by the movies made of their hostage rescues in Entebbe, Mogadishu, and London.[55] Hollywood has shown some interest in imaginary rescues by the U.S. Navy Seals and the antiterrorist unit, Delta Force, but not in actual rescue attempts, like the 1980 Operation Eagle Claw in Iran that ended in a calamity of malfunctioning helicopters, colliding aircraft, eight dead—and no one rescued.[56]

But a closer, colder scrutiny of the terrorist/antiterrorist distinction reveals an ambiguity that both sides of the divide have sought to eliminate. This has been most tragically borne out in the killing ruins of Beirut, where all the violent players—state, antistate, and nonstate—seemed to pause from their endless cycles of violence only long enough to argue who struck the first blow when, and thus to determine who is the *real* terrorist and the *real* antiterrorist. Israel, Syria, Iran, and their Lebanese understudies reach back to originating myths (of "Judea and Samaria," a "Greater Syria," or the *"dar al-Islam"* of the *jihad*) to justify their own actions—a "surgical" air strike, an indiscriminate shelling, a refugee camp massacre, a car-bombing, or a kidnapping—as an antiterrorist action taken against terrorist foes.

At a less abstract, much more personal level, the distinction between retaliation and revenge, deterrent and destructive violence, combatant and noncombatant becomes almost meaningless. When asked by a visiting Arab-American delegation to release their hostages because they were innocent, the Hizballah captors of U.S. citizens Joseph Cicippio and Terry Anderson replied that their family members killed by sixteen-inch shells from the U.S. battleship *New Jersey* in 1984 and American bombs dropped from American planes piloted by Israelis had been just as innocent.[57] When terrorism persists, when its acts of violence intensify, accelerate, and accumulate, the word games behind it become superannuated. People *forget* the original reasons, and blood feuds and revenge cycles take over. In "civilized" countries, it often becomes the task of intelligence agencies to carry out the "necessary" retributions that the public would not or could not sanctify. Cases like the Israelis' secret assassination campaign against PLO agents (that mistakenly killed an innocent Palestinian in Norway); former CIA director William Casey's support for the car-bombing of Sheikh Fadlallah, a Lebanese leader of Shiism implicated in the bombing of the Marine barracks and the kidnapping and murder of CIA station chief William Buckley (the bomb missed him but killed eighty others); or the KGB's retaliatory kidnapping and mutilation of a relative of Hizballah terrorists (resulting in the release of three Soviet envoys) are only the exposed skirmishes of what is probably a much deeper and wider intelligence war.[58] In "*decivilized*" countries, like Lebanon, Colombia, and El Salvador, where feudal terror has resurfaced and spread, antiterrorist forces have not solved the terrorist "problem": they have become just one among many warring militias and guerrilla groups.

## PURE TERRORISM

Very little attention has been paid to the relationship between the nuclear balance of terror and modern terrorism. A few experts in the field have envisaged an ultimate bonding of the two, where a handful of terrorists steal or make their own nuclear device—or chemical weapon, biological contagion, or computer virus—to hold millions at a time hostage. But it is another kind of terrorist fusion—not this think-thank, worst-case scenario of what could be called hyper-terrorism—that warrants serious consideration.

First, we need to consider a possible paradox: has the nuclear stalemate, by bringing into an already violent family of nations a guarantee of limited peace—or more precisely, a state of nonwar based on massive retaliation—served as the stepfather to conventional terrorism? Historical parallels with another epoch point toward a possible answer. The classic foundations of colonization—a new mobility of power, technological superiority, and the cultivation of a pervasive fear of retribution—reappeared as attributes of the superpower system of nuclear terror. And like earlier apologists of colonization, those who have made a dogma of nuclear deterrence celebrate the stasis of a nuclear "peace" while denying any responsibility for the displacement of persistent rivalries and conflicts into new forms of violence.[59] Social critic Paul Virilio has tenaciously pursued this trend toward, in his words, "*pure war,*" declaring that "The art of deterrence, prohibiting political war, favors the upsurge, not of conflicts, but of *acts of war without war.*"[60] In the global pure war that ensued, terrorism has emerged as its most virulent expression, triggering in turn an antibody reaction, antiterrorism, that has proven, I believe, to be more devastating than the original "infection."

Socio-terrorists and anarcho-terrorists may of course claim, as did the Red Brigades in Italy and the Tupamaros in Uruguay, that this is the very purpose of terrorism—to reveal the repressive face of the state. However, this moral imperative of terrorism, treated as a truth that can be proven only by deed, is exposed as nothing more than a blood-soaked truism when the state provoked reveals its violent core once again—and nothing changes. To be sure, at world-historical moments like the French, Russian, or Chinese revolutions, when governments lose the ability and the will to rule (usually in the aftermath of a major war) and some other group, class, or people is mobilized and ready to take power, then terrorism can indeed take on an important and usually spectacular role in transforming societies. But it should be clear from the weight of the cases outlined above that the heroics of terrorism, acting as a substitute for a mass movement, have only served to fortify the worst aspects of the modern state: its propensity for surveillance and secrecy, vigilantism and surrogate violence.[61] To push the family analogy one step further: fostered by the displacement of superpower violence and orphaned by the masses in whose name they act, the modern terrorist in some ways resembles the repressed child who grows up into a serial killer, unable to distinguish the guilty parent from the innocent bystander. Conversely—sometimes perversely— we constitute and preserve our own "normalcy" by the terrorist's deviance.

This is not to belittle the moral turpitude of the terrorist—or the oppressive, alienating conditions that can give rise to terrorism. It is, rather, to highlight how pervasive and potentially universal terrorism—in all its guises—really is. As stated at the outset, the fact that terrorism kills people should not be buried under a pile of words. But, contrary to prevailing moral and materialist views, the meaning and power of terrorism will not be found—to put it morbidly—under a pile of its victims. A new form of *pure terrorism*, as immaterial and diffuse as Virilio's pure war, has emerged as an international political crisis in which the violent intimidation and manipulation of a global media audience creates a pervasive state of insecurity and fear. This means that the critical production and distribution of the terrorist threat is not *territorial*, as is the case in conventional war, but *temporal*: its power is increasingly derived from the instantaneous representation and diffusion of violence by a global communication network. But before we assign villainy to the disseminators of terrorist violence—as did British Prime Minister Margaret Thatcher when she repeatedly called the media the "oxygen of terrorism"—we should recognize the *receptive* and *interpretive* power of a mass audience for whom (and often in whose name) terrorist rituals of violence are committed.[62]

Take again the bracketing terrorist acts of the 1980s, the murders of Aldo Moro and Colonel Higgins. Of the Red Brigade kidnapping of Moro, Claire Sterling wrote, "For speed, mobility, reconnaissance, logistics, staying power, and refinements in psychological warfare, it was a matchless performance."[63] True, but in stating the obvious she misses the more important point. The real terror network does not go through Moscow or Libya or Iran, but through a nonplace, an electronic cyberspace that reproduces and contextualizes the terrorist act for the global audience. In a manner, Sterling mimics the terrorist, attributing a surplus of power to the "heroic" individual as the author of violence, when it is the interventionary power of governments, the representational practices of the media, and the conformist interpretations of the audience that reconstitute and magnify the force of terrorism. The day after the

Red Brigades released the photograph of Moro holding the April 20 issue of *La Repubblica* in his hands, it appeared on the front pages of over forty-five major newspapers around the world.[64] I am sure that the video of Colonel Higgins hanging from a noose "captured" an even wider audience. The journey from the original terrorist deed to its propagandized destiny remains, I believe, the most important and understudied area of terrorism.[65]

## THE FUTURE: POSTMODERN OR NEOMEDIEVAL?

In the Middle Ages, power was fragmented along overlapping lines of religious, class, and national loyalties; a tenuous order was regularly shaken and reconfigured by kidnappings, hostage takings, and assassinations; and, aside from rare and brief rebellions, a peasant majority was terrorized into a fatalistic subservience. Now, on a single day we can read of Latin American drug "lords" and their retinues, equipped with small arms, antitank weapons, and air forces challenging the sovereignty of states; of Shiite plots, hatched in Iran and Syria, to attack Israeli and American targets and to overthrow the secular government of Egypt; and of warring fiefdoms in Lebanon, one side calling on Christian nations to help break a five-month old sea blockade, the other side vowing to fight "the new crusade" and to kill hostages should any Western power intervene.[66]

Is modern terrorism a containable "crisis," or is it a telling sign of a major shift "back to the future," from a world order based on the eminent domain of nation-states to a segmented and sectarian system of warring economic, religious, and political powers? Is the new terrorization of global politics a harbinger of a reterritorialization, as was the religious and civil terror that presaged the Thirty Years' War of the seventeenth century? Or, has it already arrived, in the form of a postmodern simulacrum of the Middle Ages, played out in C³I omnideterrence centers, covered by ABC News Simulations with Peter Jennings, and—when necessary—fought out with secret and privatized armies? In short, as the model for the new global castle, does modern terrorism eliminate the global village of the interdependency die-hards, substituting instead something between Disneyland and Beirut—a world that combines high technology, brutality, and organized chaos?

These speculations run against the grain of peace-mongering that has marked the turn of this decade. Perhaps there *are* reasons to be more optimistic, to discern emerging alternatives to national identities built upon violent antipathies. As a sign of the fractured state of the world order, hope for global solutions—sometimes in the guise of a new nostalgia—has gained ground. Full of promise are the globalist adherents of *nove myshlenie* ("new thinking") that advise Gorbachev, the democratic parties in East/Central

Europe, and the transnational social movements with various shades of Green in their eco-politics.[67] More peculiar and still popular have been the New Age schemes, that range from the *est*-ian exhortations to think our way beyond war, to the apocalyptic musings of Ronald Reagan, which took on a science-fiction character at one of his last question-and-answer sessions when he spoke longingly for the arrival of a *truly* alien threat to bring the world together in a final fight for good against evil.[68]

Contrary to the globalists, I believe that there are—and there will remain—irreconcilable differences and *many* evils at large in the world. Hence my hopes are on a smaller scale and come with a longer time span. For alternative models to terrorism in the name of national liberation, social change, and other forms of self-determination, I look to the remarkable yet incomplete accomplishments of the Palestinian *intifadah,* the journey of Polish Solidarity and Baltic national movements from underground to parliamentary status, the self-liberation of Central and Eastern Europe, and the fledgling democratization of formerly repressive regimes in Latin America. In these cases terrorism was confronted in all its forms and rejected in favor of a (relatively) nonviolent resistance. They have done more to devalue the currency of terrorism than all of the official dealers in the anti-terrorist discourse. They also provide, I might add, an important lesson for everyone who profits by the terrorist discourse, a lesson once taught by history's most successful practitioner of nonviolence who upon discovering that his house of prayer had become a den of thieves left the chief priests alone—but threw out all the moneychangers.

But we are left with a much more secular concern: what to do? I have no global solution for the problem—and I would hope that the diverse and complex array of terrorism presented in this chapter serves as a sufficient repudiation of national policymakers as well as global salvationists who think that there is one. We can no more remedy the problem of terrorism than we can wipe out difference in the world; and were that possible, it would lead not toward a better world but a final solution. Alternatively, I offer a much more modest yet potentially radical prospect, that through the deconstruction of the terrorist discourse we make possible a new constructive power to mediate global political violence.

## Notes

1. Terrorism was on the top of the agenda at the first National Security Council meeting of the Reagan administration. On the next day, 27 January 1981, President Reagan stated: "Let terrorists be aware that when the rules of international behavior are violated, our policy will be one of swift and effective retribution." To punctuate the point, Secretary of State Alexander Haig announced the following day at his first press conference that "international terrorism will take the place of human rights" as the number one priority of the Reagan administration. George Bush, who as Vice President headed the Task Force on Combatting Terrorism, which formulated U.S. policy, announced in his inaugural address that terrorism and drugs would be his administration's primary targets. For a breakdown and explanation of terrorist incidents

from 1980–88, see *Patterns of Global Terrorism: 1988* (Department of State Publications, March, 1989), pp. 1–11 and 85.

2. Probably the best of a very large lot is *Inside Terrorist Organizations*, ed. David Rapoport (New York: Columbia University Press, 1988). The Rand Corporation churns out an enormous amount of material on the subject, including the very helpful if intimidating (with over 3,500 entries from 1968 to the present) *Chronology of International Terrorism*. In the Rand collection, I found articles by Brian Jenkins on the multiple strategies of terrorism, Jeffrey Simon on the perception of terrorist threats, and Bruce Hoffman on extreme right-wing terrorism the most useful. For those who need a quarterly fix of terrorist discourse, there is *Terrorism: An International Journal*, edited by Yonah Alexander.

3. See Claire Sterling, *The Terror Network: The Secret War of International Terrorism* (New York: Holt, Rinehart, and Winston, 1981); Christopher Dobson and Ronald Payne, *Terror! The West Fights Back* (London: Macmillan, 1982); Benjamin Netanyahu, *Terrorism: How the West Can Win* (New York: Farrar, Straus, & Giroux, 1968); Yossi Melman, *The Master Terrorist: The True Story of Abu-Nidal* (New York: Avon Books, 1968): and *Fighting Back: Winning the War Against Terrorism*, ed. Neil C. Livingstone and Terrel E. Arnold (Lexington, MA: Lexington Books, 1986).

4. Paul Wilkinson, *Terrorism and the Liberal State* (London: Macmillan, 1977); Walter Laqueur, *Terrorism* (Boston: Little, Brown and Company, 1977); and *Terrorism, Legitimacy, and Power: The Consequences of Political Violence*, ed. Martha Crenshaw (Middletown, CT: Wesleyan University Press, 1983) are good examples of this genre. *Terrorism and International Order*, by Lawrence Freedman and other British international relations generalists (London: Royal Institute of International Affairs, 1986), offers a more philosophical and historical analysis. Official U.S. policy in the 1980s has vacillated between the conspiracy and liberal camps, but the most astute synthesis is Secretary of State Shultz's "Terrorism and the Modern World," an October 1984 address at the Park Avenue Synagogue in New York (Bureau of Public Affairs, Current Policy No. 629). For a critical examination of the liberal attitudes toward terrorism, see Richard Rubenstein, *Alchemists of Revolution: Terrorism in the Modern World* (New York: Basic Books, 1987); and for a refreshingly anarchistic view, see Noam Chomsky, *Pirates and Emperors: International Terrorism in the Real World* (New York: Claremont, 1986). Finally, I believe two works stand out from the crowd, effectively using literary theory and cultural analysis to say something new about terrorism: Robin Wagner-Pacifici, *The Moro Morality Play: Terrorism as Social Drama* (Chicago: University of Chicago Press, 1986); and Khachig Tololyan, "Cultural Narrative and the Motivation of the Terrorist," in *Inside Terrorist Organizations*, op. cit., pp. 217–33.

5. *Taking the Stand: The Testimony of Lieutenant Colonel Oliver North* (New York: Pocket Books, 1987), pp. 26–27.

6. After Colonel Higgins's captors released the video of his hanging, 58 percent of those polled were for negotiations, 39 percent against; 40 percent supported a commando rescue attempt even if lives might be lost, while 50 percent were opposed; and 33 percent advocated the bombing of terrorist hideouts in Lebanon even if innocent people were killed, while 60 percent were against it. See *Time*, 14 August 1989, p. 15.

7. This is something I attempted in an earlier essay on terrorism: "Arms, Hostages and the Importance of Shredding in Earnest: Reading the National Security Culture," *Social Text*, no. 22 (Spring 1989).

8. Shultz, "Terrorism and the Modern World," pp. 5–6.

9. Hedley Bull, "International Relations as an Academic Pursuit," *Australian Outlook* (Vol. 26, No. 3, December 1972), pp. 264–5. While I clearly believe current world politics fully warrant Bull's classical stance of "political nihilism," I believe it can be positively supplemented by "postclassical" or "postmodern" approaches. My own efforts to do so include a Nietzschean and Foucaultian genealogical study of neglected and forgotten possibilities for diplomacy in *On Diplomacy: A Genealogy of Western Estrangement* (Oxford: Basil Blackwell, 1987); and a Bakhtinian dialogical analysis of espionage in "Spy vs. Spy: The Intertextual Power of International Intrigue," *International/Intertextual Relations*, ed. J. Der Derian and M. Shapiro (Lexington, MA: Lexington, 1989). Against charges that postmodernist and poststructuralist approaches are nihilist (like classical realism?), I have found the best theoretical defense to be William Connolly's account of a "projectional interpretation" that "draws part of its sustenance from an always-already-operative attachment to life as a protean set of possibili-

ties exceeding the terms of any identity in which it is set. . . . It then strives to thaw perspectives which tend to stay frozen within a particular way of life, to offer alternative accounts of threats to difference created by the dogmatism of established identities, and to advance different accounts of danger and possibilities crowded out by established regimes of thought." (From *Politics and Irony* forthcoming from St. Martin's Press).

10. William Hazlitt, quoted in *The Complete Works of Shakespeare* (London: Collins, 1981), p. 277.

11. The expansion and acceleration of interdependence was recently highlighted in an event that warranted only a few inches in *The New York Times* (7 January 1990, p. 15), when world financial markets dipped on the news (later proven false) that Gorbachev had canceled some upcoming meetings with foreign leaders to deal with domestic problems. For theoretical analysis of radical changes in international relations, see Paul Virilio, *Défense populaire et luttes écologiques* (Paris: Editions Galilee, 1978); R.B.J. Walker, *One World, Many Worlds: Struggles for a Just World Peace* (Boulder, CO: Lynne, Reiner, 1988); and J. Der Derian, "The (S)pace of International Relations: Simulation, Surveillance, and Speed," in *International Studies Quarterly*, June 1990.

12. *Semiotics* in this context refers to systems of sign usage—including words, visual images, codes, or any signifying practices ("languages")—that convey relations of power and constitute meaning.

13. For those still unfamiliar (or just familiar enough to be contemptuous) with "deconstruction," it can be described as a skeptical (or in some hands, subversive) reading of texts—any verbal or nonverbal sign-systems—that elicits the paradoxes, indeterminacy, and contradictions of any language-generated reality.

14. With an additional dash of hyperbole, French social critic Jean Baudrillard levels a similar charge: "Hence the stupidity and the obscenity of all that is reported about the terrorists: everywhere the wish to palm off meaning on them, to exterminate them with meaning which is more effective than the bullets of specialized commandoes. . . ." See "Our Theater of Cruelty," *In the Shadow of the Silent Majorities and Other Essays* (New York: Semiotext(e), 1983), p. 117.

15. *New York Times*, 25 June 1985, p. 1. More recently in (unusually) clearer prose, former Secretary of State Alexander Haig echoed Weinberger in an editorial article: "We cannot allow a hostage crisis to paralyze the Government to the neglect of everything else. . . . But it is crucial to realize that we are in a war—a twilight war, to be sure, a war of unusual tactics—but one that requires continuing, strenuous efforts, not just a spasmodic reaction to the headlines." (*New York Times*, 15 August 1989, p. 21).

16. Weinberger's belief that the United States should not use military force unless fully supported by the American people and Congress and only as a "last resort" became a matter of public record after his 18 November 1984 speech to the National Press Club. This view would seem to preclude preemptive or retaliatory antiterrorist operations, and, indeed, Weinberger was opposed to the sending of the Marines to Lebanon and the hijacking by F-14 Tomcats of the Egyptian plane carrying the *Achille Lauro* terrorists. In his major statement on terrorism, Secretary of State Shultz was much less equivocal on the equation of war with terrorism and the need for military retaliation: "We now recognize that terrorism is being used by our adversaries as a modern tool of warfare. It is no aberration. We can expect more terrorism directed at our strategic interests around the world in the years ahead. To combat it, we must be willing to use military force." See Jane Mayer and Doyle McManus, *Landslide: The Unmaking of the President, 1984–1988* (Boston: Houghton Mifflin, 1988), pp. 52–54, 140–2; and Shultz, "Terrorism and the Modern World," p. 5.

17. Brian Jenkins, *International Terrorism: The Other World War* (Santa Monica, CA: Rand, 1985), p. 12.

18. Although it is obvious that I am referring to *international* war and *international* terrorism, I have avoided the word because it is a misnomer: war and terrorism fought on individual, tribal, class, and other terrain can have multilevel effects. Probably *global* is a better modifer for the phenomena under discussion, but I do not want to arbitrarily delimit the area to be investigated.

19. For a persuasive account of the roots of violence in "mimetic desire," and the historical attempt to control violence in substitutive rituals of sacrifice, see Rene Girard, *Violence and the Sacred* (Baltimore: Johns Hopkins University Press, 1977).

20. For instance, see Georges Sorel's study of how the myth of violent collective action in the form of a general strike can act as a revolutionary force, in *Reflections on Violence*, trans. T.E. Hulme and J. Roth (New York: Collier, 1961).

21. See N. Cohn, *The Pursuit of the Millennium* (London: Paladin, 1970); David Rapoport, "Fear and Trembling: Terrorism in Three Religious Traditions," *American Political Science Review*, 38:3, September 1984, pp. 658–77.

22. *New York Times*, 17 June 1906.

23. Although Richard Rubenstein presumes in the label of "anarcho-communism" what needs to be historically demonstrated, his opening chapter to *Alchemists of Revolution*, "The Bogeyman, the Hero, and the Guy Next Door," is the best study to date of the complex psychological, political, and historical factors behind terrorism.

24. Sergey Nechaev, *Catechism of the Revolutionist*, in *The Terrorism Reader*, eds. W. Laqueur and Y. Alexander (New York: Penguin, 1987), pp. 68–72.

25. See Laqueur, *Terrorism Reader*, pp. 47–49 and pp. 395–97, for useful bibliographical notes.

26. Saint-Just, *Fragments sur les institutions republicaines*, ed. A. Soboul (Turin: Einaudi, 1952), p. 49, quoted by F.E. and F.P. Manuel, *Utopian Thought in the Western World* (Oxford: Blackwell, 1974), p. 567.

27. W. Laqueur, *Terrorism* (London: Weidenfield and Nicolson, 1978), p. 17.

28. Karl Marx, *Political Writings Volume III*, "The Civil War in France" (New York: Vintage, 1974), pp. 228–31.

29. Ibid., p. 230.

30. Leon Trotsky, "Terrorism and Communism," *The Basic Writings of Trotsky*, ed. Irving Howe (New York: Vintage Books, 1965), pp. 142–53.

31. Ibid., p. 146.

32. Ibid., p. 151.

33. V.I. Lenin, "Where to Begin?" in *Selected Works* (Moscow: Progress Publishers, 1968), pp. 38–39.

34. Ibid., 459.

35. See also Lenin's 1920 essay, "Left-Wing Communism—An Infantile Disorder," in which he attacks the "Socialist-Revolutionary Party" since it "considered itself particularly 'revolutionary,' " or "Left" because of its recognition of individual terrorism, assassination—something that we Marxists emphatically rejected." *Selected Works*, p. 521.

36. See Leon Trotsky, *Their Morals and Ours* (New York: Pathfinder Press, 1969), where he uses the exigencies of the civil war to defend the Decree of 1919—which called for taking hostages of relatives of commanders suborned from the Czar's Army—against "the institution of family hostages [by which] Stalin compels those Soviet diplomats to return from abroad. . . ." (p. 37–39).

37. See, for example, Eric Wolf, *Peasant Wars of the Twentieth Century* (New York: Harper and Row, 1969).

38. Franz Fanon, *The Wretched of the Earth* (Hammondsworth, England: Penguin, 1967).

39. Judging from the prehistory of the key players, like Shackley, Clines, and Secord, reexposed in the Iran-Contra affair, it would seem that fiction rang truer than fact, or at least Eliot Abram's version of it. See below.

40. *Arizona Republic*, 7 April 1989, p. 1.

41. See *The International Narcotics Control Strategy Report* (Department of State Publications, March 1989). It is interesting to note that the United States is not included in the "Country and Regional Summaries" (pp. 19–24), nor in the list of "Worldwide Production Totals" (p. 15), in spite of the fact that the United States has increased its annual rate of marijuana production over the last decade to rival Colombia and Mexico as a major supplier. Since Section 481(h)(2)(A) of the Anti-Drug Abuse Acts of 1986 and 1988 requires that the president certify whether major drug-producing and drug-transit countries have "cooperated fully" with the United States "to enforce to the maximum extent possible the elimination of illicit cultivation," the question arises whether the United States should cut off aid to itself, or at least the marijuana-producing states within the United States.

42. See *International Narcotics Control Strategy Report*, op. cit.; and Michael Massing, "Dealing with the Drug Horror," *New York Review of Books*, 30 March 1989, pp. 22–26. The *New York Times* does, however, report a rise in police officers killed in drug-related incidents to

14, out of a total of 78 for 1988 ("A Record 14 Officers Killed in '88 in Drug Incidents," 3 September 1989, p. 22).

43. A sampling of this school would include Alfred McCoy's classic study, *The Politics of Heroin in Southeast Asia* (New York: Harper and Row, 1972); Peter Maas, *Manhunt: The Incredible Pursuit of a CIA Agent Turned Terrorist* (New York: Random House, 1986); Edward S. Herman, *The Real Terror Network: Terrorism in Fact and Propaganda* (Boston: Southend Press, 1982); and Jonathon Kwitney's *Crimes of Patriots* (New York: Simon & Schuster, 1987).

44. See *Report of the Congressional Committees Investigating the Iran-Contra Affair* (Random House, 1988), pp. 130–31 and pp. 318–21.

45. Both narco-terrorism and the war against it can also be the occasion of insurgency and counterinsurgency on the sly: Juan E. Mendez, executive director of Americas Watch, has recently reported on the collusion between the Colombian military and the drug cartels in attacks on members and sympathizers of the leftist group *Union Patriotica* and guerrilla movements (*New York Times*, 31 August 1989). In Peru, it would appear that the Maoist group *Sendero Luminoso* (Shining Path) has set up protection "rackets" with coca growers and tactical alliances with narco-traffickers.

46. President Bush confirmed this suspicion six months later in a speech, in which he stated that the cocaine cartels "are taking on the pretensions of a geopolitical force" and so "they must be dealt with as such by our military." Address by George Bush at the Commonwealth Club of San Francisco, 7 February 1990 (White House Office text).

47. See Michael Massing, "Dealing with the Drug Horror," *New York Review of Books*, 30 March 1989, pp. 22–26.

48. The State Department's Bureau of International Narcotics Matters spends about $100 million a year, of which only $3.6 million goes to crop substitution and development assistance, while $45 million goes to eradicating crops, and $35 million to law enforcement and interdiction. See Massing, op. cit.

49. One folly could well beget another: on 18 May 1989, the *Washington Times* reported that "House Democrats said yesterday that they will try next week to take money from President Bush's Strategic Defense Initiative research to pay for full funding of the war on illegal drugs." (p. 2).

50. *Patterns of Global Terrorism: 1988*, p. v.

51. Shultz, "Terrorism and the Modern World," Current Policy No. 629, p. 2. President Reagan added some hyperbolic flourishes to say much the same thing at an address to the American Bar Association in July 1985: "So, there we have it: Iran, Libya, North Korea, Cuba, Nicaragua—continents away, tens of thousands of miles apart, but the same goals and objectives. I submit to you that the growth in terrorism in recent years results from the increasing involvement of these states in terrorism in every region of the world. . . . [A]nd we're especially not going to tolerate these attacks from outlaw states run by the strangest collection of misfits, looney tunes, and squalid criminals since the advent of the Third Reich." (quoted from "The New Network of Terrorist States," Bureau of Public Affairs, Current Policy No. 721, pp. 2–3).

52. See, in particular, the section of the CIA's Nicaragua manual, *Psychological Operations in Guerilla Warfare* (republished by Random House in 1985), on "Implicit and Explicit Terror" which instructs the *contras* to "Kidnap all officials or agents of the Sandinista government and replace them" (pp. 52–55).

53. Shultz, "Terrorism and the Modern World," p. 3.

54. Although *antiterrorism* and *counterterrorism* are often used interchangeably in both the official and academic terrorist discourses, I prefer to use only the term *antiterrorism* to describe violent operations against terrorism. *Counterterrorism* (the preferred term of the U.S. State Department) implies, I believe, a competing structure (in the manner that Gramsci refers to a "counter-hegemony" or Foucault to a "counter-justice") that could, or intends to, take the place of terrorism, although the stated policy is to deter and if possible *negate* terrorism rather than replace it with something else. For the official U.S. policy of counterterrorism—based on no concessions, retaliation, legal prosecution, and law enforcement assistance—see the introduction to *Patterns of Global Terrorism*, pp. iii–iv. For a theoretical discussion of the anti/counter distinction, see A. Gramsci, *Selections from Prison Notebooks*, ed. and trans. Q. Hoare and G. N. Smith (London: Lawrence and Wishart, 1971), pp. 206–76; and M. Foucault, "On

264 /  JAMES DER DERIAN

Popular Justice: A Discussion with Maoists," in *Power/Knowledge*, ed. C. Gordon (New York: Pantheon, 1981), pp. 33–35.

55. Although the roles of antiterrorist and counterinsurgency forces, as well as the rationales of low-intensity conflict and covert action, often overlap, I will focus only on antiterrorism since the other topics are well covered elsewhere. For a reasonably sober-minded assessment of the various military units involved, see James Adams, *Secret Armies* (New York: Bantam, 1989); and for a more analytical account of the doctrine of low-intensity conflict, see Michael Klare and Peter Kornbluh, eds., *Low-Intensity Warfare* (New York: Pantheon, 1988).

56. Nor do you hear much in the antiterrorist lore of the Egyptian attempt to rescue a hijacked airliner in Malta that resulted in fifty-seven of the ninety-eight passengers and crew dead. Antiterrorism, like its evil *doppelganger*, relies heavily on the myth of invincibility; hence, much is made of its vaunted capabilities, and very little of its shortcomings—except through the blatant failures or occasional press leak.

57. "The Captors' Reasons," *New York Times*, 27 August 1989.

58. See Bob Woodward, *Veil: The Secret Wars of the CIA 1981–1987* (New York: Simon and Schuster, 1987), pp. 396–8, 416.

59. This begs the question of whether Western leaders have been too quick to dismiss as opportunist the claims of Southern leaders who have discerned a legitimating affinity between anticolonial struggles and some modern forms of terrorism. A critical reading of the biennial UN General Assembly debates on international terrorism over the last two decades could possibly shed some light on this question.

60. Paul Virilio, *Pure War* (New York: Semiotext(e), 1983), p. 27. See also Virilio's *Défense populaire et luttes écologiques*, where he describes nuclear deterrence as being at the same time the catastrophic process of *"une colonisation totale"* (pp. 35–36).

61. "One cannot use violence against what is already violence, one can only reinforce it, take it to extremes—in other words, to the State's maximum power." Virilio, *Pure War*, p. 51.

62. "We can find a sociological, historical and political equivalent to this diabolical conformity, to this evil demon of conformity, in the modern behaviour of the masses who are also very good at complying with the models offered to them, who are very good at reflecting the objectives imposed on them, thereby absorbing and annihilating them. There is in this conformity a force of seduction in the literal sense of the word, a force of diversion, distortion, capture and ironic fascination. There is a kind of fatal strategy of conformity." See Jean Baudrillard, *The Evil Demon of Images* (Sydney: Power Institute, 1987).

63. Sterling, *The Terror Network*, p. 80.

64. Actually Moro's hands are not visible, which at the time raised some doubts of the authenticity of the photograph. The artist Sarah Charlesworth has captured this terrorist cybernet in her presentation of forty-five photographic facsimiles of newspapers that carried the image of the hostage Moro. Part of a much larger series, *Modern History* (1977–79), the collection was at the International Center of Photography in the summer of 1989. In the exhibition she goes beyond the obvious, Sterlingesque point that the Red Brigades made effective use of the media. Charlesworth's blanking out of all written text save the bannerheads of the newspapers reveals the power of context in terrorist discourse. For example, the Roman newspaper that originally received the photograph, *Il Messaggero*, filled two-thirds of the front page with it, with no other news pictures to distract the reader, while *l'Unita*, the newspaper of the Italian Communist Party, ran a much smaller one with two other photos of the forces of law and order, the *carabinieri*, busy at the scene. The *London Times* ran a small, tightly cropped photo of Moro, dwarfed by what *seems* to be a large photo of the Queen holding her new grandson, until one moves down the gallery wall, past the *Irish Times*, the *New York Times*, and the *Baltimore Sun* with multiple news photos as well, to the *Toronto Globe and Mail* which has the smiling monarch blown up three times the size of Moro. Stripped of the verbal signs, the newspapers reveal their ability to impart powerful meanings before the first caption or article is attached, through the image's cropping, placement, size, and relation to other photographs. The viewer / reader is drawn into the process, to see how even the subtlest aspect of media coverage of terrorism becomes an indispensable part of the reterritorialization of global political conflict.

65. To be sure, there are many works on media coverage of terrorism. For example, see Alex Schmid and Janny de Graaf, *Violence as Communication: Insurgent Terrorism and the Western News Media* (Beverly Hills, CA: Sage, 1982); and *Terrorist Spectaculars: Should TV*

*Coverage Be Curbed?* (New York: Priority, 1968). But I believe Jean Baudrillard is the first to get inside the relationship of the global audience, the media, and terrorism, what he sees to be a circle of simulation that is not only ruptured from material referents but now engendering a political *hyper*-reality. See *A l'ombre des majorités silencieuses* (Paris: Cahiers d'Utopie, 1978), *Simulacre et Simulation* (Paris: Galilee, 1981), and *Les Stratégies fatales* (Paris: Bernard Grasset, 1983); the edited translations in the Foreign Agent series (New York: Semiotext(e), 1983), *In the Shadow of the Silent Majorities* and *Simulations*; or *Jean Baudrillard: Selected Writings*, ed. Mark Poster (Stanford, CA: Stanford University Press, 1988).

66. See "Colombians Seize Drug Ring Suspect and 134 Aircraft" (p. 1); "Egypt Arrest 41; Sees Shiite Plot" (p. 6); and "France Says It Plans No Military Role in Lebanon" (p. 7) in *New York Times*, 22 August 1989.

67. It would appear that antiterrorism is fast becoming (after disarmament) a primary site for cooperation with the Soviet Union. Confronting an increase in terrorist incidents (for instance, Aeroflot has suffered at least eleven hijackings since 1973, compared to the next highest airlines, TWA, Air France, and Kuwaiti, which have all been hijacked twice), the Soviet Union has set up a new hostage rescue unit and called for more intelligence-sharing on terrorism with Interpol and the CIA. There have also been high-level discussions on how jointly to combat terrorism: in January 1989 a group of ten American and ten Soviet experts met in Moscow; in September, 1989, Lt. General Fjodor Sherbak, former deputy head of the KGB, and Maj. General Valentin Zvezdenkov, former head of KGB counterterrorism, met at the Rand Corporation for closed-door talks with William Colby, former CIA Director, and Ray Cline, former CIA Deputy Director; and in 1990 Secretary of State James Baker and Soviet Foreign Minister Eduard Shevardnadze hold a second round of official talks on terrorism. See Glenn Schoen and J. Derleth, "KGB Fields New Hostage Rescue Unit," *Armed Forces Journal International* (October 1989), p. 22; and Robin Wright, "U.S. and Soviets Seek Joint War on Terrorism," *Los Angeles Times*, p. 1.

68. The speech was to the National Strategy Forum in Chicago in May 1988, and his response was to someone who asked what he thought was the most important unsolved problem in international relations. The last part of his reply was: "But I've often wondered what if all of us in the world discovered that we were threatened by a power from outer space—from another planet. Wouldn't we all of a sudden find that we didn't have any differences between us at all—we were all human beings, citizens of the world—wouldn't we come together to fight that particular threat?"

For their commentary and help I would like to thank Ruth Abbey, Hayword Alker, Jr., Jean Bethke Felshtain, Jeneen Hobby, Bruce Hoffman, Kiaran Honderich, Michael Klare, M. J. Peterson, and the students from my seminar on Critical and Poststructural Theories of International Relations.

# 12 / Multilateral Institutions and International Security

## MARGARET P. KARNS AND KAREN A. MINGST

### SECURITY AND INTERNATIONAL ORGANIZATIONS

Prior to World War II, international security was conceptualized almost exclusively in terms of questions of war, peace, and armed conflict. National security involved protecting the nation and its territory from external attack or internal subversion. The Charter of the United Nations, however, embodied a broader definition—one that encompassed economic and social well-being, respect for human rights, literacy, adequacy of food, and protection from diseases—along with the more traditional avoidance of use of force. Over the postwar period, that definition has been further broadened to include the security of a safe, nontoxic environment and the security of political and civil rights as well as social and economic rights. International organizations have played prominent roles in broadening the definition of security, and more importantly, in efforts to address the multitude of persistent threats to that security.

Following World War II, a large number and variety of international organizations were created, designed by the victors to eliminate war and its causes and to create a liberal international political and economic order. As the dominant power, the United States played a key role in both the planning phase during the war and in the early days of the organizations' development. In particular, the U.S. government energetically pushed for the creation of the UN as the successor to the failed League of Nations. The United States also promoted the establishment of regional security organizations such as the Organization of American States (OAS) and the North Atlantic Treaty Organization (NATO) and specialized functional organizations such as the International Atomic Energy Agency (IAEA).

Over time, multilateral institutions have become increasingly prominent features of the international environment. One study lists over a thousand international governmental organizations (IGOs) alone, with 70 percent of those established since 1960, most by IGOs themselves.[1] As integral parts of the networks of complex interdependence, international organizations enlarge the possibilities and add to the constraints under which their member states develop and implement foreign policy. Common interests in enhancing predictability in interstate interactions, information sharing, and problem solving provide bases for multilateral cooperation even among states whose specific interests may differ significantly.[2]

States join IGOs to use them as instruments of foreign policy. The IGOs, in turn, establish mechanisms for creating patterns of order and cooperation among states (and other actors). They provide forums for legitimating viewpoints, principles, and norms, for coalition building, and for issue linkage. They establish regularized processes of information gathering, analysis, and surveillance. They institutionalize decision making and negotiating processes for rule creation and dispute settlement. They provide collective goods and support operational activities.[3] Not all organizations perform all of the above functions, and the manner and extent to which they carry out particular functions varies. Like any organization, international organizations are susceptible to bureaucratic growth, corruption, mismanagement, and dominance by special interests. There is nothing inherently "better" about them.[4] They are tools of their member states—instruments of policy—to be used, abused, or ignored.

International organizations depend upon the cooperation and resources of their member governments to implement decisions and recommendations whether that be a cease-fire in a war, a program to clean up an international waterway, or a famine relief effort. Thus, they not only create opportunities for their member states as instruments of policy, but also impose constraints on and influence those policies and the processes by which these policies are formed. IGOs constrain or affect member states by setting international and, hence, national agendas and forcing governments to make decisions; by subjecting states' behavior to surveillance through information sharing; by encouraging states to develop specialized decision making and implementing processes to facilitate and coordinate IGO participation; and by creating principles, norms, and rules of behavior with which states must align their policies if they wish to benefit from reciprocity.

As both instruments and influencers, IGOs are often key components of what are called international regimes—that is, "sets of implicit or explicit principles, norms, rules, and decision-making procedures around which actors' expectations converge in a given area of international relations."[5] Regimes, therefore, encompass a variety of multilateral arrangements that provide processes for international governance, for creating order and patterns of cooperation.[6] An international regime *may* include a formal organization along with treaties, norms of international behavior, and broad principles such as the UN Charter's proscription against the use of force to settle international disputes. By studying the larger processes and sets of arrangements that a regime encompasses, we gain a better conception of the multifaceted nature of global problem solving. Examples of international regimes include the international trade regime centered on (but not limited to) the

General Agreement on Tariffs and Trade; the international food regime encompassing the Food and Agriculture Organization, World Food Program, and the International Fund for Agricultural Development as well as other arrangements; and emerging regimes for marine fisheries, deep-seabed mining, and nuclear accidents, which currently have little in the way of formal organizational arrangements.[7] In the security area, scholars disagree on whether there is a general international security regime;[8] however, a limited regime certainly exists in the nuclear nonproliferation area. The International Atomic Energy Agency provides an organizational core; the regime's rules are spelled out in the network of treaties—global (e.g., the Treaty on the Nonproliferation of Nuclear Weapons) and regional (Treaty of Tlatelolco).

International relations scholars generally agree that in the arena of relations among nation-states and nonstate actors (and, hence, of international organizations), security questions revolve first and foremost around preventing the use of armed force, ending hostilities already under way, lessening tensions that might contribute to the use of force, and controlling or eliminating the proliferation of arms. Therefore, although international organizations devote considerable energy and resources to addressing other threats to international security, we have chosen in this chapter for the sake of manageability to focus on the more conventional definition of security and the role of both formal and informal multilateral institutions in dealing with such security issues. The United Nations is the most important of these.

## International Organizations and International Security

The structure of the United Nations as outlined in the Charter includes six major bodies. The Security Council, with fifteen members, is responsible for international peace and security, with the five permanent members—the United States, the Soviet Union, France, Great Britain, and China—having veto power. The General Assembly, composed of delegates from every member state, has the power to debate any topic within the scope of the Charter. The Economic and Social Council (ECOSOC), with fifty-four members, coordinates the economic and social welfare programs of the UN itself and the specialized agencies such as the Food and Agriculture Organization (FAO), World Health Organization (WHO), and the United Nations Educational, Scientific, and Cultural Organization (UNESCO). The Trusteeship Council has only five members now and a limited role in overseeing the administration of the last non-self-governing UN trust territory. The International Court of Justice or World Court, with fifteen justices, provides a forum for noncompulsory dispute settlement and UN agency advisory opinions. The UN Secretariat, headed by the secretary-general, constitutes an international civil service.

The United Nations Charter in Article 2 (sections 3,4,5) obligates all members to settle disputes by peaceful means, to refrain from the threat or use of force, and to cooperate with UN-sponsored actions. The Security Council has primary responsibility for maintenance of international peace and security (Article 24), and the authority to identify aggressors (Articles 39,40), decide what enforcement measures should be taken (Articles 41,42,48,49), and call on members to make military forces available, subject to special agreements (Articles 43–45). More generally, under Article 34, "The Security Council may investigate any dispute, or any situation which might lead to international friction or give rise to a dispute, in order to determine whether the continuance of the dispute or situation is likely to endanger the maintenance of international peace and security." Prior to the Iraqi invasion of Kuwait in 1990, the Security Council had used its enforcement powers in only two cases—sanctions against Southern Rhodesia (now Zimbabwe) in 1966 and an arms embargo against South Africa in 1977. It has primarily relied instead on its peaceful settlement mechanisms to respond to the many situations that have been placed on the agenda over the years.

Other UN organs also have responsibilities related to peace and security. The secretary-general is authorized to bring to the Security Council's attention any and all matters that threaten international peace and security (Article 99). The General Assembly has the right to make inquiries and studies that might trigger further united action (Articles 13,14) and to be kept informed (Articles 10,11,12). On the basis of the General Assembly's right to consider any matter within the purview of the Charter, the Uniting for Peace resolution during the Korean War in 1950 established a precedent that has enabled the General Assembly to act when the Security Council was stymied by great power veto.

Regional security organizations are structured similarly to the UN, with a general assembly (e.g., the NATO Assembly) in which all states enjoy voting power, and a smaller council (such as the OAS Permanent Council or the OAU's Commission of Mediation, Conciliation, and Arbitration) designed to act on behalf of the whole membership on important or urgent security matters, as well as secretariats to service the organization's activities. The International Atomic Energy Agency, the only UN specialized agency dealing with security matters, has a similar structure, with an annual general conference, director general, secretariat, and board of governors. The distinct feature of the latter is that its members are elected according to a formula for regional representation and leadership in nuclear technology. The performance of regional and international security organizations, the UN in particular, in responding to threats to international peace and security has inevitably been affected by the changing realities of postwar international politics.[9] We turn to an examination of several key developments.

# IMPACT OF POSTWAR CHANGES ON THE FUNCTIONING OF INTERNATIONAL ORGANIZATIONS

The decline of great power unity and development of the Cold War, the decolonization process and emergence of new states, the proliferation of new issues with security implications, and the decline of American hegemony have all affected the functioning of international and regional organizations on peace and security issues.

## Decline of Great Power Unity and the Development of Peacekeeping

The UN Charter ensured that no collective measures could ever be instituted against the "Big Five"—those countries with veto power. Effective functioning of the Security Council, therefore, requires the concurrence of the five. Yet concurrence was almost impossible to achieve during the Cold War era. The sanctioning of UN forces to counter the North Korean invasion of South Korea in 1950 was made possible only by the temporary absence of the Soviet Union, which was protesting the UN's refusal to seat the newly established communist government of the People's Republic of China. Yet the procedural innovation that authorized continuance of those forces once the Soviet Union returned to its seat and exercised its veto—the Uniting for Peace resolution—provided the precedent for the General Assembly to assume responsibility for issues of peace and security when the Security Council was deadlocked by the veto. This procedure has been used subsequently to deal with crises in Suez and Hungary (1956), in the Middle East (1958), and in the Congo (1960). In all, nine emergency special sessions of the Assembly have dealt with threats to international peace when the Security Council was deadlocked.

One creative response to the breakdown of great power unity and the concern over the spread of East-West tension to regional conflicts has been the development of UN peacekeeping—a concept never mentioned in the Charter. Peacekeeping has been defined as

> the prevention, containment, moderation, and termination of hostilities between or within states, through the medium of a peaceful third party intervention, organized and directed internationally, using multinational forces of soldiers, police, and civilians to restore and maintain peace.[10]

The permanent UN military forces envisioned by the Charter were never created. Instead, ad hoc military units, drawn from the armed forces of *nonpermanent* members of the Security Council (often small, neutral members), have been used to prevent the escalation of those conflicts, to keep the great powers at bay, and to keep the warring parties apart until the dispute is settled.

The advantages of the peacekeeping approach over collective security as envisioned in the UN Charter or other means are numerous. Because peace-keeping requires the approval of the parties to the conflict, there is at least a nominal commitment to cooperate with the mandate of the forces. Troops are volunteered by member countries, so the commitment by many members is relatively small. No aggressor need be identified, so no one party to the conflict is singled out for blame. The peacekeeping forces are generally placed along a cease-fire line to separate the hostile forces, to monitor the cessation of hostilities and withdrawal of foreign troops, and to facilitate negotiated settlement once tensions subside. They can contribute to nation-building, as in Namibia in 1990, where UN peacekeepers organized elections, or prospectively in Cambodia, where proposals call for UN peace-keepers to provide a temporary administrative authority.

UN peacekeeping forces have been used most extensively in the Middle East and for conflicts arising out of the decolonization process. The Suez crisis of 1956 marked the first major example of their use. The General Assembly created the United Nations Emergency Force (UNEF I), following the British, French, and Israeli attack on Egypt for its nationalization of the Suez Canal and threat to close the canal to Israeli shipping. (The Suez Canal was built and operated from 1869 to 1956 by a company in which the British and French governments owned shares. The canal historically had served as a vital link for the British Empire.) The UN troops separated the combatants, supervised the withdrawal of British, French, and Israeli forces, and thereafter patrolled the Sinai Peninsula and Gaza Strip.

UNEF I was withdrawn at Egypt's request just before the Six-Day War in 1967. Only in 1973, following the Yom Kippur War, was UNEF II established to monitor that cease-fire and facilitate the disengagement of Egyptian and Israeli forces by supervising a buffer zone between the combatants. A separate force, the United Nations Disengagement Observer Force (UNDOF), super-vised the disengagement of Syrian and Israeli forces on the Golan Heights and a similar buffer zone.

A fourth Middle East force, the United Nations Interim Force in Lebanon (UNIFIL), was established in 1978 following the Israeli invasion and occupa-tion of southern Lebanon to monitor the withdrawal of Israeli forces and assist the government of Lebanon in reestablishing its authority in the area.

UNEF II was terminated in 1979 following the Camp David accords, whose provisions have been monitored by a non-UN Multinational Force and Observers that includes one U.S. battalion. Both UNDOF and UNIFIL remain in place, despite UNIFIL's inability to prevent repeated Israeli raids and the vulnerability of its members to attack and kidnapping by the various warring groups in southern Lebanon.

UN peacekeeping forces were also deployed in the former Belgian Congo (now Zaire) following its independence in 1960. The United Nations Operation in the Congo (ONUC) initially was designed to help the newly independent government establish law and order and to ensure the withdrawal of Belgian troops that had returned to the Congo when violence broke out. When the province of Katanga seceded, ONUC's mission expanded to restore territorial integrity of the Congo and avert full-scale war. The controversial operation, which led the UN to the brink of bankruptcy because of disputes over payment for the force, ended in 1964.

Another operation, the United Nations Force in Cyprus (UNFICYP), has been in existence since 1964 to provide a buffer zone between Greek and Turkish populations on the island of Cyprus. UNFICYP remained in place even during the Turkish invasion in 1974.

By the generally accepted definition of peacekeeping outlined above, the UN role in the Korean War (1950–53) came closer to a collective security action than to peacekeeping. The UN provided a framework to legitimate U.S. efforts to defend the Republic of Korea and mobilize other states' assistance, with a U.S. general designated as the UN commander, but taking orders directly from Washington.

The late 1980s saw a resurgence of UN peacekeeping activities, in large part because the Soviet Union for the first time became interested in its possibilities for dealing with regional conflict and Gorbachev was eager to reduce the costs of Soviet involvement in a number of such conflicts to free resources for domestic Soviet economic needs. The result was a series of initiatives that involved the UN and UN peacekeeping forces. Intense negotiations in the Security Council produced Resolution 598, which prodded Iran and Iraq to agree to a UN-supervised cease-fire in August 1988. The cease-fire has since been monitored by 350 UN military observers while the parties, working with the secretary-general, have pursued negotiations to settle the conflict. In August 1988, an agreement on the withdrawal of Cuban and South African forces in Angola opened the way to the implementation of UN Security Council Resolution 435, which had been approved in September 29, 1978. This called for a UN force (UN Transition Assistance Group or UNTAG) to oversee the transition to independence for the territory of Namibia, which had been ruled by South Africa since the end of World War I. UNTAG's key role in guiding Namibia's transition to independence was symbolized when UN Secretary-General Pérez de Cuéllar administered the oath of office to Namibian President Sam Nujoma on March 21, 1990. Also in 1988, the Soviet Union agreed to withdraw its troops from Afghanistan. The UN secretary-general played an important role in the negotiations, and fifty UN observers monitored the Soviet withdrawal. In fact, the Nobel Peace Prize was awarded to UN peacekeeping forces in 1988 in recognition of their "decisive contribution toward the initiation of actual peace negotiations."

Evaluating the relative success of the peacekeeping approach is not an easy task. One author suggests that evaluation be based on two criteria: whether the interposition of troops prevented the renewal of armed hostilities between disputing parties and whether they facilitated peaceful resolution of a dispute.[11] In several cases, armed hostilities were stopped, but permanent resolution of many disputes proved elusive. UNEF I averted war between the Arabs and Israelis for eleven years. UNEF II was one of many factors that facilitated the negotiation of the Israeli-Egyptian peace agreement at Camp David. ONUC succeeded in preventing the secession of Katanga province and, at a minimal level, helped restore order in the Congo. UNFICYP has averted overt hostilities between the Greek and Turkish communities on Cyprus, but could not prevent the coup d'état by Greek officers in 1974 or the subsequent Turkish invasion. UNDOF can take credit, at least in part, for the quietness of the Golan Heights since 1974. UNIFIL has been the victim of Lebanon's chaos. Because no country wants to be blamed for withdrawing the UN forces and causing even more bloodshed, the Security Council continues to renew its mandate. The border between Iran and Iraq has been quiet since the UN-monitored cease-fire went into effect. Negotiations even to secure an exchange of prisoners of war proved more difficult until Iraq needed to secure its border with Iran after invading Kuwait.

Thus, the record of UN peacekeeping is a mixed one. For those whose definition of success is the peaceful settlement of conflicts, only UNEF II and UNTAG would be deemed successful. If success is defined in terms of ending armed hostilities and preventing their renewal at least for a period of time, then all the operations except UNIFIL could be deemed successful. Critics might well question, however, whether a temporary halt to hostilities, even of several years, is not like putting a lid on a boiling pot. After a period of time, the conflict either erupts in renewed fighting or continues to fester. Either way, the result is a crisis. Yet since 1988 the possible roles for UN peacekeepers have significantly expanded with the new superpower interest in resolving long-standing regional conflicts. In addition to the traditional tasks of physical control of a buffer zone, controlling the movement of armed personnel and weapons, maintaining law and order, and monitoring withdrawal of foreign forces, peacekeeping is increasingly attractive for its peace-building possibilities. That can include establishing an interim administrative authority (Cambodia), holding free elections (Nicaragua, Namibia, Cambodia), organizing humanitarian and reconstruction programs (Central America, Afghanistan, Cambodia), or preserving a country's independence and neutral status (Afghanistan, Cambodia). The increased interest in peacekeeping has also revived interest in the possibility of creating a permanent peacekeeping force or having member states earmark national contingents for such purposes.

The UN has also used techniques other than peacekeeping for conflict management, including fact finding, mediation, conciliation, and arbitration. This broader record of the UN on matters of peace and security is also a mixed one, "combining quiet successes with all-too-visible failures of collective will and imagination." A 1988 report noted

> Far too often, paralyzing differences among the major powers have prevented the UN from playing more than a marginal role in addressing the most intransigent and explosive threats to world peace. Despite its readily apparent limitations, however, the UN has managed to make an important, sometimes critical, difference in resolving a wide range of disputes and conflicts, in forestalling their escalation, and establishing global arms control and disarmament norms.[12]

International organizations other than the UN have provided alternative routes for conflict management. For example, during the 1970s the Association of Southeast Asian Nations (ASEAN) developed the practice of bureaucratic and ministerial consultation for policy coordination on security issues. The technique has enabled the six member nations to coordinate their approaches in dealing with Vietnam and Cambodia. The Organization of African Unity (OAU) has been somewhat successful in resolving low-level disputes among African leaders. On several occasions the organization's officials have been the catalyst for bilateral negotiations, for example, between Morocco and Algeria in 1963. In the Shaba crises of 1977–79 between Angola and Zaire, an inter-African force for peacekeeping was established, but at the urging of the OAU president, the initiative was undertaken outside of OAU auspices. And these forces helped pave the way for the 1980–82 OAU Inter-African force in Chad, which created the conditions for an international resolution of the Chadian conflict.[13] In two situations in the late 1980s, regional organizations teamed up with the UN in peace-keeping roles: in Nicaragua, the UN joined with the Organization of American States (OAS) in monitoring elections, and in Western Sahara, the UN and the Organization of African Unity (OAU) are cooperating on a peace plan.

Given different approaches to conflict management, a clearer picture of the role of international organizations requires more careful delineation of what exactly the organization succeeded in doing. Was the conflict abated or isolated? Did hostilities cease? Was the dispute resolved? One scholar notes that of 282 disputes catalogued between July 1945 and September 1981, 44 percent were referred to the UN, 10 percent to the OAS, 9 percent to the OAU, 8 percent to the Arab League, and 2 percent to the Council of Europe. Assigning numerical values to the various categories of success, with a potential total score of 100 (meaning the organization made a major contribution on all applicable dimensions during the period), the UN received a score of 23; the OAS, a score of 34; the OAU, 20; the Arab League, 15; and the Council of Europe, 18. Aggregating different levels of conflict management, the UN was neither the most successful nor the least successful IGO. For virtually all organizations, though, there was a marked decline of success after 1970 in dealing with threats to peace. The record for the United

Nations, in particular, was worse in isolating disputes and stopping hostilities after 1970, although success in abating conflict was about even.[14] This evaluation, however, predates the resurgence of interest in UN peacekeeping in the late 1980s and Secretary-General Pérez de Cuéllar's active conciliation efforts and focuses only on peacekeeping in its traditional conflict-abatement mode.

Over the postwar period, great power differences have had a profound impact on conflict management, especially by the UN. The development of peacekeeping and regional organizations provided alternate means for responding to conflicts. Another postwar development, namely the process of decolonization and the corresponding expansion of the state system, also had important effects on the role of international organizations in conflict management.

## Decolonization and the Emergence of New States

At the close of World War II, few people would have predicted the effective end of European colonial rule in most of Africa and Asia; twenty years later it had been largely accomplished and with relatively little threat to international peace and security. The number of independent states in the international system increased from 51 in 1945 to 160 in 1990. The United Nations played a significant role in this remarkably peaceful transformation. The Charter endorsed the principle of self-determination for colonial peoples; already independent former colonies such as India, Egypt, Indonesia, and the Latin American states used the UN as a forum to advocate an end to colonialism and independence for territories ruled by Great Britain, France, the Netherlands, Belgium, Spain, and Portugal. Success added new votes to the growing anticolonial coalition. The United States strongly supported decolonization, although alliance ties to the Western European colonial powers sometimes posed sharp dilemmas for U.S. policymakers. By 1960, a majority of the UN's members favored decolonization. General Assembly Resolution 1514 condemned the continuation of colonial rule and preconditions for granting independence (such as lack of preparation for self-rule), and called for annual reports on the progress toward independence of all remaining colonial territories. By 1965, the only major territories remaining under colonial rule were the Portuguese colonies (Angola, Mozambique, and Guinea-Bissau), South West Africa (now Namibia), and Southern Rhodesia (now Zimbabwe)—which because of the unilateral declaration of independence by its white settler minority became a "threat" to international peace and security and the subject of the Security Council's first enforcement action since Korea. In sum, the UN provided an important forum for the collective legitimation of a change in international norms and the organization of the international system.[15]

The consequences of tripling the number of independent states in the system have been manifold: the agendas of international organizations became much more heavily tilted toward issues of economic development and relations between the developed countries of the industrial North and the less developed countries (LDCs) of the South. The ideological leaning of the LDCs toward a heavy governmental role in economic development and redistribution of wealth shaped programs and activities of many IGOs. Indeed, in 1974 these states championed a new international economic order (NIEO), marshalling support in the UN General Assembly for the Declaration on the Establishment of a New International Economic Order and the Charter of Economic Rights and of States Duties. The developing countries argued that the existing international economic order was structured to their disadvantage by weighted voting systems in institutions such as the World Bank and International Monetary Fund and by adverse terms of trade. The proposed norms and principles were reiterated in numerous meetings and resolutions. The NIEO dominated and polarized debate in a number of forums during the 1970s, at times making agreement on both economic and security issues impossible to achieve.

A coalition of developing countries, the so-called Group of 77 or G-77, (whose membership numbers closer to 120 today) and the related Non-aligned Movement commanded a majority of the votes in many IGOs and since 1960 has showed high cohesion across a broad range of issues. The Third World majority succeeded in securing support to amend the Charter in the 1960s to expand their representation in the limited membership UN bodies. As a result, the Security Council was expanded from six to ten nonpermanent members.[16]

In the peace and security field, the interests and sympathies of the developing countries had a powerful influence on the UN and other organizations. Regional conflicts involving LDCs proliferated as a result of decolonization, the emergence of new states, border conflicts among those states, and restive ethnic groups within and across those borders. The continuing East-West conflict raised the risk of superpower intervention. In the Middle East, for example, the G-77 has tilted toward the Arab states and the Palestinians with support from the Soviet Union, while the United States has steadfastly supported Israel. On the issue of apartheid in South Africa, the G-77 has sought to isolate the racist regime through economic and military sanctions. The United States, Great Britain, and France have resisted efforts of the G-77 to get the Security Council to take enforcement action beyond an arms embargo imposed after South Africa's bloody suppression of riots in Soweto in 1976. The South African government's staunch anticommunism made it a tacit ally in the Cold War years. The presence of Soviet-backed Cuban troops in Angola from 1975 on complicated efforts to secure Namibian independence and to press South Africa on apartheid, until changes in Soviet policy helped bring about the 1988 agreement on Cuban troop withdrawal and Soviet support for peaceful change in South Africa.

The decolonization process and increased membership in many international organizations were only two factors in the proliferation of new issues on the agendas of IGOs. The NIEO itself as outlined earlier was an umbrella for a host of issues—a model for efforts on the part of developing countries to redress what they perceived as the inequities in many aspects of the international system. We turn now to other developments that contributed to the proliferation of issues for IGO agendas.

## Proliferation of Security Issues

Many issues that have enlarged IGO agendas have both direct and indirect security dimensions. They encompass issues arising from technological developments, including nuclear energy; issues relating to the areas of global interest not under the jurisdiction of any one state—the "global commons"—such as Antarctica, the seas and seabed, as well as outer space; and developments such as terrorism and airline hijacking.

**Nuclear Energy**    Directly relevant to security and yet not included in the UN Charter are the issues surrounding nuclear technology: its development, expansion, proliferation, and control. The ink on the Charter was hardly dry before atom bombs were dropped on Hiroshima and Nagasaki. From the UN's inception, therefore, its agendas have included items relating to atomic energy. The United States proposed the Baruch Plan in 1946 to place nuclear materials under international control, but the plan was rejected by the Soviet Union. Proposals for arms control and general disarmament have abounded over the years. Only in the wake of the Cuban missile crisis of 1962, however, have there been formal negotiations in the United Nations dealing with nuclear weapons. From 1965 to 1968, the UN provided the forum for negotiators to hammer out the Treaty on the Nonproliferation of Nuclear Weapons that spells out the rules of the nuclear nonproliferation regime. Countries without nuclear weapons agreed in signing the treaty not to acquire or develop them. States with weapons technology promised not to transfer it to nonnuclear states. The treaty went into effect in 1970 and has now been ratified by 137 states. A number of key nuclear states and "threshold" nonnuclear states, however, remain outside the treaty, including France, China, India, Israel, Pakistan, Brazil, and South Africa. The UN was also the principal forum for negotiation of the Outer Space Treaty prohibiting states from orbiting nuclear weapons or other weapons of mass destruction, installing them on celestial bodies, or in any way stationing them in outer space; the 1971 Seabed Treaty that banned weapons of mass destruction from the ocean floor; and the Antarctic Treaty (1959) proscribing the testing of nuclear weapons on that continent. Other nuclear arms control treaties—such as the Test Ban Treaty (1963), the Treaty on the Limitation of Antiballistic Missile Systems (1972), and the two agreements resulting from the Strategic Arms Limitation Talks (SALT I in 1972 and SALT II in 1979)—were negotiated bilaterally between the United States and Soviet Union. Although a number of efforts have been made on a multilateral regional basis to negotiate nuclear free zone accords, only two have thus far succeeded: the Latin American Treaty of Tlatelolco (1967) and the South Pacific Free Zone Treaty (1985).

An important issue in creating a nuclear nonproliferation regime has been how to prevent the proliferation of nuclear weapons, yet enable nations to tap the potential benefits of nuclear technnology for peaceful purposes. In 1957 the International Atomic Energy Agency was established for the dual purpose of disseminating knowledge about nuclear energy and ensuring that this knowledge would be used only for peaceful purposes. IAEA was a direct outgrowth of President Eisenhower's 1953 "Atoms for Peace" address calling for such an international agency. It is unique in that the United States and Soviet Union have cooperated to establish the mechanisms of on-site inspection of nuclear facilities in countries without nuclear weapons and have worked in concert to extend the regime—a rare example of superpower cooperation.[17]

The IAEA has created a system of safeguards "to deter by threat of detection the development of weapons by states that submit to IAEA safeguards. . . . Information about countries' compliance with those norms is the collective good that the IAEA produces."[18] The agency also offers technical assistance to develop peaceful uses of atomic energy to member states accepting the safeguards. Overall, the nonproliferation regime has been relatively successful in limiting the number of new nuclear weapons states, and enabling nonweapons states to tap the benefits of nuclear power.

**Global Commons**    The UN has been the primary forum for discussion of issues involving global commons and for negotiation of treaties and conventions. Indeed, it was in the 1967 UN resolution proposing new international negotiations on the law of the sea that the seas were first referred to as the "common heritage of mankind." The seas and the seabed, which had never previously been the subject of discussion, Antarctica, and outer space have all challenged negotiators to frame legal regimes for areas that are not under the jurisdiction of any state. And each of these global commons poses security issues, some of which stem also from technological developments, especially weapons developments, as well as concern about the impact on fragile and common-use areas of the emplacement of weapons of mass destruction. The treaties previously referred to bar such weapons from Antarctica, outer space, and the seabed. But the lengthy negotiations for a new UN convention on the law of the sea that concluded in 1980 also had to consider such security-related questions as how the interests of maritime states (that is, those states with shipping interests, naval and commercial) could be reconciled with those of coastal states in protecting the resources off their shores, or their own freedom from intimidation. Rising concern over the environment led in 1977 to the conclusion of the Environmental Modification Convention. The beginnings of space exploration in the 1960s had prompted conclusion of the Treaty on Principles Governing the Activities of States in the Exploration and Use of Outer Space, Including the Moon and Other Celestial Bodies (1967). Thus, security and nonsecurity issues relating to the global commons have challenged states to devise multilateral responses and appropriate institutional and organizational arrangements.

**Terrorism**    The increase in international terrorism since the mid-1970s, sponsored both by states and by a bewildering (and ever proliferating) number of nonstate actors, has proven a difficult problem to counter. Even a definition has proven elusive. As the well-known phrase puts it: "One person's terrorist is another person's freedom fighter." Yet terrorism is also the type of problem for which IGOs can be invaluable tools because collection and sharing of information about terrorist groups is essential. IGOs also provide forums to put pressure on states whose border controls or airport security is lax or which are suspected of aiding terrorist groups. And where the cause of terrorism is an unfulfilled claim for self-determination, an IGO may be able to facilitate negotiations to settle the claim. What makes the problem of international terrorism particularly difficult to deal with is the key role played by nonstate actors who are not subject to international law nor members of IGOs. This limits the opportunities for using peer pressure on the perpetrators of terrorist actions or denying them the benefits of reciprocity that underlie much international cooperation. IGOs have been used to pressure states that support international terrorism, such as Libya, Syria, and Iran, but again only to a limited extent because they are members of the G-77, which has been reluctant to take decisive action on terrorism.
    IGOs have undertaken a variety of measures to respond to and deter the increase in international terrorism. For example, after Iran's seizure of American hostages in 1979, the United Nations General Assembly adopted the Convention against the Taking of Hostages and the Resolution on Measures to Enhance the Protection, Security, and Safety of Diplomatic and Consular Missions and Representatives (1980). The International Civil Aviation Organization (ICAO) has long been active in achieving technical agreements to protect international airline traffic and airports from terrorist attacks. These agreements include the Tokyo Convention on Offenses and Certain Other Acts Committed on Board Aircraft (1963), the Hague Convention for the Suppression of Unlawful Seizure of Aircraft (1970), and the Montreal Convention for the Suppression of Unlawful Acts against the Safety of Civil Aviation (1971). Over one hundred nations are parties to these agreements. Regional organizations, including the Nordic League, the Organization of American States, and the European Community, have drafted conventions dealing with terrorism with strong extradition provi-

sions for alleged terrorists.[19] Political differences involving the G-77 members especially have precluded agreement in the UN on such measures aimed at perpetrators of terrorism.

At root, however, the causes of terrorism are manifold and media coverage has frequently been blamed for contributing to its increase. Because much of the terrorist activity has its roots in the Middle East—in the Palestinians' quest for self-determination and their own internal conflicts over strategy, in the hostility among various Islamic groups and the resurgence of Islamic fundamentalism, and in the aftermath of the Iranian revolution—one might argue that solutions to these problems would lead to a diminution, if not end, to terrorism. In any case, neither IGOs nor states acting alone can solve the problem. Both working together can perhaps lessen its incidence and the threat to international security that it poses.

A number of new "human security" issues with serious, indirect, unanticipated security implications have appeared on the UN agenda in recent years.[20] Some of these issues have also fallen under the purview of UN specialized agencies, including the international economic development institutions, the World Health Organization, and the Food and Agriculture Organization. These issues are not always genuinely new, but thanks to media attention and the availability of IGO forums or to increased severity, they may assume greater urgency. They can also pose difficult questions. How can developing countries, in particular, be persuaded to use their scarce resources for economic development and assuring minimal quality of life for their people rather than purchasing military hardware? What are the economic and security implications of AIDS for African countries whose young adult populations are being decimated? How can international agencies ensure that food relief reaches the hungry and is not used as a political instrument of governments?

Issue proliferation has had both negative and positive outcomes. On the negative side, the international agenda is overloaded and fragmented. Some of the new items are "marginal activities" and "incremental tasks [added] without full consideration of whether they are susceptible to meaningful international action."[21] The positive ramifications may emerge in the decade ahead, as Michael Klare explains with reference to environmental issues:

> The United Nations and other international bodies are likely to play an increasing role in managing global environmental problems that exceed the capacity of any one nation to solve. Such problems—the depletion of the ozone layer, the 'greenhouse effect,' widespread deforestation, and pollution of the oceans, for example—acquired new urgency in the late 1980s and demonstrated the need for international cooperation in overcoming threats to global security. It is possible that such cooperation will legitimize concepts of 'common security,' and thereby increase the willingness of countries to cooperate in other areas, including disarmament and international peacekeeping.[22]

Functionalist logic may apply in this regard: that is, cooperation in non-security issues requiring global action may facilitate international cooperation on traditional security issues and constrain national sovereignty in ways that contribute to greater peace and security.

The proliferation of states and issues and the inevitable changes in economic well-being since World War II have all contributed to the fourth factor affecting the functioning of international organizations with respect to peace and security—the decline of American hegemony.

## Declining American Hegemony

In the immediate postwar era, U.S. support of IGOs was designed to nurture and guarantee American political and economic dominance, based on the notion of the "rightness" and universal applicability of American approaches and interests. U.S. dominance assured that there was a high degree of congruence between the U.S. world view and its strategies for multilateral cooperation.[23]

During the 1970s, however, there was a decline in the relative power position of the United States. This decline is evident in statistics showing the increased importance of world trade to the United States and the decline in both U.S. trade and gross domestic product (GDP) as percentages of world totals. Diminished U.S. shares of world monetary reserves, of official development assistance, and of contributions to IGOs reinforced the picture of lessened predominance. Even militarily, the margin of U.S. superiority declined relatively, as shown in comparisons of American and Soviet military capabilities, the increased capability of many Third World countries, and the increased share of the burden of alliance defense borne by the European members of NATO. This decline in relative power resources has affected the ability of the United States to control outcomes in many IGOs and especially in the UN and the specialized agencies. The United States found itself increasingly on the defensive. Its control over agendas slipped; its ability to mobilize votes eroded; more frequently, it found itself using vetoes (indeed, using the Security Council veto for the first time in 1970) and threatening the reduction or withholding of funds to influence IGO outcomes. This decline of U.S. influence within IGOs has been markedly demonstrated in the changing voting patterns in the UN General Assembly illustrated in Figures 12.1 and 12.2.

The effects of declining U.S. hegemony have also been felt in regional organizations. For example, despite continued American military dominance in NATO, the United States, no longer as willing to bear what it perceived to be a disproportionate share of the costs for the protection of Western Europe, has pressed its European allies to assume a greater share of the burden of collective defense. In the Organization of American States there have also been changes. From the end of World War II to the end of the 1970s, the Latin

**Figure 12.1 / The Position of the United States and the Soviet Union in Relation to the UN Majority**

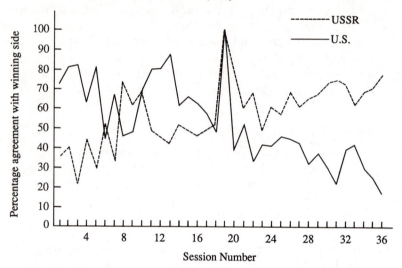

Source: Inter-university Consortium for Political and Social Research, Study Number 5512, United Nations Roll Call Data, reprinted in Harold K. Jacobson, *Networks of Interdependence: International Relations and the Global Political System*, 2nd ed. (New York: Alfred A. Knopf, 1979), p. 106.

**Figure 12.2 / United Nations General Assembly Recorded Votes, 1975–1983: Trends in the U.S. Position**

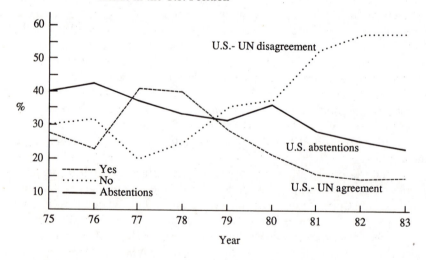

Source: *The Interdependent*, Vol. 10, no. 2 (March/April 1984), p. 4.

American countries had achieved a successful record of conflict resolution.[24] That record worsened with the erosion of consensus between the United States and Latin Americans on collective security and anticommunist norms. One indication of the decline in U.S. ability to control outcomes is the rise in complaints against the United States. Before 1965, the United States was the object of complaints in OAS deliberations only 14 percent of the time; thereafter, the figure rose to 33 percent.[25] Prior to 1965, the U.S. participated in all but one military operation and sat on every committee of investigation; by the 1970s, states were not referring cases to the OAS. In 1975, the Latin American members dropped their support for Cuba's diplomatic isolation and agreed that members could resume relations with Cuba and could choose their own form of internal organization, all over the objection of the United States. U.S. support of Great Britain in the Falkland/Malvinas conflict (1982) and unilateral 1983 invasion of Grenada suggested that since it could no longer count on the support of the other OAS members, it did not attempt to involve the organization.

The four post–World War II trends discussed above—the demise of great power unanimity, decolonization, the proliferation of states and issues on the international agenda, and the decline in the ability of the United States to influence outcomes in organizations in which it previously enjoyed "latent magnetism"[26]—have had significant impact on the role of international organizations in matters of international peace and security. They have contributed to innovation, for example, UN peacekeeping, and to the creation of new regimes and organizations, such as the nuclear nonproliferation regime and the IAEA; they have eroded the utility of some organizations, for example, the OAS; they have virtually paralyzed the United Nations at times in the 1970s and 1980s. They also pose challenges for the development of new multilateral institutions and the reform of existing ones in the 1990s.

## RESPONSES TO CHANGE AND WEAKNESS IN MULTILATERAL SECURITY INSTITUTIONS

The changes in the international political system and in the role of international institutions have contributed to a proliferation of ad hoc multilateral efforts to deal with security issues outside of the UN framework; efforts to reform the UN itself; and proposals for reform outside the UN.

### Ad Hoc Multilateralism

Ad hoc multilateral diplomacy is distinct from multilateral mediation under IGO auspices because it takes place outside the formal structures of international organizations. Such an approach may be useful under certain conditions: when available IGOs are unacceptable as mediators or conciliators to the disputing parties; when no one country has dominant interests or influence over the parties; when several countries, each important to the disputing parties, share a similar attitude about how the conflict might be resolved; when a team of diplomats are able to sustain an effective communication and coordination effort over lengthy negotiating periods. Under such conditions, a small, ad hoc group might more easily develop an acceptable resolution. Certainly, the smaller and more homogeneous the group, the easier it is to achieve consensus, and that consensus may better reflect the policy preferences of the individual members. An ad hoc multilateral group may well rely on the operational capabilities of an IGO for implementing a dispute settlement and thus on the legitimation of that settlement by the IGO's membership. During the negotiating process, however, the ad hoc group has the advantage of not being bound by the guidelines or mandate of an IGO.[27]

The Contadora Group in Central America and the Contact Group in southern Africa illustrate the potentialities and problems with ad hoc multilateral alternatives. The Contadora Group was created in 1983 by the foreign ministers of Mexico, Venezuela, Colombia, and Panama, who shared several important objectives: a desire to end the arms race in Central America, and to prohibit outside military interference, bases, and advisers; a commitment to democratization and to negotiations to attain these objectives.[28] The Contadora Group filled a vacuum created by Nicaragua's fear of U.S. influence in the OAS and by U.S. concern about Nicaragua's popularity in the UN General Assembly.[29] Hence, no established international organization was acceptable to all parties for mediating a resolution of the Central American conflicts. The Contadora negotiations, however, were viewed by the Central Americans as a way to constrain traditional U.S. hegemony and enhance the role of the Contadora states in promoting regional security. Settlement, however, eluded the group and came only when the Central Americans themselves took the initiative.

The Contact Group, composed of the United States, United Kingdom, Canada, Federal Republic of Germany, and France, worked from April 1977 to mid-1982 as an ad hoc multilateral team to deter South Africa from taking unacceptable unilateral actions and to negotiate an agreement for Namibian independence. Their efforts took place outside of the UN, but it was always understood that the UN would play a major role in Namibia's transition to independence and hence that the UN would have to approve any agreement. The group negotiated the terms of Security Council Resolution 435 (1978), but could not gain South Africa's agreement to implement the resolution. The presence of Cuban troops in neighboring Angola became a stumbling block. During the Reagan administration the United States pursued a unilateral settlement of this issue, and the Contact Group effectively lapsed. Its accomplishment, however, the transition embodied in Security Council Resolution 435, was finally put into effect beginning in April 1989 and led to Namibian independence and full sovereignty in 1990.

Thus, the Contact Group established a negotiating process where none had existed before, sustained the process over time, and defused the pressure to impose economic sanctions on South Africa.[30] The Contadora Group has promoted a regional solution to Central American conflicts, the reduction of foreign military (including U.S.) presence, and democratic rule.[31] In neither case was the ad hoc effort entirely successful.

Indeed, ad hoc multilateral diplomacy is fraught with problems. Because such efforts frequently depend on the initiatives of individual leaders, they can easily collapse when participants are drawn off to deal with other issues or leave office. Most states have resisted joining ad hoc multilateral efforts. Despite these problems, informal patterns of organization may ensure that international cooperation does not cease entirely when international institutions are paralyzed. Over the longer term, however, institutional development is critically important for establishing durable means for managing conflicts and the expanding agenda of international problems. Reform may well be necessary to adapt existing institutions to changing conditions and needs.

## UN Reform

UN reform assumed particular urgency in the 1980s, in part because of pressure from the United States, in part because of financial, bureaucratic, and political exigencies. The roots of the UN's financial problems lay in controversies over peacekeeping operations and the refusal of members to contribute that dated from the 1960s. The Soviet bloc and several Arab members refused to pay assessments for UNEF I; the Soviet Union and France refused payment for ONUC. A 1964 advisory opinion of the International Court of Justice, *Certain Expenses of the UN (Art. 17(2) of the Charter)*, ruled that peacekeeping operations should be considered "expenses of the organization" for which members could be assessed. However, the opinion has been difficult to enforce.

The immediate causes of the UN's fiscal crisis in the mid-1980s were threefold: U.S. legislation that unilaterally cut American contributions; decline in value of the U.S. dollar; and a sharp increase in the number of states in arrears. Three pieces of U.S. legislation (the Kassebaum-Solomon amendment, mandating reduced U.S. contributions to the UN budget from 25 to 20 percent unless a system of weighted voting for budget decision making was passed; the Sundquist amendment, prohibiting contributions to salaries of Soviet UN staff members; and the Gramm-Rudman Balanced Budget and Emergency Deficit Control Act, mandating cuts in federal spending, including payments to the UN regular budget and forty-three other international organizations) had the combined effect of a 50 percent reduction in American contributions to the UN in 1986. And the United States was not alone, although its actions as the single largest contributor to the UN were particularly significant. Eighteen other members, including four of the five permanent members of the Security Council, withheld about $120 million for political reasons.[32] Secondly, because the dollar is the currency of the UN, the sharp decline in its value in the 1980s resulted in an $83 million loss for the UN in 1986–87 alone. Thirdly, many states were late in paying their bills for a variety of nonpolitical reasons. Arrearages for peacekeeping were particularly high, doubling from $178 to $361 million between 1981 and 1987. Between 1985 and 1988, U.S. arrearages for peacekeeping, for example, increased by $35 million a year.[33] It is thus little wonder that the UN was on the brink of financial insolvency in the mid-1980s.

In light of the 1985 U.S. threat embodied in the Kassebaum amendment to reduce U.S. contributions to the UN unless the budget decision process was altered from a one-state, one-vote formula, the UN convened a Group of Eighteen experts to draft recommendations for "improving the . . . functioning of the Organization."[34] The group's mandate and time were limited because of the need to recommend immediate measures to meet the financial crisis. It submitted its report to the Forty-first General Assembly in October 1986. From the standpoint of meeting American concerns, the most important recommendation by the Group of Eighteen called for consensus voting during the early review of program budgets by the UN Committee for Program and Coordination (CPC). Even though programs and budgets must subsequently be reviewed by the General Assembly, "consensus voting at the CPC stage gave the United States (which, as a major power, always has a seat on the 21-member CPC) a virtual veto on projected programs without forcing a revision to the principle of one state one vote."[35] Because the CPC advises the General Assembly on program content and the size of budget requests, the requirement for consensus also responded to the criticism that the General Assembly has frequently approved new programs without regard to the availability of funding, or to put it another way: member states, especially Third World states, could no longer assume that whatever they wanted would be funded by the major contributors.[36] The adoption of the Group of Eighteen's recommendation gave the United States a virtual veto on projected programs without forcing a revision of the principle of one state, one vote.

The UN budget crisis was also closely linked to a crisis of administration in many UN agencies that was dramatized by American and British withdrawal from UNESCO in 1984. The problems were rooted in poor staff performance, overly complex internal structures, wasteful and duplicative programs, and lax financial control.[37] The Group of Eighteen recommended severe cuts in the top levels of UN staff and simplification of organizational procedures.[38]

Beneath the budgetary and administrative problems was what UN

Secretary-General Pérez de Cuéller in his 1986 Annual Report called the need for "the strengthening and revitalization of the present structure of multilateral institutions." The secretary-general noted, "We are still adjusting to the new and uneasy distribution of forces in the world" that have emerged since World War II. Although the secretary-general predictably argues that "the United Nations should be, and is, a central element in bringing . . . the necessary adjustments,"[39] the UN is now only one framework for ensuring global security, albeit the only universal-membership international organization.

With specific reference to security issues, the least revolutionary proposals for UN reform call only for the Security Council to make more effective use of powers delegated to it under the Charter, for example, to investigate situations before conflict breaks out; for the secretary-general to bring potential disturbances to the attention of the Security Council earlier; for the Security Council to hold meetings in private to establish a more conciliatory rather than confrontational atmosphere; to provide peacekeeping forces with better logistical support and training; and to establish more secure financing arrangements for peacekeeping operations.[40] Other proposals have called for establishment of a permanent UN military force as authorized but never implemented under Article 43 of the Charter. Such a permanent force of international civil servants would be trained for the task of peacekeeping, stationed together, available for duty immediately, and have a permanent infrastructure for logistical support.[41]

It has also been suggested that the UN should build on its relative success in some areas and be more selective in the range of issues it addresses at any one time and the techniques it employs. The Security Council might, therefore, concentrate on the informal negotiations and consensus building that it often does well, providing face-saving alternatives when parties are ready to terminate hostilities. This approach would renew the UN's role in providing good offices and conflict mediation and conflict management, and reduce peacekeeping.[42] In addition, the UN could strengthen cooperation with regional bodies, rationalize its arms control and disarmament agenda, develop multilateral inspection teams for impartial verification on security issues, and establish ad hoc review groups.[43]

Many proposals for UN reform have sought to provide a more effective and efficient framework for solving global problems; some have been designed to promote particular countries' interests, for example the Soviet proposal in 1960 to replace the secretary-general with a troika—a three-person executive. The revisions in UN budget decision processes and reductions in administrative staffing have helped to remedy some of the major problems in the organization and its specialized agencies. In the area of peace and security, proposals that recommend strengthening the office of the secretary-general and encouraging an active role for the secretary-general stand the best chance of producing a more effective role for the UN.[44] This is because (a) such steps require no difficult political battle for Charter amendment; (b) the office has historically commanded a high level of perceived objectivity and respect that peacemaking requires; and (c) a strong secretary-general can work for other reforms in the organization and can help to open other avenues to peaceful settlement of disputes when the contending parties are looking for a way out.[45] Both East-West and North-South conflicts have amply demonstrated the possibilities for deadlock. Yet the UN is only one among many multilateral institutions. Proposals for reform have also sought to create or strengthen other multilateral mechanisms for promoting and maintaining international peace and security.

## Reforms Outside the UN

Like the UN, regional organizations have also faced administrative and budgetary problems and are in need of reform. For example, the OAU is reportedly in shambles; over 75 percent of the secretariat are not physically present in Addis Ababa. Those that are present are unqualified; there is flagrant mismanagement of resources, compounded by the confiscatory policy of the host Ethiopian government.[46] Yet the 1989 appointment of the highly respected Salim Ahmed Salim of Tanzania as secretary-general was viewed as a step toward revitalization and reform in the OAU.

One proposal to enhance international peace and security advocates creating a transnational police force outside the UN of around five thousand individuals to be deployed at three or four base camps. This force would be authorized to engage in four different types of enforcement action: the first, broadly similar to UN peacekeeping, i.e., preventing border clashes and discouraging third-party intervention; the second, humanitarian intervention, aiding innocent victims caught between hostile forces; the third, restraining officials who resist internal implementation of norms such as those proscribing brutality and torture; the fourth, implementing arms reductions agreements. The proposed police force would have very broad powers to intervene without host country consent, and in the absence of unanimity of permanent members of the Security Council.[47] How such a force could be created and sustained is not clear.

Other proposals have called for more systemic reforms. One writer, himself a former Secretariat official, suggests that although some minor changes and improved management will solve the current UN crisis, "a change in the political climate is needed before a real revitalization of the UN can be achieved."[48] Since almost from the beginning of the post–World War II period the UN was unable to play the role in questions of peace and security for which it was designed, two other networks emerged. One, already touched upon, includes regional organizations, NATO, OAS, OAU, the Warsaw Pact. In addition, for example, the Conference on Security and

Cooperation in Europe (known as the Helsinki Conference and convened periodically since 1975) and the Mutual and Balanced Force Reduction Talks (MBFR) (under way since the early 1970s involving most European states) have provided trans-European forums for discussion of security questions. The other network has involved bilateral links between the superpowers (or other states). With the dramatic changes that have taken place in central Europe since mid-1989, new security arrangements are needed and old ones, especially NATO and WTO, need to change. Technological developments and other global changes will continue to generate new issues and challenges for multilateral problem solving, even as nations continue their struggle to adopt the previous developments. Yet any steps designed to improve the ability of the international system to manage problems of peace and security, whether they are reforms of existing organizations such as the UN or new development of new regimes, with or without formal organizations, will require the commitment of states so long as sovereign (or even semi-sovereign) states remain the key components of that system. States have all too often made commitments casually—commitments they cannot, should not, or even intend not to fulfill. This tendency is encouraged by international institutions and particularly by conference diplomacy. Inis Claude notes, "The discrepancy between promise and intention results from the tension between the urges to assume international responsibility and to maintain national freedom of action. Casual commitment represents an effort to have it both ways."[49] Renewal or strengthening of member states' commitments to existing organizations, to reform or to new arrangements, is imperative.

## Renewal of State Commitment

In 1987 Soviet General Secretary Gorbachev suggested the need for revitalization of the UN and regional groups, especially in the area of security, noting:

> We are arriving at the conclusion that wider use should be made of the institution of UN military observers and UN peace-keeping forces in disengaging the troops of warring sides, observing ceasefire and armistice agreements.

> Of course at all stages of a conflict extensive use should be made of all means for the peaceful settlement of disputes and differences between states and one should offer one's good offices, one's mediation with the aim of achieving an armistice. The ideas and initiatives concerning nongovernmental commissions and groups which would analyze the causes, circumstances and methods of resolving various concrete conflict situations appear to be fruitful.

> The Security Council permanent members could become guarantors of regional security. They could, on their part, assume the obligation not to use force or the threat of force, to renounce demonstrative military presence.[50]

To back up this verbal commitment, the Soviet Union announced that it would pay up financial arrears of $127 million, including assessments for UN peacekeeping forces it had long opposed. One assessment of the changes in Soviet policy suggested, "Gorbachev has presented a far more comprehensive and positive view of the United Nations than any of his predecessors."[51] Certainly, his speech and Soviet actions represented a new Soviet commitment to multilateral institutions.

Ironically, these Soviet proposals for renewal of the UN's role coincided with the low point in U.S. commitment. To some Americans, the UN and other international organizations were "like the sorcerer's apprentice—out of control";[52] they were "the scene of a struggle that we [the U.S.] seem doomed to lose."[53] The United States acted unilaterally in a number of situations during the Reagan administration, such as the invasion of Grenada, interventions in Nicaragua and El Salvador, and the bombing of Libya, rather than seeking multilateral action through international organizations. Some members of Congress and conservative organizations such as the Heritage Foundation contended that since the United Nations no longer reflected American priorities, it was a "dangerous place."[54] Poll data showed a significant drop in public support for the UN. In 1956, 51 percent of the American population thought the UN was doing a good job; in 1985, the figure had dropped to 28 percent; it rose again in 1989 to 38 percent. Regardless of their opinions on the job the UN was doing, most Americans (76 percent in 1986) continued to believe that the United States should not withdraw from the organization.[55]

Even before the end of the Reagan administration in 1987, however, there were signs that U.S. antagonism toward the UN was moderating. UN successes in peacekeeping and conflict management and the change in the Soviet attitude contributed to the change.[56] Reforms in UN administrative and budgetary processes, following the report of the Group of Eighteen, met most congressional concerns.

States other than the United States or the Soviet Union have also showed commitment to a changed UN. The failure of efforts to institutionalize the new international economic order has led G-77 members to temper their expectations, recognizing that a new order requires many changes that cannot be forced through by a coalition that commands a majority of votes, but whose members are economically weak. As Coate and Puchala note, "the Southern tone in North-South diplomacy has moderated. . . . Southern delegates . . . explain that their current, more restrained approach actually signifies the growing realization that the UNO is a limited mechanism for dealing with many of their most immediate concerns."[57] This new moderation and pragmatism on the part of the Third World, combined with the renewed commitment to multilateralism by the First and Second Worlds, may well provide the impetus to further changes in international arrangements for peace and security in the decade ahead.

The Iraqi invasion of Kuwait on August 2, 1990 brought immediate evidence of the new commitment by the superpowers and other states to the UN in the unanimous condemnation of Iraq's actions and imposition under Article 41 of economic sanctions. For the first time since the founding of the UN in 1945, the Charter's collective security system actually worked. The five permanent members of the Security Council, along with the nonpermanent members, were united in their insistence that the blatant violation of the Charter's prohibition on the use of force to settle disputes must not stand. The Gulf crisis also drew new attention to the UN Military Staff Committee, with Soviet insistence that it coordinate any UN military activity in enforcing the economic sanctions or ousting Iraqi forces from Kuwait itself. The consequences of the Gulf crisis for the UN's role in future threats to international peace and security are certain to be significant.

# TOWARD THE TWENTY-FIRST CENTURY

In the 1990s, as changes in the international political system solidify and some of the reforms within and without the UN system are instituted, attention might well focus on further development of formal and informal arrangements for international security. The achievement of peace and security will require a variety of both traditional and nontraditional, multilateral global and regional mechanisms. What will be the role of existing organizations such as the UN, NATO, OAS, OAU? Will multilateral institutions—new and existing—evolve with emerging international security problems in this increasingly interdependent world? Whatever form new structures take, or old ones like the United Nations assume, the difficult problems of international peace and security in the last decade of the twentieth century will demand multilateral solutions.

## Notes

1. Harold K. Jacobson, William M. Reisinger, and Todd Mathers, "National Entanglements in International Governmental Organizations," *American Political Science Review* 80 (March 1986), pp. 141–60.

2. For an elaboration, see Margaret P. Karns and Karen A Mingst, eds., *The United States and Multilateral Institutions: Patterns of Changing Instrumentality and Influence* (Boston: Unwin Hyman, 1990).

3. Collective or public goods are the benefits provided by groups, including international organizations and national governments, that serve the common interests of members of that group. Because they are provided to some members, they cannot be withheld from others in that group, i.e., they are indivisible. Examples of the collective goods provided by IGOs include information that is gathered and disseminated about other states' activities (e.g., human rights violations or compliance with atomic energy safeguards); control of nuclear proliferation; and the order that ensues from international air traffic regulations. For a discussion of collective goods, see Mancur Olson, Jr., *The Logic of Collective Action: Public Goods and the Theory of*

*Groups,* rev. ed. (New York: Schocken Books, 1971), pp. 9–16. Operational activities are things like peacekeeping, development assistance, or monitoring of nuclear power facilities.

4. Inis L. Claude, Jr., *States and the Global System: Politics, Law and Organizations* (New York: St. Martin's Press, 1988).

5. Stephen D. Krasner, "Structural Causes and Regime Consequences: Regimes as Intervening Variables," in Stephen D. Krasner, ed., *International Regimes* (Ithaca: Cornell University Press, 1982), p. 186; see also, Stephan Haggard and Beth A. Simmons, "Theories of International Regimes," *International Organization,* 41:3 (Summer 1987), pp. 491–517 for an excellent review of the regime literature.

6. See Friedrich Kratochwil and John Gerard Ruggie, "International Organization: A State of the Art of the State," *International Organization,* 40 (Autumn 1986), pp. 753–76; also Margaret P. Karns and Karen A. Mingst, eds., *The United States and Multilateral Institutions.*

7. See Oran R. Young, *International Cooperation: Building Regimes for Natural Resources and the Environment* (Ithaca: Cornell University Press, 1989) for an excellent discussion of these emergent regimes.

8. Note the contrasting arguments found in Robert Jervis, "Security Regimes," *International Organization,* 36:2 (Spring 1982), pp. 357–78; and Ernst B. Haas, "Regime Decay: Conflict Management and International Organizations, 1945–1981," *International Organization,* 37:2 (Spring 1983), pp. 189–256.

9. For discussion of these changes and their effects on the UN, see especially Inis L. Claude, Jr., *Swords into Plowshares: Problems and Progress of International Organizations* (New York: Random House, 1964); Evan Luard, *The United Nations: How It Works and What It Does* (New York: St. Martin's Press, 1979); A. LeRoy Bennett, *International Organizations: Principles and Issues* (Englewood Cliffs: Prentice Hall, 1988); and Inis L. Claude, Jr., *The Changing United Nations* (New York: Random House, 1967).

10. Jit Rikhye, Michael Harbottle, and Bjorn Egge, *The Thin Blue Line: International Peacekeeping and Its Future* (New Haven: Yale University Press, 1974).

11. Paul F. Diehl, "Peacekeeping Operations and the Quest for Peace," *Political Science Quarterly* 103:3 (1988), p. 489.

12. United Nations Association of the USA, *A Successor Vision: The United Nations of Tomorrow,* Peter J. Fromuth, general editor, (Boston: University Press of America, 1988), p. 3.

13. For more specifics on regional peacekeeping, see Michael Leifer, *ASEAN and the Security of South-East Asia* (London: Routledge, 1989); Robert O. Tilman, *Southeast Asia and the Enemy Beyond: ASEAN Perceptions of External Threats* (Boulder: Westview, 1987); I. William Zartman and Yassan El-Ayouty, eds., *The OAU After 20 Years* (New York: Praeger, 1984); and Guy Martin, "Security and Conflict Management in Chad," *Bulletin of Peace Proposals,* 20:4 (1989).

14. Ernst B. Haas, "Regime Decay: Conflict Management and International Organizations, 1945–1981," p. 203.

15. For discussion of the UN role in decolonization, see Claude, *The Changing United Nations;* Harold K. Jacobson, "The United Nations and Colonialism: A Tentative Appraisal," *International Organization,* 16 (Winter 1962), pp. 37–56; David Wainhouse, *Remnants of Empire: The United Nations and the End of Colonialism* (New York: Harper & Row, 1964).

16. ECOSOC membership has been expanded on two occasions, moving from 18 to 54 members.

17. See Joseph S. Nye, "Maintaining a Nonproliferation Regime," *International Organization,* 35:1 (Winter 1981) pp. 15–38; Benjamin Schiff, *International Nuclear Technology Transfer: Dilemmas of Dissemination and Control* (Totowa: Rowman and Alanheld, 1984), ch. 1; John R. Redick, "The Tlatelolco Regime and Nonproliferation in Latin America," *International Organization,* 35:1 (Winter 1981), pp. 103–34; Lawrence Scheinman, *The International Atomic Energy Agency and the World Nuclear Order* (Washington, D.C.: Resources for the Future, 1987).

18. Benjamin Schiff, "Dominance Without Hegemony: U.S. Relations with the International Atomic Energy Agency," in Margaret P. Karns and Karen A. Mingst, eds., *The United States and Multilateral Institutions,* p. 60.

19. For more detail, see Alona Evans and John Murphy, *Legal Aspects of International Terrorism* (Lexington: D.C. Heath, 1978); Donna M. Schlagheck, *International Terrorism: An Introduction to the Concepts and Actors* (Lexington, Mass.: Lexington Books, 1988).

20. UNA/USA, *A Successor Vision*.

21. George Davidson, *United Nations Financial Emergency: Crisis and Opportunity* (New York: Mimeo, August 1986), p. 27.

22. Michael T. Klare, "Peace Studies in the 1990s: Assessing Change in the Global War/Peace System," in Daniel C. Thomas and Michael T. Klare, eds., *Peace and World Order Studies: A Curriculum Guide* (Boulder, Colo.: Westview, 1982), p. 70.

23. See Margaret P. Karns and Karen A. Mingst, eds., *The United States and Multilateral Institutions*, pp. 11–13; Robert O. Keohane, "The Theory of Hegemonic Stability and Changes in International Economic Regimes, 1967–1977," in Ole R. Holsti, Randolph M. Siverson, and Alexander George, eds., *Change in the International System* (Boulder: Westview Press, 1980) pp. 131–62; Robert O. Keohane, *After Hegemony: Cooperation and Discord in the World Political Economy* (Princeton: Princeton University Press, 1984) pp. 31–46.

24. Jorge I. Dominguez, "Latin American International Conflicts and the Threats of War," in J.S. Mehta, ed., *Third World Militarization: A Challenge to Third World Diplomacy* (Austin, Tex.: The University of Texas Press, 1985), p. 144.

25. Ernst B. Haas, "Regime Decay: Conflict Management and International Organizations, 1945–1981," p. 213.

26. H. G. Nicholas, *The United Nations as a Political Institution*, 5th ed. (London: Oxford University Press, 1975), p. 200.

27. Margaret P. Karns, "Ad Hoc Multilateral Diplomacy: The United States, The Contact Group, and Namibia," *International Organization*, 41 (Winter 1987), pp. 122–23.

28. Bruce Michael Bagley, "Contadora: The Failure of Diplomacy," *Journal of Inter-american Studies and World Affairs*, 28:3 (Fall 1986), p. 5.

29. Susan Kaufman Purcell, "Demystifying Contadora," *Foreign Affairs*, 64:1 (Fall 1985), p. 75.

30. Karns, "Ad Hoc Multilateral Diplomacy," pp. 119–20.

31. Bagley, "Contadora," pp. 13, 21.

32. Maurice Bertrand, "Can the United Nations Be Reformed?" in Adam Roberts and Benedict Kingsbury, ed., *United Nations, Divided World: The UN's Roles in International Relations* (Oxford: Clarendon Press, 1988), p. 194.

33. Donald J. Puchala and Robert A. Coate, *The State of the United Nations, 1988*. Report to the Academic Council on the United Nations System (1988), pp. 8, 12.

34. For a review of reform proposals, see Maurice Bertrand, "Can the United Nations Be Reformed?," pp. 193–208.

35. Gene M. Lyons, "Reforming the United Nations," *International Social Science Journal*, 120 (May 1989) p. 250.

36. Bertrand, "Can the United Nations be Reformed?" p. 198.

37. Maurice Bertrand, "Planning, Programming, Budgeting, and Evaluation in the U.N.," in UNA/USA, *A Successor Vision: The United Nations of Tomorrow*, pp. 255–87.

38. For more details, see Peter Fromuth and Ruth Raymond, "U.N. Personnel Policy Issues," in UNA/USA, *A Successor Vision: The United Nations of Tomorrow*, pp. 213–54; Yves Beigbeder, "Financial Crisis and Management Reform in U.S. Organizations," paper presented at the Annual Meeting of the International Studies Association and the British International Studies Association, March 28–April 1, 1989, forthcoming in W. Junk, ed., *Essays on Inter-International Administrations* (Norwell, Mass.: Martinus Nijhoff, 1989).

39. Report of the Secretary General on the Work of the Organization, (New York: United Nations, 1986), p. 4.

40. Evan Luard, "Conclusion: The Contemporary Role of the United Nations," in Adam Roberts and Benedict Kingsbury, eds., *United Nations, Divided World: The UN's Roles in International Relations* (Oxford: Clarendon Press, 1988), pp. 220–30.

41. Paul F. Diehl, "A Permanent UN Peacekeeping Force: An Evaluation," *Bulletin of Peace Proposals*, 20:1 (1989), pp. 27–36.

42. UNA/USA, *A Successor Vision*, pp. 44–50.

43. Ibid, pp. 64–67.

44. Ibid.

45. Lyons, "Reforming the United Nations," p. 261.

46. "Gâchis à Addis Ababa," *Jeune Afrique*, 1294 (23 octobre 1985), pp. 11–17.

47. Robert C. Johansen and Saul H. Mendlovitz, "The Role of Enforcement of Just Law in

the Establishment of a New International Order: A Proposal for a Transnational Police Force," in Richard Falk, Friedrich Kratochwil, and Saul H. Mendlovitz, eds., *International Law: A Contemporary Perspective* (Boulder, Colo.: Westview, 1985), pp. 346–64.

48. Bertrand, "Can the United Nations be Reformed?"

49. Inis L. Claude, *States and the Global System,* pp. 65–66.

50. M. S. Gorbachev, "Secure World," printed in *FBIS-SOV* (17 September 1987), p. 25.

51. Edward C. Luck and Toby Trister Gati, "Gorbachev, the United Nations, and U.S. Policy," *The Washington Quarterly,* 11:4 (Autumn 1988), p. 22.

52. Robert O. Keohane and Joseph S. Nye, Jr., "Two Cheers for Multilateralism," *Foreign Policy,* 60 (Fall 1985), p. 148.

53. Jeane Kirkpatrick, quoted in ibid, p. 148.

54. For example, see Burton Yale Pines, *A World Without the UN* (Washington, D.C.: The Heritage Foundation, 1984); Abraham Yeleson and Anthony Gaglione, *A Dangerous Place: The United Nations as a Weapon in World Politics* (New York: Grossman Publishers, 1974); Daniel Patrick Moynihan, *A Dangerous Place* (New York: Berkley Books, 1980).

55. Gallup Organization, 1977, and Roper Polls, 1988 and 1989; National Opinion Research Center, 1986.

56. Donald J. Puchala and Roger A. Coate, *The State of the United Nations, 1988,* p. 24.

57. Ibid., p. 31.

# 13 / Promoting Human Rights

STEPHEN P. MARKS

## INTRODUCTION

For the first time in history, human rights, as a set of widely accepted standards defining minimum obligations of treatment of individuals and groups, has become a dimension of international affairs. This extraordinary development has taken place essentially since 1945. For the activist, it is a painfully slow process, fraught with hypocrisy, backsliding, and entrenched interests. From a broader historical perspective, however, it is one of the directions of change that is chipping away at the nation-state system and establishing new cooperative approaches that may hasten new structures of international society more conducive to peace and security than the current ones.

This chapter will explore the promotion of human rights as a factor in the shifting paradigms of international relations during the final decade of this millennium. To set the stage for this inquiry, we must first agree on what we mean by "human rights." With some general definitions in mind, we will then explore the priority issues of human rights in the coming years and conclude with an overview of the means of redressing and preventing human rights abuses.

## THE MEANING OF HUMAN RIGHTS IN INTERNATIONAL AFFAIRS

Human rights may be understood in various ways. Some observations on the distinction between the moral and empirical foundations of human rights, the process of internationalization of human rights, and the content of the current catalogue of human rights will contribute to a basic understanding of the meaning of the term in international affairs.

### Moral and Empirical Foundations of Human Rights

For many, the expression *human rights* denotes a philosophical or religious position regarding the ultimate value of the individual in society. This approach refers to the moral foundation of human rights and is usually linked to the theory of "natural rights." Another approach stresses the legal foundations of human rights: the normative basis is to be found in an authoritative source, essentially a legal source of "black letter" or positive law, applied in a system where the rule of law prevails.[1]

The modern conception of human rights is, to a large extent, based on the natural law approach as it developed in eighteenth-century Europe.[2] Its significance today as a factor in international relations, however, is due in large part to its empirical foundation, by which we mean the formal evidence that states accept the rules of human rights. A truly remarkable feature of international relations today is the acknowledgement of that empirical foundation by virtually all countries in their own constitutions, in formal pronouncements of leaders, and through ratification of international human rights treaties. This lip service to human rights can be used to hold a government accountable, to point out the gap between word and deed, whatever the nature of its political and social system.

The two approaches (moral and empirical), moreover, are not incompatible. On the contrary, it is often because of a belief system that ideas such as human rights are articulated in formal, empirically identifiable rules, accompanied by social inducements to comply with those rules. In other words, members of a society may hold a moral precept like "Thou shalt not kill" and derive therefrom the idea of the right to life. It is likely also that murder is proscribed in the laws of their society. Therefore, to say "The right to life is a human right" may mean "I have a belief system that prohibits the taking of another's life" or it may mean "Murder is prohibited by law here."

In order to understand human rights, we must not only distinguish the moral and empirical approaches[3] but also study the process whereby rights become "shaped" and "shared" within a community.[4] In response to human needs felt by the members of the community, values are consecrated as rights by authoritative bodies (e.g., the legislature) and effectively applied. This "authoritative decision," to use the terminology of the "policy-oriented perspective" of McDougal and others, covers both the "technical myth" (what the law says) and actual practice.[5]

A full understanding of the philosophical foundations of human rights would require examining a wide range of historical developments, cultural conditions of different societies, attitudes toward the ideas of right and justice, and so on. For our purposes, we shall assume that, as a subject of international and global studies, the term refers to the set of prescriptions relating to the treatment of individuals and groups that have been formally consecrated as internationally recognized human rights.

## The Internationalization of Human Rights

While theoretical debate over the nature of rights and the place of rights in the domestic legal order has long been part of political discourse, especially since the Enlightenment, human rights have really entered the political arena in the post-1945 period. During the late 1940s and through the 1950s and 1960s, the standard-setting work of the United Nations proceeded apace, and regional conventions and institutions for their implementation were adopted by the Council of Europe and the Organization of American States. This internationalization of human rights was the process whereby propositions formulated theoretically or as part of national legal systems were accepted as legitimate matters of international concern and standard setting. Among the salient developments in this process, which began well before the twentieth century, were the abolitionist movement in the eighteenth and nineteenth centuries, the minorities treaties and the constitution of the International Labor Organization following World War I, and, at the close of World War II, the "enthronement" of human rights in the Charter of the United Nations. It accelerated in the post-1945 era with the International Bill of Human Rights[6] and about one hundred treaties and other significant international instruments adopted in the United Nations system and through regional organizations.[7]

## The Content of International Human Rights

The rights recognized in those instruments are traditionally grouped in two categories: civil and political rights (CPR) and economic, social, and cultural rights (ESCR).[8] The standard references are the Universal Declaration of Human Rights (adopted in 1948), which proclaims CPR in Articles 1–21 and ESCR in Articles 22–27, and the two International Covenants on Human Rights (adopted in 1966 and ratified by over ninety countries), one on CPR and the other on ESCR. The array of international human rights is wider and deeper than these three instruments, and the distinction between the two categories is far from tight. Nevertheless, they constitute a good starting point for grasping what we mean by human rights in international affairs.

A closer look at the two covenants reveals that they contain more than the enumeration of rights belonging to one or the other category. At the risk of oversimplification, we can deepen our initial understanding of the meaning of human rights by noting that the covenants, the most widely accepted catalogue of human rights, contain forty propositions that may be grouped as follows:

### Rights of Peoples and Minorities

1. Right of peoples to self-determination
2. Right of peoples to permanent sovereignty over natural resources
3. Rights of ethnic, religious, and linguistic minorities

## Principles of Interpretation or Application

4. Principle of progressive implementation of ESCR
5. Principle of realization of civil and political rights through legislative and other measures
6. Principle of nondiscrimination in respecting and ensuring rights
7. Right to an effective remedy for violations of CPR
8. Principle of equality of rights between men and women
9. Possibility of limitations and derogations
10. Right to the highest existing standard of protection

## Civil and Political Rights

11. Right to life
12. Prohibition of torture
13. Prohibition of slavery
14. Right not to be arbitrarily arrested or detained
15. Right to humane treatment under detention
16. Nonimprisonment for debt
17. Freedom of movement and residence
18. Nonexpulsion of aliens
19. Right to a fair trial and legal personality
20. Right to privacy
21. Freedom of thought, conscience, and religion
22. Freedom of opinion and expression
23. Prohibition of war propaganda or advocacy of hatred constituting incitement
24. Freedom of assembly
25. Freedom of association
26. Right to marry
27. Rights of children
28. Rights of political participation
29. Right to equal protection of the law

## Economic, Social, and Cultural Rights

30. Right to work
31. Right to just and favorable conditions of work
32. Trade union rights and right to strike
33. Right to social security
34. Protection of family, mothers, and children
35. Right to an adequate standard of living, including food, clothing, and housing
36. Right to physical and mental health

37. Right to education, including free and compulsory primary education
38. Right to participate in cultural life
39. Right to enjoy the benefits of scientific progress
40. Right of authors to benefit from their scientific, literary, or artistic production

This enumeration does not do justice to any of the rights proclaimed in the covenants and ignores those that appear elsewhere. Its intended purpose is to provide a quick overview of what is understood by internationally recognized human rights.

A final comment will be made before we place these rights in the context of the challenges of the 1990s: this enumeration is adequate to suggest that the rights proclaimed in the covenants are fully respected nowhere and that the full realization of these rights constitutes a platform for social transformation of revolutionary proportions. Seen from this perspective, promoting human rights in their totality implies working toward a different social and international order than prevails today. This fact was not lost on the drafters of the Universal Declaration of Human Rights, who stipulated in Article 28: "Everyone is entitled to a social and international order in which the rights and freedoms set forth in this Declaration can be fully realized."

Such a social and international order fits most broad definitions of peace. Moreover, the first preambular paragraph of the same Declaration contains the claim that "recognition of the inherent dignity and of the equal and inalienable rights of all members of the human family is the foundation of freedom, justice and *peace* in the world." (Emphasis added.)

Obviously, the governments whose representatives adopted UN human rights texts did not intend to challenge fundamentally the prevailing order of which they are a part. There is thus a contradiction between the preeminent role of the nation-state in the international system, including the formulation and implementation of human rights standards, on the one hand, and the transformation of the nation-state in its domestic and international relations, implied by those standards, on the other. Perhaps it is more accurate to speak of these seemingly opposing forces (to maintain and transform the state) as the dynamic or dialectical nature of human rights. The issues discussed below are part of this human rights dialectic.

## The Political Context of Human Rights

The internationalization of human rights is inseparable from the political context of international relations. East-West and North-South relations determine, in large measure, the limits of the possible in promoting human rights. The shifts and transformations of these two international conflict formations continue to affect the province and function of human rights in the 1990s.

**Human Rights in East-West Relations**   The early years of the post–World War II era were characterized by Cold War rhetoric and policies. Human rights quickly became a frame of reference for finding fault and demonstrating the fundamental immorality of the other side. While this mutual acrimony was primarily a feature of Soviet-American relations, it was clearly reflected in the scholarly, official, and activist attitudes of the allies of the Soviet Union and the United States in Europe and their friends throughout the world. Over the last fifteen years, the Conference on Security and Cooperation in Europe (CSCE) and the Helsinki Final Act have been a central focus of the East-West confrontation over human rights. The changes in Eastern Europe in the last years of the 1980s set the stage for a very different type of human rights dialogue in the 1990s.

Most countries of Eastern Europe have now responded to economic crisis and popular dissent by moving dramatically toward granting civil and political rights to their citizens. This change challenges the ideological basis for much of the Western criticism of the social and political system of Eastern Europe and has major ramifications for the economic and strategic relations between the two blocs of a divided Europe. Among the numerous challenges posed by rapid social change in the Soviet Union, the German Democratic Republic, Czechoslovakia, Poland, Hungary, and Bulgaria is whether the West, and particularly the United States, will acknowledge its own failings regarding economic, social, and cultural rights. In any case, the potential is now obvious for a new form of dialogue in the CSCE process. Rather than a forum for mutual accusations and suspicion, the CSCE process could move in the direction of a genuine free flow of people and ideas. The economic dimension of this shift is the new challenge to the European Community as 1992 approaches. The potential at this level is to add the free flow of goods to the free flow of people and ideas.

The idea of a "common European house" is gaining ground and may take a variety of institutional forms, including establishing a permanent pan-European organization in one of the neutral countries (Finland, Sweden, or Austria) or expanding the Council of Europe. Whatever form it takes, the human rights dimension of East-West relations will be fundamentally different from what it has been in the CSCE process.

**Human Rights in North-South Relations**   The place of human rights in policy discussions between the industrialized countries of the Northern Hemisphere and the poorer countries of the Southern Hemisphere is one of confusion, ambiguity, and contradictions. The emergence of most developing countries from the first generally negative experiences with independence and development is changing the terms of the dialogue. The nature of the relationship between developed and developing countries, between North and South, may well become more open and productive in the 1990s than in the past three decades. Three lessons of the recent past tend to support this prognostic.

First, the realization that self-determination—without doubt a necessary condition for respect for human rights—does not resolve the problems of satisfying the material and nonmaterial human needs of the population of the developing country. It merely places at the helm of government a group more likely than the colonial power to act in the popular interest. All the problems of organizing and implementing a system of laws and policies designed to reconcile competing claims remain and often are magnified.

Second, the argument that economic and social conditions must be improved before a country can afford the luxury of human rights has, to a large extent, been abandoned in light of the negative effect repressive practices have had on development. Thus, it is no longer credible for a Third World leader to justify human rights abuse because of economic difficulties since respect for these rights is more and more widely acknowledged as part of "human development."[9]

Third, the artificial distinction between individual rights as a Western concept and collective rights as a socialist and Third World concept is being approached with greater sophistication. With the notable exception of the United States during the Reagan era, Western countries accept that economic, social, and cultural rights are indeed human rights and that progress in their realization has a great deal to do with the collective well-being of the population. Many students, intellectuals, and activists in the Third World aspire to greater freedom of thought, expression, and political participation and no longer regard so-called individual rights as a Western import to be looked upon with suspicion.[10]

Nonetheless, the human rights discourse between industrialized and underdeveloped countries will continue to be fraught with ambiguity, such as that surrounding the linkage between development assistance and human rights performance. In addition, the human rights discourse between North and South raises anthropological problems regarding the content of universal human rights standards in light of the anthropologist's preference for cultural relativism. Referring to the Universal Declaration and the international covenants, an anthropologist warns that "[a] careful reading of these documents reveals the cultural values that underlie the societies of the writers of the statements: the statements reflect the imposition of a Western model and definition of human rights on the world."[11] From the perspective of the culturally relative anthropologist, certain difficult questions need to be asked, such as the appropriateness of imposing so-called universal standards on societies radically different from those that have evolved from modern European experience. This problem becomes particularly acute regarding the rights and status of women. In spite of remarkable progress made by the United Nations Decade for Women (1976–1985), the three world conferences (1975, 1980, and 1985), the "Forward-looking Strategies for the Advancement of Women," adopted in Nairobi in 1985, the ratification of the Convention on the Elimination of Discrimination against Women and the functioning of the committee empowered to monitor that convention, conflicts will continue to pit traditional values, concentrated mainly in societies in the South, against movements seeking greater equality and empowerment of women, originating mainly in the North. Women's rights is but one of the problems of human rights that arise in the North-South context. Like the human rights issues affecting East-West relations in post-Stalinist Europe, those affecting North-South relations are being recast in the postcolonialist Third World. These new dimensions of international relations determine to a large degree the potential for resolving the priority human rights issues of the 1990s.

## PRIORITY ISSUES OF HUMAN RIGHTS IN THE 1990s

In suggesting priorities for human rights in the 1990s, one needs to identify the trends that pose the greatest risks and that offer the best opportunities in human rights terms.

The three sets of issues discussed below were chosen from many that respond to these criteria. They are by no means exclusive of others. In selecting these issues, I do not wish to underestimate the importance of other human rights concerns that deserve continued and sustained attention during the 1990s. The rights of women, of refugees, of children, and of workers are all covered by specific international treaties and monitoring machinery. Freedom of opinion and expression, freedom of religion or belief, the right to organize and to a fair trial also continue to require constant vigilance and the effective use of procedures put in place over the last decade and before.

By choosing the breakdown of authority, the structures of poverty, and ethnic conflict in the following analysis my aim is to identify social processes that lie at the basis of human rights violations but that cannot be fundamentally modified by simple, "quick fix" solutions through human rights procedures. Efforts to redress human rights violations under circumstances described below must, therefore, be seen as one among many dimensions of the process of social change.

### Authoritarianism and the Breakdown of Authority

Respect for human rights is inseparable from issues of governance. As Richard Falk has written, "Abuses of human rights on a systematic basis are almost always associated with certain repressive features of the governing process. In this respect, patterns of authoritarian rule, if widespread, limit greatly prospects for implementing human rights."[12]

It is, of course, a feature of the nation-state system that the apparatus of the state possesses a monopoly on the legal use of force. The understanding, based on the concept of "social contract,"[13] is that the general will of the people is expressed in the democratic state, and the individual, in exchange for abandoning autonomy, accepts the authority of the state. Therefore, *democracy*, in the sense of genuine popular participation in the political process, and *accountability*, in the sense that those in power are held responsible whenever they betray the public trust, are prerequisites for human rights within the nation-state system.

There are two major sets of circumstances under which these prerequisites are not met and major violations of human rights occur. The first is *authoritarian rule*, usually taking the form of militarism—a common phenomenon of postcolonial societies in the Third World, and Stalinism, the type of Communist party rule in industrialized socialist states in the North. These patterns of authoritarian rule, along with several others, have been analyzed by Richard Falk in his pathbreaking study of "A World Order Perspective on Authoritarian Tendencies."[14] The second circumstance jeopardizing the social contract due to lack of democracy and accountability is the *breakdown of authority*. By this we mean the weakening of the authority of either an authoritarian or a democratic government to the point that it either loses power or employs harsh means to hold on to power.

Third World militarism and Second World Stalinism, which have been so prominent in the 1970s and 1980s, have certainly not been eliminated. However, the trend in the Third World, particularly in Latin America, has been toward civilian rule and, in the Soviet Union and Eastern Europe, toward rapid de-Stalinization transforming the European scene at the opening of the 1990s.

In the 1990s the breakdown of authority seems to be a pressing human rights issue for two reasons. First, it often accompanies the transition from militarism and Stalinism to democratic rule and, therefore, is part of the pattern of social change in Eastern Europe and the Third World. Second, it is characteristic of vulnerable civilian governments contending with ethnic conflict (for example, Sri Lanka or Uganda), powerful and armed narcotics dealers (for example, Colombia), or radical and armed political opposition (for example, Peru or Mozambique).

When the breakdown of authority threatens the state, human rights are not likely to be the highest priority, even of a democratically elected civilian government. It is true that the rules of human rights themselves allow for limitations and derogations "in time of public emergency threatening the life of the nation."[15] However, there are certain standards of human rights and humanitarian treatment that, in international law, remain applicable in all circumstances, regardless of the severity of the emergency. The standards of minimal treatment under such conditions are accepted by international treaty (the Covenants of 1966 and the Geneva Conventions of 1949 and the two 1977 protocols to those conventions) and by international customary law. These include the prohibition of torture, slavery, degrading or humiliating treatment or punishment, the arbitrary deprivation of life, adverse discrimination, and summary justice.

The harsh reality under regimes made vulnerable by the breakdown of authority takes the form of death squad activity, as continues to occur in El Salvador; disappearances, notorious during military rule in Argentina and practiced in all regions of the world today; and torture, an official practice of scores of countries according to information regularly published by Amnesty International. Unfortunately, many such acts will continue to occur as societies go through violent transitions. While it is true that fragile institutions of government are at stake during such transitions, the necessary and inescapable fact is that governments must be held accountable for failure to abide by minimal human rights standards.

## Human Rights and Structures of Poverty

The decades of the sixties and seventies were times of disillusionment for proponents and protagonists of economic and social development in the economically disadvantaged countries of the Third World. The hopes and aspirations of the peoples of the Third World centered on the realization of their economic potential, finally free of foreign domination and exploitation. As their newly independent countries were, in many cases, so rich in human and natural resources, it seemed that the new society they set out to establish would prosper and establish more social justice than the European countries that had betrayed their lofty principles of human rights by their colonialist adventure.

The reality of power brought two lessons home to the leaders and especially the people of the developing world. First, it was not enough for the colonialist powers to pack their bags. The structures of poverty persist in the distorted economies they inherited and were maintained by entrenched class and ethnic interests. Second, however unjust one might claim the structures of the international economy to be, through pronouncements such as the Declaration on the Establishment of a New International Economic Order or the Charter of Economic Rights and Duties of States, rhetoric alone will not change them. In fact, indebtedness, dependency, global reach of multinationals, and other manifestations of the international division of labor favoring Western Europe, North America, and Japan (and other Asian newly industrialized countries) have only increased, further weakening the authority of civilian rule in many developing countries. As already noted, this vulnerability often results in disregard for human rights as part of an effort to suppress popular opposition to unpopular economic constraints (for example, in application of conditions set by the International Monetary Fund), to satisfy the military contemplating a return to power, by force if necessary, or, finally, to defend the institutions of the state against illegal opposition taking advantage of the weakened state of the economy to seek the overthrow of the government.

One of the principles of application of human rights holds that economic, social, and cultural rights are to be implemented "progressively" and "to the maximum" of the country's "available resources."[16] Deteriorating economic conditions are, of course, not conducive to progressive realization of these rights, and it is proving all but impossible for many poor countries to achieve much progress toward that end. Nevertheless, many means of maximizing economic, social, and cultural rights in spite of a weak economy remain untested. In fact, the development planning process, which is a high priority for most developing countries, ignores these human rights obligations. New approaches to integrating human rights and development need to be tried, simultaneously with the developing world's efforts to overcome the inequality in the international economy and mismanagement at home. Of particular importance is the role of the international financial institutions (IFIs). Suggestions have been made to incorporate human rights into the planning and execution of projects funded by IFIs.[17] Their traditional resistance to considering so-called noneconomic factors is not likely to withstand the pressure during the 1990s to pay more attention to the environment, including the human ecology of development.

The structures of poverty do not only affect human rights in the Third World. The underlying causes of hunger and homelessness in the richest countries of the West are structural and raise serious problems for civil and political rights, such as access to justice, political participation, and right to privacy, as well as economic, social, and cultural rights, of which they make a mockery. The right to an adequate standard of living, including housing, food, and clothing; the right to education; the right to participate in cultural life; the right to the highest attainable level of physical and mental health, among other rights, mean little for the underclass in the rich countries. Current trends appear to be moving toward the expansion of an underclass in the wealthy developed countries, while economic inequalities are likely to increase in socialist countries that are taking the first steps toward a free market system. The ravages of the economic and social policies, skyrocketing debt, and the widening gap between classes during the 1980s make ratification of the ESC Covenant by the United States all the more urgent in the 1990s.[18] The structures of poverty make the promotion of human rights in all parts of the world dependent upon the integration of human rights concerns in decisions regarding the allocation of resources and the processes of governance.

## Ethnic Conflict

The earliest form of oppression and what we call today human rights violations is that resulting from conquest and domination—often accompanied by wholesale massacres—of one tribe over another. Biblical stories, shifting empires in India, China, and Egypt, Roman and Islamic expansion are replete with invasion, plunder, mass murder, rape, and enslavement.

Today, massive violations of human rights linked to intolerance between two ethnic groups have not disappeared. The settlement of the Western hemisphere by the Spanish, Portuguese, Dutch, and English resulted in the decimation of native peoples. The Armenian genocide of 1917 was the first mass killing of the century based on racial and ethnic intolerance. The Nazis' ideology was one of racial hatred, and extermination of entire peoples was part of their war effort. The post–World War II world has not eliminated such practices. Massacres of tribal peoples in Latin America, genocide in Kampuchea and Uganda, and politically motivated mass killings in Indonesia in 1965 and Argentina in 1976–79 are recent phenomena of a level of brutality known in earlier times.

However, there is an important difference between tribal warfare and conquest through collective murder in the past and mass killings in the twentieth century. Such behavior is no longer accepted as the unfortunate but natural order of things. The destruction of other peoples is considered repugnant in principle and has been prohibited by law. Nevertheless, treatment of minorities and indigenous peoples and the effects of ethnic conflict stand out as priority concerns of human rights in the 1990s. Ethnic tensions—often going back hundreds of years—are sometimes fanned by governments (for example, Uganda and Kampuchea in the 1970s) and sometimes governments are powerless to prevent the escalation of violence among such peoples (for example, Lebanon since the mid-1970s). To place this dimension of world security at century's end in the human rights context, we need to understand the scope and meaning of genocide and of group rights, the effective protection of which will determine whether or not the 1990s will be a decade of collective victimization.

**Genocide**[19] Following the extermination of six million Jews and several million Catholics, Gypsies, Communists, homosexuals, and others at the hands of the Nazis in World War II, the General Assembly of the United Nations, at its first session in 1946, qualified "genocide" as an international crime. Two years later, the General Assembly adopted the Convention on the Prevention and Punishment of the Crime of Genocide. The coining of the term *genocide* (from *genos,* race, descent, kin, sex, kind, and *cide,* killing) and the international prohibition of this crime owes much to the lobbying of Raphael Lemkin.

The crime is defined in Article II of the convention as "any of the following acts committed with intent to destroy in whole or in part, a national, ethnic, racial or religious group, as such: a. Killing members of the group; b. Causing serious bodily or mental harm to members of the group; c. Deliberately inflicting on the group conditions of life calculated to bring about its physical destruction in whole or in part; d. Imposing measures intended to prevent births within the group; and e. Forcibly transferring children of the group to another group."

The hopes and expectations of the proponents of the convention were that the horrors of World War II would generate a strong enough commitment to abolishing such inhumane behavior that no nation would dare commit the crime or, if one did, other nations would move swiftly to stop the guilty party and bring those responsible to justice. Thus the states parties accepted the obligation to try persons accused of the crime, to allow an international penal tribunal to do so, or to extradite them. Disputes regarding the application of the convention were to be submitted to the International Court of Justice.

These expectations were misguided. Since the convention was adopted, several states parties to it have engaged in genocidal acts without other states parties invoking the conventions, let alone agreeing to the creation of an international penal tribunal or submitting any dispute to the International Court of Justice. The most blatant examples are Uganda under Idi Amin and Kampuchea under the Khmer Rouge.

This is not to say that there has been a lack of interest in genocide. Several non-governmental organizations such as the Minority Rights Group, the Institute of the International Conference on the Holocaust and Genocide, International Alert, the Institute for the Study of Genocide, and the Cambodia Documentation Commission have studied and called attention to acts of genocide or situations that could degenerate into genocidal behavior and have sought improvements in international action to prevent or punish genocide. The United Nations Subcommission on Prevention of Discrimination and Protection of Minorities commissioned a study from one of its members, Ben Whitaker, then director of the Minority Rights Group. His report brought out the problems of dealing with genocide and applying the convention. However, his reference to the Armenian genocide in Turkey provoked a political outburst and, for that and other reasons, the Secretariat did not follow up on his recommendations for improving the application of the convention.

The United States has been particularly conspicuous by its absence from efforts to implement the convention. President Truman submitted the convention to the Senate for its advice and consent on June 19, 1949. Every president since then, with the exception of Eisenhower, expressed support for the convention. When the Senate finally voted on February 19, 1986, by 83 to 11 for approval, it attached two reservations, five understandings, and one declaration. The major impact of those provisos was to eliminate automatic jurisdiction of the International Court of Justice, to require extradition only under separate treaties, to protect members of the armed forces from prosecution for genocidal acts committed during combat, and to require additional Senate approval before the United States would participate in an international penal tribunal. Final legislative approval was given on October 14, 1988, to amend U.S. law to comply with the convention.[20]

How will genocidal acts be dealt with in the 1990s? While the world stood by with folded arms, the Vietnamese army invaded Kampuchea on December 25, 1978, and did not leave until September 25, 1989. Throughout that occupation, the UN General Assembly called for the withdrawal of Vietnamese troops and the establishment of an independent government. However, the basic question was not answered: What could the international community have done to dislodge the genocidal regime of Pol Pot, which was removed only by the Vietnamese invasion? And with the departure of the Vietnamese troops, there is no guarantee that the Khmer Rouge will not regain power, and even resort to more massacres. This situation exemplifies the challenge of the 1990s. With over one hundred ratifications, including that of the government of Kampuchea (the Khmer Rouge), the machinery of the convention (prosecution by the capturing state, extradition, international penal tribunal, jurisdiction of the International Court of Justice over disputes) has not worked. Whitaker found that "as in attitudes to improving United Nations human rights' effectiveness generally, too often respect for State sovereignty, domestic jurisdiction and territorial integrity can, and does, take precedence over the wider human concern for protection against genocide."[21]

He went on to propose an early warning system, an international body dealing exclusively with genocide, and an international human rights tribunal. He also felt that consideration should be given to an optional protocol to the Genocide Convention to deal with ethnocide and ecocide and the killing of political and other groups not covered by the convention's definition, and that certain provisions of the convention should be amended to clarify matters relating to culpable acts of omission and the defense of superior orders. Finally he proposed that state responsibility be clarified and universal jurisdiction be recognized over the crime, as is the case in the Convention against Torture.

It is a tragic commentary on the effectiveness of international human rights law that the efforts made to establish mechanisms for dealing with genocidal behavior have not been applied. Efforts to promote human rights in the 1990s will have to face this failure.

**Minority Rights**[22]  The concept of minority rights is older than genocide. Whereas the latter applied to a "group" defined primarily in ethnic or religious terms, the concept of "minorities" relates to entities within a society having a "majority" population. When the relationship with the majority population is such that the "minority" group aspires to be fully independent, then it is claiming the right of self-determination of peoples. The meaning of the "self" in "self-determination" and of "peoples" is fraught with confusion and controversy. As a priority issue of human rights for the 1990s, minority rights requires attention in two major dimensions:

1. Several groups, or fractions within groups, refuse to be treated as "minorities" and claim the status of peoples with a right to self-determination. The Irish, Palestinians, Kurds, Basques, Tamils, Eritreans, and several tribes of Native Americans are among the "peoples" who resort to legal and illegal means to make their claims to self-determination.

2. Even when a group is acknowledged to be a minority and accepts to live within an existing state, the definition and extent of the minority's rights, its participation in governing its own affairs and in governing the larger polity, and the responsibility for preserving its identity are problematic.

The intergovernmental texts on minority rights present no ambiguity with respect to potential secessionist rights, as could be expected from such sources. The principle text is Article 27 of the International Covenant on Civil and Political Rights: "In those States in which ethnic, religious or linguistic minorities exist, persons belonging to such minorities shall not be denied the right, in community with the other members of their group, to enjoy their own culture, to profess and practice their own religion, or to use their own language."[23]

The Subcommission on Prevention of Discrimination and Protection of Minorities studied for decades the question of definition and classification[24] and appointed a special rapporteur to study the implementation of the principles set out in Article 27.[25] In his final report the special rapporteur offered the following definition: "A group numerically inferior to the rest of the population of a State, in a non-dominant position, whose members—being nationals of the State—possess ethnic, religious or linguistic characteristics differing from those of the rest of the population and show, if only implicitly, a sense of solidarity, directed towards preserving their culture, traditions, religion or language."

A working group was established to draft a declaration on the rights of members of minorities. However, alternative definitions were proposed and agreement has not been reached on the declaration.

Whatever the status of international standards regarding minority rights, the next decade will see several major powers (the Soviet Union and the People's Republic of China, in particular) seek solutions to claims of autonomy or independence by some mix of respecting and promoting minority rights and repression of secessionist movements. The Baltic Republics of Latvia, Lithuania, and Estonia; the Ukraine; Tibet; and other regions in these vast countries will require some creative and effective balancing of competing rights claims if they are not to degenerate into more violent confrontations. Numerous other countries like Yugoslavia, France, Canada, the United States, Japan, the United Kingdom, Belgium, Sri Lanka, and Nicaragua, to name a few, have equally dramatic problems with national, ethnic, linguistic, and religious minorities. The unresolved issue is whether and when groups treated as minorities may properly be considered as peoples having the right to self-determination.

**Self-Determination of Peoples**[26]   Before raising some of the problems of self-determination, a few observations must be made about the use and abuse of the concept of "people" in international human rights. Two rights of peoples mentioned in Article 1 of both international covenants of 1966 are generally accepted by governments: the right to self-determination and the right to permanent sovereignty over natural resources. Nongovernmental efforts, such as the 1976 Universal Declaration on the Rights of Peoples ("Algiers Declaration"), have sought to expand the rights considered as belonging to peoples. At the intergovernmental level, the Commission on Human Rights, through several resolutions, and the Organization of African Unity, through the African Charter of Human and Peoples' Rights, have given some normative content to the right to peace, the right to development, and the right to a clean and ecologically balanced environment.[27] The practical value of these efforts remains to be seen, although politically they may suggest a level of consensus on planetary priorities. In spite of frequent references to "peoples" in the opening words of the UN Charter, the term remains undefined and, in any case, holds different meanings in different contexts. The controversy over the meaning of the terms is strongest when people claim the right to self-determination, the frustration of which usually leads to armed conflict.

It has been argued that it is meaningless to talk about a "right" for such groups that are juridically not "determined", i.e., do not have a recognized existence as an entity with international status, and that it is illogical to talk about "self" determination when the determination is not made by the "self," i.e., the population claiming the right, but rather by others, such as the General Assembly of the UN.[28]

Others argue that self-determination is a basic principle of international law and relations that concerns peoples living in non-self-governing territories, i.e., under the trusteeship system (or the mandates system at the time of the League of Nations), colonialist domination, or foreign occupation. This second position would limit self-determination to decolonization and deny the right to "peoples" living within a fully independent state.[29] Many governments assume that the General Assembly, in adopting Article 1 of the covenants, intended to limit the right in this way; however, the legislative history is not conclusive on this point.[30] Self-determination in this sense is applied to Namibia, which became independent in 1989, and is the basis for claims to majority rule in South Africa,[31] and to an independent state for the Palestinians.[32] The South African and Palestinian cases will most certainly continue to be burning issues in the 1990s. In neither of these cases, however, is the situation one of classical decolonization, with a European metropole maintaining control over and exploiting overseas territories. The situations in Western Sahara, East Timor, Mayotte, and New Caledonia result more directly from colonist domination, and will challenge the capacity of the international community to clarify and apply the concept of self-determination in the context of decolonization.

The third, more radical approach to self-determination is based on a broader definition of "peoples," which would accept that groups with sufficient sense of identity (through common history, ethnicity, religion, language, etc.) who are victims of oppression and are excluded from control over their future may exercise a right to determine freely their political, economic, and cultural development. Their claim may be full independence or more limited forms of autonomy. The former claim is equivalent to separatist secession; the latter may be accommodated by the concept of minority rights. Prominent cases in this category include the Tamils, Kurds, Sikhs, Eritreans, Armenians, and Lithuanians.

The right to self-determination is defined in the International Covenants on Human Rights as the right by which all peoples "freely determine their political status and freely pursue their economic, social and cultural development."[33] Not only is the lack of a definition of "peoples" problematic for the practical application of this right, but the vagueness of the other words raises doubt as to the means and ends of the right. The heart of the matter, as already mentioned, is the extent to which populations located within an independent state, identifying themselves as "peoples," may modify their basic political identity through autonomy or through independence. The peaceful solution to conflicts between peoples aspiring to independence and central governments wanting to maintain territorial integrity passes through a range of forms of autonomy.[34]

Self-determination is also relevant to the transformation taking place in Eastern Europe. The government of the Federal Republic of Germany, for example, holds the view that the decision of the citizens of the German Democratic Republic to dissolve the GDR and join the FRG to form a single German state is a manifestation of "internal self-determination" consistent with Article 1 of the Covenant on Civil and Political Rights.[35] The concept of internal self-determination could also be applied to units within a federated state, such as the Baltic Republics of the Soviet Union or Quebec in Canada. In these and other federal cases, the central government will resist any interpretation of the right of people to self-determination that could be used for secession and seek an accommodation based on autonomy or minority rights. A particularly acute form of the issue is the plight of indigenous peoples.

**Indigenous Peoples**[36]  Groups that occupy ancestral land within countries that have been settled and developed by other groups, through colonialism or otherwise, have been variously called "native," "aboriginal," or "indigenous." When they are protected by the majority population that controls the state, as in Canada, the United States, or Sweden, they are confronted with painful choices regarding preservation of their cultural identity and traditional ways against the values, laws, and development planning of the majority. In cases of indifference or hostility to indigenous peoples, as well as greedy economic exploitation of resources on which the peoples rely, the issue is all too often one not only of cultural survival but of physical survival.

An awareness of the needs of aboriginal peoples can be found in the work of abolitionists during the last century and in some standards set by the ILO and others. However, the intense international concern with the plight of indigenous peoples really dates from the mid-1970s and the pioneering work of nongovernmental organizations, leading to the creation of the Working Group on Indigenous Populations of the UN Subcommission on Prevention of Discrimination and Protection of Minorities. In that forum, a complex debate has emerged between advocates of assimilation with minority rights and those who seek full land rights and self-determination of indigenous peoples treated as nations. In addition to the fundamental issue of political independence, the protection of the rights of indigenous peoples requires adequate responses to their claims to recover land, to own land collectively, and to administer land and natural resources.

These observations on genocide, minority rights, self-determination, and indigenous peoples suggest that security, survival, and identity of innumerable groups can be achieved only by creative solutions to conflicts arising out of competing group rights.

## MEANS OF REDRESSING AND PREVENTING HUMAN RIGHTS ABUSES

Insofar as the human rights problems arising from the breakdown of civil authority, the structures of poverty, and the situation of vulnerable groups affect peace in the 1990s, a strategy for peace must identify the means of coping with those problems. There are two basic approaches to coping with human rights violations. The first is to respond to violations after they have occurred by seeking means of redress for the victims. This is the curative or *protection function* of the international action for human rights. The second is to prevent them from taking place. This *preventive function* involves raising popular awareness of human rights through education and establishing permanent mechanisms for dealing with violations as they arise, the existence of which acts as a deterrent.

The preventive and curative functions cannot be clearly distinguished in practice because actions to redress past violations have a deterrent and educational value on future behavior. Nevertheless, a complex set of procedures and practices has developed in the last forty years that provides the framework for implementing a human rights strategy.

## Human Rights in Foreign Policy

Human rights have been a feature of international relations to an increasing degree since 1945, with the consequent need for all countries to have some form of foreign policy in this area. In most countries, the human rights concern of foreign policy is one of many that fall within the responsibilities of the United Nations desk in the Ministry of External Relations. This was the case in the United States until recently. The Bureau of International Organization Affairs of the Department of State dealt with the work of all the organizations of which the United States was a member, including the work of the Commission on Human Rights of the United Nations. In the mid-1970s, new structures and procedures began to modify the place of human rights in U.S. foreign policy. The initiative for this transformation was not that of the executive branch but rather of Congress.

The Chairman of the House Committee on Foreign Affairs, Donald Fraser, is credited with the principal initiatives that led to the establishment of legislation designed to use the tools of foreign relations to seek improvements in the human rights performance of other countries. The first such law was an amendment to the Foreign Assistance Act prohibiting U.S. military assistance to countries that engage in a "consistent pattern of gross violations of internationally recognized human rights."[37] This approach to human rights was extended to restrict U.S. economic aid, voting of loans in international financial institutions, and certain trade advantages. In addition, several country-specific laws were passed requiring improvements in human rights before certain advantages would be granted or restored to the target countries. The underlying premise was that the economic clout of the United States could be used to achieve results where public persuasion or quiet diplomacy were doomed to fail.

During the first years of this new approach to human rights in foreign policy, there was some hope that it could produce significant results, particularly in light of the strong emphasis the Carter administration demonstrably gave to promoting human rights worldwide. In 1976, a new unit in the State Department was created to collect facts and formulate policy. The Bureau of Human Rights and Humanitarian Affairs was given the task of preparing thorough documentation on the human rights situation in countries receiving aid[38] and of raising human rights concerns within the executive branch. The commitment from the president and the selection of dedicated outsiders to run the bureau was not enough to overcome the entrenched positions of the various national and regional desks in the department, for whom more traditional concerns, such as strategic interest and ideology, took precedence over human rights. The result was bureaucratic infighting and inconsistent positions from one country to the next.[39] Thus, while President Carter had an unwavering moral commitment to universal standards of human rights, foreign policy action with respect to Iran under the Shah and the Philippines under Marcos, to name but two examples, fell short of expectations. Furthermore, the president submitted four important human rights treaties to the Senate for advice and consent prior to ratification[40] but was soon stymied by the crisis over U.S. hostages in Iran and did not maintain the pressure. By the time he left office, human rights occupied the most prominent position it has ever had before or since in U.S. foreign policy,[41] and the laws went farther than any other country to inject human rights considerations into economic and military relations. However, the policy could not be pursued systematically or aggressively, and the laws were rarely applied with rigor.

The Reagan administration began by attempting to replace the human rights element of foreign policy with its campaign against terrorism. In spite of the president's popularity, neither the Congress nor the public would let human rights slip off the foreign policy agenda, and the administration was, as one observer put it, "brought kicking and screaming" back to a concern for human rights.[42] Both the Reagan and Bush administrations have had to maintain at least a rhetorical commitment to human rights.

Several dilemmas remain unsolved in the foreign policy area, and they are likely to plague any administration. How can a superpower demonstrate respect for the sovereign equality of states while taking coercive measures, such as withholding economic and military aid, to influence internal policies of independent states? Is it in the interest of the United States to open for international scrutiny, through participation in regimes of human rights monitoring, immensely complex domestic problems, such as treatment of Native Americans, the death penalty, surrogate motherhood, homelessness, and unemployment, when the deployment of considerable human and financial resources at home has not provided solutions? Should the United States accept international obligations in areas in which the primary responsibility lies with the states and over which direct federal authority would be in violation of the Constitution? When the authoritative determination of security and economic interests of the United States suggests policies not in strict conformity with international human rights, how can these conflicting interests be sorted out?

Those are some of the dilemmas facing anyone attempting to define and implement a human rights foreign policy. The fact that many human rights organizations have quick answers to most of these questions does not resolve the issues. The opinion- and policy-makers (Congress, the White House, the National Security Council, nongovernmental organizations, the media, the State Department officials, etc.) need to be convinced that, in light of their own priorities, a pro–human rights foreign policy should prevail. A range of techniques of conflict resolution—or at least of negotiation—will be required

to move from the ineffective policies of the 1970s and the absence of commitment of the 1980s to a meaningful human rights foreign policy in the 1990s.

## International Law

Prior to the UN Charter, human rights were not part of the rules governing
the relations among states. The body of law known as "the law of nations"
in former times and as "international law" by the nineteenth century focused on the rights and duties of the sovereign, the monarchs, and later the
sovereign states. The law of nations had little to say about the treatment of
individuals or groups, who had no rights in the international legal system.

The situation today is radically different. All governments have accepted
international obligations in the field of human rights, and a corpus of international rules relating to these rights has developed to the point where
human rights is widely recognized as a branch of international law. The
fundamental expression of international human rights obligations is in Article 1, paragraph 3, of the UN Charter, making international cooperation in
promoting and encouraging respect for human rights one of the purposes of
the UN, and in Articles 55 and 56, which contain a pledge of all member
states to "take joint and separate action in cooperation with the Organization" in order to achieve respect for and observance of human rights.

The substantive content of the rights reaffirmed in general terms in the
Charter was subsequently set out in the International Bill of Human Rights,
mentioned in the first section of this chapter. Some, including the secretary-
general of the UN, claim that the Universal Declaration is the authoritative
interpretation of the human rights provisions of the Charter, and others
argue that the Declaration has become customary international law. Whatever the force of these arguments—and there is good authority for them—
most governments have accepted legally binding obligations through ratification of a vast array of international human rights conventions of the United
Nations, its specialized agencies, and the major regional organizations
(Council of Europe, Organization of American States, and Organization of
African Unity).

How can these commitments under international law be used to promote human rights in the absence of effective enforcement? First of all, the
most significant feature of the development of this body of law is that it
provides an indisputable basis for pointing an accusing finger at individuals
and governments that violate human rights. This can be done both through
domestic courts and international forums.

**Domestic Courts**[43]   Some countries, like the Netherlands, recognize in
their constitutions that international law is binding internally. Others, like
most British Commonwealth countries, require that the provisions of an
international treaty be transformed into domestic law by an Act of Parlia-

ment. Still others, like the United States, consider that an international treaty is the "supreme law of the land"[44] and must be applied by the courts like an act of the legislature. However, a distinction is made between "self-executing treaties" that are directly applicable and "non-self-executing treaties" that require implementing legislation.[45]

Through these various means of incorporating international law into domestic law, human rights become "justiciable." Lawyers and human rights advocates can invoke international human rights standards before domestic tribunals. This can be done in several ways. The first is to bring an action before a court based on a rule of international human rights law. Among the most famous recent cases is *Filartiga* v. *Peña-Irala*,[46] in which the court found torture to be a violation of international law and granted damages of over $10 million. In another case, a district court found that indefinite detention of an illegal alien constituted arbitrary detention in violation of international human rights law.[47]

A second approach is the establishment of an independent commission with the authority to raise before any court the state's obligations under international human rights law. The Australian Commission on Equality of Opportunity and Human Rights, for example, has such power.

Initiatives like the *Filartiga* case and the Australian Commission were highly exceptional in the 1980s. With the further development and consolidation of international human rights law in the 1990s, these methods are likely to become more common.

**International Forums**   The most salient feature of international human rights law today is that virtually every country accepts it. In speeches before the General Assembly, the Commission on Human Rights, the CSCE review conferences, and innumerable other international forums, there is almost never a dissenting voice as to the universal validity of the human rights provisions of international law. The extensive network of ratifications of international conventions further attests to governments' willingness to be bound by international human rights standards, or at least to give the appearance of being bound. Even if a government's commitment to international human rights is mere rhetoric, it legitimizes critiques by international organizations, other governments, and nongovernmental organizations of that government's human rights performance.

Of course, any government under attack for human rights abuse will respond with a counterattack based on the principle of noninterference in domestic affairs. On the subject of the relation between the sometimes conflicting principles of respect for human rights and noninterference, there has been a remarkable evolution in practice.[48] A few short decades ago, names could not be named in the UN; letters sent by NGOs to governments received no response; their efforts to conduct on-site investigations were often thwarted; agenda items of international organizations were "sanitized," and euphemisms replaced clear designations of real countries and problems; major atrocities went virtually unmentioned. During the 1970s and 1980s the situation evolved, particularly in the Commission on Human Rights and the CSCE review conferences, to the point that today almost any country can be studied officially, and resolutions denouncing specific policies and practices are common. NGOs—at least the major ones—usually receive visas for investigative missions, are often sent detailed replies and comments, present criticisms to high government officials, and report frankly to major international bodies. All these efforts continue to be fraught with difficulty. However, the degree to which governments accept today to be held accountable was inconceivable in the 1950s or 1960s. Essential to this progress is the argument that the monitors are merely drawing governments' attention to the gap between their public commitments and their actual behavior. Thus, adherence by states to international standards facilitates independent criticism in international forums.

In addition, there are formal procedures for monitoring the application of international instruments. The regional system of courts and commissions on human rights allows for a judicial remedy for violations. The fact that at least a generation of lawyers and activists has applied these procedures enhances the likelihood of more audacious application of the procedures in the coming decade. The jurisprudence of these bodies is taught in law faculties, and governments are used to being held accountable before them. There is talk in the Council of Europe of merging the Court and Commission and establishing a permanent body that would be continually in session. The Inter-American Court of Human Rights has begun hearing contentious cases.[49] The African Commission on Human and Peoples' Rights has begun functioning. The quasi-judicial procedures of committees on the application of conventions and recommendations of the ILO and UNESCO and of the treaty-monitoring bodies offer more opportunities to present cases for international scrutiny. In spite of frequent disappointments, the more political bodies, such as the Commission on Human Rights and the subcommission also provide innumerable opportunities to call recalcitrant governments to task on the basis of international law. This array of international procedures is poised for the issues of the 1990s. The use to which the procedures will be put depends, in large measure, on the extent to which NGOs alert victims of abuse and their representatives to the opportunities available.

## NGO Activity

While legal documents and intergovernmental procedures are the most noticeable manifestations of human rights in international affairs, they are but the tip of the proverbial iceberg. They came into being and are kept alive by grass-roots human rights and social justice movements that proliferated after 1945 and especially in the 1980s into what today is a worldwide movement.[50] Among professional circles of scientists, journalists, lawyers, educators, health practitioners, and even the police, new commissions, committees and separate organizations have emerged with a specific human rights mandate.[51]

Human rights advocacy groups existed before the UN Charter. A significant precursor to the human rights organizations of today is the French League for Human Rights, established a hundred years ago in the wake of the Dreyfus affair. In 1922 the International Federation of Human Rights began to operate from its Paris headquarters on behalf of similar leagues in different parts of the world. During the Second World War, the International League for the Rights of Man (now the International League for Human Rights) was established in New York with similar purposes. A growing network of human rights organizations, such as Amnesty International, Human Rights Watch, the International Commission of Jurists, and many others has established a solid constituency for human rights and a set of reliable sources of human rights documentation and denunciation that governments and international institutions take quite seriously.[52]

One of the most significant features of human rights in the 1980s was the development of independent human rights commissions and other human rights groups in numerous Third World countries, as well as in many Eastern European countries.[53] These are the watchdogs, the forces of the civil society that hold the government (their own and those of other countries) accountable for their human rights practices. They create the shared community expectations that allow legal means of redress to be meaningful. They are part of the emerging network of people developing new cooperative approaches to global survival.

Their methods obviously vary. Best known among them is Amnesty International, a membership organization with sections in many countries and chapters in hundreds of cities and campuses. Chapters "adopt" prisoners of conscience on the basis of information provided by the London headquarters of the organization. Urgent action campaigns, mass mailings of postcards to heads of state and other officials in countries holding prisoners of conscience, country-specific investigations, publication of newsletters and annual reports, campaigns against torture and the death penalty, and lobbying in international organizations characterize Amnesty International's work.

The following is a partial list of the main forms of action of activist human rights organizations:

- compiling information from their own field staff or from witnesses and secondary sources regarding alleged human rights violations by the authorities of the country where the NGO is located and making the information available
- providing legal representation to victims of human rights violations to

enable them to utilize whatever legal recourses are available domestically or internationally

- disseminating information about human rights to the population and the media through campaigns and scholarly publications to alert more people to official misconduct or means of redress
- making diplomatic representations to officials from the government concerned to give the government an opportunity to resolve the problem without publicity, or to seek authorization for an on-site investigation
- conducting an investigation of alleged violations, including traveling to remote areas and interviewing victims, their families, witnesses, and officials
- presenting complaints to judicial and quasi-judicial human rights bodies, especially those of the regional organizations and the United Nations, and presenting documents and making speeches to the political bodies of these organizations
- mobilizing prestigious individuals or large numbers of citizens to address appeals to the authorities responsible for alleged violations
- providing aid and relief directly to victims

Frequently, such action is carried out at considerable risk, and human rights monitors themselves become targets for human rights abuse.[54] This is particularly true for small groups in developing countries who are all the more vulnerable as they usually belong to the political opposition. The survival of local human rights groups may depend on the contacts they have with larger and better-known groups in Paris, London, Geneva, or New York and the willingness of the latter to publicize the threats to them and to intervene on their behalf.

The proliferation of local human rights groups and the increasing sophistication of their methods are likely to continue throughout the 1990s. The capacity of these groups to influence the political process and to bring under glare of publicity governments' failure to live up to their formal commitments to human rights will probably do more than anything else to further human rights in the coming decade. The longer-term goal of creating a "human rights culture" requires more; it requires greater attention to human rights in education and new ways of raising awareness of the importance of human rights in social change in general.

## Education and Consciousness-Raising

Application of law and even of nongovernmental activism can achieve only so much. Indeed, the effective enforcement of law depends not so much upon the existence of properly worded laws as upon expectations of the community. Many of the fundamental concepts of human rights (sanctity of the human being, equality, dignity) are part of the cultural traditions of most civilizations, as evidenced in their religious, philosophical, and literary writings.[55] Socialization, therefore, may help develop community expectations of respect for human rights. Education, both formal and nonformal, is critical, for it is the privileged vehicle for transmitting the affective sensitivity to and cognitive awareness of human rights. In recent decades, "human rights education" has gained a considerable following in many countries, leading to the inclusion of human rights within traditional subjects and the development of the specialized study of the subject. A nongovernmental proposal is moving forward to make the decade from 1991 to 2000 the Decade for Human Rights Education.

Through nongovernmental organizations, people can raise their own consciousness and that of others to human rights. Without a human rights culture and political action to induce governments to comply with human rights standards, the decade of the 1990s will be one of great insecurity for millions of people. With effective use of concepts and mechanisms of human rights by individuals, grass-roots organizations, international NGOs, and intergovernmental institutions, the next decade could open the way for the twenty-first century as the human rights century, a period in which security is predicated on respect for individuals and groups rather than on sovereignty of the state.

## Notes

1. On the legal reality as a precondition for human rights, see Vasak, "Human Rights: As a Legal Reality," in Karel Vasak and Philip Alston, eds., *The International Dimensions of Human Rights*, 1982, pp. 3–10. More generally on the meaning of human rights, see Louis Henkin, *The Age of Rights*, New York: Columbia University Press, 1990, pp. 1–10.

2. R. J. Vincent, *Human Rights and International Relations*, New York: Cambridge University Press, 1986, pp. 19–36; Kenneth Minogue, "The History of the Idea of Human Rights," in Walter Laqueur and Barry Rubin, *The Human Rights Reader*, 1979, pp. 3–17. H. Lauterpacht, *International Law and Human Rights*, New York: Praeger, 1950, pp. 3–141.

3. See, e.g., Maurice Cranston, "What Are Human Rights?" in Laqueur and Rubin op. cit., pp. 17–25.

4. On this process, see Myres S. McDougal, Harold Lasswell, and Lung-Chu Chen, *Human Rights and World Public Order*, New Haven: Yale University Press, 1980, pp. 84–86.

5. McDougal, et al., op. cit., pp. 86–88.

6. By the International Bill of Human Rights, we understand the Universal Declaration of Human Rights, the International Covenant on Economic, Social, and Cultural Rights, the International Covenant on Civil and Political Rights, and the Optional Protocol to the latter.

7. Several compilations of these international texts are available, including Ian Brownlie, *Basic Documents on Human Rights*, 2d ed., Oxford University Press, 1981; Committee on Foreign Affairs of the House of Representatives, *Human Rights Documents*, U.S. Government Printing Office, 1983; and *Human Rights: A Compilation of International Instruments*, United Nations, 1988.

8. While accepted by almost every country and most authorities on international affairs, this division into two categories is occasionally challenged. Some seek to extend it with the addition of a third category of "solidarity rights," or "rights of humanity," consisting of rights to peace, development, communication in the broad sense, a balanced and healthy environment, and humanitarian assistance. See Stephen P. Marks, "Emerging Human Rights: A New Generation for the 1980s?" *Rutgers Law Review*, vol. 33, No. 2 (1981), pp. 435–52, reprinted in

Richard Falk, Friedrich Kratochwil, and Saul Mendlovitz (eds.), *International Law: A Contemporary Perspective*, London: Westview Press, 1985, pp. 501–13. The need for restraint in proclaiming new rights is argued persuasively in Philip Alston, "Conjuring Up New Human Rights: A Proposal for Control," *American Journal of International Law*, vol. 78 (1984), pp. 607–21. The U.S. government since Reagan, on the other hand, questions the category of economic, social, and cultural rights, which the Department of State finds "confused, sometimes willfully, by repressive governments claiming that in order to promote these 'rights' they must deny their citizens the rights to integrity of the person as well as political and civil rights." *Country Reports on Human Rights Practices for 1987*, U.S. Government Printing Office, 1988, pp. 3–4.

9. A recent example of the positive correlation between human rights and development is found in United Nations Development Program, *Human Development Report 1990*, New York: Oxford University Press, 1990, p. 16.

10. An eloquent and audacious formulation by Third World intellectuals of the premise that the concept of the individual is now part of the Third World mindset and thereby opening the way for deeper involvement in the struggle for human rights is Mahmoud Hussein, *Le Versant Sud de la Liberté*, Flamarion, 1989.

11. Thomas Weaver, "The Human Rights of Undocumented Workers in the United States-Mexico Border Region," *Human Rights and Anthropology*, Theodore E. Downing and Gilbert Kushner, eds., *Cultural Survival*, 1988, p. 76.

12. Richard Falk, *Human Rights and State Sovereignty*, New York and London: Holmes & Meier, 1981, p. 63.

13. Theories of the state and the legitimacy of various forms of government vary. One of the most influential theories at the time of the major human rights declarations of the eighteenth century was that of Jean-Jacques Rousseau's *The Social Contract* (1762).

14. Loc. cit., pp. 63–124.

15. On this subject see Marks, "Principles and Norms of Human Rights Applicable in Emergency Situations: Underdevelopment, Catastrophes and Armed Conflicts," in Vasak and Alston, eds., op. cit., pp. 175–212.

16. The terms are taken from the International Covenant on Economic, Social, and Cultural Rights. The obligations relating to the implementation of the covenant have been analyzed at a symposium held in Maastricht, the Netherlands, in 1986. See *Human Rights Quarterly*, vol. 9, May 1987.

17. See, for example, the symposium on "International Development Agencies (IDAs), Human Rights and Environmental Considerations," in *Denver Journal of International Law and Policy*, Vol. 17, No. 1, Fall 1988.

18. Philip Alston, "U.S. Ratification of the Covenant on Economic, Social and Cultural Rights: The Need for an Entirely New Strategy," *American Journal of International Law*, Vol. 84, pp. 365–93 (1990).

19. Among the leading references on the subject of genocide are Helen Fein, *Accounting for Genocide*, Free Press, 1979; and Leo Kuper, *The Prevention of Genocide*, Yale University Press, 1985.

20. See Public Law 100–606 of November 4, 1988, reproduced in *International Legal Materials*, vol. XXVIII, No. 3 (May 1989), pp. 759–85.

21. UN Document E/CN.4/Sub.2/1985/6 (July 2, 1985), para. 77.

22. On this subject, see the UN study by Francesco Capotorti, *Study on the Rights of Persons Belonging to Ethnic, Religious and Linguistic Minorities*, UN Document E/CN.4/Sub.2/384 (Rev. 1, 1979); and Louis Sohn, "The Rights of Minorities," in Henkin, ed., *The International Bill of Rights*, New York: Columbia University Press, 1981, pp. 270–89.

23. This article has an interesting history. The drafters of the Universal Declaration failed to reach a compromise between the attitude of governments in the New World, who favored assimilation, and those of the Old World, who maintained national and ethnic minorities, and no article referred specifically to minorities. The General Assembly referred the matter to ECOSOC and the Commission on Human Rights, which requested the Subcommission on Prevention of Discrimination and Protection of Minorities to make a thorough study. For this study the Secretariat prepared a document on "Definition and Classification of Minorities" (document E/CN.4/Sub.2/85). After its deliberation on this subject in 1951, the subcommission drafted the text, which became Article 27 of the covenant.

24. See, in particular, the UN publication *Protection of Minorities* (1967).

25. Resolution 1418 (XLVI) of June 6, 1969. The rapporteur, Francesco Capotorti, was appointed in 1971 and issued his final report in 1977. The report is contained in UN Document E/CN.4/Sub.2/384 and Add. 1–6. (1977).

26. On this subject in general, see Antonio Cassese, "The Self-Determination of Peoples," in Henkin, op. cit., pp. 92–113.

27. See above, note 8. See also, James Crawford, ed., *The Rights of Peoples*, New York: Oxford University Press, 1988.

28. This is the argument made in Fitzmaurice, "The Future of Public International Law," *Livre du Centenaire*, Institut de droit international, 1973, p. 233, note 85. Another author who focuses on the problem of defining the "self" is Michla Pomerance, *Self-Determination in Law and Practice*, Norwell, Mass.: Martinus Nijhoff, 1982.

29. The literature representing this position is quite vast. See, for example, Eisuke Suzuki, "Self-Determination and World Public Order," *Virginia Journal of International Law*, vol. 16, 1976, pp. 779–862.

30. See John Humphrey, "Political and Related Rights," in Theodor Meron, ed., *Human Rights in International Law: Legal and Policy Issues*, Oxford University Press, 1984, p. 196. Many UN pronouncements, in particular the Declaration on the Granting of Independence to Colonial Countries and Peoples, lend support to the position that the right applies only to decolonization.

31. Self-determination in the case of South Africa, of course, relates to the majority rather than a minority of the population. Among the enumerable resolutions condemning the racist régime in South Africa, a summary of the UN position on the matter is found in the General Assembly's Program of Action against Apartheid, annexed to resolution 31/6 J of November 9, 1976, which, *inter alia*, reaffirmed the legitimacy of the struggle for self-determination of the South African people. See also the Declaration on South Africa, adopted by Resolution 34/93 O of December 12, 1979.

32. In spite of opposition from the United States, Israel, and several other Western countries, the General Assembly has reaffirmed the right of Palestinians to self-determination. For example, in Resolution 3236 (XXIX) of November 1974, the Assembly recognized that "the Palestinian people is entitled to self-determination in accordance with the Charter of the United Nations," which it characterized as one of its "inalienable rights," along with the "right to national independence and sovereignty." The work of the Committee on the Exercise of the Inalienable Rights of the Palestinian People, established by Resolution 3376 (XXX) on November 10, 1975, although challenged by the United States, has sought to promote the realization of those rights. The claim has of course been challenged by supporters of Israel, e.g., Yoram Dinstein, "Self-Determination and the Middle East Conflict," in Y. Alexander and R. Friedlander, eds., *Self-Determination: National, Regional and Global Dimensions*, Boulder, Colo.: Westview Press, 1980, pp. 243–58. See also M. Halberstam, "Self-Determination in the Arab-Israeli Conflict: Meaning, Myth, and Politics," *New York University Journal of International Law and Politics*, Vol. 21, No. 3, pp. 465–87 (1989).

33. Article 1 common to both covenants.

34. On this subject, see Yoram Dinstein (ed.), *Models of Autonomy*, Transaction Books, 1981; and more recently Hurst Hannum, *Autonomy, Sovereignty and Self-Determination: The Accommodation of Conflicting Rights*, Philadelphia: University of Pennsylvania Press, 1990.

35. See Third Periodic Report of the Federal Republic of Germany submitted to the Human Rights Committee in 1990, UN Document CCPR/C/52/Add.3, para. 52.

36. On the subject in general, see International Commission on International Humanitarian Issues, *Indigenous Peoples, A Quest for Justice*, London: Zed Books Ltd., 1987.

37. Sec. 502B, Foreign Assistance Act of 1961, 22 U.S.C. § 2304.

38. This task was carried out through Annual Country Reports on Human Rights Practices, which have been expanded to cover virtually every country and not only those receiving aid.

39. See Caleb Rossiter, "Human Rights: The Carter Record, the Reagan Reaction," Center for International Policy, *International Policy Report*, 4–5 (Sept. 1984).

40. Message from the President Transmitting Four Treaties Pertaining to Human Rights, S. Exec. Doc. C, D, E, and F, 95th Cong., 2d Sess. (1978). The numerous declarations, understandings, and reservations accompanying these treaties further reflect the difficulties encountered in accommodating all the interdepartmental concerns as part of human rights foreign policy.

41. See Arthur Schlesinger, Jr., "Human Rights and the American Tradition," *Foreign Affairs*, Vol. 57, pp. 503 (1978).

42. Tamar Jacoby, "The Reagan Turnaround on Human Rights, *Foreign Affairs*, Vol. 64, Issue 5, pp. 1066–1086 (summer 1986).

43. On this subject, see Richard Lillich, "The Role of Domestic Courts in Enforcing International Human Rights Law," in Hurst Hannum, *Guide to International Human Rights Practice*, Philadelphia: University of Pennsylvania Press, 1984, pp. 223–47.

44. U.S. Constitution, Article VI, 2.

45. On this distinction, see Louis Henkin, *Foreign Affairs and the Constitution*, New York and London: Norton, 1975, pp. 156–67.

46. 630 F. 2d 876 (2d. Cir. 1980), on remand, 577 F. Supp. 860 (D.N.Y. 1984).

47. *Rodriguez-Fernandez* v. *Wilkinson*, 505 F. Supp. 787 (D. Kan. 1980), *affirmed*, 654 F, 2d 1382 (10th Cir. 1981). At the appellate level, the lower court decision was affirmed on different grounds than the one based on international human rights.

48. On this subject see Louis Henkin, "Human Rights and Domestic Jurisdiction," in Thomas Buergenthal, ed., *Human Rights, International Law and the Helsinki Accord*, Washington, D.C.: American Society of International Law, 1987; reproduced in Louis Henkin, *The Age of Human Rights*, New York: Columbia University Press, 1990, pp. 51–64.

49. The first of these was a case involving disappearances in Honduras.

50. See David Weissbrodt, "The Contribution of International Non-Governmental Organizations to the Protection of Human Rights," in Meron, ed., *Human Rights in International Law: Legal and Policy Issues*, New York: Oxford University Press, 1984, pp. 403–38.

51. Among the numerous examples are the American Association of the Advancement of Science, the National Academy of Science, Physicians for Human Rights, the Committee to Protect Journalists, and the Lawyers Committee for Human Rights.

52. Regular information on these organizations is published by Human Rights Internet through the *HRI Reporter* and regional directories.

53. Detailed information on these groups is provided in regional directories published by the Human Rights Internet.

54. Several organizations, including the Human Rights Watch Committees, the Lawyers Committee for Human Rights, and the Committee to Protect Journalists, publish regular lists of human rights monitors who have been attacked for their efforts.

55. A collection of such texts is found in Jeanne Hersch, ed., *Birthright of Man*, UNESCO, 1969.

# 14 / Global Debt and Third World Development

VINCENT FERRARO

In 1919, writing about a massive debt imposed upon Germany by the Allied Powers as reparations for a catastrophic war, John Maynard Keynes expressed contempt for the wisdom of the policy:

> The policy of reducing Germany to servitude for a generation, of degrading the lives of millions of human beings, and of depriving a whole nation of happiness should be abhorrent and detestable,—abhorrent and detestable, even if it were possible, even if it enriched ourselves, even if it did not sow the decay of the whole civilised life of Europe. Some preach it in the name of Justice. In the great events of man's history, in the unwinding of the complex fates of nations Justice is not so simple. And if it were, nations are not authorised, by religion or by natural morals, to visit on the children of their enemies the misdoings of parents or of rulers.[1]

Twenty years later, the debt, partially responsible for the rise of the Nazis, had been repudiated and Keynes's views had been confirmed.

Seventy-two years later, the world confronts another massive debt, although not one imposed by a treaty of peace. Indeed, this debt, totaling $1.32 trillion in 1989, has no identifiable demons: one cannot point to the vindictiveness of a Clemenceau, or the opportunism of a Lloyd George, or the naive idealism of a Wilson. Nonetheless, this debt has had the effect of plunging millions of people into conditions of economic despair and desperation. Most tragically, this debt will jeopardize the chances for the happiness of millions of children who will have committed no crime other than that of being born into a poor society. Ultimately, this debt, like the German debt, will not be repaid in full.

## WHAT IS THE "DEBT CRISIS"?

To be fully accurate, one should refer to the multiple debt crises that exist in the world today. For our purposes here, however, the "debt crisis" will refer to the external debt, both private and public, of developing countries, which has been growing enormously since the early 1970s. The focus of this chapter should not obscure, however, the other debt crises that trouble much of the global economy: the budget deficits of the United States government, its balance of trade deficits, and the insolvency of many of its savings and loans institutions. These crises are highly interconnected, particularly as they relate to the issues of interest rates, export values, and confidence in the international banking system. The "debt crisis," then, is a global phenomenon and any attempt to understand it fully needs a global perspective.

However, the greatest suffering thus far in the crisis is found within developing countries, and therein lies the justification for the focus of this chapter. But even within the developing world, our attention can be directed toward a variety of problems depending on how one chooses to think about debt. One can focus on the integrity of the international financial system, in which case one's emphasis is on the countries with the largest debts, such as Mexico or Brazil. Alternatively, a primary concern can be the desperate human costs of the debt, which would direct attention to sub-Saharan Africa, for example. Yet another perspective, the strategic dimensions of the problem, would concentrate on debtors like Turkey or South Korea.

This chapter will pay primary attention to what have been termed the most heavily indebted nations within the developing countries. This focus is not neutral since it generally refers to those nations with the largest debts and whose threat of default represents a serious concern to lending agencies.[2] The bias of the focus, however, should not divert attention from the smaller countries, particularly those in Africa, whose debts are crushingly large to their people even though the banks and international lending agencies consider them less important or threatening.[3]

The accelerating magnitude of debt for the most heavily indebted nations is staggering. In 1970, the 17 heavily indebted nations had an external public debt of $17.923 billion—which amounted to 9.8 percent of their GNP. By 1987, these same nations owed $402.171 billion, or 47.5 percent of their GNP. Interest payments owed by these countries went from $2.789 billion in 1970 to $36.251 billion in 1987. Debt service, defined as the sum of actual repayments of principal and actual payments of interest made in foreign currencies, goods, or services on external public and publicly guaranteed debt, accounted for 1.5 percent of their GNP and 12.4 percent of their total exports of goods and services in 1970. In 1987 those figures had risen to 4.3 percent and 24.9 percent, respectively.[4] (See Table 14.1.)

# WHAT ARE THE CAUSES OF THE DEBT CRISIS?

The conventional explanation is that the debt crisis of the 1980s was due to a number of highly contingent circumstances that were essentially unpredictable at the time many of these loans were made. For example, William R.

Table 14.1 / Selected Debt Statistics of the 17 Most Heavily Indebted
Developing Nations

|  | Total external debt (millions of $U.S.) | Total long-term debt (as a % of GNP) | | Debt service (as a % of exports) | |
| --- | --- | --- | --- | --- | --- |
|  | 1987 | 1970 | 1987 | 1970 | 1987 |
| Argentina | 56,813 | 23.8 | 65.5 | 21.6 | 45.3 |
| Bolivia | 5,548 | 49.3 | 115.6 | 11.3 | 22.1 |
| Brazil | 123,932 | 12.2 | 33.7 | 12.5 | 26.7 |
| Chile | 21,239 | 32.1 | 103.6 | 19.2 | 21.1 |
| Colombia | 17,006 | 22.5 | 45.3 | 11.7 | 33.4 |
| Costa Rica | 4,727 | 25.3 | 95.9 | 10.0 | 12.1 |
| Côte d'Ivoire | 13,555 | 19.5 | 124.1 | 7.1 | 19.6 |
| Ecuador | 10,437 | 14.8 | 93.2 | 8.6 | 20.7 |
| Jamaica | 4,446 | 73.1 | 141.2 | 2.8 | 26.6 |
| Mexico | 107,882 | 16.2 | 69.6 | 23.6 | 30.1 |
| Morocco | 20,706 | 18.6 | 117.9 | 8.7 | 29.9 |
| Nigeria | 28,714 | 4.3 | 111.3 | 4.3 | 10.0 |
| Peru | 18,058 | 37.3 | 31.2 | 11.6 | 12.5 |
| Philippines | 29,962 | 21.8 | 69.4 | 7.5 | 23.2 |
| Uruguay | 4,235 | 12.5 | 44.2 | 21.7 | 24.4 |
| Venezuela | 36,519 | 7.6 | 67.8 | 2.9 | 22.6 |
| Yugoslavia | 23,518 | 15.0 | 32.2 | 10.0 | 13.3 |

Source: World Bank, *World Development Report, 1989* (Washington, D.C.: World Bank,
1989), Tables 21, 23, and 24, pp. 204–5, 208–9, and 210–11.

Cline, of the Institute for International Economics, summarized the causes
as follows: "The external debt crisis that emerged in many developing countries in 1982 can be traced to higher oil prices in 1973–74 and 1979–80,
high interest rates in 1980–82, declining export prices and volume associated with global recession in 1981–82, problems of domestic economic
management, and an adverse psychological shift in the credit markets."[5]

The story actually begins earlier than 1973 because debt has been solidly
entrenched in the finances of developing countries for many years. The
United States was a heavily indebted country in the nineteenth century, and
poorer countries have always needed outside infusions of investment capital
in order to develop their resources. The logic of indebtedness is commonplace and not especially arcane: one incurs a debt in hopes of making an
investment that will produce enough money both to pay off the debt and to
generate economic growth that is self-sustaining. An important characteristic of developing country debt prior to 1973 was that it was largely financed
through public agencies, both bilateral and multilateral. These agencies,
such as the World Bank, presumably guided the investments toward projects
that held out genuine promise of economic viability and success.

After the oil crisis of 1973–74, however, many commercial banks found themselves awash with "petrodollars" from the oil-producing states, and these private banks were eager to put this windfall capital to productive use. The banks assumed that sovereign debt was a good risk since there was a prevalent belief that countries would not default.[6] Many developing countries, reeling from oil price increases, were eager to receive these loans. These countries assumed that loans were an intelligent way to ease the trauma of the oil price increases, particularly given the very high inflation rates at the time. Other developing countries, the oil-exporting ones (Colombia, Ecuador, Mexico, Nigeria, and Venezuela, for example), saw the loans as a way to capitalize on their much-improved financial status, and they assumed that oil prices would remain high in real terms for an extended period of time.

In retrospect, it is easy to point out that these actions did not conform to the typical logic of indebtedness. These loans were being used to pay for current consumption, not for productive investments. The money was not being used to mobilize underutilized resources, but rather to maintain a current, albeit desperate, standard of living. Moreover, these loans were being made in an unstable economic environment: since the unraveling of the Bretton Woods agreement in 1971 (precipitated by the U.S. termination of the gold standard), global economic relationships had been steadily worsening. The developing countries began to experience a long-term, secular decline in demand for their products as the developed countries tightened their economic belts in order to pay for oil and as they initiated tariffs and quotas to reduce their balance of payments deficits.

The proof of the wrongheadedness of the lending in the 1970s became dramatically apparent in 1981. Interest rates shot up, and global demand for exports from developing countries plummeted. The very deep global recession of 1981–82 made it impossible for developing countries to generate sufficient income to pay back their loans on schedule. According to the United Nations Conference on Trade and Development (UNCTAD), commodity prices (for essential foodstuffs, fuels, minerals, and metals) dropped 28 percent in 1981–82, and between 1980 and 1982 interest payments on loans increased by 50 percent in nominal terms and 75 percent in real terms.[7] In 1982 Mexico came to the brink of what everyone had thought impossible just two years earlier—a default.[8] This critical situation marked the beginning of what is conventionally termed the debt crisis. Private banks abruptly disengaged from further lending because the risks were too great. In order to prevent a panic that might have had the effect of unraveling the entire international financial system, a number of governmental and intergovernmental agencies, led by the United States, stepped in to assure the continued repayment of the Mexican loans.

At this same time the International Monetary Fund (IMF) emerged as the guarantor of the creditworthiness of developing countries. The IMF had performed this role in the past, but primarily with regard to its "own" money—that is, money lent by the IMF to assist countries in addressing balance of payments problems. This new emphasis on creating conditions primarily to assure payments to private institutions, while in theory not a new undertaking, was different in character and content from what the IMF had done in the past, largely because of the enormous amount of money involved. Unfortunately, the IMF, in spite of the unprecedented situation, did not perceive that its responsibilities had changed in any significant way, and gave its seal of approval for additional loans only to those countries that accepted its traditional policies, which are generally referred to as stabilization programs of "structural adjustment."

Programs of structural adjustment are designed to address balance of payments problems that are largely internally generated by high inflation rates, large budget deficits, or structural impediments to the efficient allocation of resources, such as tariffs or subsidies. The IMF structural adjustment programs highlight "productive capacity as critical to economic performance" and emphasize "measures to raise the economy's output potential and to increase the flexibility of factor and goods markets."[9] A fundamental assumption in a structural adjustment program is that current consumption must be suppressed so that capital can be diverted into more productive domestic investments. A further assumption of an IMF stabilization program is that exposure to international competition in investment and trade can enhance the efficiency of local production. In practice, these programs involve reduced food and transportation subsidies, public sector layoffs, curbs on government spending, and higher interest and tax rates.[10] These actions typically affect the poorer members of society disproportionately hard.[11]

When one is dealing with a particularly inefficient economic system, structural adjustment is perhaps acceptable medicine; and there were many examples of gross inefficiency, not to mention outright corruption, in many of the countries that were soliciting IMF assistance. In this respect, the IMF programs were probably regarded as the correct approach by the public and private agencies that were being asked to reschedule or roll-over loans. But the critical difference between the traditional IMF role and its new role as guarantor of creditworthiness is that the suppression of demand previously designed to free capital for domestic investment simply freed capital to leave the country.

Moreover, the approach assumes that it was primarily inefficient economic management in the developing countries that led to the debt crisis. From this point of view, the developing countries had gorged themselves on easy money, with the debt crisis being the rough equivalent of a fiscal hangover. Indeed, according to Stephen Haggard, the IMF believed that a large majority of the failures of adjustment programs were due to "political constraints" or "weak administrative systems," as opposed to external constraints that were largely beyond the control of the developing countries, for example, high interest rates.[12]

Table 14.2 / Impact of Exogenous Shocks on External Debt
of Non–Oil-Developing Countries

| Exogenous change | Amount (billions of $U.S.) |
|---|---|
| Oil price increase in excess of U.S. inflation (1974–82 cumulative) | 260 |
| Real interest rate in excess of 1961– 80 average: 1981 and 1982 | 41 |
| Terms of trade loss, 1981–82 | 79 |
| Export volume loss caused by world recession, 1981–82 | 21 |
| Total | 401 |
| Total debt increase, 1973–82 | 482 |

Source: Adapted from William R. Cline, *International Debt: Systemic Risk and Policy Response* (Washington, D.C.: Institute for International Economics, 1984), p. 13.

It is extraordinarily difficult to determine the validity of this perspective. Clearly, some loans have been used in inappropriate ways.[13] Nonetheless, developing countries cannot be accused of fiscal irresponsibility in such matters as the increase in interest rates or the global recession in 1981–82. The assessment of culpability is in some respects crucial and in other respects irrelevant: crucial, because one would like to understand the crisis so that a repetition of a similar crisis can be avoided in the future; irrelevant, because the current situation is so desperate that solutions must be found no matter where the blame for the crisis actually lies. In the final analysis, blame rests on a system of finance that allowed developing countries and banks to engage in transactions reasonable only in the context of wildly optimistic scenarios of economic growth. Additionally, much blame rests on policies of the United States government that were undertaken with insufficient regard for their international financial implications.

William Cline attempted to distinguish between the internal and external causes of the debt crisis by looking at figures for the effects of oil price and interest rate increases in order to determine the degree to which each was responsible for the crisis. His figures, reproduced in Table 14.2, should be treated as only suggestive because there is a high degree of "double-counting" (loans were taken out in some cases to cover earlier loans) in many of these figures. Nonetheless, as a rough approximation, the data suggest that external factors were significantly more important than the internal causes of inefficiency and corruption.

The IMF stabilization programs, with their nearly exclusive emphasis on the internal economic policies of heavily indebted countries and relative disregard for the factors that Cline identifies, have failed to encourage the very type of economic growth that might have helped the developing countries to grow out of their indebtedness. In fact, these programs have had exactly the opposite effect: they have further impoverished the heavily indebted countries to a point where their future economic growth must be seriously doubted. Many observers have come to share Jeffrey Sachs's assessment of structural adjustment programs: "The sobering point is that programs of this sort have been adopted repeatedly, and have failed repeatedly."[14]

This failure of traditional techniques to alleviate the debt problem suggests that perhaps the conventional interpretation of the debt crisis is incomplete or misleading. Indeed, much evidence suggests this inference. Perhaps the most compelling evidence is the fact that periodic debt crises seem to be endemic to the modern international system. There have been cycles of debt and default in the past, and some of the same debtors have experienced similar crises in almost regular cycles.[15] Thus, the debt crisis of the 1980s cannot be ascribed solely to the contingent circumstances of oil prices and U.S. monetary and fiscal policy, at least as the conventional perspective portrays these factors. This explanation must be supplemented by factors that are more structural and deep-seated.

There are at least two issues relatively unexplored by the conventional explanation of the debt crisis that deserve greater attention, and they both relate to the vulnerability of the developing countries to changes in the world economy over which they have little direct control: their sensitivity to monetary changes in the advanced industrialized countries and their dependence on primary commodities as sources of their export earnings. The first consideration is perhaps the more dramatic.

It is no mere coincidence that the United States experienced its own very serious debt crisis in the same year that panic arose over the external debt of developing countries.[16] The massive government debt of the United States and its related balance of trade deficit precipitated a deliberate strategy of economic contraction that had global effects. Interest rates in the United States had achieved very high levels in 1979, but the inflation rates at the time were also very high. After the deep economic recession of 1981–82, the inflation rate had declined markedly, but the interest rates remained high.[17] Interest rates remained high because they were necessary to bring in foreign money to finance the extraordinary U.S. budget deficits created by the tax reductions pushed by the Reagan administration and passed by Congress. In turn, the high interest rates inflated the value of the dollar, reducing U.S. demand for developing country exports and further diminishing the ability of the indebted countries to repay their loans.

The United States, however, did not experience a debt "crisis" because it was able to reassure its creditors that its promises to pay were plausible. But the high real interest rates forced upon the developing countries as their loans were turned over created a situation where no similar guarantees could be offered. As it became obvious that the debtor countries could not meet the increased payments, the private banks tried to pull back, bringing about the very crisis they wished to avoid. Only very persistent efforts by official governmental agencies managed to stabilize the situation enough to avoid a precipitous default. In a very real sense, however, it was the actions of the United States that created the immediate crisis, and not some event or pattern of events in the developing world itself.

Similarly, this debt crisis aggravated an already bad situation with respect to the ability of the developing countries to pay back their loans. Many of the developing countries were extremely poor prior to the crisis, which was one reason why they took out such massive debts in the first place. There was no evidence before 1973 that this condition of relative poverty was changing in any but a few of the developing countries, the newly industrializing countries such as South Korea, Singapore, and Taiwan. In fact, most of the traditional measures of economic development suggest that most developing countries were falling farther behind the advanced industrialized countries at an increasingly faster rate.

The developing countries will always be relatively poorer than the advanced industrialized countries as long as they rely heavily on primary commodities, such as copper and rubber, for export earnings. Trade may be a stimulus to growth, but trade is not an effective way to overcome relative poverty if the values for primary commodities fail to keep pace with the value of manufactured products. This relationship between the values of manufactured exports and the values of primary commodities exports (the terms of trade) has been carefully examined by many economists, and some economists, such as Raul Prebisch, have argued that the international division of labor is systematically biased against the interests of countries that rely heavily on the export of primary products. This debate, which has been extended into what has been termed a theory of dependency, is a difficult one to resolve with clear empirical evidence. Some recent evidence, however, suggests that raw materials producers have indeed suffered relative economic losses in the twentieth century. Enzo R. Grilli and Maw Cheng Yang analyzed the terms of trade between primary commodities and manufactured goods since 1900 and found that "the prices of all primary commodities (including fuels) relative to those of traded manufactures declined by about 36 percent over the 1900–86 period, at an average annual rate of 0.5 percent."[18]

Thus, the developing countries are at a structural disadvantage compared to the advanced industrialized countries. The newly industrializing countries of East Asia are the exceptions that prove this rule. Because they have been able to expand manufactured exports, they have improved their relative economic situation tremendously in recent years. Other countries have been less successful, and the recent resurgence of protectionist measures against manufactured products from the developing world will make this type of transition only more difficult. Ultimately, the solution to the debt crisis, and the underlying poverty that spawned it, must address this terms of trade issue. This imperative will be discussed in further detail below. Clearly, however, the solutions to the debt crisis will require a perspective that looks at the problem as more than a temporary aberration precipitated by bad luck and incompetence.

## WHAT ARE THE COSTS OF THE DEBT CRISIS?

The explosion of debt has had numerous consequences for the developing countries, but this section will focus on only three consequences: the decline in the quality of life within debtor countries, the political violence associated with that decline, and the effects of the decline on the developed world. The next section will explore separately the most publicized cost of the debt crisis, the possibility that it might have instigated a global banking crisis.

The first, and most devastating, effect of the debt crisis has been the significant outflows of capital to finance the debt. According to the World Bank: "Before 1982 the highly indebted countries received about 2 percent of GNP a year in resources from abroad; since then they have transferred roughly 3 percent of GNP a year in the opposite direction."[19] In 1988, the poorer countries of the world sent about $50 billion to the rich countries, and the cumulative total of these transfers since 1984 is nearly $120 billion.[20] The problem has become so pervasive that even agencies whose ostensible purposes include aiding the indebted countries are draining capital: in 1987 "the IMF received about $8.6 billion more in loan repayments and interest charges than it lent out."[21]

This capital hemorrhage has severely limited prospects for economic growth in the developing world and seriously skewed the patterns of economic development within it. The implications for growth are summarized in Table 14.3.

The decline in average growth, from 6.1 percent a year to 1.1 percent a year, is even worse than it seems. Given the rate of population increase in these countries, a 1.1 percent increase in GDP translates into a net decline in per capita GDP. In other words, the populations of these countries were significantly worse off economically during the period of the debt crisis; and this decline further jeopardizes opportunities for future economic growth given its implications for domestic demand and productive investment. The terms of trade statistics, which reflect the relative movement of export prices to import prices, are similarly grim: developing countries are getting much less in return for their exported products when compared to their costs for imported items. In short, these countries must export even more of their products in order to maintain current levels of imports. The total effects for

Table 14.3 / Effects of External Debt on Economic Growth and Trade

| | Gross domestic product (Average Yearly Growth) | | Terms of trade (1980 = 100) | |
|---|---|---|---|---|
| | 1965–80 | 1980–87 | 1985 | 1987 |
| Argentina | 3.5 | −0.3 | 90 | 81 |
| Bolivia | 4.5 | −2.1 | 84 | 51 |
| Brazil | 9.0 | 3.3 | 89 | 97 |
| Chile | 1.9 | 1.0 | 79 | 77 |
| Colombia | 5.6 | 2.9 | 98 | 70 |
| Côte d'Ivoire | 6.8 | 2.2 | 96 | 86 |
| Ecuador | 8.7 | 1.5 | 94 | 61 |
| Jamaica | 1.3 | 0.4 | 95 | 100 |
| Mexico | 6.5 | 0.5 | 98 | 73 |
| Morocco | 5.4 | 3.2 | 89 | 106 |
| Nigeria | 6.9 | −1.7 | 90 | 54 |
| Peru | 3.9 | 1.2 | 81 | 69 |
| Philippines | 5.9 | −0.5 | 92 | 98 |
| Uruguay | 2.4 | −1.3 | 87 | 97 |
| Venezuela | 3.7 | 0.2 | 93 | 54 |
| Yugoslavia | 6.0 | 1.5 | 111 | 116 |
| Averages | 6.1 | 1.1 | 92 | 84 |

Source: World Bank, World Development Report, 1989 (Washington, D.C.: World Bank, 1989), Tables 2 and 14, pp. 166–67 and 190–91.

the quality of life in the highly indebted countries were summarized by the United Nations Conference on Trade and Development: "Per capita consumption in the highly-indebted countries in 1987, as measured by national accounts statistics, was no higher than in the late 1970s; if terms of trade losses are taken into account, there was a decline. Per capita investment has also fallen drastically, by about 40 percent between 1980 and 1987. It declined steeply during 1982–83, but far from recovering subsequently, it has continued to fall."[22] Jeffrey Sachs portrays the situation in even starker terms: "As for the debtor countries, many have fallen into the deepest economic crisis in their histories. Between 1981 and 1988 real per capita income declined in absolute terms in almost every country in South America. Many countries' living standards have fallen to levels of the 1950s and 1960s. Real wages in Mexico declined by about 50 percent between 1980 and 1988. A decade of development has been wiped out throughout the debtor world."[23]

Sachs is not overstating the case. Before the debt crisis, global poverty had reached staggering proportions. One can document the extent of poverty in the world by pointing out statistics on Gross National Product, per capita income, or the number of telephones per thousand in a particular country. But these statistics obscure too much in their sterility. As Joseph Collins points out in the following chapter, in 1988 one billion people were considered chronically underfed. Millions of babies die every year from complications from diarrhea, a phenomenon that typically causes mild discomfort in the advanced industrialized countries. Millions of people have no access to clean water, cannot read or write their own names, and have no adequate shelter.

And this misery will only continue to spread. The debt crisis has a self-reinforcing dynamic. Money that could have been used to build schools or hospitals in developing countries is now going to the advanced industrialized countries. As a consequence, fewer babies will survive their first year; those who do will have fewer opportunities to reach their intellectual potential. To raise foreign exchange, developing countries are forced to sell more of their resources at reduced rates, thereby depleting nonrenewable resources for use by future generations. Capital that could have been used to build factories and provide jobs is now sent abroad; as a result, the problems of un- and underemployment will only get worse in poor countries.

A second effect of the decline in living standards in the heavily indebted countries concerns the increased potential for political violence. There have been over twenty violent protests in recent years specifically against the austerity measures imposed by the IMF, with over three thousand people killed in those protests.[24] The most recent outburst occurred in Venezuela, where about three hundred people were killed. Harold Lever posed the problem well in 1984: "Will it be *politically* feasible, on a sustained basis, for the governments of the debtor countries to enforce the measures that would be required to achieve even the payment of interest? To say, as some do, that there is no need for the capital to be repaid is no comfort because that would mean paying interest on the debt for all eternity. Can it be seriously expected that hundreds of millions of the world's poorest populations would be content to toil away in order to transfer resources to their rich rentier creditors?"[25]

Political violence will only continue in the future, but its implications are hard to predict. Political instability may make it more difficult for democratic regimes to survive, particularly in Latin America, and may lead to the establishment of authoritarian regimes. Similarly, popular pressures may lead to regimes radically hostile to market economies, thus setting the stage for dramatic confrontations between debtor countries and the external agencies that set the terms for debt rescheduling or relief. Finally, political violence can spill over into international security issues. One can only imagine what sustained political conflict in Mexico would do to the already troubling issues of drug smuggling and immigration between Mexico and the United States. Debt-related issues have unquestionably complicated political relations between the United States and the Philippines over military bases, and the extraordinary impoverishment in Peru (a decline in real GNP of between

15 to 25 percent from September 1988 to September 1989) has certainly led to an increase in the drug-related activities of the Shining Path.[26]

Debtor governments will find themselves forced to demand certain concessions on debt repayment in order to maintain their legitimacy, and these concessions will invariably be cast at least in terms of lower and more extended payments, if not reduction or outright debt forgiveness. If the debt crisis is not resolved in terms that address the inevitable political consequences of declining living standards, then the prognosis for recovery is dim, even if debtor governments, banks, and the international lending agencies agree upon acceptable financial terms. The political dynamics of the debt crisis must be considered an integral part of the solution: to ignore the violence and protest as less important than the renegotiated interest rates will produce agreements that have little hope of success.

A final cost of the debt crisis has been one experienced by the developed countries themselves, in particular by the United States. Increasing poverty in the developing countries leads to a reduction of economic growth in the developed countries. The debtor countries have been forced to undergo a dramatic decline in imports in order to increase the foreign exchange earnings needed to pay back their debts. The decline in the average annual growth rate for imports of the seventeen most heavily indebted countries is dramatic: the average annual growth rate for these countries in 1965–80 was 6.3 percent; in 1980–87 that figure had fallen to −6.0 percent, for a total shift of −12.3 percent.[27] One estimate is that the seventeen most heavily indebted nations decreased their imports from the developed world by $72 billion from 1981 to 1986.[28]

The United States has been profoundly affected by this decline in imports because most of its exports to the developing world have historically gone to the Latin American states most seriously affected by the debt crisis. The United Nations Conference on Trade and Development suggests that this decline in U.S. exports is a more important explanation for U.S. trade difficulties than for the deficits of other countries: "Because of this import compression by the highly-indebted developing countries, United States exports to them actually declined by about $10 billion between 1980 and 1986. . . . As a result, the United States recorded a negative swing in its trade balance of about $12 billion between 1980 and 1986; the corresponding negative swings for the other developed market economy countries were much smaller: about $3 billion for Japan, $2.4 billion for the Federal Republic of Germany and $1.6 billion for the other EEC countries."[29] These declines seriously aggravated an already bad trade situation for the United States. The absolute declines were quite large; and if one extrapolates losses from an expected increase for export growth based on recent history, the declines are quite significant. Richard Feinberg translated the export loss to the United States in terms of lost jobs when he testified before the Senate: ". . . roughly 930,000 jobs would have been created if the growth trend [of U.S. exports to the Third World] of the 1970s had continued after 1980. In sum, nearly 1.6 million U.S. jobs have been lost due to recession in the Third World."[30]

This final point deserves more sustained attention than it has yet received: it is also in the interests of the advanced industrial nations to seek an equitable solution to the debt crisis. No one's long-term interests are served by the increasing impoverishment of millions of people. The financial health and stability of the richer countries depends crucially on debt resolution terms that allow and foster the economic growth and development of the poorer countries.

## HOW REAL WAS THE THREAT OF AN INTERNATIONAL BANKING COLLAPSE?

The global cost most talked about in lending circles was that of a massive default by the debtor countries that might have had the effect of unraveling the international financial system. The point at which the debt crisis actually made it to the front pages of newspapers in the advanced industrial countries was in 1982, when it became clear that Mexico was unable to meet its financial commitments. The size of the Mexican debt, coupled with the overexposure (lending in excess of capital assets) of the private banks that had provided loans to Mexico, raised the possibility of a widespread banking collapse, reminiscent of the bank failures in the 1930s. Table 14.4 gives some idea of the extent of overexposure in 1982.

The threat of a banking collapse was perhaps overstated at the time since these types of measures only imperfectly reflect the vulnerability of banks to a profound crisis of confidence. Nonetheless, it was clear that some of the most important banks in the United States stood to lose a great deal of money if one of the major nations defaulted on its loans. Under even normal conditions, a banking collapse is always possible since banks rarely have enough capital to cover their commitments. Indeed, it is generally considered inefficient to maintain this much available capital. Banks generally have nothing to fear from their overcommitment of resources since it is almost never the case that people wish to question the financial integrity of banks. In 1982, however, it became clear that psychological confidence in the banking system had lost some important underpinnings, and only the rapid intervention of governmental institutions averted events that might have completely undermined public confidence. Since that time, most private banks have stopped lending money to developing countries. Table 14.5 details the extent to which the largest private banks have reduced their vulnerability.

In addition, the major private lenders have increased their reserve holdings to cover possible losses on their loan accounts. Citicorp first announced that it was enlarging its loss reserve in 1987. As of September 1989, many

Table 14.4 / Exposure as a Percentage of Capital, Major Banks, End-1982

|  | Argentina | Brazil | Mexico | Venezuela | Chile | Total |
|---|---|---|---|---|---|---|
| Citibank | 18.2 | 73.5 | 54.6 | 18.2 | 10.0 | 174.5 |
| Bank of America | 10.2 | 47.9 | 52.1 | 41.7 | 6.3 | 158.2 |
| Chase Manhattan | 21.3 | 56.9 | 40.0 | 24.0 | 11.8 | 154.0 |
| Morgan Guaranty | 24.4 | 54.3 | 34.8 | 17.5 | 9.7 | 140.7 |
| Manufacturers Hanover | 47.5 | 77.7 | 66.7 | 42.4 | 28.4 | 262.8 |
| Chemical | 14.9 | 52.0 | 60.0 | 28.0 | 14.8 | 169.7 |

Source: William R. Cline, *International Debt: Systemic Risk and Policy Response* (Washington, D.C.: Institute for International Economics, 1984), p. 24.

Table 14.5 / Exposure of U.S. Banks in the Debtor Countries

|  | End-1982 | End-1986 | End-1988 |
|---|---|---|---|
| **Nine major U.S. banks** |  |  |  |
| Percentage of bank capital in: |  |  |  |
| Developing countries | 287.7% | 153.9% | 108.0% |
| Latin America | 176.5 | 110.2 | 83.6 |
| **All other U.S. banks** |  |  |  |
| Percentage of bank capital in: |  |  |  |
| Developing countries | 116.0% | 55.0% | 21.8% |
| Latin America | 78.6 | 39.7 | 21.8 |

Source: Jeffrey D. Sachs, "Making the Brady Plan Work," *Foreign Affairs*, Vol. 68, no. 3 (Summer 1989), p. 89.

banks had created reserves to cushion potential losses from loans to developing countries (see Table 14.6).

The net effect of these two actions—the sharp reduction in loan exposure and the creation of reserves against potential losses—has insulated the major banks from any threat of a banking collapse precipitated by a widespread default on loans by developing countries. Indeed, these actions have been partially responsible for the revival of the stock prices of these banks, signaling renewed investor confidence in the banks as well as supplying new capital to offset the equity losses generated by the creation of the reserve holdings. The strengthened position of the major banks led William Seidman, Chairman of the Federal Deposit Insurance Corporation, to assert in 1989 that the banks would remain solvent even if they were forced to "write-off 100 percent of their outstanding loans" to the six largest debtor countries.[31]

The newly protected position of the banks alleviates the threat of a collapse, but leaves the developing countries with fewer sources of external

338 / VINCENT FERRARO

Table 14.6 / Selected Reserves against Third World Loans, September 1989

| Bank | Medium- and Long-term Third World loans (in millions of $U.S.) | Reserves against Third World loans (in millions of $U.S.) | Reserves as percentage of loans |
|---|---|---|---|
| Citicorp | 8,854 | 2,600 | 30 |
| BankAmerica | 7,400 | 2,460 | 33 |
| Manufacturers Hanover | 6,800 | 2,400 | 36 |
| Chase Manhattan | 6,400 | 3,000 | 46 |
| Chemical Banking | 4,600 | 1,246 | 27 |
| Bankers Trust | 3,110 | 995 | 32 |
| J. P. Morgan | 2,800 | 3,000 | 100 |

Source: Sarah Bartlett, "The Third World Debt Crisis Reshapes American Banks," *New York Times*, 24 September 1989.

assistance. Banks are not apt to enter into any new or extensive commitments to developing countries now that they do not necessarily need to protect the loans already made. If there were a serious downturn in global economic activity that would further imperil the ability of the developing countries to raise the money to pay back their debts, the only alternative for the debtors would be public assistance, either bilateral or multilateral. In short, while the gains from debt repayment will still be private, the costs will be shifted onto the public sector.

This shift now appears to be the strategy of the major banks. In response to new proposals for debt reduction, the banks, represented by an organization called the Institute for International Finance, have demanded certain conditions for accepting these proposals. In the words of Walter S. Mossberg of *The Wall Street Journal*, "The banks indicated they would be willing to make major debt reductions and new loans only if they receive new loan guarantees, tax breaks, and other financial sweeteners from the U.S., other countries, the World Bank and the International Monetary Fund."[32] The institute also asserted that "any government effort to force debt forgiveness 'would be contested in the courts' as 'an unconstitutional taking of property' unless the government pays the banks compensation."[33] The truculent tone of this position confirms that the banks no longer fear an imminent collapse of the international financial system.

## SOLUTIONS

One fact is undeniable: someone is going to have to pay for past debts. It could be the people in debtor countries, or the banks, or the people in advanced industrial countries. Most likely it will be some combination of these three groups. In the last seven years, there have been various proposals, which, unfortunately, usually reflect only the special interests of the groups proposing them. Generally speaking, these solutions fall into three categories: repudiation, minor adjustments in repayments, or reduction.

Debt repudiation, in the sense of a unilateral cessation of repayment, has already occurred in a number of countries: Bolivia, Brazil, Costa Rica, Dominican Republic, Ecuador, Honduras, Nicaragua, Panama, and Peru.[34] With the exception of the Peruvian cessation, however, most of these actions have been taken with assurances that the stoppages were only temporary. Peru announced that it was unilaterally limiting its debt repayments to a percentage of its export earnings; since Peru took this action, other nations have indicated that they will act similarly. There have been no serious proposals for a widespread and coordinated repudiation of global debt.

Economist Jeffrey Sachs offers several reasons for this absence of a general repudiation.[35] First, debt repudiation is a dramatic and abrupt act. Most nations would prefer to defer such decisions as long as there are advantages to muddling through, and growth prospects are sufficiently ambiguous to make this muddling a viable course. Second, debtor countries fear retaliation from commercial banks. If the banks were to cut off non-debt-related activities such as trade credits, the situation could be made even worse. Third, the debtor countries fear retaliation from creditor governments and multilateral lending agencies. Grants from development banks could be affected, and trade relations would probably be seriously disrupted. Finally, the leaders of most of the debtor countries have interests in maintaining good relations with the richer countries, and repudiation would jeopardize these interests.

Repudiation would also seriously disrupt global economic relations, probably far beyond the immediate losses of the debts themselves. Retaliations would follow, because it would be politically impossible for lenders not to react and because there would be a conscious effort to warn other potential defaulters against similar action. The escalation of economic warfare would have the effect of sharply reducing international economic interactions in trade, investment, and exchange. Such an outcome is in no one's interest.

The vast bulk of activity since 1982 has involved adjusting the timing and method of repayment. The number of specific proposals is bewildering.[36] One can read about debt-equity swaps, in which businesses or properties in the debtor country are purchased at a discount by the banks as partial repayment; debt-for-debt swaps, where bonds are offered as discounted repayments; exit bonds, which are long-term bonds tendered essentially as take-it-or-leave-it offers to creditors who have no interest in investing any further and wish to cut their losses; or cash buy-backs, where the debtor country simply buys back its loan at a deep discount.[37] Some of these proposals, notably the debt-for-nature swaps, where the debtor country promises to protect the environment in return for purchases of the debt by outside groups, are creative and could have important effects.

This array of proposals is referred to as a menu approach to debt repayment, and its logic is superficially sound. It was the logic of the plan offered by Secretary of the Treasury James Baker in 1985. By providing a number of different options, repayments can be tailored to the specific circumstances of a country, thereby easing the burden. Critical to the success of the menu approach is the assumption that countries will "grow out of" their debt. Yet the evidence suggests that this assumption is not entirely sound. This approach further assumes the repayment of debts on terms that are essentially dictated by the creditors. No lender is obligated to accept any one of these possibilities. Moreover, the opportunities for swaps and buy-backs are limited: there are, after all, a relatively small number of investment opportunities in poorer countries, and the debt crisis itself has further limited those possibilities. Finally, some of these swaps can actually increase the drain on the capital of a country, particularly if profit remittances on successful investments turn out to be very high.

The final proposals have to do with debt reduction, and these only became a real possibility in the spring of 1989 with the announcement of a new plan, dubbed the Brady Plan, after U.S. Secretary of the Treasury Nicholas Brady. The plan calls for a total reduction of about 20 percent of global debt, with the IMF and the World Bank offering guarantees for the repayment of the other 80 percent of the debt.[38] This approach recognizes that many of the menu approaches were, in fact, schemes for debt reduction on a case-by-case basis. This formal recognition of the need for systematic debt reduction is a hopeful sign, but the plan clearly does not go far enough.[39] In market terms, developing country debt is already selling on the secondary market at about $0.35 to the dollar.[40] In other words, debt reduction has already occurred in the marketplace, and any plan that incorporates reductions must take this into account.

There are some serious problems with debt reduction. Debt reduction could reduce the incentive for debtor nations to make economic changes that could lead to greater efficiency. Or it could set a precedent that would have the effect of reducing, or even eliminating, the possibility for any future bank lending for economic development projects. Finally, debt reduction could have the effect of saddling public lending agencies, like the World Bank, with enormous burdens, thereby vitiating their future effectiveness.

These concerns are genuine. Counterposed to these possibilities, however, is the stark reality of hundreds of millions of people living in desperate conditions with no hope of relief in the near- or medium-term future. Any plan for easing the debt burden, therefore, must try to incorporate a number of legitimate, but competing, concerns of varying importance. First, the repayment of the debt itself has ceased to be the central concern. Private banks obviously have an interest in the repayment of the debt and, to the extent possible, these interests must be accommodated. But the security of the international banking system is no longer at risk, and that, as a legitimate public concern, can no longer dictate possible necessary actions. The central concern now is the reestablishment of economic growth in the heavily indebted countries and their reintegration into the international economic system. Only after sustained economic growth returns to the heavily indebted countries can the international community even begin to determine manageable rates and methods of debt repayment.

Second, the International Monetary Fund must fundamentally reassess its policies. Programs of structural adjustment may be appropriate for the original purpose of the IMF—to assist nations having temporary difficulties in maintaining currency values because of transient balance of payments difficulties. But these programs are profoundly counterproductive in current circumstances and, indeed, are guided by a wildly inappropriate perspective. The current inflows of capital to the IMF from the heavily indebted countries are more than a gross embarrassment; they are conclusive evidence for the IMF's misunderstanding of the causes of the debt crisis. The IMF should shift its perspective to more creative or appropriate ways of stabilizing or depressing interest rates rather than raising them, or ways of preventing capital flight from developing countries, or any number of issues that concern the specific conditions of economic growth. The mechanical application of a "model" of economic growth is wrongheaded.

Third, the resolution of the debt crisis depends upon a clear recognition that much of the debt, as formally constituted, will not, because it cannot, be repaid. Some countries, like those in sub-Saharan Africa, ought not to repay their debts. Other countries, particularly the heavily indebted ones, can pay something on their debts, and perhaps the appropriate percentage is about half. Viewed in this light, the real question becomes one of allocating the costs of this nonpayment of debts. The current emphasis of forcing the poor to pay with broken lives and broken spirits is demeaning to both rich and poor, and ill serves the long-term interests of rich as well as poor.

Finally, there are genuine issues of responsibility that deserve to be made explicit. The debt "crisis" is only a symptom of an international economic system that tolerates growing and abysmal poverty as a normal condition. This need not, and should not, be the case. The developed countries have a responsibility to create conditions whereby the poorer countries can interact more productively in international economic activities: their single most important contribution to this end might be in the area of reducing trade restrictions on the products of poorer countries. Similarly, the developing countries have a responsibility to see that money is more effectively utilized within their own borders. The obscene personal profits accumulated by such leaders as Marcos of the Philippines and Mobutu of Zaire should not be fostered by the strategic interests of other countries. The banks should also face up to the fact that their single-minded pursuit of profits almost led them to the brink of bankrupty. The lesson to be learned from this experience is

342 / VINCENT FERRARO

that for economic growth to occur, close attention must be paid to the mutual interests of all parties involved.

## Notes

I wish to thank Jens Christiansen, Stephen Ellenburg, Anthony Lake, Tammy Sapowsky, Dan Thomas, and Sharon Worcester for all their assistance in the writing of this essay.

1. John Maynard Keynes, *The Economic Consequences of the Peace* (London: Macmillan and Co., Limited, 1919, reprinted in 1924) pp. 209–10.

2. The original classification was used in the context of the initiative of James Baker in 1985, which identified fifteen heavily indebted nations: Argentina, Bolivia, Brazil, Chile, Colombia, Côte d'Ivoire, Ecuador, Mexico, Morocco, Nigeria, Peru, Philippines, Uruguay, Venezuela, and Yugoslavia. This classification is used by the IMF and UNCTAD. The World Bank in 1989 added Costa Rica and Jamaica. In 1990, the World Bank changed the classification again, dropping Colombia, Jamaica, Nigeria, and Yugoslavia and adding the People's Republic of the Congo, Honduras, Hungary, Nicaragua, Poland, and Senegal. This chapter uses the 1989 classification and data.

3. For an analysis of the economic catastrophe faced by many African nations, see Richard J. Barnet, "But What About Africa?: On the Global Economy's Lost Continent," *Harper's*, Vol. 280, no. 1680 (May 1990), pp. 43–51.

4. World Bank, *World Development Report, 1989* (Washington, D.C.: World Bank, 1989), Table 24, p. 211.

5. William R. Cline, *International Debt and the Stability of the World Economy*, Policy Analyses in International Economics, No. 4 (Washington, D.C.: Institute for International Economics, September 1983), p. 31.

6. Jeffrey Sachs cites Citicorp Chairman Walter Wriston as justifying the heavy bank activity with the observation that "countries never go bankrupt." Jeffrey D. Sachs, "Introduction," in *Developing Country Debt and the World Economy*, edited by Jeffrey D. Sachs, A National Bureau of Economic Research Project Report (Chicago: University of Chicago Press, 1989), p. 8. Sachs also points out Wriston's self-interest in this belief as international operations accounted for 72 percent of Citicorp's overall earnings in 1976.

7. United Nations Conference on Trade and Development, *Trade and Development Report, 1988*, UNCTAD/TDR/8 (New York: United Nations, 1988), pp. 92–93.

8. For an excellent analysis of the Mexican debt crisis, see Adhip Chaudhuri, "The Mexican Debt Crisis, 1982," Pew Program in Case Teaching and Writing in International Affairs, Case #204 (Pittsburgh, PA: University of Pittsburgh, 1988).

9. International Monetary Fund, *Annual Report, 1989* (Washington, D.C.: International Monetary Fund, 1989), p. 17.

10. Cheryl Payer, *The Debt Trap: The International Monetary Fund and the Third World* (New York: The Monthly Review Press, 1974), p. 33.

11. See, for example, Kathy McAfee, "Why the Third World Goes Hungry: Selling Cheap and Buying Dear," *Commonweal*, Vol. 117, no. 12 (15 June 1990), pp. 380–85.

12. Stephen Haggard, "The Politics of Adjustment: Lessons from the IMF's Extended Fund Facility," *International Organization*, Vol. 39, no. 3 (Summer 1985), p. 506, citing Tony Killick, et al., *The Quest for Economic Stabilization: The IMF and the Third World* (New York: St. Martin's, 1984), p. 261.

13. The Philippines is one such example. See Penelope Walker, "Political Crisis and Debt Negotiations: The Case of the Philippines, 1983–86," Pew Program in Case Teaching and Writing in International Affairs, Case #133 (Pittsburgh, PA: University of Pittsburgh, 1988). See also Tyler Bridges, "How Our Loan Money Went South," *Washington Post*, 19 March 1989, p. C2. One should not make too much out of such cases without remembering that political corruption, such as the HUD scandal in the United States, afflicts the rich as well as the poor.

14. Jeffrey Sachs, "Introduction," op. cit., p. 29.

15. See Peter H. Lindert and Peter J. Morton, "How Sovereign Debt Has Worked," in *Developing Country Debt and the World Economy*, edited by Jeffrey D. Sachs, A National

Bureau of Economic Research Project Report (Chicago: University of Chicago Press, 1989), pp. 225–37; Albert Fishlow, "Lessons from the Past: Capital Markets During the 19th Century and the Interwar Period," *International Organization*, Vol. 39, no. 3 (Summer 1985), pp. 383–440; Tim Congdon, *The Debt Threat: The Dangers of High Real Interest Rates for the World Economy* (Oxford: Basil Blackwell, 1988), pp. 109–10.

16. The following discussion relies heavily on the explanations offered by Jan Joost Teunissen, "The International Monetary Crunch: Crisis or Scandal?" *Alternatives*, Vol. 11, no. 3 (July 1987), pp. 359–96, and Gerald Epstein, "The Triple Debt Crisis," *World Policy Journal*, Vol. 2, no. 4 (Fall 1985), pp. 625–58.

17. "Real interest rates charged to less developed countries (LDCs) jumped from 1% in 1980 to between 6.73 and 8.50% in 1981–84. . . ." James R. Barth, Michael D. Bradley, and Paul C. Panayotacos, "Understanding International Debt Crisis," *Case Western Reserve Journal of International Law*, Vol. 19, no. 1 (Winter 1987), pp. 31–52, footnote 4, as quoted in *Current Readings on Money, Banking, and Financial Markets, 1990 Edition*, edited by James A. Wilcox and Frederic S. Mishkin (Glenview, IL: Scott, Foresman/Little, Brown Higher Education, 1990), p. 360.

18. Enzo R. Grilli and Maw Cheng Yang, "Primary Commodity Prices, Manufactured Goods Prices, and the Terms of Trade of Developing Countries: What the Long Run Shows," *The World Bank Economic Review*, Vol. 2, no. 1 (1988), p. 34.

19. World Bank, *World Development Report, 1989*, p. 17.

20. *New York Times*, 18 September 1989, p. D1.

21. *New York Times*, 11 February 1988, p. D1.

22. United Nations Conference on Trade and Development, *Trade and Development Report, 1988*, UNCTAD/TDR/8 (New York: United Nations, 1988), p. 101.

23. Jeffrey Sachs, "Making the Brady Plan Work," *Foreign Affairs*, Vol. 68, no. 3 (Summer 1989), p. 91.

24. Susan George, "The Debt Crisis: Global Economic Disorder in the 1990s," speech given at Smith College, Northampton, MA, 10 April 1989.

25. Harold Lever, "The Debt Won't Be Paid," *New York Review of Books*, Vol. 31, no. 11 (June 28, 1984), p. 3. Emphasis in the original.

26. The statistic on the decline in the Peruvian GNP comes from Jeffrey D. Sachs, "A Strategy for Efficient Debt Reduction," *Journal of Economic Perspectives*, Vol. 4, no. 1 (Winter 1990), p. 20.

27. World Bank, *World Development Report, 1989* (Washington, D.C.: World Bank, 1989), Table 14, p. 191.

28. James D. Robinson 3d, "It's Time to Plan a Third World Revival," *New York Times*, 28 August 1988, p. F3.

29. UNCTAD, *Trade and Development Report, 1988* (New York: United Nations, 1988), p. 66.

30. Statement by Richard E. Feinberg, Vice President, Overseas Development Council, before the Subcommittee on International Debt of the Committee on Finance, United States Senate, Washington, D.C., 9 March 1987, mimeo, pp. 6–7.

31. As quoted in Jeffrey Sachs, "A Strategy for Efficient Debt Reduction," op cit., p. 21. For statistics on the dramatic increases in the values of bank stocks, see Mark Fadiman, "Bad News Is Good News for Big Bank Stocks," *Investor's Daily*, 27 September 1989.

32. Walter S. Mossberg, "Major Banks Vow to Fight Any Effort to Force Third World Debt Forgiveness," *The Wall Street Journal*, 12 January 1989, p. A16.

33. Idem.

34. Jeffrey D. Sachs, "Introduction," *Developing Country Debt and the World Economy*, op cit., p. 26.

35. His arguments are summarized from his introduction to *Developing Country Debt and the World Economy*, op cit., pp. 26–27.

36. For a comprehensive analysis of many of the proposals, see *Analytical Issues in Debt*, edited by Jacob A. Frenkel, Michael P. Dooley, and Peter Wickham (Washington, D.C.: International Monetary Fund, 1989).

37. Peter T. Kilborn, "Debt Reduction: Ways to Do It," *New York Times*, 6 April 1989, p. D1; see also International Monetary Fund, *Annual Report, 1989* (Washington, D.C.: International Monetary Fund, 1989), pp. 26–27.

38. Peter T. Kilborn, "Greenspan Backs Shift on Debt," *New York Times*, 17 March 1989, p. D1.

39. The Brady Plan has not yet had a significant effect on debtor-creditor relations. In the Mexican case, it is not yet clear what the total effect will be. For one view that the 1989 debt restructuring agreement was less than optimal, see Jorge C. Castaneda, "Mexico's Dismal Debt Deal," *New York Times*, 25 February 1990, p. F13.

40. Jeffrey Sachs, "Making the Brady Plan Work," *Foreign Affairs*, Vol. 68, no. 3 (Summer 1989), p. 90. The range of discounts is quite wide. In July 1989 Peru's debts were discounted by 97 percent; Chile's by a little more than 35 percent. See Peter B. Kenen, "Organizing Debt Relief: The Need for a New Institution," *Journal of Economic Perspectives*, Vol. 4, no. 1 (Winter 1990), p. 9.

# 15 / World Hunger: A Scarcity of Food or a Scarcity of Democracy?

JOSEPH COLLINS

In 1974 Henry Kissinger, then U.S. Secretary of State, proclaimed in n address to the United Nations World Food Conference that "in ten years lot one child shall go to bed hungry." Nevertheless, in 1984 more children vent hungry than a decade before, with malnutrition being invariably the crucial factor in the deaths that year of more than 15 million children under ive years of age.[1] And in the 1980s the number of hungry people increased five times faster than in the previous decade.[2] By 1988, according to a World Bank calculation, at least one billion human beings were chronically underfed.[3] All statistics about hunger are gross estimates since the data are scarce and inadequate and at times suppressed by embarrassed governments. The United Nations Food and Agriculture Organization (FAO) places the number of the hungry at about 550 million by 1988. World Bank estimates are considerably greater, in part because it uses a standard of energy (calories) needed to sustain an active working life and not just a diet adequate to prevent stunted growth and serious health risks. There may be a tendency both to exaggerate nutritional requirements and to underappreciate the extent to which poor people manage by one way or another to acquire food.[4]

Even the most circumspect estimates of those who suffer from malnutrition to a greater or lesser degree and from associated diseases are truly alarming while underscoring the pervasive apathy about the unmitigated scandal that hunger is for the human race at the end of the twentieth century. In the words of one respected scholar of world hunger, "The exact number of people suffering from hunger is unimportant, it is enough to know that the number is huge."[5] Since at least as far back as the late 1940s, conventional wisdom in government and scholarly circles, amplified by the mass media, has been that increased food production, particularly through new technologies, constituted the appropriate response to chronic world hunger. The "war against hunger" has been repeatedly defined as a war to boost food production in a race against population growth. This war has been waged with considerable financial and political backing by the U.S.

government (and most other governments), foundations such as Rockefeller and Ford, and international financial institutions led by the World Bank.[6]

By the late 1970s the results of this narrow technical focus, at least in the short term, were clear: significantly more food per person was being produced. The world's output in grains alone was two pounds a day—more than 3,000 calories and ample protein—for every man, woman, and child on earth.[7] And that calorie estimate, enough for even working adults, does not include the many other nutritious foods people eat: beans, nuts, fruits, vegetables, root crops, seafoods, and grass-fed meats.

Approaches to greater production centering on varieties of seeds that yield more in response to increased inputs, especially synthetic fertilizers and, for the most part, regulated watering through irrigation, have been widely celebrated as successful. Popularly such technologies have been hailed as the "green revolution."[8]

On a global basis, it has become an indisputable fact of our times that hunger can no longer be blamed on a shortage of food.[9] The telling fact is that in the early 1980s the number of hungry people was accelerating precisely at a time when global food stocks were building up to record levels.[10] The additional food required by the world's hungry to close their dietary gap is small. Based on the cautious calculations in 1987 of the Food and Agriculture Organization[11] (FAO) and estimates by the International Food Policy Research Institute, only 15 to 20 million tons of cereal grains annually (out of a then-total production of some 1,660 million tons) would be sufficient to raise the diets of the present number of the world's undernourished[12] to adequate levels.[13]

Production of food grains significantly increased not only in the industrial countries but also in many nations in the Third World. By the mid-1980s, green revolution seeds were being sown on roughly half the total rice and wheat acreage.[14] The production of these key grains together with other food staples in the Third World during the 1960s and 1970s followed, for a variety of reasons, a clearly upward trend, with an average annual growth rate of 2.6 percent.[15] Over this period the growth of food production was slightly faster than the unprecedented rise in population.[16]

Even in countries where chronic hunger is widespread, by the 1970s enough food was available to wipe out hunger. Nowhere does an absolute shortage of food explain chronic hunger. One hypothetical question highlights how misleading it is to think that absolute food shortages even in Third World countries are the root cause of hunger: how much of the food now available within Third World countries would it take to make up for the total food lacking in the diets of each country's chronically hungry people? According to the World Bank, the answer for country after country with widespread hunger is a tiny percentage.[17] In India, home of over a third of the world's hungry people,[18] a mere 5.6 percent of the country's food supply, if eaten by the hungry, would make an active life possible for everyone.[19] For Indonesia, with the second greatest number of undernourished people in the world,[20] only 2 percent of the country's food supply would make the difference.[21] For the Philippines, where 70 percent of the children are thought to be undernourished, only 1.9 percent of the total food supply would make up the entire deficit in the diets of all the hungry.[22] A redistribution of only 1.6 percent of the total food supply of Brazil, the world's second-largest food exporter (after the United States), would meet all the needs of the 86 million Brazilians estimated in 1984 to be undernourished.[23]

## AFRICA'S "FOOD CRISIS" AND THE REALITIES OF HUNGER

The 1980s witnessed a worldwide explosion of awareness of hunger and starvation in Africa. A flood of commentaries, in official, scholarly, and media circles, argued that the drought exacerbated a preexisting general decline in African food production. Repeatedly stated, with considerable self-assurance, was that in sub-Saharan Africa, in contrast to virtually everywhere else, food production per person was lagging behind population growth. Typically, the 1983 FAO World Food Report stated that "Africa South of the Sahara is losing the race to keep food production ahead of population growth."[24] Moreover, the fact that tropical Africa, starting in the 1970s, became a significant net importer of basic foods, notably cereal grains, was "readily understood" by many prominent analysts of world hunger as flowing from lagging local food production.[25]

In fact, evidence for stagnation in per capita food production in much of Africa is both very thin and subject to significant bias.[26] The reasons for this conclusion are instructive.

Given the self-assurance of the claims about African food production, one might assume that the data upon which these conclusions were based were reasonably well-founded and accurate. But as British analyst Philip Raikes has convincingly argued, "Nothing could be further from the truth."[27]

There are few countries in sub-Saharan Africa where the level of food production is known within any reasonable parameters.[28] For instance, in Tanzania, by no means the African country with the least effective agricultural ministry, government production estimates for important food crops vary by a factor of up to three for the same year.[29] FAO production estimates for staple food production in Tanzania also vary considerably. The 1982 FAO Production Yearbook shows Tanzanian corn production in 1982 to have been 0.8 million tons. Yet the 1984 edition of the Production Yearbook puts the figure for Tanzanian corn production in 1982 at 1.55 million tons. In 1985 the FAO expert most qualified to estimate corn production in Tanzania was of the opinion that total corn production was well over 2 million tons and had been for some years.[30] Such messy data for Tanzania are hardly exceptional. Raikes compared estimates of corn production for

1982 in the 1982 and 1984 FAO Production Yearbooks for the twenty largest sub-Saharan countries and found that only five remain unaltered. Eight are revised between 1 and 10 percent, another five between 11 and 50 percent, and two by over 50 percent. As Raikes notes, "While this gives some idea of the degree of uncertainty, there is no reason to suppose that because figures have not been revised, they must necessarily be accurate."[31]

Part of the problem of obtaining reliable agricultural statistics, something especially true in much of Africa, is that most staple food production comes from a large number of marginal small peasant farms, the vast majority of which are covered by no system of registration or crop reporting. It is near impossible to produce even reasonably accurate estimates of the area cultivated, much less of actual harvests. Just one of the many other complications in estimating production is that peasant farmers often intercrop, that is, grow one crop (or more) between the rows of another. Moreover, many peasant farm families consume part, even much, of the food they produce, making even more unlikely that such unmarketed production is officially counted. Where marketing is not government-controlled, the many small- to medium-size traders in food crops are likely to underreport their sales in an effort to minimize taxation. Where the government theoretically monopolizes marketing, much (and perhaps most) will be illegally marketed privately and therefore is even more likely to go unreported. Officials whose greatest interest might well be what food the government has at its disposal often tend to estimate food production from the portion of it which is marketed through government channels, or to let this figure greatly shape the estimation.

Important for any consideration of whether food shortages are at the root of the chronic hunger in Africa is that all these problems (and doubtlessly others) point to a high probability of a significant downward bias in the reporting.[32]

Government policymakers (in Africa as well as elsewhere in the Third World) and international agency officials strongly prefer chronic hunger to be diagnosed in terms of inadequate and declining production. Raikes argues that such a diagnosis "points to conclusions which most policy-makers would like to draw in the first place: that more food needs to be imported and that rapid technical change is needed to increase aggregate production. . . . Finally . . . there is some reason to suspect dramatization and exaggeration of 'food gaps' by governments anxious to increase or maintain levels of food aid."[33]

None of this is to underplay the difficulties confronting African food producers. Arguably, many of the very policies that bias food supply statistics downward in fact thwart and distort Africa's food potential.[34] The point is that even in sub-Saharan Africa, where often official statistics might at first suggest otherwise, chronic hunger cannot be blamed on an absolute scarcity of food. (Famine or starvation relatively suddenly or for a short time affecting all or much of a population is usefully distinguished from chronic or enduring undernutrition. In Africa in the 1980s a number of major famines resulted precisely from acute food shortages due to armed conflicts, including food blockades and "scorched earth" policies as weapons of war.[35])

Ground-breaking historical research carried out in the 1970s and 1980s revealed that frequently there have been major famines in which millions of people died while local food output and availability remained high and undiminished.[36] Indeed, some famines, such as the Bangladesh famine of 1974, have occurred in periods of peak food availability.[37] Famines have been caused not by scarcity of food but by large numbers of people being unable to acquire it.

What can be learned from more than three decades in numerous countries around the world of the pursuit of the single-minded "production solution"? Most fundamentally, more and more people can (and do) go hungry no matter how high the aggregate levels of food production, not only on a global basis but in the very countries in which they live.

Large numbers of people go hungry most of the time or seasonally without any shortage of food. People eat only when they have access to the resources to produce (and keep) enough food to feed themselves, or to a livelihood that gives them enough money to purchase the food they need. Failing both, they go hungry unless they have the political power to lay claim to subsidized or free food. The chronically hungry are those who are deprived of enough land and other food-producing resources, those who cannot find regular employment at adequate wages, those who cannot keep enough of what they produce due to excessive rents or taxes, those who get prices too low for their produce or handicrafts.

It is not that production is unimportant—a patently absurd position. Nor that production will not eventually have to increase if populations continue to grow. Even if it were not for other good reasons, it is therefore crucial that public policies encourage, even mandate, a shift to sustainable food-producing technologies away from ones that are based on the "mining" of largely nonrenewable resources.[38]

Rather, what is crucial for the hungry is how democratic or how tightly concentrated is the distribution of economic power, especially access to food-producing and/or income-generating resources. Indeed, hunger is a problem not of supply but of distribution; the fundamental solution, however, lies not with redistributing food but with redistributing economic power.

Likewise, programs such as food stamps and mother-child food supplementation schemes at best treat the symptoms of malnutrition and not the causes.[39] Therefore, if they work at all, they are sustainable only as long as they are funded. They do not lead to a situation in which they are no longer needed. Distributive reforms that enhance the economic base of poor individuals and households may.

Inequalities in economic power operate on every level, from the household, to the village, through the national level, to that of international commerce and finance. Inequitable control is often most strikingly manifest at the village level in the access to agricultural land; few aspects of economic life more directly affect the food well-being of so many hundreds of millions of human beings. A 1975 World Bank study cited a United Nations survey of 83 Third World countries that found that typically only 3 percent of all landowners control a staggering 79 percent of all farmland, depriving most rural families of owning any land at all.[40] Land-deprived families working in agriculture, for the most part, either cannot grow food for themselves (or retain enough of it after paying steep rents to landlords) or cannot earn enough money to purchase even their food necessities. The fact that in many countries the portion of families who are land-deprived has grown faster than population growth since the early 1960s goes a long way in explaining widening poverty and therefore hunger.

When a new production technology—such as hybrid seeds that yield more in response to irrigation, fertilizers, and pesticides—is introduced into a social system riddled with inequalities, it should be assumed that the beneficiaries will be those who already possess land, money, creditworthiness, political influence, or some combination of these.[41] By the mid-1970s, abundant documentation from around the world[42] confirmed that development strategies that avoid the social-political issues of who controls land and other productive assets, attempting instead simply to get more produced, set into motion processes that actually worsen the plight of the poor majority. Enhancing the productive capacity of the land (invariably irrigated largely at public expense) attracts a new class of "farmers"—moneylenders, merchants, bureaucrats, military officers, speculators, and multinational agribusiness companies—who rush in and take control of the land. Land values soar—up, for instance, three- to fivefold in only a few years in the green revolution areas of India. As land values rise, so do rents, driving tenant farmers into the ranks of the landless. Seeing new profit possibilities, landlords evict tenants and cultivate the land themselves with new machinery and seasonal farmworkers.[43]

In northwest Mexico, the birthplace of green revolution technologies, the average farm size over about twenty years jumped from 200 to 2,000 acres, with over three-quarters of those working in agriculture deprived of owning, or even renting, any land at all.[44] In India, the portion of the rural work force that is landless doubled in the two decades following the introduction of high-response seeds.[45] And while more landless rural people are created by the expansion of larger operators, thanks to greater mechanization they must compete, by and large, for fewer jobs and therefore probably lower real wages. In the very areas of northwest Mexico where agricultural production boomed, the average number of days of employment for a farmworker shrank from 190 to 100.[46]

Narrow production strategies have produced more food in many countries, but hunger has only widened and deepened. A series of major studies conducted in the mid-1970s for the International Labor Organization document that in seven South Asian countries—Pakistan, Bangladesh, India, Sri Lanka, Malaysia, the Philippines, and Indonesia—where the focus has simply been on getting more food produced and where food output per person has in fact risen, the rural poor were found to be absolutely worse off than before. The study concludes that "the increase in poverty has been associated not with a fall but with a rise in cereal production per head, the main component of the diet of the poor."[47] In-depth investigations by the United Nations Research Institute for Social Development (UNRISD) of the impact of green revolution technologies in twenty-four different Third World countries have confirmed this consistent pattern—a decline in well-being, including nutritional status, for much of the rural majority even as agricultural production bounds ahead.[48]

Increasing food production while ignoring who is in control of that production is not even a neutral strategy. It does not "buy time"—feed more people until the difficult questions of control can be addressed. In fact, it tends to marginalize larger numbers of people from control over productive resources and therefore from consumption, while further enriching the minority and making them more willing and able than ever to resist democratization of economic power.

The 1990s, it is widely assumed, will witness a second "revolution" in agricultural production based on developments in biotechnology in which the molecular constitutions of living organisms are manipulated for some sought-after end. In addition to other concerns about biotechnology (and they are many and varied[49]), it no longer can responsibly be claimed that greater food production is the key to ending hunger.

The tightening of control over productive resources generates a concentration in income and, as a consequence, a limited internal market for what is produced from those resources. Even the vital needs of millions of nearby human beings will not count: through no fault of their own, they cannot express their needs in money, the only language an increasingly globalized market understands. Those who monopolize productive resources, far from advocating redistributive reforms, see their future in terms of catering to the upscale tastes of already well-fed high-income consumers at home and especially in industrial countries.

Particularly indicative of the bypassing of the vital needs of hundreds of millions of people has been the clearly noticeable trend to use food staples for animal feed to satisfy the burgeoning demand for more grain-fed meat, poultry, eggs, and milk in the diets of the world's better-off.[50] Worldwide, by the 1980s, more than 40 percent of all grain went to livestock, up from a third a decade earlier.[51] Indeed, despite persistent widespread hunger and increased numbers of people, the 1970s in most of the Third World witnessed an explosion in the demand for livestock feed. On average, the demand for feed in the Third World grew 75 percent faster than the demand for food.[52] During the 1970s, the fastest growth in the use of food for animal feed was in Central America, a region known for widespread malnutrition; feed production more than doubled during the decade.[53] Rapid growth of feed use occurred also in Western Asia, Northern Africa, and East and Southeast Asia.[54]

Mexico, where two-thirds of the people are economically marginalized and therefore chronically undernourished,[55] has been a dramatic case of the language of the market. The area planted in the foods most consumed by the poor majority—corn and beans—did not expand, despite the growth in population, over the 1960s and 1970s.[56] Over the same period, the percentage of Mexico's grain production fed to livestock increased as much as eight times, to virtually half the total output. Not only does just a fraction of the nutrients fed to livestock return to humans, but at least 25 million Mexicans are too poor ever to eat beef, and even poultry and dairy foods are largely beyond their reach.[57]

# THE 1980s

The 1980s witnessed a severe further undermining of the power of the poor majority in numerous countries, especially in Latin America and Africa, to lay claim to adequate food. Measures taken by governments attempting to pay off enormous debts to foreign creditors became a major new factor in the hunger equation.

In the 1970s, Third World governments found it easy to borrow hundreds of billions of dollars. The borrowing was totally undemocratic: the vast majority had no say in the process, nor did the loans support broad-based development. Much of the borrowed money was squandered on show-case projects—conference centers, high-tech medical centers, and administrative buildings—with little hope of generating enough foreign exchange to pay off the loans and interest.[58] Some went to import consumer goods, invariably for the better-off. On average, 15 to 20 percent of the borrowing was sunk into arms purchases and other military expenditures, guaranteed not to produce goods that might help repay the loans. And, of course, healthy chunks simply disappeared due to graft and corruption.

The money pushed out by banks loaded down with huge deposits, especially from oil-exporting countries, seemed cheap; during much of the 1970s, interest rates were actually below the rate of inflation.[59] But the interest rates were in most cases adjustable, meaning that the cost of using the borrowed money could change over time. And it did. In the Reagan era, as the United States stepped up Pentagon spending and lowered rates of taxation on the wealthy, heavy borrowing by the deficit-strapped U.S. government fueled higher world interest rates. The billions of increased interest payments for Third World borrowers came on top of a sharp run-up in the prices of imported oil, making it necessary for many Third World countries to borrow billions of dollars on top of the already snowballing loans.

By 1982, many governments could no longer afford to service their debts. Unable to obtain even short-term credits for imports, they turned to the lender of last resort, the International Monetary Fund (IMF). But the IMF lends only when a government agrees to reorganize its economy the IMF's way so that the banks can be repaid. This reorganization is formally called structural adjustment.

Instead of penalizing the wealthy and the military, the burden of structural adjustment has fallen squarely on the poor and the middle class. The IMF prescription to spend less ("demand management") means drastically cutting consumption; for the poor, often the majority, who already live on the edge, consumption cuts mean increased malnutrition, illness, and indeed even higher mortality rates. Sweeping devaluation of the local currency makes vital imports far more expensive. Imported basic foods, medicines, spare parts, and essential farm inputs become impossible luxuries, out of reach of the majority of urban poor and small farmers. Government spending on health and other social services is slashed. Government subsidies for transportation, water, electricity, and cooking fuel are dramatically curtailed and in some cases totally eliminated. In countries that tried to keep basic food affordable for the poor, consumer subsidies for basic staples have been removed. Bank credit is tightened and made so expensive that local businesses fail, thereby driving up unemployment.

Governments are also mandated to step up dollar earnings through further gearing their economies for production for export. For most countries, this means more deforestation and pouring more topsoil, water, and labor into the production of raw or semi-processed agricultural goods. With the IMF directing dozens of countries to export, world markets cannot possibly absorb the flood, so prices plummet. By the late 1980s, commodity prices sank to their lowest levels in sixty years (while prices of many manufactured goods and chemicals imported from industrial countries to produce those agricultural goods increased). Low prices on world markets push countries to export even more, just to try to keep revenues from falling. This vicious, debt-induced circle creates pressures to increase cash crop production further at the expense of crops for local consumption as well as at the expense of the environment.

Governmental pressures (including aid-financed programs) on peasant households to grow cash crops for export diverts labor, especially women's labor, away from food production for the family. Moreover, women seldom have a say over the disposal of money from cash-crop sales. Especially in African societies, this is the man's domain, and men tend to spend the money on things other than food. When women are obliged to labor long hours on cash crops, child care and cooking suffer as well.[60] Poor women and children, invariably the least powerful members of society, are the most harmed.

Between 1982 and 1987 the IMF-directed measures resulted in Third World countries transferring to the banks $140 billion more in interest and principal payments than they received in new loans. They also resulted in a significant widening and deepening of hunger.

The nature of the adjustment of the debt-ridden economies of most Latin American nations greatly worsened the already widespread unemployment. The International Labor Organization reported that official unemployment in Latin America rose by 40 percent between 1980 and 1984.[61] The total number of jobless in Latin America increased by at least two-thirds during the same period. Huge numbers of people desperately seeking work drive down wages for everyone. The purchasing power of farmworkers in Latin America who did find work fell sharply throughout the 1980s to levels below those of two decades earlier.

The purchasing power of millions of Mexican households plunged as the government decreed IMF-prescribed policies to pay off the foreign banks and as Mexican elites (illegally) spirited an estimated $90 billion[62] into foreign real estate and bank accounts. A survey carried out in greater Mexico City in 1984 estimated that 40 percent of the population was malnourished and that those with nutritional deficiencies ate mostly corn tortillas, bread, beans, and rehydrated milk, all of which were at the time subsidized. In 1986 these subsidies were eliminated as part of the IMF-required cutbacks.[63] While official statistics have not been made available, no one doubts that in the 1980s an even greater percentage of Mexicans fell into malnutrition as the country stepped up its export of food and other agricultural products to higher-bidding foreigners in an effort to pay the interest on the foreign debt.

The buying power of Peruvian workers who could find work fell precipitously in the early 1980s as debt-repayment austerity measures were applied. A Peruvian worker earning the minimum wage in 1980 had to work 17 minutes in order to buy a kilo of rice; but just four years later it took 2 hours and 5 minutes of work. A can of powdered milk cost 17 minutes of labor in 1980, but 83 minutes in 1984.[64] It is hardly surprising then that a former governor of Peru's Central Bank declared that the IMF adjustment policies mean "the death of some 500,000 children."[65]

Brazil's military dictatorship contracted the Third World's largest debt, a great part of the loans going for military ends. Yet in the 1980s ordinary Brazilians paid dearly, falling behind even in meeting the gargantuan interest payments. As previously noted, Brazil became the world's second-largest exporter of food, while by 1985 the government estimated, on the basis of surveys, that two out of three Brazilians were underfed, double the percentage arrived at by a respected household survey carried out in 1961.[66] Infant mortality rose by 12 percent between 1982 and 1984 alone, after years of decline.[67]

In mineral-rich Zaire, where the public debt and the private fortune held outside the country by dictator Mobutu are both estimated to be $6 billion, malnutrition has been on the rise since 1983. By the mid-1980s, reportedly half of the children in some areas were dying before reaching the age of five. One survey found that in the two largest cities the average daily calorie consumption had reached starvation levels.[68] Throughout sub-Saharan Africa, policies mandated for debt-burdened countries caused economies to contract, shrinking the employment and purchasing power of millions of Africans.

With some years' distance from the 1980s, it might be more widely recognized how much the day-in and day-out hunger widened in so many societies, in the face of a steady buildup in world stocks of grain (with the exception of 1984, since a 1983 acreage-restriction program in the United States had the intended result of reducing grain production). By the end of the decade, the United Nations International Children's Emergency Fund (UNICEF) charged that "adjustment" measures had taken a yearly toll of an "extra" half million children's lives.[69] This widening of long-term undernutrition went on little reported in the world's media, in contrast to their intense, albeit fleeting, focus in the mid-1980s on famines in African countries torn by war and civil war.[70]

# THE 1990s

The decade of the 1990s has opened without any sign of a letup in the pressures working against ever larger numbers of people being able to secure the food they need. The food riots triggered by the debt-driven austerity policies in so many countries in the mid-1980s, destabilizing a number of regimes, could become more frequent and acute as the victims of the policies grow ever more numerous. These victims may well decide that they will not quietly watch themselves and their children starve.

Moreover, many Third World countries, most notably in sub-Saharan Africa, have been made significantly more dependent in the 1980s on importing food, largely as a result of governments being told that they can export their way out of the debt crisis and that they can import "cheap" grains.[71] Also a factor in this increased dependence on imports is chronic food "aid," which has in many cases undermined local food producers and virtually everywhere (as intended by many donors) created demand in recipient countries for products they cannot reasonably grow themselves (e.g., wheat in tropical countries).

Any further softening of world markets for exports of Third World countries, resulting from competition among producers and worldwide economic recession or worse in the 1990s, could very well sharply increase hunger. More loans for food aid and even grants of food aid would be neither adequate nor desirable.

Food policy analyst Susan George finds the increased dependence of so many Third World countries on imports of cereal grains for their urban populations especially distressing at a time when bilateral sales agreements are increasingly used between major suppliers and clients (for example, the U.S. and the USSR), thus substantially reducing the size of markets from which smaller and financially weaker countries must buy. Any future climatic or commercial shock, including sharply rising prices for petroleum that directly affect fertilizer and fuel costs, could send prices on these "residual" markets skyward (in no small measure thanks also to commodity speculators), creating even greater hardship for needy purchasers.[72]

The 1980s also saw "free-market" policies reintroduced in societies that had previously taken farmland, other food-producing resources, food itself, and employment/job security out of the marketplace. Most notable among these is China, home to one-fifth of humanity, which over the 1950s and 1960s had eliminated the once recurrent and devastating famines[73] and significantly slowed its rate of population growth.

The market, by definition, responds to economic power and not to need. The more widely dispersed is purchasing power, the more the market will in fact respond to human needs and preferences. But the market left to its own devices will concentrate wealth and purchasing power. Every gain in power over resources sets the stage for potential further gains. Concentrating land into ever fewer hands, food speculation, ignoring the vital need to be part of production and therefore consumption of those who cannot pay, increased exports in the face of growing hunger—all are normal marketplace behavior. Unless ground rules are established and enforced to counteract the tendency toward excessive concentration, the 1990s, in societies that have re-introduced free-market policies, should more than glimpse the negative consequences, including even chronic hunger. China, without different ground rules, could become more like India, a country of widespread chronic hunger in the face of considerable production, even "surpluses."

Some of the ground rules seemingly needed if a market society is to eliminate hunger include land tenure rules to keep ownership from becoming concentrated, and tax and credit policies geared to the needs of smaller farmers. Also needed are tax, credit, and social welfare policies that actively disperse buying power.[74]

## POPULATION AND POWERLESSNESS

A population "explosion" is frequently advanced as the fundamental cause of hunger. This Malthusian paradigm dominates the popular understanding in the United States of the hunger problem. The world's population has indeed "exploded," more than doubling just since 1950, with 85 percent of that growth occurring in the Third World.

A few have argued that rapid population growth is no problem, claiming that the historical record shows that it should stimulate higher technological development and thereby in the long term promote economic development and higher standards of living.[75]

But, on several grounds, population growth *is* a major problem. Obviously, if populations were to continue to grow at rates similar to those of the recent past in much of the Third World *and* if the resource depletion inherent in elite-driven agricultural production systems and consumer lifestyles commonplace in the "developed" world were to remain unreformed (and only emulated in the Third World), pressures on the world's environment would become unsustainable. Just as obviously, increased population densities in the Third World without both democratizing changes in terms of access to productive resources and improvements in productive techniques would mean greater poverty and therefore greater hunger.

There are also ethical grounds that should compel us to reject any suggestion that population growth in most countries at this time is not a grave problem. Not to do so implies that the impact of population growth can be judged solely as to how it affects *human* well-being, ignoring any responsibility toward the integrity of the larger ecosphere. Moreover, to argue that population growth is not a problem because of infinite human ingenuity to discover new techniques to substitute for any depleted resource is to ignore that at this point in history, in most places, human efforts to support ever larger numbers threaten other forms of life and the natural world's delicate, interacting balance. In addition, high population densities can also render changes in access to resources, for instance, making reforms redistributing access to agricultural land more difficult.

Nevertheless, to suggest that until population growth is curbed there is little use in doing anything else to confront the problem of hunger is tragically wrongheaded. As we have seen, in a world of huge unmarketable surpluses of food, sheer numbers of people are not the real cause of hunger and chronic malnutrition. Diminishing population growth would have no effect on the proportion of hungry people because population growth is not the primary cause of their food poverty.

Rapid population growth is rooted in economic insecurity generated and perpetuated by antidemocratic power structures.[76] Indeed, rapid population growth can perhaps best be understood to result largely from efforts by the poor to cope in the face of the concentrated economic power of an elite. For example, for rural families deprived of land assets, children from a remarkably early age can enhance the survival income of the family by laboring on other people's land and through other economic activities. Hunger, the most dramatic symptom of pervasive poverty, and rapid population growth often occur together not because hunger is caused by high population density but because they have a common cause.

Studies of the societies that have lowered their fertility rates[77] point to democratizing shifts in power relations in key and interrelated aspects of family, community, and national life that have made lowered fertility both desired by many families as well as possible for them. Among the most significant democratizing shifts are those that have led to the enhanced power of the poor—especially poor women—through the provision of basic literacy, education, employment, and old-age security; the heightened power of peasants to provide food and income for themselves because reforms have widely dispensed access to land, credit, markets, and other economic resources; the bolstered power of consumers to secure adequate nutrition where deliberate policies have been implemented to keep basic food staples within the reach of all; the enhanced capacity of people to protect their health as medical services are made accessible to all; and the heightened power of women to make effective their choice to limit family size through birth control.

Policy strategies therefore to slow and eventually halt population growth and to eradicate hunger are complementary, not competitive. *In fact, they are overlapping and in large measure identical.*

The right to eat is not in effect the right to charity nor necessarily the right to government provision of food. Fundamentally, the right to eat is the right to participate in control over economic resources and therefore, among other things, to produce enough food or be able to buy enough food for one's needs. Wherever political rights for all citizens flourish, people are most likely to see to it that they share in control over economic resources.

## Notes

1. Estimate by UNICEF. See *The State of the World's Children 1989* (New York: Oxford University Press, 1989), p. 87.

2. Estimate by the World Food Council, President's Report to the Fifteenth Ministerial Session (Rome: World Food Council, 1989), p. 3.

3. Based on extrapolations from World Bank studies; see *Poverty and Hunger: Issues and Options for Food Security in Developing Countries* (Washington, D.C.: World Bank, 1986) and Shlomo Reutlinger and Marcelo Selowsky, *Malnutrition and Poverty: Magnitude and Policy Options*, World Bank Staff Occasional Paper No. 23 (Baltimore: Johns Hopkins University Press).

4. For a discussion of some of the methodological problems, see Amartya Sen, *Hunger and Entitlements* (Helsinki: World Institute for Development and Economics Research), p. 6, and Thomas T. Poleman, "Quantifying the Nutrition Situation in Developing Countries," *Food Research Institute Studies*, vol. XVIII, no. 1, 1981.

5. Keith Griffin, *World Hunger and the World Economy* (London: Macmillan, 1987).

6. See Andrew Pearse, *Seeds of Plenty, Seeds of Want*, especially Chapter II (Oxford: Clarendon Press, 1980).

7. For calculations, see Frances Moore Lappe and Joseph Collins, *Food First: Beyond the Myth of Scarcity* (New York: Ballantine Books, 1978), p. 13.

8. For a critical discussion of the range of issues associated with the green revolution, see

Frances Moore Lappe and Joseph Collins, *World Hunger: Twelve Myths* (New York: Grove Press, 1986), Chapter 5, and Lappe and Collins, *Food First*, Part IV, and below.

9. World Food Council, President's Report to the Fifteenth Ministerial Session (Rome: World Food Council, 1989), p. 3.

10. World Food Council, The Cyprus Initiative Against Hunger in the World (Rome: World Food Council, 1989), p. 10ff. In fact, OECD countries as well as the U.S. government in the 1980s have been pursuing policies intended to reduce "surpluses." A 1983 U.S. government acreage restriction program reduced grain harvests by over 100 million tons (approximately by 30 percent).

11. United Nations Food and Agriculture Organization, *Fifth World Food Survey, 1987* (Rome: FAO, 1988).

12. Throughout this chapter *undernourished* and *hungry* are used interchangeably. Most often, the literature here cited employs these terms to refer to those who regularly consume below 90 percent of the energy standard developed jointly by the Food and Agriculture Organization and the World Health Organization. The standard is based on the caloric intake required to replace energy expenditure and to provide for growth in childhood. Standards were set on an individual country basis by accounting for observed demographic patterns in body weights, age, and sex structure. For example, the standard for a U.S. "reference man" in his twenties weighing 155 pounds and not especially active is 2,700 calories (kcal) per day and for a U.S. "reference woman" in her twenties and weighing 127 pounds is 2,000 calories (kcal) per day. The world average is 2,350 (kcal) calories per person per day. Calories adequate to cover energy needs are generally sufficient to meet protein needs, except for people (especially young children) subsisting on low-protein root crops and plantains.

13. World Food Council, The Cyprus Initiative Against Hunger in the World (Rome: World Food Council, 1989), p. 10.

14. Frances Moore Lappe and Joseph Collins, *World Hunger: Twelve Myths* (New York: Grove Press/Food First Books, 1986), p. 47.

15. Leonardo Paulino and John Mellor, "The Food Situation in Developing Countries," *Food Policy*, vol. 9, no. 4 (November 1984), p. 292. There are good reasons to judge these estimates conservative. See discussion of African food production statistics below.

16. Ibid.

17. World Bank, *Poverty and Hunger*, p. 19ff. Based on the calculation of the aggregate caloric deficit in the diets of the hungry as a percentage of the total caloric value of all the food produced.

18. The FAO, using its minimal standard, estimated in the early 1980s that of the 435 million hungry in the Third World, 201 million were in India; see FAO, *Dimensions of Needs* (Rome: FAO, 1982). Other studies estimate the number of chronically hungry people in India closer to 300 million; see, for instance, U.S. Department of Agriculture, *Agricultural Outlook* (December 1985).

19. World Bank, p. 20.

20. FAO, *Dimensions of Needs*, Part III.

21. World Bank, p. 20.

22. Ibid.

23. See World Bank, *Poverty and Hunger*, 20, for percentage. Rank as food exporter, see FAO Production Yearbook, 1988.

24. *FAO World Food Report, 1983* (Rome: FAO), p. 9.

25. See, for example, Paulino and Mellor, p. 298.

26. Highly recommended is Philip Raikes, *Modernizing Hunger* (London: James Currey and Portsmouth, New Hampshire: Heinemann), Chapter 2.

27. Ibid., p. 17.

28. Ibid., p. 18.

29. FAO estimates also vary considerably.

30. Raikes, *Modernizing Hunger*, p. 18.

31. Ibid., p. 18.

32. See also Sara S. Berry, "The Food Crisis and Agrarian Change in Africa: A Review Essay," *African Studies Review* 27, no. 2 (June 1984).

33. Raikes, *Modernizing Hunger*, p. 20.

34. See Lappe and Collins, *World Hunger*, p. 13.

35. United Nations World Food Program estimated that in 1987 almost three-quarters of the 79 emergency operations were in response to war situations. Angola, Mozambique, Ethiopia (and Eritrea), and the Sudan were particularly affected by war-created famine in which food denial was often used as a weapon of war.

36. See Amartya Sen, *Food, Economics and Entitlements* (Helsinki: World Institute for Development Economic Research, 1986).

37. M. Alamgir, *Famine in South Asia: Political Economy of Mass Starvation in Bangladesh* (Boston: Oelgeschlager, 1987).

38. See "Toward an Agriculture We Can Live With" in Lappe and Collins, *World Hunger*, p. 60ff.

39. Per Pinstrup-Andersen, *Approaches to Targeted Food, Nutrition and Health Programmes* (Rome: World Food Council, 1989).

40. World Bank, Assault on World Poverty (Washington: World Bank, 1975), p. 244. See also Milton J. Esman, *Landlessness and Near Landlessness in Developing Countries* (Ithaca: Center for International Studies, Cornell University, 1978).

41. Andrew Pearse dubs this marked phenomenon the "talents-effect" after the well known parable in Matthew, Chapter 25. See chapters 15 and 16 in Lappe and Collins, *Food First: Beyond the Myth of Scarcity*.

42. United Nations Research Institute for Social Development, multi-volume study, *The Social and Economic Implications of the Large-Scale Introduction of New Varieties of Food Grains* (Geneva: UNRISD, 1975); see the excellent overview of this authored by Andrew Pearse. See also Keith Griffin and A. R. Khan, *Landlessness and Poverty in Rural Asia*, prepared for the International Labor Organization, Geneva, Switzerland.

43. Lappe and Collins, *Food First*, p. 136ff.

44. Cynthia Hewitt de Alcantara, *Modernizing Mexican Agriculture* (Geneva: UNRISD, 1976), p. 30.

45. For an explanation of preference for the term "high-response seeds" rather than the much more commonplace "high-yield seeds," see Lappe and Collins, *Food First*, p. 129ff.

46. Hewitt de Alcantara, op. cit., p. 318. Between only 1973 and 1983, the number of tractors throughout the Third World doubled, in the face of surging numbers of landless laborers. Calculated from *FAO Production Yearbooks* (Rome: FAO, 1975 and 1984).

47. See Griffin and Khan, *Poverty and Landlessness*.

48. See UNRISD, *op. cit.*, and Pearse, *Seeds of Plenty*.

49. Biotechnology for Third World agriculture will reinforce trends associated with the green revolution, especially exacerbated inequalities, further impoverishment of poorly capitalized producers with severely restricted access to credit to purchase commercial inputs, and dramatically heightened dependence on factors outside national control. Alarmingly, even more than green revolution technologies, which were developed in quasi-public international research centers, biotechnologies will be in the hands of private corporations seeking monopolistic profits for patented genetic material and processes. See Frederick H. Buttel, Martin Kenney, and Jack Kloppenburg, Jr., "From Green Revolution to Biorevolution: Some Observations on the Changing Technological Bases of Economic Transformation in the Third World," *Economic Development and Cultural Change* 34, no. 1 (October 1985), pp. 31–55; and Frederick H. Buttel and Jill Belsky, "Biotechnology, Plant Breeding, and Intellectual Property: Social and Ethical Dimensions," *Science, Technology, and Human Values* 12, 1 (Winter 1987), pp. 31–49.

50. For a discussion of the "meat mystique," see Frances Moore Lappe, *Diet for a Small Planet*, Part II (New York: Ballantine Books, revised 1982).

51. Lappe and Collins, *World Hunger: Twelve Myths*, p. 58; based on calculations in FAO *Food Balance Sheets*.

52. Pan A. Yotopoulos, "Competition for Cereals: The Food-Feed Connection," *Ceres* 17 (September-October 1984), p. 23.

53. Paulino and Mellor, p. 295.

54. Ibid., p. 295.

55. According to the National Nutrition Institute of Mexico, 66 percent of the Mexican population is nutritionally deficient. Reported in *La Jornada* (Mexico City daily), June 16, 1985.

56. Steven Sanderson, *The Transformation of Mexican Agriculture* (Princeton: Princeton University Press, 1986), Tables 4.7 and 4.8.

57. Billie R. DeWalt, "Mexico's Second Green Revolution," *Mexican Studies I,* no. 1 (Winter 1985), p. 49.

58. See, for example, Kathie L. Krumm, *The External Debt of Sub-Saharan Africa* (Washington, D.C.: World Bank, 1985), p. 11.

59. Susan George, *A Fate Worse Than Debt* (New York: Grove/Food First Books, 1988), p. 28.

60. J. Hanger and J. Morris, "Women and the Household Economy," in Robert Chambers and J. Morris, eds., *Mwea: An Irrigated Rice Settlement in Kenya,* Afrika-Studien No. 83, IFO, Munich.

61. George, *A Fate Worse than Debt,* p. 121.

62. Ibid., p. 20.

63. Ibid., p. 139.

64. Ibid., p. 136.

65. Ibid., p. 135.

66. Ibid., p. 137.

67. Susan George, "Debt the Profit of Doom," *Food First Action Alert* (San Francisco: Institute for Food and Development Policy, 1988), p. 2. See references for this in George' *A Fate Worse than Debt,* p. 133.

68. George, *A Fate Worse Than Debt,* p. 108.

69. UNICEF, op. cit., p. 1. Actually the estimate is 650,000 for only sixteen countries (ten in Africa, six in Latin America), 400,000 in the African countries. See also Ralph R. Sell and Steven J. Kunitz, "The Debt Crisis and the End of an Era in Mortality Decline," *Studies in Comparative International Development,* 1987.

70. For a critique of the relationship of U.S. policies to the war-inflicted famines in the Horn of Africa, see John Prendergast, "Perestroika for U.S. Policy in the Starving Horn of Africa," *Why,* Spring 1990.

71. U.S. farm policy in the 1980s continued to make the United States a major "dumper" of grain on the world market, selling way below production costs, with U.S. taxpayers covering the difference. (In 1988, for instance, the United States was selling corn overseas at about $1.10 a bushel when it cost between $2 and $3.50 to produce.) Farmers in Third World countries are often unable to compete.

72. Susan George, "On the Need for a Broader Approach," *Food Policy* (February 1985), p. 78.

73. The last (and major) famine was 1959–62. Carl Riskin, *Feeding China: The Experience since 1949.* World Institute for Development Economics Research, Helsinki, Working Paper 27 (November 1987).

74. Sweden, a developed democratic nation, gives some example here. Even though overall wealth is still tightly concentrated in Sweden, some time ago Swedes decided that farming and food were too important to be left to the market alone. In Sweden, therefore, only working farmers are permitted to own farmland, and sales of farmland are closely monitored by country boards to ensure that prices paid are not so high as to eliminate family farmers from the competition. See Mark B. Lapping and V. Dale Forster, "Farmland and Agricultural Policy in Sweden: An Integrated Approach," *International Regional Science Review,* 7, no. 3 (1982), pp. 297, 299. Moreover, wholesale food prices are not allowed to fluctuate with the market, wreaking havoc on the family farm. Instead, they are periodically set when farm representatives, government officials, agribusiness executives, and consumer food cooperative officers sit down at the negotiating table. See Lappe and Collins, *World Hunger: Twelve Myths,* p. 83.

75. Julian Simon is a prime exponent of this view. See Julian Simon, "Resources, Population, Environment: An Oversupply of False Bad News," *Science* 208 (27 June 1980): 1434, and *The Ultimate Resource* (Princeton, New Jersey: Princeton University Press, 1981).

76. For a fuller development of the "power-structure" paradigm, see Frances Moore Lappe and Rachel Schurman, *The Missing Piece in the Population Puzzle* (San Francisco: Food First Books, 1989).

77. China, Sri Lanka, Colombia, Chile, and Cuba as well as the Indian state of Keraia are among the most often cited.

# 16 / The Environment and International Security

JESSICA TUCHMAN MATHEWS

The 1990s will demand a redefinition of what constitutes national security. In the 1970s the concept was expanded to include international economics as it became clear that the U.S. economy was no longer the independent force it had once been, but was powerfully affected by economic policies in dozens of other countries. Global developments now suggest the need for another analogous, broadening definition of national security to include resource, environmental, and demographic issues.

The assumptions and institutions that have governed international relations in the postwar era are a poor fit with these new realities. Environmental strains that transcend national borders are already beginning to break down the sacred boundaries of national sovereignty, previously rendered porous by the information and communication revolutions and the instantaneous global movement of financial capital. The once sharp dividing line between foreign and domestic policy is blurred, forcing governments to grapple in international forums with issues that were contentious enough in the domestic arena.

Despite recent headlines—the polluted coastlines, the climatic extremes, the accelerating deforestation and flooding that plague the planet—human society has not arrived at the brink of some absolute limit to its growth. The planet may ultimately be able to accommodate the additional five or six billion people projected to be living here by the year 2100. But it seems unlikely that the world will be able to do so unless the means of production change dramatically. Global economic output has quadrupled since 1950 and it must continue to grow rapidly simply to meet basic human needs, to say nothing of the challenge of lifting billions from poverty. But economic growth as we currently know it requires more energy use, more emissions and wastes, more land converted from its natural state, and more need for the products of natural systems. Whether the planet can accommodate all of these demands remains an open question.

Individuals and governments alike are beginning to feel the cost of substituting for (or doing without) the goods and services once freely provided by

An earlier version of this article appeared in *Foreign Affairs*, Spring, 1989, Volume 68, Issue 2. Copyright 1989 by the Council on Foreign Affairs, Inc.

healthy ecosystems. Nature's bill is presented in many different forms: the cost of commercial fertilizer needed to replenish once naturally fertile soils; the expense of dredging rivers that flood their banks because of soil erosion hundreds of miles upstream; the loss in crop failures due to the indiscriminate use of pesticides that inadvertently kill insect pollinators; or the price of worsening pollution, once filtered from the air by vegetation. Whatever the immediate cause for concern, the value and absolute necessity for human life of functioning ecosystems is finally becoming apparent.

Moreover, for the first time in its history, humankind is rapidly—if inadvertently—altering the basic physiology of the planet. Global changes currently taking place in the chemical composition of the atmosphere, in the genetic diversity of species inhabiting the planet, and in the cycling of vital chemicals through the oceans, atmosphere, biosphere, and geosphere are unprecedented in both their pace and scale. If left unchecked, the consequences will be profound and, unlike familiar types of local damage, irreversible.

## EFFECTS OF RESOURCE DEGRADATION

Population growth lies at the core of most environmental trends. It took 130 years for world population to grow from one billion to two billion: it will take just a decade to climb from today's five billion to six billion. More than 90 percent of the added billion will live in the developing world, with the result that by the end of the 1990s the developed countries will be home to only 20 percent of the world's people, compared to almost 40 percent at the end of World War II (see Figure 16.1). Sheer numbers do not translate into political power, especially when most of the added billion will be living in poverty. But the demographic shift will thrust the welfare of developing nations further toward the center of international affairs.

The relationship linking population levels and the resource base is complex. Policies, technologies, and institutions determine the impact of population growth. These factors can spell the difference between a highly stressed, degraded environment and one that can provide for many more people. At any given level of investment and knowledge, absolute population numbers can be crucial. For example, traditional systems of shifting agriculture—in which land is left fallow for a few years to recover from human use—can sustain people for centuries, only to crumble in a short time when population densities exceed a certain threshold. More important, though, is the *rate* of growth. A government that is fully capable of providing food, housing, jobs, and health care for a population growing at 1 percent per year (therefore doubling its population in seventy-two years), might be completely overwhelmed by an annual growth rate of 3 percent, which would double the population in twenty-four years.

Figure 16.1 / World Population Growth, 1750–2100

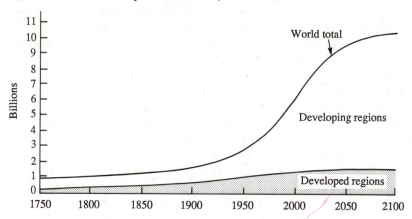

Sources: Thomas W. Merrick et al., "World Population in Transition, *Population Bulletin,* Vol. 42, No. 2 (1986), Figure 1, p. 4, and *World Resources Report 1988–1989,* World Resources Institute, p. 16.

Today the United States and the Soviet Union are growing at just under 1 percent annually (Europe is growing only half that fast). But Africa's population is expanding by almost 3 percent per year, Latin America's by nearly 2 percent, and Asia's by somewhat less. By 2025 the working-age population in developing countries alone will be larger than the world's current total population. This growth comes at a time when technological advance requires higher levels of education and displaces more labor than ever before. For many developing countries, continued growth at current rates means that available capital is swallowed up in meeting the daily needs of people, rather than invested in resource conservation and job creation. Such policies inescapably lay the foundations of a bleak future.

An important paradox to bear in mind when examining natural resource trends is that so-called nonrenewable resources—such as coal, oil, and minerals—are in fact inexhaustible, while so-called renewable resources can be finite. As a nonrenewable resource becomes scarce and more expensive, demand falls, and substitutes and alternative technologies appear. For that reason we will never pump the last barrel of oil or anything close to it. On the other hand, a fishery fished beyond a certain point will not recover, a species driven to extinction will not reappear, and eroded topsoil cannot be replaced (except over geological time). There are, thus, threshold effects for renewable resources that belie the name given them, with unfortunate consequences for policy.

The most serious form of renewable resource decline is the deforestation taking place throughout the tropics. An area the size of Austria is deforested each year (see Table 16.1). Tropical forests are fragile ecosystems, extremely

**Table 16.1 / Annual Rates of Tropical Deforestation, 1976–1980** (*millions of hectares per annum*)

| | Closed forests | | | | Open woodlands[a] | |
|---|---|---|---|---|---|---|
| | All tropical | | Moist tropical | | | |
| | Area | Percent of total | Area | Percent of total | Area | Percent of total |
| Africa | 1.33 | 0.61 | 1.20 | 0.59 | 2.34 | 0.48 |
| Asia-Pacific | 1.82 | 0.59 | 1.61 | 0.61 | 0.19 | 0.61 |
| Latin America | 4.12 | 0.61 | 3.30 | 0.54 | 1.27 | 0.59 |
| Total | 7.27 | 0.61 | 6.11 | 0.57 | 3.8 | 0.52 |

[a]Projections for 1981–85.
Sources: For all tropical closed forests and open woodlands, see Jean Paul Lanly, Tropical Forest Resources, *FAO Forestry Paper No. 30* (United Nations Food and Agriculture Organization, Rome, 1982), Table 6d, p. 80 and Table 6e, p. 84. For tropical moist forests, see Alan Grainger, "Quantifying Changes in Forest Cover in the Humid Tropics: Overcoming Current Limitations," *Journal of World Forest Resource Management*, Vol. 1 (1984), Table 8, p. 21. Original table from *World Resources Report 1988–1989*, World Resources Institute, p. 71.

vulnerable to human disruption. Once disturbed, the entire ecosystem can unravel. The loss of the trees causes the interruption of nutrient cycling above and below the soil: the soil loses fertility; plant and animal species lose their habitats and become extinct; and acute fuelwood shortages appear (especially in the dry tropical forests). The soil erodes without the ground cover provided by trees and plants, and downstream rivers suffer siltation, causing floods and droughts, and damaging expensive irrigation and hydroelectric systems. Traced through its effects on agriculture, energy supply, and water resources, tropical deforestation impoverishes about a billion people.[1] This pattern is endemic throughout Central America, much of Asia, sub-Saharan Africa, and South America.

The planet's evolutionary heritage—its genetic diversity—is heavily concentrated in these same forests. It is therefore disappearing today on a scale not seen since the age of the dinosaurs, and at an unprecedented pace. Biologists estimate that species are being lost in the tropical forests 1,000 to 10,000 times faster than the natural rate of extinction.[2] As many as 20 percent of all the species now living may be gone by the year 2000. The loss will be felt aesthetically, scientifically, and, above all, economically. These genetic resources are an important source of food, materials for energy and construction, chemicals for pharmaceuticals and industry, vehicles for health and safety testing, natural pest controls, and dozens of other uses.

The only reason that species loss is not a front-page issue is that the majority of species have not yet been discovered, much less studied, so that none but a few conservation biologists can even guess at the number and kinds of species that are vanishing. The bitter irony is that genetic diversity is disappearing on a grand scale at the very moment when biotechnology makes it possible to exploit fully this resource for the first time.

Soil degradation is another major concern. Both a cause and a consequence of poverty, desertification, as it is generally called, is causing declining agricultural productivity on nearly two billion hectares, 15 percent of the earth's land area. The causes are overcultivation, overgrazing, erosion, and salinization and waterlogging due to poorly managed irrigation. In countries as diverse as Haiti, Guatemala, Turkey, and India, soil erosion has sharply curtailed agricultural production and potential, sometimes destroying it completely. Though the data are uncertain, it is estimated that the amount of land permanently removed from cultivation due to salinization and waterlogging is equal to the amount of land newly irrigated at great expense each year.[3]

Finally, patterns of land tenure, though not strictly an environmental condition, have an immense environmental impact. In 1975, 7 percent of landowners in Latin America possessed 93 percent of all the arable land in this vast region. In Guatemala, a typical case, 2 percent of the population in 1980 owned 80 percent of the land, while 83 percent of farmers lived on plots too small to support a household. At the same time, even in Costa Rica, with its national concern for social equity, 3 percent of landowners held 54 percent of the land.[4] These large holdings generally include the most desirable land and are often inefficiently used or not used at all. The great mass of the rural population is pushed onto the most damage-prone land, usually dry or highly erodible slopes, and into the forests. Some of this land is so environmentally fragile that it should not be used at all. Some of it could be sustainably farmed, but, lacking ownership, these farmers have no reason to undertake the hard labor necessary to ensure the soil's long-term productivity. Land reform is among the most difficult of all political undertakings, but without it many countries will be unable to create a healthy agricultural sector to fuel economic growth.

Environmental decline occasionally leads directly to conflict, especially when scarce water resources must be shared. Generally, however, its impact on nations' security is felt in the downward pull on economic performance and, therefore, on political stability. The underlying cause of turmoil is often ignored; instead governments address the poverty and instability that are its results.

In the Philippines, for example, the government regularly granted logging concessions of less than ten years. Since it takes thirty to thirty-five years for a second-growth forest to mature, loggers had no incentive to replant. Compounding the error, flat royalties encouraged the loggers to remove only the most valuable species. A horrendous 40 percent of the harvestable lumber never left the forests but, having been damaged in the logging, rotted or was burned in place. The unsurprising result of these and related policies is that out of 17 million hectares of closed forests that flourished early in the century, only 1.2 million remain today. Moreover, the Philippine government received a fraction of the revenues it could have collected if it had followed sound resource management policies that would have also preserved the forest capital. This is biological deficit financing writ large.[5]

Similarly, investments in high-technology fishing equipment led to larger harvests but simultaneously depleted the stock. Today, ten of fifty major Philippine fishing grounds are believed to be overfished; the net result of heavy investment is that the availability of fish per capita has actually dropped. These and other self-destructive environmental policies, combined with rapid population growth, played a significant role in the economic decline that led to the downfall of the Marcos regime. So far, the government of Corazon Aquino has made few changes in the forestry, fishery, and other environmental policies it inherited.[6]

Conditions in sub-Saharan Africa, to take another case, have reached catastrophic dimensions. In the first half of the 1980s, export earnings fell by almost one-third, foreign debt soared to 58 percent of GNP, food imports grew rapidly while consumption dropped, and per capita GNP fell by more than 3 percent. A large share of those woes can be traced to Africa's dependence on a fragile, mismanaged, and overstressed natural resource base (see Table 16.2).

Exports of mineral and agricultural commodities alone account for a quarter of the region's GNP, and nearly three-quarters of the population makes its living off the land, which also supplies, as fuelwood, 80 percent of the energy consumed. The land's capacity to produce is ebbing away under the pressure of rapidly growing numbers of people who do not have the wherewithal to put back into the land what they take from it. A vicious cycle of human and resource impoverishment sets in. As the vegetative cover— trees, shrubs, and grass—shrinks from deforestation and overgrazing, soil loses its capacity to retain moisture and nourish crops. The decline accelerates as farmers burn dung and crop residues in place of fuelwood, rather than using them to sustain the soil. Agricultural yields then fall further, and the land becomes steadily more vulnerable to the naturally variable rainfall that is the hallmark of arid and semiarid regions, turning dry spells into droughts and periods of food shortage into famines. Ethiopia is only the most familiar case. The sequence is repeated throughout the region—with similarly tragic results.[7]

When such resource and population trends are not addressed, as they are not in so much of the world today, the resulting economic decline leads to frustration, resentment, domestic unrest, or even civil war. Human suffering and turmoil make countries ripe for authoritarian government or external subversion. Environmental refugees spread the disruption across national borders. Haiti, a classic example, was once so forested and fertile that it was

Table 16.2 / Sub-Saharan Africa Today

| Indicator | Africa | All developing countries |
|---|---|---|
| Only region with declining per capita GNP, 1980–86 | −3.05 | — |
| Highest foreign debt as percent of GNP, 1986 | 58% | 37%[a] |
| Highest annual rate of population growth, 1980–86 | 3.1 | 2.0 |
| Highest infant mortality (infant deaths per 1,000 live births), 1986 | 113 | 67 |
| Lowest life expectancy, 1986 | 49 years | 57.3 years |
| Only region with declining per capita agricultural production | √ | — |
| Only region with declining per capita food consumption | √ | — |
| Highest percentage of population severely malnourished (less than 80% of FAO/WHO caloric requirement, 1980) | 25 | 16 |
| Highest proportion of soils with fertility limitations | 81 | — |
| Highest percentage of productive drylands desertified | 84 | 61 |
| Heaviest reliance on fuelwood as energy source | 80 | — |
| Lowest percentage of arable land potentially irrigable | 5 | — |

[a]Average for 109 developing countries
Source: J. T. Mathews, *Africa: Continent in Crisis,* World Resources Institute, 1988.

known as the "Pearl of the Antilles." Now deforested, soil erosion in Haiti is so rapid that some farmers believe stones grow in their fields, while bulldozers are needed to clear the streets of Port-au-Prince of topsoil that flows down from the mountains in the rainy season. While many of the boat people who fled to the United States left because of the brutality of the Duvalier regimes, there is no question that—and this is not widely recognized—many Haitians were forced into the boats by the impossible task of farming bare rock. Until Haiti is reforested, it will never be politically stable.

Haitians are by no means the world's only environmental refugees. In Indonesia, Central America, and sub-Saharan Africa, millions have been forced to leave their homes in part because the loss of tree cover, the disappearance of soil, and other environmental ills have made it impossible to grow food. Sudan, despite its civil war, has taken in more than a million refugees from Ethiopia, Uganda, and Chad. Immigrants from the spreading Sahel make up one-fifth of the total population in the Ivory Coast.[8] Wherever refugees settle, they flood the labor market, add to the local demand for food, and put new burdens on the land, thus spreading the environmental stress that originally forced them from their homes. Resource mismanagement is not the only cause of these mass movements, of course. Religious and ethnic conflicts, political repression, and other forces are at work. But the environmental causes are an essential factor.

## GLOBAL CHANGE

A different kind of environmental concern has arisen from humankind's new ability to alter the environment on a planetary scale. The earth's physiology is shaped by the characteristics of four elements (carbon, nitrogen, phosphorous, and sulfur); by its living inhabitants (the biosphere); and by the interactions of the atmosphere and the oceans, which produce our climate.

Humankind is altering both the carbon and nitrogen cycles, having increased the natural carbon dioxide concentration in the atmosphere by 25 percent. This has occurred largely in the last three decades through fossil-fuel use and deforestation. The production of commercial fertilizer has doubled the amount of nitrogen nature makes available to living things. The use of a single, minor class of chemicals, chlorofluorocarbons, has punched a continent-sized "hole" in the ozone layer at the top of the stratosphere over Antarctica, and caused a smaller, but growing loss of ozone all around the planet. Species loss is destroying the work of three billion years of evolution. Together these changes could drastically alter the conditions in which life on earth has evolved.

The greenhouse effect results from the fact that the planet's atmosphere is largely transparent to incoming radiation from the sun but absorbs much of the lower energy radiation re-emitted by the earth. This natural phenomenon makes the earth warm enough to support life. But as emissions of greenhouse gases increase, the planet is warmed *un*naturally. Carbon dioxide produced from the combustion of fossil fuels and by deforestation is responsible for about half of the greenhouse effect. A number of other gases, notably methane (natural gas), nitrous oxide, ozone (in the lower atmosphere, as distinguished from the protective ozone layer in the stratosphere), and the synthetic chlorofluorocarbons are responsible for the other half (see Figure 16.2).

Despite important uncertainties about aspects of the greenhouse warming, a virtually unanimous scientific consensus exists on its central features. If present emission trends continue, and unless some as yet undocumented phenomenon (possibly increased cloudiness) causes an offsetting cooling,

**Figure 16.2 / Past and Future Warming Contribution for Primary Greenhouse Gases (Warming per Decade)[a]**

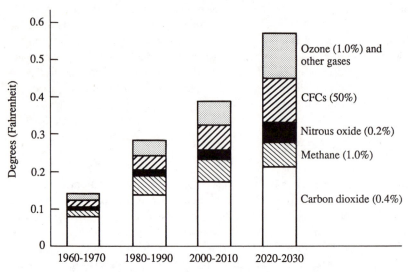

[a]Figures in parentheses indicate annual rate of increase of each gas as of 1986.
Sources: World Resources Institute, based on radiative forcing estimates in V. Ramanathan et al., 1985. *Journal of Geophysical Research* 90: 5547–5566. Annual rates of increase in atmospheric concentration from U.S. EPA, D. A. Lashof, and D. Tirsak, eds., 1989. *Policy Options for Stabilizing Global Climate.*

the planet will, on average, get hotter because of the accumulation of these gases. Exactly how large the warming will be, and how fast it will occur, are uncertain. Existing models place the date of commitment to an average global warming of 1.5° to 4.5°C (3° to 8°F) in the early 2030s. The earth has not been this hot for two million years, long before human society, and indeed even Homo sapiens, existed (see Figure 16.3).

Hotter temperatures will be only one result of the continuing greenhouse warming. At some point, perhaps quite soon, precipitation patterns are likely to shift, possibly causing dustbowl-like conditions in the U.S. grain belt. Ocean currents are expected to do the same, dramatically altering the climates of many regions. A diversion of the Gulf Stream, for example, would transform Western Europe's climate, making it far colder than it is today. The sea level will rise due to the expansion of water when it is warmed and to the melting of land-based ice. The oceans are presently rising by one-half inch per decade, enough to cause serious erosion along much of the U.S. coast. The projected rise is one to four feet by the year 2050. Such a large rise in the sea level would inundate vast coastal regions, erode shorelines, destroy coastal marshes and swamps (areas of very high biological productivity), pollute water supplies through the intrusion of salt water, and put at

Figure 16.3 / Average Global Temperatures

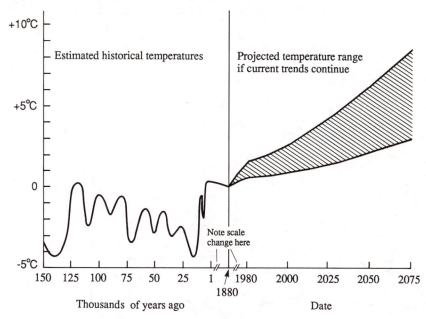

Sources: *Ozone Depletion, the Greenhouse Effect, and Climate Change*. Hearings before the Subcommittee on Environmental Pollution of the Committee on Environment and Public Works, U.S. Senate. June 10–11, 1986, p. 94; and the World Resources Institute.

high risk the vastly disproportionate share of the world's economic wealth that is packed along coastlines. The great river deltas, from the Mississippi to the Ganges, would be flooded. Estimates are that a half-meter rise in Egypt would displace 16 percent of the population, while a two-meter rise in Bangladesh would claim 28 percent of the land where 30 million people live today and where more than 59 million are projected to live by 2030[9] (see Figure 16.4).

Positive consequences would be likely as well. Some plants would grow more quickly, fertilized by the additional carbon dioxide. (Many of them, however, will be weeds.) Rainfall might rise in what are now arid but potentially fertile regions, such as parts of sub-Saharan Africa. Conditions for agriculture would also improve in those northern areas that have both adequate soils and water supplies. Nonetheless, as the 1988 drought in the United States vividly demonstrated, human societies, industrial no less than rural, depend on the normal, predictable functioning of the climate system. Climate undergoing rapid change not only will be less predictable because it is different, but may be inherently more variable. Many climatologists believe that as accumulating greenhouse gases force the climate out of equilib-

**Figure 16.4 / Coastal Impacts of Sea-Level Rise in Bangladesh**

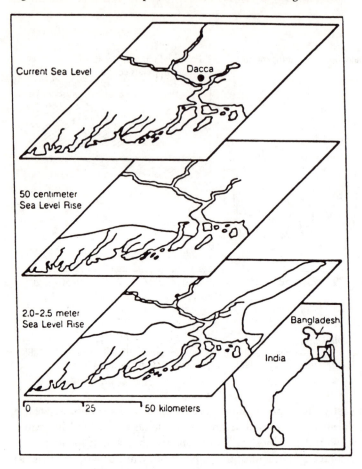

Sources: United Nations Environment Programme (UNEP). *The Green-house Gases,* UNEP/Global Environment Monitoring System Environment Library No. 1 (UNEP, Nairobi, 1987), p. 31, and *World Resources Report 1988–1989* World Resources Institute, p. 174.

rium, climate extremes—such as hurricanes, droughts, cold snaps, and typhoons—will become more frequent and perhaps more intense.[10]

Since climate change will be felt in every economic sector, adapting to its impact will be extremely expensive. Developing countries with their small reserves of capital, shortages of scientists and engineers, and weak central governments will be the least able to adapt, and the gap between the developed and developing worlds will almost certainly widen. Many of the adaptations needed will be prohibitively costly, and many impacts, notably the effects on wildlife and ecosystems, will be beyond the reach of human correction. A global strategy that relies on future adaption almost certainly means greater economic and human costs, and vastly larger biological losses, than would a strategy that attempts to control the extent and speed of the warming.[11]

Greenhouse change is closely linked to stratospheric ozone depletion, which is also caused by chlorofluorocarbons. The increased ultraviolet radiation resulting from losses in that protective layer will cause an increase in skin cancers and eye damage. It will have many still uncertain impacts on plant and animal life, and may suppress the immune systems of many species.

Serious enough in itself, ozone depletion illustrates a worrisome feature of humans' newfound ability to cause global change. It is almost impossible to predict accurately the long-term impact of new chemicals or processes on the environment. Chlorofluorocarbons were thoroughly tested when first introduced, and found to be benign. Their effect on the remote stratosphere was never considered.

Not only is it difficult to anticipate all the possible consequences in a highly interdependent, complex system, the system itself is poorly understood. When British scientists announced the appearance of a continent-sized "hole" in the ozone layer over Antarctica in 1985, the discovery sent shock waves through the scientific community. Although stratospheric ozone depletion had been the subject of intense study and debate for more than a decade, no one had predicted the Antarctic hole and no theory could account for it.

The lesson is this: current knowledge of planetary mechanisms is so scanty that the possibility of surprise, perhaps quite nasty surprise, must be rated rather high. The greatest risk may well come from a completely unanticipated direction. We lack both crucial knowledge and early warning systems.

## CONCLUSION

Absent profound change in our relationship to the environment, the future does not look bright. Consider the planet without such change in the year 2050. Economic growth is projected to have quintupled by then. Energy use could also quintuple; or if post-1973 trends continue, it may grow more slowly, perhaps only doubling or tripling. The human species already consumes or destroys 40 percent of all the energy produced by terrestrial photosynthesis, that is, 40 percent of the food energy potentially available to living things on land.[12] While that fraction may be sustainable, it is doubtful that it could keep pace with the expected doubling of the world's population. Human use of 80 percent of the planet's potential productivity does not seem compatible with the continued functioning of the biosphere as we know it. The expected rate of species loss would have risen from perhaps a few each day to several hundred a day. The pollution and toxic waste burden would likely prove unmanageable. Tropical forests would have largely disappeared, and arable land, a vital resource in a world of ten billion people, would be rapidly decreasing due to soil degradation. In short, sweeping change in economic production systems is not a choice but a necessity.

Fortunately, this grim sketch of conditions in 2050 is not a prediction, but a projection, based on current trends. Like all projections, it says more about the present and the recent past than it does about the future. The planet is not destined to a slow and painful decline into environmental chaos. There are technical, scientific, and economical solutions that are suitable to many current trends, and enough is known about promising new approaches to be confident that the right kinds of research will produce huge payoffs. Embedded in current practices are vast costs in lost opportunities and waste, which, if corrected, would bring massive benefits. Some such steps will require only a reallocation of money, while others will require sizable capital investments. None of the needed steps, however, requires globally unaffordable sums of money. What they do demand is a sizable shift in priorities.

For example, family-planning services cost about $10 per user, a tiny fraction of the cost of the basic human needs that would otherwise have to be met.[13] Already identified opportunities for raising the efficiency of energy use in the United States cost one-half to one-seventh the cost of new energy supply. Comparable savings are available in most other countries.[14] Agroforestry techniques, in which carefully selected combinations of trees and shrubs are planted together with crops, can not only replace the need for purchased fertilizer, but also improve soil quality, make more water available to crops, hold down weeds, and provide fuelwood and higher agricultural yields all at the same time.[15]

But if the technological opportunities are boundless, the social, political, and institutional barriers are huge. Subsidies, pricing policies, and economic discount rates encourage resource depletion in the name of economic growth, while delivering only the illusion of sustainable growth. Population control remains a controversial subject in much of the world. The traditional prerogatives of nation-states are poorly matched with the needs for regional cooperation and global decision making. And ignorance of the biological underpinning of human society blocks a clear view of where the long-term threats to global security lie.

Overcoming these economic and political barriers will require social and institutional inventions comparable in scale and vision to the new arrangements conceived in the decade following World War II. Without the sharp political turning point of a major war, and with threats that are diffuse and long term, the task will be more difficult. But if we are to avoid irreversible damage to the planet and a heavy toll in human suffering, nothing less is likely to suffice. A partial list of the specific changes necessary suggests how demanding a task it will be.

Achieving sustainable economic growth will require the remodeling of agriculture, energy use, and industrial production after nature's example—their reinvention, in fact. These economic systems must become circular rather than linear. Industry and manufacturing will need processes that use materials and energy with high efficiency, recycle byproducts, and produce little waste.[16] Energy demand will have to be met with the highest efficiency consistent with full economic growth. Agriculture will have to rely heavily upon free ecosystem services instead of nearly exclusive reliance on synthetic substitutes. And all systems will have to price goods and services to reflect the environmental costs of their provision.

A vital first step, one that can and should be taken in the very near term, would be to reinvent the national income accounts by which gross national product is measured. GNP is the foundation on which national economic policies are built, yet its calculation does not take into account resource depletion. A country can consume its forests, wildlife, and fisheries, its minerals, its clean water, and its topsoil, without seeing a reflection of the loss in its GNP. Nor are ecosystem services—sustaining soil fertility, moderating and storing rainfall, filtering air, and regulating the climate—valued, though their loss may entail great expense. The result is that economic policymakers are profoundly misled by their chief guide[17] (see Figure 16.5).

A second step would be to invent a set of indicators by which global environmental health could be measured. Economic planning would be adrift without GNP, unemployment rates, and the like, and social planning without demographic indicators—fertility rates, infant mortality, literacy, life expectancy—would be impossible. Yet this is precisely where environmental policymaking stands today.

Development assistance also requires new tools. Bilateral and multilateral donors have found that project success rates climb when nongovernmental organizations distribute funds and direct programs. This is especially true in agriculture, forestry, and conservation projects. The reasons are not mysterious. Such projects are more decentralized, more attuned to local needs and desires, and have a much higher degree of local participation in project planning. They are usually quite small in scale, however, and not capable of handling very large amounts of development funding. Often, too, their independent status threatens the national government. Finding ways to make far greater use of the strengths of such groups without weakening national governments is another priority for institutional innovation.[18]

More broadly, bilateral and multilateral aid donors must be convinced to view environmental considerations as an essential, constructive element of successful development lending, rather than a hurdle to be surmounted before a loan agreement can be signed. Though evidence supporting this truism is pouring in from the donors' own analysts—from hydroelectric projects that lose their capacity in years instead of decades due to deforesta-

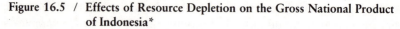

**Figure 16.5 / Effects of Resource Depletion on the Gross National Product of Indonesia***

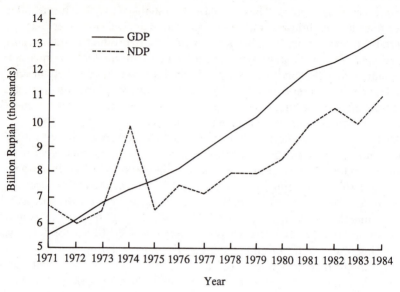

*Gross domestic product (GDP) and net domestic product (NDP) in constant 1973 rupiah.
Results of a case study of Indonesia. NDP, net domestic product, is derived by subtracting estimates of net natural resource depreciation of only three sectors: petroleum, timber, and soils. Annual growth of GNP falls from 7.1% to 4.0%. From R. Repetto et al., *Wasting Assets: Natural Resources in the National Income Accounts;* and the World Resources Institute, Washington, D.C., 1989.

tion, to African livestock projects with a 100% failure rate—the needed transformation in understanding is proceeding slowly, and unevenly.

Better ways must also be found to turn the scientific and engineering strengths of the industrialized world to the solution of the developing world's problems. The challenges include learning enough about local constraints and conditions to ask the right questions, making such research professionally rewarding to the individual scientist, and transferring technology more effectively. The international centers for agricultural research, a jointly managed network of thirteen institutions launched in the 1960s, is a successful model that might be improved upon and applied in other areas such as energy, forestry, and soil management.

On the political front, the need for a new diplomacy and for new institutions and regulatory regimes to cope with the world's growing environmental interdependence is even more compelling. Put bluntly, our accepted definition of the limits of national sovereignty as coinciding with national borders is obsolete. The government of Bangladesh, no matter how hard it tries, cannot prevent tragic floods, such as it suffered in 1988. Preventing them requires active cooperation from Nepal and India. The government of Canada cannot protect its water resources from acid rain without collaboration with the United States. Eighteen diverse nations share the heavily polluted Mediterranean Sea. Even the Caribbean Islands, as physically isolated as they are, find themselves affected by others' resource management policies as locusts, inadvertently bred through generations of exposure to pesticides and now strong enough to fly all the way from Africa, infest their shores.

The majority of environmental problems demand regional solutions that encroach upon what we now think of as the prerogatives of national governments. This is because the phenomena themselves are defined by the limits of watershed, ecosystem, or atmospheric transport, not by national borders. Indeed, the costs and benefits of alternative policies cannot often be accurately judged without considering the region rather than the nation.

The developing countries especially will need to pool their efforts in the search for solutions. Three-quarters of the countries in sub-Saharan Africa, for example, have fewer people than live in New York City. National scientific and research capabilities cannot be built on such a small population base. Regional cooperation is required.

Dealing with global change will be more difficult. No one nation or even group of nations can meet these challenges, and no nation can protect itself from the actions—or inaction—of others. No existing institution matches these criteria. It will be necessary to reduce the dominance of the superpower relationship, which so often encourages other countries to adopt a wait-and-see attitude (you solve your problems first, then talk to us about change).

The United States, in particular, will have to assign a far greater prominence than it has heretofore to the practice of multilateral diplomacy. This would mean changes that range from the organization of the State Department and the language proficiency of the Foreign Service, to the definition of an international role that allows leadership without primacy, both in the slogging work of negotiation and in adherence to final outcomes. Above all, ways must soon be found to step around the deeply entrenched North-South cleavage and to replace it with a planetary sense of shared destiny. Perhaps the successes of the UN specialized agencies can be built upon for this purpose. But certainly the task of forging a global energy policy in order to control the greenhouse effect, for example, is a very long way from eradicating smallpox or sharing weather information.

The recent Soviet proposal to turn the UN Trusteeship Council, which has outlived the colonies it oversaw, into a trusteeship for managing the global commons (the oceans, the atmosphere, biological diversity, and planetary climate) deserves close scrutiny. If a newly defined council could sidestep the UN's political fault lines, and incorporate, rather than supplant, the existing strengths of the United Nations Environment Program, it might provide a useful forum for reaching global environmental decisions at a far higher political level than anything that exists now.

Today's negotiating models—the Law of the Sea Treaty, the Nuclear Nonproliferation Treaty (NPT), even the promising Convention to Protect the Ozone Layer—are inadequate. Typically, such agreements take about fifteen years to negotiate and enter into force, and perhaps another ten years before substantial changes in behavior are actually achieved. (The NPT, which required only seven years to complete these steps, is a notable exception.) Far better approaches will be needed.

Among these new approaches, perhaps the most difficult to achieve will be ways to negotiate successfully in the presence of substantial scientific uncertainty. The present model is static: years of negotiation leading to a final product. The new model will have to be fluid, allowing a rolling process of intermediate or self-adjusting agreements that respond quickly to growing scientific understanding. The recent Montreal agreement on the ozone layer supplies a useful precedent by providing that one-third of the parties can reconvene a scientific experts group to consider new evidence as it becomes available. The new model will require new economic methods for assessing risk, especially where the possible outcomes are irreversible. It will depend on a more active political role for biologists and chemists than they have been accustomed to, and far greater technical competence in the natural and planetary sciences among policymakers. Finally, the new model may need to forge a more involved and constructive role for the private sector. Relegating the affected industries to a heel-dragging, adversarial, outsiders role almost guarantees a slow process. The ozone agreement, to cite again this recent example, would not have been reached as quickly, and perhaps not at all, had it not been for the cooperation of the chlorofluorocarbon producers.

International law, broadly speaking, has declined in influence in recent years.[19] With leadership and commitment from the major powers, it might regain its lost status. But that will not be sufficient. To be effective, future arrangements will require provisions for monitoring, enforcement, and compensation, even when damage cannot be assigned a precise monetary value. These are all areas where international law has traditionally been weak.

This is only a partial agenda for the needed decade of invention. Meanwhile, much can and must be done with existing means. Four steps are most important: prompt revision of the Montreal Treaty, to eliminate completely the production of chlorofluorocarbons no later than the year 2000; full support for and implementation of the global Tropical Forestry Action Plan developed by the World Bank, the UN's Development Programme, the Food and Agricultural Organization, and the World Resources Institute; sufficient support for family planning programs to ensure that all who want contraceptives have affordable access to them at least by the end of the decade; and, for the United States, a ten-year energy policy with the goal of increasing the energy productivity of our economy (i.e., reducing the amount of energy required to produce a dollar of GNP) by about 3 percent each year. While choosing four priorities from dozens of needed initiatives is highly arbitrary, these four stand out as ambitious yet achievable goals on which a broad consensus could be developed, and whose success would bring multiple, long-term global benefits touching every major international environmental concern.

Reflecting on the discovery of atomic energy, Albert Einstein noted "everything changed." And indeed, nuclear fission became the dominant force—military, geopolitical, and even psychological and social—of the ensuing decades. In the same sense, the driving force of the coming decades may well be environmental change. Humans are still utterly dependent on the natural world but now have for the first time the ability to alter it, rapidly and on a global scale. Because of that difference, Einstein's verdict that "we shall require a substantially new manner of thinking if mankind is to survive" still seems apt.

## Notes

1. FAO, WRI, The World Bank and the United Nations Development Programme, "The Tropical Forestry Action Plan," FAO, Rome, June 1987, p.5.

2. E. O. Wilson, ed., *Biodiversity*, National Academy Press, Washington, D.C., 1988, pp. 3–18.

3. World Resources Institute and International Institute for Environment and Development, *World Resources Report 1986*, Basic Books, New York, 1986, Chapters 4 and 8. Also, see M.W. Holdgate, et al., *The World Environment 1972–1982*, United Nations Environment Programme, Dublin, 1982, p. 267.

4. A. Maguire and J.W. Brown, eds., *Bordering on Trouble: Resources and Politics in Latin America*, Adler & Adler, Bethesda, 1986, p. 397.

5. E.L. Boado, in R. Repetto and M. Gillis, eds., *Public Policies and the Misuse of Forest Resources*, Cambridge University Press, Cambridge, 1988.

6. G. Porter and D.J. Ganapin, Jr., *Resources, Population and the Philippines' Future*, World Resources Institute, Washington, D.C. 1988, pp. 35–44 and 45–53.

7. J.T. Mathews, "Africa: Continent in Crisis," White Paper prepared for International Foundation for the Survival and Development of Humanity, World Resources Institute, August 1988.

8. N. Myers, *Not Far Afield: U.S. Interest and the Global Environment*, World Resources Institute, Washington, D.C., 1987, pp. 29–30.

9. United Nations Environment Programme (UNEP), "The Changing Atmosphere," UNEP Environment Brief No.1, UNEP, Nairobi, undated.

10. G. Titus, ed., *Effects of Changes in Stratospheric Ozone and Global Change*, Vol. 1, *Overview*, U.S. Environmental Protection Agency, Washington, D.C., 1986.

11. J.T. Mathews, "Global Climate Change: Toward a Greenhouse Policy," *Issues in Science and Technology*, Spring 1987, pp. 57–68.

12. P.M. Vitousek, et al., "Human Appropriation of the Products of Photosynthesis," *BioScience*, Vol. 36, No. 6, 1986, pp. 368–73.

13. N. Sadik, "The State of World Population 1989," United Nations Population Fund (UNFPA), 1989, p. 19.

14. A.H. Rosenfeld, "Conservation, Competition and National Security," testimony on the Role of Conservation in the National Energy Picture, Subcommittee on Energy and Power,

Committee on Energy and Commerce, U.S. House of Representatives, Nov. 4, 1987. Also, W.U. Chandler, et al., "Energy Efficiency: A New Agenda," American Council for Energy Efficient Economy, Washington, D.C., 1988. Also, W. Keepin and G. Kats, "Greenhouse Warming: Comparative Analysis of Nuclear and Efficiency Abatement Strategies," *Energy Policy*, Vol. 16, No. 6, 1988, pp. 538–61.

15. R. Winterbottom and P.T. Hazlewood, "Agroforestry and Sustainable Development: Making the Connection," *Ambio*, Vol. 16, No. 2–3, 1987.

16. G. Speth, "The Greening of Technology," *The Washington Post*, Nov. 20, 1988.

17. R. Repetto, et al., *Wasting Assets: Natural Resources in the National Income Accounts*, World Resources Institute, Washington, D.C., 1989.

18. P. Harrison, *The Greening of Africa: Breaking through in the Battle for Land and Food*, Penguin Books, New York, 1987, pp. 278–318.

19. W.P. Bundy, "The 1950s Versus the 1990s," in E.K. Hamilton, ed., *America's Global Interests: A New Agenda*, W. W. Norton & Co., New York, 1989, pp. 33–81.

# Bibliography

Brown, Janet W. *In the U.S. Interest: Resources, Growth, and Security in the Developing World*. Westview Press, Boulder, 1990.

Brown, Seyon. "Inherited Geopolitics and Emergent Global Realitites" in E.K. Hamilton, ed. *America's Global Interests: A New Agenda*. W. W. Norton & Co., New York, 1989.

Kennan, George F. "Morality and Foreign Policy," *Foreign Affairs*, Vol. 64, Winter 1985/1986.

Leonard, H. Jeffrey. *Environment and the Poor: Development Strategy for a Common Agenda*. Transaction Books, New Brunswick, 1989.

Maguire, A. and J.W. Brown, eds. *Bordering on Trouble: Resources and Politics in Latin America*. Adler & Adler, Bethesda, 1986.

Mathews, J.T., ed. *Preserving the Global Environment: The Challenge of Shared Leadership*. W. W. Norton & Co., New York, 1990.

Myers, Norman. *Not Far Afield: U.S. Interests and the Global Environment*. World Resources Institute, Washington, D.C., 1987.

Myers, Norman. "Environment and Security," *Foreign Policy*, Number 74, Spring 1989.

PRIO/UNEP Programme on Military Activities and the Human Environment. "Environmental Security—A Report Contributing to the Concept of Comprehensive International Security." Peace Research Institute in Oslo, Norway, 1989.

Renner, M. *National Security: The Economic and Environmental Dimensions*. World Watch Paper #89, Washington, D.C., 1989.

Scientific American Special Issue. "Managing Planet Earth," *Scientific American*, September 1989.

Westing, A.H., ed. *Global Resources and International Conflict: Environmental Factors in Strategic Policy and Action*. Oxford University Press, Oxford/New York, 1986.

World Commission on Environment & Development. *Our Common Future*. Oxford University Press, Oxford/New York, 1987.

World Resources Institute. *World Resources Report 1990–1991*. Oxford University Press, Oxford/New York, 1990, and previous volumes, 1988–89, 1987, 1986, published by Basic Books, Harper & Row, New York.

# 17 / Catastrophic Climate Change

DAVID A. WIRTH

For the past several years scientists have issued ominous warnings about the future of the earth's climate. Emissions of natural and synthetic gases are increasing the heat-trapping capacity of the atmosphere through a phenomenon known as the greenhouse effect. Predictions of dramatic global change arising from the continued dumping of industrial byproducts into the atmosphere and forest loss of massive scale can no longer be ignored. Compelling scientific evidence and the projections of computer models now strongly suggest that world climate patterns, previously regarded as reliably stable, could be thrust into a state of turmoil.

The projected effects of this worldwide climatic disruption dwarf many of the environmental problems of the past and augur political, economic, and social disturbances on an enormous scale. Global warming could have catastrophic consequences for the habitability and productivity of the whole planet. The accompanying strain and upheaval on the international scene in turn could have serious foreign policy consequences for all countries.

Broad scientific agreement exists on the underlying theory of climate change, although the timing and magnitude of the effects of greenhouse warming remain subjects of considerable debate. Some of these, such as a rise in the sea level, have been established with greater certainty than others. Nonetheless, the range of consequences is sufficiently clear and the magnitude of the resources at stake so enormous that policy action is required sooner rather than later. Once a crisis has been reached, it will be too late to act.

The international political and legal system, despite some promising recent progress on global environmental issues, such as stratospheric ozone depletion, remains ill equipped to offer a solution that will assure the integrity of the earth's climate. Although the greenhouse theory of warming has been accepted for about a century, policymakers have only recently become aware of its significance for the global environment. The international community cannot afford to continue to delay elevating the greenhouse effect to the top of the foreign policy agenda. Arresting the impending climate instability will require a concerted international agenda and a reorientation of energy and development priorities in virtually all countries of the world.

Heading this agenda for action should be a global multilateral agreement that, at a minimum, sets strict, binding targets for global emissions of carbon dioxide.

## CAUSES OF GREENHOUSE WARMING

Human activities, such as the burning of fossil fuels, since the Industrial Revolution have dramatically altered the composition of the global atmosphere. A number of gases, emitted in small but significant amounts, absorb infrared radiation reflected from the surface of the earth. As the concentrations of these heat-absorbing gases increase, average global temperatures will rise.

Emissions of carbon dioxide ($CO_2$) are the single largest cause of elevated terrestrial temperatures from the greenhouse effect, accounting for approximately one-half of the problem. Concentrations of $CO_2$ in the range of 280 parts per million (ppm), together with water vapor in the atmosphere, established the preindustrial equilibrium temperature of the planet. Since the middle of the nineteenth century, atmospheric $CO_2$ levels have increased by about 25 percent to approximately 350 ppm and are continuing to rise by approximately .4 percent per year (see Figure 17.1).[1] Elevated $CO_2$ concentrations result primarily from the intensified burning of fossil fuels—coal, oil, and natural gas—which liberates the chemical in varying amounts. Coal burning releases the most $CO_2$, while the combustion of quantities of natural gas and oil needed to produce the same amount of energy results in only about 56 percent and 78 percent as much $CO_2$, respectively.[2]

The world's forests are vast storehouses or "sinks" for carbon. Worldwide loss of forest cover, by releasing this vast stockpile of carbon into the atmosphere as $CO_2$, aggravates the greenhouse problem. Deforestation in Third World countries is particularly severe, with the destruction of tropical forests in developing countries like Brazil and Indonesia exceeding 40 to 50 million acres annually from activities such as burning, logging, and conversion to agricultural and pasture land.[3] Indeed, the release of $CO_2$ into the atmosphere as a result of deforestation worldwide amounts to about 2.8 billion metric tons annually.[4] As temperature rises, the rate of plant respiration and decay also increases, releasing more carbon dioxide and methane, respectively. There is great concern that these so-called feedbacks will further accelerate and exacerbate the effects of climate warming.[5]

Concentrations of a second important greenhouse gas, nitrous oxide ($N_2O$), have also been rising, probably because of heavier fossil fuel use, greater agricultural activity, and other ecological disturbances. Average global atmospheric levels of $N_2O$ are approximately 310 parts per billion (ppb) and are increasing at an annual rate of .25 percent.[6] Both $CO_2$ and $N_2O$, unlike some conventional pollutants, are very stable compounds. $CO_2$

Figure 17.1 / Carbon Dioxide Concentrations since Preindustrial Times

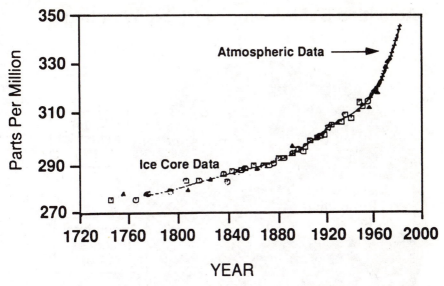

Sources: Friedli et al., 1986; Keeling, 1983; Siegenthaler and Oeschger, 1987; Neftel et al., 1985; and the Environmental Protection Agency.

remains in the upper atmosphere for decades after its release and $N_2O$ for considerably more than a century.[7] Consequently, without major reductions in emissions of these gases with long atmospheric lifetimes, their concentrations will continue to grow.

A group of volatile chemicals known as chlorofluorocarbons (CFCs) is believed to be currently responsible for about 17 percent of the global warming trend during the period from 1980 to 1990.[8] These chemicals, unlike $CO_2$, are strictly synthetic and are not known in nature. After their use as refrigerants, propellants, solvents, and thermal insulators, they are often released to the atmosphere. A related class of bromine-containing chemicals called halons is found in fire-extinguishing systems. Average global atmospheric concentrations of CFC-11 and CFC-12, two of the most commercially important chlorofluorocarbons, are approximately .28 ppb and .48 ppb, respectively.[9] Atmospheric concentrations of CFC-11 and CFC-12 are growing at a rate of approximately 4 percent annually as a result of increased world production in recent years.[10]

Although their concentrations are small relative to that of $CO_2$, molecule for molecule CFCs are up to 12,000 times more potent in absorbing infrared radiation.[11] After release, CFCs and halons reside in the atmosphere for close to a century, or sometimes more, because of their great chemical stability at low altitudes. Consequently, an immediate 70 to 85 percent

Figure 17.2 / Anthropogenic Sources of Greenhouse Gases*

# Activities Contributing to Global Warming

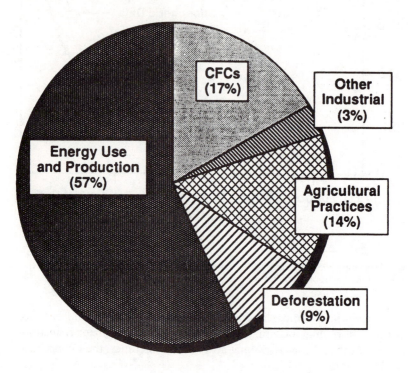

*Estimated values based on average values found in literature.
Source: The Environmental Protection Agency.

reduction in emissions of CFC-11 and CFC-12, for example, would be necessary merely to stabilize their atmospheric concentrations.[12] With their long atmospheric lifetimes, CFCs and halons eventually reach the upper atmosphere. There they are the principal culprits in the worldwide loss of the protective stratospheric ozone layer, a global environmental problem distinct from, although related to, the greenhouse effect. Loss of stratospheric ozone, which shields life on earth from harmful levels of ultraviolet solar radiation, can increase the risk of skin cancer and cataracts and undermine the productivity of terrestrial flora and aquatic ecosystems.

Methane ($CH_4$), the principal component of natural gas, is another significant climate-modifying chemical. It has an atmospheric residence of about ten years.[13] Average global concentrations of methane are approximately 1.7 ppm and are increasing by about 1 percent per year, the highest rate of any naturally occurring greenhouse gas, for reasons that are not now

Figure 17.3 / Annual Fossil Fuel $CO_2$ Emissions, by World Regions (1950–1981)

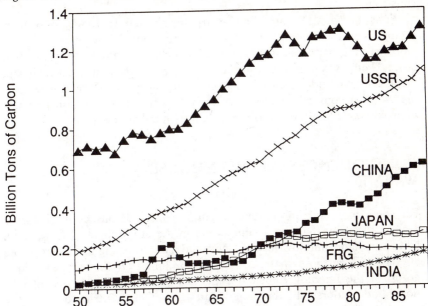

Sources: Rotty, personal communication, 1987; and Oak Ridge National Laboratories.

clear.[14] Animal husbandry and rice cultivation have been identified as major sources of increased methane emissions. Ruminant livestock emit methane from digestive processes, while flooded rice paddies generate methane from the anaerobic decomposition of organic matter. Coal mining, which releases methane from coal seams, and landfills, which produce methane from the anaerobic decomposition of garbage, are also significant sources, with a large potential for rapid growth in the future.

Low-level ozone is another greenhouse gas. Although ozone in the stratosphere is beneficial, this highly unstable chemical is the leading component of photochemical smog pollution at the earth's surface (see Figure 17.2).

While greenhouse gases are dispersed relatively quickly throughout the global atmosphere after release, industrial emissions of these heat-absorbing chemicals are highly concentrated in the developed world (see Figure 17.3). In 1986, 23 percent of total global fossil-fuel-related $CO_2$ emissions of more than 20.4 billion metric tons originated in the United States—the single largest emitting country and one of the highest per capita contributors among industrial countries to the greenhouse problem. The second biggest contribution came from the Soviet Union, with 18 percent of total industrial $CO_2$ emissions. Western Europe emitted 14 percent of this total, Japan 5 percent, and the People's Republic of China 10 percent. Other developing countries together accounted for about 20 percent of total industrial $CO_2$ emissions.[15]

Emissions of CFCs are likewise strongly skewed. In 1986, use of these chemicals in the United States accounted for roughly 26 percent of total global atmospheric releases of approximately 770,000 metric tons. The Soviet Union was responsible for about 13 percent, the remainder of Europe 36 percent, and industrialized Asian countries 8 percent. The entire developing world accounted for no more than 13 percent of the global total—approximately half the contribution of the United States alone.[16]

## CONSEQUENCES OF GREENHOUSE WARMING

For some time, an international scientific consensus has been coalescing around the view that the accumulation in the atmosphere of $CO_2$, $N_2O$, CFCs, methane, and low-level ozone could have sweeping and far-reaching effects on the earth's climate. For instance, in June 1990 the science working group of the Intergovernmental Panel on Climate Change—the international body endorsed by the United States and other countries to review the science of global warming—made the following categorical assertion:

> "We are certain of the following: . . . emissions resulting from human activities are substantially increasing the atmospheric concentrations of the greenhouse gases: carbon dioxide, methane, chlorofluorocarbons (CFCs) and nitrous oxide. These increases will enhance the greenhouse effect, resulting on average in additional warming of the Earth's surface."[17]

By as early as the year 2030, the heat-retaining capacity of the atmosphere may have increased by an amount equivalent to doubling preindustrial concentrations of $CO_2$. Within the next century, average global temperatures may have risen by as much as 5° to 10°F compared with preindustrial times.[18] The absolute magnitude of these temperatures, as well as the rapidity of temperature change, will exceed any previously experienced in human history.

The effects of a greenhouse-driven climate disruption will be characterized with complete certainty only after significant damage has already occurred. However, among the most dramatic effects likely to ensue from greenhouse warming is an unprecedented rise in sea level resulting from thermal expansion of the oceans and melting of glaciers and polar ice. Over the past century the average global sea level has increased less than six inches. By contrast, by the middle of the next century sea-level rise will have accelerated considerably, producing a total increase of up to 1 to 7 feet by 2075, depending on the degree of global warming that occurs.[19]

The impact of sea-level rise in the United States is likely to be severe. The anticipated increase in the elevation of the oceans could permanently inundate low-lying coastal plains, accelerate the erosion of shorelines and beaches, increase the salinity of drinking water aquifers and biologically sensitive estuaries, and increase the susceptibility of coastal properties to storm damage. An increase of five to seven feet in sea level would submerge 30 to 80 percent of America's coastal wetlands, which are crucial to the productivity of commercially important fisheries.[20] Extensive existing coastal development may prevent the widespread formation of new wetlands. Even in undeveloped coastal areas, the rapidity of the predicted sea-level rise will mean that existing wetlands would be lost faster than new ones can be created.

The increase in elevation of the oceans will also seriously affect the approximately 50 percent of the earth's population that inhabits coastal regions. Entire countries, such as the Maldives, could disappear. A rise in sea level of only three feet could flood an area of the Nile Delta that constitutes 12 to 15 percent of Egypt's arable land, produces a similar portion of the Egyptian annual Gross National Product (GNP), and is home to a comparable percentage of the country's more than 50 million people.[21] In Bangladesh, a three-foot rise would inundate 11.5 percent of the country's land area, displace 9 percent of the more than 110 million people in this densely populated country, and threaten 8 percent of the annual GNP.[22]

The range of uncertainties associated with local climatic changes is substantially larger than for global averages. The dramatic anticipated increases in global temperature are virtually certain to cause a wide variety of modifications in regional climates. In middle latitudes, where the continental United States lies, summertime temperature increases are expected to exceed the global average by 30 to 50 percent.[23] Forests, many of them economically productive, could begin to die off as early as the year 2000 if they prove unable to adjust to rapidly shifting climatic zones.[24] Regions of agricultural productivity could shift at the expense of the American Midwest, which currently has some of the most fertile soils in the world. A warming of only 3.6°F could decrease wheat and cereal yields by 3 to 17 percent.[25] Computer models, such as those developed at Princeton University's Geophysical Fluid Dynamics Laboratory and the National Aeronautics and Space Administration's Goddard Institute for Space Science, predict continental drying in middle latitudes. This means that parched soils, scorching droughts, and massive heat waves, like those that devastated crops in the Midwest in the summer of 1988, could become commonplace. Water levels in the Great Lakes could drop by a foot, interfering with navigation for ocean-going vessels.[26] Extreme temperatures have been shown to elevate human mortality. Some models also project perturbations of atmospheric and ocean circulation patterns. The impact of these changes is highly unpredictable.

Countries with tropical climates could experience especially severe consequences. Semiarid areas, like much of sub-Saharan Africa, might suffer from even lower rainfall. Many semiarid areas are already marginal for agriculture, are highly sensitive to changes in climate, and have had severe droughts and famines for the last several decades. Tropical humid climates could become hotter and wetter, with an increase in the frequency and severity of tropical storms. Floods, which between 1968 and 1988 killed more than 80,000 people and affected at least 200 million more, could worsen. Natural disasters such as floods, now unusual, could become increasingly common.

While there is little disagreement over greenhouse theory, some controversy—on occasion quite acrimonious—surrounds the question of whether the planet is already experiencing greenhouse-driven warming as measured against a background of natural temperature variability. A number of well-respected experts assert that climate disruption caused by the greenhouse effect is already evident. They point to a trend in global temperatures, which in 1988 were at or near the record for the period of instrumental data. Moreover, the five warmest years in this century all occurred during the 1980s, and the rate of global warming for the past two decades was higher than any in recorded history.[27] Others, citing a still unexplained cooling trend earlier in the century, question the causal relationship between greenhouse theory and elevated temperatures.[28]

Occasionally the science of global warming is contrasted with that of stratospheric ozone depletion, which is said to be quite certain. However, it is interesting to note that for the better part of a decade, the policy debate over stratospheric ozone was dominated by a focus on precisely the sort of scientific uncertainties that now characterize the greenhouse issue. In any event, because there is a lag on the order of decades between emissions of greenhouse gases and their effects, the level of heat-absorbing chemicals already released into the atmosphere may have irrevocably committed the world to an additional increase of .9° to 2.7°F over the next fifty years, even if the atmosphere's composition were stabilized today.[29]

## SECURITY IMPLICATIONS

The greenhouse effect, if unchecked, is likely to cause unpredictable disturbances in the balance of power worldwide, exacerbating the risk of war. The projected climatic turmoil and its accompanying impacts are sufficiently dramatic in quality, magnitude, and rapidity that policymakers should give the most serious consideration to the security implications of the ongoing failure to anticipate and arrest greenhouse warming. The oil crises of the 1970s, like the Persian Gulf crisis, were widely perceived as a national security issue because excessive dependence on foreign oil threatened the American economy. Prevention of global climate perturbation demands the immediate attention of the nation's leaders for the same reason. But so far, the implications of the greenhouse phenomenon have not played the slightest role in long-term strategic planning by the government.

The odds are strongly stacked against every country in the game of climate roulette. Contrary to some speculation, it is very unlikely that any region of the world will be a net "winner" from climate change. The very concept of "winning" implies the existence of a stable warmer climate, which will not occur unless the warming trend is halted. There is no natural endpoint to climate disruption from the greenhouse effect. Even the limited goal of a steady-state warmer climate will require major policy reform. Otherwise, greenhouse gas concentrations and global temperatures will continue to increase indefinitely, nullifying any short-term benefits. Moreover, no single country will be able to guarantee that the phenomenon is arrested at an optimal point for that country. The only way to ensure that there will be *any* winners is to guarantee that *all* countries are winners by reversing the global buildup of greenhouse gases in the atmosphere.

Even if a stable warmer climate were identified as a policy goal, the rate of climate change resulting from greenhouse gases already in the atmosphere would be faster than ever experienced in human history. This climate alteration would undoubtedly result in decades of destruction from an inability to alter human behavior, such as agricultural techniques, fast enough to take advantage of new weather patterns. The transition to warmer climates is expected to be turbulent, accompanied by an increase in the frequency, intensity, duration, and geographic extent of extreme weather events like droughts and storms. Moreover, sea-level rise would be certain to entail net harm the world over. No region or individual country should place the health and well-being of its public and environment at stake in what amounts to a crapshoot.

While all countries are likely to be losers in the global climate gamble, some countries have more at stake than others. The United States has a particularly large investment in the status quo. Its current preeminence in world affairs ultimately derives from the strength of the nation's economy. The productivity of the country's natural resources, such as the incomparably valuable farmland of the Midwest, was an essential prerequisite to America's economic well-being in the latter half of the twentieth century. Impending climate change means that this productivity can no longer be taken for granted. The greenhouse effect threatens the overall health of the American economy and could require a massive diversion of resources to nonproductive adaptive activities.

The United States has one of the most productive agricultural sectors on earth, producing nearly 50 percent of the world's corn and nearly 60 percent of its soybeans. The United States is also the world's leading exporter of wheat and corn. Climate models, however, suggest that this pattern could change dramatically if the Midwest became 10 to 20 percent drier and crop yields were reduced.[30] The drought of 1988 demonstrated that falling crop yields are a very real possibility. The difference between summer 1988's events and the effects of greenhouse-induced climate change would be that the latter is permanent and worsening, not just an isolated calamity.

Adapting to future climate change is also likely to require significant resources in the United States. Fighting the effects of a rising sea level on the heavily developed coasts of the United States, where about 75 percent of the population of the United States resides in 1990, will be phenomenally expensive. Maintaining threatened developments along American shorelines by diking cities, pumping sand, and building bulkheads and levees could cost $73 to $111 billion by 2100 for a three-foot rise.[31] Seven of the ten most populous cities in the United States are located either on the coasts or on coastal estuaries that would be severely affected by sea-level rise.

The effects of greenhouse warming will also be felt in other parts of the world, creating disruptions of global scale with inevitable adverse impacts on the United States and its political and economic security. Loss of low-lying territory could create refugee problems of an unprecedented scale. Inundation of just the tiny island country of the Maldives would require the relocation of nearly 200,000 people. Competition over territory and natural resources launched by those displaced by sea-level rise could create or exacerbate regional strife. Pressure from the 10 million individuals in Bangladesh who would be uprooted by a three-foot sea-level rise could heighten regional tensions. Famine created by greenhouse-driven crop failures could also generate regional clashes. Such an acceleration in regional showdowns could destabilize the world political balance in highly unpredictable ways, placing United States security interests at risk.

In addition to these strategic considerations, the economic and social dislocations caused by global warming could undermine the development strategies of Third World countries, condemning hundreds of millions of people to decades more of poverty. Moreover, the pressure on Third World governments to deal with these disturbances would likely hinder their ability to formulate and implement policies to reduce further emissions of greenhouse gases. This may be one of the most catastrophic "feedbacks" associated with global climate change. It underscores the need to pursue policies to mitigate the amount of warming sooner, rather than later. Waiting until the consequences of climatic change have been manifested will severely impair the efficacy of later policies implemented to slow the pace of climatic change.

## ARRESTING CLIMATE CHANGE

The worst effects of a greenhouse-induced climate cataclysm can be averted. And the sooner action is taken, the more effective it will be. Conversely, the longer a policy response is delayed, the greater the warming that will have accumulated and the more radical the measures that will be required to prevent further climatic upheaval.

CFCs and halons are by far the easiest component of the greenhouse problem to eliminate. Besides their major contribution to the global warming phenomenon, these chemicals are also the principal culprits implicated in the destruction of stratospheric ozone. In contrast to other greenhouse gases, reductions in emissions of CFCs and halons are now required by the regulatory structures of the Vienna Convention for the Protection of the Ozone Layer[32] and the Montreal Protocol on Substances That Deplete the Ozone Layer.[33] Aside from representing a diplomatic milestone for international cooperation on protecting stratospheric ozone, the Montreal protocol—the more significant and prescriptive of the two multilateral treaties—is also an important precedent for a multilateral strategy on the more challenging issue of greenhouse warming. But despite the fact that these instruments help to address the global warming problem in an indirect, incremental manner, they are far from a comprehensive greenhouse gas regime. Indeed, the Montreal protocol does not specify that alternatives to the CFCs and halons controlled by the government must or even should be greenhouse friendly.

The Montreal Protocol, signed in September 1987, requires an incremental 50 percent reduction in the consumption of five ozone-depleting CFCs by the end of the century. Beginning in July 1989, consumption of these substances was to be frozen at 1986 levels. A reduction of 20 percent must be achieved beginning four years later, and an additional 30 percent beginning in July 1998. The agreement permits each country to implement these requirements as it chooses through recycling, destruction, or abandonment of unnecessary uses of these chemicals. However, the overall strategy is to stimulate the development of alternatives to existing CFCs by constricting supply. The Montreal Protocol contains groundbreaking trade incentives for broad participation, including a ban on imports of controlled substances from countries that are not party to the accord. Its provisions dealing specifically with developing countries resolve delicate equity issues by allowing Third World countries a ten-year grace period to make required reductions. As of mid-1990, the obligations of this multilateral treaty were in force for fifty-seven countries.

Despite the precedential importance of the Montreal Protocol, the reduction schedule in the agreement was recognized as inadequate even from the day of its signature. Moreover, soon afterwards a seasonal thinning of 50 percent of the ozone layer over Antarctica—the ozone "hole"—was conclusively connected to CFCs.[34] Widely accepted scientific evidence documents that average global losses in stratospheric ozone of about 3 percent—two to three times that previously predicted by computer models—have already occurred.[35] Even if CFCs and halons are phased out within five to seven years, the long atmospheric lifetimes of these chemicals mean that the environment could take up to a century to recover. Further, even if production of these dangerous chemicals were to be eliminated altogether, they would continue to seep out of the existing stock of refrigerators, air conditioners, insulation, and other repositories. It is now clear that emissions of CFCs and halons must be virtually eliminated because of the overwhelming risks these chemicals pose to climate and stratospheric ozone.

In light of these scientific findings, major initiatives have already been undertaken to strengthen the Montreal protocol and, through it, domestic control measures. The amended agreement requires a total phase-out by industrialized countries in consumption of CFCs, halons, and a related ozone-depleting chemical, carbon tetrachloride ($CCl_4$), before the end of the century. Consumption of another potent ozone depleter, methyl chloroform ($CH_3CCl_3$), is to be completely terminated by 2005. Developing countries, as in the original agreement, will receive a grace period for making required reductions. The amended agreement also creates a multilateral fund of up to $240 million "for the purposes of providing financial and technical co-operation, including the transfer of technologies, to [developing countries]."

To stabilize global concentrations of $CO_2$, it will be necessary to cut global emissions of this gas by at least 60 percent.[36] Particularly in the industrialized world, the burning of fossil fuels releases most of the excess $CO_2$ in the atmosphere. Because no economical technology for removing $CO_2$ from waste gas streams is now available, reducing releases of $CO_2$ will require a lower total energy consumption and a shift in energy sources toward low- or non-$CO_2$-emitting technologies. Greenhouse impacts should be an explicit part of all future decision-making processes in the energy sector. Reductions in fossil fuel use will also help to ease other environmental problems associated with current patterns of energy use, such as acid rain and local air pollution.

Even with the most optimistic assumptions about economic growth, major reductions in $CO_2$ emissions from industrialized countries can be achieved with energy conservation, efficiency technologies, and renewable energy sources. For example, the 1,200 kilowatt-hours per year used by a typical frost-free refrigerator can be reduced to only 180 with a state-of-the-art model. Current technology can light an office building with an expenditure of only .55 watts per square foot, as little as one-fifth of today's average. It is now possible to produce motor vehicles—which currently account for more than one-fourth of greenhouse gases released in the United States— that have fuel economies of up to 98 miles per gallon, two to five times as efficient as those now on the road.

Efficiency improvements have meant that the amount of energy used in the United States today is about the same as in 1973, despite a 40 percent increase in GNP during the same period.[37] Application of existing efficiency technologies could reduce United States $CO_2$ emissions by 14 to 18 percent by the end of the century.[38] In California alone, a steady improvement in efficiency of 3.4 percent per year was achieved between 1973 and 1985 with only mild encouragement from state and local governments through policy measures to encourage conservation and efficiency. Through a strategy mandating or aggressively promoting efficiency improvements, national progress could be much faster.

Nuclear energy has been proposed in some quarters as the preferred solution to the problem of greenhouse warming. Although atomic power is a $CO_2$-free technology, its other risks currently make it the least attractive alternative to fossil fuels. Nuclear energy carries the inherent danger of weapons proliferation. The current generation of nuclear reactors still entails the unacceptable danger of accidents and suffers from a critical lack of public confidence in an increasingly large number of countries. The problem of disposing of waste that will remain hazardously radioactive for many hundreds of thousands of years has yet to be adequately solved. Of the alternative strategies for reducing $CO_2$ emissions, nuclear energy is among the most expensive. Moreover, to reduce $CO_2$ emissions by 50 percent by the year 2020 solely through the expansion of the nuclear industry would require bringing a new plant on line somewhere in the world at the rate of almost one a day starting in the mid-1990s—clearly a practical impossibility. While the nuclear option may be worthy of consideration as part of the public debate on ultimate solutions to the greenhouse problem, increased reliance on nuclear power at present would be both politically unfeasible and irresponsible when major, cheap reductions in $CO_2$ emissions are available with existing efficiency and conservation technologies.

Reversing deforestation and creating new forested areas will help to offset current levels of $CO_2$ emissions. New forests, in absorbing $CO_2$ from the air during photosynthesis, will contribute to climate stabilization by serving as supplementary reservoirs for carbon. Aggressive policies to conserve existing forests and create new forested areas will yield other significant environmental benefits, including erosion control and the preservation of a rich diversity of species whose genetic potential is only now becoming accessible to humankind.

The fundamentals of the greenhouse phenomenon are now well understood and the need for swift policy responses firmly established. But in the United States, as in every country, the intransigence of entrenched interest groups can create policy lethargy. Moreover, it may be difficult to muster a political constituency in support of subsidies for overseas transfers of greenhouse-friendly technologies and assistance to poorer countries for combating the greenhouse phenomenon. But there are also likely to be substantial opportunities for those astute businesses and considerable advantages for those farsighted countries that anticipate the need for policy responses sooner rather than later.

While these responses are being implemented, the development and dissemination of technologies to combat climate disturbance—such as CFC-free, energy-efficient refrigerators and low-methane strains of rice—should be a high priority. Increased basic research to resolve remaining uncertainties concerning the magnitude, rate, and effects of greenhouse warming should also be undertaken.

## THE ROLE OF DEVELOPING COUNTRIES

An equitable response to the special needs of developing countries is crucial to removing greenhouse threats to the global climate. On the one hand, developing countries have caused little of the problem, and industrialized countries must bear the bulk of the blame for past and current emissions. On the other hand, as economic development accelerates, Third World countries may account for the preponderance of greenhouse gas emissions by the middle of the next century. An international solution that provides incentives for the participation of developing countries while fairly distributing the responsibility for implementing solutions is essential to a successful global strategy for combating greenhouse warming.

The consequences of the greenhouse effect strongly suggest that it is in the self-interest of Third World countries to reexamine expeditiously their energy priorities. Developing countries, with fewer resources to adapt to environmental disturbances, stand to suffer disproportionately from a rapid climate change. For example, the productivity of common rice varieties falls off dramatically at temperatures just a few degrees higher than those currently prevailing in many rice-growing areas.

Tapping the tremendous potential for conservation and improved end-use efficiency in the developing world would contribute to a solution for greenhouse warming while meeting much of the Third World's growing energy needs.[39] This strategy also avoids other serious environmental and social problems, such as land degradation, local air pollution, and population displacement, that accompany the building of fossil-fuel-fired power installations. By the year 2020 it may be possible to achieve a universal standard of living far beyond that necessary to satisfy basic needs with little or no increase in global energy consumption from today's levels. However, many developing countries use energy in a highly inefficient manner. Macroeconomic policies in many developing countries, such as electricity price subsidies, discourage conservation and efficiency improvements. Firms in Brazil, where electricity prices are subsidized, have manufactured energy-efficient air conditioners for export but cheap, inefficient models for domestic consumption.

Investments in efficiency gains are extremely attractive from many points of view. They require less capital and less foreign exchange than do comparable amounts of new power supply, contributing to overall economic productivity. Through efficiency and conservation, developing countries could avoid at least $1.4 trillion in power supply expansion costs between now and the year 2008.[40]

Efficiency investments represent a major opportunity for donors like the

United States and the World Bank to assist developing countries in making energy choices that both avoid mistakes made earlier in the developed world and reduce risks to the entire planet from greenhouse warming. Unfortunately, much of current foreign aid directed to the environmentally sensitive energy sector often exacerbates the threat of greenhouse warming by emphasizing conventional energy sources, such as massive fossil-fuel-fired power plants.

For instance, the World Bank, which controls an annual energy lending portfolio of roughly $4 billion, is one of the principal donors supporting power-generation projects in the Third World. Through measures such as pricing reforms and improvements in the operation of existing power plants and distribution systems, the bank has already made a commitment to encourage conservation and the efficient use of energy. There is, however, considerably more that the bank can do.

The bank requires preparation of a "least cost" plan to precede investments in the energy sector. Current methodologies for these studies primarily address strategies for increasing energy supply. Support for demand-reduction measures, such as end-use efficiency improvements, which are often economically as well as environmentally superior to investments in supply, have not consistently been considered as alternatives to conventional power-generation projects in bank energy-sector strategies. Expanding the universe of alternatives to include demand-reduction options would simultaneously help developing countries reduce the rate of growth in their power-generating capacity and reduce greenhouse-gas emissions without sacrificing the energy needed for economic development. Additional staff trained in strategies for encouraging end-use efficiency improvements would significantly increase the bank's capabilities in this crucial area.

Forest policy is another area where development assistance can provide benefits to Third World countries while simultaneously cutting emissions of greenhouse gases. While there has been great concern in North America and Western Europe about destruction of tropical forests, donor countries historically have devoted little capital to conservation of this crucial resource and have earmarked even less for the creation of new forest areas. Case studies have documented that projects financed with little regard for the integrity of natural resources by donors such as the World Bank have seriously exacerbated forest loss in key countries such as Brazil and Indonesia. Industrialized countries can also help to reverse tropical deforestation and encourage reforestation through changes in domestic policies. Developed countries provide the primary market for tropical hardwoods, virtually all of which are harvested at an unsustainable rate and in an unsustainable manner. Firms based in industrialized countries often reap the profits of this trade. Governments of industrialized countries should consider controlling trade in tropical woods and compensating exporting countries for lost revenues through alternative investments.

The Third World debt crisis may also present major opportunities for encouraging better forest management in developing countries. As the market value of such debt has fallen, a number of private banks have sold debt owed to them by Third World governments to private conservation organizations, which have then forgiven the debt in return for specific promises by the governments concerned, such as a commitment to conserve a particular area and to support its maintenance with a stream of payments in local currency. Such "debt for nature" swaps are already in place in Bolivia, Costa Rica, and Ecuador, and more are under negotiation. Governments of creditor countries can adopt policies, such as tax incentives, that encourage private banks to sell debt for swaps. Then it may even be possible to inject environmental policy considerations, such as forest preservation or energy efficiency, into negotiations between debtor country governments and creditor banks involving potentially massive amounts of debt. Creditor governments can also reduce interest or principal on sovereign debt in return for promises of policy reform in these critical sectors.

## CONCERTED INTERNATIONAL ACTION

Coordinating policies on the international level to fight greenhouse warming will maximize environmental and foreign policy benefits. Unilateral reductions in releases of greenhouse gases by large emitters such as the United States and the Soviet Union will go a long way toward arresting global climate disruption. However, a multilateral consensus strategy will further the crucial goals of creating incentives for universal participation and establishing an equitable balancing of responsibility for solving the problem. These and other international political, legal, and institutional challenges are likely to endure over time, even as the science of the global warming issue evolves.

Existing international mechanisms are an important part of such a strategy. A reassessment of the Montreal Protocol, a process that is provided for by the document itself, is the most expeditious way to eliminate the contributions CFCs and halons make to the global warming problem. The World Bank's institutional structure includes mechanisms for member countries to redirect priorities in the critical energy and forest sectors. But existing mechanisms by themselves are highly unlikely to be adequate for the task of crafting a comprehensive greenhouse gas regime.

The remainder of the greenhouse problem could be handled most effectively through a multilateral treaty, with standards binding under international law that would require each country to take prescribed actions to reduce and halt greenhouse warming. An international agreement designed to arrest global climate change should satisfy several basic requirements. First, it must require reductions in releases of greenhouse gases of a magnitude and speed sufficient to stabilize the earth's climate. The most important gas to control is $CO_2$, for which global reductions of at least 60 percent are necessary. Participating countries should accomplish these reductions by means of environmentally and economically sound technologies that do not present unacceptable risks to public health or world security. The creation of new forested areas might be encouraged by allowing credits against reductions of $CO_2$ emissions that would otherwise be required and by provisions establishing or promoting forestry programs. Because the agreement could be expected to cover a large number of emissions sources, it should require strict mechanisms for enforcement through reporting of emissions, on-site audits, and internationally controlled remote sensing.

Second, the responsibility for making reductions must be distributed equitably. Among the criteria that could be applied is relative national wealth as measured by per capita GNP. Another test could be per capita emissions of $CO_2$, with the highest reductions required of those countries with the highest emissions per unit of population. Another possibility would be to require the imposition of a fee for carbon emissions, either as a primary mechanism for achieving reductions or as a supplementary measure to generate revenue. Any of these formulas would require proportionally greater cutbacks by the wealthiest countries and leave the poorest countries with the fewest constraints on $CO_2$ emissions.

A treaty should also require a commitment from wealthier countries for increased research into non-$CO_2$ energy supply technologies and development assistance to help poorer countries meet the requirements accepted by them in the agreement. One mechanism for generating the necessary capital is to require countries to contribute to a fund in proportion to their $CO_2$ emissions. The resources of the fund, which could be financed by a carbon fee, could be used to fund forest protection and reforestation programs, as well as to develop and disseminate energy efficiency and conservation technologies and environmentally benign renewable energy sources. Restricting access to this fund to those countries that accepted the obligations of the treaty would create incentives for broad participation.

The first step toward international negotiations on a global climate treaty was taken with the establishment of the Intergovernmental Panel on Climate Change (IPCC), which met for the first time in November 1988. The IPCC was created under the auspices of the United Nations Environment Program (UNEP) and the World Meteorological Organization with a mandate to study the climate change issue and report to the Second World Climate Conference in the fall of 1990. More than thirty-five countries participate in IPCC activities, which are distributed among three "working groups": a science working group; a working group studying social and environmental impacts of climate change; and a Response Strategies Working Group (RSWG). The RSWG, beginning with its meeting in Geneva in October 1989, has begun to examine possible elements for inclusion in a framework convention on climate change. Although the original scope of the IPCC's activities did not include preparation for the adoption of a formal treaty, a number of recent directives clearly authorize the negotiation of a greenhouse-gas convention. These include the final statement of an international meeting hosted by the government of Canada in 1988,[41] the declaration of an international meeting sponsored by the government of the Netherlands in March 1989,[42] a decision of the UNEP governing council taken at its May 1989 meeting,[43] the communiques of the Group of Seven industrialized countries from their 1989 and 1990 gatherings,[44] the declaration of a ministerial conference on pollution and climate change hosted by the Dutch government in November 1989,[45] and the final statement of a ministerial conference sponsored by the government of Norway in May 1990.[46]

Optimism about the prospects for a treaty to limit emissions of greenhouse gases through a global convention arises to a great extent from progress on CFCs and halons in the Montreal Protocol. However, most of the existing mandates for the negotiation of a global warming treaty consciously limit action to a "framework" or "umbrella" instrument analogous not to the 1987 Montreal Protocol, but to the 1985 Vienna convention. Unfortunately, this precursor to the Montreal Protocol establishes only a structure for cooperation in research and exchange of information. It does not mandate reductions in emissions of CFCs or halons, nor does it require any other measures that directly benefit the environment.

There is a serious risk that precious time will be lost in protracted negotiation over these "framework" functions, which in any event have already been largely performed by the IPCC process. Instead, a greenhouse-gas convention should contain minimum global goals commensurate with environmental necessity, such as a commitment to reduce global emissions of $CO_2$ by at least 60 percent on a specified timetable. The implementation of these goals could be taken up in negotiations on ancillary agreements similar to the Montreal Protocol, when complicated issues such as the distribution of national obligations for reductions could be addressed.

Industrialized countries, and in particular the United States, must take the lead in identifying global solutions to this global problem. Developed nations are primarily responsible for past and current threats to the global climate, and these are the countries with the resources to combat it. If the industrialized world does not seize a leadership role, there is scant likelihood that other, far poorer countries can be convinced either of the seriousness of the problem or of the necessity to mobilize the political will efficaciously to respond.

As of mid-1990, debate on the greenhouse issue, both internationally and domestically within the United States, fails this test. The most ambitious policies currently under serious international consideration would merely level off emissions of $CO_2$ by the end of this century or the beginning of the next. The United States, citing scientific uncertainty, has rejected even this modest goal. Moreover, the United States and others have resisted simultaneous negotiation of the "framework" convention and protocols, raising the possibility of an endlessly protracted procedure for the adoption of a multilaterally agreed strategy. Faced with international gridlock, some countries, such as the Federal Republic of Germany, have chosen to act on a unilateral basis, and others, such as eighteen European nations, have opted for coordinated regional measures. Some states of the United States, such as Connecticut, New York, and Vermont have taken an analogous approach, in part to prod inertial federal policies.[47]

Considering the importance of the resources at risk, it would be nothing short of reckless to continue with business as usual. A failure to respond to the threat of greenhouse warming would amount to an affirmative decision to wager the health and well-being of current and future generations against overwhelming odds.

## Notes

This work was supported in part by the Rockefeller Foundation's Study Center in Bellagio, Italy through the author's appointment as a scholar-in-residence. The author gratefully acknowledges the assistance of Eric L. Washburn in the preparation of this article.

1. J. M. Barnola, D. Raymond, and Y. S. Korotkevich, et al., "Vostok Ice Core Provides 160,000-Year Record of Atmospheric $CO_2$," 329 Nature 408 (1987).

2. G. Marland, T. A. Boden, R. C. Griffin, S. F. Huang, P. Kanciruk, and T. R. Nelson, Estimates of $CO_2$ Emissions from Fossil Fuel Burning and Cement Manufacturing, Based on the United Nations Energy Statistics and the U.S. Bureau of Mines Cement Manufacturing Data, ORNL/CDIAC–25–NDP–030, (Oak Ridge, TN: Oak Ridge National Laboratory, May 1989).

3. World Resources Institute, World Resources 1990–1991, (Oxford: Oxford University Press, 1990).

4. Ibid.

5. Intergovernmental Panel on Climate Change, Policymakers Summary of the Scientific Assessment of Climate Change, Report to IPCC from Working Group 1, (Bracknell, UK: IPCC Group at Meteorological Office, March 1990). Also see D. Lashof, The Dynamic Greenhouse: Feedback Processes that May Influence Future Concentrations of Atmospheric Trace Gases and Climatic Change, 14 Climatic Change 213 (1989).

6. Ibid.

7. D. Lashof and Ahuja, "Relative Contributions of Greenhouse Gas Emissions to Global Warming," 344 Nature 529 (1990).

8. Scientific Assessment of Climate Change.

9. Ibid.

10. Ibid.

11. Ibid.

12. Ibid.

13. Ibid.

14. Scientific Assessment of Climate Change; Blake and Rowland, "Continuing Worldwide Increase in Tropospheric Methane, 1978 to 1987," 239 Science 1129 (1988).

15. Estimates of Carbon Dioxide Emissions.

16. World Resources 1990–91.

17. Scientific Assessment of Climate Change.

18. Ibid.

19. J. G. Titus, ed., Greenhouse Effect, Sea Level Rise and Coastal Wetlands (Washington, D.C.: U.S. Environmental Protection Agency, 1988).

20. Ibid.

21. United States Environmental Protection Agency and United Nations Environment Program, Effects of Changes in Stratospheric Ozone and Global Climate, (4-volume proceedings of conference held at Leesburg, Virginia, June 16–20, 1986).

22. Ibid.

23. Ibid.

24. World Meteorological Organization and United Nations Environmental Program, De-

*veloping Policies for Responding to Climatic Change* (1988) (report of conferences held at Villach, Austria, September 28–October 2, 1987, and Bellagio, Italy, November 9–13, 1987).

25. *Effects of Changes in Stratospheric Ozone and Global Climate.*

26. Ibid.

27. Intergovernmental Panel on Climate Change, *Scientific Assessment of Climate Change* (1990).

28. Greenhouse Effect and Global Climate Change: Hearing Before the Senate Committee on Energy and Natural Resources, 100th Cong., 1st Sess. 39 (1988) (statement of Dr. James E. Hansen, Goddard Institute for Space Studies, United States National Aeronautics and Space Administration); Houghton and Woodwell, "Global Climatic Change," *Scientific American,* April 1989, at 36 (1989).

29. I. Mintzer, *A Matter of Degrees* (World Resources Institute, 1987).

30. J. Smith and D. Tirpak, *The Potential Effects of Global Climate Change on the United States* (Washington, D.C.: U.S. Environmental Protection Agency, Dec. 1989).

31. Ibid.

32. Senate Treaty Doc. No. 9, 99th Cong., 1st Sess. (1985), reprinted in 26 *International Legal Materials* 1516 (1987).

33. Senate Treaty Doc. No. 10, 100th Cong., 1st Sess. (1987), reprinted in 52 Fed. Reg. 47,515 (Dec. 14, 1987); 26 Int'l Legal Materials 1550 (1987).

34. United States National Aeronautics and Space Administration, *Ozone Trends Panel Report* (1988) (consensus findings of panel of more than 100 scientists).

35. Ibid.

36. *Scientific Assessment of Climate Change.*

37. United States Department of Energy, *United States Energy Policy 1980–1988* (1988); Oak Ridge National Laboratory, *Federal Roles to Realize National Energy-Efficiency Opportunities in the 1990s* (1989).

38. Natural Resources Defense Council, *Cooling the Greenhouse: Vital First Steps to Combat Global Warming* (1989).

39. J. Goldemberg, T. Johansson, A. Reddy, and R. Williams, *Energy for a Sustainable World* (1987); J. Goldemberg, T. Johansson, A. Reddy, and R. Williams, *Energy for Development* (1987); World Bank, *End-Use Electricity Conservation Options for Developing Countries* (1986) (Energy Department Paper No. 32).

40. United States Agency for International Development, *Power Shortages in Developing Countries: Magnitude, Impacts, Solutions, and the Role of the Private Sector* (1988).

41. The Changing Atmosphere: Implications for Global Security (statement from international meeting sponsored by Government of Canada in Toronto, June 27–30, 1988), reprinted in 5 *American University Journal of International Law and Policy* 515 (1990).

42. Declaration of the Hague (statement from international meeting sponsored by government of the Netherlands in the Hague, March 11, 1989), reprinted in 5 *American University Journal of International Law and Policy* 567 (1990), 30 *Harvard International Law Journal* 417 (1989), 12 *International Environment Reporter (BNA)* 215 (1989).

43. G.C. Dec. 15/36, 44 U.N. GAOR Supp. (No. 25) at 164, U.N. Doc. A/44/25 (1989), reprinted in 19 *Environmental Policy and Law* 118 (1989).

44. Economic Declaration (statement of Group of Seven major industrialized nations in Paris, July 16, 1989), reprinted in 5 *American University International Journal of Law and Policy* 571 (1990), 19 *Environmental Policy and Law,* 183 (1989), *New York Times,* July 17, 1989, p. A7, col. 1; Houston Economic Declaration (statement of Group of Seven major industrialized nations in Houston, July 11, 1990), reprinted in *New York Times,* July 12, 1990, p. A15, col. 1.

45. Noordwijk Declaration on Atmospheric Pollution and Climatic Change (statement of ministerial conference sponsored by government of the Netherlands in Noordwijk, Nov. 7, 1989), reprinted in 5 *American University Journal of International Law and Policy* 592 (1990), 19 *Environmental Policy and Law* 229 (1989).

46. Bergen Ministerial Declaration on Sustainable Development in the ECE Region (statement of ministerial conference sponsored by government of Norway in Bergen, May 16, 1990).

47. D. Lashof and E. Washburn, *The Statehouse Effect: State Policies to Cool the Greenhouse* (1990).

# 18 / A Policy Framework for World Security

ROBERT C. JOHANSEN

As we stand amidst the extraordinary fluidity of the vast political, economic, and environmental changes of the 1980s and 1990s and attempt to lay plans for enhancing U.S. and global security over the next decade, we would do well to heed the historians and experts on military strategy who have repeatedly warned that generals (and others) tend to overlook inconvenient realities and to prepare defenses that are more appropriate for the last war than for the next one, or that respond more to wishful thinking than to real problems.

The momentous changes in security needs that have arisen in recent years are no less profound, when both military and nonmilitary dimensions of security are taken into account, than the changes that accompanied the end of World War II in 1945. But instead of a contemporary equivalent to the new thinking symbolized by the San Francisco Conference of 1945, which established the United Nations, we find a tepid, almost casual response from the United States, Great Britain, and other countries from which international leadership ought to come. Their leadership has not proposed, for example, ways to graft a third generation of world institutions onto the first two generations—the League of Nations and the United Nations–Bretton Woods systems.

Policymakers in many capitals seem snared in perhaps the oldest and most widely honored maxim of international relations throughout the world: "If you want peace, prepare for war." This is not the place to debate whether preparations for war throughout history have more often led to war than to peace.[1] But it seems increasingly clear to people not closely wedded to the vested interests of traditional policies, that if we want peace we must prepare for peace. This can be done by strengthening norms and institutions *against* war, not organizations and arsenals for the conduct of war. As Seyom Brown has warned, "The instruments the United States has been relying upon for prosecuting the cold war—and, indeed, the predominance of cold war geopolitics in the overall definition of U.S. world interests—have become woefully insufficient tools. . . ."[2]

What new tools, what harmonization of national interests with the human interest, what more imaginative mentality could truly come to grips with the security challenges that press upon people throughout the entire world community? In the preceding chapters the authors have recommended a variety of specific initiatives to enhance security. Here I will try to integrate these recommendations and move beyond them, to chart the long-range direction that policy must follow if the people of the United States and the world are to survive, and to survive with dignity for themselves and respect for each other. My intention is to develop principles that can inform the policies of *all* nations, but to show how the United States in particular can change its own direction to chart a fundamentally new path and set an example for other nations.

At the heart of a new security concept must be a transformation of views on the role of military power. This transformation was anticipated to some degree in the envisaging of "common security" by people like Willy Brandt and Olof Palme, and reflected in the reports of the well-known international commissions that they, and later Gro Harlem Brundtland, headed.[3] As the Palme Commission concluded, the destructiveness of modern war, even so-called conventional war, has become so horrendous that "war is losing its meaning as an instrument of national policy, becoming instead an engine of senseless destruction that leaves the root causes of conflict unresolved." The changes in warfare and the growth of planetary interconnectedness "have made traditional concepts of national security obsolete." Once humanity has become proficient in building weapons of mass destruction, nations "can no longer hope to protect their citizens through unilateral military measures." Rather than traditional security thinking, *common security* policies are needed. They are rooted in the recognition that "all states, even the most powerful, are dependent in the end upon the good sense and restraint of other nations." In sum, "true security requires a cooperative effort, a partnership in the struggles against war" as an acceptable human institution.[4]

In contrast, U.S. policy remains based on "discriminate deterrence,"[5] which rationalizes the continued development and deployment of a long list of more sophisticated weapons. U.S. security managers continue to over-emphasize the importance of high-tech military hardware as a response to future security problems, despite Soviet initiatives for demilitarization, the de facto disappearance of the Warsaw Treaty Organization, and the alarming rise of nonmilitary security threats rooted in economic and environmental problems. Current U.S. security thinking is characterized by continuing emphasis on nuclear weapons and strategic doctrines that are virtually unusable because they are morally unacceptable, risk self-destruction, or are impractical (Star Wars weapons); by preparing military instruments for overt or covert action in Third World contexts where U.S. military involvement often is self-defeating; and by overlooking the possibility that the U.S. nuclear arsenal will be outflanked by poorer, more desperate countries with other kinds of weapons of mass destruction or by nonmilitary security threats, like environmental decay, economic decline, or migratory pressures that simply cannot be managed by military might.

Even if the threat of a major military attack on the United States were a problem, which seems unlikely in the foreseeable future, to deploy new nuclear and space-based weapons would probably only speed the proliferation of weapons elsewhere and stimulate deeper planetary militarization. Most new U.S. weapons eventually will only increase counterthreats to the United States and make U.S. economic decline more likely. Unwilling to make bold decisions to address global security needs, officials seem to doom themselves, as of this writing, to some military procurement activities likely to be no more helpful than pouring concrete for the useless bunkers named after the pre–1939 French minister of war, André Maginot.

Despite some reductions in U.S. and world military expenditures, these are a far cry from a new orientation that would attempt to encompass the security of all nations and reduce the role of military power in international affairs generally. Many governments, including the United States, continue to operate in the mode of adversarial security, rather than common security. Most national security managers do not acknowledge that people's security in the future will rest on finding alternatives to the military postures that have characterized the nation-state system up to now—not on their modernization. Symptomatically, more attention is devoted in Washington to naming one or more alternatives to replace the Soviet Communist government as a security threat than to finding an alternative to the international security system that has produced recurring threats throughout its existence. This system never has and presumably never will prevent war permanently. Yet permanent prevention of major war must be the aim of any serious future security policy.

Political leaders of course rhetorically acknowledge obvious dangers, from the possibility of a planetary hothouse to a nuclear winter. But the policies undertaken for meeting the vast array of challenges before us, despite many unexplored diplomatic opportunities to demilitarize international relations and address nonmilitary security threats, remain maladaptively confined to modest revisions in traditional security thinking. Washington's potential intellectual and moral power remains unutilized.

## WORLD SECURITY IN THE 1990s AND BEYOND

To avoid remaining enmeshed in an outmoded worldview, it is essential to develop basic guidelines to orient citizens' actions, to inform political leaders, and to hold them accountable to what the commonweal needs and the new realities demand. The preceding chapters make clear that the concept of security must be (1) deepened to include an understanding of how military threats against an adversary produce a boomerang effect that increases one's own insecurity and (2) broadened to include many security threats that are not military. In other words, a useful security concept in the postmodern age must emphasize both *common* security and *comprehensive* security.

## Common Security

As the preceding brief quotations from the Palme Commission's report indicate, an adequate concept of security must expand to include not only one's own nation and its allies, but, surprisingly, all of one's adversaries and neutral bystanders as well. In an environmentally fragile age endowed with nuclear and nonnuclear weapons of mass destruction, either we hold security in common with all other nations or we cannot achieve it at all. If the United States seeks to enhance its security by building new weapons that increase the threat, even inadvertently, to an adversary, the latter will usually try to develop more weapons to increase the threat to the United States. If the adversary possesses advanced industrial and technological capacities, as in the case of the Soviet Union, the weapons deployed will be similar to those built by Washington. If the adversary lacks an equivalent industrial base, it will, in desperation, resort to unorthodox weapons and methods of attack that are usually labeled "terrorist." Yet regardless of the labels used to describe the techniques of destruction, military defense against or ability to repel determined attackers is becoming increasingly difficult and unsatisfactory. As a result, no country can, in the long run, increase its own security while ignoring or increasing the insecurity of other societies.

Even if continually advancing U.S. technologies of destruction remain beyond the capabilities of U.S. adversaries, in the absence of security policies designed to reduce reliance on the threat-system of international relations, one adversary or another in the future will be able to bring catastrophe home to U.S. citizens by launching nuclear weapons, delivering suitcase bombs, or engaging in chemical, radiological, biological, environmental, economic, or migratory warfare (discussed below). The world's societies are so intertwined and easily despoiled that more armaments do not lead to more security. On the contrary, arms buildups impede the growth of security by siphoning off resources and attention from the new security requirements: to enhance the common security of all countries, including adversaries, and to address nonmilitary security threats, to which we now turn.

## Comprehensive Security

To be successful, new security policies must be far more comprehensive in giving attention to nonmilitary problems than policymakers have done in the past. If the first duty of government is to provide safety for its people, this duty includes protection against whatever dangers may kill people or disrupt a society, be they environmental jeopardy or economic deprivation, as well as the threat of invasion by foreign armies. As Michael Renner has written, "National security is a meaningless concept . . . if it does not encompass the preservation of livable conditions within a country."[6] Human activity that thins the layer of ozone in the stratosphere, for example, or thickens the density of carbon dioxide in the atmosphere probably constitutes a more clear and present danger to national security than the unlikely possibility of a Soviet nuclear attack.

The entrance of environmental concerns into the security equation is far more complex and beyond the reach of contemporary policies than can be addressed by simply employing even enlightened traditional diplomacy. As Jessica Tuchman Mathews points out in Chapter 16,[7] traditional diplomacy is too slow and cumbersome to meet pressing environmental problems. A global authority with veto-free decision-making powers is required, as leaders from twenty-four nations recently recognized in the path-breaking Declaration of the Hague. In this statement they called for what might be described as a globally representative environmental security council to render binding decisions on vital issues affecting the biosphere through veto-free voting procedures. They expressed willingness to limit their national sovereignty to protect the planet.[8]

The environmental security threat is far removed from traditional security thinking, which is based on ideas about sovereignty that make a spatial distinction between friend and foe. But the humans who thin the ozone and intensify atmospheric carbon dioxide do not line up on one side of a national border, wear national uniforms from other countries, and fire away at the United States. Since a territorial distinction between friend and enemy no longer applies, we must change our ideas about what constitutes a true security community. It is no longer the community or nation within a traditional state.[9]

The presence of security friends and foes on *both* sides of one's national borders should help us disengage from lining up traditional defenses, but because of mental inertia, it has yet to do so. We still do not seem to recognize that weapons cannot suppress an economic or environmental security target. To pour billions of dollars into making ICBMs mobile is as irrelevant today as was building stationary concrete bunkers for meeting security needs of the 1930s. More arms are as outdated against today's security threats as were efforts to thicken castle walls after the invention of gunpowder and cannons.

Immigratory and migratory "warfare" also cannot be addressed by military means. Until major progress is made in implementing the principle of equity, some governments are likely to face virtually irresistible pressures for migration or immigration. These will be rooted in the efforts that millions of impoverished people, reflected only in small part by today's boat people and more than 12 million other refugees, will make to achieve lives of larger decency.[10] The quest for more equity will override, at least in the minds of many, traditional barriers to travel and immigration. The rich will be at war with the poor when the latter will no longer accept the arbitrariness of national boundaries that keep them on de facto "national reservations," outside the boundaries enclosing food surpluses and economic prosperity. As this occurs, world civilization will increasingly appear to be a morally unacceptable system of global apartheid in which 80 percent of the world's people are prevented from sharing their birthright by the 20 percent of the world's most prosperous people.[11] If capital does not move to poverty-stricken people, then poverty-stricken people may move to regions of prosperity.

Similarly, the bleeding of the U.S. economy during the Reagan and Bush administrations' enormous deficit spending on unnecessary military hardware will harm the well-being of U.S. people far more than the compensations of "standing tall" before what can only be considered virtually nonexistent traditional military threats during the 1980s and 1990s. As Paul Kennedy's lengthy historical study has demonstrated, mature great powers decline because they spend so much on military purposes that they destroy the economic health on which their power depends. In times of challenge, leaders have repeatedly made the *wrong* decisions for their own good.[12]

For security policy to encompass the subjects that are essential for it to be truly effective, it must extend even beyond economic and environmental threats, and attend to human rights, psychological, and even spiritual dimensions of personal security. The political, economic, and psychological changes required to build a safe world are of such a large order of magnitude that people with deep personal insecurities, no matter how well hidden, will be unable to provide reliable political help. As many feminists have pointed out, personal psychological security contributes to and probably is essential for national and global security.[13] High levels of personal security facilitate openness to new ways of thinking and to new forms of identity that transcend gender, racial, class, national, and generational lines. These forms of identity are essential to sustain a prudent security policy in the future.

## THE NEED: A PRINCIPLED FOREIGN POLICY

To interrupt the inertial tendencies to remain unresponsive to changing security needs, it is essential to develop a principled foreign policy, designed to implement clearly desirable humanitarian values.[14] Embracing key principles for the conduct of nations can produce several positive results. First, central principles give overall direction and constancy to policy. Because they are publicly discussed and supported, officials are less tempted to depart from preferred conduct in opportunistic political machinations. Awareness of central principles reduces the damage arising from partisan politics when elected officials and candidates, in the interest of obtaining votes, fan the flames of adversarial nationalism, reinforce exaggerated fears of foreigners and unfamiliar ideologies, and suggest that jingoism, militarism, economic protectionism, and the stifling of dissent are congruent with patriotism.

Moreover, just as a principled policy may reduce the disruption of narrow-minded nationalism and domestic political partisanship, so the establishment of a principled policy can alleviate the conflict-generating tendency in international relations to believe that one's own nation may legitimately give higher priority to its *interests* than to other peoples' *rights*. This tendency is one manifestation of what could be called "national partisanship" in an age of global interdependence. It makes a virtue of the kind of behavior in a global context that would be widely condemned as a vice if practiced in a domestic legal context. National partisanship violates the well-established principle that no party should be the final judge in its own case. In a world where the entire species becomes an important constituency in decision making, any national perspective, however bipartisan it may be from the standpoint of domestic politics, is partisan from a global perspective.

The hallowed idea that politics should stop at the water's edge loses its meaning in the postmodern world, because domestic bipartisanship could be the worst form of national partisanship in a planetary context. A government might with bipartisan support decide to launch a genocidal war, or more commonly, consume energy at an irresponsibly high level that intensifies the greenhouse effect. Similarly, domestically partisan debates over the appropriate principles to follow in foreign policy could be healthy,[15] if they lead the public to consider the partisanship of national policies from the standpoint of the species.

Finally, by articulating and honoring an explicitly principled code of conduct, Washington can more readily encourage other governments to follow suit.[16] To have a peaceful and just world order, people and governments must increasingly move away from an us-versus-them mentality toward common standards of conduct and fair play. The expansion of human identities that this implies need not be seen as an unwise sacrifice of legitimate national interests. As in domestic society, one person willingly gives up his or her "right" to act in disregard for the law in return for other persons' compliance with it. Washington can advocate legitimate U.S. rights most effectively amidst the advocacy of rights by other governments when all operate within a global political structure that requires disputes to be settled through political and legal means.

The growth of such a structure can be aided enormously by relying on an explicit code of conduct, not only to dampen illegitimate demands that Washington might otherwise be tempted to make, but also to demonstrate, in a less adversarial manner, what may be excessive in the demands of others. An international judgment by many nations, for example, articulating the same principles of fair play that the U.S. Congress might use to guide U.S. policies, can more effectively moderate nationally partisan claims from Moscow, Tokyo, Baghdad, or Tripoli, than can the United

States acting as a mere party—not a neutral judge—in a dispute with other nations.[17]

Five basic principles or guidelines are useful in shaping a U.S. policy that will enhance security for people in the United States and all other nations: reciprocity, equity, environmental sustainability, democratization, and demilitarization.

## Reciprocity

Reciprocity, the first and most fundamental guideline, simply means that a government willingly evaluates its own actions by the same standards that it holds for other nations' behavior. A national government that respects the principle of reciprocity does not insist on a right for itself that it does not willingly grant to others, nor does it specify a duty for others that it does not accept for itself.[18] This principle is almost universally endorsed, in rhetoric at least, by people regardless of nationality, religion, or ideology. But in practice it is violated frequently. Still, its universal endorsement provides a basis for attempting to hold governments accountable to a fundamental ordering principle.

If rigorously respected, this principle could by itself eliminate most wars. For example, if the United States denies that the Soviet Union, Libya, Iran, Syria, Vietnam, or other governments do not have any right to support armed insurrection in other countries or to finance clandestine movement of arms or military forces across borders, then the United States must not claim that "right" for itself, as it did in trying to overthrow the Nicaraguan government. To pose a second example, if the United States claims a right, as it has done in the Carter Doctrine, to use force to maintain access to the oil fields of the Middle East, then may malnourished societies claim a right to use force to gain access to the wheat fields of Kansas, or to let starving people migrate to the United States to obtain food?

A concern with reciprocity also can drain heated ideological hostilities from many conflicts, because the focus in disputes could be on principles of good conduct, rather than on the ideological goals of the government. Ideologically diverse governments can live peacefully with one another as long as the fundamental principles of world policy are supported.

A rigorous respect for reciprocity is also an effective antidote to one of the most serious dangers associated with a principled foreign policy: namely, that its proponents may assume a moralistic attitude, based on the assumption that their policies are more virtuous than the policies of other governments. They may insist on their own way, evangelize for the "right" point of view, and use military threats to implement their policies. To nullify this common yet poisonous tendency, reciprocity should be authoritatively interpreted wherever possible by multilateral institutions or a third party to a dispute. Moreover, application of the other proposed principles, such as democratization and demilitarization, helps guard against the danger that a policy inspired by a moral vision will take on a self-righteous or aggressive tone. The proposed combination of principles can avoid the excesses of unprincipled "arrogance of power"[19] on the one hand and of legalism and moralism, so well described by George Kennan many years ago,[20] on the other.

## Equity

The second guideline, to advance equity throughout global society, arises from a moral desire for more justice, an economic need for more economic rationality and global productivity, and a political need for more international cooperation and willingness to sacrifice for the good of all. This guideline pertains especially to economic opportunity, to meeting basic human needs, and to fairer distribution of political influence and economic resources throughout the world. As Nicole Ball and Vincent Ferraro have each pointed out in Chapters 9 and 14, a more equitable distribution of political and economic resources would advance development programs designed to meet the needs of all people, as well as reduce the political power of military and authoritarian forces that threaten democracy in the poor countries.

Poverty must be abolished because the worldwide cooperation needed to build a durable security system cannot be achieved with the planet divided, economically half slave and half free.[21] Poverty also leads to degradation of the biosphere, because poor governments often feel forced to cut development costs by accepting low environmental standards to attract capital or by destroying rain forests to earn cash. Yet the forests produce oxygen and absorb carbon dioxide, a process essential to all those on earth who are concerned about human life in the long run. As a result, the abolition of poverty becomes a security goal for the rich even if they have little moral concern for justice or the well-being of the poor.

The world economy now functions so inefficiently that it harms all nations, rich and poor alike. Today's economic structures leave approximately 1 billion people living in poverty, facing serious shortages of food, and often leading unproductive lives. In part because the world community has not eliminated glaring inequities, the North's industrial capacity remains underutilized while the South urgently needs goods that the North could produce. Meanwhile, the creative power of many of the earth's people, who happen to live in the South, is lost. In addition, poverty adds pressures on limited food resources, tillable land, and timber supplies. Overfishing, overgrazing, desertification, and loss of topsoil cause a declining standard of living, eventually, for the species everywhere.[22] Poverty also stimulates unwanted population growth that would be reduced if more equitable, higher standards of living were attained throughout the world.

As the Brandt Commission concluded a decade ago, the whole world community has a responsibility to generate more substantial funds for economic development and equity. All states, it said, should contribute to a capital fund for development, based on a sliding scale related to national income, and support what "would amount to an element of universal taxation."[23] The purpose of such progressive taxation would be nothing less than to abolish global poverty. Although taxes are disliked everywhere, using them in a global plan to end poverty not only would be a concrete step toward democratizing global economic structures (which Joseph Collins has demonstrated in Chapter 15 is necessary to abolish hunger), but would also turn out to be a money-saving way of alleviating economic and political conditions that, once addressed, help in achieving war prevention and environmental protection.

Reform of the international monetary system and development banks should aim to achieve more equitable burden sharing in establishing more stable exchange rates, adjusting balance of payments deficits, expanding international liquidity, and dealing with the debt that keeps many societies buried in poverty.[24] With a serious international program to share resources and conserve energy and resources, hunger and poverty could be abolished within two decades by using only a modest fraction of total world military expenditures or of the likely increase in income of the richest one-third of the world's population. Indeed, annual world military expenditures today equal the total yearly income of the poorest half of humanity. Moreover, because present environmental decline is in part a consequence of poverty, advances in equity, which seem a prerequisite to increasing worldwide sensitivity to environmental protection, will directly meet future security needs.

The political necessity for more economic equity is no less important than the economic arguments for it. A greater degree of equity within and among countries would increase all peoples' stake in avoiding traumatic disruptions of global society. It would encourage people, many of whom are now alienated from prevailing political and economic institutions throughout the world, to support what would become a politically more stable and fair international system.

## Respect for Nature: Environmental Sustainability

A deeper respect for nature is essential to maintaining a healthy biosphere, without which a life of human dignity cannot continue. Environmental issues pose planet-enveloping dangers with the prospect of such irretrievable damage that they constitute the most serious long-range security problem in the world today. The World Commission on Environment and Development has concluded that life support systems for the entire species face severe danger from pollution, resource depletion, and population pressure.[25] These dangers cannot in most cases be treated at all through the traditional security instruments of military strength. Only the transfer of massive financial resources and brainpower from the military to environmental purposes and only truly cooperative, multilateral efforts to protect the ozone layer of the stratosphere and to halt climatic change induced by global warming will enable the species to enhance its security.

This principle suggests that the current flurry of fragmented activity on environmental issues should be given a coherent purpose to clarify what we wish to achieve. The goal is a sustainable world society, one that "satisfies its needs without jeopardizing the prospects of future generations." This means that each generation is responsible for ensuring "that the next one inherits an undiminished natural and economic endowment."[26] This third principle relates directly to the previous one, because the goal of environmental sustainability is rooted in a concept of intergenerational *equity*.

Severe though the dangers are, the Worldwatch Institute has estimated that $77 billion a year over one decade could reverse adverse environmental trends in the four key areas of protecting topsoil on croplands from further erosion, reforesting the earth, raising energy efficiency, and developing renewable sources of energy. This amounts to only 8 percent of current annual world military spending. The global amount spent on developing new military technologies, estimated at $100 billion in 1986 alone, exceeds all governments' expenditures on developing new energy technologies, increasing agricultural productivity, controlling pollution, and improving human health.[27]

Exciting possibilities for managing environmental problems, through reformulating the nature and location of sovereignty, emerged from the meeting convened by the prime ministers of France, Norway, and the Netherlands at the Hague in March 1989. Acutely aware of the twin problems of global warming and ozone depletion, the governments declared that international cooperation must occur on an unprecedented scale to avoid ecological disaster. The Hague Declaration calls for a strong international institution within the United Nations system to avert climate and ozone depletion. The new agency must, according to the governments meeting at the Hague, be endowed with power to make binding decisions, even when unanimity cannot be achieved among all members. If any government would violate community decisions, its case would be referred to the World Court.

Some of the largest polluters and consumers of energy, like the United States, were not even invited to the Hague meeting because of the conferees' desire to build support for progressive ideas before approaching those governments most likely to resist initiatives. Yet, in a July 1989 meeting of the Group of Seven, which includes the major industrialized democracies— Canada, France, Italy, Japan, the United Kingdom, the United States, and West Germany—these major economic powers reflected at least some openness to institution building. In their final communiqué they declared that "the increasing complexity of the issues related to the protection of the atmosphere calls for innovative solutions. New instruments may be contemplated."[28] The Hague Declaration, of course, expressed intentions, not a plan of action, let alone legally binding agreements. The public and Congress should press the United States to set a positive example by seeking to turn this declaration into a plan of action.

Benefits from cooperation on managing environmental problems might produce added gains from spilling over into other areas of security. Successful environmental management could build trust, suggest models for representation and veto-free deliberations in strengthened international institutions, and establish community-wide enforcement.

## Democratization

Democratization, the fourth principle, aims to increase every government's accountability to the people, regardless of their nationality, who are affected by every particular government's decisions, regardless of the country in which the respective decisions are made. Ensuring that all governments become and remain accountable to the people who are affected by their decisions is not merely a desirable political goal. It is essential for security in the future. Without governmental accountability, major decisions, whether made at national, regional, or global levels, will lack sufficient legitimacy to avoid unacceptable risks and disruptions of international life. To enhance global security through deepening democracy requires progress in both "horizontal" and "vertical" accountability.

**Horizontal Accountability**  "Horizontal accountability" refers to a government's responsibility that extends across national borders. Traditionally, scholars and politicians alike have not recognized a need for any horizontal accountability beyond what could occur through normal diplomatic representation. But increasingly, more reliable representative mechanisms are needed to enable citizens to influence the decisions that are made in neighboring societies and that directly affect them.

Horizontal accountability, of course, is little more than an expansion to a wider geographic domain of the more familiar idea of vertical accountability of a government to its people within domestic society. The principle of governmental accountability, so important in the revolutionary founding of the United States, has been virtually ignored in modern times, during which the locus of many political decisions relevant for U.S. citizens has moved beyond the boundaries of the United States to Tokyo, Brussels, Bonn, and Moscow. Yet, if we are to maintain a democratic way of life domestically, the relevance of horizontal democratization throughout the international arena is growing dramatically. As interdependence increases, the number of decisions that affect U.S. citizens and yet occur outside the United States also increases. If the political, economic, and environmental decisions that affect

U.S. people increasingly occur outside the United States while U.S. political institutions remain constant, then the element of democracy in U.S. political life declines, even though fair elections, a free press, and competing political parties remain operational as they have in the past.

If people in other lands pollute the atmosphere, then U.S. citizens suffer environmental degradation without representation. Alternatively, if U.S. economic policies cause worldwide inflation, then people in other lands suffer inflationary "taxation" without representation. To take yet another example, those who plan, build, and operate the nuclear plant at Chernobyl might reasonably be held accountable to standards established by all those who are likely to be affected by its operations or possible breakdown, whether they live in Sweden, Italy, the Soviet Union, or elsewhere. For a forward-looking security policy at century's end, the principle of accountability must be international, as well as national and local.

Most U.S. citizens are unaware of the extent to which they are letting the democratic U.S. way of life slip through their nationalistic fingers by failing to support internationalist solutions to contemporary problems. In a world where decisions and influences that affect our lives occur outside our national political institutions, to think that we live in a democratic society just because national institutions are democratic is a dangerous deception. The economic security of the U.S. public depends on decisions made in Tokyo or Brussels as well as on Wall Street. The security of U.S. citizens depends on military decisions made in Moscow or Tel Aviv as well as in Washington. The society relevant to our lives now is global as well as national and local, so advocates of democracy must aim to remodel sovereignty and overcome the profoundly inadequate—in terms of representativeness, authority, and power—institutions at the global level.

Of course the United States is well represented, perhaps unfairly overrepresented, in many of the international institutions that do exist. In areas where none exist, Washington in the past has often gotten its way by exerting economic and military strength in an international system in which the strong have dominated custom and practice. But as military force becomes less applicable to problem solving and less widely accepted as legitimate, and as economic power becomes more widely diffused throughout the world, the United States will want to ensure that its voice is heard in international institutions that are reliable and democratic and that guarantee rights for global minorities as well as majorities.

**Vertical Accountability**  A healthy concern for cross-border government accountability at the global level also means concern for accountability at the national and local levels, since global representation and decisions cannot fully implement the democratic principle unless the structure beneath them facilitates representative government. As Stephen Marks has demonstrated in Chapter 13, authoritarian governments are less likely to serve the interests of their people, including security in the broadest sense, than are more popular, responsive governments. As a result, the growth of "people power," in ousting dictators or pressing for democratic reforms in the Philippines, Poland, Hungary, East Germany, Czechoslovakia, Rumania, the Soviet Union, China, Nepal, and elsewhere, is conducive to global security. The growth of democracy aids the growth of peace because democratic societies have related more peacefully to each other than they have to authoritarian societies or than authoritarian societies have to each other.[29]

To encourage democratic accountability, Washington could be more consistent in attempting, through nonviolent means, to discourage authoritarian government and to facilitate the growth of representative government wherever possible. Forming transnational alliances with nonviolent demonstrators and building effective international support for the right of indigenous people to humanize their own governments may often serve U.S. security better than external U.S. military pressure. Moreover, initiatives to create an international human rights court and to coordinate international sanctions against those who violate fundamental international protections against arbitrary imprisonment, torture, and execution could give visibility and added strength to those who might organize peoples' power and conduct nonviolent demonstrations against authoritarianism.

Centuries of political experience demonstrate the need to maintain strong protection for minorities wherever majorities rule. Reinforcing such protection at every opportunity will not only encourage minorities to accept and support majoritarian procedures, but also prevent the deepening of fears and hostilities among ethnically diverse populations. The industrialized countries might find it in their interests to establish effectively functioning global, democratic institutions as quickly as possible, so their durability and fairness will be well established when needed. The prosperous societies pursue a perilous course toward the year 2000, when, as Jessica Tuchman Mathews points out, the developed countries "will be home to only 20 percent of the world's people."[30]

Some useful instruments to protect minority rights are already available, but are not yet being used. These exist in the UN human rights covenants and protocols which codify rights and enable individual citizens to bring grievances against their own governments to an international hearing for possible redress of injuries. The United States should implement these covenants itself and support efforts by regional and global authorities, whether through the UN Human Rights Commission, regional commissions, or nongovernmental organizations like Amnesty International, to monitor government performance. Such efforts, of course, serve the well-being of all people, whether or not they feel themselves part of a minority. In addition, to the extent that the international community can protect human rights through international institutions, it will have removed one of the main rationales for war and against demilitarization: namely, to use force in protecting people against mistreatment by brutal governments.

## Demilitarization

The fifth principle, global demilitarization, is inspired by the desire to reduce the role of military power in international relations generally, not merely to reduce arms of one sort or another. It is far more comprehensive and far-reaching than arms control, which, as it has been practiced for four decades, has merely meant limited management of the arms buildup. To be sure, one way of hemming in the use of military force is to eliminate arms that exacerbate tensions and insecurities. So demilitarization includes gradual reduction of arms, but it goes far beyond arms control—the mode in which Washington seems stuck—to aim at eventual elimination of national armed forces for purposes other than maintaining domestic tranquility and monitoring borders for purposes of regulating activities like trade and immigration. In addition, demilitarization extends beyond even major reductions of armed forces, to include steps to demilitarize the political economy, the habits of political and educational institutions, and the social and psychological patterns that sustain collective violence as well. Demilitarization includes the dismantling of national and international military culture and its replacement with a culture of legal obligation and nonlethal forms of dispute resolution.

Demilitarization is necessary because it seems impossible to achieve a lasting, just peace within a balance of power system that is endowed with unilaterally employed national armed forces, continuing weapons development by national military organizations, and the prospect of yet unimagined weapons of mass destruction and environmental vulnerabilities always close at hand. In addition, demilitarization is required because military institutions, regardless of ethnic or ideological setting, organize and train people, as well as shape economic and political institutions, in ways that are antithetical to democratic processes and the other proposed policy principles themselves. Hierarchical, undemocratic institutions discourage democratic culture and respect for all members of the human species. Military governments generally inhibit progress in all areas of concern, from equity to demilitarization. Demilitarization can begin to address the discouraging consequences described by Nicole Ball, which flow from the military rulers who have directly or indirectly governed approximately three-fourths of the societies in Africa, Asia, South and Central America, and the Middle East since 1945.[31]

Because military power remains a central preoccupation of officials in current thinking about security, despite some scaling down of expenditures, the principle of demilitarization will be examined here in greater detail to

416 / ROBERT C. JOHANSEN

suggest ways to transform the international system in the long run without jeopardizing security in the short run.

# DECREASING THE ROLE OF MILITARY POWER AND INCREASING THE ROLE OF NONMILITARY INFLUENCES

Because of its influence, resources, and relatively unthreatened security position in world affairs, the United States could be a path-breaker in reducing the role of military force. To succeed, its political leadership would need consciously to adopt policies aimed at changing the international code of conduct. Although steps toward such a goal obviously will require international negotiations along the way, there is no need to delay important initiatives until after negotiations have occurred. The most effective course is likely to be found by taking independent actions that are not contingent upon first negotiating precise formulas for arms reductions. Conditional steps, with an invitation to the Soviet Union or others to reciprocate, can avoid the delays of long negotiations and cut through suspicion and distrust.[32] Through independent initiatives the United States could stimulate global learning and mobilize transnational, populist political pressures for progressive change, not only in the body politic at home, but also in other societies throughout the world.

To reduce reliance on arms and simultaneously to take account of a country's fears of its adversary, as successful political leaders everywhere must do, requires the strengthening of world security institutions. They must eventually enable national governments to transcend not the conflictive element of relations among diverse peoples that characterizes today's security system, but its *militarily* adversarial nature. World security institutions must also provide reliable assurances that security can indeed be enhanced and eventually maintained by dependable UN or other global institutions, acting in concert with regional, national, and popular public efforts to create and maintain a less violence-prone code of international conduct. The United States could increase worldwide security while demilitarizing the balance of power by developing a concrete diplomatic program to reduce the role of military power and to strengthen nonmilitary forms of dispute settlement and of deterrence to war.

A carefully orchestrated U.S. effort to diminish reliance on military force could focus on three goals: to reorient military power toward nonoffensive defenses and gradually reduce all national armed forces; to denuclearize world security policies; and to curtail external military interventions and the projection of military power throughout the world.

## Developing Nonoffensive Defenses

In recognition of the mutuality of security in today's interdependent world, the United States and other like-minded governments could ask all countries to confine themselves more strictly to defense by halting the development and deployment of weapons which by their speed, stealth, destructive power, or range are extremely threatening to other countries. As a first step, the United States or the Soviet Union could announce that it will conditionally halt the testing and deployment of all additional missiles and aircraft of intercontinental range, and of all weapons for use in space, including both antisatellite and ballistic missile defenses. If the other superpower reciprocates, the moratorium could be extended indefinitely and expanded to include all other nations.[33] Weapons that are particularly well suited for first-strike uses, such as the Trident D-5 and M-X missiles and Stealth B-2 bomber, should be phased out altogether, as defensive capabilities would be increasingly emphasized in all weapons systems, both nuclear and conventional.[34]

As a step away from adversarial military relationships, U.S. allies in Europe could take a stronger lead in constructing an all-European security regime, as Thomas Risse-Kappan suggests in Chapter 6, to encompass members of both NATO and the Warsaw Treaty Organization. Limits could be placed on national arms for all countries in the region. This could ensure that a unified Germany would be a threat to no one. Such a step can be taken without risk because the prospect of Soviet aggression against Western Europe is virtually out of the question in the foreseeable future. The most sensible long-term goal for the United States is to spin a growing web of norms, laws, security institutions, and political and economic arrangements that could make East-West violent conflict as unthinkable twenty years from now as it became for Germans and French, archenemies for many decades, within twenty years after the close of World War II.

## Denuclearizing Security Policies

One of the most important ways of making military postures less offensive is to end the proliferation of all weapons of mass destruction, beginning with nuclear arms. To underscore that a strengthened nuclear nonproliferation regime will not be an inequitable one in which the nuclear "haves" enjoy privileges over the "have-nots," the United States and Soviet Union must downgrade the importance they assign to nuclear arms. Although the heads of government in the United States and Soviet Union have both advocated, on occasion, the complete elimination of nuclear weapons, their bureaucracies do not seem to take this idea seriously.[35] To be sure, verification problems arise as arms reductions move toward very low levels of nuclear weapons. Yet, intense efforts to verify the abolition of nuclear arsenals and delivery systems, plus worldwide measures to make it unlikely that anyone could take political advantage of any clandestine nuclear arms, probably could reduce risks to an acceptably low level.

In Chapters 2 and 3, Walter Clemens and Kosta Tsipis both disagree with this idea and favor indefinite retention of nuclear arms by the United States and the Soviet Union. But I am not persuaded that such a policy will enhance U.S. or world security. Moscow and Washington seem unlikely to attack one another with either conventional or nuclear arms in the foreseeable future, regardless of the state of their nuclear arsenals. The most likely prospect for using nuclear weapons grows from the spread of nuclear weapons to additional countries. The best defense against this most likely prospect is to be found in preventing additional countries from obtaining nuclear arms and delivery systems, and from disarming those with a rudimentary, clandestine arsenal already in existence. Such goals can most likely be achieved only if there is a universal move to delegitimize the *possession* as well as the testing of all nuclear arms.[36] It is unrealistic to assume that any country may keep nuclear weapons indefinitely without expecting that eventually every country that wants them may obtain them.

If U.S. officials would support a universal effort to abolish nuclear arms, and if most countries would agree to such a ban, it is very unlikely that the remaining would-be nuclear powers could successfully produce and hide weapons from modern surveillance techniques and on-site inspection. But even if some unsophisticated and extremely small number of weapons might possibly be hidden, their use could be deterred, to the extent that one believes deterrence works, with the extremely destructive nonnuclear arms that now exist and, in the long run, through nonmilitary incentives to dismantle them. When all the arguments are weighed carefully, a plausible case can be made that the risks the world will face are higher with an indefinite continuation of nuclear deterrence and the further spread of nuclear arms and other nonnuclear weapons of mass destruction, than with the abolition of all nuclear arms and worldwide, intense efforts to verify abolition.[37]

## Establishing a Noninterventionist Regime

Friendlier relations between Moscow and Washington, of course, will not in themselves eliminate the problem of military intervention by regional or global hegemonies in many regions of the world. Interventions have in recent years occurred in Cambodia, Lebanon, Chad, Kuwait, the Sudan, the Western Sahara, Angola, Namibia, Sri Lanka, Central America, and elsewhere, as well as in Vietnam and Afghanistan. Yet the growing awareness among governments in the East and West, North and South, that military interventions often produce higher costs than benefits suggests the importance of attempting to establish a noninterventionist regime.

To encourage comprehensive limits on future interventions, Washington or Moscow could publicly pledge not to send any of its armed forces, even if invited, to a selective list of nonaligned countries in return for a similar promise from the other. If an extranational peacekeeper is required in such countries, it could be provided under UN auspices. Once Moscow and Washington agree to establish a noninterventionist regime, they and other sympathetic countries might encourage guarantees from remaining states that their armed forces would not intervene, possibly in return for strengthened UN peacekeeping capabilities paid for by the countries presently spending the most on national military power.

Noninterventionist policies and a more formal nonintervention regime could be buttressed by declaring a moratorium on the establishment of new foreign military bases and the addition of forces or weapons to existing bases. Again, the moratorium should be followed by an invitation to other nations with foreign bases to reciprocate. Negotiations thereafter could specify guidelines to maintain the moratorium and to remove long-range weapons. International inspectors could verify that armed forces on foreign territory were for defensive purposes until most bases could eventually be phased out.

A future security policy for the United States, in addition to designing a worldwide campaign to reduce the armed forces of national governments and constrict their offensive capabilities, needs to upgrade and institutionalize nonmilitary influences that would gradually bridle the military option and construct a legally constituted international security system to replace the military instrument in security maintenance. The proposed policy direction can be illustrated by efforts to: establish a permanent UN peacekeeping force; create a global monitoring ability; and enhance global reliance on legal processes as a technique of conflict resolution.

## Establishing a Permanent UN Peacekeeping Force

The creation of a permanent global police force would help set the institutional stage for educating publics and governments about the possibilities of gradually curtailing national uses of military power.[38] Even in its infancy, such a force could help, as have ad hoc UN peacekeeping forces, to deter border violations and small-scale aggression by militarily adventurous states. What is proposed here would differ from past UN peacekeeping in two ways: This police force would be permanent, and it would consist of individually recruited persons instead of contingents from various national military forces. Because a permanent global police force would be more thoroughly integrated and efficient, more readily available, less subject to charges of unreliability due to allegedly divided loyalties, and better able to build useful precedents over time, it is an important step in the process of domesticating the international system. It can help people learn that non-adversarial enforcement by the world community, on behalf of norms endorsed by the global community, is possible now in limited domains, and can be expanded in the future.

## Creating a UN Monitoring and Research Agency

The creation of an international monitoring agency under the auspices of the UN could help bring the weight of the entire world community into the process of encouraging compliance with arms restraints and of assuring that no government could avoid detection if it violated international limitations on military forces. Such an agency could utilize surveillance by high-altitude aircraft, satellites, and other means. Most nations already favor such an idea, which France first proposed in 1978.[39] Moscow has endorsed the creation of a verification agency to check compliance with disarmament accords.[40] The United States remains opposed, but Congressman Robert Mrazek has introduced legislation to establish a commission to study the formation of an international satellite monitoring agency and to create a global network that would contribute to the common security of all nations.[41] Strong endorsement of such an agency, from people both outside the United States and within, could probably overcome current U.S. opposition to such an agency.

By lifting verification questions from the adversarial hands of U.S. and Soviet intelligence operations, UN agencies and other countries could draw upon impartial information to exert leverage against destabilizing military deployments. The prospect that worldwide attention would be drawn instantly to violations of arms agreements would increase the obligatory quality of treaty rules. In addition to monitoring arms agreements, such an agency could help deter clandestine tests of missiles or warheads anywhere on earth, observe cease-fire lines in the Middle East, discourage illegal arms shipments and infiltration of arms across borders in Central America or elsewhere, hamper covert operations to manipulate political events in small countries, and in general help resolve questions of fact that U.S. or Soviet intelligence services by themselves are incapable of resolving to the satisfaction of each other and the international community.

## Expanding the Use of International Courts

Finally, the United States could expand the international use of the most widely accepted domestic instrument for solving disputes between individuals and groups: processes of legal settlement and impartial adjudication. Because the United States is a powerful and wealthy country relatively satisfied with the status quo, legal instruments on balance can be very useful in protecting its interests. Yet the United States has not established a positive record of respect for the International Court of Justice and for legal norms against the use of force, as demonstrated when the United States walked out of the Court after Nicaragua made claims against Washington's use of force in Central America. New Soviet interest in accepting the compulsory jurisdiction of the Court, as well as the demonstrated ineffectiveness of military power in many contexts, provides a new opportunity and more solid basis for Washington to endorse the principle that all countries should accept without qualification the compulsory jurisdiction of the International Court of Justice or regional courts in all disputes with countries similarly accepting compulsory jurisdiction.

## SPECIES SECURITY: THE KEY TO U.S. SECURITY

The contributors to this volume have demonstrated that a fundamental transformation of security policies and world security institutions must occur to bring real safety to the postmodern world. To chart a purposeful course toward common security and comprehensive security, we need a clear vision of the values—reciprocity, equity, environmental sustainability, democratic accountability, and demilitarized security—to implement in a principled world policy. These ends must be clear, not only to develop the most useful means for their attainment, but also to motivate and shape the forces necessary for change. Focusing on explicit goals, the benefits of which should flow equitably to all people, can help us recast our understanding of how to relate to other people and to the planet. If we honor these principles in our personal and national political lives, we will demonstrate what world politics and security can be.

Moreover, keeping these principles in mind will help the United States exercise "leadership without primacy."[42] The United States will need to become more skilled at multilateral diplomacy, since few of its security needs can any longer be met by itself or even in cooperation with others through traditional forms of bilateral diplomacy. As Margaret Karns and Karen Mingst point out in Chapter 12, multilateral diplomacy exercised through international organizations enables governments to set common agendas, gather information to open new paths, create norms, monitor behavior, and force decisions.

To hold all countries accountable to higher standards than in the past, students and scholars, public officials, journalists, political parties, and the public at large could create indicators for measuring not only the general environmental health of the planet, as Mathews aptly suggests in Chapter 16, but also for evaluating the behavior of national governments in each of the other areas of concern defined by the five principles proposed here. They together might provide a calculus of human progress or regress.

A truly effective foreign policy, which can be distilled from the preceding chapters, not only must set new policy directions, but also must draw upon moral inspiration to guide its direction and to enhance its political strength. To serve the human interest in justice and peace does not compromise national prudence; it is prudence of the long run. In our era as never before in history, what is ethically desirable to do in relating to one's neighbor converges with what is politically prudent for oneself. That is the full meaning of the preceding chapters' emphasis on the mutuality and comprehensiveness of security. A truly realistic U.S. security policy recognizes that species security provides the firmest foundation for U.S. security. Such a policy can be pursued effectively through legal, political, economic, environmental, psychological, and educational means, but not, as in the past, through chronic preparations for war.

## Notes

1. Although one nation or another may benefit for a limited time from high levels of military preparedness, international society as a whole suffers in the long run from chronic preparations for war. For elaboration, see Robert C. Johansen, "Do Preparations for War Increase International Peace and Security?" in Charles W. Kegley, ed., *The Long Postwar Peace* (New York: HarperCollins, 1991), pp. 224–44.

2. Seyom Brown, "Inherited Geopolitics and Emergent Global Realities," in Edward K. Hamilton, ed., *America's Global Interests* (New York: W. W. Norton, 1989), pp. 196–97.

3. See Independent Commission on International Development Issues, Willy Brandt, chairman, *North-South: A Programme for Survival* (Cambridge, MA: MIT Press, 1980); Independent Commission on Disarmament and Security Issues, Olof Palme, chairman, *Common Security: A Blueprint for Survival* (New York: Simon & Schuster, 1982)); World Commission on Environment and Development, Gro Harlem Brundtland, chairman, *Our Common Future* (New York: Oxford University Press, 1987).

4. The Palme Commission on Disarmament and Security Issues, *A World At Peace: Common Security in the Twenty-first Century* (Stockholm: The Palme Commission, 1989), pp. 6–7.

5. See the Report of the Commission on Integrated Long-Term Strategy, Fred C. Ikle and Albert Wohlstetter, co-chairmen, *Discriminate Deterrence* (Washington: Government Printing Office, 1988).

6. Michael G. Renner, "What's Sacrificed When We Arm," *World Watch*, Vol. 2 (September-October, 1989), p. 9.

7. See Chapter 16, pp. 376–78.

8. The group included Australia, Brazil, Canada, Egypt, the Federal Republic of Germany, France, Hungary, Ivory Coast, India, Indonesia, Italy, Japan, Jordan, Kenya, Malta, New Zealand, Netherlands, Norway, Senegal, Spain, Sweden, Tunisia, Venezuela, and Zimbabwe. Those at the Hague meetings have solicited additional signatures since the meeting. The original twenty-four nations have been joined by Austria, Belgium, Czechoslovakia, Denmark, Ireland, Luxembourg, Pakistan, Portugal, and Switzerland. China, the United States, and the Soviet Union were not invited because they were unlikely to endorse the declaration. See Hilary F. French, "An Environmental Security Council?" *World Watch*, Vol. 2 (September-October 1989), p. 7.

9. See R. B. J. Walker, "Security, Sovereignty and the Challenge of World Politics," unpublished essay, p. 18.

10. For the past three decades or more, the aggregate number of refugees has varied between 10 and 15 million. The people included are not always the same ones because repatriation and resettlement do occur. Nonetheless, "such high absolute totals over a period of several years are historically unprecedented." Leon Gordenker, *Refugees in International Politics* (New York: Columbia University Press, 1987), p. 52. See also Gil Loescher and Laila

Monahan, eds., *Refugees and International Relations* (New York: Oxford University Press, 1989).

11. On the apartheid analogy, see Gernot Kohler, "Global Apartheid," *Alternatives: A Journal of World Policy*, Vol. 4 (1978–79), pp. 250–70.

12. *The Rise and Fall of the Great Powers: Economic Change and Military Conflict from 1500 to 2000* (New York: Vintage, 1987).

13. Betty Reardon, *Sexism and the War System* (New York: Teachers College, 1985).

14. These ideas build upon "global humanism" discussed in Robert C. Johansen, *The National Interest and the Human Interest: An Analysis of U.S. Foreign Policy* (Princeton: Princeton University Press, 1980), pp. 3–37.

15. See Richard Falk, "Lifting the Curse of Bipartisanship," *World Policy Journal*, Vol. 1 (Fall 1983), pp. 127–58.

16. Soviet leaders apparently adopted this approach in concluding that they could increase the pressures on Washington to abide by the ABM treaty by taking the unusual step of a public admission that the Soviet construction of a radar at Krasnoyarsk, which Gorbachev stopped, would have violated international law. In this case, at least, law-abiding behavior even by an adversary can compel U.S. compliance more effectively than would have more Soviet military power martialed against the United States.

17. Even in the highly charged atmospheres such as surround U.S. feelings toward Libya on issues of terrorism, a principled policy would help the United States, its allies, and its adversaries avoid confusion between a U.S. hostility to Muammar Qaddafi and a balanced, universal antiterrorist policy. A principled opposition to terrorism, if defined in ways that do not make the terrorist label merely a propaganda weapon to condemn one's foes, could be joined by most nations, regardless of ideology or region, including Arab societies. But the latter would not be willing to join an effort in which they appeared to be supporting a U.S. policy that was anti-Libyan, anti-Palestinian, or anti-Arab.

18. This principle represents a modest international expression of Immanuel Kant's categorical imperative in which each person should behave in ways that, if everyone else behaved in the same way, would result in his or her own happiness.

19. J. William Fulbright, *The Arrogance of Power* (New York: Random House, 1967).

20. *American Diplomacy 1900–1950* (Chicago: University of Chicago Press, 1951).

21. Evidence to support this view is found in the analyses in this book by Joseph Collins, Steven Marks, and Vincent Ferraro.

22. For the negative impact of poverty on the environment, see Alan B. Durning, *Poverty and the Environment: Reversing the Downward Spiral* (Washington, D.C.: Worldwatch, 1989).

23. Independent Commission on International Development Issues, Willy Brandt, chairman, *North-South: A Programme for Survival* (Cambridge, MA: MIT Press, 1980), p. 274.

24. For a promising set of suggestions, see Walter Russell Mead, *The United States and the World Economy* (New York: *World Policy Journal* Reprint, 1989), especially pp. 425–68; and Robert L. Ayres, *Banking on the Poor: The World Bank and World Poverty* (Cambridge, MA: MIT Press, 1983). For different perspectives, see Ashok Bapna, ed., *One World One Future: New International Strategies for Development* (New York: Praeger, 1985); Paul Taylor and A.J.R. Groom, eds., *Global Issues in the United Nations' Framework* (New York: St. Martin's, 1989); David Steele, *The Reform of the United Nations* (London: Croom Helm, 1987); and Kenneth W. Dam, *The Rules of the Game* (Chicago: University of Chicago Press, 1982).

25. World Commission on Environment and Development, note 3.

26. Lester R. Brown, Christopher Flavin, and Sandra Postel, "Picturing a Sustainable Society," in Lester R. Brown, ed., *State of the World 1990* (New York: W. W. Norton, 1990), pp. 173–90.

27. Michael Renner, note 8.

28. Article 45, "Key Sections of the Paris Communique by the Group of Seven," *New York Times*, 17 July 1989, p. A7.

29. Bruce Russett, "Toward a More Democratic and Therefore More Peaceful World," in Burns Weston, ed., *Alternative Security* (Boulder: Westview, 1990).

30. See Mathews, Chapter 16.

31. See Ball, Chapter 9.

32. I am referring here to "graduated reciprocation in tension reduction," the approach

suggested by Charles E. Osgood in *An Alternative to War or Surrender* (Urbana: University of Illinois Press, 1962).

33. Such a blanket moratorium is verifiable with a high degree of confidence by using the monitoring equipment the United States, the Soviet Union, and other countries now have in operation. The intrusive inspection accompanying the INF treaty suggests that further means are available, if needed, to assure permanent reliability.

34. See Dietrich Fischer, *Preventing War in the Nuclear Age* (London: Croom Helm, 1984).

35. Theodore B. Taylor, "Go Cold Turkey," *Bulletin of the Atomic Scientists,* July/August, 1989, pp. 26–31.

36. Rather than advocate such an effort, Walter Clemens writes (see Chapter 2) that India, Pakistan, and presumably all other would-be nuclear countries "must be persuaded that their domestic needs as well as their external security do not require nuclear weaponry." Yet to critics this argument might appear to be an ethnocentric judgment against the less wealthy countries and a denial of the principle of reciprocity. What is the basis for arguing that the United States, which has fewer serious security problems than either India or Pakistan, is entitled to possess nuclear weapons indefinitely, even though it is not in the interest of other countries to have them?

37. One added problem with the indefinite continuation of nuclear deterrence is that it is likely to stimulate the development of other weapons of mass destruction, as has already occurred with the effort by Israel's rivals to obtain poison gas to offset Israeli nuclear capability.

Kosta Tsipis is one of the many national security experts who reject the idea of abolishing nuclear weapons because of "its impracticality" (see Chapter 3). He seems comfortable with the continuation of deterrence: "Assured destruction makes deterrence both possible and obligatory." Deterrence "is in reality *an existential fact* because there is *no other choice.*" Deterrence between the United States and the Soviet Union "remains the inescapable steady state those two countries find themselves in." Yet upon reflection these sweeping assertions are not reassuring. Are the proliferation of nuclear weapons and the increased risks that attend proliferation any less "impractical" than effots to abolish nuclear weapons? What are the precise calculations that lead one to conclude that the risks of verifying nuclear disarmament are more dangerous than the risks of proliferation? By what calculus of moral obligation does one conclude that threatening massive destruction with nuclear weapons is "obligatory" or indeed that there is "no other choice"? If deterrence is an "inescapable steady state," why do so many worry about its unsteadiness? Even if deterrence has seemed stable between the United States and the Soviet Union, what destabilizing consequences may flow from the legitimacy that Moscow's and Washington's policies give to the procurement by others of nuclear and nonnuclear weapons of mass destruction?

38. For elaboration of this point, see Robert C. Johansen, "The Reagan Administration and the U.N.: The Costs of Unilateralism," *World Policy Journal,* Vol. 3 (Fall, 1986), pp. 601–41.

39. For further discussion of this idea, see Department of Disarmament Affairs, Report of the Secretary-General, *The Implications of Establishing an International Satellite Monitoring Agency,* Study Series 9 (New York: United Nations, 1983).

40. Speech of Eduard A. Shevardnadze before the General Assembly, reported by Paul Lewis, "Soviets Press Offer on Disputed Radar," *New York Times,* 28 September 1988, p. A3.

41. H.R. 4036, 100th Congress, 2nd Session.

42. See Mathews, Chapter 16, p. 377.

# About the Contributors

Nicole Ball is a visiting fellow at the National Security Archive in Washington, D.C. and the author of *Security and Economy in the Third World* (1988).

Peter A. Clausen is a director of research for the Union of Concerned Scientists and writes frequently on nuclear policy and arms control topics. He was previously an analyst with the CIA and the Department of Energy, and holds a Ph.D. in political science from UCLA. He is the author of a forthcoming book on U.S. nonproliferation policy.

Walter C. Clemens, Jr., is professor of political science at Boston University and adjunct research fellow at the Harvard Center for Science and International Affairs. His books include *Baltic Independence and Russian Empire* (1990), also published by St. Martin's Press, *Can Russia Change?* (1990), *The USSR and Global Interdependence* (1978), and *The Superpowers and Arms Control* (1973).

Joseph Collins is the cofounder of and a senior researcher at the Institute for Food and Development Policy in San Francisco. He is the author of *World Hunger: Twelve Myths* (1986) and *The Philippines: Fire on the Rim* (1989).

James Der Derian is an associate professor of political science at the University of Massachusetts at Amherst. He is the author of *On Diplomacy: A Genealogy of Western Estrangement* (1987) and *Antidiplomacy: Speed, Spies, and Terror in International Relations* (1990).

Daniel Deudney is a Hewlett Fellow in Science, Technology, and Society at the Center for Energy and Environmental Studies at Princeton University. He is a coauthor of *Renewable Energy: The Power to Choose* (1983) and the author of numerous articles and monographs.

Richard A. Falk is the Albert G. Milbank Professor of International Law and Practice at Princeton University and a member of the New York State Bar.

He is the author or coauthor of numerous books and articles, including *Indefensible Weapons* (1982), *International Law: A Contemporary Perspective* (1985), and *The Promise of World Order* (1987).

Vincent Ferraro is chair of the International Relations Program and a professor of politics at Mount Holyoke College in South Hadley, Massachusetts. He is the author of many articles on strategic doctrine and the international political economy.

Donald L. Horowitz is the Charles S. Murphy Professor of Law and a professor of political science at the Duke University School of Law. He is the author of *Ethnic Groups in Conflict* (1985) and various other works.

Robert C. Johansen is the director of graduate studies at the Institute for International Peace Studies and a professor of government at the University of Notre Dame. He is the author of numerous articles and *The National and the Human Interest* (1981).

Margaret P. Karns is director of the Center for International Studies and a professor of political science at the University of Dayton. She is the coauthor, with Karen Mingst, of *The United States and Multilateral Institutions* (1990).

Michael T. Klare is an associate professor of peace and world security studies at Hampshire College in Amherst, Massachusetts, and the director of the Five College Program in Peace and World Security Studies. He is the author of *American Arms Supermarket* (1985) and coeditor of *Low-Intensity Warfare* (1988).

Allan S. Krass is professor of physics and science policy at Hampshire College in Amherst, Massachusetts. He is the author of *Verification: How Much Is Enough?* (1985) and *The Verification Revolution* (1989).

Stephen P. Marks is visiting professor of law and director of the Program in International Law and Human Rights at the Benjamin N. Cardozo School of Law of Yeshiva University in New York City. He also teaches at the New School for Social Research and Columbia University, where he is adjunct professor. He is the author of numerous articles about human rights and international organizations.

Jessica Tuchman Mathews is vice president of the World Resources Institute. She served on the National Security Council from 1977 to 1979 as director of the Office of Global Issues. The author acknowledges a great debt to colleagues at W. R. I.

Karen A. Mingst is a professor of political science at the University of Kentucky. She is the author of *Politics and the African Development Bank* (1990) and, with Margaret Karns, the coauthor of *The United States and Multilateral Institutions* (1990).

Thomas Risse-Kappen is an assistant professor of government in the peace studies program at Cornell University. He received his Ph.D. from the University of Frankfurt, West Germany, and his previous affiliation was with the Peace Research Institute, Frankfurt. He has written extensively on European security issues, and his books include *The Zero Option: INF, West Germany, and Arms Control* (1988).

Daniel C. Thomas is a Ph.D. candidate in Government at Cornell University and former Associate Director of the Five College Program in Peace and World Security Studies. He is the author—with Michael Klare—of *Peace and World Order Studies: A Curriculum Guide* (1989).

Kosta Tsipis is the director of the Program in Science and Technology for International Security and a professor of physics at the Massachusetts Institute of Technology. He is the author of *Arsenal: Understanding Weapons in the Nuclear Age* (1984) and *New Technologies: Defense Policy and Arms Control* (1989).

David A. Wirth is an assistant professor of law at Washington and Lee University. He is author of numerous articles on international environmental issues.